1942

OSPREY
PUBLISHING

And when Alexander saw the breadth of his
domain, he wept for there were no more
worlds to conquer.

Attributed to Plutarch

RICHARD HARGREAVES

1942

HITLER'S GAMBLE FOR VICTORY

OSPREY PUBLISHING
Bloomsbury Publishing Plc
Kemp House, Chawley Park, Cumnor Hill, Oxford OX2 9PH, UK
Bloomsbury Publishing Ireland Limited,
29 Earlsfort Terrace, Dublin 2, D02 AY28, Ireland
Bloomsbury Publishing Inc.
1359 Broadway, 12th Floor, New York, NY 10018, USA
E-mail: info@ospreypublishing.com
www.ospreypublishing.com

OSPREY is a trademark of Osprey Publishing Ltd

First published in Great Britain in 2026

A catalogue record for this book is available from the British Library.

ISBN: HB 9781472874962; eBook 9781472874979; ePDF 9781472874955; XML 9781472874931;
Audio 9781472874948

26 27 28 29 30   10 9 8 7 6 5 4 3 2 1

Image credits are given in full in the List of Illustrations (pp.7–8)

Maps by www.bounford.com
Index by Mark Swift

Typeset by Lumina Datamatics Ltd
Printed and bound in Great Britain by Clays Ltd, Elcograf S.p.A.

Osprey Publishing supports the Woodland Trust, the UK's leading woodland conservation charity.

To find out more about our authors and books visit www.ospreypublishing.com. Here you will find
extracts, author interviews, details of forthcoming events and the option to sign up for our newsletter.

For product safety related questions contact productsafety@bloomsbury.com

CONTENTS

ACKNOWLEDGEMENTS

As with my previous works, this book is the result of more than a decade's research in the archives, libraries and museums of Europe – letters, diaries, official and personal papers, contemporary newspapers, memoirs and testimonies, monographs and studies, and military histories – in a good half-dozen languages. As a result, it has also drawn upon the knowledge and assistance of many organisations and individuals including: the staffs of the Bundesarchiv in Freiburg; the Department of Documents at the Imperial War Museum, London; NIOD in Amsterdam; the National Archives in Kew; the British Library; and Hampshire Library Service. Jan-Hendrik Wendler helped with rare unit histories; Jason Mark and Yan Mann kindly shared their expertise on the Eastern Front; members of the Eastern Front Research Forum pointed me in the direction of sources and frequently helped with translation. Michael Miller helped with SS, SD and police authorities; Prit Buttar, Tom Houlihan, Bill Russ, Iain Ballantyne and many more provided general advice, support and proofreading. The book which follows is all the richer for their input.

LIST OF ILLUSTRATIONS AND MAPS

ILLUSTRATIONS

An 88mm flak cannon engaged in ground combat against Soviet armour outside Kharkov. (Author's collection)

German assault troops scramble over the Tatar Wall, one of the historic defences brought back into use by the Red Army to hold the Kerch peninsula in the Crimea. (Author's collection)

German troops comb through a smashed goods yard on the barren northern shore of Severnaya Bay. (Author's collection)

German soldiers by the waters of Severnaya Bay with warehouses burning on the waterfront in the last week of June. (Author's collection)

Two Germans crawl along a ravine to avoid the shrapnel of Soviet guns while delivering food to their comrades at the front. (Author's collection)

A Panzer Mk3 follows German armour moving across the Don steppe in formation. (Author's collection)

Troops of the *Grossdeutschland* motorised infantry division leave a village in flames as they support the drive to the Don. (NARA)

Rommel's favourite Italian division, the *Ariete*, manoeuvres in formation. (Author's collection)

Erwin Rommel (second right) confers with his chief-of-staff Fritz Bayerlein, *Afrika Korps* intelligence officer Friedrich von Mellenthin and *Afrika Korps* commander Walther Nehring. (Battlefield Historian Collection (BHC) 01314)

A British Grant tank passes a knocked-out – and long-obsolete – Panzer Mk2 destroyed in the battle of the Cauldron, 6 June. (BHC 01269)

Armour burns in the Cauldron, 5 June. (BHC 01280)

Columns roll into Egypt past a Panzer Mk3 of 21st Panzer Division at the end of June. (BHC 01358)

A dead soldier lies next to a knocked-out Panzer Mk3 at Alamein. (BHC 01356)

Assault troops supported by a Panzer Mk3 attack a fortified position in central Rostov, 26 July. (Author's collection)

Pack horses and *Gebirgsjäger* (mountain infantry) file along a mountain pass ferrying supplies to the front line; the animals died at the rate of 30 a day. (Author's collection)

Elements of a panzer division move through the Caucasian steppe with the mountains around Pyatigorsk in the distance, circa 10 August. (Author's collection)

A panzer commander watches the oil wells of the Kuban burn. (Author's collection)

Weary German infantry march through the Caucasus foothills. (Author's collection)

16th Panzer Division races towards the Volga, 23 August. (Author's collection)

A mortar team and infantry from 577th Infantry Regiment approach Stalingrad's Barrikady gun works, 16 October. (NARA)

Battalion commander Karl-Heinz Fricke raises the German ensign on the burned-out façade of the Univermag department store in Stalingrad's Red Square, 26 September. (NARA)

MAPS

INTRODUCTION:
46° 39' NORTH, 47° 47' EAST

How much longer will the war last? There's still no end in sight.

Anonymous German civilian, September 1942

A little after mid-day on Wednesday 16 September 1942, Fritz Euler brought his assorted column of vehicles to a halt following a monotonous eight-hour drive across near featureless terrain. Nothing but sand, dunes and the occasional scrub bush. The men called it the Russian Sahara, even giving the paths and dirt tracks – you could not call them roads – suitable African names: Tripoli Strasse, Benghazi Strasse, Tobruk Strasse and, of course, Rommelweg (Rommel's Way). Over the past three days, Euler and his men had crossed this 'desert', a wild ride dozens of miles ahead of the vanguard of their parent 16th Infantry Division. Now they stood on the edge of the vast Kalmyk steppe, their mission almost complete. Here the steppe gave way to lush, cultivated fields irrigated by the lower reaches of the Volga. The river itself – here half a mile wide – lay within sight, but dense vegetation on the west bank prevented Euler and his comrades from observing the shipping moving along it.

Fritz Euler's motley assortment of men and machines – pioneers, motorcyclists, an interpreter, medics and signallers equipped with a couple of half-tracks (armoured vehicles with wheels at the front, caterpillar tracks at the rear) armed with 20mm cannon, three anti-aircraft guns, half a dozen trucks carrying water, petrol and food, an ambulance, and some armoured cars – would never reach the Volga. It stopped here, three miles outside a village the Germans knew as Zhadovka, the Soviets Dzhakuevka and which today is called Volzhskoe. It came to a halt on the edge of an anti-tank ditch guarded by bunkers, machine-gun posts and perhaps as many as 300 troops, who appeared alarmed at the sight of German troops so far behind the front line. Both the defences and their defenders were too strong for Euler's force. Regarding his mission – to scout for Soviet troops in the steppe – as complete, Fritz Euler turned around but not before making an observation. Perhaps, he mused, his men 'had advanced furthest east of all the units in the army'. Euler's makeshift force or *Kampfgruppe* (battle group) stood just four miles from the Volga, 20 miles north-northwest of Astrakhan – more than 1,500 miles east of Berlin.[1]

Euler's force was one of three which 16th Infantry Division dispatched into the unknown in mid-September 1942. Barely three weeks earlier, the division had been committed around Maykop, one of the hubs of oil production in the western Caucasus. But those directing Germany's campaign in the East were concerned by the widening gap between the forces starting to invest Stalingrad, and those spread along a front which meandered for a good 350 miles on both sides of the central ridge of the Caucasus mountains. The motorised infantry division was hauled out of the line and ordered to redeploy in Kalmykia and plug that gap by advancing on Astrakhan, near the mouth of the Volga.

For men from Hanover, Westphalia and the Rhineland, Kalmykia – its people descended from Mongols who'd left their native land in present-day northwest China in the 14th century – was an alien land, its landscape African, its populace and their customs and religion Asian. Only its capital Elista, a 'city' of around 8,000 souls, possessed any trappings of Western civilisation: 'huge pink, sky blue or snow-white' government buildings – a cinema, theatre, railway station – jarred with the more typical Kalmyk mud huts. It was, one 23-year-old Berliner wrote, 'one of the strangest places I've ever got to know, a total surprise slap bang in the middle of the desert'. Camels pulling carts jostled for space in the streets – some fine avenues, others no better than tracks in the sand – with motor vehicles. Elista was 'a chaotic confusion of a past which has not yet been abandoned and a future summoned too soon'.[2]

Elista sits in the Yergeni hills, the boundary of the catchment areas of the Sea of Azov to the west, the Caspian Sea to the east. As the 16th Infantry pushed towards the latter along the 'highway' to Astrakhan, 200 miles away – its commander Sigfrid Henrici reckoned his men would cover the distance in a mere 36 hours – the green, undulating landscape began to give way to the vast Kalmyk steppe, an area the size of Hungary, extending as far as the southern outskirts of Stalingrad in the north, Astrakhan, the west bank of the Volga and its delta to the east, and the shores of the Caspian Sea and edge of the Caucasian foothills. This was a land of sand and dunes, as bleak as Libya or North Africa – with temperatures to match. The terrain was monotonous – 'sand, sand and yet more sand'. What roads and tracks existed were mostly mined, the defenders dug in among the dunes which straddled them. Settlements were few, clustered around wells, and often hidden behind a fog-like 'mist', sandstorms stirred by the near-constant strong east wind. Kurt Wendt remembered 'driving through clouds of sand for hours on end, nothing to see to your left or right but sand, steppe grass, roaming herds of sheep and camels, feeling the sand in your eyes, tasting it on your tongue'.[3] The division's operations officer, Kurt Ritter und Edler von Kienle, struggled to adjust to the topography of the steppe. Convinced there was a large settlement on the edge of a lake not marked on the charts, he sent off a reconnaissance unit to find it. A few hours later the scouts returned: they had found no such village, and wasted the afternoon chasing a mirage. Despite Henrici's predictions, it took four days to advance the 80 miles from Elista to Utta, the last substantial 'town' on the road to Astrakhan. From Utta – '15 clay huts, two wells, nothing more…'[4] – he continued east along the highway to the next village, Khulhuta. The road – and village – were showered with leaflets calling on the 34th Guards Rifle Division to surrender: 'We will take Stalingrad by bombing, we will enter Astrakhan playing the accordion.' Intelligence suggested that although the approaches to the city were well fortified, the morale of its defenders was poor.[5] The Red Army was thrown out of Khulhuta, but it was as far east as Henrici dared push his men. It became the easternmost border of the Third Reich.

Life for troops at Khulhuta mirrored the existence of their comrades dug in at Alamein (see Chapter 6). The men spent their days under the blazing sun, painstakingly and slowly developing their trenches, with only half a flask of salted coffee as their daily quota.[6] With no bushes or trees, finding wood to make a fire proved challenging, and the wind moving unimpeded over the undulating sand ensured the flames licked everywhere – except under the pans or canteens soldiers tried to heat. They were at least spared the plague of flies which dogged soldiers in North Africa, but the constant breeze blew the fine desert sand into every cup, on to every plate, such that every bite was accompanied by a crunch as teeth ground the grit.[7] The infantrymen were fascinated by the native populace: the Kalmyks lived a life as primitive as any people in Europe in the mid-20th century. Those who settled lived in single-room huts made entirely of mud. They slept on the bare ground, fur skins their only bedding. Nomads moved around in horse- or camel-drawn caravans. Life depended on the few wells and springs. There were no bushes or trees, so they had access to neither building material nor firewood. Dried dung acted as fuel, set alight using a flint and iron.

Kalmykia reminded Hans Doerr, chief-of-staff of LII Corps, of the adventure novels of Karl May. 'For a moment you forgot that there's Europe with civilisation and culture.'[8] 'The Kalmyks were still a little mistrustful when they saw German soldiers for the first time,' Kurt Wendt remembered. 'They shut themselves off from modernity.'[9] But, hostile to the Bolsheviks, the people of Kalmykia began to warm to their new masters. They began exchanging milk and butter for tobacco and tea and, as time passed, sharing information about wells, desert tracks and Soviet dispositions with the Germans.[10]

With his front stuck at Khulhuta, Sigfrid Henrici sought ways of outflanking the Soviet troops on the Elista–Astrakhan highway. In Utta, three long-range reconnaissance units commanded by energetic young leaders were formed to probe the Kalmyk steppe. Two – one under Fritz Euler, the other led by Walter Gottlieb – would head north, the third, commanded by Jürgen Schliep, would go south. Their mission: to locate Red Army forces, cut the north–south railway lines and, if possible, reach the shore of the Volga or Caspian Sea. The maps issued to the scouting parties were, Walter Gottlieb remembered with considerable understatement, 'not very good': the most detailed, 1:300,000. 'It looked like a map of the Sahara,' one officer recalled. 'A large area with a red line running from west to east for a road – in reality a primitive dirt road – parallel to it a few thin black lines and some perpendicular to it – a dirt track (in reality camel tracks, or paths for light vehicles in places through desert sand) and a few blue spots for salt water pans or wells.'[11]

Gottlieb's group – motorcycles, trucks and a couple of anti-tank guns – rolled out of Utta in the small hours of 13 September. Fritz Möbius remembered the advance:

> It's the crack of dawn. It's cold when we pull down our tents and the wind blows across the steppe with an unpleasant sharpness…
>
> In the ditches on the left and right [of the road], already half buried by sand, there's the Ivans' equipment: Ammunition pouches, gas masks, gas mask tubes and broken rifles. On our left, a sandy desert. The tops of the dunes almost shimmer white under the rising sun.
>
> We then turn to the northeast. Around 9am we enter a Kalmyk settlement. The curious inhabitants come up to us and stare in admiration at our vehicles. They're all small, stocky figures, but very strong and muscular. Their hair is jet black, the skin colour yellow rather than dark brown. Their faces are often covered with pockmarks. With their slit eyes, they smile at us and beg for tobacco. An old woman in particular stands out – she must have been at least 70 years old. She wears a fur cap, even though the thermometer shows it's at least 25° Celsius. Her slight frame is wrapped in shimmering dark-blue clothes, which almost reach as far as her ankles and is adorned with a lace collar which was once white. On her feet fur shoes and a pair of young girl's white socks. All in all, she presents such a strange sight, particularly when she holds out her claw-like hands for tobacco, that the men take photographs of her from every angle.

Twenty-four hours ahead of Fritz Euler, Walter Gottlieb's detachment advanced to within 25 miles of Astrakhan, navigating via long-winded negotiations with native

Kalmyks found clustered around every well. The men were close enough to observe thick black clouds of smoke rising from the city after the latest Luftwaffe raid – and close enough to the Volga to see its sparkling waters a dozen miles to the east. 'From high sand dunes one has an extensive view reaching the river. Sand and salt marshes make the terrain almost inaccessible,' Gottlieb reported. He turned around.[12]

The terrain south of the highway was no less barren as Jürgen Schliep found out. His foray relied on wells for success, the water vital not just for his men, but to cool the engines of his trucks in temperatures upwards of 40° Celsius. At the first watering hole, the Germans were warmly welcomed by the native Kalmyk population who informed Schliep he had missed Soviet cavalry by a matter of hours. The vehicles soon caught up with the Russians. Their fate is vague. Schliep was under strict instructions not to take any prisoners, but nor could he allow the enemy to escape and opened fire with his 2cm flak.

Over sand and steppe grass, the reconnaissance troop continued southeast into the wilderness, the motorcycles struggling to make headway as they rode over the fine sand. 'We could see the salt lakes glistening in the sun from far away,' Schliep recalled. 'In the past, when people talked about a mirage, I could never really imagine it. In the Kalmyk steppe I experienced it several times.' The men were ordered to wave, rather than shoot, at any Soviet aircraft which appeared. Thanks in part to using captured Red Army vehicles, the ruse worked, although without any radio contact with his headquarters, Jürgen Schliep was left with 'a somewhat uncomfortable feeling' advancing so far ahead of the rest of his division.

By the third day of the patrol, the group had reached the village of Zenzeli, 55 miles southwest of Astrakhan, and with it the railway line running north–south. Before long a goods train appeared from the direction of Baku, its petrol and oil tankers promptly shot up by Schliep's guns, resulting in 'an impressive firework display', while pioneers blew up the tracks to put the line out of action.

As Schliep pondered his next move – probably a thrust south along the line – his small group came under attack, first from the Red Army, then an Il-2 ground-attack aircraft. He shook both off with a wild drive into the steppe, but it was a sufficient scare to prompt his return to Utta. Out of radio contact with his masters, and with a long-range reconnaissance aircraft unable to locate the group, 16th Infantry Division's staff had feared the reconnaissance party was lost. Jürgen Schliep surprised them when he emerged from the steppe after three days, unscathed. He had not lost a single man or vehicle.[13]

The tentacles 16th Infantry Division extended through the Kalmyk steppe in mid-September marked the high-water mark of Hitler's bid for victory. Save a final lunge towards the capital of the Caucasus, Ordzhonikidze, at the beginning of November, never was Hitler's empire larger. The German soldier stood – albeit precariously – on the Volga in the centre of Stalingrad after three weeks of bitter fighting for the city. He stood on the northern shore of the Black Sea at Novorossiysk. He stood just 70 miles from Alexandria after a 350-mile advance through Cyrenaica in five breathless weeks spanning the end of May to the beginning of July when he put the British Eighth Army to flight. He had triumphed over the elements and raised the German ensign on Europe's highest mountain, Elbrus, in the central Caucasus. More than one million square miles of Soviet territory – including half of its farmland – and two in every five Soviet citizens were now under the rule of the swastika. A large map published in the Nazi Party mouthpiece *Völkischer Beobachter* as the war entered its fourth year reminded readers of the vast empire over which Germany and the Axis powers now presided. The newspaper went on to list the accomplishments of 1942 alone: the Soviet winter offensive 'smashed'; a 'successful' U-boat campaign off the eastern seaboard of the United States; the Crimea was now 'clear of the enemy'; the Mediterranean was 'dominated' by Axis forces; and in the East, the German Army's 'victorious advance' continued.[14] Ignoring the distances involved – well over 1,300 miles separated the Axis spearheads – Hitler and even some sober military commanders considered the possibility of the thrusts meeting somewhere on the African–Asian–European border and pushing on into Mesopotamia, depriving both the Soviet Union and Britain of their sources of oil.[15] As he embarked on the summer offensive to the Volga, confident panzer division officer Joachim Stempel was convinced 1942 would be the year of victory. 'Perhaps we'll even meet Marshal Rommel somewhere,' he mused. 'Over the Caucasus, Iran down to Syria, Arabia and into Egypt! Well, dreams!'[16] Paul Meixner, the naval officer in charge of logistics in North Africa, pictured the swastika flying over the Suez Canal, the Volga, the Caucasus as far as the Soviet–Turkish border. 'If we still succeed this summer, namely before the onset of winter, then 1942 has been very successful and justifies the highest hopes. Then we will not have "victored" ourselves closer to death – as the English reckon – rather we've achieved very, very tangible successes, secured food and oil supplies for an unlimited period and faced the English in their key positions.'[17]

If the German people were impressed by the successive victories, the frequent triumph of German arms, they were growing increasingly weary of rationing and never-ending restrictions and the ever-lengthening casualty lists – both at the front and at home, caused by ever-heavier British air raids. Above all, the always-listening ears of the security services found their fellow countrymen wished for peace, recording observations such as: 'Who thought after the tremendous successes at the beginning of the war that it would take such a course and last so long?' or 'How much longer will the war last? There's still no end in sight!'[18]

And therein lay the rub. However many countries Germany conquered or subdued, however many battles it won, however grave the losses its foes suffered, there was no *Endsieg* – final or ultimate victory. And it could not go on like this. The winter battles had demonstrated that the German Army was neither infallible nor invincible and that both the Soviet Union and the British Empire were far from beaten. Having needlessly declared war on the United States, Nazi Germany now faced a war on two fronts against three major powers. The balance of power was increasingly shifting in the Allies' favour. The summer campaigns of 1942 in North Africa and the Soviet Union offered the final throw of the dice, the *possibility* of victory – no more, whatever the bombastic pronouncements of Adolf Hitler in public or private – demanding superhuman efforts not just from the regular German soldier, the *Landser*, but his Italian, Romanian, Hungarian, Croatian and Slovakian allies. It would take an equally determined effort by the Allied powers to stop them.

Before there could be any thought of unleashing a second summer offensive in the Soviet Union, the German Army had to end the 1941 campaign.

1

UNFINISHED BUSINESS

Everything to come must be easier!

Dietrich von Choltitz

Shortly after dawn on 10 March, radio operator Max Lagoda was conducting final checks on a Junkers 88 at a Luftwaffe airbase outside the city of Nikolaev in Ukraine. The twin-engine aircraft was the newest and best bomber in the German Air Force, but the only payload Lagoda's machine carried was a camera. Stripped of bombs, the Junkers had been equipped with two fuel tanks, one beneath each wing, to increase the aircraft's range by 50 per cent. It would need it. Ahead lay a mission of more than 2,000 miles. The Junkers' crew – 22-year-old Lagoda plus two comrades – had been comprehensively briefed the previous day: cross the Black Sea to photograph the harbours at Sochi, Sukhumi, Poti and Batumi, then follow the railway line through Georgia to Tbilisi, eastwards to Baku, before turning north along the Caspian coast to Makhachkala. From there the aircraft would begin its long run for home via the Caucasus – the oil town of Grozny, the spa resort of Pyatigorsk, the towns of Mineralnye Vody and Armavir, and finally the great city of Rostov on the Don.

Over Batumi the Junkers encountered 'a true wall of flak' but came through unscathed. Jettisoning the external fuel tanks, the bomber climbed to its maximum altitude – more than 29,500 feet, higher than Everest – as it continued to the Georgian capital. The two Jumo engines struggled for oxygen but the 'propellers spun like clockwork'. The sky was clear – of clouds and foe. 'We assumed that here, far beyond the Caucasus, no-one expected a German aircraft,' Lagoda recalled as the Junkers passed over Tbilisi. Nevertheless, observers posted along the railway line to Baku sighted the solitary German and telephoned their reports such that the anti-aircraft guns in the port were ready when the Junkers appeared overhead. Again they could not harm Lagoda and his fellow aircrew, but the flak was sufficiently ferocious to force their aircraft to make several passes over Baku to photograph its airfields. Even from nearly 30,000 feet, Max Lagoda recognised the city's importance. He could clearly make out the oil wells pumping away – 'a tremendous resource which we had to take away from the Russians'. Half a dozen Soviet fighters scrambled to intercept – but could not reach the Junkers' altitude. At any rate, the Germans were well on their way to Makhachkala, 200 miles to the north. Once again the flak fired harmlessly. The aircrew observed tankers in harbour and also making their way through the Caspian Sea to Astrakhan at the head of the Volga delta. With no orders to follow them, the Junkers turned northwest, first towards Grozny and the heart of the regional oil industry, then over the Caucasian foothills to Mineralnye Vody and Armavir, following the main railway line through the northern Caucasus to Rostov, where there was lively traffic on both sides of the Don. Finally, the Junkers turned west on a 300-mile leg home to Nikolaev. The aircraft could begin descending, allowing crew to remove their oxygen masks and breathe normally below 10,000 feet. At 3.45pm, the Junkers touched down at its base and rolled to a stop on the standings, where a vehicle from the unit's photographic section was already waiting to take films for developing and then assessment. The crew reported to ground technicians about the machine's performance, then returned to their quarters where 'rewards' – extra rations – were waiting for them in recognition of the sortie's length: a bar of chocolate, cigarettes, milk and white bread.[1]

During its nine hours in the skies of the southern Soviet Union, the route of Max Lagoda's aircraft had encompassed a vast area, more than 100,000 square miles, and yet it was barely one third of the land Hitler sought to occupy through his summer offensive in 1942. Distant objectives such as Grozny and Baku, the shores of the Black and Caspian Seas, the peaks of the Caucasus, may have fired imaginations, but it was not cities, geographical features and land that the Nazi dictator wanted but the rich oilfields of the Caucasus.

Adolf Hitler looked south in 1942 not merely because he needed oil – in typically dramatic fashion he told his generals, 'If we don't get our hands on the oil of the Caucasus, the war will be over in three months and Germany will lose'[2] – but also because German arms could not attack in three directions as they had done the previous summer. Indeed, as the winter of 1941–42 drew to a close, many senior officers wondered whether the German Army could defend itself, let alone take the offensive. From the thousands of reports pouring daily into the army's operational headquarters – a sprawling collection of more than 200 concrete bunkers and wooden huts on the northwest shore of the Mauersee in East Prussia – from front-line units, staff officers had come to a bleak conclusion: three out of five of the 162 German divisions in Russia were barely able to defend themselves, while fewer than a dozen could be considered fit for offensive action.[3] Nearly 3,500 panzers and self-propelled guns had been lost since crossing the Soviet frontier. German industry could not keep pace; its army in Russia was short of more than 2,000 armoured vehicles as spring began, with just 140 working panzers along the entire front. There were shortages everywhere: rifles, machine-guns, anti-tank guns, field guns, howitzers. Only one in ten of the 75,000 vehicles lost had been replaced. A quarter of a million horses had died, leaving the army 160,000 animals short. The Luftwaffe too had been denuded, though Germany's factories had replaced more than three quarters of the 2,800 aircraft it had lost in the East to date. It embarked on the second year of the war roughly on an equal footing with its foe – though with 500 fewer machines than the previous summer and without a good 1,500 experienced aircrew.

And then there was the human element. The German Army suffered one million casualties in the East in the first nine months of campaigning, a quarter of them dead or captured – two in every 25 men who marched into Russia. Add the number of wounded, and one third of the Wehrmacht had become a casualty on the Eastern Front. At Hitler's headquarters deep in the forests of East Prussia, such losses were deemed 'within acceptable limits – and much lower than losses in the great battles of the World War'. Replacements had been sent from the Reich, but too few: 600,000 too few to be precise. Even the best infantry divisions were short of nearly 2,500 men; those which had suffered the most in the winter fighting lacked nearly 7,000.[4]

Numbers tell only half the story. The first year in the Soviet Union had cost the army some of its finest experienced officers and non-commissioned officers – men blooded in Spain, Poland, France and the Balkans. Those who were left were exhausted. Hermann Oehmichen, a staff officer sent to inspect troops involved in some of the most bitter fighting outside Moscow, found men completely apathetic and unable to carry or operate their weapons. Instead of fresh units confident of victory, he kept seeing the 'remnants of companies, miles apart, limping two by two, leaning on their rifles, their feet wrapped in rags. If you spoke to them, they didn't listen or started crying.'[5] In Gotthard Heinrici's Fourth Army, which had been driven back a good 80 miles from the gates of Moscow during the winter fighting, 'there is just a handful of troops who survived from 22 June until today,' the general conceded to his family in early May. 'For many, including me, the period between the beginning of the campaign and today was one continuous battle, without relief, without leave, without rest. There was nothing like it in World War 1.'[6] Oskar Munzel, commanding 6th Panzer Regiment near Kharkov, had come to a similar conclusion. 'Our army today is no longer the army of

22 June,' he confided in a friend on the General Staff in Berlin. The infantry were worn out, the panzers not the 'sharp sword' they had been the previous summer. Worse still was a widespread feeling in the regiment 'that the war with Russia was a mistake and that those at the top only realised it too late – or not at all.'[7] Refitting in rural Brittany, Horst Rocholl's unit was preparing to return to the East. It had spent the winter converting from the German Army's last cavalry to its newest panzer division, the 24th. 'The mood in which we'll go into battle this time will be different,' the 34-year-old doctor told his mother in Kassel. 'The feelings which drive every single one of us are not those of June 1941 – optimism and certainty that our arms would once again be victorious because they were always victorious – rather the determined necessity to do our duty even if it is extremely hard and bitter.' Rocholl and his comrades were under no illusions about the challenges facing them, nor did they shy from them. 'Today we know our enemy, we know the way he fights, we know how hard is the struggle which lies ahead of us. We will nevertheless go into the new struggle calmly because we're so firmly convinced that we must be victorious for the world must not sink into misery, our people must live if the lives of all of us are to have any meaning.'[8] Machine-gunner Hans König noticed a distinct change in the mood of the ranks of 295th Infantry Division, deployed in eastern Ukraine. One year before, the men had sung heartily as they trained in southern Poland: 'And spring has come again and you haven't heard my prayer' or 'Grey soldiers, in the howl of shells, have forgotten how to laugh.' After their experiences during the winter, the infantrymen no longer sang, König recalled, 'they just hummed occasionally'. Replacements arrived – 'men' of 16 or 17, or perhaps veterans who had recovered from their wounds. 'But the gaps were not yet closed.' At 20, Günther Köpke was one of 900 replacements the division received that spring. He didn't share the apprehension and misgivings of his more experienced comrades. 'Every day, we "newbies" and "youngsters" impatiently await the order to attack and advance in line with the old motto: Germany is victorious on all fronts.'[9]

The German people in the spring of 1942 were preoccupied by their day-to-day existence – *Alltag*. It had been the harshest winter in half a century in parts of the Reich. In Cologne heavy snowfalls had brought the city to a near halt in January and February – trains did not run, coal was not delivered, electricity usage was restricted, schools closed. Food, already strictly rationed, was in even shorter supply – meat especially.

The bitter weather merely compounded the gloom in Germany that winter. Russia had not been beaten – and the cost was already fearful. The *Völkischer*

Beobachter may have declared 'Stalin's winter war a complete failure', but the death notices in the newspapers – there were three every day in the principal journal of the charming university city of Freiburg – suggested otherwise. Some Freiburgers had died 'for Führer, people and Fatherland', others 'in the bitter struggle against Bolshevism'. Most were simply 'unforgettable' or 'beloved' sons, brothers, husbands. Such a toll, and such sentiments, were mirrored across Germany.

It was not the only long shadow cast over the Reich in the spring of 1942. The British bombing offensive had reached a new intensity; the devastation of the historic Hanseatic city of Lübeck on Palm Sunday had shaken Germans to the core. Rumours of 'enormous losses – hitherto unheard of' reached every corner of the land. Sixteen months earlier, Germany had threatened to *coventrieren* – 'coventrate' – British cities in the wake of the devastating raid on the Midlands city. Now London responded in kind. Its bombers would *lübecken* the Reich. The German people believed them. They looked to the coming summer 'with a great deal of anxiety', the agents of the Security Service noted as they surreptitiously monitored public opinion, 'because they assume this attack on Lübeck is merely the beginning of the continued, deliberate bombardment of other cities in the Reich'. In the days and weeks since, there had been heavy raids on Cologne, Hamburg, Dortmund, Essen, interspersed with lesser attacks, while a bold daylight strike at Augsburg, deep in Bavaria, provoked widespread shame. The city, after all, was the home of Messerschmitt. Perhaps even worse than the physical destruction wrought by the bombers was the emotional effect of the near-constant raids. Many of Cologne's inhabitants went to bed each night fully dressed, convinced the sirens would sound. 'Everybody is gradually going under,' the Swiss consul, Franz-Rudolf von Weiss, observed. 'Going to bed in the evening, you never know whether to put on your burial shroud' was a common quip in the city.

And yet, as von Weiss's compatriot Hans Gremminger, consul in Munich, noticed, with the advent of spring 'there was a certain change in mood'. Spring brought hope. But a *different* hope than that in 1941. 'There wasn't the distinct lift there was a year ago,' Gremminger reported. 'The tremendous, fateful struggle in Russia weighs ever more heavily on people.'[10]

In the industrial city of Stalino – today it has reverted to its historic name, Donetsk – nurse Ingeborg Ochsenknecht's 'heart stopped' at the first sight of spring flowers in the grounds of her military hospital. 'Several sisters sang with joy as they worked, the patients too suddenly seemed less ill,' she remembered. 'Nature had woken up and with it too the hopes of better chances for the German Army and for our soldiers. With a single act, there seemed to be a spirit of optimism everywhere.'[11]

It was a feeling shared by almost every German on the Eastern Front. They had overcome the very worst that the Soviets – and Nature – could throw at them. 'Once again we place all our faith and hope in this summer, knowing that the Russians will be completely finished off and face destruction,' one wrote home to his family. Spring in Ukraine was not like spring in Germany. True, the snow was gone. Soldiers working outside were bronzed by the sun. A warming wind was blowing across the land, gradually thawing and softening the soil – but not drying it out. The Russians called it *rasputitsa* – the season between the winter and the spring, when the roads were impassable. Germans, with typical soldiers' humour, called it 'Russki asphalt'. Vehicles sank to their axles on tracks and roads. Horses foamed at the mouth, sweated, shook as they struggled to pull carts. The mud spilled over the tops of boots, turning legs to hundredweights. 'And yet spring is here,' wrote one exhausted non-commissioned officer. 'And after it comes summer! The summer, which belongs to us!'[12]

Adolf Hitler certainly believed so. Propaganda Minister Joseph Goebbels found him filled with 'joy at the onrush of spring. He tells me that he has never awaited it with such fervour in his life.' For the Führer there was no question of consolidating Germany's position in Russia in 1942. His only considerations were where to strike and when. On 5 April – the day the *Völkischer Beobachter* proclaimed the Soviets' winter offensives had been 'a complete failure' – Hitler issued his latest directive for the conduct of the war, the 41st. The Red Army had all but bled itself white over the winter, he argued. Moscow was throwing men aged 50 or even 60 into the fray. All that the Reich needed to do was await better weather and allow the ground to dry out and once again 'superior German troops and their leadership' would 'seize the initiative and impose their will upon the enemy', destroying the enemy's armies and depriving them of the raw materials needed to power their war effort. First Germany would strike south and, having dealt the Soviet Union a mortal blow there, would switch attention to crushing Leningrad – besieged since September – and join forces with the Finns. The plan had been thrashed out the previous week when Hitler was closeted with Franz Halder, the highly strung Chief of the General Staff. German arms would push east to the city of Voronezh and follow the course of the River Don then on to the Volga, where they would meet forces advancing east from Rostov around the city of Stalingrad, trapping and smashing the Red Army in southern Russia. Then – and only then – would the main offensive be launched over the mountains to the Black and Caspian Seas, seizing the oilfields of the Caucasus. 'The Soviet Union would then feel its Adam's apple squeezed, so to speak.' Hitler called these 'limited goals', but the distances and spaces involved were vast: Voronezh was 100 miles from

German lines, the lower reaches of the Don more than 350. As for the strike south, the closest Black Sea ports of the Caucasus were still 200 miles distant, Baku more than 700 miles – and with Europe's highest mountain range standing in the way. Some senior officers – including Fedor von Bock, who would command the offensive initially – thought it beyond Germany's capacity. Others argued that 1942 should be used to consolidate the front, re-build and re-equip the army ready for the concerted onslaught by the Allied powers in 1943. And some, like Germany's intelligence chief Wilhelm Canaris, believed that there was now no hope of winning the war.[13]

If the summer campaign – originally codenamed *Siegfried*, but subsequently renamed *Blau* (Blue) – did succeed, it would probably cost three quarters of a million dead and wounded, but then, the Führer predicted, 'the war will have all but been won by us'. Before Germany could celebrate victory in the East, however, there was unfinished business to attend to. The winter battles had left gaps, salients and anomalies along the entire front. The north and centre of the Eastern Front had witnessed the most severe fighting, but the Soviets had made inroads in Ukraine and Crimea. Ambitious amphibious landings to relieve the besieged naval base of Sevastopol had ended in partial success – or partial failure; Sevastopol was still invested, and the liberating Soviet armies were bottled up east of the fortress city on the Kerch peninsula. South of Kharkov, the Red Army had forged a huge salient 50 miles or more wide which might serve as the springboard for future operations. It would have to be eliminated and the Crimea conquered ahead of *Blau*.[14]

After a winter of bitter fighting which only died down in the second week of April, the front in the eastern Crimea came to rest in the Parpach isthmus, a 12-mile-wide neck of land. To the east of the line, the Kerch peninsula, occupied by three Soviet armies – some 20 divisions and tank brigades, over 200,000 men in all. To the west, one German army, the Eleventh, torn between holding the Parpach front and keeping eight Soviet divisions in check in the other unconquered part of the Crimea, the fortress city and port of Sevastopol.

The army could spare just three divisions to hold the enemy at bay at Parpach, including the Bavarians and Sudeten Germans of the 46th Infantry Division in the centre of the line. At the turn of the year, the men of the 'leaping deer' division had – unjustly – 'forfeited their military honour' for withdrawing during the Red Army's Crimean counter-offensive. The division had quickly regained its honour thanks to its dogged resistance in the weeks since. To reservist officer Max Fuchs the Crimea was a land worth fighting for. A few days ago, the company commander had been granted leave to explore Yalta and the riviera in the spring sunshine. It had proved inspiring – Fuchs had visited parks and palaces, chief among them Livadia, from the days of the tsars. Fuchs, a forestry official before the war, was convinced that once conquered, the Crimea would be turned into a gigantic resort for the KdF – *Kraft durch Freude*, 'Strength through Joy', the Nazis' expansive tourism and leisure organisation. 'So much blood cannot have been spilled on the Crimea for us to entrust this beautiful land to other nationalities.'[15]

To re-take Kerch – German forces had captured the city in November 1941 then lost it the following month – the Eleventh Army under Erich von Manstein would have to overcome four lines of defences: the fortified front line, followed a couple of miles to the rear by the principal defensive obstacle, the Parpach line – a huge 35ft-wide anti-tank ditch running the width of the peninsula, watched over by numerous strongpoints, protected by barbed wire, minefields and steel barriers. The isthmus was littered with the burned-out and wrecked hulks of Soviet tanks, victims of the winter fighting, which now served as ideal nests for snipers. Further east lay a secondary defensive line and finally, 18 miles outside Kerch, an ancient rampart known as the Turkish or Tatar Wall. The Germans were outnumbered two to one in tanks and at least three to one in men. The Parpach line should have proved unassailable. Banners taunted the Germans: 'Come on, we're waiting!'[16]

To break the stalemate, Manstein used the same ploy which had brought Germany victory in the West two years before: strike the enemy at his weakest point, where he least expected it, in force. He selected the boggy ground by the Black Sea coast, a four-mile stretch of front held by two under-par units of Stepan Cherniak's Forty-Fourth Army, including the 63rd Mountain Rifle Division, whose morale was uncertain at best. At the same time as the direct onslaught, assault boats would put infantry and pioneers ashore behind the anti-tank ditch to take it from the rear. Under a protective umbrella of the Luftwaffe, 'the like of which has never existed', pioneers would bridge the gap, allowing a specially formed motorised battle group to race into the Soviet rear. The plan – given the codename *Trappenjagd* (Bustard Hunt) – was a gamble. It would be aided to a good degree by Soviet mistakes and shortcomings.

The troops of the Crimean Front were not the Soviet Union's elite. The winter battles had worn men and machines down. Supplies were spasmodic – everything came across the Kerch Strait separating the Crimea and the Caucasus. The Germans mined the waters. The Luftwaffe attacked shipping or the trains moving matériel to the front line. Fuel and food were in short supply: men sometimes ate the meat of dead or wounded horses, and drank from the peninsula's freshwater lakes. There was little wood not just for fires but for erecting barbed-wire fences, building positions and trenches – not that the men were particularly inclined to do so. Little thought was given to defence, only attack, as war correspondent Konstantin Simonov observed when he visited the front in late February. 'Everything forward, forward, forward!' was the watchword. 'It was like an incomprehensible and terrible mania, the likes of which I have never experienced before or since,' Simonov noted. There were too many men packed in the front lines 'senselessly bunched up'. But just half a dozen miles to the rear the journalist found 'neither troops nor anti-tank strongpoints, nor trenches nor artillery positions. Between the front and Kerch lay an almost deserted zone.' Konstantin Simonov left for Moscow at the beginning of March with 'a bad omen that things would come to an unfortunate end'.[17]

The attackers bore the expectations of the entire Reich. Clearing the Kerch peninsula was the German Army's first offensive of the year on the Eastern Front. After the setbacks and trials of the winter, much was expected of the ordinary German soldier, the *Landser*. Victory in the Crimea could set the tone for the possible triumph of German arms in the East in 1942. Company commander Erich Bärenfänger was itching to take the offensive again. 'The hard winter months have not worn us down, on the contrary, we've become the old hands and grown stronger,' he told his parents in Menden, near Dortmund. Having studied the plans, the terrain and his foe, the 27-year-old was convinced the impending attack would 'make the world sit up and listen. We'll inflict a second Dunkirk on the Russians... I've never been as confident during the fighting on the Crimea as I am now. We are strong again, well rested, and our faith in the Führer is our faith in victory.'[18]

As Thursday 7 May 1942 turned to Friday 8 May, the assault waves of 28th and 132nd Infantry Divisions moved forward to their jump-off positions. Some men ate their iron rations – meant to sustain them in the field for a few days; others talked. A few veterans managed to grab some fitful sleep. The line was filled not just with infantry, but artillery and mortar observers, pioneers, messengers, radio operators. The tips of cigarettes glowed in the darkness. One company commander in 49th Infantry Regiment eagerly awaited the moment of attack for it would bring 'release from the tension of waiting, but also overcoming all fears from previous defensive battles, where we had pressed ourselves into foxholes in mortal fear while the tank tracks of the T-34 ploughed through the position next to and behind us. Today it was our turn again.'[19]

Before dawn on Friday, a doctor with *Kampfgeschwader* 77 watched a succession of Heinkel He111 bombers take off from Kherson airfield in southern Ukraine for the hour-long flight to the Crimea. 'Finally, we're off again,' he recorded enthusiastically. 'I wouldn't like to be sitting in a Russian trench right now. It will also give our brave infantry a big lift when squadron after squadron flies behind enemy lines and drops 100,000 kilogrammes of bombs.'[20]

A few minutes later Heinz Topp found 20 Junkers Ju88 bombers lined up on the runway at Yevpatoria on the northern end of Kalimata Bay, ready for the first of five sorties they would carry out against Soviet defences at Parpach this day. The aircraft flew low over German positions to make a point to their infantry brothers then ran into heavy Soviet anti-aircraft fire as they continued over enemy lines, making for the Crimean Front's headquarters. 'It was a marvellous sight when all 20 aircraft were diving,' Topp told his brother. 'Everywhere there was smoke and fug after the attack. Nothing more could be seen of the village where the enemy headquarters were located.'[21]

A couple of minutes after sunrise, Manstein's artillery joined battle, the *Nebelwerfer* multiple rocket launchers howling as they spewed their projectiles at the Soviet lines. 'To our rear a never-ending ripple of flashes from the firing batteries,' one infantryman wrote. 'The earth shakes. The tremendous air pressure from the *Werfer* rounds has an oppressive effect on eardrums and lungs. Like giant balls of fire, rocket projectiles trailing a comet tail pass over us with a loud squeal. Our tension is released at this sight.' A German gunner was mesmerised by the 'tremendous magic' of 'fire-breathing rocket launchers, flares of all kinds, shells of every calibre' rising over his head. 'The planes hum in the air against the rising sun. The aircraft glow in the sunlight as if they were on fire. I haven't seen anything like it in the war.'[22]

Fifteen minutes into the bombardment, the assault troops moved out. They found the battlefield shrouded in mist. Mixed with the smoke from the shells, it reduced visibility to just 50 metres at times. The outlines of pioneers led the attackers through the gaps they had cleared in the Russian minefields. White flares – signalling the infantry to move forward – bathed the battlefield in a ghostly light.[23]

Just as Stepan Cherniak had predicted, the unreliable 63rd Mountain Rifle Division 'did not offer any resistance and a gap was torn in the front an hour after the beginning of the attack as it treacherously surrendered'.[24] Within another 30 minutes, supported by the mobile artillery of *Sturmgeschütze* assault guns, the attackers had a foothold on the eastern side of the Parpach Line. There they joined the pioneers and infantry ferried ashore nearly a mile behind the man-made ditch – with minimal losses – by a flotilla of small assault boats.

So far *Trappenjagd* was proceeding according to plan – for both sides. Soviet intelligence had predicted where Manstein would attack, that it would almost certainly be accompanied by overwhelming air support and possibly an amphibious landing. But it had glibly brushed the threat aside. 'The enemy will

Operation *Trappenjagd*: The German counter-offensive
on the Kerch peninsula, 8–17 May

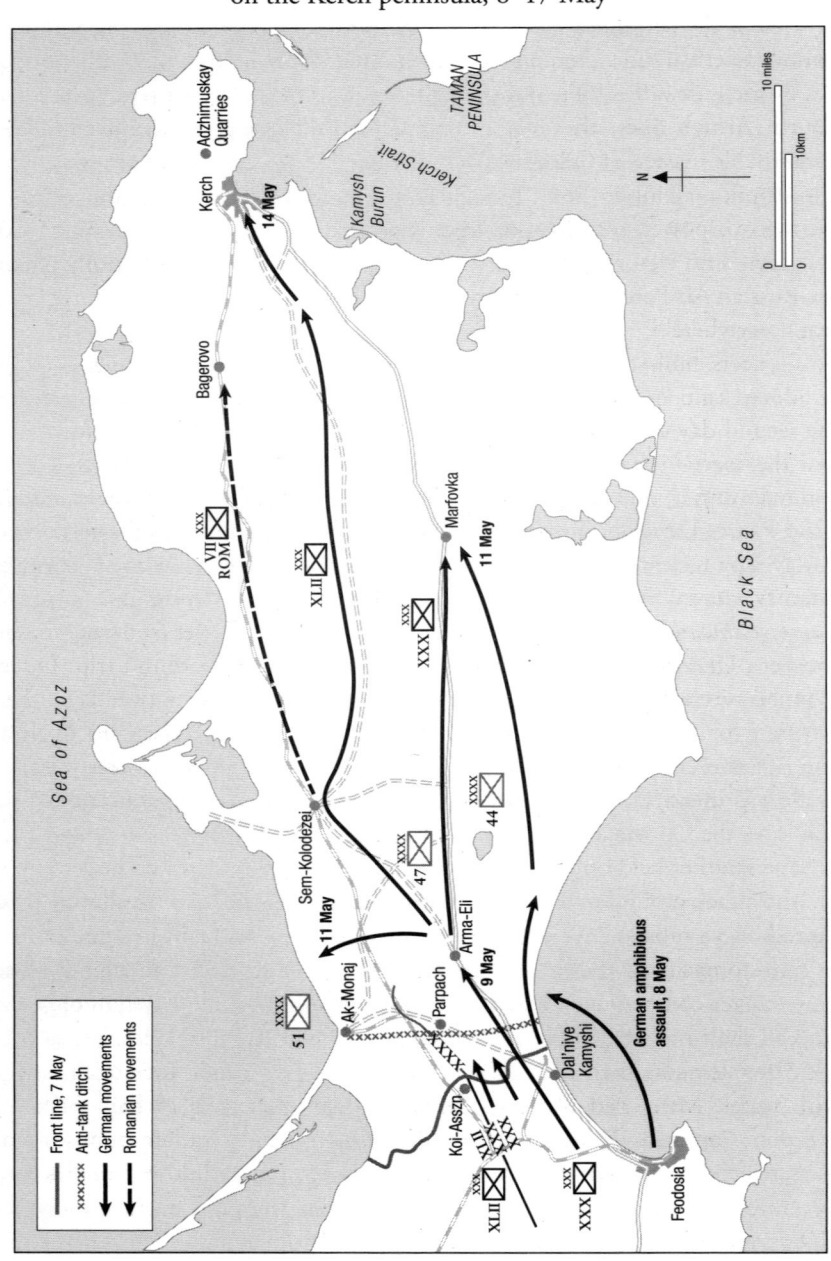

achieve success on the first day of his offensive,' the report declared, 'then they will be completely wiped out by our counter-attack.'

Except the counter-attack never came. When Cherniak tried to commit his armour to crush the German penetration, the tanks were systematically knocked out by the Luftwaffe. There were never fewer than 80 German aircraft over Forty-Fourth Army's lines, the general complained. 'The enemy was a completely unassailable master' of Crimean skies, he fumed. The Kerch peninsula was, wrote fighter pilot Heinrich Setz, 'ploughed up in the truest sense of the word' by German air power. Despite more than seven hours in the cockpit of his Me109, Setz scored no victories this day – but many of his comrades did, 'really picking the Russian Air Force to pieces'. By mid-day, the Red Army was 'streaming to the rear everywhere'.[25]

Pioneers built their bridge over the Parpach ditch, while other engineers bulldozed sand and soil into the enormous trench to fill it in. By late morning on the second day of the offensive, the Germans felt confident enough to commit first the specialist motorised unit, *Brigade Groddeck* – named after the colonel commanding it, one Karl-Albrecht von Groddeck – followed by the armour of 22nd Panzer Division. Both were through the Parpach line by mid-afternoon on 9 May, a path cleared for them once again by German aircraft. 'I don't believe the infantry have ever had such Luftwaffe support,' wrote a doctor in *Kampfgeschwader* 77, whose Heinkel bombers flew four sorties from their base in southern Ukraine this Saturday – each mission a 350-mile round trip. Indeed, German aircraft completed nearly 4,000 sorties on the first two days of the offensive for minimal losses. The man co-ordinating the massed assault, Wolfram von Richthofen – cousin of Great War 'ace' the Red Baron – was convinced the battle was already decided. 'As long as the weather doesn't hamper us, no Russian will leave the Crimea alive.'[26]

The weather held only until the late afternoon of 9 May, when heavy rain set in. The attack ground to a halt almost immediately as the brown-yellow clay soil turned into a morass. 'We were under fire up to our knees and in some cases up to our stomachs in the water and mud for two days and two nights,' Erich Bärenfänger complained. 'We could not lie down and could barely move at all. And all the time we had no food supplies.' Soldiers on both sides fought more with the elements than they did with each other. Trenches and foxholes filled with water. Men tried using spades and cooking utensils to bail them out. Weapons jammed. Runners could not bring up food or ammunition, nor messengers deliver reports. Radios failed in the damp conditions, vehicles could not move over the waterlogged ground and, when night fell, no man moved for it was impossible to get your bearings.[27]

When the ground dried out the next day, the Germans resumed the attack where it had stalled. Brigade Groddeck's ad hoc motorised troops smashed through the Turkish Wall with little difficulty, while 22nd Panzer Division made solid progress towards the Sea of Azov to cut off the thousands of troops still holding the front at Parpach. Realising their precarious position, the Soviets attempted to escape encirclement by retreating along the coastal road. Vehicles broke down, became stuck in the mud, or were shot up by regular low-level passes by Luftwaffe fighters. Artillery batteries were abandoned when they ran out of ammunition. It was more than some Soviet soldiers could endure. A gunner with 240th Artillery Regiment was astonished to see large numbers of enemy troops – perhaps two battalions strong – emerge from their foxholes and surrender. 'They are obviously happy and claim that only the commissars in their rear prevented them defecting earlier,' he wrote. 'They laugh, hug us, sometimes kiss our boots, want us to help them.' A few sharpshooters remained hidden, ready to take the fight to the enemy from behind. If captured, they faced summary execution. Most Red Army men fled. 'There was nothing but a mass of healthy and wounded soldiers streaming to the rear – a chaotic, disorganised torrent of soldiers from various units,' one official German report observed. 'No-one directed the retreat and German aircraft constantly disrupted it.' The Luftwaffe, the political officers of the three Soviet armies complained, 'basically bombed everything'. Their generals were the first to flee, leaving 'the wounded at road junctions where they were trampled – no help was rendered'. The fields of the eastern Crimea presented 'a dreadful sight,' one Romanian artilleryman wrote. 'Many burned tanks, people burned, dead horses, cars, destroyed carts, visions of [the] apocalypse.' War correspondent Felix Lützkendorf described it as 'a Soviet catastrophe. A hurricane of destruction has struck down anything which dared to resist it: heavy vehicles, tanks, guns with their carriages, have been whirled into the air by this hurricane like the lightest of toys.' Wolfram von Richthofen was ecstatic. 'They're fleeing, disintegrating,' he noted gleefully. 'Everyone's trying to save his skin.' They hoped to do so by reaching Kerch and somehow crossing the narrow strait to reach the apparent safety of the Caucasus.[28]

Few found salvation. Most found chaos and death. Kerch's naval commander, Alexandr Frolov – a rear admiral at just 39 and out of his depth – was 'seized by panic' while his men had abandoned the city for the hills surrounding it. Corps commander Mikhail Shapovalov was dispatched to restore order in the port. He established blocking units, their ranks ordered to shoot deserters and stragglers, but they were swept away by the avalanche of beaten soldiers – remnants of at least four divisions, each one abandoned by its commanders – making for the harbour.[29]

Among those stumbling around the city was Crimean Front's Lev Mekhlis, whose actions and interference had contributed to the disaster. The 53-year-old commissar had sought to place the blame for the collapse on the front's commander, Kozlov, almost from the moment Manstein unleashed his offensive. Neither man distinguished himself. Indeed, Stalin ordered another of his cronies, Semyon Budyonny to cross the Kerch Strait and take command as his generals on the spot had 'lost their heads'. Suitably admonished, Crimean Front's commanders tried to rally their men at the Turkish Wall, but the front had disintegrated. Forty-Seventh Army collapsed under relentless air attack. Communications broke down. Units broke down and splintered into scattered groups. Early on the evening of 14 May, with some German troops fighting in the outskirts of Kerch and some having bypassed the port to the north, Lev Mekhlis reported to Moscow that the game was up: 'Units are falling back without orders. There will be little evacuation of equipment and men. The command post is moving to Yenikale. We have disgraced the country and must be damned. We'll fight to the last man. The enemy air force has decided the outcome of the battle.' A few hours later, a furious Stalin reprimanded the Crimean Front once again. 'Kerch is not to surrender,' he demanded. 'Organise a defence along the lines of Sevastopol.'[30]

After the never-ending fanfares through the summer and autumn of 1941 which had ended with failure outside Moscow, Goebbels wondered whether to 'make a big fuss' over Kerch. In the end, he decided he should. The victory was 'tremendous – it far exceeds expectations'; the news would 'make a deep impression on the German people'. Announcing 40,000 prisoners, plus nearly 200 tanks, 600 guns and over 250 aircraft destroyed, Kerch was not merely a victory, but a signal to the world. 'Now the defenders have turned attackers and their first great thrust has led to complete success,' the *Völkischer Beobachter* declared. 'The German soldier has shown to the entire world that his attacking spirit is as alive as ever.' The German public reacted as Joseph Goebbels had hoped. 'Now we're advancing in the East again,' people said. They discussed the war – and especially the victory at Kerch – 'with enthusiasm not seen for a long time'.[31]

Victory was certain, but still the battle raged. German troops had reached Kerch on 14 May, but their first forays into the city were driven back under heavy fire both from houses and from Soviet gunboats in the bay which turned their main armament upon the town. War correspondent Felix Lützkendorf settled down for the night in a home on the outskirts and awaited reinforcements. 'Suddenly, the thunder of a huge detonation jolted us from our sleep,' he recalled.

'The air pressure lifted us up and threw us back to the ground. The whole house shook down to its foundations.' Window panes shattered and glass whirled around. A bright glow of fire flared up over the centre of Kerch. Grenades and shells exploded. White and green flares rose over the harbour. Machine-gun and rifle ammunition crackled. The noise was tremendous – 'like the roar of an enormous waterfall'. German artillery joined in this hellish concert, raining shells on the harbour. In time, the Germans would determine that the initial explosions were caused by the Russians blowing up their magazines and ammunition dumps. For now, Lützkendorf and his comrades sat on a garden wall 'and silently watched the monstrous spectacle of the burning and exploding city'.[32]

For the Red Army soldiers in the city, this was no spectacle. It was 'akin to being in hell'. One Russian pilot flew over a ten-mile stretch of the waterfront at Kerch and saw nothing but the detritus of a wrecked army and an assortment of small boats waiting just offshore to save them. Desperate soldiers jumped into the water and began swimming towards them. Others built makeshift rafts and attempted to paddle across the strait – but the current was against them and merely carried them into the arms of the Germans. Kerch was no Dunkirk. There was no organised evacuation: the weak-willed naval commander Alexandr Frolov had already crossed the narrows, along with many of Crimean Front's leaders. By night, at least, there was a slim hope of slipping away in a motley flotilla of small craft – naval launches and motor boats, tugs, barges, fishing vessels. But in daylight, escape was impossible. German artillery and the Luftwaffe rained shells and bombs down on Kerch's quays and jetties. The ferocious bombardment stripped the blossom off trees in the full bloom of spring and razed the fine villa selected for the port's future German harbourmaster. From a hill above the harbour, which offered a clear view both of Kerch and the far shore, Manstein watched Russian motor launches attempt to approach the beach to rescue their comrades, only to be driven off by withering German fire.[33] 'Left to their own devices,' corps commander Mikhail Shapovalov wrote, desperate Russian soldiers 'throw themselves into the water, build "ferries" from the wood that they happen to find or from car tyres. Without any permission they swim and no-one holds them back. There are thousands of such swimmers, heading to a certain death. The enemy opens terrible fire on them.'

Men quickly became indifferent to the fate of their comrades and de-sensitised to the horrors, as one Red Army officer observed walking around the harbour:

> One wounded man sits alongside a line of others. He has no hands and both his feet are injured. Someone steps over him, he's covered in dust, he's helpless, too tired to scream and he simply looks around dolefully so that someone might help him.

Beside him there's another man with his foot in plaster, both eyes damaged – the right eye is hanging on by a nerve thread, the other, the left one, stares blankly, it's full of blood. No, this is no longer an eye, but a strange, bloody red ball without a pupil.[34]

The Crimean Front's medics worked selflessly in appalling conditions to tend to such men on the piers and jetties as bombs and shells crashed around them, then accompanied patients on fishing boats and barges. Doctors and nurses stuffed their pockets with whatever surgical instruments they could lay their hands on, then ran the gauntlet of crossing the strait. Not only were most of the front's medical staff saved, but over 40,000 wounded – nearly 5,000 of them seriously injured – were ferried to the relative safety of the Taman peninsula.[35]

With the sea the sole hope of salvation, thousands of Red Army men trapped on the peninsula made a determined effort to bludgeon their way to the coast. East of Kerch they found the lines of 49th Infantry Regiment standing in their way, as one of its soldiers recalled: 'The Russians approached in dense brown masses. The machine-gun and rifle fire grew to a never-ending rattle. Individual bursts of fire or even shots were no longer distinguishable. We thought we were standing in a burning ammunition depot. Numerous wounded horses stood around or reared up repeatedly in their death throes.'

Another German soldier was astonished to see Soviet troops advancing 'calmly and evenly, as if on a field exercise'. The men of the 49th waited until the enemy was upon them, before opening fire at point-blank range. 'Despite the devastating effect of our machine guns in their ranks, the survivors continued the death march,' the infantryman recorded. The survivors attacked until the last man was gunned down. 'We breathed a sigh of relief but at the same time shuddered at the horror of the final hour.'[36]

When they realised that there would be no escape by sea, Red Army soldiers fought with the desperation of men 'with their backs to the wall', Joachim Senholdt of 22nd Panzer Division remembered. Soviet snipers in particular 'reaped a bloody harvest – men killed by shots to the head were being reported constantly'. Every beach, every headland, every strip of coast had to be cleared. In the few settlements, buildings were turned into makeshift fortresses whose defenders hurled Molotov cocktails at passing German armour. Senholdt's division was forced to abandon at least one assault on the lighthouse at the easternmost tip of the peninsula. 'It was a brutal fight, often hand-to-hand. The Red Army troops had nothing more to lose – most of them were certain their lives were at an end.' The lighthouse finally fell around 9am on 19 May.[37]

Other Soviet troops chose to continue the struggle from the quarries of Adzhimushkay, carved out of the limestone on the northeastern edge of Kerch over the past century. During the winter it had been turned into an underground barracks, complete with quarters, a hospital, a prison, an armoury, even a cinema, extending for hundreds of metres underground. At first the defenders – estimated to be 13,000 strong – resisted by day, on the surface, but as the ring around Adzhimushkay tightened, so they fell back to the bewildering network of caves and catacombs. Each night raiding parties would leave the quarry and seize food, weapons and ammunition. Any German soldier encountered was killed. Commissars and political leaders assured the men that their government would not abandon them, that the Red Army would return to Kerch as it had done in December, that the Germans would fall back. Slogans were painted on the cave walls: *Smert nemetskim okkupantam* – Death to the German occupier. They warned anyone who considered surrendering that they faced inhuman treatment at the hands of their captors. 'Every attempt by us to convince the Red commanders of the insanity of further resistance was answered with a blaze of fire and the murder of deserters and the wounded,' 42nd Infantry Regiment reported. Yet surrender they did. By early June, with food and water running low – some desperate men resorted to licking the chalk walls of the caves – nearly 9,000 officers and men had been rounded up. There were scores of entrances and exits, each systematically blown up by German pioneers, who placed more than 28 tonnes of explosive at points around the quarry complex. Poison gas was also pumped into the caves, with some success. After three weeks of clearing out the quarries, 42nd Infantry Regiment reported that 'an inhumane battle which was forced upon us moves towards its inglorious end for the enemy'. In fact, the last defenders of Adzhimushkay held out until 30 October. Of the original 13,000 men, there were just 48 alive.[38]

The German war machine had trumpeted victory at Kerch long before then. Its troops had reached the easternmost point in the Crimea at 9.15 on the morning of 19 May and immediately raised the swastika in triumph. It was sufficient for Erich von Manstein to declare the battle over. At a cost of fewer than 2,000 dead, he had defeated a Soviet force 250,000 men strong. Upwards of 30,000 of them lay dead on the Kerch peninsula. Another 170,000 had been taken prisoner.[39]

Despite the rapid victory, when he stood his ground at Kerch, the Russian soldier had 'fought for his life' – certainly more doggedly than in 1941, 28th Infantry Division reported. The fact that he had been beaten all the same was a good omen for the 'new fighting season... It shows that if they can be hit hard, the Russians can be dealt a devastating blow. The enormous success of the attack on the Kerch peninsula therefore allows us to look to the future course of the Russian campaign optimistically.'[40]

In Berlin, Joseph Goebbels had come to a similar conclusion – though with less magnanimity. 'The first great victory over the Soviet armies this year!' he celebrated in his diary. 'We breathe a sigh of relief and we feel as if our entire nation is breathing a sigh of relief too. And while we are breathing a sigh of relief, our enemies will have an apprehensive feeling.'[41]

No senior Soviet commander at Kerch escaped Stalin's fury in the aftermath of defeat. All were demoted and dismissed, condemned to spend the rest of the war in lesser roles, often on secondary fronts. But they were spared the kangaroo courts their predecessors faced for similar failures the previous summer. It proved of little consolation for Crimean Front's disgraced commander Dmitry Kozlov. 'My disgrace has lasted almost 25 years,' he told a friend shortly before his death in 1967. 'I very much regret that I did not lay down my head there. I would not have to listen to injustices and insults, for the dead do not suffer shame...'[42]

The dead were everywhere. The narrow waters and the headland were 'littered with corpses,' one Soviet report noted. 'A sweet smell of corpses hangs over the battlefield,' a soldier in 49th Infantry Regiment recalled, counting around 800 Russian dead in an area the size of about four football pitches. 'Some of those who were killed are blue-black; as if pumped up, they burst out of their uniforms. Others have already collapsed... There's one squashed into the ground. These were men who were worried about their wives and mothers somewhere; they will wait and never know where their men were.' Catholic priest Johannes Stelzenberger noted that battle-hardened veterans of his 28th Infantry Division were shocked by the sights at Kerch. 'Corpse after corpse lies on the beach and in the gorges. They lie on top of each other on the jetty. Were they hoping to be saved when they were hit by bombs and shells? How could the survivors hold out here, because the bloated and blue-black-looking dead must have been here for days?' Josef Hödl went to pay his respects to his 46th Infantry Division comrades killed on the peninsula the previous autumn. As he approached the cemetery, he noticed 'the foul, sweetish stench of decomposition. The Russians had dug up many of our comrades before they retreated. Desecration of corpses! Wild dogs had eaten the limbs and what was left was scattered over the terrain. Finally birds pecked at the decaying body parts lying all around. A gruesome sight!' Appalled, Hödl set about silently re-burying his comrades 'or what was left of them'. Fighter pilot Armin Köhler commandeered a staff car and drove to Kerch to inspect the havoc wrought by his *Jagdgeschwader* 77. He rather wished he hadn't. The road to the town was lined with the bodies of Russian soldiers which had already turned black in the May sun, as well as dead horses and shot-up tanks. The air was filled with the stench of pestilence, but it was sights at Yenikale, at the tip of the peninsula, which shook the 32-year-old to the core:

What the eye sees is indescribable. The ravines in the valley are a field of bits of equipment, people and animals. Russian cavalry was wiped out here. There are thousands of vehicles with their crews, destroyed, for kilometre after kilometre, vehicle after vehicle, all burned-out. Countless vehicles are completely shot-up, bits of vehicle are mixed up with the corpses of men and the carcasses of horses. We are only able to breathe through a damp cloth.

Hands, heads, feet, legs are lying around, burned, torn up, torn to pieces. Radio equipment, radios, records, electrical cars, tool trucks, ambulances with medicine, boxes from the typing pool, telephones, guns, quadruple machine-guns, equipment and clothes, sleeping blankets – chaos, all separated into their constituent parts. It's as if someone had cut them up into numerous parts then thrown everything on the ground. Scenes of misery on the beach and in the villages. Lord, what sort of people wanted this? They should be sent here, I believe, they'd soon lose their appetite for it.

The dead lie piled up on top of each other, tangled up, as far as where the landing stage runs into the sea. In the houses – dead, the streets are full of dead, dead on the vehicles and ships, the beach is strewn with the dead, the entire steep coast, which is full of caves, wherever you look: dead Russians. Men with half their heads, squashed skulls, swollen to the point that they are unrecognisable. And in the midst of them, the worst of all – those still alive! Wounded! They yell, moan, whimper. It tears at the heart. I don't know what was running through my mind, but I know one thing: war is mankind's most terrible evil. When I ask an infantry corporal why they've left the injured among the dead, he tells me: 'They'll all die a wretched death!' Twice they were asked by the Germans to surrender and they fought on each time. We too suffered heavy losses. In the water too there are a vast number of corpses which the sea washes on to the beach.[43]

The Bavarians of 46th Infantry Division had entered the ruins of Yenikale on the morning of 20 May. The town and surrounding terrain were 'littered with destroyed vehicles, guns, ammunition and equipment,' one corporal wrote. 'Countless *panje* carts and horses are lying around. It reminds us of Dunkirk. And everywhere countless corpses of Red Army soldiers. They give off a pervasive stench. We'd not expected so many dead Russians.' The division swept through Yenikale, searching every house, rounding up 'suspicious' civilians and the occasional Russian soldier in hiding. By mid-morning they were done. 'It's all over,' the corporal continued in his diary. 'German *Landsers* are standing all over the Kerch peninsula. We lie in the sun and take a rest until fresh orders arrive.'[44]

Three hundred miles to the north, the men of Sixth Army could only dream of such an idyll.

At 6.30 on the morning of Tuesday 12 May the guns of three Soviet armies opened up along a 15-mile front to the east of Kharkov. Forty minutes into the barrage, the Red Air Force joined battle, followed by infantry and tanks at 7.30am. The attackers made particularly rapid progress on their left wing, where the troops of 76th Rifle Division had crossed the Donets during the night, giving them a head start when the main offensive assault began. By the day's end, the spearhead was barely a dozen miles from Kharkov.[45] It boded well for Soviet fortunes in the summer of 1942.

Like Hitler, the winter ended for Joseph Stalin with much unfinished business to resolve. The Germans had been driven back by the succession of blows the Red Army had delivered since December, but they were not beaten, 'still less finished off'. Nevertheless, the Soviet leader or *vozhd* was convinced that 'the initiative is now in our hands' – and he intended to maintain the pressure. 'We can't stay on the defensive and do nothing until the Germans strike the first blow!' he told his generals. 'We must launch several pre-emptive strikes.'[46]

The Red Army in the spring of 1942 was not the sword Joseph Stalin believed it to be. In the first nine months of the war with Germany, it had suffered over six million casualties – more than half of them now prisoners in German hands. The group of armies – known collectively as a 'front' – defending the Moscow axis had effectively been destroyed twice in 1941. And yet there were still well over five million men under arms – for every two Axis soldiers on the Eastern Front, there were three Soviets facing them, achieved by ruthless mobilisation of the Soviet Union's manpower resources. The Germans estimated the Red Army could call on nearly 550 divisions or brigades, just shy of 60 of them armoured formations. It had made good the losses of 1941 and even had more than one million men in reserve, enough to form more than 70 new divisions and tank brigades. In raising them, however, training had been cut to a bare minimum, while the junior officer and non-commissioned officer cadres had been decimated, invariably pitchforked into battle before they had completed their education. Soviet factories – in many cases re-born, having been dismantled in the face of the advancing Germans, then reassembled beyond the Ural mountains – were producing war matériel at an impressive rate: upwards of 700 of the mainstay T-34 tank and 1,200 aircraft a month.[47] It remained to be seen if the Red Army's leaders knew how to exploit its numerical superiority.

The concept behind the counter-offensive at Kharkov was simple enough: two pincers would strike from bulges in the lines either side of the city, one driving westwards from a small salient to the east, the second driving north and west out of the much larger salient to the south. These pincers – the Northern and Southern Shock Groups – would meet, if all went well, around the fifth day somewhere west of Kharkov, liberating the city, trapping or smashing numerous German divisions and creating a huge dent in the enemy's lines from which to launch further thrusts westwards across Ukraine.

The attackers possessed more men – twice the number of infantry – more guns, mortars and aircraft than their opponent, and five tanks for every two German panzers. And yet none of the Soviet units was at full strength. They were sorely in need of vehicles, anti-tank guns, machine-guns, even rifles. They were not short of morale, however. 'We will fight and destroy the Fascist snakes until our land is purged of the Fascist occupiers,' one junior non-commissioned officer urged his comrades. His words echoed the May Day address by their leader when Joseph Stalin had called on his soldiers 'to smash the Fascist-German army and exterminate the German occupiers to a man'. The Red Army possessed the means to do so. The year 1942 would be that of 'the final rout of the Fascist-German troops and the liberation of Soviet soil from Hitler's scoundrels'. Dzhek Altausen was convinced the attack was the first of many which would deliver the Soviet Union a great victory. 'This summer will go down in history as the period of the greatest battles the world has ever seen,' he told his family. 'Much blood will be shed, many, very many difficulties will still have to be overcome, but victory is near, it is coming, it cannot fail to materialise.' In some units morale bordered on over-confidence. 'Now all we need to do is throw our helmets at the enemy.' But Fifty-Seventh Army's commander, Kuzma Podlas, warned a subordinate: 'Don't let yourself be tricked by such thoughts. The Fascists are still strong.'[48]

By 11 May, Marshal Semyon Timoshenko reported to Moscow that the troops under his command – more than three quarters of a million men – were ready to begin the offensive the next day. Behind the lines, the men were fed supper at 8pm before bedding down for the night at 9pm. Their commanders wanted them to get nine hours' sleep before the artillery barrage began. It was already light when 226th Rifle Division's commander Alexander Gorbatov rose at 4am and quietly headed to his forward observation post east of Kharkov. 'My deputy, Lieutenant Colonel Likhachev, reported that everything was ready. Watches were checked. Five minutes left before the artillery preparation...'

Among the German units facing the onslaught from the Soviets' northern pincer was 79th Infantry Division. Half an hour before the preparatory barrage was due to begin, a deserter crossed the Alsatians' lines, giving them sufficient time to

Operation *Fridericus*: The German counter-offensive south of Kharkov, 17–23 May

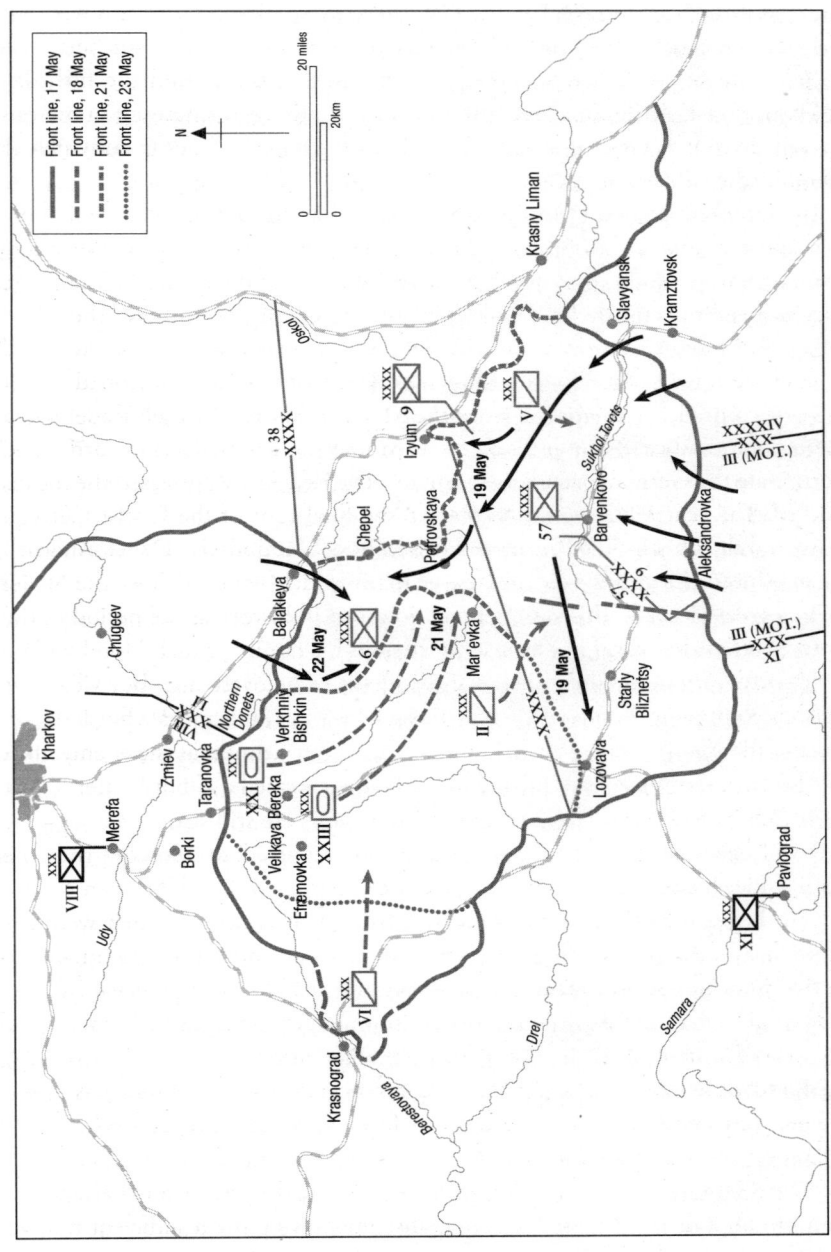

fall back from the primary positions. Otherwise, the forewarning availed them little. 'The hellish battle lasted about six or seven hours,' 22-year-old Joseph Schmitt wrote to his wife one month later. 'Shells were landing all around us, and some men were wounded at the very outset.' The men cowered in foxholes, cut off from any leaders – or orders. When Soviet armour appeared, a few outposts continued to hold out (one kept the attackers at bay for three days), but otherwise the Germans retreated – and did not stop. Schmitt's company fell back eight kilometres on the opening day of the offensive, while no Red Army division advanced further that Tuesday than Alexander Gorbatov's: a good six miles by nightfall.[49]

The southern pincer, bursting out of the salient anchored in the east at the town of Izyum which straddles the Donets, also made rapid headway initially. It smashed through thinly held German lines, such as 113th Infantry Division's, which faced two Soviet rifle divisions and elements of a cavalry corps. Faced with such overwhelming force, one artilleryman wrote, 'all our men could do was flee to escape Russian captivity. Every gun had to be left behind and was lost. And so we became a unit without weapons.'[50] Franz Gehrig's 530th Grenadier Regiment was driven out of its positions after firing every round of ammunition, leaving the 'road to Kharkov practically open to the Russians'. Yet to the company commander, his foe failed to press his advantage. 'We've as good as run out of ammunition and don't have any reserves,' he recorded in his diary. 'We were lucky that the enemy was lacking in courage, otherwise he would have advanced as far as Kharkov and could have held a parade.'[51]

Eight hundred miles away in the woodland of East Prussia, the Chief of the General Staff Franz Halder was untroubled by the enemy's attack, dismissing the gaps in the German front as mere 'blemishes', and forbidding the senior officer on the spot to fritter away his reserves plugging these gaps. 'We're not dealing with "blemishes" here,' army group commander Fedor von Bock snapped, perhaps with a degree of exaggeration – certainly with a good deal of frustration. 'Our existence is at stake.'[52]

The German lines east of Kharkov continued to crumble on 13 May – except in the town of Ternovaya, where the defenders were simply bypassed – until late in the morning. Franz Halder relented and released two of the panzer divisions held in reserve for an offensive to crush the Izyum salient. Coupled with German air power hastily diverted from operations in the Crimea, they blunted the assault by the Northern Shock Group. It got to within eight miles of Kharkov – but no further. Having pushed the Germans back no more than 15 miles along a 30-mile front, the northern offensive had largely run its course after just four days.

The Southern Shock Group struck with much less force than its northern counterpart, but it still punched a hole more than 20 miles wide in the German lines – then failed to exploit it. On 15 May, the entire German front southwest of Kharkov could have collapsed. Instead, the attackers seemed preoccupied with seizing the town of Krasnograd and the main railway line. A scratch force of Germans and Romanians plugged the gap. The opportunity went begging. By the fifth day, the Southern Shock Group's assault had ground to a halt. Worse, the Luftwaffe was now unleashed against the stalled Soviet forces. 'It dominates the skies and clobbers the enemy,' a relieved officer in 71st Infantry Division noted. 'Hundreds of [Russians] choose surrender as a way out to escape destruction.'[53]

Equally worrying as the failure of the offensive were growing reports from scouts and spies that the Germans were massing forces for a counter-stroke against the base of the Izyum salient, held by the Ninth and Fifty-Seventh Armies. When Fyodor Kharitonov, Ninth Army's commander, tried to warn Timoshenko, he was curtly dismissed. 'Do your job,' the marshal rebuked him. 'Or are you afraid, Comrade Kharitonov? Since when did you become timid?' Fifty-Seventh Army sent two teenage girls behind German lines. They returned having eavesdropped on enemy officers' conversations and reported that the Germans would launch a counter-attack within hours. Kuzma Podlas believed them. The staff of the Southern Front did not. 'This is fiction,' the front's senior commissar Leonid Korniets snapped, suggesting Podlas should be dismissed. 'Such "data" sows panic in the troops. I regard it as cowardice.'[54]

Moscow – still being fed overly optimistic reports by Timoshenko – deemed the time right to announce the 'victory' at Kharkov to the Soviet people. The Red Army had advanced three dozen miles in places, liberated 300 towns and villages, captured more than 1,200 German soldiers and killed ten times as many, as well as wiping out 400 panzers. 'The offensive,' the official communiqué concluded, 'continues.'[55]

At first light the next day, Sunday 17 May, a 45-mile stretch of the front south of Izyum rippled with flashes as the barrels of German guns hammered the Soviet Ninth Army. It was the first blow of Operation *Fridericus*, a strike by two corps into the flank of the southern salient aimed at cutting it off by reaching German lines 50 miles to the north, trapping the bulk of four Soviet armies in the process.

The attackers had been issued their iron rations – 300g of bread, 200g of canned meat, 150g of soup in tablet form and a sachet of *Ersatz* coffee granules – there were no field kitchens to serve hot meals, as the rising smoke might betray the German build-up. And they had been read a stirring order of the day from Ewald von Kleist, First Panzer Army's commander: 'We are on the eve of decisive days – decisive not only for our army group, which alone can redress a serious situation, but also for this summer's operations and, by the same token, for the entire campaign against the Soviets.'[56]

From dawn until last light the Luftwaffe dominated the skies over the salient – the Red Air Force reckoned its foe flew upwards of 1,000 sorties in support of Kleist's counter-stroke: bombers, Stukas, fighters, fighter-bombers. They struck at river crossings and troop concentrations. Even small groups of troops.[57] An officer in 257th Infantry Division watched as Stukas pummelled Soviet positions at the base of the neck on the southern salient. German infantry jumped up from their foxholes and advanced, accompanied by anti-aircraft guns which directed their 20mm barrels at enemy strongpoints. 'The first line of Russian positions was destroyed under a hail of bombs and shells,' the officer reported. 'Despite this, Soviet soldiers – those who survived all this hell – put up fierce resistance.' One battalion held out to the last man. The Germans found 450 dead Russians in its positions.[58]

Resistance this Sunday morning was sporadic at best. Many more units panicked at the sight of attacking German infantry and armour bearing down on them. At Ninth Army's headquarters, Fyodor Kharitonov was summoned to the radio by an anxious operator. Daniil Yegorov, the commander of 150th Rifle Division, was calling. 'I am involved in fierce fighting! There are up to 100 enemy tanks in the division's sector. I've suffered heavy losses. The combat units are being bombed by enemy aircraft.'[59] The official Soviet account talks of officers and men performing 'miracles of heroism'.[60] The Belgian Fascist volunteers of the *Légion Wallonie* were held up for 12 hours by Soviet troops doggedly holding on to one village – reduced to rubble by a Stuka raid. The enemy, the *Légion*'s future commander Léon Degrelle conceded, 'defended themselves with marvellous courage' before succumbing in the mid-afternoon to a concerted infantry and panzer attack. But in most places, the Russian lines had been broken by mid-morning. By mid-day, Fyodor Kharitonov no longer had full control of his army. And by nightfall, the Germans were 15 miles inside his lines – and pushing ever deeper. Pausing after their exertions during the day, the Belgians resumed their advance once night fell. Degrelle continued:

Large, burning haystacks lit up the hills as we slipped through the Russian minefields. Thousands of men advanced in this way, crawling along, since the bright flames drew sharp silhouettes. From time to time, a soldier hit a mine and was thrown in the air, torn to pieces. In the valley, artillery teams would be blown up – four or six horses at a time, along with their cannon.[61]

Semyon Timoshenko recognised both the threat and the objective of the German attack, demanding Moscow send reinforcements. But he refused to call off his offensive, convinced he could hold off the lunge into his southern flank *and* deliver a great victory at Kharkov. He could not. 'The advance stopped, staffs held one urgent meeting after another, liaison officers kept moving between neighbouring units,' gunner Lev Maidanik remembered. 'For the first time we could hear – whispered in the back of our minds – that ominous word: encirclement.' The battered Ninth Army rapidly disintegrated. Largely leaderless, it retreated in chaos towards the Donets, rear services compounding the chaos, their vehicles and carts becoming tangled up with the fighting units trying to reach the river's left bank. The river was in flood in many places, the few bridges were invariably unsuitable for armour and heavy military traffic, pontoon ferries were overwhelmed. Troops massed at crossing points, which became a magnet for German air attacks. 'Carts creaked,' remembered Nikolai Lyashchenko, the youthful commander of 106th Rifle Division – just turned 32.

> The wounded moaned, cursing the Nazis. Officers urged on their subordinates with hoarse voices. Infantry helped the gunners push the guns… And again, the Junkers bombed… The battalion's laundry and medical battalions were hit. The mass of men dashed towards the water with a heartbreaking scream, the wounded horses whinnied furiously. Wagons turned over, destroying everything in their path, horses gone mad ran along the gullies. It took a lot of time to restore at least some form of order and begin running a ferry using improvised means… Doctors ferried the wounded on a flat-bottomed boat which had appeared from nowhere and on rafts. Women swam, holding on to the logs. Officers and soldiers crossed the river. Everyone hurried to the other side. On a hillock, the shooting by the artillery, which had already fought one duel with enemy tanks, spurred everyone on. There was less chaotic screaming and noise.[62]

Ninth Army's commander Fyodor Kharitonov would be dismissed for his failure – and arrested for cowardice on the orders of Moscow, where Joseph Stalin was still insisting the enemy attack would falter. 'The Germans will soon be played out,' he assured Timoshenko.[63] They would not. The counter-stroke continued. On 22 May, the narrow neck of the Izyum salient was broken. Three Soviet armies were trapped.

Over the next six days, some 200,000 Russian soldiers tried to bludgeon their way out of a pocket three dozen miles wide and 60 deep. Salvation lay only in breaking through the corridor linking German forces north and south of Kharkov – initially a mere ten miles wide at its narrowest point around the small town of Chepel – assisted by their comrades in the east extending their hands across the Donets. Except that the breakouts and break-ins were never co-ordinated; most were blunt – sheer weight of numbers was seen as the key to success – invariably unsupported by air power, frequently unled and often unplanned.

At first there was some semblance of order in the pocket. Men retained their soldierly bearing, obeyed their officers and commissars. But companies, battalions, regiments, brigades, divisions became blurred, all too often troops grouped in an amorphous mass, hoping to bludgeon their way to freedom. Lev Maidanik, who'd fought with 131st Tank Brigade, joined around 1,000 troops from various units and branches – infantry, cavalry, mortar troops, gunners and tank crews – concentrating to break out in a huge, gently sloping field which extended beyond the horizon. 'There were cars, tractors, field and anti-aircraft guns, tanks, armour, mobile kitchens, carts and other vehicles everywhere,' he wrote. 'Despite our worries we still believed, wanted to believe, that our leadership would find a way out of the situation.'

There was nothing subtle about most attempts to break out of encirclement: the Russian troops merely charged the German lines head-on. It seemed to work. 'It became clear that people were breaking through,' Maidanik wrote.

> Even panzers got out of the way of the enraged mob, as German tank crews knew there would certainly be a soldier with an anti-tank grenade or a Molotov cocktail. The mob killed captured German machine gunners, taking very heavy casualties as usual. German soldiers knew all this and were justifiably afraid of the enraged masses, just as they were afraid of the frost, fighting at night, and forests, and just as we were afraid of being surrounded.

Yet all too often such breakouts foundered. The escaping Soviets failed to exploit their initial success. German troops rallied; reinforcements or scratch units were thrown in at the decisive moment to plug the gaps in the line. The Russians regrouped and attacked again. The tactics were the same, the men increasingly desperate. Often drunk, sometimes linking arms, they walked or ran towards German lines with the shrill cry of 'Urra!' ringing across the battlefield. Heinz Krapp's company of motorcyclists lost 56 men fending off 'utterly-desperate Russians – thousands upon thousands of them. They charged past us, drunk and bellowing like animals, running senselessly into the fire of our machine-guns. The dead lay there on top of each other in their thousands.' Machine-gunner Anton Hörmann and his 389th Infantry Division comrades held a night-time attempt to break out at bay. With every fifth round fired a tracer, it looked 'as if someone was swinging a glowing wire fence around to form waves'. Hörmann thought the sight 'wonderful', but he knew it also 'spread death a thousand times over'. The next morning a bulldozer was needed to clear a route through to the

389th's lines. It did so, leaving 'dead Russians in heaps by the side of the road'. Heinz Krapp's motorcyclists ambushed a breakout attempted by trucks carrying female soldiers which ran into machine-gun fire and were 'completely wiped out. The vehicles went up in flames. No-one escaped. Everyone, whether wounded or dead, burned. Hundreds of charred corpses were on the road next to the vehicles. A terrible sight!'[64]

By day, the Luftwaffe dominated the battlefield. Its aircraft struck at every crossing point, every troop concentration sighted, however small – some Russian accounts even claim enemy fighters chased individual soldiers. Lev Maidanik's 131st Armoured Brigade was caught redeploying on a 'dark green carpet' of steppe. Once the German aircraft had passed, the terrain 'looked as if it had been ploughed, with craters everywhere, black and grey,' Maidanik remembered. 'On the ground lay many corpses, some horribly disfigured, human body parts were mostly charred. Bloody pieces of clothing hung from the branches of bushes.' The Luftwaffe's intervention often tipped the balance of battle the Germans' way. After two days of holding off break-out attempts by 'Russians who enjoyed a tenfold superiority,' Alfred Rimmer was convinced the lines of his 64th Motorised Infantry Regiment could not withstand a third day of assaults with supplies of ammunition exhausted. 'All of us had already wished our lives goodbye,' he wrote. Then the Luftwaffe attacked, leaving 'dead everywhere and masses of booty'.[65]

Viennese doctor Josef Artner tried to set up his first-aid post as close to 384th Infantry Division's lines as he could. Speed, he reasoned, saved lives. But it also frequently put the lives of his men in danger. On at least one occasion, his unit found itself in no man's land, facing Russian soldiers who had come charging out of a wood screaming 'Urra!'

> We froze in horror, knowing that the war would soon be over for us in the most terrible way imaginable. We stretched out our hands once more and surrendered ourselves to our fate.
>
> Suddenly we heard tremendous gunfire behind us. Between us and the Russians there were numerous impacts in the earth and in the splintering rain of the German flak guns behind us, the attacking Red Army soldiers were simply mown down.

Kharkov was Artner's baptism of fire. 'I had never seen such terrible injuries,' he recalled.

> The injured were shouting for help everywhere. One man's arm had been torn off – it was two metres away from him – another's leg had been severed and

another's shoulder splintered. And then the horribly scarred faces! While you tried to bandage one, others bled to death in the deadly hail of splinters all around. It was hell. In many cases, you were better helping as a priest than a doctor.[66]

After intense fighting involving his 113th Infantry Division on the pocket's northwest perimeter, Karl Bühler, who had just celebrated his 30th birthday, told his family: 'I have to wonder why I am still among the living.' It was, he reasoned, 'more through luck than judgment'. During one attack a Russian shell landed next to his squad. 'The *Unteroffizier* lying on my left was killed instantly and half of the thigh of the man on my right was torn off... All I suffered were bruises.' Soviet soldier Dzhek Altausen assured his family he was invincible. 'You have to believe in life and fight for it until the last second. Rejoice that luck is by my side,' he told them. 'And I am convinced that it will be the same in the future. I wish you courage, live in hope and in faith in the glorious future that awaits our Motherland.'[67] It was his last letter home.

Lev Maidanik made his own luck. Hiding in a ravine after his failed attempt to break out, the tank man told himself: 'For me captivity means death...' He joined a group of soldiers who forced their way through to the Donets. The river was in flood in many places, its currents, eddies and whirlpools too much, even for the strongest swimmers who tried, but failed, to reach the left bank. But Lev Maidanik was in luck. He found a bridge which was still standing – despite a wall of horse cadavers which had built up against the pilings having been carried downstream by the floodwater. 'A few planks remained in place and from the centre onwards the bridge was practically intact,' Maidanik remembered. The men filed over it 'one after the other – a long chain of tired and emaciated warriors' and soon found themselves among comrades once more.[68]

The bloodletting could not last forever. The Russians were running out of time, space and men. The pocket had shrunk by two thirds in just a few days, while failure to break out quickly turned once-proud warriors into a defeated rabble, resigned to being taken prisoner, as Lev Maidanik observed. After failing to break out, many men discarded their weapons, some threw away their caps, even their belts. 'Stooping, they stare at their feet, as if looking for something on the ground,' Maidanik wrote. 'Everyone has a concentrated look, and everyone is silent. Only the sound of hobnail boots and boots hitting the ground can be heard.'

Clearing out the pocket wasn't merely a question of letting Russian soldiers batter themselves to death against the encircling wall. German panzer and infantry divisions exerted pressure on the trapped enemy armies from every direction. For Soviet units on the western perimeter such as 270th Rifle Division – perhaps 50 miles from salvation when the pocket was closed – there was little hope. Yet it fought bravely, its men ignoring the leaflets showered on them by the Luftwaffe which called on them to surrender, and continuing to press eastwards. They'd covered around one third of the distance to Izyum when German armour found them and began to literally steamroller the division, crushing its carts, trucks and vehicles in a 'terrible meat grinder'. After one unequal, increasingly desperate three-hour struggle for high ground overlooking one of the rivers furrowing the pocket, the last Russian defenders destroyed their secret documents and sent a final radio message: 'Fascists are surrounding our dugout. The shells have taken a heavy toll of them. There are few Germans left, but there are only two of us here. We are firing our last rounds of ammunition. Goodbye, dear comrades!'[69]

The fighting was as bitter in the villages and small towns as it was in the open terrain. Retreating Soviet troops invariably carried out a 'scorched earth' policy to leave nothing to their enemy. 'The Russians set fire to everything that could burn,' wrote Captain Dragan Jurak, a supply officer serving with a Croatian artillery unit fighting alongside the Germans. 'It's a method that's been used since the Napoleonic campaign.' And what the Red Army did not destroy, the Germans and their allies did. 16th Panzer Division sent panzers specially equipped with flamethrowers to root out troops trying to hide in any buildings. Houses burned. Knocked-out vehicles burned. Riderless horses galloped through the streets, sometimes dragging their dead masters in their stirrups. And yet, as Wolfgang Werthen observed, the enemy did not give in. 'From behind corners of houses and overturned vehicles, from hatches and cellar windows, the Russians were still fighting back, firing their carbines, throwing hand grenades, seized by hatred and the desire to fight,' he noted. Eventually, the Russian soldiers surrendered, waved 'passes' – propaganda leaflets dropped by the Luftwaffe calling on them to give up – asked their captors for cigarettes and were generally treated with suspicion by the Germans, who feared it was all an act and the prisoners actually wanted to kill their enemy. As the fighting died down, Werthen watched civilians cautiously emerge from their hiding places. 'An old woman stood in front of her burning house,' he wrote. 'As one of the flamethrower panzers rolled over her oven, she collapsed to her knees and beat her hands plaintively in front of her chest; her young daughter tried to comfort her.'[70]

The mountain infantry of 1st *Gebirgs* Division were thrown into the closing stages of the fighting to clean out the pocket, arriving at their positions on its southeastern edge along the River Bereka at mid-day on Whit Monday, 25 May.

Augsburger Albert Arnhard's breath was taken away by the scene before him beneath gathering storm clouds:

> ... a battlefield littered with destroyed or abandoned Russian military equipment such as trucks, tanks, carts, Stalin organs, guns and everything else. In addition, there is the roar of battle from every weapon. Guns crack like thunderstorms, but there's no rain, tanks burn like pans of pitch. The pressure of the encircled mass of the enemy can literally be felt, flowing and ebbing, wriggling like a big fish in a net.

The noise of battle was on a scale the mountain troops had never experienced before as the division's guns added to the tumult. Riderless horses galloped around the battlefield. German aircraft – so low that the brightly coloured sharks' mouths painted on the noses could clearly be seen – strafed anything Russian which moved. The enemy's attack faltered. Instead, a never-ending column of deserters and prisoners streamed past the mountain troops' positions to the rear. 'What we had before us,' Arnhard believed, 'was probably the last throw of the dice.' The fighting died down. The night was quiet.[71]

When the sun rose shortly after 4.30am on 26 May it heralded a day of battle like no other in the fields, woods and villages south of Kharkov. Late the previous evening, the remnants of Sixth and Fifty-Seventh Armies had moved out, heading southeast through 'terrain strewn with corpses'. Towards dawn Fifty-Seventh Army's group was somewhere near the small town of Stepok, about 20 miles west of Izyum, when it was attacked by 50 German aircraft. Men abandoned their vehicles and rushed temporary bridges thrown across a stream, or else sought shelter in one of the many ravines. Their commander, Kuzma Podlas, and his chief-of-staff, Andrei Anisov, were lost in the confusion. Their bodies were discovered a few days later by German troops. Attempting to hold off German machine-gunners, the two senior officers saved their last bullets for themselves. The Germans spent the rest of the day combing out the riverbank, rooting out at least 2,000 prisoners. Soviet Fifty-Seventh Army ceased to exist.[72]

Outside Chepel, Joachim Stempel's 14th Panzer Division found itself battered by relief attempts from the east. First came Soviet infantry – 'a mass of earth-brown figures' – sweeping westwards to break into the pocket and mown down in waves by artillery and machine-gun fire. Next came tanks, 'an armada of T-34s', approaching the division's lines, unfazed by Stukas plunging at them, hurling bombs and ploughing up the open ground with their cannon. 'It is unbelievable, the strain is indescribable!' Stempel wrote. Yet his comrades remained confident. 'Just let them come! We'll do it!' When the Russians came within range of 14th Panzer's armour, the tank crews opened fire. 'Hit! Hit! Hit! Unbelievable! Twelve T-34s are left burning amid a mass of tanks now driving around wildly! They burn in front of us like gigantic torches, standing out in red and black against the sky! The other Soviet tanks turn, turn around, try to reach the cover behind them. Our panzers follow and shoot!'

A few miles to the west, 1st *Gebirgs* Division found itself facing another mass of Russians, led by a cavalry charge, swarming towards its positions. Artillery cut down the galloping riders. The infantry, trucks and cars behind them did not follow. Once again, the Bavarians told themselves that perhaps now the fighting in the pocket really was over. They were sorely mistaken, for with twilight came the opening salvo of a fresh barrage – and a fresh attempt to break out. From his foxhole, Albert Arnhard watched a 'human avalanche' bypass his squad hiding on the edge of a hollow and simply crush his regiment's front line. The Russians seemed not to notice the 88mm flak guns turned against them, tearing gaps in their ranks. Trucks packed with troops – many of them drunk on vodka – stopped for nothing; even when the rear was ablaze with barrels of fuel exploding, sending jets of flame into the night, the driver in the cab continued 'rolling over their own dead and wounded'.[73]

After thwarting the attack on Kharkov from the east, 23rd Panzer Division had been diverted to help crush the ever-shrinking pocket south of the city. As its armour bore down from the north, scouts alarmingly reported: 'Masses of Russians in front!' Under remorseless defensive fire, the attacking Soviet troops quickly became a leaderless mob who abandoned hope of breaking out and instead tried to surrender – only for Russian guns to direct their barrels at their own lines. Junior officer Ernst Rebentisch watched as Russian shells 'tear huge gaps in the massed ranks of unarmed soldiers, who are thinking only of saving their skin by being captured. The barren meadows and fields are strewn with dead, with whimpering Red Army men crawling forwards, with weapons and equipment.' A short distance away from the fallen soldiers, their officers and commissars 'often huddled together in groups' and also dead, having taken their own lives. At dusk, massed Soviet infantry 'some of them drunk and unarmed' made a fresh attempt to smash through 23rd Panzer's positions. 'They were gunned down in rows, but still they advanced,' Rebentisch wrote.[74]

The fall of night also brought an end to 14th Panzer's intervention at Chepel. The Red Air Force joined battle, only to be knocked out of Ukraine's sky by Messerschmitt Me109 fighters. As the sun went down, the terrain was bathed in a flickering orange-yellow light from the fires of still-burning Soviet tanks, cottages and huts. Joachim Stempel and his comrades were exhilarated. 'This is a day of battle! Everyone is utterly enthralled!'[75]

The leftovers of Sixth Army reached the safety of Red Army lines in the small hours of 27 May. Just four tanks escaped encirclement, with several thousand exhausted but relieved soldiers – Soviet accounts claim 22,000, contemporary reports suggest just 3,000 men – trailing behind them.[76]

Darkness brought no relief to the mountain infantry. The night of 26–27 May was described by one officer as 'a hell of fire and fighting' which 'matched a natural catastrophe for its fury and wildness'. Wild screams and cries announced the coming onslaught. Under the flickering glow of flares, the Germans watched the Russians – the first rows arm in arm, mostly drunk – approaching their lines.[77] The assault on the senses – shells crashing, the trill sound of officers and commissars sounding whistles to spur the men on, the fires, the white signal flares arcing over the battlefield, the strings of tracer skipping over the ground at an unholy rate, the constant flicker on the horizon of artillery muzzle flashes – was too much for Albert Arnhard. After an hour of battle, with ammunition expended, with the regiment's rear lines overrun, he and a handful of comrades shared their last rounds, and awaited the end as they watched the outlines of a 'wild black mass' silhouetted against the flames advance towards their position.

They never reached it. Arnhard's small group was saved by the sudden, unexpected appearance of machine-gunners, freshly supplied with ammunition. The Russians were scythed down. Cries of 'Urra!' turned to moans and whimpers. 'They're crawling towards us, one by one,' the mountain troops celebrated – as they picked off the wounded enemy. And in the middle of these horrors 'individual horses stand like silhouettes in the red night,' Arnhard noted. 'Calmly, as if stunned, they look around, try to graze, and collapse.'

But the breakout had passed its climax. Fighting would continue throughout the night, but with less intensity. When dawn came on 27 May, all that was left in front of 1st *Gebirgs* Division's lines were dead Russians and drunken Red Army troops stumbling among the bodies.[78] Hubert Lanz, the division's commander, could remember 'no comparable sight' in two world wars. 'Dead Soviet soldiers lay literally in heaps.' Lanz was filled 'with a certain pride' at his men's hard-fought victory – and filled with horror at the sight of their corpses 'with their skulls smashed in or unrecognisable'.[79]

Both sides would claim the other butchered the wounded, killed and mutilated prisoners in the Kharkov pocket. The fighting repeatedly degenerated into hand-to-hand combat. Men grabbed whatever weapon they could lay their hands on: spades, rifle butts, grenades. Doctor Josef Artner wandered past a German strongpoint which had been overrun by the Soviets. 'A scene of horror presented itself,' he recalled. 'Corpses, mutilated beyond recognition with bayonets, skulls split, faces trampled.' Drunken Russian soldiers seized outposts held by infantry accompanying 23rd Panzer Division; the defenders were 'beaten to death with spades' after they had surrendered.[80]

But there were also instances when Soviet and German soldiers went beyond what might be called 'the fury of battle'. Infantryman Anton Hörmann watched the crew of a knocked-out panzer escaping their burning vehicle, only to be shot dead; given their encirclement, the desperate Russians could not take prisoners. And Ivan Chilyushin, serving with a Red Army reconnaissance unit, came across the charred corpses of three Soviet tank crew, tied up with telephone cable, plus several bodies stabbed and mutilated, their skulls smashed in. 'Here is a crime the soldiers of my unit cannot forgive the Germans or forget until their last breath,' Chilyushin seethed. 'We will take revenge, revenge until we destroy all of them to the bitter end, when we completely destroy Hitlerism.'[81]

In late May 1942 that seemed a distant dream. The exhortations of Stalin – the call for victory in 1942, 'the final rout of the Fascist-German troops and the liberation of Soviet soil' – the confidence of officers convinced all they had to do was hurl their helmets at the invader and he would retreat, died with thousands of Red Army soldiers in the plains, woods and river valleys around Kharkov. When the battle finally petered out in the closing days of the month, one in three of the 750,000 Russian soldiers who had begun the offensive on 12 May was a casualty. Nearly 30 rifle and cavalry divisions had been destroyed, alongside more than a dozen Soviet armoured brigades and a good 1,200 tanks. Some 170,000 Red Army men were killed or captured by the Germans; just 22,000 escaped from the Izyum pocket – roughly equivalent to German losses in the entire battle. Having reported to their captors, where commissars and officers were separated from the rank and file, most prisoners lay down on the grass and fell asleep. 'I found their behaviour strange,' Romanian officer Gheorghe Avram remembered. 'Many had torn off their epaulettes and ranks, displayed a degrading humility to the victors, swore and denounced their commanders and especially the commissars.'[82]

No man who fought at Kharkov would ever forget it. 'History has never seen such a battlefield,' staff officer Helmuth Groscurth told his brother. The fields southeast of Kharkov had been turned into a 'graveyard of tanks – burned and torn apart by anti-tank shells,' Gheorghe Avram, commanding a platoon of Romanian infantry, recalled. There were 'tank crew burned in open turrets, heaps of infantrymen who fell in rows as they attacked, huge craters caused by explosions large enough to swallow a peasants' hut whole'. It wasn't real, Avram convinced himself. It was all some macabre film. Croatian junior officer Dragan Jurak 'could have never imagined seeing so many dead people in one place'. But that was only the beginning of the horrors. The pocket presented 'an image of desolation invoking a feeling of dread, an image one never forgets'. He continued:

> I have seen destroyed houses, roads and ditches and fields of green wheat trampled into the ground, many broken carts, car wrecks, broken machine-guns and guns of all types, mortar tubes everywhere; parts of clothing and footwear and other war matériel; remains of archives, the papers being carried through the air over the fields and ditches by the wind. There lay huge, destroyed tanks, like slain monsters, destroyed tractors and all this mixed with multitudes of dead people and dead horses.[83]

In the heat of late May – daytime temperatures now regularly topped 20°C – those cadavers blackened in the sun, bloated, eviscerated bodies gave off a sickening sweet smell, noticed even by those who flew over the battlefield, such as 21-year-old fighter ace Walter Krupinski. 'We could see hundreds of horses still lying there for days,' he recalled, 'and in the cockpit we could even smell the stench from the carcasses.' The ground was littered with cadavers 'as far as the eye can see,' First Panzer Army's commander Ewald von Kleist reported. There was no path through them – only over them, as Paul-Hans Voss's signals unit found. 'Corpses, mountains of corpses for miles on end,' he wrote. 'We drive over them, there is no other way. We just can't get the many dead out of the way. It's horrible: death, blood and destruction, annihilation everywhere… Whenever I fall asleep for a moment, I see dead people. Torn, twisted, dismembered corpses. Burned, shrunk to the size of a child.'

Joachim Stempel was haunted by many sights: a Russian soldier walking around with no lower jaw, another who had lost both eyes, a third dressed in only his underpants, shot at least three times yet somehow still standing. The Kharkov pocket was, the 22-year-old told his father, General Richard Stempel, commanding the 371st Infantry Division, 'a scene of horror!' And one Soviet battalion commander said simply: 'It is impossible to describe this hell – only those who have experienced it themselves will understand and believe.'[84]

In many respects, Kharkov was in reality the 'last battle of 1941'. It mirrored the great battles of encirclement the previous summer and autumn. 'The situation at the front is the same as it was at the beginning,' one Russian cavalryman fumed. 'People are being thrown to the lions, turned into cannon fodder, and there are no results…' The commander of a Red Army artillery regiment complained: 'If we continue to fight like this, we'll kill all our men and still not achieve success.' Many Germans shared their enemy's bleak assessment. 'Nothing has changed since the beginning of the war,' 3rd Panzer Division concluded after the battle. 'The Russians are fighting with manpower and are achieving success at the expense of colossal casualties.' Tank commander Ernst-Alexander Paulus told his father Friedrich, in charge of Sixth Army, which had been so sorely tested in the opening days of the Soviet offensive, that the battlefield was littered with wrecked enemy tanks. 'The Russian command has no idea how to use them competently.' But III Panzer Corps' commander Eberhard von Mackensen was not so dismissive. His foe was 'more fanatical, more ruthless and more united' than in 1941. 'The Red Army risks everything. It takes clear decisions on a grand scale and commits everything to attain these ends. In carrying out these decisions, the leadership and troops follow them far more than last year. The Red tank arm and cavalry show guts and a will to fight to the point of destruction.' German victory at Kharkov, he reported, 'was achieved at the last breath'.[85]

For Joseph Stalin, defeat at Kharkov was a 'catastrophe' on a par with the devastating blows inflicted on the Russian Army a quarter of a century before in East Prussia. Semyon Timoshenko – unfairly – laid the blame squarely at the door of the unfortunate Fyodor Kharitonov, whose warnings had been ignored and whose Ninth Army had been all but wiped out – casualties of more than 30,000 – by the German counter-stroke. He was not merely dismissed, but arrested for cowardice on Moscow's orders.[86] Much of the responsibility for the defeat rests with Timoshenko himself, a man promoted beyond his abilities, who missed opportunities, misled Moscow and ignored or overruled subordinates. Stalin tolerated his friend's shortcomings, but his patience was wearing thin. 'Maybe the time has come for you to wage war by losing less blood, as the Germans are doing,' he told the flailing marshal. 'If you won't learn how to fight better, all the armaments produced in our whole country won't be enough for you.'[87]

Kerch and Kharkov. Only Sevastopol remained to be cleared up before the Germans unleashed their summer offensive.

Hailed by both sides as the strongest fortress in the world, Sevastopol had served as Russia's principal naval base and home of the Black Sea Fleet for more than 150 years. It had been left in ruins after an 11-month siege during the Crimean War, which ended with the city in enemy hands and what was left of the fleet scuttled in harbour. Its ordeal nine decades later began on the opening day of the war in the East when it was bombed by the Luftwaffe. It was the beginning of November before German troops made their first attempt to seize the city in a failed *coup de main*. Conventional attempts proved no more successful. A hastily prepared offensive in mid-November 1941 was easily parried by the defenders. A more concerted effort was made one month later courtesy of an assault which was better planned but with attacking forces which were still far too weak. When it was finally called off after a fortnight – the troops were needed elsewhere in the Crimea to deal with the Soviets' amphibious landings – the Germans had suffered nearly 9,000 casualties and barely dented Sevastopol's defences.

And there, more or less, the front remained for the next five months, wending its way in a rough semi-circle for 21 miles from Belbek in the north to Balaklava in the south. The terrain – hills, cliffs, escarpments, ravines and gorges, caves, plateaux and steep-sided valleys – was 'made for defence', war correspondent Theo Janssen observed. The rocky ground made digging in difficult – but it also made trenches and earthen fortifications invulnerable to all but the heaviest fire. Fritz Lindemann, commanding 132nd Infantry Division, likened the battlefield to Verdun a generation earlier, 'except that it's all on rocky ground, plus steep crags and grotesque rock faces which are impossible to climb. Elsewhere there's scrubland stretching for up to ten kilometres, impenetrable apart from the few paths.' As one German soldier remarked, 'it was almost as if the devil had created the terrain'.[88]

Man added to the natural obstacles by digging anti-tank ditches and barriers, unrolling barbed wire and laying around 150,000 mines. There were more than 200 miles of trenches linking some 3,600 concrete and earth bunkers and gun positions. And above all, there were 20 or so major fortifications, fortifications from 19th-century brick batteries to the most modern, Maginot Line-esque underground fortresses armed with heavy naval guns and protected by the thickest armour.[89]

The Soviet command split the defensive zone into four sectors, numbered anti-clockwise from I in the south to IV holding the front at Belbek. It entrusted them to Admiral Filipp Oktyabrsky, commander of the Sevastopol Defence Region, and the Primorsky (Coastal) Army of Ivan Petrov, a mishmash of soldiers, sailors from sunken ships and naval infantry, some 90,000 men in total, all but 20,000 of them in the fighting units. What the defenders lacked was hardware. When Sevastopol's factories were combed for men who could bear arms to form workers' units, they were equipped with 'any weapon found' – often five grenades each, hunting rifles or blades. There were fewer than 50 tanks in the fortress – and one in five was out of action. Although there were around 600 artillery pieces along the front, ammunition was in short supply. Air power could not compensate – there were only 115 aircraft covering the Sevastopol sector.[90]

Investing the city was the Eleventh Army, seven German and two Romanian divisions led by the ablest of the Wehrmacht's generals, Erich von Manstein. Many of his units were still understrength after the 1941 campaign and fighting over the winter, but in every respect the Axis forces still enjoyed a superiority over their opponent: nearly two to one in men, a marked advantage in artillery – nearly

800 pieces distributed among more than 200 batteries – and a sixfold superiority in the skies.

With the advent of spring at Sevastopol, nature came back to life. Under the warm Crimean sun, the barren scrub was quickly covered with grass; trees and bushes were green with leaves. The sun shone more brightly in the cloudless sky, and a warm, shimmering haze hung above the soldiers in the trenches. After months in the line, Werner Hofmann's company was given a few days' leave in an 'idyllic mountain village' inhabited by Tatars hostile to the Soviet regime. The men drank real, not *Ersatz* coffee, enjoyed cakes, figs, schnapps, and in the evening sang soldiers' tunes accompanied by an accordion, while local girls performed folk songs played on guitars. Even those in the trenches appreciated the advent of spring, observed Ivan Laskin, commanding the largely untested 172nd Rifle Division. 'They began to emerge from their dugouts and trenches more often, met each other more frequently, shared memories of home, brides and wives. Jokes, the colourful language of soldiers, and laughter were often heard.' And although every unit was understrength and ammunition limited, Soviet morale was evidently good – 132nd Infantry Division did not record a single deserter crossing its lines since the beginning of May. Nor did the defenders show any signs of attempting to break out. Mentally and physically they were prepared to hold the fortress, although the catastrophic defeat at Kerch had shaken them. The landings on the peninsula over the winter should have been the catalyst for Sevastopol's relief. Any hope of lifting the siege had been shattered. After Kerch, the defenders of Sevastopol knew that they were next.[91]

The final chapter in the long siege of Sevastopol – Operation *Störfang* (Sturgeon Trap) – began at first light on Tuesday 2 June, as Manstein's guns cleared their throats. Never before had the Germans concentrated such a preponderance of artillery: upwards of 800 pieces, plus another 100 Romanian guns. Over the next five days, nearly 2,500 tonnes of shells would rain on the city, systematically hammering every known defensive position – each one given a specific number by the gunners directing the bombardment. As the first shells impacted, the Luftwaffe appeared over Sevastopol. With the fighting at Kharkov now over, Wolfram von Richthofen was able to throw more than 700 machines – predominantly bombers and dive-bombers – at the city, especially the barracks and quarters supposedly occupied by the defenders. To bomber pilot Werner Baumbach, 'from the air Sevastopol looked like a painter's battle panorama', but accompanied by a cacophonous soundtrack. 'The screaming descent of the Stukas and the whistling of falling bombs seemed to make even Nature hold her breath.' The soldiers of 50th Infantry Division watched 'with terrified joy' as the 102 artillery barrels deployed along their front began 'spitting fire with a terrible fury'. Great War

Operation *Störfang*: The fall of Sevastopol, June–July

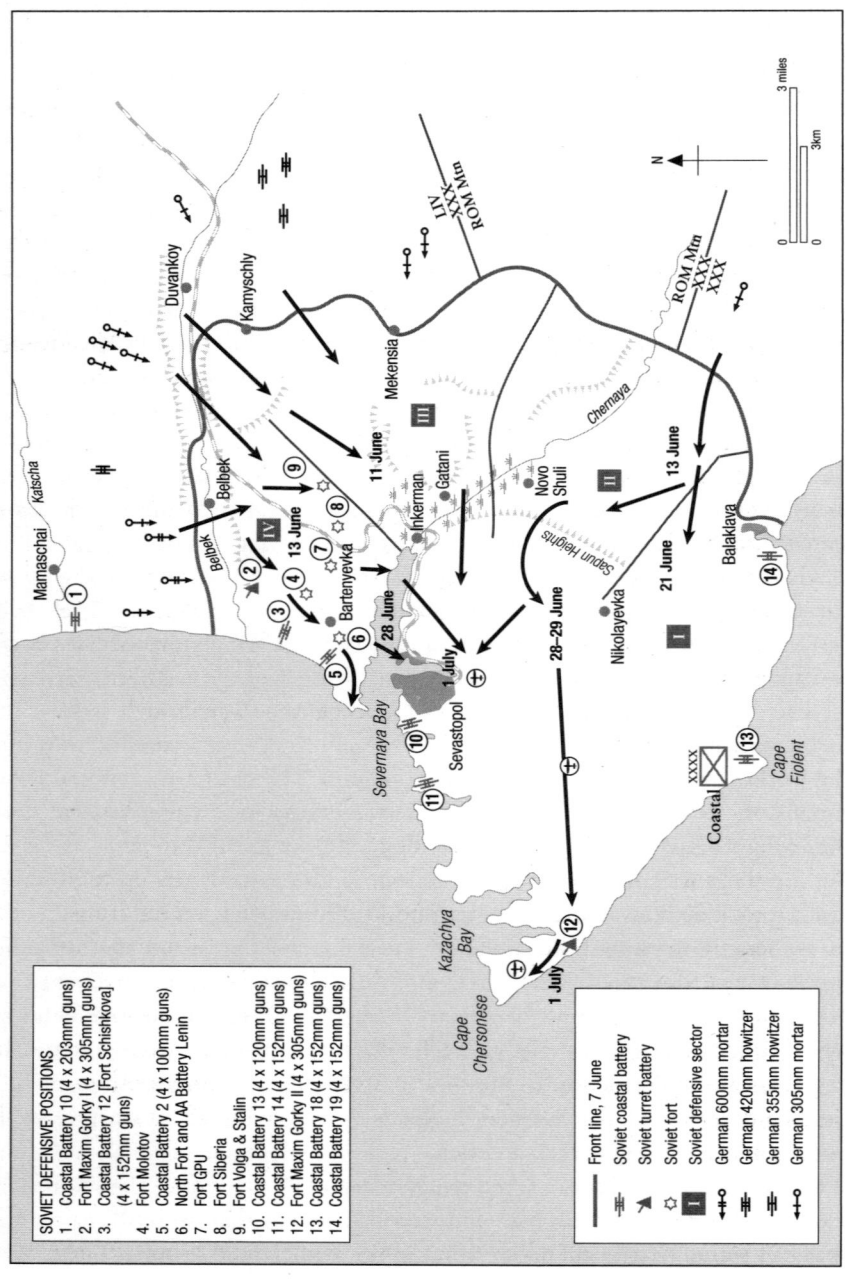

SOVIET DEFENSIVE POSITIONS
1. Coastal Battery 10 (4 x 203mm guns)
2. Fort Maxim Gorky I (4 x 305mm guns)
3. Coastal Battery 12 [Fort Schishkova]
    (4 x 152mm guns)
4. Fort Molotov
5. Coastal Battery 2 (4 x 100mm guns)
6. North Fort and AA Battery Lenin
7. Fort GPU
8. Fort Siberia
9. Fort Volga & Stalin
10. Coastal Battery 13 (4 x 120mm guns)
11. Coastal Battery 14 (4 x 152mm guns)
12. Fort Maxim Gorky II (4 x 305mm guns)
13. Coastal Battery 18 (4 x 152mm guns)
14. Coastal Battery 19 (4 x 152mm guns)

	Front line, 7 June
	Soviet coastal battery
	Soviet turret battery
	Soviet fort
	Soviet defensive sector
	German 600mm mortar
	German 420mm howitzer
	German 355mm howitzer
	German 305mm mortar

veterans were reminded of Verdun, the Somme and Flanders. They watched the village of Kamyschly and a 195-metre hill they dubbed the Trapeze disappear in clouds of grey smoke which lingered in the still June air.[92]

A short distance to the south, the ground beneath 25th Rifle Division 'shook from hundreds of explosions,' its commander Trofim Kolomiets recalled. 'It was like being at the epicentre of a nine-point earthquake.' One of his men complained: 'A few more days and the Germans will leave nothing left of Sevastopol.'[93]

It seemed that way to war correspondent Petr Sazhin, who attempted to walk from Kamyshovaya Bay in the west of Sevastopol towards the burning centre of the city after nightfall. The main road was littered with debris from the day's bombardment: corpses which no-one cleared, some cans of engine oil, a box of unknown goods, a broken wheel. Every now and then an incoming shell forced Sazhin and his companions to hit the ground. 'Gasping from the heat and the acrid, bitter smell of wormwood and gunpowder, bypassing craters and corpses, we made our way towards Sevastopol.'[94]

Though the city burned 'from end to end', the reports reaching the Coastal Army's commander Ivan Petrov were encouraging; his regiments and divisions were telling his headquarters they had suffered minimal casualties.

'Is that true? Are you reporting correctly? Are your statements correct?' he barked down the telephone at one divisional commander.

'I would not have the guts to lie to you, Comrade Commander-in-Chief,' came the response.[95]

Each day the bombardment grew heavier, but hellish though it was, the Germans had yet to play their trump card: three mighty siege weapons, including the world's largest artillery piece. Twenty miles northeast of Sevastopol, outside the historic town of Bakhchysarai, soldiers, labourers and engineers had been preparing since April for the arrival of Dora, a gigantic railway gun capable of hurling shells weighing between five and seven tonnes at targets up to 30 miles away. It took 60 railway wagons to transport the leviathan from the army's ranges in Pomerania to the Crimea, where a specially laid line, running through a specially created – and well-disguised – cutting lay ready to accommodate Dora. Assigned to operate the mighty weapon were the 250 men of *Schwere Artillerie Abteilung* (*E*) 672 – Railway Heavy Artillery Detachment 672. With the attendant engineers and construction troops – who also built a dummy position with a cardboard replica of the monster – guards and anti-aircraft units, the whole operation needed well over 4,000 men.

At first light on 5 June, one gunner watched in awe as Dora – 'her barrel like a chimney' – belched a seven-tonne armour-piercing shell at nearly twice the speed of sound. 'I had the feeling that now no-one could touch us any more.

When it roared, that crashing, that unbelievably-long streak of fire, the shaking of the ground, you can't describe it. Anyone who's not experienced it can hardly imagine it.' The shell arced through the Crimean sky for 30 seconds or more before crashing down nearly 16 miles away, throwing up 'an enormous explosive cloud'. It missed its target – an anti-aircraft command post just north of Severnaya Bay dubbed Fort Molotov by the attackers – by 400 metres.[96]

Not one of the 15 shells Dora fired this day hit its target – seven aimed at Fort Molotov, eight at a suspected underground ammunition depot on the north shore. It took at least 35 minutes – and on one occasion more than two hours – to load a new shell. A handful landed within 20 metres of their intended target. Most missed – and by some distance. Observers reported large explosive clouds when the shells impacted and one crater nearly 30 metres wide.[97] Otherwise, Dora was a failure.

It came as no surprise to Karl Justrow, from the German Army's weapons inspectorate, who remembered the 'Paris cannon' from 1918 which had hurled shells at the French capital from nearly 80 miles away. Even with a target as large as the metropolis to aim at, only three in every five shells had landed within the city's limit. 'Dora with its armour-piercing shells was used against concrete targets only a few square metres in size,' he wrote. 'The prospect of a direct hit was almost zero from the very outset.'[98]

The cumbersome 60cm mortars – officially known as the 'Karl device', but named Thor and Odin by their crews – proved only slightly more effective when they belatedly joined battle on 6 June. In practice, their two-tonne shells could smash through concrete up to eight feet thick at ranges of more than 2½ miles. At 5pm on the final day of the preliminary barrage, Thor began lobbing rounds from a hilltop down on Maxim Gorky I, lynchpin of the defence on the northern shore. One of its crew watched excitedly as a shell landed on one of the fort's two armoured cupolas. 'The turret slowly rises out of the smoke, the structure is shattered, missing, a dark black colour, battered, it sits crookedly on its bearings,' he recalled. 'Thor's hammer has struck!'[99]

It was one of the few successes the heavy artillery scored at Sevastopol. Indeed, the whole preliminary bombardment was largely a failure. Despite the tremendous expenditure of ammunition – well over 40,000 shells, and nearly 24,000 incendiary bombs, ten for every high-explosive one dropped – the barrage had barely made an impression on the city's defences beyond smashing many of the tractors and trucks used to haul shells from the underground ammunition dumps to the guns on the front line; for the remainder of the battle, men and horses would have to bear the burden. The five-day bombardment's greatest achievement was to reduce the city to rubble. 'Sevastopol, as we were used to seeing and imagining it, as it had been after the two previous assaults and seven months of siege, no longer existed,' wrote Nikolai Krylov, Petrov's chief-of-staff. More than 4,500 buildings were destroyed and another 3,000 damaged, burying 138 inhabitants, there was widespread disruption to water and electricity supplies, and more than 500 fires raged. 'There is no town left,' one junior officer told war correspondent Boris Voyetekhov. 'The streets are nearly all blocked by avalanches of rubble. You hear nothing but bursting bombs and shells. It is Pompeii.'[100]

After five days of hammering Sevastopol's defences, Manstein was ready to commit his infantry. From captured German documents the Soviets knew the precise time of his assault. Five minutes before 3am on 7 June, hundreds of Red Army artillery pieces opened fire on the enemy's suspected jump-off positions. They hit empty ground. The attackers had yet to occupy their lines – they were working to Berlin time, two hours behind Moscow.[101]

The attackers were still performing their final checks and preparations. Under cover of darkness pioneers removed mines, as they had done on preceding nights. Cigarettes – a gift from the Bulgarian general staff – were generously distributed among troops in 50th Infantry Division's first assault wave. 'We made good use of them – they seemed to calm our nerves,' one infantryman wrote as he watched the bombardment. 'The mood was confident. Of course we would finish off Sevastopol! No man could withstand this torrent of shells which was pulverising the Russians!'[102]

The barrage unleashed this Sunday surpassed any on the Eastern Front, a bombardment ten times heavier than the one five days earlier when the battle opened. In the pale light before sunrise, Sevastopol appeared to be surrounded by a ring of fire as muzzles flashed along a 21-mile front. 'It's truly a concert in hell,' one artillery officer observed to war correspondent Theo Janssen. The reporter was mesmerised. 'Wherever you look, shells are exploding in and behind the Soviet line!'[103] A Red Army major on the receiving end remembered, 'a true firestorm. Everything disappeared in a roar of continuous explosions.'[104] Ivan Laskin wrote that the earth shook 'with renewed vigour'. He continued:

> A whirlwind of fire raged through all of our positions. The sky darkened as a result of the explosions from thousands of bombs and shells. And the aircraft continued to appear, wave after wave. Bombs rained down on us almost continuously. Huge chunks of earth, trees with roots were flung into the air… Over one thousand guns and mortars simultaneously fired at a narrow section of four to five kilometres; around 100 bombers bombed it. A huge cloud of dark grey smoke and dust rose up and soon obscured the sun. A bright sunny day became gloomy, like during an eclipse. I'd been at war for a year, but I'd never experienced such strong enemy fire.[105]

It wasn't Thor, Odin or Dora which troubled Laskin's men and their comrades as much as the *Nebelwerfer* multiple rocket launchers which were deployed en masse for the first time at Sevastopol. Dubbed 'infernal machines' by Soviet troops, four *Werfer* units – 21 batteries with 576 barrels in all – were arrayed around the fortress. Individually, the effect of their mortar bombs impacting was far less devastating than an artillery shell. But *collectively* the shock wave, the shrapnel spiralling through the air, the blast wave from so many shells exploding close together in rapid succession, caused blood vessels to burst while the banshee cry of the *Werfer* as it left the launcher was every bit as terrifying as the sirens on the Stukas diving at Soviet positions. 'It couldn't be any worse in Dante's hell,' one commissar complained.[106]

Overhead, a crewman in a Heinkel He111 bomber observed that 'hardly a second passes without there being a flash somewhere – impacts and shooting'. He pitied the infantry about to attack 'in this volcano of fire, steel and death'. Stukas plunged into this volcano, but regimental commander Rudolf Buhse could only hear the howl of the sirens mounted on their undercarriage – the 'trumpets of Jericho' – such was the 'thick veil of smoke, dust and haze over the battlefield'.[107]

Buhse's parent 22nd Infantry Division moved out first, assaulting the centre of the northern front. A flak gunner providing cover watched his comrades storm the first enemy line:

> Then the trench which has just been taken goes up in the air – with the *Landsers* who've leapt into it: Ivan laid mines under it and now he's pressed the button. A Russian marksman causes one fatality among our gunners. The next man jumps into his seat. The sun in the sky stings, the thermometer rises to 60°C, we're tormented by unimaginable thirst. Clayey, yellow water in a crater doesn't compare with a cool glass of beer in the slightest, but it quenches our thirst. Shells exploding, the Stukas' 'trumpets of Jericho', the strange retching of the rocket launchers, all this is drowned out by background noise which grows ever louder until it becomes an infernal concert in which the heavy mortars, the fortress artillery and Russian naval guns also take part. In the middle of all this, our 2cm guns also boom. Sweat, oil and dust make our faces unrecognisable. It is an arduous struggle for every foxhole, for every bunker, for every heap of rubble.[108]

Despite the hellish preparatory bombardment, Buhse quickly found there was still 'plenty for the infantry and pioneers to do'. The concentrated firepower 'made the fight easier for the attacking infantry, but it could not spare them'. He continued:

> Every metre of ground was a fire- and steel-spitting hell, in which the Russians, relentless and unflinching, crouched like faceless, mechanically-functioning parts

of a giant machine in their foxholes and very narrow trenches which were several metres deep, shooting as long as they had a rifle in their hands, even if they had long since been bypassed and lay behind the German infantry who continued to storm forward.[109]

On the 22nd's left, 50th Infantry Division stepped off to attack the Kamyschly Ravine and the Trapeze Heights towering above it. At the first sign of Stukas, the massif's defenders abandoned the defensive positions which extended all over the hill and hid in communication trenches in the valley floor, occupying their posts again when the raids had ended – before the Germans could exploit the attack. Cheers of 'Hurrah!' and hoarse cries of 'Urra!' echoed off the valley sides as the Germans stormed the hill... and Soviet troops counter-attacked. The terrain favoured the defender – the slopes were 'impossibly steep', the rock-hard soil proved impenetrable to entrenching tools, affording men no cover when shells impacted. Bunkers and trenches were carved out of the rock. Superbly camouflaged, all too often they were only discovered by German troops when they were directly on top.

In the mid-day and afternoon sun the craters in the rocky terrain where troops sheltered 'turned into gigantic frying pans' while 'crawling over the glowing rocks was already like the pain of being in Dante's Inferno'. Canteens had long been emptied of their coffee. Men gasped for water like fish on dry land. Some hallucinated, suffered heat stroke, babbled incoherently.[110] Soviet fighter-bombers strafed the summit, 'spewing death and destruction'. Shells, shrapnel and explosive fragments whirled around the peak, followed seconds later by harrowing cries of '*Pomoshch!*' (Help!) and '*Raneni!*' (Wounded!) – the Trapeze Heights were still in Russian hands.

By mid-afternoon, such misfortune and the relentless German assaults eventually drove the defenders from the summit. The attackers found the peak gave way to a plateau, covered with shrubs, bushes and tree stumps, while the ground itself, one radio operator recalled, had been 'churned up as if moles had been through it' and so hammered by artillery shells that it looked like a lunar landscape. 'In heat similar to Africa, without a drop to drink, with everything damp from sweat, with dear [valuable] rifles in dirty hands, with eyes stuck together, numb to the bone', the Germans continued their attack over the hill. The Russians struck back, some behaving 'as if they were drunk'. Mortar fire drove them back to their lines and, with light fading, the Germans dug in for the night to secure their hard-won prize.[111]

Progress was even slower in 132nd Infantry Division's front on the extreme right wing of the German attack. Even before his infantry comrades jumped out of their positions, it was apparent to anti-tank gun commander Gottlob Bidermann that despite the ferocity of the German bombardment, Maxim Gorky I and its ancillary forts had not been subdued. 'Shell bursts of all calibres began to explode around us,' he remembered.

> Helpless to react, we could only cower in our shallow trenches, pray for survival and wait out the storm… Shrapnel filled the air, hissing and whistling overhead. We were showered with hunks of stone and earth as massive shells exploded nearby, tossing brown-black geysers skyward and leaving us numb with fear. The earth trembled, dirt filled our eyes, it became difficult to breath. We lay motionless, pressed against the earth in our trenches as rocks and dirt rained on dull grey-green helmets. Our hands were clapped tightly over our ears and we squeezed our eyes shut in vain attempts to block out the unexpected horror that had descended on us.[112]

With the Soviet defence revolving around Maxim Gorky I, the attack made sluggish progress, eventually capturing the village of Belbek mid-afternoon but advancing little further despite support from armour. Soviet accounts talk of 'an avalanche' of German tanks – 50 or 100 – approaching their lines through the Belbek valley. The 'tanks' turned out to be assault guns. Their numbers were few – and became fewer after Ivan Sharov's anti-tank battalion knocked out four of them before falling back. An exhausted Sharov – black from head to toe with smoke and his blood-stained face encrusted with dust – later appeared at the forward observation post of Ivan Laskin's 172nd Rifle Division.

'Are you injured, Comrade Sharov?' Laskin inquired. 'Your face is bleeding.'

'Almost everybody's bleeding over there. Even if one of them is not wounded by a grenade or a bullet, it's from splinters or stones flying around.'[113]

Laskin decided to head to the front to see how his units were faring, beginning with Vladimir Shashlo's 747th Rifle Regiment holding high ground overlooking Belbek. To Laskin, Belbek had become a modern-day valley of death, 'covered in the corpses of German soldiers and officers'. But its defence had taken its toll. 'Our defensive strip was unrecognisable,' Laskin continued. 'The plantation had been completely destroyed, the land one huge blackish crater. Stooped, we walked through collapsed trenches, where the dead lay. When we finally reached Shashlo, the entrances to his observation post were buried by earth, but he had telephone contact with all his units. I spoke to him through the door. His regiment was holding on.'[114]

The offensive in the north at least made ground, albeit far less than Manstein had hoped. But on the southern end of the 21-mile siege front, the attack stalled almost completely. The light infantry of 83rd *Jäger* Regiment stormed two heavily fortified hills to the east of Balaklava Bay, running headlong into an enemy 'who clings to every metre of the rocky bedrock extremely bitterly'. After initial success seizing one of the peaks within the first hour, by the end of the second, Soviet snipers and a counter-attack had reduced the hill's conquerors to a handful of men. All attempts to relieve them failed – at great cost. Casualties were left where they were struck down. Those that could crawled into hollows or shell holes to escape the glare of the sun – temperatures as high as 50°C were recorded in the middle of the day – and Russian fire. Evacuating them was impossible as the entire battlefield could be observed by the enemy. Any man lightly wounded who tried to make a break for German lines was immediately cut down. By nightfall, the last three Germans on the heights fell back under the cloak of darkness to the positions from which they had attacked 16 hours earlier, while troops from the regimental supply column moved out to recover the dead, wounded and any equipment which might be saved. The sun was rising on 8 June before they were finished.[115]

Night prompted a counter-attack against 50th Infantry Division's makeshift positions on the rear slope of the Trapeze Heights. The cry 'The Russians are coming!' was passed along the line. The Germans 'unleashed a hell of steel and crashing' at the oncoming brown masses. Anti-tank gun shells – fired at a range of just 150 metres – tore huge gaps in the Soviet ranks and then, when the counter-attack faltered and the men took shelter in the scrub, at individual bushes. Soon, one German non-commissioned officer wrote, 'more than half the attackers had been dealt with and lay bleeding on the ground'.[116]

Darkness allowed Ivan Laskin and his superior Ivan Petrov to take stock of the first day's battle. 'Officers now learned if there were men left in companies, battalions, batteries,' Laskin recalled.

> Soldiers now stood up, looking for their officers and comrades. The terrain was unrecognisable. Men could not find the trenches and trails they had walked on before and did not recognise each other immediately when they met. Faces were black with dust, only their teeth shone. Many people's voices had changed from the smoke, dust, burning and nervous shock. Everyone's mental and physical strength was badly worn down.[117]

Laskin's division had fought as well as any this Sunday. Ivan Petrov was delighted with its performance. 'We did not make a mistake when we deployed your division in this threatened and decisive sector!' he gushed. 'Thank the soldiers for their steadfastness.'[118]

Erich von Manstein had followed the attack from his observation point on the rocky massif above the Tatar village of Cherkez Kermen, which afforded a panoramic view of the entire battlefield. His memoirs betray no hint that his offensive had failed, only praise for the 'spirit of German arms, the bravery, the initiative, the self-devotion of the German soldier' facing a foe who 'resisted bitterly'. The Russians, said regimental commander Dietrich von Choltitz, had fought 'with the courage of desperation'. The staff of 28th Infantry Division, on the southern end of the German front, blamed the terrain, the heat, the well-camouflaged defences, and the fact that the enemy knew the time of the assault. Its men had never fought over such ground before. They had underestimated the demands it made of them – and they had underestimated a fanatical foe.[119]

7 June was just the beginning. The next morning the assault resumed much as it had begun 24 hours earlier: a ferocious barrage, followed by an infantry assault which gnawed at Soviet lines, but failed to break through them. Ivan Laskin's positions were pummelled by a barrage 'so enormous, and the smoke and dust raised by it so dense that our companies literally walked through a grey veil,' one German battalion commander remembered. By the afternoon, Laskin's division was on the verge of collapsing, he warned his superior, Ivan Petrov. 'Slowly but surely the enemy is eating his way through the division's defences. I have no reserves.'

'Will the division be able to hold its main front until nightfall?' the general asked.

'Yes,' Laskin assured him.[120]

Ivan Laskin's lines bent, his men fell back, but his front did not break. And so it continued for nearly a week at tremendous cost to both sides.

Soviet propaganda taunted the Germans for the failure to make headway. 'You are spilling torrents of blood on the heights of Sevastopol,' one leaflet scattered over German lines declared. 'You face two possibilities: to die ingloriously for Hitler's criminal and hopeless cause, or to surrender to the defenders of Sevastopol and save your lives.' Instances of desertion were few, but the attackers were bleeding to death before Sevastopol. Erik Hansen's LIV Corps, battering the northern front, bore the brunt of the fighting – and with it, the brunt of the losses. After a few days, Hansen's companies were reduced to just 25 men, suffering the effects of excessive strain and the relentless, bitter fighting.[121]

With markers on charts of Sevastopol in the briefing room at Führer headquarters in East Prussia barely moving, Hitler sent his senior military adviser, Alfred Jodl, to the Crimea to investigate the 'failure' and, if necessary, 'make heads roll'. Jodl was 'fobbed off' by Manstein and corps staff and sent to 28th

Infantry Division's command post. 'Here, in this division, no-one has failed,' its furious operations officer snapped. The men hadn't failed. The leadership had. The attacks had been badly planned. The defensive lines on the hills south and southeast of Sevastopol were impenetrable. Even now, Jodl was not satisfied and moved further up the line to 83rd *Jäger* Regiment, led by an old colleague, Hartwig von Ludwiger, who was no less indignant at the criticism. He showed Jodl the terrain and outlined the difficulties his men faced. Alfred Jodl returned to East Prussia. Heads did not roll.[122]

Still Erich von Manstein was worried. When he visited Wolfram von Richthofen's command post to discuss the course of the battle, it was hardly surprising that he appeared 'with an even longer face than mine,' the Luftwaffe general observed. Both men were not merely depressed, but beginning to consider the unthinkable: that Sevastopol might not fall. 'If time wasn't an issue, then events would be in our favour since we would kill all the Russians here in time.' But time *was* an issue. Both the troops and aircraft were needed elsewhere in support of the summer campaign, while the ten-day bombardment of the fortress had almost exhausted the Luftwaffe's stockpile of bombs; on airfields shared by several formations, armourers from different units frequently 'stole' bombs for their aircraft at night. Nor could Manstein's quartermaster keep pace with the artillery moloch. At the current rate of consumption, the guns would run out of shells before the end of June. 'The spectre of failure quite seriously threatens now,' Richthofen noted gloomily.[123]

With his leaders contemplating defeat, the German soldier delivered the first signal success of the assault on its seventh day. Fort Stalin – a thorn in the side of the attackers for the past week – fell to a dawn attack from the relatively fresh troops of 16th Infantry Regiment, which paid for the capture of the anti-aircraft position with heavy casualties among its junior officers. It was, nevertheless, a fillip to German morale. When a young soldier with a shattered arm was being ferried back to his lines on a handcart for treatment, his artillery commander touched his bandaged head and spoke a few words of encouragement. '*Ach, Herr Oberst*, this isn't so bad,' the soldier responded. 'We've got Stalin.'[124]

The fall of Stalin denied the defenders one of the two strongpoints upon which the defence of the front north of Severnaya Bay was anchored. Far more formidable was the second, the complex of modern bunkers, underground passageways and galleries of Coastal Battery No.30, labelled Maxim Gorky I by the Germans. Stalin was little more than a reinforced field fortification. Battery No.30 owed its design more to the Maginot Line. The complex was more than three storeys deep, a small town with water, a power station, a hospital, canteens, machinery rooms with ammunition elevators, an arsenal, and subterranean galleries and passageways, one more than half a kilometre long linking the central bastion with the two armoured turrets and their four 305mm guns. A heavy mortar round had smashed one of the cupolas during the preliminary bombardment, but the eastern turret continued to shoot with apparent impunity, the crash of its two working barrels distinctive amid the hellish cacophony of the Sevastopol concert.

As with Stalin, the fall of Maxim Gorky I required a staged attack, codenamed *Tatzelwurm* after a mythical reptile with a cat's head. Maxim Gorky I was the prize, but first outlying forts had to be knocked out. Fort Siberia fell within minutes of the attack being unleashed late on the morning of 17 June, but pioneers armed with flamethrowers were needed to end resistance at nearby Fort Volga, already badly battered by the fortnight-long bombardment, compounded by a *Nebelwerfer* mortar barrage ahead of the assault. Now jets of fire swept through the trenches and narrow embrasures into the bunkers. Most of the defenders were flayed alive, a few tried to escape only to be gunned down, while the infantry following in the pioneers' wake finished off any survivors.

With the lesser outposts subdued, German infantry advanced rapidly in the rear of Maxim Gorky I. No attempt to take the fort was made until after a 30-minute Stuka bombardment in the early afternoon. 'Maxim Gorky suffered the hell of destruction,' a war correspondent wrote. 'The landscape was churned up and ploughed, heavy bunkers were turned upside down.' An excited artillery observer reported: 'Armoured dome off its mountings, Maxim Gorky's head has been smashed in.' But beyond damaging the still-functioning turret, the fort was largely intact – as the Bavarians of Otto Hitzfeld's 213th Infantry Regiment found as they approached from the east. They had made half a dozen failed attempts to storm the complex already; Hitzfeld needed encouragement from Erich von Manstein – 'Who will take Maxim Gorky if the 213th can't do it!' the general told him – to make a renewed assault. As it turned out, the fall of the fort owed as much to the accompanying pioneers as it did the Bavarian infantrymen. The garrison – at least 300 strong in the central bastion – as well as the crews of the two disabled turrets had no intention of surrendering, as a frustrated Otto Hitzfeld recalled: 'We asked them to come out through the cupola; nothing would happen to them. No success. We tried yelling from the lowest level of this huge barracks, again no success. We sent captured Russians into the galleries, asking the garrison to surrender. Once more no success. The commissars still in the barracks shot the Russians we sent in.'

Instead, every room, magazine, compartment and subterranean gallery or passageway had to be cleared. Each one was sealed by a steel door, which pioneers blasted open, then tossed hand-grenades inside. When the smoke cleared, there were a few pistol shots before the attackers moved on to the next section of the fortress, leaving the compartment or passageway littered with corpses. Occasionally, the Germans intercepted messages from the defenders: 'The Germans are hammering at the steel door, calling on us to surrender. We can no longer open the hatches to shoot any more. There are just 46 of us left.' Then, half an hour later: 'We're now down to just 22. We're getting ready to blow ourselves up and end communications. Farewell!' At times, the Germans resorted to methods which would not have been out of place in medieval sieges. To eradicate the garrison of one of the 305mm turrets, explosive charges were used to punch a hole through the 20 centimetres of armour plate. A funnel was inserted and 600 litres of petrol and flammable oil poured in. Flares set the mixture ablaze and rocked the gun position with an explosion which filled the subterranean passages with smoke and fire. Two men used the cover the smoke provided to escape. Their comrades perished minutes later as the flames reached the magazine.

The resulting explosion was the trigger for 118 men to surrender – though they reckoned there were still 114 men, women and even a child in the bowels of the fort, led by a dogged major, Georgy Aleksander. By the time he resolved to break out – after more than a week trapped in the depths of Maxim Gorky – there were only around 50 defenders left, including five female medics.

Aleksander removed his naval uniform, put on civilian clothes, burned his papers and led his group down a drain into the Belbek valley, intending to break through to the partisans in the mountains beyond Sevastopol. It took them two days to dig their way out of the fort, only for one of the female medics who was suffering from tuberculosis, to cough loudly, alerting the Germans. After a short skirmish – the breakout group had weapons but no ammunition – the survivors, including Aleksander, were taken prisoner. He would pay for his decision to remove his uniform with his life. After a thorough interrogation by the captors, Georgy Aleksander was executed as a partisan on the orders either of Manstein or his staff.[125]

By the time Georgy Aleksander was captured on 25 June, the Germans were masters of the northern shores of Severnaya Bay. The first troops – elements of 22nd Infantry Division – had reached the water's edge within hours of the fall of Maxim Gorky I. A junior officer surveyed the scene: 'Severnaya Bay lies before us, beyond it the city of Sevastopol. Ghostly red flames twitch in the night sky and are reflected in the water. Several shot-up ships and boats are burning on the opposite shore. Large and small fires rage in the city and in the midst of this more shells impacting flash.'[126]

Ivan Petrov committed his last reserves – a brigade of naval infantry, fresh but not fully ready for action – in a final attempt to turn the tide of battle. Seven times they battered the German lines, advancing nearly a mile and almost succeeding in breaking through on four occasions. 'We heard the screams of the wounded and the orders of officers and commissars, who repeatedly drove the attacking waves forward,' one German officer reported. The defenders also intercepted a radio message from Ivan Petrov urging on his men: 'Congratulations! German resistance broken. Push through with all forces!' Except German resistance wasn't broken. Despite hand-to-hand fighting in their trenches at times, the Germans' lines swayed, but never gave way. After the seventh and final failed assault and 15 hours of bitter fighting, the naval brigade was a spent force. It left behind a field of dead – and the conviction that Soviet resistance on the northern shore was crumbling.[127]

All that remained for the defenders to do was fall back to the caves and galleries carved out of the rock on the northern shoreline which served as magazines, warehouses and ultimately shelters for the civilian populace. German troops began combing their way through the catacombs from east to west. The defenders were relatively few in number, but resisted doggedly, usually to the last man. A few tried to escape by swimming across the bay to join their comrades on the south bank. Most drowned in the attempt. In Sukharnaya Balka, a small inlet near the eastern end of the bay, the defenders chose death over dishonour by blowing themselves up. Entire slabs of the cliff – some up to 150 metres long – were lifted up then crashed into the water, along with anyone unfortunate enough to be standing on them. One German officer described the scene:

> First there's a strong earthquake and the ground shakes, then there's a tremendous blast which lifts us up in the air and throws us to the ground. At the same time, the earth opens up and spews out an unbelievable mass of fire and rock like a volcano. An enormous explosion fills the air. Shaken by something impossible to comprehend, dazzled by the flash of fire, we hold our hands in front of our faces and try to get away from the steep slope on the shaking earth. The entire sky is filled with fire, smoke and a mass of rock. Chunks of rock and pieces of iron crash into the bay in front of us and turn it into a seething boiling kettle. After all this, out of the black-red sky which arches over the terrible event, a dense white shower of ash falls.

One Soviet eyewitness reckoned as many as 200 German troops were searching through the galleries when they were detonated. 'The blast wave hurled them into the middle of the bay.' Long after the initial detonations, ammunition continued to explode. The ground trembled with each after-shock. Tongues of flame licked out of fissures in the ground which belched dense yellow sulphurous clouds.[128]

Such sights and such horrors were not uncommon in the siege of Sevastopol. The final battle changed the face of the city, the landscape and the men fighting over it forever. The panorama of the battlefield assumed hellish proportions. What foliage and plant life there was had either been killed by the bombardment or turned grey by the dust and ash from the constant fires burning in the port. When there was an apparent lull in battle, such as following the fall of Maxim Gorky I, the Luftwaffe took advantage by subjecting Sevastopol to a ferocious bombardment from dawn until dusk. First German bombs turned the city to rubble; then, from mid-day, incendiaries caused fires to rage – as many as 500. Sevastopol burned from end to end. An enormous cloud hung over the city, 'torn open only by the bright tongues of flame from the burning oil tanks in the port,' a soldier in 50th Infantry Division wrote. 'The thunder from this tremendous storm devoured every other sound.' It brought all regular life in the city to an end while a huge black cloud spilled over the harbour. It could be seen more than 90 miles away in Feodosia. 'The city was unrecognisable,' naval officer Aleksandr Evseev noted. 'It had died. Only recently a gleaming, beautiful Sevastopol, now in ruins. Instead of getting his hands on a city, all that's left is a pathetic yet magnificent mass of stones, rubble and ash.'[129]

And yet men were prepared to die defending it in their thousands – to the astonishment of those assaulting the city. Otto von Hentig, the German Foreign Ministry's liaison officer at Manstein's headquarters, repeatedly heard troops praise the Soviet soldier at Sevastopol. 'No Frenchman, no Englishman, not even we could have withstood that,' they said, acknowledging 'the bravery and, in many cases, unheard-of courage not only of the soldier, but also the commissar and politruk. The pistol of the politruk or the commander cannot have been the only thing that drove the people forward or caused them to endure.' Praise for the defenders of Sevastopol was not limited to the soldier. The Red Air Force at Sevastopol was tiny compared with its foe, but fought skilfully, regularly reinforced with fresh aircraft flown in from the Caucasus. 'They have the newest birds and their pilots have also learned a great deal,' wrote Luftwaffe ace Heinrich Setz. 'Those chaps really have nerves. They see their comrades falling from the sky in flames every day and they fly every day just as bravely.'[130]

Having watched the defence of the Kerch peninsula crumble in little more than a week, the Soviet leadership was not prepared to see a repeat at Sevastopol. At the beginning of the German onslaught it had warned – rather than reminded – the defenders that the fortress was to be held 'at all costs'. Once battle was joined, there were exhortations almost daily to resist. The Coastal Army's newspaper *For the Motherland* urged its readers to 'be a hero of the Great Patriotic War! This is what your wife, your children, your mother, your sisters call on you to do. The Motherland and the holy duty of protecting your native land are calling to you to do this.' There was praise from Stalin for 'the Red Army, Red Navy, officers and commissars, courageously defending every inch of Soviet soil, striking at the German invaders and their Romanian henchmen. The selfless struggle of Sevastopol is an example to the entire Red Army and the Soviet people.' The pages of the Communist Party organ *Pravda* informed the city's defenders that 'all the Soviet people, the peoples of freedom-loving countries are breathlessly watching the fierce battle... The selfless struggle of Sevastopol's citizens is an example of heroism for the entire Red Army, for the entire Soviet people.' And Ivan Petrov tried to assure his men that if they continued to hold on, their foe would 'bleed to death. The enemy is committing his final reserves in the struggle. The German troops are tired of attacking and are badly demoralised.'[131]

They were – but so were their foe. The line between victory and defeat was a fine one. When 47th Infantry Regiment was ordered to clear out a 200-metre-long tunnel which once carried the main Simferopol–Sevastopol railway line, it was surprised by a counter-attack involving three fresh Soviet battalions which had been ferried to the city just three days beforehand by warship. Rudolf Buhse's sorely weakened regiment 'defended itself with machine-guns, rifles and hand-grenades, but what use were they against these hordes of attacking Russians?' Buhse scraped together every man he had – rifles were thrust into the hands of the ranks of the supply column – drummed up a couple of assault guns and a few panzers and struck back. 'The Russians were caught completely off guard,' Buhse remembered. 'They thought they were the victors.' Resistance was stubborn, but once broken, collapsed. 'The Russians were soon gripped by panic-stricken flight.' The railway tunnel was captured and with it nearly 800 prisoners – three times more men than Rudolf Buhse led.[132]

Deserters crossing the lines reported that the constant barrage and bombardment – and the absence of the Red Air Force, coupled with a growing shortage of ammunition to respond to the Germans – gnawed at the defenders' morale daily. They began to realise that they would die defending Sevastopol – or perhaps fall into German hands, but there would be no evacuation. On the other hand, with nothing to lose – and with political officers acting ruthlessly against any signs of dissent or desertion – the defenders fought with far greater determination than they had at Kerch.[133]

And so the daily shower of leaflets dropped by the Luftwaffe – nearly three million in the final month of the siege – calling upon Soviet soldiers and sailors to surrender, promising fair treatment in captivity, largely fell on fallow ground. Given the shortage of paper in the city – its defenders frequently didn't have enough to even roll a cigarette – the German flyers proved a useful substitute for toilet paper. As the siege progressed, they were much in need. Sevastopol's defenders were plagued by stomach cramps, 'dashing out of their bunkers every five minutes for calls of nature', as the water supply either failed or was polluted. The city drew much of its water from natural and man-made underground reservoirs or springs. When caves, galleries and bunkers collapsed under the weight of the German barrage or were blown up by retreating troops, killing soldiers and civilians sheltering within, decomposing bodies subsequently contaminated the supply.[134]

Water – or rather lack of it – tormented every man who fought at Sevastopol. Where creeks and streams had run during the winter, now there was only 'a cracked and crusted layer of mud'. 'The battle carved runes on the faces of the men,' an officer in 50th Infantry Division observed. His men were dogged by lack of sleep, irregular – and often awful – food, thirst and heat exhaustion. 'The heat during days of battle was oppressive, the nights brought little relief,' anti-tank gun commander Gottlob Bidermann remembered. 'We lived only for cigarettes, cold coffee and tea, every now and then iron rations which were handed out daily to those in the front line. We did not have time to wash and shave.' The strain of battle was just as great on aircrew, some of whom flew more than half a dozen sorties every day. 'Not every man is up to the enormous physical and nervous strain,' fighter squadron commander Gordon Gollob wrote. 'It is prudent – and humane – to relieve pilots who are no longer stable in good time before they infect others and kill themselves.'[135]

The nights at Sevastopol, remembered Romanian artillery officer Alexandru Pantazopol, were 'a fevered spectacle':

> As soon as a Soviet aircraft was reported, German searchlights would sweep the sky in every direction until they caught the enemy plane in their beams and then its fate was sealed. Every searchlight focused on it, and anti-aircraft artillery of every calibre fired until it was shot down. On other occasions, the plane trapped in the searchlight beams – blinding the pilot – was directed into the surrounding hills, where it crashed into the rocks and exploded.[136]

Company commander Friedrich Haag spared his parents nothing of the horrors of Sevastopol in a letter home to the picture-postcard small town of Schorndorf, near Stuttgart. 'It's not sights – which you almost get used to in this terrible bloodbath, the mutilations, men bleeding to death, groaning, men silently collapsing – rather often the scenes on the fringes of battle, which I cannot shake,' he wrote.

I saw a beautiful white horse grazing by a roadside ditch. An artillery shell took away its right leg beneath the ankle joint. It continued to graze, swinging its bloody stump back and forth slowly, in untold misery, then it looked up with a gaze which made your blood curdle, shook its head, unable to understand, and continued grazing.

I don't know if I've captured the misery of this sight; for me it was the perfect example of all this madness. Then I said to one of my men – and this too is typical: 'Put down that horse!' The soldier, who'd been in battle not ten minutes earlier, said: 'I don't have the heart, *Herr Leutnant*.' Such experiences are more depressing than the 'chaos of battle' and personal danger.[137]

New arrivals pitchforked into this hell often broke down. Gottlob Bidermann watched them run around 132nd Infantry Division's trenches holding their hands up in the hope of being shot by a Soviet sniper – so they might get sent back to Germany to recover. One German officer who came to Sevastopol from the peace of occupied France struggled to comprehend the ferocity of the battle. 'I have to ignore any kind of compassion and get used to it, like the soldiers who have been fighting on the Eastern Front for so long,' he recorded in his diary. 'It is necessary to put aside reflection on this issue. The only good thing is that mothers cannot see what their children are like, nor wives their husbands.'[138] Junior officer Hermann Bousset struggled to preserve his humanity:

Man gets used to everything, to all the images of the most horrific destruction. It is a kind of self-protection. I fight against growing used to this numbness, otherwise I no longer have a yardstick. Instead, I try to summon up the courage and strength to see and recognise fate in all its tragedy – and still endure it... War is a question of character in addition to a question of nerves and luck; especially if the war lasts longer.[139]

Bousset survived the inferno of Sevastopol, but around 25,000 men on both sides were killed during the final battle. They were afforded little dignity. At night, burial parties and stretcher bearers tentatively moved out on to the battlefield, temporarily pausing their work when flares lit up the landscape, even though each side enforced an unofficial truce and never shot at them – one of the few acts of humanity in Sevastopol. But the casualties were too numerous, the June nights too short. 'The dead still lay everywhere. In some places they were piled up in mountains,' remembered Walter Winkler. He watched a wounded Russian soldier in a bloody, shredded shirt which he tied to his rifle and waved in no man's land. 'He had been forgotten or not found during the night, and no-one dared to help him now because the shooting had already resumed.' Occasionally women stumbled among the corpses, perhaps trying to find their husbands, brothers, fathers, sons. But this proved increasingly difficult as the dead lay unburied, often for days on end. Limbs stiffened, faces and hands turned black under the midsummer sun as temperatures on the ground often topped 40°C, stomachs 'collapsed like mummies' or bloated so much that the 'seams on their uniforms burst'. 'Trucks drove over the corpses as if they were rags,' battalion commander Diedrich Bruns remembered. 'It is inconceivable how indifferent we became to these gruesome sights.' Chlorine or lime was poured on the bodies, but it could not disguise 'the awful smell of decomposition' plaguing the battlefield, nor keep the swarms of flies which gorged on the corpses or cadavers of horses, and gutted cattle. 'There is such a stench in the hot air that people are sick,' one Soviet marine wrote. 'There is no escape from it anywhere. Sailors who have never suffered from lack of appetite do not touch their food.'[140]

Loss of the northern shore did not merely free up German forces for a final assault on Sevastopol; it deprived the defenders of key port facilities. Throughout the siege, they relied on the lifeline across the Black Sea to the Caucasus. Ships would bring in food, ammunition and troops and take away casualties and civilians, completing the offloading and embarkation long before sunrise. When the re-supply worked, vessels could be turned around in just three hours. Warships would even hammer the German positions with their guns as they departed. It was a well-honed operation, but with the nights shortening and harbour facilities smashed, the port was no longer running smoothly. And it could not keep pace with the demands of the front; Soviet artillery was consuming upwards of 600 tonnes of high explosive every day, but receiving only 200 by sea.[141]

If the unloading was delayed, it was punished mercilessly. Minutes after the steamer *Abkhazia* was sighted still at a wharf in Sukharnaya Balka, the Luftwaffe responded with three waves of attacks. Some accounts say the crew abandoned the ship to her fate, terrified that the ammunition still aboard would explode, others that they worked tirelessly to transfer wounded evacuees ashore. *Abkhazia's* death throes were protracted. After listing nearly 90 degrees to starboard she finally broke from her moorings in the middle of the afternoon and rested on her side a few metres off the jetty. She joined a growing graveyard of ships peppered around Severnaya Bay. In places their bows or sterns rose from the water. A fully laden schooner lay on her side, her masts extending across the surface of the bay. There was a large capsized steamer, the upturned hull perforated by shells and now a refuge for seagulls. Barges and tugs had been sunk at their moorings, a tanker cut in half, the waves now lapping at her innards. When the steamer *Georgia* fell victim to the Luftwaffe on 13 June, it put an end to merchant ships running the gauntlet. For the remainder of the siege, the re-supply of Sevastopol was performed solely by warships (carrying troops) and submarines (delivering ammunition, medicine and food).[142] It would not suffice.

With inadequate supplies and resources, dwindling numbers of increasingly exhausted troops, the Luftwaffe dominating the skies and German forces regrouping for a final onslaught, it was obvious to any clear-headed commander that Sevastopol's fall was inevitable. Moscow for once stirred and promised to come to the city's aid, landing several thousand soldiers and marines on the Kerch peninsula again. The operation was scheduled for the first days of July.[143] Filipp Oktyabrsky was perhaps the only man who believed the fortress would hold out that long, though he was hardly certain in his judgment. His mood in the final week of June 1942 veered between confidence and resignation. One minute he was attempting to rally his commanders, assuring them that the Germans were exhausted, 'choking to death' at the gates of Sevastopol, their divisions reduced to the size of battalions, their reserves used up. 'Victory will be ours,' he declared, then corrected himself. 'Victory is already ours.'[144] The next he was reporting to superiors that 'the line cannot be held',[145] then changed his mind, assuring them 'we'll last another ten to 15 days' after ordering final efforts made to comb out the rear services and send any man capable of bearing arms to the front[146] – though it was of little consequence when divisions were reduced to between 400 and 600 men, brigades half that size. Oktyabrsky refused to contemplate any large-scale evacuation of the Primorsky Army, to say nothing of the civilians, yet ordered units to surrender their banners to headquarters so the flags could be saved – even if the men who fought under them could not.[147]

Late on Sunday 28 June, 20 men – divisional and regimental commanders, senior commissars – crammed into Ivan Petrov's command post, a one-time dining room in the guardhouse of the barracks at Chersones. All were weary and exhausted. There were no smiles or quips. The men discussed the state of their troops and the situation in their sector. 'The picture was far worse than any of us had previously thought,' Ivan Laskin recalled. For the first time, the evacuation of Sevastopol seemed a genuine possibility. 'The Supreme Command will take all measures to evacuate us and not leave us in the lurch,' Ivan Petrov assured his comrades. 'And we will fulfil our duty to the Motherland till the end.' Filipp Oktyabrsky was the one dissenting voice. There would be no evacuation because Sevastopol would not fall, he insisted. 'We must hold on to this line, we have nowhere else to retreat from.'[148]

Two hours later the Germans launched their final assault on the fortress.

The night of Sunday 28 June to Monday 29 June was warm, clear, star-filled. The sound of bombs exploding in the docks drowned out the noise of pioneers dragging more than 100 small assault boats to the water's edge on the north shore of Severnaya Bay. Neither the pioneers operating the motorboats, nor the assault teams of infantry climbing into them spoke a word, while a smokescreen prevented prying eyes 250 metres away on the southern shoreline seeing anything. In a few minutes, the boats would cross the bay and land infantry in the Soviets' rear, the first act in the last major set-piece attack of the siege, Operation *Fackeltanz* – Torch Dance.

The boat assault was, battalion commander Otto Hitzfeld conceded, 'a tremendous gamble, but the idea somehow attracted us'. He watched from the waterfront as the boats set off under a stunning display of fireworks: tracer fire, the muzzle flashes of artillery, signal flares. 'It was a magnificent spectacle.'

The boats raced through a thin veil of mist caused by gunsmoke and dust which sat upon the bay's calm waters and, four minutes later, disembarked their passengers before turning around to pick up the next wave. To Otto Hitzfeld, the crossing ran 'so assuredly, so perfectly, as if it were a peacetime exercise'. A few minutes later flare signals reported the troops had the high ground overlooking the southern shoreline.[149]

Almost simultaneously, the artillery of XXX Corps opened fire on the Sapun Heights to the southeast of Sevastopol 'with a ferocity never before experienced… which lit up the night' and continued until sunrise. 'We got used to everything, but we had never experienced anything like this before,' one Soviet brigade commander recalled. His own guns were largely silent due to lack of ammunition.

With shells still crashing down, the assault waves of 170th Infantry Division moved across a narrow strip just 800 metres wide. Darkness, smoke and dust hindered every step they took – and prevented any clear observation of the attack's progress from German lines. First light brought little clarity: the dawn mist mixed with dust and smoke from exploding shells and obscured the view, while signal flares added to, rather than cleared up, any confusion. Three German battalions were thrown against the heights. Only one succeeded in gaining a foothold on the lower reaches of the ridge and decided to continue the assault. Shortly after daybreak, the Germans had ejected the defenders from the peak. Reinforcements were hurriedly thrown up the mountain by the Germans to bolster the solitary battalion, followed by a Stuka raid against the reverse slope to pin down any counter-attacking Russian troops. The anti-aircraft guns were silent. They had no shells. By mid-morning, the Russians were in headlong retreat towards the city. The Sapun Heights were lost. Novo Shuli – the village key to Sevastopol's fresh water supply – was seized by Romanian troops. Some

Soviet units lost four in every five men this Monday. Battalions were wiped out, brigades reduced to 150 men, others eliminated, and artillery regiments left with just a single cannon. Nevertheless, occasionally the attacker was reminded Soviet resistance was not entirely broken. Trofim Kolomiets was stunned by the naivety – or arrogance – of German troops filing down the main road from the Sapun Heights as if the battle were won, the enemy wiped out. They marched in peacetime formation, their colours supposedly flying. Kolomiets' shattered 25th Rifle Division could still bring five machine-guns and five 45mm artillery pieces to bear. 'In five minutes the road was littered with Nazi corpses.'[150]

With Soviet lines crumbling at both ends, coastal artillery commander Petr Morgunov urged Oktyabrsky to fall back to the secondary command post, Battery No.35 – branded Maxim Gorky II by the Germans – a couple of miles south of Cape Chersonese, as the enemy might break through to the city at any moment. 'You are exaggerating the forces of the Hitlerites, they have suffered heavy losses and we will last a few more days,' the admiral assured him, convinced he could hold out for another 24 hours.

For once, Filipp Oktyabrsky allowed himself to be persuaded. At 10pm he moved his command post to the coastal fort. It was a decision which triggered a total collapse of Soviet leadership and order in Sevastopol as first senior, then middle-ranking, and finally junior officers followed the lead of their commander and fell back towards Chersonese.[151]

As Sevastopol's leaders settled into their new command post, the men of 50th Infantry Division were closing in on the city centre from the east. By midnight, they had reached Inkerman, a small town on a limestone ridge which rose vertically above the mouth of the Chernaya river and eastern shore of Severnaya Bay. For more than a millennium, monks had worshipped in caves, while in more recent times rock had been quarried from the same limestone cliffs. In Soviet times, those cavernous galleries had been used to store the Crimea's famous sparkling wine. During the siege, the caves had been partitioned to create an underground shelter for ammunition, supplies and civilians, plus a makeshift hospital with 500 beds – though now treating at least 2,000 casualties – while the champagne was used for cooking or, when boiled, in tea and coffee. Soviet engineers rigged explosives throughout the subterranean maze, but the hundreds of civilians taking refuge never expected their comrades to detonate them without first evacuating the caves. Shortly after 1am on the last day of June 1942, they were proved wrong.

Medic Alois Fendt was accompanying infantry combing through Inkerman when there was 'a roar of thunder underground, the mountain shook, part of it was lifted in the air, and was torn apart along a 300-metre stretch,' he recalled.

'An enormous cloud of rough and fine dust mixed with smoke and gun smoke bubbled above the hill.' Men were swept away by a relentless landslide of rock, or else tottered and fell into the caverns opened up as the ground parted, 'swallowed like the whale once swallowed Jonah'. For a quarter of an hour dust and ash rained down on the German troops while dense clouds of smoke obliterated the moon. When the dust settled Walter Winkler and his comrades tentatively approached the 'open wound' left by the explosion. 'As if a shell had torn a body apart, the innards of the Inkerman rock were now revealed,' he wrote. 'Out of rooms where bottles of Crimean champagne were stored in their millions, there were foaming streams, out of others black smoke and, as far as the view was not blocked by rubble, we saw people, animals, vehicles, bedsteads and ammunition in a terrible jumble.' The walls and partitions separating the different galleries and sections of the complex collapsed. Those not killed under the rubble were often burned alive by the fires or choked on the acrid smoke which followed in the flames' wake. 'I saw rocks sliding apart before my eyes, boulders break off and the whole ravine strewn with rocks,' remembered Valya Kotlyarova, sheltering with her family. She heard her mother and sisters calling her name from somewhere deep in the caverns – they'd been blown into the basement, where thousands of bottles shattered, flooding the gallery knee-deep with sparkling wine. The galleries echoed with screams and crying. In a stampede to find the exit, people were crushed, trampled or even drowned in the champagne. Valya Kotlyarova found her father, dead, buried beneath a rockslide. When she and her surviving family members finally heard soldiers trying to dig them out, the voices turned out to be German.[152]

Organised defence had all but collapsed in Sevastopol as thousands of soldiers and sailors followed the example of their leaders and streamed towards Cape Chersonese. Communications broke down. Command structures shattered. After a month of near-constant fighting, men collapsed mentally and physically. Units splintered. They streamed towards Kamyshovaya and adjacent Kazachaya Bays, 'hoping for personal good fortune to get on board' the ever-shrinking flotilla of boats running the gauntlet to enter harbour at night.[153] 'On the move were masses of military equipment, ambulances, guns, carts, vans, field kitchens and yet more vehicles, cars packed with the quartermaster's goods,' one Soviet artilleryman recalled. The carriageway and roadside ditches were strewn with all manner of things:

> ... sacks of uniforms, scattered piles of bags, torn, with rice, sugar, flour and raisins. Boxes of tinned food, dried fruit, butter, condensed milk and even wine. Fireproof crates, sealed and open. Half-burned, untouched staff correspondence

lying around like white snow. There's paper money, in bundles and in bulk: 10, 30, 50 and 100 roubles. In some places, there's so much money that you walk over it like in the woods after a heavy leaf fall.[154]

War correspondent Petr Sazhin was caught up in the same torrent of soldiers, civilians and vehicles heading west. There were fires everywhere – some burning furiously, others barely flickering. 'People were walking in tattered uniforms, with bloody bandages, walking, sheltering in the balkas from the squally fire,' he wrote. 'Some, having passed through seven circles of hell, here, on the eighth and perhaps the last, were hit by bombs and remained forever.' At times the column was agitated, at others sullen and depressed. Unlike most of his fellow travellers, Petr Sazhin possessed hope. He held a pass from Sevastopol's commanders permitting him to leave the besieged city.[155]

There were still some Soviet troops determined to defend the city to the last round. Sailors holding Malakhov Hill just east of the city centre had no wish of repeating the fate of their forebears who had surrendered the height to the French 90 years before. Normally Malakhov was a green oasis in the heart of Sevastopol. Now it was churned up and cratered by bombs and shells which had swept every bush from its slopes. The bunkers and dugouts had largely collapsed, while the original 18th-century fortifications were barely recognisable from the effects of 20th-century artillery fire. Three times before mid-day the defenders were driven from the hill. Three times sailors counter-attacked and re-took the high ground. Led by a veteran reservist, the sailors forced their way into the trenches and killed the Germans occupying them with grenades and knives and, on occasions, even resorted to strangling their foe. After the third successful assault, the sailors sent their final signal: 'Malakhov Hill is surrounded. Suffering heavy losses. Come to the rescue.' No help was forthcoming. Instead, the Germans committed armour to support their infantry trying to dislodge the sailors, but the panzers fell victim to the final rounds in the barrels of anti-tank guns and rifles, even grenades thrown at point-blank range. Finally, the attackers turned to persuasion. In broken Russian, the Germans resorted to promises of good treatment in captivity. 'Bullets, grenades and a harsh word in Russian flew back towards the invaders,' the reservist colonel commanding the sailors recalled. 'There was not a single case of surrender, no-one even thought about it.'[156] 30 June ended, as it had begun, with Malakhov Hill in Soviet hands. The height was strewn with Russian and German corpses.

Seven miles to the west, Ivan Laskin entered the new headquarters of Filipp Oktyabrsky for the evening conference with fellow commanders. Staff officers were running to and fro, carrying bundles of paper to be burned, pausing only to direct Laskin to a room dimly lit by a kerosene lamp where senior officers were gathered around Ivan Petrov. 'The command and headquarters of the army,' he told them, 'are being evacuated tonight by submarine, and you and General Kolomiets are on an aircraft.'[157]

On the other side of the lines, Georghe Manoliu reported to the command post of Franz Lindemann's 170th Infantry Division to receive orders for the coming day's assault on the city centre.

'My orders are for our army to attack and gloriously enter Sevastopol,' Lindemann told him.

'And my 4th Mountain Division?'

'We have enough German troops, I think your division will be given another mission, it will probably remain in reserve.'

The German offered his ally a glass of champagne to toast the coming attack.

'*Herr General*, I did not come to the city of Sevastopol to drink champagne, and for my division to be in the second line,' Manoliu snapped. Romanian troops, he protested, would remember the snub 'from private to marshal'. Before midnight Georghe Manoliu had fresh orders: his mountain infantry would take part in the last assault.[158]

By midnight on 30 June–1 July, the streets leading down to Kamyshovaya Bay, to say nothing of the quays, jetties and wharves, were a seething mass of noisy, desperate, scared people – civilians, sailors, soldiers. 'Everyone was waiting for something,' naval officer Ivan Zaruba remembered. Unable to reach the waterfront, he made for Battery No.35 instead. Come the morning, with no more boats entering the bay and rumours swilling around, the mob began to disperse, confident it would find salvation on the Chersones peninsula.[159]

It was now the first day of July. The sporadic sound of battle faded. Under the milky-white light of the moon, deserters dared to cross the lines and surrender to the Germans. Behind the front artillery pieces moved forward, ready to support the final assault on the city by the infantry, who settled into their jump-off positions. For perhaps the last time, they studied the silhouette of Sevastopol. 'For some of us, our hearts beat faster,' one German machine-gunner recalled. 'This land and naval fortress, which we'd fought for over the past eight months, was within sight, almost touchable.'[160]

On the Chersones peninsula, 13 Soviet-built Douglas Dakota transporters flown by specialist crews set down on the last airfield in the fortress and were immediately surrounded by guards. As the doors opened and ladders were thrown out, hundreds of troops and civilians began pressing forward, convinced salvation had arrived.

Ammunition and food were hurriedly offloaded. Any hopes of an orderly embarkation and evacuation of Sevastopol's leaders were dashed almost immediately as the major directing the whole operation panicked and scrambled on to the first aircraft. The lines of guards trying to hold back the crowd swayed, buckled and finally broke. Before the third transporter took off, fighting had broken out on the airfield between the evacuees and the thousands more seeking salvation.

One aircraft, well away from the rest, had been reserved for the most senior officers. Around 1am Filipp Oktyabrsky, his senior commissar Kulakov and several staff left one of Battery No.35's observation posts to embark. It was not the admiral's finest hour. Wearing a civilian coat – supposedly to protect himself from 'enemy agents' – Oktyabrsky was quickly recognised by his men. Incensed not only that he was abandoning them – but abandoning his uniform – the troops pressed forward, hurling insults and threats at the admiral. Shots rang out. A commissar stepped forward, hoping to appease the baying mob. The political officer sacrificed his place on the aircraft to explain that Oktyabrsky was leaving Sevastopol to organise the evacuation. At 1.40am, Filipp Oktyabrsky, a handful of commissars, staff officers, brigade commanders and two divisional leaders, Ivan Laskin and Trofim Kolomiets, departed for Krasnodar in the Caucasus. In all, the 13 aircraft ferried more than 230 senior officers and nearly 50 wounded men, plus 3½ tonnes of important cargo to safety.[161]

Around the same time, Ivan Petrov was making his way down to the shoreline with his chief-of-staff Krylov, the coastal artillery commander Petr Morgunov and numerous staff officers and political workers. Waiting a short distance offshore were submarines *Shch-209* and *L-23*, ready to transport yet more of Sevastopol's military leaders to the safety of the Caucasus. Tugs were berthed at a jetty, prepared to ferry the men to the boats. Also waiting at the water's edge: a large crowd, growing larger by the minute. The sight of their leaders evidently fleeing Sevastopol proved incendiary. 'Off with you!' they screamed 'Leave us to our fate!' or 'Let's shoot everyone!' Petrov's adjutant demanded a minesweeper's captain surrender ten of his men, armed with machine-guns, to 'tame' the crowd. And perhaps they were needed. One soldier broke through the cordon, aimed his machine-gun at Petrov and yelled: 'You, you sons of bitches, you're leaving us and running.' His burst of fire missed the general but wounded the staff officer standing next to him.

'Did we ever dream that Sevastopol would end like this?' Petrov confided in his friend Petr Morgunov.

Even now the general hesitated. In the chaos, he'd become separated from his son Yuri, a junior staff officer. As a tug waited to ferry him to one of the two submarines, he turned to Morgunov again. 'I will not get on the boat – I will go back for my son.' Morgunov persuaded the general to leave; Yuri would follow – and, amazingly, he did, having been somehow found in the crowd on the quayside.

The submarines weighed anchor around 3am, bound for Novorossiysk – a journey they made entirely submerged. They safely delivered more than 200 of Sevastopol's defenders.[162]

Sevastopol's agony began again at first light with one more annihilating barrage, now concentrated squarely on the city centre. The bombardment, one machine-gunner remembered, 'turned into a proper hurricane. The city was hidden by clouds of smoke and dust, and flames which hung like a veil in front of us.' Each time the heavy mortars added to the bombardment, 'the earth shook to its very foundations' and the air filled with an 'infernal roar' before the shells impacted 'with unimaginable force'. Twenty of those rounds were fired thanks to the calculations of Berliner Alfred Hennecke, who passed on his figures to the gunners operating one of the two Karl heavy mortars. All but two shells came down on the shipyard in Yuzhnaya Bay in the heart of the city; the remainder were fired only for the benefit of the newsreel cameras. As the bombardment continued well into the morning, Hennecke's observations became increasingly difficult. 'Nothing could be seen of the city through the smoke and dust,' he recalled as the city was reduced to nothing more than a 'burning sea of houses'.[163]

Even when the barrage ended, an enormous cloud continued to hang ominously over Sevastopol, accompanied by an 'eerie silence'. The Russians did not respond. Through his binoculars, Hennecke watched 'infantry stroll into the city without firing a shot. All life in the rubble seemed to be extinguished.'[164]

The houses on the outskirts were still 'relatively intact', one machine-gunner remembered, 'but after that begins one single field of ruins with numerous fires'.[165]

The further the men of 50th Infantry Division pushed into the city, the more civilians – mostly women, children and the elderly, all distraught, impoverished, poor, filthy – began to emerge from cellars and underground shelters. Captain Ivan Stojanov, a Bulgarian observer accompanying the division, was shocked by their appearance. 'The people seemed to be like animals,' he wrote. 'When they rushed to loot a flour store, they were more like a pack of starving dogs than people.'[166]

The troops of 50th Infantry Division soon stood at the head of Yuzhnaya Bay – location of the city's central station, 'now recognisable only as a mess of bent track and wrecked points,' one officer recalled. The surrounding area had been pummelled by 1,500 tonnes of artillery shell in the past seven days alone. 'Barely a house had been spared as a result,' the officer continued. 'Streets which had been ploughed by shells were half buried by ruins.'

A few hundred yards away, the Romanians were making equally rapid progress this Wednesday morning. Georghe Manoliu had chosen not to follow orders and wait until nearly mid-day before throwing his mountain infantry into the fray. His scouts moved out at 7am, the rest of his men an hour later. Their day's work was completed before noon, not least to the surprise of the Germans who sent Manoliu clear instructions 'to raise the Romanian national flag on the tallest building in Sevastopol and report the time when it was executed.'

A reply came back almost instantaneously: 'Your order was executed at 10.30am, when the national flag fluttered on top of the war memorial from 1854–1855.'[167]

50th Infantry Division had to wait a little longer for their iconic flag-raising moment, storming the Panorama Heights just west of the central station. The statue of Eduard Totleben, the Baltic German who had led the city's defence in 1854–55, was decapitated by a German shell (the head was recovered and subsequently dispatched to Berlin for display). At 1.10pm, German soldiers scaled the dome of the panorama museum – stripped of its famous painting which had been partially damaged earlier in the battle – and unfurled their battle ensign. 'The Panorama Heights are taken. At the same time, the neighbouring divisions reach their objectives. The city has been occupied. The swastika and the Romanian flag fly over the port – Sevastopol has fallen!'[168]

The report was a little premature. Troops were still pushing into the city, advancing on both sides of Yuzhnaya Bay. As they swept downhill from the Panorama Heights, the attackers raised the Reich's battle ensign on the minaret of the Tatar mosque. 'The heat and acrid smoke became unbearable,' a soldier in 46th Infantry Division wrote.

> Entire streets were aflame and had to be avoided. Of once fine large buildings, all that was left were the remnants of walls. Entire buildings repeatedly collapsed with a tremendous crash, throwing up clouds of dust and ash. The soldiers were afraid of ammunition and petrol tanks detonating or catching on fire as a result of the tremendous heat, as a fresh sea breeze blew towards them.[169]

Finally, in the middle of the afternoon, the attackers pushed into Lenin Square, the symbolic centre of Sevastopol, just a few yards from the mouth of Yuzhnaya Bay. Infantrymen, their faces blackened by soot, their uniforms covered in dust, and equally filthy panzer crews, who'd climbed out of their vehicles, filled their lungs with the fresh sea air. With its neo-classical houses, largely intact apart from broken window panes, the square had suffered less than the rest of the city – especially the opposite shore of the bay. 'Wherever we look here there's devastation and more devastation,' one non-commissioned officer wrote. 'The bulwark, the jetties, cranes, all are just one desolate tangle of iron, wood, earth and lumps of stone, overturned and burned-out railway carriages, an upturned locomotive, deep craters caused by explosives, battered sea walls, bent and broken railway tracks demonstrate the destructive effect of our bombing attacks.'[170]

The soldiers of Ernst Maisel's 42nd Infantry Regiment were resting in the square when an open-topped staff car suddenly appeared. Accompanied only by his driver, Erich von Manstein wanted to inspect his prize. The men hurriedly presented arms, while Maisel presented the city to the general.[171]

His – and their – triumph was proclaimed to the world a few hours later. The closing bars of Liszt's *Les Préludes*, which always preceded good news from the Eastern Front, blared out of radio sets and loudspeakers throughout Germany. 'Sevastopol has fallen,' a special communiqué announced. 'German and Romanian battle flags fly over the fortress, city and harbour. As of mid-day, German and Romanian troops have captured the hitherto strongest sea and land fortress in the world after a bitter 25-day struggle.' At the same time, Hitler made Manstein a field marshal and awarded his men a special badge acknowledging the ferocity of the ten-month battle for the peninsula, the Crimean Shield.

That night the conquerors of Sevastopol pitched tents close to the southern shore of Severnaya Bay. 'Flares light up the night on the spits of land and in the rear area, individual shots resound in the distance,' one soldier recalled. 'Apart from that we can hear nothing but the calming, sleep inducing crash of the surf and regular footsteps of the guards.'[172]

Even the Nazi propaganda machine conceded that the battle for Sevastopol wasn't over quite yet. 'The remnants of the beaten army have fled to the Chersones peninsula,' the special announcement had concluded. 'Pressed into the narrowest area, they face their doom.' For once the official communiqué spoke the truth. There were now thousands of soldiers – many of them wounded – compressed into a narrow spit of land covering no more than a couple of square miles. German artillery lined up on the far side of the bay rained shells down on the airfield. 'You could see the heads and legs of soldiers flying everywhere,' one commissar remembered. The terrain was covered with wounded men, begging for water or, worse, to be shot to spare them the endless torment. The ever-shrinking number of men still uninjured were often unarmed – they'd abandoned their weapons after firing their last rounds.[173]

Before the day ended, German troops had penetrated the outer defences of Battery No.35 and sealed off its command post – several hundred yards from the gun positions. The garrison set about smashing up radios, telephones, range-finding and fire-direction equipment, with crowbars and sledgehammers. Oil was drained from generators and diesel engines, the air conditioning plant wrecked, while a demolition team wired crates of explosives and depth charges to several kilogrammes of dynamite. A little after midnight, first one turret, then the second was blown up – with scores of men still in the bowels of the battery. 'It was a nightmare,' remembered Ivan Zaruba, captain of the cruiser *Chervona Ukraina* sunk the previous autumn. 'People were suffocating from poisonous gunpowder and smoke, many, mad, fought, shot and cursed everyone and everything. And that was the flower of the Primorsky Army. What a terrible fate!'[174]

With the airfield at Chersones under fire there would be no evacuation by transport aircraft that night – or ever again. Instead, the 500 or so senior military and political officers left in the city made their way down to the waterfront in Golubaya Bay, just south of Battery No.35. Once again a crowd had gathered on the quay. And once again anger in the crowd swelled when they realised they were being abandoned by their leaders. When a handful of motor launches – too small to embark the 500 officers, let alone their men – appeared offshore, the seething masses surged. The line of guards broke. A stretcher bearing a wounded soldier was knocked into the sea. Some soldiers jumped into the water and attempted to swim out to a launch. Petr Novikov, the most senior officer present, succeeded in embarking in one of the boats, accompanied by at least a dozen other commanders and politruks, but many more officers remained ashore, voluntarily or unable to force their way through the mob.

After two chaotic hours, the three boats departed for Novorossiysk – a good 230 miles away across the open waters of the Black Sea – only to be intercepted by German E-boats around dawn. The boats fought a running battle for more than three hours until two of the Soviet craft were left dead in the water.

With his boat awash and surrounded by the dead and dying, Petr Novikov and three dozen comrades were rescued by the Germans and taken to Yalta. As he awaited treatment for his injuries, he tried to rally his fellow prisoners. 'Brothers, we bled them white good and proper. That eases the pain of our defeat a little.'[175]

Mopping up the remnants of Sevastopol defenders was taking far too long for the liking of Adolf Hitler, who voiced his 'considerable displeasure' to Manstein. The new field marshal, in turn, demanded his commanders redouble their efforts. Normally found at Eleventh Army's headquarters directing its heavy artillery, Robert Martinek decided to influence the fighting at Cape Fiolent, a headland on the southern outskirts of the city. There was little sign of fighting on the 'completely flat, barren peninsula' – the artilleryman's staff car roamed the battlefield 'as if on manoeuvres' while exhausted soldiers slept in their foxholes. 'Not a shot was fired.' Leaving his car behind, Martinek and his operations officer Kurt Pickart began walking across 400 metres of no man's land towards the old fort on the headland. They did not get far before coming under rifle and machine-gun fire. 'The *Landsers* around us were awake, and you could see how happy they were, that a general, who had no business here at the front, was taking cover,' Pickart recalled. His commander was undeterred, bringing up a couple of assault guns and ordering a mortar battery to fire at the seaward side of the old fortification. 'Everyone, listen to my orders,' Martinek ordered. 'Fix bayonets.' The stunned Pickart described what happened next:

> When the first shot landed on the fort and shrapnel was flying around our ears, the general – I could hardly keep up with him – stormed out with a *Reichskriegsflagge* under his arm. And everyone followed him with cries of 'Hurrah', the assault guns shooting constantly. Then the entrances to the fort opened and hundreds of Russians swarmed out, their hands raised, and surrendered.

While Martinek raised the German ensign on a mast inside the fortress, the scratch assault force took around 20,000 Soviet troops prisoner – only a handful tried to flee in rafts and small boats. As the prisoners were being processed, 105th Infantry Regiment's commander Friedrich-Wilhelm Müller arrived to take charge of the mopping-up operation, allowing Robert Martinek to return to headquarters. There he was greeted by an ebullient Maximilian Fretter-Pico, in charge of XXX Corps.

'Once again you can see what a great regiment Müller has,' he gushed. 'It's just being reported that he took Cape Fiolent.' Martinek said nothing. Only later did he confide in his operations officer: 'So you see, Pickart, that's how you miss out on earning a Knight's Cross.'[176]

There never was an organised evacuation from Sevastopol, nor even an attempt to improvise one. Filipp Oktyabrsky was not prepared to risk his fleet for an army which *might* be saved. But that was not the impression given. Perhaps accidentally, perhaps deliberately, a rumour swirled around the peninsula that 14 ships were on their way, and the crowds began to move towards the jetties and shoreline. 'Everyone talked about these 14 – they waited for days and nights and fought to the last man,' one Soviet colonel recalled.[177]

Captain Aleksandr Evseev was one of thousands of soldiers and civilians desperate to reach Sevastopol's westernmost bays, convinced salvation lay on the water. 'It seemed there was no possibility of reaching the sea, but people nevertheless made their way there,' he wrote. 'They crawled, ran, spent a long time lying on the ground, waiting for the barrage or air raid to end, avoiding areas subjected to methodical enemy fire.'

Above Kamyshovaya Bay, the penultimate inlet before the open waters of the Black Sea, he took a final look at the city. 'Its ruins were masked by fire and smoke,' he wrote. 'Sevastopol had already been set on fire several times and everything that could burn had burned. These explosions were clearly ammunition dumps, paying a final salute to a city which had suffered for so long. Sevastopol drowned in pillars of crimson flame and smoke.'

The naval officer headed towards the waterfront. The roads were crammed with trucks, carts, tractors and, above all, soldiers. In the moonlight Evseev watched three small boats round the headland at Chersones and enter the bay, and clambered aboard one with two comrades for a journey of more than 200 miles through open waters. 'Only the situation around Sevastopol could make us attempt to sail over such a long distance from Sevastopol to the Caucasus. We preferred death in the sea we knew to destruction by the Germans on land.'[178]

Chersones peninsula, the westernmost tip of Sevastopol, was the last refuge for most troops hoping, somehow, to avoid captivity. One nurse gave up trying to estimate how many people were crammed into the peninsula. 'A frightful number!' she wrote. 'Military – officers of all ranks, sailors and soldiers, wounded – women with children, large and small. All merged into one continuous mass, burned by the sun and finished off by the Nazis.'[179] The Luftwaffe sowed discontent, scattering hundreds of thousands of leaflets, such as this one:

Your hopes for Sevastopol have been smashed. Your comrades have raised the white flag and surrendered! As of today, Sevastopol is in German hands!

Your situation is hopeless, your resistance senseless.

No Red Army soldier, no commissar, no communist needs fear for his life. Give up your senseless resistance. Give up![180]

Abandoned by their leaders, short of ammunition and food, exposed to the remorseless sun by day, it quickly became 'impossible to call these men an army,' noted one observer. 'These were the remnants of various types of troops from the garrison, slowly withdrawing to this small, free piece of land on the Crimean peninsula... But it was not a crowd seized by panic, rather it had lost the will to fight.'[181]

There were still occasional pockets of resistance. Four riflemen and a political officer held off three panzers and two dozen infantry until their ammunition ran out, then threw themselves off a cliff into the Black Sea, crying: 'Long Live the Motherland! For Stalin!'[182] The remnants of 172nd Rifle Division made a stand on the edge of Chersones airfield to the last bullet. No-one gave orders or co-ordinated the defence; the men simply stood their ground and took aim at the onrushing Germans. 'Hit the bastards, there's nothing else to be done,' one commissar urged. 'And as long as there's still at least one round left we'll hit them.' He was subsequently wounded and taken prisoner, supposedly telling his captors, 'I've nothing to say to you, only that I am a Bolshevik, a commissar, and I know that you are doomed, that you will be destroyed.' Taunted and beaten repeatedly with a rifle butt, the commissar was finally shot. His comrades died almost to a man, leaving the runway strewn with corpses.

They had died defending an airfield no longer in use, but perhaps bought a little time for those hoping to escape by sea. But that time was limited. In the small hours of 3 July, eight motor launches reached Golubaya Bay, although only five were able to get close to shore. The operation rapidly descended into disorder just like the previous night's. The water from the shore as far out as the boats – perhaps as far away as 500 yards – was a mass of bobbing heads, men all desperately trying to reach the boats. Between 350 and 400 people were hauled aboard before the boats raised anchor and made for the Caucasus. When the sun rose a few hours later, it revealed a gruesome scene. On the shore, like abandoned bonfires, lay partially burned carts, wrecked cars, barbed-wire posts, wrecked field guns. There were machine-guns and rifles scattered around, harnesses for horses, ammunition, equipment. And everywhere a smell of burning and the unmistakeable stench of gunpowder. The true horrors were reserved for the waters. Waves carried corpses, five or six deep, along several hundred metres of shoreline. There were hundreds of dead on wrecked makeshift rafts. 'This is a nightmare,' wrote one observer, 'but real.'[183]

No more concerted attempts were made to rescue Sevastopol's defenders. Nearly 3,000 people – soldiers, civilians, sick and wounded – had been saved by boat and aircraft in the first days of July, more than half of them the city's military and political leaders of various ranks.[184] Left behind were at least 32,000 soldiers and between 20,000 and 42,000 civilians. It was now clear to them there would be no evacuation – the official Soviet communiqué had already announced they had been 'saved'. The only hope now was to break through the German lines and somehow join forces with the partisans in the mountains beyond the city. As soon as night fell on 3 July, groups of 200 to 250 men tried to slip away from Chersones or, more typically, bludgeon their way past the Germans under the cover of acrid smoke swirling around the peninsula. Of the 2,000 troops who attempted to break out, no more than one in ten succeeded – the rest were 'mown down by machine-guns as if by a scythe' – and most of those were subsequently picked up by the German authorities.

As Saturday 4 July dawned, conditions on the peninsula were hellish. The shore was lapped by corpse-filled waters. A few soldiers and sailors had dismantled the wooden piers and struck out to sea on makeshift rafts or planks in the hope they might be picked up by the Red Navy, only to be strafed by Luftwaffe fighters. On land, the suffocating stench of decay from corpses piled up in the trenches hung over the headland. There was barely a man who was not wounded. They had received no fresh food or water for perhaps four days or more. Yet when the Germans once again showered Chersones with leaflets calling on them to surrender, the men gave no answers. 'This time the Germans decided to wipe us off the face of the earth,' one Soviet soldier recalled. 'There had never been such a bombardment, artillery and mortar bombardment. We ran out of ammunition. Enemy aircraft were bombing, fighters were flying almost level with the ground, strafing with machine-guns. Every man who held the line in the trenches huddled on the ground.' The attackers quickly swarmed over Battery No.35 and a neighbouring older fort, before pressing on to the lighthouse at the head of the peninsula. There, a little after 7.30am, the swastika was raised.[185]

A few hours later corps commander General Erik Hansen took the salute in Lenin Square, hurriedly cleared of rubble. No-one was certain if the plaza was entirely secure, or clear of mines, but it at least looked 'almost presentable' for the cameramen. Parading for Hansen, whose LIV Corps had borne the brunt of the fighting on the northern side of the encircling ring, were German soldiers, airmen and sailors, plus Romanian mountain infantry, whose ranks were showered with praise by Bucharest for writing 'one of the most glorious pages in the history of our nation, thereby earning the gratitude of the homeland'.[186]

Celebrations continued the next day as Erich von Manstein welcomed a select group of officers and soldiers on the terrace of Nicholas II's magnificent villa in Livadia on the southern outskirts of Yalta. Sevastopol was only two hours' drive away, but the contrast between the ruined city and the glistening white limestone palace with its lush grounds, palm trees and finely kept gardens could not have been greater. Only senior commanders or recipients of Germany's highest decorations received invitations to the two-hour private celebration of victory in the Crimea. 'Bravery, faith and the will to win – from the Führer down to the last soldier – led to our victory,' Manstein told his guests. After the newly promoted field marshal's brief welcome, pioneers and a couple of regimental bands marched on to report, before entertaining guests with four marches, a tattoo, a tribute to the fallen. After a '*Sieg Heil*' for the Führer and the German and Romanian national anthems, guests sat down at long tables laid out in the grounds, each one laid with white sheets and a lavish cold buffet washed down with Crimean sparkling wine – recovered from the galleries at Inkerman. As the veterans of Sevastopol ate to the music of 16th Infantry Regiment's band, celebrations were interrupted by several Rata fighter-bombers passing low over

Livadia, dropping their bombs just beyond the palace and in neighbouring Yalta. While everyone else fled into the apparent safety of the Tsar's palace, regimental commanders Otto Hitzfeld and Ernst Maisel remained seated, continuing to enjoy the meal convinced that nothing could happen to a pair of veteran front-line warriors.[187]

In Yalta, Stuka commander Herbert Pabst had been sunbathing on a roof terrace when he was wakened by the explosion of flak clouds in an otherwise unscarred sky. As guns crashed and shrapnel rained down, Pabst saw Russian aircraft attacking in three waves. 'They came from the sea, and go back to sea, just as we do,' he wrote. 'They got wind of the victory celebration and savoured a little of it.'[188]

Victory at Sevastopol had cost the Axis forces nearly 6,000 dead – German divisions lost on average 500–600 men killed – and nearly 30,000 wounded in the final month's assault. One regiment which suffered more than 1,250 casualties – one in five of them killed or taken prisoner – complained the battle left it 'completely worn-out, reduced to a tiny rump'. The Luftwaffe had destroyed four enemy aircraft for every one it lost in conducting nearly 24,000 sorties over the city.[189] Soviet losses in June and July 1942 alone amounted to at least 95,000 men captured and upwards of 20,000 dead.

Newsreel footage and propaganda accounts suggested the heavy guns and mortars had been Sevastopol's downfall. There were whoops of appreciation as the camera panned to show the size of the mortar, while the sight of the gigantic Dora gun in action left cinemagoers 'flabbergasted'. Audiences applauded every time the 'colossus technical wonder' or 'super gun' – appeared and watched in amazement as the crew readied the gigantic gun for action 'like tiny figures'.[190] The reality on the ground was very different. Of the half a million shells fired at Sevastopol in June and July 1942, fewer than 250 came from the barrels of the Karl heavy mortars or Dora. Neither proved to be accurate or effective – and certainly did not justify either the effort expended or the propagandistic laurels. 'We repeatedly heard from the propaganda department that the fortress could only be captured with the help of this cannon,' a soldier in 22nd Infantry Division fumed. 'That's a lie!'[191]

For many German participants, Sevastopol was the greatest test they had faced. 'The soldiers don't hold back or mince their words,' Joseph Goebbels wrote after hosting a reception for 70 veterans later that summer. 'We can probably say the battle for Sevastopol has been the hardest which the Wehrmacht has been forced to fight in this war.' And yet, once again, German arms had triumphed. The terrain was against the *Landser*, the summer heat debilitating, while his foe had fought 'with extraordinary skill, a great deal of guile and fanatical courage'.

And so their leaders drew the same conclusions as at Kerch and Kharkov: Germans arms were still superior to their foe's. 'Even if there's more bitter fighting, Russian resistance will be broken once and for all.'[192]

As with the fall of Tobruk (see Chapter 2), Joseph Goebbels was determined that the German people hear the authentic voice of the Sevastopol warrior. A special courier aircraft brought Dietrich von Choltitz to Berlin to address the nation on the radio. Short, middle-aged, rotund, monocled, the Prussian aristocrat was not your typical Nazi hero. He and his regiment, drawn largely from northwest Germany, had fought bravely, however, seizing Fort Stalin and leading the assault across Severnaya Bay. Over 30 minutes, Choltitz described the confidence and eagerness of his men to attack, the formidable terrain and defences, and above all an enemy who fought 'bitterly' and 'doggedly', refusing to surrender. Even when cut off or surrounded, Soviet positions, bunkers, dugouts and shelters had to be eliminated 'one-by-one... until there was no man left alive'. Choltitz left his listeners in no doubt about the ferocity of the battle. He told of heavy German losses, of 'wild, determined Bolsheviks' and desperate men blowing up underground caverns, taking everything – and everyone – with them into the gates of hell. Dietrich von Choltitz's regiment had seized Rotterdam in May 1940 then fought its way through Ukraine and finally spent ten months in the Crimea, eight of them before Sevastopol. 'Of all the tasks we have faced, this latest one was the hardest. Everything to come must be easier!'

The broadcast brought many listeners to tears. Choltitz spoke calmly, honestly, clearly, all of which made it unusually human and powerful. In the days which followed he received countless letters from mothers, fathers and wives of soldiers in the East, all of them thanking him for describing the war as it was, as their loved ones described it, not some glorified propaganda account. 'It eclipses every war report to date,' one German commented, while another praised the report as 'an epic which no poet could compose better'.[193]

The prize lay in ruins. The siege had ravaged Sevastopol. More than half a million shells – from the seven- and two-tonne rounds of the mighty Dora and Karl to the 390,000 10.5cm shells fired by light field howitzers – were expended in the final month of battle, while in excess of 20,000 tonnes of bombs had been dropped on the city over the same period. 'You have to have seen Sevastopol, burning, completely destroyed,' company commander Max Fuchs noted. The city was scarred everywhere: smashed bunkers, field positions churned up by shells, a succession of bomb craters, crushed guns, the remnants of crashed aircraft, abandoned military equipment, tossed into the roadside ditches by the retreating Red Army, and cadavers and corpses, contorted in their death throes, now beginning to decompose. The English Cemetery had been turned into a defensive stronghold, its fine marble monuments to fallen Britons smashed, while graves were ripped open by shells, tossing the remains on the surface. 'Nothing is more desolate than a dead harbour,' wrote Herbert Caspers, a war correspondent with the German Navy, as he surveyed the port with its wrecks jutting out of the water, the hideously contorted forms of cranes on the jetties, their twisted steel still towering above the bay. The oil tanks, dry docks, power station lay in ruins. 'All life has been extinguished.' Nothing larger than half a dozen motorboats could be salvaged – but it was pointless, for Severnaya Bay was so heavily mined it would be weeks before any vessel could use the port.[194] The Chersones peninsula was just as desolate. 'I have never seen such a battlefield in my entire life,' SS officer Ludolf von Alvensleben wrote after touring it.

> There are thousands of totally-destroyed motor vehicles in the area. Heavy weapons of all kinds, rifles and ammunition, in short, everything an army needs for battle, are lying around at random. The ground is churned up, one shell next to another, with the enemy field positions in between. Tens of thousands of dead Russians, the cadavers of countless horses pollute the air. I saw a *Landser* eating his breakfast in total contentment just five metres from the already completely decomposed corpse of a Russian soldier. An endless number of Russian soldiers and vehicles plunged on to the steep coast. The bodies cannot be recovered yet and are continuously washed against the rocks.[195]

When Alvensleben wrote his report, fighting in Sevastopol had only just ended. The Germans may have trumpeted victory on 1 July and celebrated in style in Livadia a few days later, but Soviet sailors and soldiers continued to offer desperate, if uncoordinated resistance in the caves, rocks and crevasses of Chersones for at least another week. Manstein's men still faced as many as 6,000 troops and civilians scattered across the peninsula. What was left of 109th Rifle Division gathered in a dugout near the lighthouse. A colonel told the men they faced three choices: 'drown ourselves, shoot ourselves or go into captivity, but we might escape from captivity and could still be useful to the Motherland'. The soldiers wrapped their Communist Party cards in celluloid and buried them in an iron ammunition crate under rocks and surrendered to the Germans a few hours later. Nearby, under a white flag a German demanded a group of Red Army troops huddled at the foot of a cliff surrender. The Soviets shot him dead. Fighting repeatedly flared up in the depths of the supposedly conquered Battery No.35. Every attempt to break out on land ran into a near-impenetrable cordon. As for those who hoped to flee by sea, German and Italian motor boats patrolled the waters off the headland. Their guns poured fire at the caverns. Landing parties were sent ashore to root soldiers out. Explosives were lowered down cliff faces and detonated in an attempt to bring the caves down on the last defenders. A Great War veteran confided in his Italian comrades that he'd never experienced such horrors, not even at Verdun. The last concerted resistance at Chersones ended on 12 July. An interpreter lambasted Private F. P. Zemlyansky, captured in the ruins of Battery No.35, and his comrades for 'delaying sending German troops to the Caucasus through their senseless resistance'. When he finished, a Red Army officer addressed the men: 'My dear comrades, defenders of Sevastopol, we are now prisoners of the enemy, but we have not surrendered, we have defended our sacred lines steadfastly and honestly. And if any of us manage to stay alive, tell our fellow countrymen that we have fulfilled our military duty to the end, let people know about it!' Staff Sergeant N. L. Anishin was surprised by the initial reception of his captors: 'The German command spares you, because you have fought bravely.' The prisoners would be spared little.

Around 40,000 Soviet troops fell into German hands in the first days of July 1942 – 'so many prisoners that we could not believe our eyes,' remembered I. V. Antonyuk of 8th Marines Brigade, while a Red Army communications officer recalled seeing lines of captured soldiers 'as far as the eye could see, all the way to the horizon'. Doctors, officers and commissars were separated while Crimean Tatars in German uniforms moved through the columns singling out Jews, Communists and other foes. Marines seemed particularly loathed by Sevastopol's new masters, who regarded them as the kernel of the city's resistance. They were frequently hauled out of the line and shot on the spot at point-blank range, while in Kamyshovaya Bay some prisoners were driven into the water at gunpoint, then executed ten at a time.

With selection complete, the prisoners were marched through the ruins of Sevastopol in columns four deep. A 14-year-old girl watched 'an endless black ribbon' shuffling along through the rubble, wounded almost to a man, many of them shell-shocked, their filthy uniforms in tatters. Romanian troops took pot-shots at the long file of prisoners, while German guards spurred their captives on by striking men with rifle butts and shooting anyone who failed to keep pace. Junior officer Gottlob Bidermann watched as the Russian prisoners 'moved around supporting each other, hobbling around with the aid of sticks, surrounded by swarms of flies, covered in bloody bandages. It was a long, wretched column which struggled under the sweltering sun of the Crimea, through the land of Iphigenia, towards the prison camps and wells.' When faced with oncoming traffic, no attempt was made to move the prisoners to the roadside. German vehicles simply crushed those men in their path. 'People were flattened like frogs on the asphalt,' one horrified eyewitness remembered. 'Human life meant nothing to the occupiers.' Any man who tried to break rank was shot.[196]

In the camps, they received rudimentary treatment from captured doctors and medics who had been put to work, while other prisoners toiled in the broiling July heat to repair roads or restore the water supply. Bulgarian observer Captain Ivan Stojanov saw only 'happy faces' among the prisoners, men 'completely satisfied with their fate', while civilians seemed 'glad to have escaped the wrath of the commissars'. Max Fuchs, on the other hand, encountered nothing but 'bony skeletons, anxious and haggard' in the streets of Sevastopol. He handed out sweets and tobacco to stunned civilians who 'couldn't believe that we wouldn't kill them.'[197]

Max Fuchs' empathy was not widely shared. 'The life of one German soldier is worth more than 100 dodgy Russians,' one military police commandant sneered.[198] An officer in 50th Infantry Division was convinced that 'the majority of the Russians left in Sevastopol were our enemies'. Commissars were handed over to the security services – which meant certain death – while Jewish soldiers were executed. Civilians fared little better. More than 35,000 had stayed behind in Sevastopol's ruins. There was no running water, just a couple of fountains still operating, no sewage system intact, no fresh food and no working medical facilities. Hitler had demanded all but the ethnic German and indigenous Tatar population deported – giving Manstein's staff just six hours to draw up a detailed plan, before scaling down his original idea by ordering only the 'rabble in the big cities' rounded up instead.[199] A school in the outer suburbs was turned into a makeshift prison for supposed enemies of the Reich. Any civilian who tried to flee Sevastopol invariably ended up there. But there was no 'big city rabble'. Not in Sevastopol, nor anywhere else in the Crimea. The majority of inhabitants who remained were worn out, scared, cowed, starving. What remained of Sevastopol's Jewish population was handed over to an SS detachment which established itself a few days after the city's fall. It quickly began executing Jews in an anti-tank ditch on the edge of Sevastopol – sometimes in groups of 30, on one occasion as many as 300 men murdered in a mass shooting. Jewish women and children were spared shooting – but not death. They were piled into the back of 'gas vans' where they were killed by the exhaust fumes. When the screams inside faded, the trucks drove out to the ditch where the corpses – 'a ball of people, all tangled up with each other' – joined the decomposing bodies of men.[200] Foreign Office official Otto von Hentig was appalled. The crimes being committed daily in Sevastopol 'utterly shook the Army's reputation'. The administration did not listen. Four months after Sevastopol's fall, Hentig complained that the German occupation of the Crimea had 'brought only hunger, unemployment, a shortage of housing, more worries and unrest'.[201]

For the conquerors of the Crimea, there was a little rest before the battle resumed. Some followed the bulk of Manstein's Eleventh Army north to besiege Leningrad; others were dispatched to the central front or joined the summer offensive in southern Russia. Max Fuchs' company was given five days' leave on the coast. 'These are wonderful days,' he wrote. 'I lie naked on the magnificent sand all day long. We fish using hand-grenades. Baked, they taste marvellous.'[202] Before being transferred to the Caucasus, Josef Wimmer enjoyed a few days at 50th Infantry Division's rest home in Yalta:

There was an almost unnatural silence, no mortars, no machine-gun fire and no sound of orders being given here. Only the blue sea crashing in rhythmic intervals against the beach before roaring off again. Sometimes gentle gusts blew through the park, moving the pine, palm and almond trees. Their shadows moved almost rhythmically and seemed to dance over the wonderfully-laid-out flowerbeds. There were many vines on the mountain slopes. I stared at the blue-black sea. Somewhere, far in the distance, lay the Caucasus, Turkey, Syria, Arabia and the Indian Ocean. As I was all alone, I forgot where I was. The quiet and silence overwhelmed me. How beautiful life really could be.[203]

2

ROMMELING AGAIN

We don't comprehend our victory yet. Only our eyes can see that something tremendous has happened.

Officer in 15th Panzer Division

There was still a little residual snow on the sleepers at Oberalm station on the southern outskirts of Salzburg, even though May was just three days away. Adolf Hitler stood on the gravel, dressed in a long black winter coat. The Führer engaged in light-hearted small talk with his substantial entourage – all standing half a dozen paces behind their leader – as he waited for two rather drab diesel locomotives to haul Benito Mussolini's special train into the siding. Barely had the train ground to a halt than the Duce stepped off it and Hitler was seizing his hands, shaking them vigorously. The Italian dictator exchanged platitudes with his German counterpart. But the brief smile he gave the newsreel cameras was weak, almost awkward. 'This is a meeting which was wanted by the Germans and for which, as usual, they've not given us any idea of the agenda,' the Duce's son-in-law and Italian Foreign Minister Galeazzo Ciano had bitterly observed in his diary as the train made its way north from Rome. The agenda, as Mussolini and Ciano would learn over the next two days, was the Axis conduct of the war in the Mediterranean in 1942.[1] The goals were Suez and the Nile Delta to unhinge the entire British position in North Africa and the Middle East – but there were two obstacles in the way: Malta and Tobruk.

After swinging furiously for more than a year, the pendulum of war in North Africa had momentarily come to a stop. It had swung Italy's way, briefly, in the autumn of 1940, as Mussolini's troops limply invaded Egypt, before the British spectacularly drove them back to the Gulf of Sirte in the winter of 1940–41.

The collapse prompted German intervention – initially to give the Italians backbone. But the force dispatched, the *Afrika Korps*, and the man dispatched to lead it, Erwin Rommel, resolved to attack, not merely defend. Rommel's bold thrust in March and April 1941 pushed the British some 600 miles – back into Egypt. Libya's coastal towns fell: Agheila, Benghazi, Derna. But not Tobruk. Its garrison doggedly held out, thwarting two attempts by Axis troops to storm it – and thwarting any onward drive into Egypt, for there could be no thought of advancing on the Suez Canal and the Nile Delta with a British fortress in the rear of the Axis lines. Worse was to come. Having deprived Rommel of his prize, the British eventually – and bloodily – lifted the siege of Tobruk in the closing weeks of 1941. Their winter offensive finally ran out of steam with the now grandly titled *Panzerarmee Afrika* back at the foot of the Gulf of Sirte. The German-Italian forces did not remain there long. In mid-January 1942 they struck east again – and once again the tide of war in the desert flowed with the Axis; after a fortnight, Rommel's troops stood just west of Tobruk once more after a 350-mile lunge through Cyrenaica which recaptured much of the ground lost over the winter. And there, for three months, the pendulum of war stopped.

Rommel's staff would attribute the rapid success of the counter-stroke – at least in part – to the arrival of a single convoy in Tripoli, delivering more than 70 panzers and vehicles, plus ammunition and supplies of all kind. 'It was just like a victory in battle,' the *Afrika Korps*' chief-of-staff Fritz Bayerlein later wrote.[2]

Logistics dictated the course of battle in North Africa as in no other theatre of war. Food, fuel, ammunition, vehicles, all came from the European continent. In a quiet month, the Axis forces in North Africa required nearly 50,000 tons of supplies and upwards of 1,000 vehicles. On the offensive, *Panzerarmee Afrika* consumed as much as 1,500 tons *a day*. Troops could be – and were – flown to North Africa, nearly 6,000 in April 1942 alone. But all bulk supplies came by sea from Italy, either from Taranto or, more usually, Naples. Whatever the port of embarkation, the destination was almost always Tripoli – and the route took shipping within range of British naval and air forces based in Malta. Of every five Axis ships sunk on the North Africa run, four were lost because Malta was in enemy hands. Berlin and Rome agreed. Malta had to be neutralised. The German Navy and the Italians especially favoured invasion. As the head of Italy's armed forces, Ugo Cavallero, put it simply: 'If we take Malta, Libya will be safe.' The Luftwaffe favoured bombing the island into submission – and by the end of April 1942, it was convinced it had done just that. Over a five-week period, the island had been pummelled by more than 6,500 tonnes of bombs dropped during nearly 12,000 sorties by German and Italian aircraft. Of the 151,000 tons of supplies shipped to North Africa that month, all but 1,000 reached their destination.³ 'We were convinced that Malta had been bombed to the point it was ready for invading,' one pilot recalled.⁴

Erwin Rommel had already decided his next course of action: 'to attack and destroy the British army in the field' before swiftly moving on to dispatch Tobruk. He would do so as soon as possible – probably at the end of May.⁵ And he would do so against the advice of most of his staff.

Time, Rommel knew, worked against the Axis. Despite having to sail around the Cape of Good Hope – a 12,000-mile journey – the British appeared to be able to build up their forces more quickly than Rommel could his own. 'It was obvious that the English would try to destroy my army with all means at their disposal as soon as they felt they were strong enough,' he wrote.⁶ That, his staff assured him, would not be until September – but by then the *Panzerarmee* too would be much stronger, and in a much better position to strike. 'Everyone advised him that it was better to wait until autumn,' recalled Siegfried Westphal, one of the few staff officers urging the general to strike sooner rather than later. 'Rommel was undecided – a very rare occurrence for him.' The Italians tipped the balance in favour of attack – but not intentionally. Their newly arrived chief-of-staff in North Africa suggested it would be irresponsible to drive on Tobruk in the spring. Rommel exploded. 'To suggest to him that his behaviour was possibly irresponsible, when he was consumed day and night by the Libyan question, was going too far,' Westphal wrote. 'His back was up. Rommel was determined to begin now.'⁷

Rommel wanted Tobruk. The Italians wanted Malta. But the question facing the Axis leadership was not Malta *and* Tobruk, rather Malta *or* Tobruk, for the forces were insufficient to mount both operations – at least not simultaneously. Over the final two days of April 1942, Hitler and Mussolini would decide how and where to strike first.

From Oberalm station, it was little more than a ten-minute drive for the two Axis leaders to the first venue for their talks: the Schloss Klessheim, a baroque palace on the western outskirts of Salzburg. Converted by the Nazis into a guest house for foreign dignitaries, it had been re-decorated with furniture, carpets and ornaments from France – 'they probably didn't pay much for them,' the Italian Foreign Minister acidly observed. The foppish but insightful Ciano was closeted with his Nazi opposite number, Joachim von Ribbentrop, while his master conferred with the Duce in a neighbouring room. Hitler treated his guest to a *tour d'horizon* – 'the same old record,' as Ciano put it. The Führer assured the Duce that he remained master of the situation. America was nothing but a 'big bluff': 'You can't build 200,000 aircraft or complete two ships every day'; Britain would throw in the towel if it continued to lose 600,000 or 700,000 tons of shipping every month. As for the Eastern Front, the German soldier of 1941 had proved himself far more resilient than the Frenchman of 1812 – despite having to endure the worst winter in a century. 'There were days,' Hitler told his ally, 'when pure military leadership failed and a brave heart was needed.' The storm, however, had been weathered. '*We* won – the soldiers *and I* won,' he declared, dismissing many of his generals as weak – physically and mentally. Now, the Russian winter offensive had run its course. In the coming spring and summer the Germans would deliver the knockout blow, lunging into the Caucasus. 'When Russia's sources of oil are exhausted, she'll be brought to her knees.'

Ribbentrop served the same dish to Ciano, who found his hosts particularly ingratiating – the more unctuous the Germans were, the worse their predicament. He also found that the winter had drained the German leader – for the first time, grey hairs were noticeable. The Duce, too, had aged visibly. Mussolini was tired, his face pale. No longer did he possess his pre-war zest – nor public support, for that matter. The cult of the Duce had attributed all of Fascist Italy's successes to him; now the Italian people blamed him for every setback or misfortune to befall them or Italian arms.

One thing had not changed since the last meeting between Führer and Duce in the summer of 1941. However much Mussolini banged the *mare nostrum* drum, Italy remained the lesser of the Axis powers. 'Hitler talks, talks, talks, talks,' Ciano noted – at one point the Führer spoke for 100 minutes without stopping. There was no subject not touched upon: war and peace, religion and philosophy, art, history. Mussolini, accustomed to talking, not listening, sat silently and frequently stared at his watch. The Führer's entourage struggled to stay awake; some even dozed off. 'The Germans, poor people, have to endure this every day.'[8]

Talks the following day a dozen miles away at the Führer's alpine retreat on the Obersalzberg outside Berchtesgaden were at least rather more structured. Aerial photographs of Malta were laid out, possible landing sites for paratroopers and gliders discussed, dates for an invasion suggested, possibly as early as mid-June. Hitler promised 'lavish' support for the operation – codenamed *Herkules* by the Germans, *C3* by the Italians: paratroopers, transport aircraft, barges to put tanks ashore. Supporting *Herkules*, however, was not the same as committing to it – and Adolf Hitler did not. He was terrified of the invasion miscarrying and the effect that might have on world opinion. An offensive in North Africa, on the other hand, presented no such pitfalls – people were used to the see-saw nature of the conflict there. 'No concrete plans' surrounding the Libya operation – codenamed *Theseus* – were discussed. Tobruk might fall, Hitler suggested, Rommel might even push into Egypt – the Suez Canal 'would be a worthwhile future objective'.[9] That was as far as discussion of Axis strategy in the Mediterranean in 1942 went. It was summed up neatly by the German Navy's liaison officer at Hitler's headquarters: *First Libya, then Malta.*

The two-day summit was typical of Hitler's conduct of the war. The Italians had arrived in Salzburg prepared to lobby for the invasion of Malta, convinced that 'the fate of Libya – and with it the Axis powers' entire position in North Africa – rests on the outcome of this year'.[10] And, as usual, Hitler held the floor, imposing his will on the Duce, issuing vague objectives, vague directives.

The talks at Schloss Klessheim and on the Obersalzberg merely reinforced the impression of the dilettante conduct of the Mediterranean campaign. Hitler, one naval staff officer observed, regarded the theatre 'as a sideshow, where successes were regarded as a gift from the gods'. There never was a grand strategy. There never was a combined Italian-German staff directing operations. There were German generals. German admirals. Italian generals. Italian admirals. There were liaison officers. They talked. They discussed. They stated the case for their plans and operations. But an overall plan? Never.[11]

Benito Mussolini returned to Rome 'satisfied' – meetings with the Führer almost always lifted his spirits. But he was not entirely fooled by the gloss Hitler had applied to Germany's situation. 'The German war machine remains formidable,' he confided in his foreign minister, 'but it's also suffered a great deal.' The joint official communiqué, naturally, described two days of talks held in 'a spirit of close friendship', concluding with 'complete agreement' between Rome and Berlin about the future course of the war. There was not. The German Navy was disappointed that *Herkules* had been postponed. Ugo Cavallero was more than disappointed. To him, failure to invade Malta would be a cardinal error. 'If it's not carried out,' he warned, 'by the autumn the English will again be able to build up superior forces in Africa and the situation in the Mediterranean will worsen once more.'[12]

Ugo Cavallero's fears were well-founded, but despite his insistence, *Herkules* would never be carried out. Within a month, Adolf Hitler had all but cancelled the operation. And by then, Erwin Rommel had all but finished his preparations for *Theseus*.[13]

Africa. The word had a 'strange alluring power,' flak gunner Rudolf Hubalek remembered. As he waited to board a Junkers Ju52 transport at Trapani in western Sicily, he conjured up images from his childhood of 'green palms, camels and nomadic Arabs in the desert sand, a white *burnous* [cloak] thrown over their shoulders, or scantily-clad blacks in the jungle, elephants and lions'. He wasn't the only German soldier attracted by dreams of 'tropical nights, palm trees, the sea air, natives, oases, pith helmets'. Panzer driver Horst Sonnenkalb imagined 'yellow and white sand dunes, camel trains, green palms and perhaps a mirage'. Instead, he was 'astonished and disappointed at the same time' by his first taste of the real Africa. 'It was cold – we shivered like pups. Very quickly we had to get used to the harsh weather conditions. Heat during the day, cold at night, salty drinking water, huge swarms of flies, sandstorms which sometimes lasted for three days – that was Africa.'[14]

Like most Axis soldiers fighting in North Africa, Horst Sonnenkalb came by sea. The journey across the 'big pond', as the men dubbed it, took a day and a half by sea from Taranto, as much as twice as long from Naples – the usual ports of departure. Radio operator Erhard Naumann joined the liner *Oceania* for the crossing to Tripoli. The mood aboard was comradely, almost congenial. 'When we found our cabins, we found small groups of Germans and Italians laughing and joking together everywhere,' he recalled. 'Very few thought that very shortly we'd begin a very dangerous journey.' Throughout the 36-hour crossing from Taranto, Naumann and his comrades wore an uncomfortable cork lifejacket and were expected to fall in three times a day for roll call. 'The rest of the time we could wander around on deck and refresh ourselves from times to time with a glass of lemonade. Although we'd left the harbour behind, there could be no talk of "enjoying a day at sea".'[15] Just 60 miles from Libya, the *Oceania* was torpedoed by the British submarine *Upholder*, which then claimed a second scalp when it attacked another converted liner, the *Neptunia*. When Erhard Naumann's battalion formed up for roll call once more, just 714 of its 800 men stood before their commander.

Air transport – a three-hour flight from Sicily to Tripoli, under two hours from Crete to eastern Libya – was equally fraught with danger. Flak officer Helmuth Köhrer climbed into one of 13 Ju52 transporters for a flight to Derna in May 1942. Only six aircraft completed the two-hour journey; they were pounced on by 30 British fighters. The sluggish Junkers had only a couple of machine-guns each to fend off their attackers. Their crews fought bravely – three fighters were shot down. But otherwise, it was a slaughter. 'The Ju burns so quickly,' a horrified Köhrer wrote. 'The soldiers sitting inside – mostly from the supply service or men returning from leave – were so desperate that they preferred to jump into the sea from fifty metres than remain in the burning aircraft.' The air-sea rescue service was able to recover nearly half the men, but at least 70 men and aircrew perished.[16]

Troops arriving in Tripoli were quickly dispatched to an old Italian barracks just outside the Libyan capital to train and acclimatise. The distance from the city gave the camp its nickname: 'KM 5' – *Kilometer* 5. It gave the impression of a typical transit camp – rickety beds, run-down barracks – and was plagued by rats. Staff advised new arrivals like flak gunner Rudolf Hubalek: *Don't use the blankets you've been given or better still burn them immediately!* Or: *Stay out of the camp until roll call!* The Austrian took their advice and headed straight into the nearby metropolis. Tripoli in the spring of 1942 bore substantial scars of war. Almost every house had been damaged in some form by the many British air raids. 'It was particularly desolate in the port – there were several wrecks on the bottom, only the top of their masts rising from the water,' Hubalek recalled. The bazaar, as expected, was the scene of lively activity: women veiled in *burkas* hurriedly finishing their shopping; German soldiers bargaining with Arab traders, who swore and called out in the name of Allah. 'This was all part of the way they did business here,' the flak gunner wrote. 'You didn't get anywhere without haggling. Extortionate prices were asked for all sorts of souvenirs – and even if you paid a fraction of the asking price, you'd still almost certainly been cheated.'[17]

After surviving the sinking of the *Oceania*, Erhard Naumann spent six weeks at KM 5 – and made the most of Tripoli's distractions. 'I must say that my life here in Tripoli is a thousand times better than the dull life in the barracks,' he told his family. He bathed in the Mediterranean, visited a tavern on the beach, took advantage of the German cinema, watched life go by in the Piazza Italia – the city's largest square – and wandered through the winding alleys and lanes of the Arab quarter, which was off-limits after nightfall. Sheikhs sat in front of their apartments and plied their trades, sometimes as shopkeepers, sometimes as craftsmen. 'You can get anything from them from razors to sewing needles,' Naumann wrote – but like Rudolf Hubalek, he always bartered. The bazaar and alleys met most of the needs of a visiting German soldier, but not all. A soldiers' rest home – 'General Rommel' – provided 'everything you could possibly wish for: cigarettes, coffee, beer, wine, chilled fruit juice and sometimes even chocolate.'[18] Perhaps not quite *everything*. To satiate the men's sexual urges, a brothel 'staffed' by Italian prostitutes, was established in the Via Tassoni. Italian and unlicensed bordellos, however, were out of bounds.

The German soldier could not remain in Tripoli or KM 5 indefinitely. Sooner or later he would have to head for the front – which in the spring of 1942 meant an 800-mile journey by truck to the front line at Gazala. For several days, individual vehicles or columns headed along the Via Balbia, a 1,100-mile coastal highway from Libya's western border with Tunisia to its eastern frontier with Egypt. Built by the Italians in the 1930s, it now served as the lifeline for Axis and British troops alike.

For German troops heading up the line, it was a journey of three or four days by truck. The drivers were the unsung heroes of the desert campaign, never credited in any official communiqué or order of the day, yet essential to the smooth functioning of the front line. 'They drove on red-hot highways, drove through cold nights and raging sandstorms for hundreds, even thousands of kilometres,' junior officer Werner Kost eulogised. 'They repaired their cars in 50-degree heat. And how often! Because eight to ten punctures a day were not uncommon. Tyres burst like balloons. Car jacks sank deep into the sand.'[19] For newcomers like Rudolf Hubalek and his flak gun crew, the lengthy ride was an adventure. 'We scanned the landscape constantly: we wanted to take in all that was new, missing nothing,' he remembered. 'These new sights were a sight for sore eyes – this coastal strip was like one big oasis.' There were few towns along the route – a handful of desert fortresses and walled cities such as Misrata. 'On the map, the journey seemed to be very short, but the individual towns were separated by hundreds of kilometres,' Hubalek wrote. At first the Via Balbia – named after Libya's Fascist governor in the 1930s who had been shot down by his own troops flying over Tobruk during the opening days of the war – was flanked by the lush coastal strip. But beyond Sirte it became increasingly barren and the journey increasingly monotonous.

The sole highlight was the pseudo-ancient *Arco dei Fileni* – the Philaenus arch – straddling the Via Balbia between the small port of Ra's Lanuf and Agheila. Built as a monument to Fascism and the pioneers behind the coastal highway, the 100ft-high arch was a homage to the altars of the Philaenus brothers, two pillars which marked the border between the domains of Carthage to the west, Cyrene to the east. More than two millennia later, the triumphal arch marked the boundary between the districts of Tripolitania and Cyrenaica.[20] It was getting dark as Hubalek and his comrades arrived at the arch. Nearby there were several graves. 'The simple wooden crosses glistened in the twilight,' the flak man wrote. 'On some hung a steel or pith-helmet, turned white by the sun's rays, moving in the evening wind.' Nearby there was a small memorial stone: *The first dead of the Afrika Korps.*[21]

The next morning the monotony resumed. Western Cyrenaica was no less drab than eastern Tripolitania. The truck passed the ancient fort of Agedabia, reduced to ruins and surrounded by burned-out vehicles, shot-up tanks and small mounds where the fallen were buried. The terrain was 'terribly desolate': camel thorn bushes brushed by the wind rising in the desert and driving a wall of sand before it in the afternoon – a *ghibli*, or sandstorm. Towards Benghazi the desert gave way to the foothills of the Jebel Akhdar, the lush mountainous plateau which dominated eastern Cyrenaica. Where once the desert extended to the sea, here there were steep cliffs and *wadis* – river valleys – up to the southern shore of the Mediterranean. As Libya's wettest region, it was also its most vibrant. 'Spring in Cyrenaica is rather beautiful,' Hubalek wrote. 'The lush green of the meadows and flowers in a kaleidoscope of colours are good for the eye after the monotony of the desert.' Beyond the ancient city of Barce, the Via Balbia 'clung magnificently on the edge of precipices which made you dizzy, snaked its way up again, then back into the floor of a valley. Rugged rocks towered on both sides.'[22] And then, towards Derna, the Jebel Akhdar began to taper out and the desert encroached once more. Fifteen miles southeast of Derna, Rudolf Hubalek reached his destination: Martuba airfield, home of the fighters of *Jagdgeschwader* 27. Hubalek and his comrades would protect the airfield against attacks from the air or on the ground.

In mid-May, the sun rose over the front line in Libya a little after 5.30am. Nights when the temperature fell below 10°C had passed. Now it stayed in the high-teens – warm enough for Rudolf Hubalek to wear only his shorts and steel helmet as he manned his 2cm flak gun. Dawn was by far the most pleasant time of day. Visibility extended four, even six miles if the soldier carrying out his first duty of the new day – the 'spade walk' to the latrine – cared to look about him. Not that there was much to see. The brief spring in the Libyan desert had given way to the relentless summer. 'The finest days of 1942 in our part of the world are over,' supply officer Hellmuth Frey told his family back in Pforzheim. 'Where there were masses of flowers like in our Alpine gardens in spring, now there is desert once more, steppe like on the parade grounds in Germany. Even the scrawny plant stalks cannot shield the view of the bare earth.'[23]

By noon temperatures had climbed to the mid-40s Celsius. 'If you have to walk around for just five minutes in the intense mid-day heat, you quickly get a headache,' 21-year-old Erhard Naumann wrote home to Leipzig:

> If you go inside your tent, it's even worse because the oppressive heat takes your breath away. Outside in the shade is best because there's often a breeze. But if it's a southerly, then it's as if you're standing in front of an oven. The funny thing is that you have very little thirst, you're just tired, you want to lie down and sleep, sleep and sleep some more.[24]

Not only did the mid-day heat exhaust the men; it caused the air to glimmer, limiting visibility and creating mirages, 'making expanses of water, oases with palms or larger objects seem like tanks or motor vehicles, only to disappear when you got closer,' company commander Adalbert von Taysen remembered. And away from the coastal strip, the heat could also stir up sand and dust storms. Men caught in the open desert when a sandstorm struck were left dehydrated and battered. 'It's as if the body has been electrocuted, nerves tingle,' von Taysen wrote.[25] Those who crawled into their tents or vehicles found they offered little escape from the storm; the fine sand still blew in through the gaps and cracks. After the *ghibli* had passed, every weapon, every vehicle had to be cleaned, ready for use once more. The men themselves, however, had little chance to wash. Those posted near the coast bathed in the Mediterranean. Those serving inland had no such relief. The four litres of water each man was allocated each day was solely for drinking or cooking. What little water was left, if there was any, was used to wash, shave and clean clothes. When there was washing water, it was carefully measured out. 'Each man began to wash his head and scrubbed himself down to his feet,' panzer gunner Otto Henning recalled. 'Then we washed our underwear. We had no water for rinsing, but there was no problem drying – we generally just put the wet underwear back on. It had a slight cooling effect.' The results were not clean by European standards, Henning admitted: 'The main thing was to get the sand out because everything here is grey anyway.'[26]

In Europe, such poor sanitation might have caused an outbreak of disease. Rarely was this the case in Libya – few germs thrived in the dry desert air. But what did spread disease and illness – dysentery especially – were flies which gathered in swarms wherever there were watering holes or large groups of men. And when disease struck, it quickly spread. At times perhaps two thirds of a unit could be laid low by diarrhoea. 'No-one escapes from it,' panzer company commander Harald Kuhn wrote. 'You really don't know if you'd rather live or die. If you've crouched down 70 times in a day then you know what it's like.'[27]

When not spreading disease, flies tormented the soldier in North Africa. 'If anyone claims that flies are not wild animals, let them come here and be tormented by them and they'll admit that these are the wildest creatures in God's animal kingdom,' Kuhn wrote.[28] Kuhn and his comrades had to contend with scorpions, rats, field and jumping mice, horn and sand vipers, even tarantulas. Before going to bed the men searched their tents thoroughly – and when they woke in the morning checked their boots to make sure nothing had scurried into them overnight. Snake bites were rare – the creatures normally slithered away if men approached, and only attacked if someone stood on their tails. Troops weren't even particularly worried about scorpion stings, which were more common, but less dangerous. But no diary, letter or memoir of a German soldier in Africa fails to mention flies – and almost all draw parallels with a biblical plague. 'Barely have you poured a cup of coffee before there are a dozen of these creatures in the cup,' Erhard Naumann wrote. 'It's impossible to drink half a litre of coffee without first getting rid of at least 30 flies from the cup even if we cover it with a newspaper or waft our hands over it. But anyone who thinks he should pour the coffee away if there are flies in it would inevitably die of thirst here.'[29] Otto Henning cursed them:

> They flew into our mouths, the corners of our eyes, our noses, ears without warning. We ran around with mosquito nets over our heads. When eating a slice of bread you had to wave your hand over it – and when you bit they flew into your mouth. It's hard to believe but the flies drove me mad. Our mosquito nets were tied at the neck but somehow they managed to creep inside the net and angrily buzzed around in front of my face. It literally drove me to despair. If you wiped your sweaty arm with your spare hand, you got a hand full of flies. In the heat you could watch the beads of sweat forming on the body and the flies swarming down on these beads in their lust for something damp.

If the troops moved they perhaps enjoyed half a day's grace in their new location before the flies found them again.[30] The only practical defence were nets issued when the men picked up their tropical uniforms: one net for the camp bed, one to wear during the day. Junior officer Ralf Ringler marvelled at the other 'wonderful things' he received: 'a tropical helmet, a tent, a sleeping bag, a pair of tropical boots, a pair of tropical shoes, long trousers, short trousers, breeches, coat, blouse, cummerbund made of sheep's wool – some shaking of the head at this point – glasses to shield the dust and much, much more.' Ringler also received 'the usual trappings of an officer' – binoculars, a map case, pistol, haversack. But only Luftwaffe ground personnel and flak gunners received steel helmets – something which baffled the Austrian infantryman as he collected a cap with a large visor. 'Apart from the pure psychological effect, a steel helmet provides real protection against the many small bomb, shell and stone splinters. At the very least it gives the wearer a feeling of safety and security. No-one would complain about being too hot in the sun – on days of battle we have entirely different things on our minds.'[31]

A steel helmet was indispensable, but newly arrived troops quickly realised that much of their standard-issue kit, especially clothing, was superfluous. 'There were no dress regulations in our group – in fact I think the same goes for the rest of the *Afrika Korps*,' panzer gunner Otto Henning recalled:

> Everybody put on what they regarded was suitable from their tropical equipment. Long trousers, short trousers, breeches, running shorts, 'Africa shoes' or 'Africa boots', a khaki shirt or string vest, but always a cap. The cap was needed should you run into a strange officer and have to salute, otherwise without headgear you'd have to raise your right arm and give the Hitler salute. Only new boys wore our tropical helmets – and which one of us wanted to be seen as a newcomer?[32]

Most men hoped for a draft to Africa – 'a little war,' as Ralf Ringler put it – to escape the mincing machine of the Eastern Front. 'These brave troops looking for a comfortable theatre of war will soon learn otherwise,' Hellmuth Frey drily observed. Soldiers transferred to Africa from Russia brushed aside advice from *Afrika Korps* veterans, known simply as *Afrikaner* – Africans. 'Why's the old man served up this old rubbish for us, experienced Russian veterans?' one flak gunner fumed. '*Herr Kamerad*,' an *Afrikaner* explained, 'you'll be amazed at the tremendous differences between war in Russia and here in the desert!' A few weeks later the Eastern Front veteran agreed: 'The war here in Africa is waged more fairly, but it's damned harder than in Russia.'[33]

In early and mid-May 1942, however, there was little war at all being waged. The odd skirmish, a few raiding parties to test the respective defences. Otherwise, life on the Gazala front settled into a drab routine. The landscape was drab. The work was drab – Otto Henning and his colleagues had turned into labourers, digging foxholes for each other and building walls of sand to protect their vehicles.[34] And the food was especially drab. It was, complained Harald Kuhn, 'the saddest chapter' of life in the desert.

> Bread, tinned beef like leather, or sardines and dried vegetables, occasionally a lemon to provide fresh vitamins. The same fare day after day, week after week, month after month. What we would do for a little fresh meat, fresh vegetables or fruit every now and then to say nothing of eggs! The best you can hope for is bartering a couple of onions or a melon from an Arab for an extortionate price.[35]

Tinned food provided by the Italians proved particularly unpopular. 'Donkey meat – hard, tough and not meant for German stomachs,' Otto Henning fumed. The cans were stamped 'AM' – *amministrazione militare* (military administration). The men invented every possible nickname: *alter Mann* (old man), *armer Mann* (poor man), *armer Mussolini* (poor Mussolini), *angeschwemmter Matrose* (washed-up sailor); nor were the quips restricted to the Germans. The Italians branded the cans *arabo muerto* (dead Arab), *asino e manzo* (donkey and beef). 'Treats' included a tube of cheese, squeezed like toothpaste, or perhaps powdered jam. When the latter was mixed with the salty desert drinking water and spread on bread 'it was enough to make you throw up,' Henning remembered.[36]

When the day's work was done, the men sat down and talked, joked, played skat – a popular card game – read, penned letters home. As it did wherever the German soldier fought, the military postal service, the *Feldpost*, delivered mail from home – but it could be delayed for weeks if the army was on the move. Parcels from Germany brought not just news from loved ones, but cakes, soap, biscuits, toiletries, newspapers. Home was not the only source of news. For soldiers, a *Propaganda Kompanie* of journalist-soldiers based in Benghazi produced a weekly newspaper, *Die Oase* (The Oasis) – a mix of news from the African front and stories from the homeland. Luftwaffe personnel received a 16- or 20-page pictorial news magazine, *Adler von Hellas* (Eagle from Hellas) each week. Beyond the news features, there were jokes, crosswords, short stories. Daily news – as well as a diet of light entertainment and classical music – came courtesy of the radio, tuned in to Berlin or Cologne or, more usually, the Belgrade transmitter. Shortly before 10pm, the dial was fixed on Belgrade before it signed off for the night. The last song of the day, by popular request, was always the wistful *Lili Marleen*. This sentimental tale of a soldier hoping his lover – the eponymous Lili – would still be waiting for him under a lamp outside the barracks aroused a longing for home. It became the *Afrika Korps'* lullaby. 'Truly a real tearjerker – but evening after evening it was listened to with the same devotion as a living link with the homeland,' Heinz-Dietrich Aberger of Machine-Gun Battalion 8 remembered. Rudolf Hubalek hummed the tune as he stood watch at his gun emplacement on the edge of Martuba airfield. 'How wonderful a lamp in front of our barracks would be now,' he wrote. 'In fact, how wonderful it would be without total darkness. How wonderful a barracks with beds and straw sacks, or even mattresses, would be right now instead of the stony desert floor.'[37]

Rudolf Hubalek was fortunate. Stationed on an airfield, he enjoyed permanent, if rudimentary, quarters built from the ruins of old barracks, bomb crates, aircraft wrecks, tents – 'anything usable which we found in the desert'.[38] Martuba was also blessed with a cinema – a large tent which could hold up to 200 men – with daily screenings: the weekly newsreel, a short cultural documentary and the main feature. Each week the programme changed as new films were delivered from the Reich. Inside the tent 'it was oppressively hot – temperatures of almost 40°C,' Stuka gunner and war correspondent Hans Gross wrote, 'but that did not dampen the enthusiasm.' He continued: 'A film show in the desert cinema! This is the social event of the week in every unit. No *Ritterkreuz* winner and no private misses this pleasure. Side-by-side they spend two entertaining hours which make them forget the desert routine with all its enemies and dangers.'

Nearer the front, a mobile cinema sporadically visited the units: the projector set up on the back of a truck, the canvas rammed into the sand. 'We had to wait impatiently for darkness to fall, sat or lay on the ground in a semi-circle and chatted with one another like at a children's performance,' Otto Henning recalled. Guards were posted and if they heard an aircraft approaching, the showing was suspended, and darkness engulfed the desert cinema. The audience waited for the danger to pass, often filling the time with a chorus of whistles. 'If the English pilots didn't give us any rest, then we'd only see half the film and had to make up the rest,' Henning wrote.[39]

Rudolf Hubalek could set his watch by the enemy air raids on Martuba: 10am each day. A dozen or so Douglas Boston bombers flew over the airfield – invariably too high for Hubalek's 2cm flak gun – dropped their bombs and turned around. Stone walls were built around the Me109s to shield them from shrapnel when the British attacked. But there was little such protection for the men. 'Most of the time we lay like sitting ducks,' Hubalek wrote. 'We envied the soldiers on the Eastern Front – at least they could always find some natural cover somewhere.' At night, Martuba was plagued by low-flying enemy fighters and bombers, whereupon the drab desert war was suddenly resplendent with colour. Hubalek wrote:

> An eerily-beautiful firework display filled the heavens. Parachute flares hung in the sky, one after another, lighting up the entire area as bright as day. Our 2cm high-explosive shells flew into the air like glowing balls. The Italians used green and white tracer, the Tommy's was red. The burning incendiaries fell like hail, fizzled and sparked in the bright glow of the magnesium light, while detonating high-explosive bombs flashed a fiery glow like sheet lightning.[40]

By the second half of May 1942, it was clear to every man in the *Panzerarmee Afrika* that such attacks along the entire front were becoming increasingly frequent. Either the British were intending to strike or, as Hellmuth Frey correctly surmised, they were convinced 'something fishy is going on' and were trying to ascertain Rommel's plans.[41]

Since early February, the front in the Libyan desert had rested some 40 miles west of Tobruk, anchored at its southern end by the remote fortress of Bir Hakeim and on the coast in the north near the fishing village of Gazala, which gave the line its name.

In the ensuing three months, the Gazala line had grown into the most impressive position the British ever constructed in the Western Desert. Infantry brigades held defensive 'boxes' – each heavily fortified, liberally provided with anti-aircraft and anti-tank guns, sown with minefields, surrounded by wire entanglements and able to survive with food, fuel and ammunition for several days should they be cut off. The boxes were widely dispersed – the defenders of one could not come to the aid of another if attacked. The gaps between them were open desert, once again heavily planted with a million mines. To the rear, where there were more boxes and strongpoints, the Eighth Army held the bulk of its armour in reserve. All in all, the Gazala line presented a formidable

Operation *Theseus*, 26–27 May (top) and the German capture of Tobruk, 14–21 June (bottom)

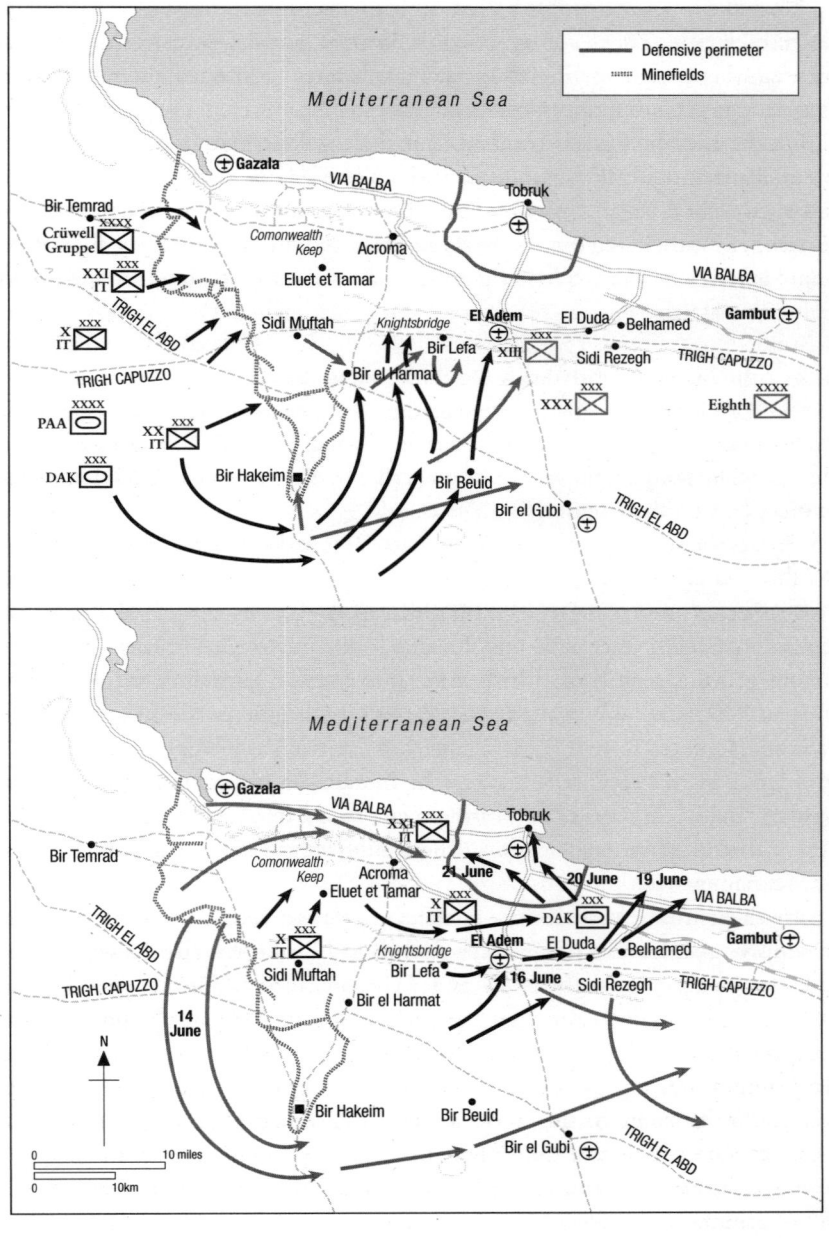

obstacle – one which would 'cause us a great deal of trouble', Rommel conceded, if attacked.[42] That was why he had no intention of running into it head-on.

Beyond the southernmost box at Bir Hakeim was the expanse of the desert – perfectly passable tank country. It was a cardinal mistake. 'Any position with an open southern flank is bound to lead to disaster,' Rommel wrote.[43] It was a weakness he intended to exploit to the full.

On the opening day of the offensive, Italian and German troops would assault the northern end of the Gazala line. It was a feint. The clouds of dust suggesting columns of tanks advancing would actually be stirred up by trucks driving around in circles. Rommel's armour – the *Afrika Korps* and Italian XX Motorised Corps – would actually be marshalled far to the rear, striking south into the desert after nightfall, past the end of the British line, then swing left and make for the coast north of Acroma, 15 miles west of Tobruk. Cut off from their supplies, the bulk of the British Eighth Army would be trapped and annihilated in a gigantic battle of encirclement in the Cyrenaican desert. With the kernel of the British forces destroyed, Rommel could take Tobruk and, if it fell, he could push on to the Egyptian border. But he could not cross it. His Italian masters determined he must halt on the frontier.[44]

Theseus was a calculated gamble, perhaps Rommel's last card before the weight of Allied matériel tipped the balance decisively against the Axis. He would attack a foe superior in men – over 100,000 Britons, South Africans, Indians and Free French, to 90,000 Germans and Italians – and matériel. He had no accurate picture of the strength of British armoured forces – estimates varied between 700 and 900 tanks – but reckoned the British outnumbered his 560 German and Italian tanks three to two,[45] while Eighth Army certainly enjoyed superiority in artillery and armoured cars. At least in the air the opposing sides were more evenly matched: around 600 British aircraft facing nearly 550 Axis opponents – 350 of them fighters, including 120 Messerschmitt 109s, superior to anything challenging them in the skies of the Western Desert.

It was qualitative superiority of machines like the Me109 which Rommel was convinced would offset the enemy's numbers. Admittedly, the 200-plus Italian tanks at his disposal – the M13 and M14, branded 'rolling coffins' by their crews – were the poorest on the Libyan battlefield. Worse still, Italian troops possessed no anti-tank gun worthy of the name. Their ally, fortunately, did; in the 88mm, Germany had the best weapon of its type of the war – although the smaller 50mm anti-tank gun was also highly effective. And above all, so far the German panzer had been more than a match for British armour. Enemy tanks were either unreliable and under-armed (Crusaders and Valentines), or sluggish and obsolescent (Matildas). But in the late winter and spring of 1942, Eighth

Army's tank divisions had begun to receive the new American-built M3 'Grant', superior to anything in *Panzerarmee Afrika's* inventory of Panzer Mk IIIs and IVs, except for four special long-barrelled Panzer IVs... but they arrived in Libya without any ammunition. By the end of May, nearly 250 Grants were spread among the armoured brigades and divisions of Eighth Army. Rommel, as we shall see, claimed he had no warning of their presence. He had – and had either chosen to overlook the fact, or dismiss them as inferior, as he dismissed all non-German armour.

As early as February 1942, Rommel's staff had learned of the impending arrival of new American tanks thanks to a remarkable intelligence coup which was exploited through the winter and spring. German and Italian codebreakers could both decipher dispatches sent by American military attachés through copying classified documents at the embassy in Rome. It was the reports sent from the legation in Cairo which proved to be the richest seam of information. Colonel Bonner Fellers enjoyed almost unfettered access to all manner of the most sensitive information relating to the desert war. Combined with his observations – of the battlefield, British commanders (the American's judgment was often scathing), equipment and the course of the fighting – Fellers' reports played a key role, first in the advance to the Gazala line and now the build-up to *Theseus*. It would serve Rommel well – he called it his 'good source' – until the dying hours of his summer offensive.

Eye-opening though the 'good source' was (one staff officer called it 'stupefying in its openness'), it did not provide a complete picture either of Allied intentions or their order of battle. 'Had we known the full facts,' his head of intelligence, Friedrich von Mellenthin, conceded a decade later, 'even Rommel might have baulked at an attack against such a greatly superior enemy.'[46]

If British strength was unquantifiable, Rommel knew he could count on the German soldier. He was well trained, well equipped, and in May 1942 he longed to attack. 'If only we'd begin the advance again, if only to get out of this sandy terrain,' one junior officer confided in Hellmuth Frey. Flak officer Helmuth Köhrer agreed. 'No *Afrikaner* minds as long as we go. Just none of this sitting about for a long time in the desert, in this desolation.' Köhrer put the thought of fighting in temperatures of over 50°C to the back of his mind. 'Heat? Don't worry about it!' he recorded in his diary. 'Rommel has said: "Heat's just a question of mind over matter!" and if that's what he says, then that's how it will be. The spirit of Rommel is our spirit.'[47] Morale in Libya had never been bad, Hellmuth Frey observed, but in May 1942 there was 'total confidence in victory. When you weigh up the forces on the two sides, then our superior leadership, better training and morale of our troops give us the advantage.'[48] The men of

Machine-Gun Battalion 8 certainly thought so. They had no doubt about the outcome of the impending offensive – or its objective, for that matter – as they struck up a new song:

> When we march into Cairo
> With a cheer and a roar
> Parading past Rommel
> Then even the old pharaohs will be silent!
>
> When we climb the pyramids
> And the Nile entices us to bathe
> And when all the barrels are silent
> Then the *Afrika Korps* has reached its goal![49]

Late on the morning of Tuesday 26 May, under a baking sun, the soldiers of 15th Panzer Division gathered for a drumhead service. For days the tension had been unbearable. It was obvious the offensive was imminent. Flak and artillery batteries had received their full quotas of ammunition; the fuel tanks of vehicles brimmed with petrol. Water rationing was introduced – and strictly enforced. Eight litres for vehicles to keep their engines cool, just three litres a day for the men to drink.

The division's panzers were lined up as if on parade, their gun barrels elevated at an angle. A stack of ammunition boxes covered with Germany's battle ensign, the *Reichskriegsflagge*, served as the altar, from where the division's protestant chaplain led the service. A regimental band struck up Martin Luther's *Ein feste Burg ist unser Gott* (*A Mighty Fortress is our God*) before proceedings ended with every man reciting the Lord's Prayer.[50]

Theseus' first blow was struck that afternoon. Despite Rommel's grandiose plans to deceive the British, the attack provoked little response. The British fell back to their fortified boxes as planned, without being unduly concerned.[51]

While the diversionary attack was heading towards the British lines, the bulk of the German-Italian force was moving to its jump-off positions far to the south. Flak gunner Rudolf Hubalek watched 'a wall of dust' rolling towards his flak unit. 'The desert droned with thumping, the rattle and clatter of engines, the air shook with the rattling, crunching and squealing of steel tracks.'[52] By 8.30pm, all the pieces were in place. The *Panzerarmee Afrika* headed into the darkness.

No man who took part in 'the great march' would forget it. Never had there been a night-time manoeuvre on such a scale. An entire army was on the move. Infantry mounted panzers, soldiers clung to the running boards of trucks or sat on mudguards as Rommel's phalanx – described variously as 'an armada', 'a wild, reckless hunt', 'a horde' and, by one Italian officer, 'a gigantic block relentlessly pushed across the endless white plain of the desert by some mysterious, superior power' – struck into the desert. To the north, around Gazala, the flash of Italian guns lit up the horizon for an instant. To the southeast, there was an occasional flare as the Luftwaffe tried to locate the fortress of Bir Hakeim. The silence of the desert was torn apart by the roar of engines, the rumble of gun carriages, the whirr and clank of tank tracks. Yet for all the noise, the men were gripped by a strange feeling 'that we were enveloped by the silence and spoke quietly – as if to prevent the enemy hearing the sound of our voices'. The ground trembled under the weight of 10,000 vehicles whose tracks and wheels first ground the loose desert soil to dust, then whipped it up into a man-made sandstorm, moving inexorably across the heart of Cyrenaica. One junior officer described the scene:

> A misty grey, which swallows up all shapes and contours, spreads across the ground and the endless expanse of the desert absorbs any light from the sky. If this is the first time you've seen a division or the entire *Afrika Korps* racing along on the march, then at first you believe it's a wild, completely disorganised horde. Only gradually do you realise that extremely sensible order and discipline rules this enormous war machine. Every unit has its fixed place, ensuring it's ready for battle and most effective in action.

Oil drums containing dim lights marked the route of advance but they were often obscured by the dust. Vehicle commanders relied on the keen eyes of their drivers or the soldiers riding the mudguards to maintain contact with the truck or panzer in front. When that failed, they turned to maps, luminous compasses or the stars to guide them.[53]

After an hour's pause in the pre-dawn southeast of Bir Hakeim, the columns wheeled left to begin rolling up the British defensive line, once again 'in a swirling cloud of smoke and dust'. As night hesitantly gave way to a breathless, clear day, revealing a barren landscape, devoid of any life, Rommel's staff intercepted a signal sent by a worried British unit: 'Enemy panzer columns are bearing down on us. It looks like it's the whole bloody *Afrika Korps*.'[54]

In fact, it was the Italian armour of the *Ariete* Division which scored the first victory of the new offensive, all but wiping out an Indian motorised brigade inside half an hour – with horrific results: a pile of tanks, trucks, guns and equipment littered the battlefield, the dead, half-naked, often burned alive, still in the vehicles, now fair game for the flies. Buoyed by success, the *Ariete* now focused on the fortress of Bir Hakeim, held by more than 3,500 Free French and Foreign Legionnaires. The *Ariete* proved themselves to be bold warriors, running the gauntlet of 50,000 mines sown around the strongpoint. French guns, many of them Great War vintage, took a fearful toll of the weak Italian armour – although so pungent was the black smoke from the burning tanks littering the battlefield that it provided a useful smokescreen for those still running. One attacking wave was finally brought to a halt inside French lines in hand-to-hand fighting. The second ground to a halt in one of the minefields. The battalion commander leading the assault had two tanks shot out from under him; he was taken prisoner when his third tank of the day was crippled. Hauled out of his blazing vehicle, 'wounded, terribly burned and almost naked', Lieutenant Colonel Pasquale Prestisimone protested to his captors that he had been failed by his leaders. 'They assured us that everything in Bir Hakeim would be over in minutes...' French officers rifling through Prestisimone's papers found documents confirming the Italian colonel's statement: Rommel had expected the isolated fortress to fall by 9.15am. '*Quel mépris et aussi quelle méprise,*' remarked the outpost's commander, Marie-Pierre Kœnig. *What contempt and also what a misunderstanding...*

Sixty comrades followed Pasquale Prestisimone into French captivity; a similar number were dead on the battlefield. After a 90-minute battle, the *Ariete* called off its attack. 'All around Bir Hakeim, the desert is now strewn with black carcasses, overturned vehicles, burned-out tanks,' one French officer recorded. 'So many victories of which the desert keeps track. So many comforting spectacles for the besieged.' The Italians counted their losses: more than 30 tanks before Bir Hakeim alone, nearly half the *Ariete*'s armour in the first day of battle. *Theseus* was not running to plan.[55]

By the time the Italians broke off their assault on Bir Hakeim, the far right of Rommel's hook was barely 15 miles from Tobruk; scything through the enemy's rear area, 90th Light Division overran numerous supply dumps, a few British stragglers and the headquarters of 7th Armoured Division, taking its commander prisoner. But to the west, the bulk of the *Afrika Korps* collided with 4th Armoured Brigade. Bobby Feakins was driving an armoured car sent ahead of British lines to scout for the enemy when it was hit by a German shell. Its commander and two radio operators were killed instantly, the latter decapitated, their heads taken clean off, their hands still holding their mouthpieces. 'The inside of my armoured car was just nothing but blood and flesh, bits of body all over the place,' he recalled.[56] A company from 5th Panzer Regiment shot up four enemy tanks in quick succession, forcing the rest to turn about. An unharmed major clambered out of one stricken tank brandishing a bottle of whisky, which he promptly shared with his captors, who found the disabled vehicle packed with cigarettes, condensed milk, canned meat, tea and other delights. 'We lived well on it for several days,' the panzer commander remembered. They sent their prisoner in the direction of a collection point.[57] The *Afrika Korps* was about to be surprised by the appearance of the first American-built Grant tanks – a surprise, Rommel conceded with considerable understatement, 'not to our advantage'. Despite its cumbersome design – its main gun was mounted in a rather unwieldy side turret which restricted its arc of fire – the Grant's firepower outmatched the Panzer III, mainstay of the *Afrika Korps*, and promptly decimated its ranks. Driver Horst Sonnenkalb counted 32 panzers in his regiment knocked out in under an hour by the new American tanks. 'Ten of them were aflame – the crews died horrible deaths in their vehicles,' he remembered. 'But there was no time for thinking, pondering, reflecting.' The men of 15th Panzer Division quickly adapted to combating their new foe: remain hidden, then drive quickly and hit the Grant from the side. Thus did the *Afrika Korps* slug its way north. By early afternoon it had crossed the Trigh Capuzzo, a desert track which bisected the battlefield east–west, still intent on reaching the coast road more than 20 miles distant – and with it encircling British forces in the Gazala line. The British had other ideas. That afternoon their armour counter-attacked with vigour. Horst Sonnenkalb once again found himself in a duel to the death with enemy tanks.

> Distance 800 metres! Armour-piercing shell, fire at will! At times temperatures in the panzer were 40 to 50°C. The gunlayer and loader worked like clockwork. Turret and cannon aimed, fix target! As driver I had stopped the panzer, applying the brakes. Panzers should only shoot when stationary. The gunlayer pressed the electrical release button, the cannon roared, direct hit. No-one got out of the enemy tank. We only saw an enormous tongue of flame and a large black cloud of smoke.

Reconnaissance unit commander Hellmuth Schroetter watched German columns roll back in the face of the British advance. 'There were moments,' he recalled, 'when we believed it was the end of *Panzerarmee Afrika*.' Walther Nehring certainly feared as much. Watching the enemy rout his supply columns, he turned to his flak commander Alwin Wolz, demanding 'a front of flak. Your cannon shoot further than the enemy tanks. Form a front out of flak using every gun at your disposal.' Wolz rounded up his guns – equally, if not more, effective against armour as against aircraft – and formed a two-mile 'flak front' exactly as Nehring desired. No quarter was given in the ensuing battle, as Rudolf Hubalek recalled.

> Howling shells whizzed over our heads and exploded very nearby. Gunsmoke left a disgusting taste in our mouths, red-hot pieces of shrapnel and shattered lumps of rock whistled and whined around our ears.

The crouched figures of soldiers lost the ground beneath their feet, tottered and fell over. Bodies were ripped to shreds, still-breathing bodies littered the battlefield. A gun in 3rd Platoon received a direct hit, lumps of flesh; bloody remains and silver braid from his uniform were all that were found of the platoon leader.

Amid this infernal noise, the screaming and whimpering of the wounded. 'Medic... Mediiicccc...'

A shiver ran down my spine every time I heard such a cry. Today that cry still reverberates in my ears – an echo from another world.

At one point Wolz's cannon mistook German panzers for enemy armour and began engaging them. But otherwise, his guns brought the British onslaught to a standstill – although not before some had 'forced their way up to the very muzzles of the guns and wiped out the crew'. At dusk the *Afrika Korps* ordered its men to 'regroup, dig in' and prepare for 'all-round defence'.

In fact, there was little co-ordinated leadership of *Panzerarmee Afrika* that night. Erwin Rommel had spent the day ranging around the battlefield, urging, cajoling, ordering his men forward. He did so at tremendous personal risk. An attempt to reach 90th Light Division at mid-day had been thwarted by British tanks. At other times the command vehicles came under fighter-bomber attack and, as darkness set in, a ferocious artillery barrage – 'a proper witch hunt,' Rommel's worried interpreter Wilfried Armbruster noted in his diary. When night fell with a red glow on the horizon from the still-burning tanks, Rommel's staff was scattered across the battlefield. Worse, the general was separated from his radio trucks. His panzer divisions were alone in the desert, split from most of their infantry and, more worryingly, their supply columns – now at the mercy of the British. His plan, Erwin Rommel conceded, had not worked. Not only had he failed to encircle the British, but he had underestimated the strength of his foe – badly. He had not reckoned with the new Grant tanks – 90th Light Division's official war diarist branded them 'monsters' – which 'tore huge gaps in our ranks'; that first day of battle cost the Germans more than one third of their armour. 'There's no denying,' Rommel wrote later, 'that night I was extremely worried.'[58]

A German Foreign Ministry official urged liaison officer Giuseppe Mancinelli to intervene with his masters in Rome 'before Rommel with his "recklessness" led us to complete disaster', while Rommel's chief-of-staff, Alfred Gause, suggested falling back to the army's starting point on the 26th, pretending the foray had merely been a 'reconnaissance mission'. Rommel tore a strip off him, making it quite clear to his subordinate that 'he – and he alone, no other – took decisions'.[59] The decision he took was to push on to the sea and cut off the British troops in the Gazala line. At first light, Rommel scanned the horizon in search of the rest of his forces. He saw only British troops on the move, and they soon made their presence felt by showering the general's cluster of command vehicles with shells – a barrage which achieved little beyond shattering the window of the bus the staff had commandeered. It was a less than propitious beginning to another difficult day.

However much Rommel might wish to lunge to the Mediterranean, his options for doing so this Thursday were limited: 15th Panzer Division had barely 20 working tanks which were all but out of ammunition, while 90th Light was locked in a struggle for its very existence with British 'monsters' and was being hounded by the enemy air force. Only 21st Panzer was capable of carrying out Rommel's intentions. It pushed north, brushing away half-hearted attempts by the British to halt its progress and reaching the high ground not five miles from the Mediterranean. 'We look at the blue sea, like a promise,' war correspondent Lutz Koch wrote:

> Before us is the glistening strip of the Via Balbia. Alongside the road, vehicles gathered and on the road, vehicles moving in both directions. Vehicle after vehicle is hit under the thunder of our guns and the first shell from our heavy flak lands in the middle of a truck, shattering it and tearing it apart in a single surge of fire.[60]

That was as close as any German got to the sea – or to halting traffic on the Via Balbia – on 28 May. With no other units able to support the exposed men of 21st Panzer Division, Rommel called them back. He had decided to corral his forces and go over to the defensive – at least until they had fuel and ammunition. To that end the *Panzerarmee* commander spent the latter part of the day rounding up his scattered supply trucks under enemy and, on one occasion, friendly fire. 'Bullets fizzed around our eyes,' his interpreter wrote at one point. At another: 'Enemy tanks broke through causing our group to flee.' Several ammunition and fuel trucks were shot up before Rommel restored some semblance of order after nightfall. Of the 16 British tanks which attacked his makeshift column, 14 now lay knocked-out in the desert.[61]

In the small hours of 29 May, a line of 1,500 vehicles began to snake along a narrow alley cleared through one of the Gazala minefields, Rommel at their head. His memoirs state simply that 'everything ran smoothly'. It most definitely did not. The British struck at his flank. Rommel calmly ordered the enemy encircled. The *Ariete* Division began to give way, prompting panic. British artillery joined in the hellish concert and began to inflict casualties. 'Then Rommel personally led our group to the *Afrika Korps*,' Armbruster wrote admiringly. 'The journey was unbelievable. We were encircled and yet everything turned out fine.' Shortly after mid-day, the column got through.[62] 'That saved our bacon,' machine-gun battalion commander Hinrich Warrelmann wrote, 'otherwise we wouldn't have been able to hold out.'[63] Rommel's arrival could not have been more timely. His flak sat in 'the hollow of death', the barrels of its 88mm guns silent for lack of ammunition, 20 fresh mounds of sand next to them for those killed over the past three days. Now the guns had the shells and the panzers had the fuel they needed. And for the first time since the battle began, the army commander could finally begin to grasp the situation. For the past few days, all manner of rumours had electrified *Panzerarmee Afrika*. 'The *Afrika Korps* is surrounded. As soon as it's fired all its ammunition, it will have to surrender.' 'The Tommies have bagged our entire supply column.' Every day there was fresh talk that Rommel, Nehring or Crüwell – leading the feint in the north – was dead. 'One rumour often contradicted another and so you questioned their believability,' Heinz-Dietrich Aberger recalled, 'but there was still a certain discomfort.' Only one thing was certain, one flak officer noted: 'We're Rommeling again.'[64] In fact, the disparate German and Italian units were beginning to mesh in an area no more than eight miles wide and eight miles long, bordered on all sides by desert tracks. History has come to know it as the *Hexenkessel* – the witch's cauldron, or simply cauldron. To the west, the British were safe in their boxes on the Gazala line, unthreatened, and unthreatening, but an obstacle to *Panzerarmee Afrika*'s freedom of movement. The isolated fortress of Bir Hakeim stood firm in the south – and threatened Rommel's rear columns. And to the north and east there were at least three British armoured and one motorised brigade. The kernel of the Italo-German army in North Africa was encircled, albeit not tightly.

Only now did Erwin Rommel abandon his original plan to strike at the ocean and encircle the Gazala positions. Instead he would form a wall of armour and anti-tank guns in the east, a wall he was sure the British would 'bang their head against and wear themselves out', and strike west with his mobile forces, overrunning the Gazala boxes: first the British at Got el Ualeb, then the Free French at the southern end of the line.[65]

The box at Got el Ualeb, held by British 150th Brigade, was thoroughly camouflaged, well fortified with minefields, tanks dug into the sand, and deep slit trenches, but above all, doggedly held. Its defenders forced their attackers to contest every single strongpoint and dugout for three days. A stunning dive-bomber raid and an all-out armoured assault, personally directed by Rommel, finally brought about the box's surrender; 3,000 prisoners fell into Axis hands, while more than 100 British tanks and vehicles were destroyed or captured.[66]

The Free French at Bir Hakeim proved no more willing to yield to the Italo-German onslaught than the British at Got el Ualeb. As the 90th Light and *Trieste* divisions regrouped for the attack on the end of the Gazala line, a small Italian staff car with a white strip stopped a few hundred metres from one of the outposts of Bir Hakeim and two men, waving a white flag, walked towards French lines. Blindfolded, they were led to Marie-Pierre Kœnig's command post where they presented their credentials as representatives of the *'grande vincitore della Libia'* – great conqueror of Libya, namely Rommel. Unable to speak French, the two Italians harangued Kœnig in their mother tongue, repeating three words: *circondati, esterminati, capitolare* – surrounded, exterminated, capitulate. The French commander stood firm. 'I am very sorry, gentlemen. Go and tell your general that we are not here to surrender.' The two parliamentarians were led back to their vehicle. *'Siete grandi soldati,'* one told his escort. 'You are great soldiers.'

As soon as they departed, Kœnig's headquarters sent a message to every unit under his command: 'General Rommel has asked us to surrender, threatening us with extermination. General Kœnig refused. Do your duty.'

Rommel persisted. The next day he sent in two captured British troops on foot under white flags carrying an ultimatum written on a signal pad, possibly by the general himself.

> To the troops of Bir Hakeim.
> Further resistance means useless bloodshed. You will suffer the same fate as the two [sic] English brigades in Got Ualeb which were destroyed the day before yesterday.
> We will cease fighting if you raise white flags and come across to us without your weapons.
>
> – Rommel, *Generaloberst*

Kœnig was incensed – not by the demand but by the fact it was addressed to his men, not their commander. Convinced he could hold out for at least another eight days, once again he rejected the demand. 'Our mission is to hold on at all costs until victory is final,' he told his staff. 'Explain this to all, officers and men alike. And good luck to all!' Not all his men were impressed. 'It's easy to say that it's our duty to remain calm and stick together,' junior officer Roger Malfettes observed. 'We are told that we have to hold on at all costs until victory, but, surrounded and stuck as we are, it will be difficult.'

No white flags appeared over Bir Hakeim. The RAF, however, did. The Desert Air Force hounded the gathering enemy vehicles, leaving 60 ablaze in the June sun, black columns of smoke climbing into the sky. When Rommel's assault belatedly began, following a heavy artillery barrage, his troops got no closer than within 300 yards of Bir Hakeim's outer defences. A combination of heat, exhaustion and withering French fire caused the attackers to break off the battle. It would be the first of many failed attempts to seize Bir Hakeim.[67]

While the Germans and Italians unsuccessfully tried to eliminate Bir Hakeim, the British were 'unbelievably quiet' on the eastern flank of the cauldron. The *Afrika Korps* used the apparent lull to repair its battered armour. It had begun the offensive with more than 300 panzers; after a week's fighting barely 120 were still in working order. But Rommel knew that the British too were exploiting the pause in battle. They were massing their armour and artillery for a concerted effort to deliver *Panzerarmee Afrika* an annihilating blow. By 4 June, Erwin Rommel was convinced there was 'something in the air' and began re-positioning his forces.

His timing was almost perfect. Shortly before 3am on 5 June, the eastern horizon flashed with lightning – heralding the beginning of the British offensive, Operation *Aberdeen*. The artillery barrage crashed down not on the armour and men of the *Ariete* Division as intended, but on the stone and sand of the empty desert. It was, Rommel's intelligence officer Friedrich von Mellenthin later wrote, 'a fitting prelude to the events of the day'.

When it came – a few hours later – the British attack was brave but disjointed. Two armoured and two infantry brigades threw themselves against *Panzerarmee Afrika*. When they did finally grapple with the *Ariete*, they drove the Italians off a ridge on the southern end of the front following bitter fighting. But when the British armour began to deploy – 32nd Army Tank Brigade in the north, 22nd Armoured Brigade in the east – so *Aberdeen* began to come apart.[68]

Friday 5 June and Saturday the 6th would prove to be the greatest days of battle in the summer campaign. The cauldron boiled. From six or seven thousand feet above the desert, airmen watched as the two British brigades advanced into battle – 'an enormous white wall, an ominous cloud' moving across the desert. On the eastern rim of the cauldron, 22nd Armoured smashed into the flak and anti-tank guns of 15th Panzer Division. Rudolf Hubalek and his comrades realised – too late – that the bulk of the British force was bearing down on their 2cm flak guns, not the much more powerful 88s as planned. 'The gigantic steel colossi seemed to be amused by our gleaming peas,' he wrote. 'What did it matter that our fire was well aimed – the bullets bounced off the armour plate like table tennis balls?' Hubalek's unit fell back, regrouped, dug in and waited for the British to renew their attack. Through the shimmering mid-day air, the flak men watched the enemy armour form up to advance, before a furious artillery barrage plastered the desert, intending to smash the German lines.

> Salvoes of exploding shells spewed out death a thousandfold. We lay pressed to the bottom of our foxholes as dense gunsmoke and drifting smoke darkened the sky and made it very difficult for our lungs to breathe. Sweat glistened on every one of my pores. My tortured senses meant I could do nothing.
>
> My soul wallowed in apathy. Nothing mattered to me. Death would come as a relief.
>
> Through the veil of smoke I watched as a lifeless bundle wrapped in canvas was dragged away. Direct hit!
>
> In the radio car, there was a curled up figure lying over the key. Death had again reaped a rich harvest.[69]

Nineteen-year-old anti-tank gunner Günter Halm remembered 'black dots in the shimmering heat rolling towards us. As if electrified, we shot up, all our lethargy was gone. In a flash the guns and ammunition were ready for battle.' As Halm and his comrades waited for 40 British tanks – led by two command vehicles, clearly identifiable from their pennants – to close within range, an armoured car passed their gun line heading towards the advancing column. The gunners realised it was Rommel, binoculars around his neck. A few minutes later, the general returned. 'Lads, they're coming from behind us,' he urged the gunners. 'Don't let one of them through.' They responded by knocking out the two command tanks. It seemed to unnerve the British. Their attack faltered. The entire armada turned around and disappeared into the desert, at which point Rommel reappeared, thanked the gunners for their efforts, and drove out into the desert after the withdrawing enemy.[70]

Such actions were typical of the cauldron – and typical of Rommel's style of leadership. 'Rommel's in his element right now – he's "Rommeling" again,' Hellmuth Frey observed. 'He's always in front. First he appears here, then there. Perhaps this type of leadership is right in the desert.' The general was, Rudolf Hubalek wrote, 'what I expected an army commander to be: brave, decisive, successful, prudent, encouraging, hard, thoughtful and fair.' But not everyone was convinced. 'When we saw that Rommel preferred to be way up front, directing individual tanks and raiding parties instead of with his staff, making decisions that the overall situation required, then we asked ourselves whether he really was such a great army leader,' one panzer company commander complained. Thanks to his propaganda image, Erwin Rommel was viewed as a great army leader by the German public, however. 'He'll crack it again this time,' people told themselves. The terse daily official communiqué gave little away about the new offensive: 'German and Italian troops have attacked enemy positions.' 'A bitter battle is under way.' 'The fighting continues.' Counter-attacks were repulsed, X-number of enemy tanks knocked out, prisoners captured, aircraft shot down. The ordinary German filled in the blanks. He dreamed of Egypt, Suez, even of linking up with the forces of Japan.[71]

And the ordinary German soldier in North Africa dreamed of Germany. 'We long so much for these and our fear of being disappointed is tremendous,' flak battery commander Helmuth Köhrer recorded in his diary. But Köhrer was also apprehensive about returning to the Fatherland – the desert had changed him. 'Sometimes we wonder: should we go on leave at all when here, across the steppes, tracks, mountains and desert sand, we've turned into a seamless entity, condemned to a fate which so often demands the lethal use of our last ounce of strength.' His melancholy was perhaps fuelled by the ever-growing numbers of crosses, normally by the side of the Bedouin tracks crossing the desert. 'After a few hours there's already a grey dust on top of the red mounds – that same grey dust which makes the living and the dead of a small, proud hand-picked army facing a bitter struggle in a strange, incomprehensible land look the same.'[72] Rudolf Hubalek helped to bury his battery commander in a strip of canvas covered with sand and stone. 'The shifting sand will soon have flattened this resting place,' he observed. 'Perhaps the simple wooden cross will still stick out of the ground. Perhaps we'll still be able to read the faded letters which were written with indelible pencil: *Oberleutnant* Peter Serson, killed 6 June 1942, aged 24.'[73] Lieutenant Alberto Coglitore felt he had a duty 'for reasons of hygiene, humanity and Christian piety' to bury the dead, albeit makeshift fashion, if time and circumstance allowed, even the enemy's fallen. Imprinted in his mind was the sight of the corpse of one Indian soldier, still rigidly in position, still seemingly aiming his rifle at enemy lines. 'His khaki shirt is covered in dried blood, his face has already turned blue and shrunk,' Coglitore wrote. 'Hundreds of flies and insects buzz with ravenous anger around that small, motionless body.' The Indian was laid to rest in a grave specially shaped to fit his contorted position.[74]

Hellmuth Frey was haunted by a visit to a first-aid post established in a desert hut, where two surgeons struggled by day and night to operate on at least two dozen patients. 'Never is war with all its cruelty more evident than in a hospital,' he recorded in his diary. 'Anyone who has the chance to visit the operating "theatre" of a hospital during a great battle gets his fill of war. Most of the faces are filled with pain and terror.' And yet, however primitive the conditions, the injured received the best possible treatment under the circumstances. Ju52 transport aircraft waited to carry the badly wounded to hospitals 1,000 kilometres behind the front in a matter of hours, while three hospital ships crossed the Mediterranean every week. British wounded – as well as captured Germans – were often treated in the hospital at Tobruk, though it could not cope with the scale of casualties from the Gazala fighting. One British surgeon remembered 'shattered bodies lying on the floor, head to head with not an inch between them, waiting for their turn'. Neither the facilities nor the staff could cope, physically but especially mentally, with the never-ending horrors: 'faces that look like smashed pulp, heads where the brain oozes out, the little room set aside for the dying, the stink, the filth, the flies, the absolute shambles following a night's work...'[75]

All too often, however, there was no-one to save. Shrapnel and armour-piercing shells turned the innards of a tank into a charnel house. Alfons Selmayr, a doctor serving with 21st Panzer Division, came across a knocked-out English personnel carrier – 'an horrific sight. Badly wounded, torn limbs and dead and between them tins of canned food.' His comrades ignored the gruesome sights and hurriedly gathered up the tins. Appalled by their contempt for the dead, the doctor quickly put a stop to the scavenging, vowing never to eat the cans' contents. 'But two hours later I was really enjoying tinned peaches.'[76] Such indifference to death and carnage was commonplace. 'We cold-bloodedly walked past the bodies of our comrades who had been torn to shreds,' Rudolf Hubalek wrote.

> We were only seized by horror later, when we remembered such sights. Did that make us creatures without pity? We had to forget Death, to not think about him, even when he randomly tore gaps in our ranks.
>
> There was no point getting too worked up about our life on earth. It rested in God's hands; he watched over and safeguarded it – and took it – that too was his will.[77]

Shells of the feared 88mm flak/anti-tank guns travelled faster than sound – there was no warning or incoming howl. They would take a head clean off or slice an unfortunate soldier in two. Death at least was instantaneous. Shrapnel shells which burst in the air and sent shards of hot metal spiralling across the desert would maim, but not necessarily kill. Albert Parker, acting as an unofficial ambulance driver, collected one comrade who was 'like a rag doll – no arms, no legs and smoking (on fire)'. In Bir Hakeim, marine Paul Leterrier was struck by shrapnel from a shell which embedded itself on the inside of his left thigh. 'It seemed to sizzle like a piece of butter in a hot frying pan. It smelled like roast pig! I tried to remove it, but I burned my fingers. However,

I had to get it out at all costs as I was literally sizzling and the glow, melting the flesh, kept sinking in. I chose the lesser evil and burned my fingers, but I managed to pull it out.'[78]

The skies over the cauldron were as contested as the sand and stone. Neither side enjoyed superiority, but when it was able to concentrate forces, the effects were both impressive and devastating. Chaplain Giovanni Rosso was impressed by the sight of Stukas 'swooping down in front of us in an infernal carousel. Hundreds of huge columns of smoke blackened the sky like the great summer storms and for five minutes the entire desert seemed shaken by a huge earthquake.' Italian fighter pilot Federico Vallauri was proud of the support he and his comrades gave to his countrymen on the ground. 'If you knew what it means to see my tracers end up in a truck, an armoured car or jeep and watch them catch fire,' he wrote to his family, 'think above all, what it means to our good soldiers to see tall columns of smoke rising from the enemy lines.' Paul Walentan's supply column was pounced on twice in one afternoon by the RAF. 'The minutes between 2.15 and 2.25pm were the most terrible of my life,' he recorded. 'Fifteen Tommy fighters attacking at low level, no cover. I'm lying under the car, the aircraft cannons and machine-guns barking for all they're worth. One of my comrades next to me had his arm torn off and his buttocks were also injured. Shreds of flesh are flying around.' Two hours later, the enemy aircraft returned, blowing up two vehicles, leaving one man dead and Walentan drenched in petrol – which caught fire. He was bandaged up at a first-aid post and sent to the rear.[79]

The strain on aircrew was tremendous. On the airfield before dawn for briefings and pre-flight checks, they rarely stood down until an hour after dusk, having flown four or five sorties on some days. Their existence quickly became exhausting, relentless, monotonous. 'For days the same thing,' Stuka rear gunner Hans Gross wrote. 'Only the targets change depending on how the fronts move.' Gross remembered hearing a 'muffled sound of engines from dawn until dusk' as his Stuka flew over the cauldron three or four times every day, 'delivering death and ruin' – the sky was scarred by 'flames and dark clouds of smoke rising above tanks, vehicles and tents'. After each sortie, Gross and his pilot clambered out of the cabin drenched in sweat, their uniforms clinging to their skin. Temperatures in the cockpit reached 50°C, while the glass canopies were as hot to touch as an iron.[80]

On the ground, the heat produced a shimmering haze hovering above the surface of the desert, making it difficult to distinguish friend from foe – a problem compounded by the use of captured vehicles on both sides; Rommel's own staff used two British command cars. It tricked fliers as well as soldiers: a Luftwaffe reconnaissance plane reported sighting 1,000 vehicles in the cauldron; on closer inspection they turned out to be oil drums, distorted by the haze. Come the early afternoon, the heat stirred up the obligatory sandstorm – 'a large black wall' moving inexorably across the desert. 'The air was oppressive and the temperature rose to 55°C,' Günter Halm remembered. It was the heat, not the sand, which could kill, but the experience of being lashed by winds driving dust at speeds of 50 or 60 miles an hour was far from pleasant. 'The sand ground in our teeth and stuck to our skin everywhere,' Halm wrote. 'We hardly dared breathe because there was sand in every breath. We thought we'd suffocate. Minutes became an eternity. We had the feeling of being close to the end of the world.' When the storm subsided, the men brushed the sand from their uniforms and cleaned their weapons. 'In the relentless heat, any movement was painful but we had to be ready for action once more as quickly as possible.' But in the afternoon, the sky grew increasingly dark as a storm brewed. 'Lightning cast the battlefield in an eerie light and occasionally the thunder in the heavens drowned out the thunder on the ground,' Heinz-Dietrich Aberger of Machine-Gun Battalion 8 recalled. 'Even old colonial Italians and Arabs could not recall experiencing rain at this time of year – and here, in the hottest part of North Africa.'[81]

The storm perfectly suited the 'apocalyptic scenario' in the cauldron. 'The sky ahead became a sea of flames as all their guns opened up,' one British gunner remembered. 'It was carnage.' His comrades talked of 'absolute chaos' and 'the beginning of the end'. By nightfall on 6 June – a day, Rudolf Hubalek remembered, dominated by a 'rain of fire and death, a gurgling, seething, hellish noise, comparable with no natural sound' – *Aberdeen* had been smashed. The British had been broken – mentally and physically. 'The first time they met the Germans they would go in with tremendous dash and courage, and very few of them would come out. One by one, the morale of these proud regiments was broken,' one British tank commander recalled. 'It was more than flesh and blood could stand always to be asked to fight at such fearful odds.' The two attacking armoured brigades had lost nearly half their tanks, while a brigade of Indian infantry ceased to exist. It could – and perhaps should – have been a British triumph. But the attackers were hampered by confused command, confused orders, confused communications. And when the fate of the Eighth Army hung in the balance, at least three armoured brigades played no, or little, part in the battle, nor too the divisions and brigades still rigidly holding the northernmost stretch of the Gazala line. Rommel was scathing of his foe's timidity. 'They should have thrown every unit at their disposal into the battle,' he wrote. 'What use is numerical superiority if you let your forces be beaten bit by bit by an enemy who concentrates his units to create superiority at the decisive point?'[82]

The battle of the cauldron was not yet over. But it had been won. And there was now no hope of relief for the defenders of Bir Hakeim, who faced the full wrath of *Panzerarmee Afrika*.

Forty miles from the coast and centred on an old desert fortress, built at the point where two Bedouin tracks met, Bir Hakeim was not 300 yards long and barely 100 yards across at its widest point. As at Got el Ualeb, the desert was sown with mines. The defenders – six battalions of French infantry, two of them drawn from the Foreign Legion – mostly wore British uniforms but bore French arms. They dug slit trenches and built emplacements, protected by sandbags, for their assorted artillery pieces, anti-tank guns and mortars.

The second attempt to overrun Bir Hakeim proved no more successful than the first. The featureless terrain offered 90th Light Division no cover, nowhere to hide. At dusk on 6 June, it called off its attack, still a good half mile from the old redoubt at the heart of the French position, brought to a halt by ferocious defensive fire. After dark, the Axis ring tightened while pioneers continued to clear lanes through the minefields ready for a renewed assault in the morning, preceded by an artillery barrage and Stuka raid. This time Rommel was convinced Bir Hakeim would fall within a day. Again he was to be sorely disappointed.

Late in the morning, senior non-commissioned officer Nico Tocci in the *Pavia* Division waited for the signal to attack, watching as ten aircraft at a time struck at the desert outpost.

> Lying on the ground in the small foxholes which we've dug among the mines lying all around us – and which none of us dares touch – I look up at the shocking spectacle of dive bombers over our heads, dropping their deadly bombs a few hundred feet above the ground which then, after a tremendous hiss, explode with a deafening roar, a clap of thunder, a crater of shrapnel, sand, smoke and, almost crashing, the plane roars over our heads with the gust of a hurricane. With hearts trembling, soldiers have to summon the strongest courage and when all the noise subsides, but smoke and dust still obscures visibility, we hear the cry of Captain Cascone: 'Forward, infantrymen of the *Pavia*!'

Tocci and his men advanced straight into furious French fire – the bombardment had evidently done little to wear down the defenders. Cascone was cut down and the attackers were forced to leap back into the foxholes they'd just dug. They stayed there; the moment any man raised his head above the desert floor he was subjected to accurate bursts of automatic fire from the French lines. Once again the Axis attack had miscarried.[83]

The courage and obstinacy of the defenders of Bir Hakeim were beginning to earn them the worldwide fame and admiration hitherto reserved for Rommel and his seemingly invincible arms. Marie-Pierre Kœnig was the hero of the hour – but he did not appreciate the attention. 'It's very nice being called the "lion of Bir Hakeim" and other rubbish,' he protested. 'I am a soldier, not a clown. I ask that the defence of Bir Hakeim is *not* romanticised.'[84]

Nowhere was the impact of the Luftwaffe more apparent in the North African campaign than at Bir Hakeim. The fortress was subjected to at least half a dozen air raids daily, ten Stuka attacks on one day – 1,300 sorties in all throughout the siege. The dive-bombers faced a wall of flak, but ran the gauntlet and dropped their bombs repeatedly. 'Suddenly clouds of sand explode, enveloping the fort,' war correspondent Hans Gross wrote. 'Down below Death reaps his harvest! The effects must be awful. Everywhere acrid smoke and dust spreads across this beacon of destruction beneath us.'[85]

The effects *were* awful. 'Hell and its eternal fire are nothing compared to what we endured for three days and three nights,' remembered Cameroonian non-commissioned officer Raphaël Onana. A British officer could not get the sound of the Stukas' droning engines out of his head. 'This sensation persists even when it's peaceful – but such moments are so short,' he recorded in his diary, which was later recovered by the Germans. Even when enemy infantry attacked, the eyes of the garrison troops were fixed on the sky. 'The fear of air attacks has turned to terror,' the diarist noted. So loud was the howl of the trumpets of Jericho and so close were the German troops encircling Bir Hakeim that the sirens even gnawed at the nerves of the attackers. 'Privately,' one gunner wrote, 'each man is glad not to be in the area of the attacks.' With no breeze, the smoke-filled air rarely cleared and the acrid smell from shells and bombs exploding mixed with the foul stench of decomposing corpses lying in the open; the sight of their comrades' lifeless bodies decaying caused some defenders to lose their minds. After their initial success in the opening days of the siege, the RAF now only intervened sporadically, often adding to, rather than easing, the garrison's misery by bombing Allied lines. Only with the fall of night was there respite from the aerial onslaught – but not from the battle. Flares cast the desert in an eerie glow, while machine-gun tracer raced through the night and gave the defenders no rest. 'The moans and cries of wounded men, scattered all over the minefield, calling for help,' filled the battlefield, Nino Tocci wrote. 'The battlefield is alive with shadowy figures searching, rummaging, soldiers quietly call out, looking for friends, helping those with minor wounds; stretcher bearers bring back those most seriously injured.' Other men ignored the dead and wounded, moving among them in search of water, food and ammunition so they could continue the battle.[86]

So frustrated was Rommel by the obstinacy of the defenders of Bir Hakeim that he ordered his flak – the same flak which had saved the *Afrika Korps* on the first day of battle – to attack the fortress *alone* when the supporting infantry and panzers failed to materialise. Alwin Wolz and his staff protested. Bir Hakeim simply 'could not be "rommeled" with cries of "Horrido and Hurrah!"' Rommel's response was to dismiss Wolz and his adjutant. The attack failed, just as Wolz had warned.[87]

The desert fortress could not hold out indefinitely, however. With no water, no saliva and bone-dry throats, the defenders were resorting to desperate measures – drinking urine. 'We collected it in our overheated bowls,' Raphaël Onana remembered. 'After a few minutes in the sun, so that it settled a little, we opened our eyes, pinched our noses, and off we went!' It tasted 'perfectly awful. But at least we had a few drops of liquid in our mouths and throats, which made the pangs of thirst less cruel.'[88] By 9 June, after being besieged for a fortnight, the defenders no longer expected relief. 'I pray to God that he will protect me. No-one protects us. Our only hope now is God,' the British diarist noted. The next day:

> Another hellish day. Water, water, water! This is the cry from the wounded, the cry from the survivors. How can we hold out! At 9am an air raid, another one at 10am and machine-guns shoot all day long. The stench from the dead is impossible to bear and breaks all our will to resist. The RAF has as good as disappeared; perhaps this is for the best because it has inflicted too many casualties on our side. At 11pm we receive orders to surrender our trucks and artillery. We must try to escape as best we can. But in which direction? No-one is bothered about us any more. We have reached the end.[89]

They had. When the Germans fatally penetrated Bir Hakeim's defensive ring that same day following an all-out assault, the fortress's commander Marie-Pierre Kœnig decided the time had come to abandon the strongpoint and link up with British forces to the west.

It was a move the Germans expected. 'Dig yourself a deep hole because there's a chance the French want to break out during the night!' one *Afrika Korps* veteran advised Otto Henning. Henning did. But the French did not come Henning's way. Having been given absolution by military chaplains, the defenders of Bir Hakeim moved out down a path cleared through the minefield surrounding the fortress. It proved too narrow for the number of men and vehicles trying to escape. Many of the latter ran on to mines. The explosions alerted the Germans and soon bursts of tracer were racing past the fleeing garrison. Yet the breakout largely succeeded, helped by two factors: firstly, they broke out to the west, not east, as the besiegers had anticipated; and secondly, a dense mist descended in the final couple of hours before dawn. As much as three quarters of the garrison slipped away, joining up with a motorised brigade and hastening through the desert night to El Adem more than 30 miles away. At first light, Rommel's forces moved in on the fortress. 'Everything is silent and really amazes us,' Sergeant Major Mario Venieri wrote. The Italian and his comrades found around 500 men, most of them wounded, and vast quantities of equipment – much of it destroyed. 'Embraces and tears of joy are the scenes of a battle won.'[90]

The 16-day siege of Bir Hakeim was over. Rommel's rear was free. He began regrouping his forces, moving them to the northern edge of the cauldron to destroy the British Eighth Army and drive on Tobruk.

Bir Hakeim's new occupiers were unimpressed by what they found – 'a rocky nest with only a couple of wrecked buildings and knocked-out military equipment,' wrote Otto Henning. Nor were they particularly impressed by the troops they captured – but they were impressed by the effects of a fortnight's air attacks on the defenders. Hellmuth Frey came across a Swiss Foreign Legionnaire who 'now turns white at the mere mention of the word "Stuka"'. Horst Sonnenkalb was surprised to find Germans among those captured at Bir Hakeim, Rhinelanders – 'soldiers from our German homeland. They had offered us a tough fight in the ranks of the Foreign Legion, side by side with soldiers from other countries.' *What path, what fates,* he wondered, *had led them to join the Foreign Legion?*

Hitler decreed that such men – if they had not been killed in battle or if they were not required for interrogation and intelligence gathering – were to be 'shot immediately on the orders of the nearest German officer'. He demanded the same fate befall any Jewish troops captured at the fortress. Neither instruction was carried out. Hitler's order was burned – 'We didn't want anything to do with such methods,' Siegfried Westphal observed. Instead, the men 'were treated just like every other prisoner of war,' Horst Sonnenkalb recalled.[91]

After the war, much would be made of such actions. The campaign in North Africa was one of rules, of order, a 'clean' conflict – unlike the fighting on the

Eastern Front – in short, as Rommel's posthumous memoirs were titled, 'a war without hate'. Battalion commander Hinrich Warrelmann certainly felt no animosity towards his foe. In quiet moments, the officer and his machine-gunners decided it was 'insane that here the English and Germans were fighting, while Bolshevism had to be recognised as the enemy of the entire world. In the end we always commented that we had to do our duty and, as soldiers, could not act differently.' Supply officer Hellmuth Frey was impressed that the British 'let ambulances with German wounded come through the lines unscathed. They even gave the lightly wounded drinking water.' When British gunners realised an Italian chaplain, Father Matrone, was recovering the dead, they ceased shelling his truck. Matrone became disorientated, strayed into no man's land and, as night fell, felt himself drawn to the groans of a wounded British soldier, surrounded by several comrades. They fled when the Italian priest approached, but Matrone remained with the injured soldier, gave him absolution and stayed by his side until he died. On another occasion, however, though his ambulance was clearly marked with the Red Cross, chaplain Giovanni Rosso's vehicle was peppered with machine-gun fire.[92] Early in the battle, Rommel's troops captured a British order stipulating that 'no food, sleep, drink, civility or comfort of any kind' be shown to German prisoners. 'Friendly actions, such as the giving of a cigarette, would seem to the German mind an admission of weakness, and would ruin the chances of successful interrogation.'[93] Medical officer Angelo Toscano was forced to watch an interrogation of Italian prisoners by a British captain. Water and food had been laid out on a table before them – but the captives could only indulge themselves once questioned. Toscano protested vigorously, but all his remonstrations achieved was to be forced to leave the cell at gunpoint. Alfons Selmayr, a doctor with 5th Panzer Regiment, was incensed. 'And this when it's 40°C in the shade,' he recorded in his diary. 'Rommel now orders that giving water to English prisoners is to be stopped immediately until this order is rescinded. These lords, who think they have the monopoly on humanity, will quickly think better of it.'[94]

They did. The matter was quickly dropped by both sides and the war without hate resumed.

It was now time to destroy the Eighth Army. With the ruins of Bir Hakeim still smouldering, 15th Panzer, 90th Light and the *Trieste* Divisions began to make for El Adem, 15 miles south of Tobruk, ready to wheel left when they got there and aim for the coast west of Tobruk, cutting off all Commonwealth troops between the port and Gazala – at least two entire divisions.

Standing in Rommel's way, three armoured and two motorised brigades; despite the mauling they had suffered in the cauldron, the British still outnumbered *Panzerarmee Afrika*. In two days of battle, the Germans and Italians turned that statistic on its head. The British had evidently learned little from *Aberdeen*. 'I don't care how many tanks you British have so long as you keep splitting them up the way you do,' Rommel told a captured brigadier. 'I shall just continue to destroy them piecemeal.'[95] Attacks were once again brave but disjointed, command was confused, even fractious, and the British command naive to the point of criminality. In one encounter, upwards of 150 British tanks closed to within 500 feet of Otto-Friedrich Senfft von Pilsach's company of 35 panzers before opening fire. The Germans seized the initiative. Shells left the barrel of every panzer – and struck every enemy tank 'with terrible effect,' one non-commissioned officer remembered. 'Before the English tank crews could recover from the shock, our next shells were already approaching or striking their vehicles.' The enemy turned about and fled, leaving more than a third of his tanks burning or immobile. The British had been lured into a trap by repeated fake radio messages: *Need immediate help, being attacked by 150 enemy tanks, have no ammunition and no fuel.* Their tank crews were ordered not to shoot so they could seize the entire panzer company intact.[96] The *Ariete* Division parried another British assault. The men watched it coming and waited as 'a long, high white curtain' – a smokescreen – moved across the desert ahead of the British tanks. It prevented the Italian gunners from picking out individual targets, but it also gave them plenty of forewarning of the approaching onslaught. 'We all lean forward out of our foxholes and positions, our eyes trying to penetrate that fog out of which enemy tanks will appear in a few minutes, our hands on our weapons ready to fire, at the most propitious moment,' Lieutenant Alberto Coglitore wrote. The self-propelled artillery and tanks of the *Ariete* opened fire as soon as the British armour emerged from the veil of mist. Coglitore continues:

All our 47/32 pieces, accompanied by machine-guns and rifles, shoot blindly, almost madly, to help form a dense barrage of fire to stop the enemy attack by tanks, followed by infantry units: a hailstone of bullets falls on the enemy, who cannot reach our line and retreats – constantly pursued by our fire. When the roar of battle dies down, and the curtain of fog has thinned and dispersed, we can see numerous knocked-out enemy tanks in front of us, many of them are aflame sending thick, acrid black smoke up into the clear sky.[97]

Rommel was particularly impressed by the defenders of 'Knightsbridge', a dreary defensive box to the east of the cauldron, who were 'subjected to the co-ordinated fire of every gun we could bring to bear on it. These troops virtually embodied the qualities and flaws of the British soldier: extraordinary bravery and doggedness combined with their inability to think for themselves.'[98]

There was an equally determined last stand by what remained of Eighth Army's armour outside the small town of Acroma, 15 miles west of Tobruk. Horst Sonnenkalb's Panzer III was struck seven times by a self-propelled gun. Suffering first- and second-degree burns and cuts, Sonnenkalb was the only man to clamber out of the wrecked panzer, having the presence of mind to grab a box of bandages as he escaped. He sat in the desert trying to bandage his wounds as burned scraps of his uniform hung off his body. A passing staff car stopped to pick him up, its occupants offering him two gulps of cognac to ease his pain, before taking him to a first-aid post. In little more than a week, Horst Sonnenkalb was back with his unit.[99]

His comrades finally punched their way through the main defensive position outside Acroma on the afternoon of 14 June, leaving 45 British tanks burned-out wrecks; their crews entered captivity with 'deep depression written over their faces'. The road to the coast was open. Scouting ahead of the *Afrika Korps*' armour, Hellmuth Schroetter pushed north to the edge of the escarpment which rose above the coast west of Tobruk, by the end of the day. 'Before us in the setting sun, the coastal plain,' he wrote. 'A look of longing from my men across the sea meant: The homeland is over there, to the north!' And below on the plain, a mass of vehicles, mostly trucks, evidently abandoned. There was no way down from the jebel – besides, Schroetter only had a handful of men at his disposal to round up the booty. He passed his report up the line to Rommel.

The British were giving up the Gazala line. The last two divisions holding the northern tip of the now-redundant position, South African 1st and British 50th, received orders to break out and re-join the Eighth Army somewhere east of Tobruk. Fighter pilot Federico Vallauri observed 'a swarm of vehicles and men. At last, they were retreating having caused us so many headaches.' All evening long Rommel impressed on his panzer divisions the need to reach the coast, blocking the Via Balbia and cutting off the retreat. The best the panzers could manage was to bring the coastal highway under sporadic fire. The thunder of the guns mixed with the crash of explosions as the Commonwealth troops blew up their ammunition dumps. But it was mid-afternoon on the following day before the armour of 15th Panzer Division finally reached the southern shore of the Mediterranean. By then, however, the bulk of the South African 1st Division had escaped to the east. The other final defenders of the Gazala line, British 50th Division, also avoided capture and annihilation, smashing through Italian units as they struck south into the desert – and the rear of Rommel's army. They left behind a good 400 shot-up or abandoned vehicles; the bulk of the division escaped and re-joined the battered Eighth Army near the Egyptian frontier.[100]

The haul of prisoners, as a result, was much smaller than anticipated. 'Rommel is bitterly disappointed that thousands of Tommies have escaped from him,' Hellmuth Frey noted. But the *Panzerarmee* commander could console himself by surveying the detritus of the Eighth Army abandoned on the Via Balbia. 'Evidence of the British defeat lay by the roadside and on the roads,' Rommel wrote. 'Masses of equipment were lying around, while burned-out vehicles, blackened and empty, were stuck in the sand. Entire columns of British trucks also fell undamaged into our hands, waiting for repair details if they hadn't already been immediately put to use by my troops.'[101] Frey organised a 'booty detail' to round up equipment abandoned on the shore west of Tobruk. The final battle here had clearly been desperate: hastily dug foxholes a yard apart in the dunes; strips of canvas, scraps of uniform, laundry, clothes, weapons, helmets strewn across the beach. 'I was surprised by the amount of books and magazines that they've left behind – not least the frequent number of copies of the Bible or New Testament,' the reservist wrote. He grabbed a pith helmet, and then, while his mechanics dismantled engines on abandoned vehicles, swam in the Mediterranean with two fellow officers.

> Peace! You would never have believed that a few hours before men were fighting on this beautiful beach. While the waves break on the coast with the same force as they did yesterday, our troops are in battle another 50 kilometres on against new enemies at El Adem. The muffled sound of guns comes from the fortress of Tobruk. The advance on the fortress is in progress. Hopefully this time we'll succeed![102]

Nestling at the foot of a steep escarpment which ran down from the desert plateau, Tobruk had little to recommend it, Dr Wolfdieter von Langen – considered an expert on North Africa – told readers of German newspapers. There was a cosmopolitan milieu, a blend of African-Arabian and Italian cultures, in Libya's other towns and cities. There was none of that in Tobruk. Italian colonial settlers, von Langen explained, 'used the adjective "*bruttissima*" to describe Tobruk – the superlative of ugly'. As a garrison town, it had largely been off limits before the war. There were no sights, no vegetation beyond a few pathetic palm trees. 'Amenities' consisted of a cinema and a bar. In short, Tobruk possessed nothing to occupy a visitor 'longer than the wait until the next steamer sailed. No-one chose to stay in Tobruk of their own free will.'[103] What Tobruk did possess – and the sole reason the warring nations fought over it – was a natural harbour: sheltered, wide, deep. It was the finest port in North Africa between Tripoli and Alexandria.

However much they hated being drafted to Tobruk, the Italians had recognised its importance and gone to great lengths to defend it. In the mid-'30s they'd begun work on a fortified belt ten miles outside the port, running for more than 30 miles in a semi-circle. Every 500 or 600 yards stood a small strongpoint for a mortar or anti-tank gun and a machine-gun, and a garrison of up to 40 men. An anti-tank ditch ten feet wide and four feet deep was intended to halt the progress of armour, while the terrain was sown with mines and covered with dense barbed-wire entanglements to prevent infantry assaults. A captured British order suggested Tobruk's defenders were prepared for a lengthy siege as they had been in the spring and summer of 1941; once again Tobruk would be 'a thorn in the enemy's side – a very active and virulent thorn which never stops pricking him'. But the Tobruk of June 1942 was not the Tobruk of April or May 1941. Many of the minefields and barbed-wire barriers had been stripped out to bolster the now-redundant Gazala line, while six months of inattention had caused the anti-tank ditch to fill with sand in places. The Australian troops who had so doggedly held Rommel at bay were gone. In their place, a 35,000-strong garrison – at least one third of the defenders were rear area troops, serving the port and Eighth Army's supply needs – comprising South Africans, Indians, Scots and any stragglers from units beaten at Gazala who found themselves in the port. After 15 months of war, much of Tobruk was in ruins – there was hardly a building undamaged. Houses were reduced to empty shells, their furnishings long-since ripped out, or burned out. In their place, war correspondent Alan Moorehead found makeshift warehouses, decontamination centres to de-louse the troops, first-aid posts. The YMCA still functioned, distributing meals to weary soldiers. The harbour was littered with wrecks, funnels and masts rising above the water. Tobruk, wrote Moorehead, was an 'accursed' place, 'hideous'. Darkness hid the horrors of war, but did not end them as Axis bombers raided the port. Even a civilian observer like Moorehead could tell the town was 'doomed'. Senior officers concurred. As one reported, the defenders and defences of Tobruk were 'in a very poor state'. But then the plan was not to hold Tobruk, but evacuate it. Just days before it was invested, the decision was reversed by Churchill. 'As long as Tobruk is held, no serious enemy advance into Egypt is possible,' he insisted from London. 'We went through all this in April 1941.' The fortress's commander, South African general Hendrik Klopper, possessed virtually no combat experience, but plenty of confidence. He was convinced his men would make 'a good stand', he told a friend. 'There is a general feeling of optimism, and I think there is every reason for it, although we expect to put up a strong fight.'[104]

Tobruk had been surrounded since the small hours of 18 June when panzers reached Gambut, three dozen miles east of the port. In doing so, they not only cut the garrison off from the bulk of Eighth Army but overran the airfield. The RAF pulled back to the east, effectively abandoning the skies over Tobruk to German and Italian aircraft. The panzers continued towards the Egyptian frontier, seizing supply dumps, rounding up scattered British units and suggesting to Tobruk's defenders that the *Panzerarmee* intended to drive on Alexandria. Unlike at Gazala, this feint seemed to work. On the afternoon of 19 June, Rommel ordered his armour to turn around and make for jump-off positions to the southeast of Tobruk. They did so unopposed – and unnoticed by the enemy.

Shortly before dusk that Friday, a small Fieseler Storch courier plane set down at Derna. When it taxied to a stop, Albert Kesselring climbed out and strode across the airfield to the mechanics' tent where the aircrew were gathered. 'Airmen! Tobruk is the city of fate in the war in Africa,' the field marshal told them. 'At 5.45am tomorrow you will fall upon the outer fortifications. The panzers of General Rommel will penetrate the fortress belt at the same time. Bomb well – just like you bombed the English Mediterranean fleet!' Kesselring moved on. Pilots and observers studied the map of Tobruk and its fortifications one last time before retiring to their tents to sleep.[105]

Outside Tobruk the men of 5th Panzer Regiment huddled around their commander as he outlined the plan of attack using a captured English map while the Belgrade transmitter signed off for the night as usual with *Lili Marleen*. In the pale moonlight, clouds of sand drifted across the desert, driven by the last panzers and vehicles moving to their starting positions. When they did, 'extremely bright rockets of all colours streaked in every direction across the sky with momentary flashes – like fireworks,' Italian assault engineer Sergeant Antonio Di Paolo remembered; it gave the night a 'strangely festive' feeling. Wrapped in blankets to shield them from the cool desert night, a few men wrote letters home. Infantrymen stuffed their pockets with cartridges of ammunition and hand-grenades, put two days' worth of food, plus bandages, in their haversacks, filled two canteens with water. The only light in the foxholes and slit trenches was the dull glow of cigarettes as men crouched, full of tension, waiting for dawn. The mood was wistful, almost pessimistic. 'Last year's siege which we'd experienced and taken part in did not allow any optimistic thoughts,' infantryman Hans Greim recalled. 'We waited for morning to come with mixed feelings.' One Italian pioneer threw himself on his knees, prayed, crossed himself, and then ran off into the desert. Flak officer Josef Hissmann moved among his men. 'There's a strange calm among the company this evening,' he observed:

Tobruk weighs heavily on the men – the fortress is to fall tomorrow. Fear? Well, depending on your point of view. When life and death is at stake, every soldier feels the enemy in front of him, his comrades at his side, superiors or laws above them and fear inside. The air crackles with tension. Somewhere in the dark is Tobruk, somewhere is home. Somewhere and sometime there's peace, eternal peace.[106]

Even Erwin Rommel had his doubts. Publicly, he had bombastically declared: 'Tomorrow, Tobruk falls!' Privately, however, he feared another repulse. Numerous attacks in 1941 had stalled in Tobruk's fortifications; parts of its outer ring of defences were 'literally soaked in blood'. Put simply: 'We *knew* Tobruk.'[107]

Hans Gross was woken at 3am and driven with his crew to his Junkers Ju88, waiting on the standings at Derna. It was a breathless morning. No breeze to stir the dust on the airfield – but also no breeze to disperse the clouds of sand kicked up as the bombers took off. As the engines warmed up, fiery jets shot out of exhaust pipes. A grey, blurry day was beginning to emerge from the deep blue of the African night and as the stars started to fade, a golden strip glowed on the horizon. Larks performing their first song of the day hovered over the pathetic camel thorn bushes. As the Ju87s and 88s joined formation over the Mediterranean, the first blood-red rays of the sun struck the sea. The flight time to Tobruk was no more than 20 or 25 minutes. The harbour appeared out of the milky haze, but this morning it was not the bombers' target. They headed for the anti-tank ditch – 'like a line drawn with a ruler' – on the high jebel plateau outside the town and the series of small forts with armoured cupolas which ringed Tobruk. On the ground, the drone of 50 approaching bombers struck 'a jarring chord shattering the harmony of the approaching day,' war correspondent Lutz Koch wrote. In the air, Hans Gross watched as the Stukas – each loaded with a single 1,000kg bomb known by the men as 'Satans' because of their terrible effect – plunged towards the African earth. Erhard Jähnert's commander took the lead – the first of nine aircraft to dive upon a fort on the southern anti-tank ditch surrounding the port. The 24-year-old Jähnert soon followed, evading 'pretty lively' flak as his dive reached a near-impossible 80-degree angle. His leader's bomb struck the corner of the enemy fortification. Jähnert's landed squarely in the middle and knocked it out. 'What should have been done by nine Ju87s had been achieved by two,' the pilot recalled. Flashes of fire on the ground were quickly followed by mushroom clouds climbing into the morning sky. In some places, the armoured cupolas were smashed; in others the forts were left in ruins or their defenders stunned. The assault lasted five, perhaps ten minutes. When it was done, the Junkers headed back to Derna and Tmimi to re-arm and refuel, passing over advancing panzers, whose crews and mounted infantry waved at them. The Ju87s and 88s and their crews faced at least two, perhaps as many as five, sorties this day, against fortress Tobruk. The Luftwaffe would continue its relentless assault, wrote Gross, 'until this city is ours and with it the strongpoint before Egypt has fallen.'[108]

As the bombers turned away from Tobruk, the German guns opened fire. There were 'flashes and crashes' along the entire British line, followed by smoke, dust and clouds which formed an almost impenetrable wall. 'Tobruk had become a brazier,' wrote Ettore Bastico, Rommel's elderly Italian superior. 'Tall columns of smoke leapt from the upset earth and the flames, blown by the wind, spread from one end of the city to the other. The originally-clear sky soon became dirty and dark.'[109] Lieutenant Alberto Coglitore's company of *Bersaglieri* elite light infantry watched this 'unforgettable spectacle both amazed and overjoyed, while our ears hear the howl of the dives, the hiss of bombs falling, striking their targets and throwing up gigantic columns of dust and smoke. The earth trembles; fresh waves of Stukas hammer the fortifications while the shells of the Italo-German artillery, which is located behind us, hiss over our heads.' It was, Coglitore wrote, 'a superb spectacle of power, a hellish carousel of hissing, bursting, roaring, smoke and flames.'

To observers like Antonio Di Paolo, the opening barrage was like nothing he had experienced in the desert to date – 'a true inferno' which left the entire landscape enveloped in a dense cloud of grey and blackish smoke. 'How can they survive that hell?' Di Paolo and his comrades asked themselves. Yet too much blood had flowed at Tobruk to dismiss the enemy as finished. The assault engineers, charged with removing mines and clearing gaps in the wire, were expected to suffer the heaviest casualties. 'Many of us silently wondered if we would really return to base,' Di Paolo recalled. An elderly non-commissioned officer had written a farewell letter, begging Di Paolo: 'Sergeant Major, do me the courtesy, keep it in your pocket, if I don't come back, send it to my family.'[110] For the first kilometre of their advance, the *Guastatori* – sappers – need not have worried: there was no response from Tobruk's defenders. But as the Italian engineers reached the outer wire, Commonwealth troops emerged from their bunkers and foxholes and poured fire down on their attackers. 'The enemy reaction was growing by the minute,' Di Paolo remembered. 'Machine-gun bursts were throwing up puffs of earth all around us.' He immediately realised that the assault engineers should have used the cover of night – or the preparatory barrage – to clear the way for the main assault, just as the neighbouring Germans had done.[111] Sporadically, orange flares signalled to German gunners to move the barrage forward as their pioneers cleared gaps through minefields, cut through barbed-wire entanglements, and built crossings over the anti-tank ditch. With the obstacles cleared, Rommel's armour moved in. 'What a scene as the panzers now advanced in long columns with the rays of the rising sun behind them,' Kurt Wolff, a junior officer on the staff of 5th Panzer Regiment, enthused. 'The rattle of machine-guns echoed across the battlefield, on the right the flak took up position, on the left behind us the light field howitzers, the panzer cannons roared.' The German armour quickly overran British artillery and anti-tank gun positions and knocked out enemy tanks threatening the flanks; their burning hulks lit the way in the gloom of sand and smoke for the infantry following behind to mop up bunkers and strongpoints. 'We advance into this inferno, our eyes always fixed on our compasses because the dust which has been whirled up by the bombs has deprived us of any visibility,' infantryman Hans Greim wrote. 'The earth groaned and there was exploding and shaking in the air like on doomsday.' Company commanders led their men from the front, rushing positions with cries of 'Hurra!' Resistance was spasmodic. In places, the fighting was hand-to-hand; in others, stunned defenders – mostly Indians – were sent to the rear of the German lines, their bodies shaking with fear, struggling to put one foot in front of the other, 'their blank, hollow eyes describing the hell from which they had just escaped,' Kurt Wolff noticed.[112]

Unable to fall back due to ferocious enemy fire – such a move would also cause them to lose face with their German ally – the *Guastatori* resolved to press ahead, 'eating sand, bayonets in front of us to feel for mines and pull them out,' Antonio Di Paolo recalled. It took individual acts of bravery to clear the barbed-wire barrier which blocked the way beyond the minefield and anti-tank ditch. Already wounded three times, 19-year-old corporal Giovanni Leccis watched as a comrade moving up to the wire with a pipe bomb was gunned down. Leccis grabbed the device and detonated it under the entanglement, blowing the first gap in the line. He was attempting to repeat the feat to broaden the hole when he was struck in the chest by an anti-tank shell.[113]

Soon the attackers had driven a wedge more than a mile wide through Tobruk's outer ring of defences. 'The spirit of attack seized each man and the importance of the name Tobruk made the heart forget everything else, even life, such that the attack was more like a storm than a battle to take a fortress following a well-thought-out plan,' Kurt Wolff wrote. Only once was there a concerted attempt to halt their advance, a brief but brutal clash with British tanks. After their encounter with panzers and Stukas, 50 blazing hulks were left on the plateau. Wolff surveyed the scene: 'The desert at Tobruk is one of the most desolate parts of Libya. The sun blazed and the men sat in their panzers covered in sweat, dusty, dirty, grimy, only the eyes on their faces were bright. No-one knew for sure: was this the beginning? Was this the first decision?'[114]

It was. A confident Rommel turned to Lutz Koch: 'Today, the troops have crowned their previous achievements with the capture of fortress Tobruk!' By late morning his men could see the Via Balbia, the coastal highway, glinting in the sun. By mid-day the armour of 21st Panzer was rolling along it, heading northwest led by their commander, Georg von Bismarck, his voice hoarse from trying to shout orders above the noise of battle. Rommel had 'the key to Tobruk' in his hands.[115]

Alberto Coglitore's company of *Bersaglieri* had waited tensely in front of the anti-tank ditch all through the morning. The infantrymen were itching to attack, convinced that 'this time, Tobruk will be ours!' So close was the enemy that they could see the tell-tale khaki helmets of their foe. But no orders to attack ever came. Instead, Coglitore was told to escort the British into captivity. Outflanked by breakthroughs elsewhere on the Tobruk front, the troops facing the *Bersaglieri* had ceased fire and decided to capitulate. In broken French, Coglitore spoke with a demoralised British officer. 'He is bewildered by the rapid and unexpected course of our attack.' The Briton surrendered a shoulder bag with documents, topographical maps and a wedding photograph. Coglitore returned the portrait. 'We look into each other's eyes for a moment and I glimpse a flash of smug appreciation as I give it back to him to hold close to his heart. He thanks me, while I walk away holding the rest of the contents of the bag that is sent to the regimental command for the usual search.'[116]

Further east, Lieutenant Ennio Calabresi advanced through Sidi Mahmud – 'a hell of burning wagons, shattered trenches' – in the centre of the defensive ring. Prisoners captured by the *Ariete* – mostly Indians – were in an 'obvious state of shock'. Their mood contrasted sharply with the victorious *Bersaglieri* who were filled with 'euphoric joy'. Calabresi continued: 'Above all there was a sense of amazement at the fact that in a few hours – and victoriously – they had eliminated the nightmare which haunted the "old guard" involved in months of siege the previous year.'[117]

Panic seized the defenders. A depot for thousands of vehicles was set on fire. Demolition parties began blowing up fuel and ammunition dumps. A black wall of smoke rose from the burning fuel tanks west of the harbour and spread over the town, turning day to night. Italian assault engineer Lieutenant Manilo Leone could see Tobruk's defenders 'setting fire to huge fuel depots, plunging the vehicles they had started off the ridges after draining their oil pans of lubricating oil so that their cylinders would seize and bayoneting large metal boxes of biscuits.'[118]

By early afternoon, German armour stood on the slopes of the escarpment overlooking the heart of Tobruk. In echoes of the advance on the Channel ports two years before, the guns of the panzers engaged ships in harbour hurriedly trying to make for open water. At least one sank, half a dozen were set on fire, but a handful escaped, trailing a smokescreen across the port as they made their getaway.

The attackers now brazenly advanced over open ground in massed formation. It was, one pioneer conceded, 'almost reckless. Our mood was cocky. But not a single Tommy appeared in the air.' A group of machine-gunners mounted panzers and rode down the hill into the centre of the port. 'Now we saw the town which was so hotly and bitterly fought over,' one wrote. 'It was just a few dozen buildings – and most of those were wrecked. The port stretched into the heart of the town, masts and funnels rising from the water bore witness to the number of sunken ships.' Italian assault engineer Manilo Leone realised it would be weeks, perhaps months, before the town might serve the Axis cause. 'Tobruk was a heap of rubble, sunken ships lay on the bottom of the harbour, the statuette of a Madonna stood intact among the ruins of a small church,' he remembered.

Driver Vittorio Vallicella was struck by the 'thousands of prisoners of every race – frightened, exhausted, wounded' filing past him out of Tobruk. The 23-year-old continued through the rubble and debris towards the harbour, pausing to throw up at the sight of piles of bloated corpses covered by swarms of flies. It was dusk by the time Vallicella reached the waterfront. 'A red sun sets over a crystal clear, calm sea,' he wrote in his diary, 'casting light on waters sprinkled with the corpses of many young men killed in a long and terrible war.'

With nightfall, the armour of 5th Panzer Regiment formed a corral in front of the Mussolini School. The men gathered around their commander's tank and drank newly 'liberated' Scotch whisky. In the flickering light of the still-blazing fuel dump, the men could see that their faces were dusty and covered in oil. 'Only our eyes still shone brightly,' Kurt Wolff wrote. He continued:

> What a night! And what a day! Tobruk, which the *Afrika Korps* had struggled so bitterly for, finally in our hands! All around fire, burning tanks, burning ships, but in the middle of all this, the corral of a German panzer detachment which had earned the highest honours.

Some mentioned the past year. The dead stood next to us, pale, yet still alive. Who wanted to feel grief on such a day? We had won a battle, victory was now in our hands.

Everybody thought of home. We were so far away, yet longing bound us closer to it than reality. In our hearts, we sang a song about the Fatherland.[119]

That night 'Tobruk was submerged into an utter chaos of fire and explosion,' Alan Moorehead wrote, as ammunition 'cooked off' or the remaining British troops continued their demolition work. Water hydrants were smashed, petrol tanks were set ablaze, sending thick black smoke rolling across the harbour, and dumps of shells, mortar rounds, hand-grenades and bullets were destroyed 'with such an unbelievable crack' that they could be distinguished by the thunderous artillery barrage. Yet still this act of mass sabotage was beyond the means and, above all, the limited time the demolition teams possessed. No German or Italian account of the fall of Tobruk is complete without reference to the vast booty the troops seized. Silhouetted against the fires still raging through the night, shadowy figures cautiously moved through the streets of Tobruk, a torch in one hand, a rifle in the other: the forage for the spoils of war was on. 'There were things which reminded us of the land of milk and honey,' one soldier in the 90th Light Division wrote: sausages, beef, pork and mutton, tins of corned beef, mixed vegetables, potatoes, preserved fruit, sacks of raisins, tea, cans of smoked ham, butter, margarine, tinned milk, chocolate, cheese, thousands of cigarettes, boxes of pipes and tobacco, gin, whisky, bottle upon bottle of red wine, a handful of bottles of champagne. There were even crates of Munich's famous Löwenbräu beer – exported to Portugal and from there to North Africa. 'I saw before me all the good things one could wish for stocked and piled up,' war correspondent Antonio Lovato of *La Stampa di Torino* wrote. Only one product was missing, which he could not find until an English officer directed the journalist towards a particular warehouse. Within 'there was enough tea for 100 cities'. On a more practical level, the new occupiers of Tobruk looted shoe polish, toothpaste, toothbrushes, underwear, woollen blankets, lambskin sleeping-bags and shoes – those with soft soles from Australia were particularly prized. A plunder detail of assault engineers led by Lieutenant Manilo Leone found a tank recovery vehicle and fell upon 30 lorries packed with food supplies: crates of tinned Argentinian meat, cans labelled 'meat and vegetables', tins of potatoes, carrots, beans, chickpeas, peas, turnips and biscuits, cans of beer, bottles of whisky, and 'Springbok' brand cigarettes in boxes of 25. An officious colonel from the Italian Army's commissariat, the *Intendenza*, attempted to stop Leone leaving with his haul, claiming the booty for his department, only to be cut down to size by a general on Rommel's staff, who rebuked him: 'Don't touch my *Guastatori*, they wage war, unlike the *Intendenza*.'

The night-time forays were not without their casualties, however. Eleven of Vittorio Vallicella's comrades were killed when they tried to remove boxes of cigarettes from a supply dump and triggered a mine. 'It was no wonder this tragic episode so badly affected me,' the driver wrote.

> Just remember what our unit had gone through: in battle constantly by day and night since May 26th, little food, terrible thirst, constantly under fire from British guns, subjected to incessant bombing and machine-gunning by aircraft. Starving, they came upon large supplies of food in Tobruk which were a godsend to many – they never gave a thought to the English leaving booby traps.

Despite such incidents, the booby traps and demolitions had been far from complete. Seven 'booty details' were dispatched to seize anything usable, put an end to any 'trophy hunting' and tally the spoils. They reported back to a delighted Hellmuth Frey.

> Hundreds and thousands of trucks and other vehicles fell into our hands. Food and clothes for weeks. Several thousand cubic metres of petrol. An abundance of equipment. We'll not go hungry in the coming weeks.
>
> I have English equipment from pith-helmets to tennis shoes. All brand-new. It's impossible to put a value on what the English have lost here. Our *Landsers* are in heaven. Every vehicle is buckling under the burden. But you can't begrudge the men that. Since May 26th they've been in battle constantly – and, of all things, at the hottest time of year. And yet we've done it. Our goal, which for months we've striven for, is reached. And the troops have been richly rewarded with booty which exceeds all expectations.[120]

By the time many Italian units scoured the Tobruk battlefield for booty, 'there was nothing left but wreckage, completely stripped of any usable accessory,' Giuseppe Mancinelli lamented. It was a typically selfish act by the Germans, the general observed, who never failed to portray themselves as the sole protagonists of the war in North Africa 'surrounded by a crowd of modest supporting actors and extras to be paid with a few crumbs, perfectly adequate for their modest stage performances'.[121]

Erwin Rommel had yet to see his prize. He spent the night camped at a road junction outside Tobruk, dining in his staff car on a menu of tinned lobster followed by a banana from Australia, accompanied by a bottle of Canadian Black Horse beer – all courtesy of the supply dumps 'liberated' by his troops. He slept little that night. It was still not light on Sunday morning when the general drove into town. Drunken prisoners wandered around, waving at the general's convoy, happily calling out: 'The war's over.' As for Tobruk itself, Rommel thought it a 'wretched hole, razed to the ground or turned to rubble. Everywhere there were burning vehicles and scenes of devastation and chaos.'

His victory was not yet complete, however. Only the harbour and town were in Axis hands. What was left of Tobruk's defenders had fallen back to the west, where they were massing for a breakout. A company of motorised flak was sent to investigate. With the guns of the company lined up facing a deep wadi where there was 'a huge concentration of tanks, vehicles and khaki-coloured soldiers', the company commander and an English-speaking doctor were sent forward, furiously waving a white nightie. They were led to Hendrik Klopper, commander of Tobruk. Hours before, the South African had assured his superiors he would 'resist to the last man and last round'. But as dawn approached and he reappraised his situation – his artillery had just 15 minutes of ammunition left – he had decided to capitulate. 'I am sorry boys, but we have to pack up,' he told his staff. 'It is foolish to carry on. Gentlemen, I propose to surrender to save useless bloodshed.' Sweating profusely, with a rolled-up travelling rug tucked under his right arm, Klopper appeared 'completely broken'. He shook his head repeatedly, muttering 'Your Stukas, your Stukas…' As an endless column of prisoners – South Africans wearing Boer hats, plus Britons and Indians – was marched off to a collection point, Klopper was taken to meet Erwin Rommel to formally surrender the fortress. Rommel asked the South African to ensure order was maintained as his command was dissolved. In return, Klopper demanded black and white officers be separated in captivity. Rommel turned him down flatly: black and white troops fought for the same cause, wore the same uniform; they would share the same camps.

And so 35,000 Commonwealth troops – all but 5,000 of them front-line warriors – entered captivity. War correspondent Domenico Bartoli of *Corriere della Sera* was led to a hotel where five generals and four British colonels were waiting to be taken away. 'One wears short trousers and has bare knees. They don't talk, they don't say anything. They are sad and at the same time content, those who were masters of Tobruk.' Their men emerged 'from every bunker: Englishmen, Scots, Indians, Australians, South African and blacks,' Hellmuth Frey observed. White troops were dejected; black troops grinned. 'For them captivity means escape from the hell of North Africa.' But not all the vanquished were browbeaten. One English prisoner told his Italian captors that Mussolini was 'a great statesman, but that if he had travelled abroad, he would not have waged war on England'. Ennio Calabresi watched Scottish troops, dressed in kilts and permitted the honour of bearing arms, 'marching proudly and impeccably with bagpipes, kilts, towards the rallying point for prisoners'. A little later fellow Italians marched down the same road, 'showing obvious signs of fatigue' as they pulled an anti-tank gun.[122]

Amid the tumult, there were brief moments of reflection. Above the noise of battle, the weak peal of the bell of St Francis church summoned Italian soldiers to Mass. Outwardly, the church had survived the siege. Inside, it was strewn with rubble, its benches singed by fire. The soldiers found prayer books discarded by the port's defenders. As a priest from a pioneer unit led the service, the building shook with each explosion. Tiles fell from the roof and dust spilled through holes in its walls as neighbouring buildings fell down. The road outside trembled with the clatter of armour moving through the town. 'Tobruk has been recaptured, the tricolore has returned to fly over the fortress and on the mast which impales the valiant St George,' soldier Luigi Grossa proudly wrote to his family. 'Here, after 14 months of enemy occupation, Tobruk is again Italian and we have now healed a plague in our current war, we have vindicated all our dead who fell in its defence, later during the siege and now in its recapture.' Stunned infantry commander Robert Witzke told his family in Westphalia: 'It is unbelievable that Tobruk fell into our hands so easily this time. Lord God. Tobruk is ours! What that means will only really become apparent in the near future.' A junior officer in 15th Panzer Division concurred as he stared at the wrecked ships in the port. Acrid black smoke billowed from the still-burning oil tanks drifting over the cobalt-blue waters of the harbour. 'We don't comprehend our victory yet,' he recorded in his diary. 'Only our eyes can see that something tremendous has happened.'[123]

War correspondent Lutz Koch immediately grasped the scale of the victory. The fall of Tobruk was 'a worldwide sensation' – and he told Erwin Rommel as much, urging the general to lend him his personal Heinkel so he could fly to Germany with recordings, photographs and footage of the victory. Rommel agreed.

After a 1,500-mile journey from Cyrenaica to Berlin, via Athens and Vienna, Koch was ushered into a room in the Propaganda Ministry to face questions from German and foreign correspondents. 'The beard's real and the dust isn't make-up. You must excuse both, they belong to the desert,' Koch introduced himself. 'I've come directly from Tobruk to be here with you. I was with Rommel only yesterday…'

Koch spent this Monday regaling first the international press corps then Joseph Goebbels with his account of Tobruk's fall before being invited to the

Reich Chancellery where he faced 'a thousand questions' from Hitler. Everything the Führer heard from the war correspondent confirmed his views. 'A nation which wants to rule an empire,' he told Koch, 'cannot live forever by retreating.'[124] The reporter was still closeted with Hitler at 9pm when his 40-minute report, sprinkled with recordings from the battlefield and two interviews with Rommel, was broadcast – right in the middle of the light entertainment programme which always drew the largest audience. At the programme's end the audience heard a brief announcement from the Führer's headquarters: Erwin Rommel was now a field marshal – the youngest in the German Army. He reacted to the news, his interpreter observed, 'like a small child'.[125]

The fall of Tobruk was not merely a defeat for Britain, but a humiliation. Churchill learned of the news from Roosevelt as the two leaders conferred in Washington. 'Defeat is one thing,' he wrote. 'Disgrace is another.' Many of the troops entering captivity thought surrender was a stain on their honour. They felt Klopper had capitulated prematurely and accused him of every sin from cowardice to treachery.[126]

Even before the announcement of Tobruk's fall, Italians were supposedly strutting around 'with puffed-up chests' thanks to the encouraging news from North Africa, according to observers in the Ministry of Popular Culture. 'That feeling of inferiority which many felt and which kept most in awe, which humiliated and diminished all the virile, proud feelings of Italian spirit, that Italy was an extra on the stage of the great war, a pawn moved around by others, has vanished.' No longer was Italy 'a supporting actor' but rather 'a protagonist of rank and great possibilities'. In the space of a month, the mood in Italy had been transformed, helped, in part, by an improving food supply. But it was the capture of Tobruk which gave Italians 'a new lively, optimistic mood'. The official report of public morale was almost lyrical:

> National pride, for so long hidden or disappointed because of the apparent uncertainty of our operations, has revived vigorously, finding the slightest pretext to manifest – and extend – itself. In discussions we only talk about Italian soldiers, Italian officers, Italian leadership, Italian valour, Italian resistance, and it is a general belief, expressed and affirmed at every step, that we could have only achieved such a resounding success against an enemy so powerfully armed and entrenched with soldiers like ours...

For the first time in months, perhaps years, the Italian people enjoyed 'a restful feeling of protection, of security for the present and for the future'.[127]

The public response in Germany was similar, eclipsing the reaction to recent victories in Russia at Kerch and Kharkov. The first news from Tobruk – a terse military communiqué, trumpeted across the Reich via loudspeakers on Sunday afternoon, even interrupting the semi-final of the third wartime cup at Berlin's Olympic Stadium – provoked 'indescribable' scenes of jubilation. Most Germans regarded Tobruk's capture as impossible. Its fall 'had an almost cathartic effect,' the official monitors of public opinion observed. For a brief moment, everyday concerns were pushed into the background, while Rommel was 'the hero of the hour', and not just in Germany, as Goebbels observed:

> Rommel is not only exceptionally popular among the German people but in the entire world, the most popular army commander that we have at our disposal at present. The English have also turned him into some form of legend, in part so that they can better explain their own defeats. But that can only help to popularise Rommel around the world. It's good that we've got an army commander whose name is respected around the world and brings fear and anxiety to the enemy.

It was, the propaganda minister lamented, 'a shame that we don't have more Rommels. We could use them on the Eastern Front.' For now, however, Erwin Rommel was needed in North Africa. The German people fully expected the new field marshal to 'exploit his victory and advance into Egypt as far as the Suez Canal'.[128]

Which was precisely what Erwin Rommel intended to do. But there was one major obstacle to such intentions: Rommel was permitted to advance as far as the Egyptian frontier, but no further. There he should wait while Malta was dealt with, once and for all – as agreed before Gazala and Tobruk. In Berlin, the Naval Staff, in Rome, the head of the *Comando Supremo*, Ugo Cavallero, and in Africa, Alfred Kesselring all pushed hard for *Herkules* 'if victory at Tobruk is not to be a mere episode, rather the first act in a major operation which might decide the outcome of the war'.[129] But there were other counsels urging Rommel to press on. 'As we've now got Tobruk, we don't need Malta any more,' Hitler's senior military adviser Alfred Jodl opined.[130] As for the Führer himself, he bent Mussolini's ear – the Duce, after all, was supreme commander in the Mediterranean. 'The goddess of military fortune only extends her hand to commanders once,' he wrote to his Italian ally. 'Those who do not grasp it firmly at such a moment will never be able to do so again!' Failing to strike now would only store up problems for the future. 'I have always pursued a beaten foe as long and as completely as I was able to,' Hitler continued. The moment had come to hound the British 'until the last breath of every soldier', to advance 'as far into the heart of Egypt as possible'. The Führer offered the Duce a glittering prize: with the offensive about to be unleashed in Russia, he would bring about the collapse of 'the entire oriental edifice of the British Empire'. 'If at this uniquely historic hour I may give you a piece of advice from the heart, Duce, then it is this: order the continuation of the operation for the total annihilation of British forces as far as your leaders or Marshal Rommel believe they can go with the military forces available.'[131]

Adolf Hitler's advice mirrored Erwin Rommel's intentions. The high morale of his men, the vast booty, the enemy's disarray, and, perhaps, belief in his own invincibility convinced him that a thrust 'into the heart of Egypt' was called for. 'What counts now is utterly destroying our foe,' he declared to his men in an order of the day. 'We will not rest until we have beaten the last remnants of the British Eighth Army.'[132]

Rommel did not wait for instructions from Rome or Berlin. And he did not listen to Ettore Bastico – newly promoted Marshal of Italy and ostensibly his superior in position and rank. The elderly Italian urged caution, suggesting nothing more than a tentative advance into Egypt until Malta was in Axis hands.

'Without Tobruk, the British are on their knees. Destroyed,' Rommel insisted.

Bastico stood firm. Men and machines were exhausted after four weeks of battle, and rich though the booty at Tobruk had been, it had not made good the Italo-German army's losses. 'I will never give the order to continue,' he insisted.

Rommel snapped. 'My flanks and front are clear. Nobody can stop me.' He removed his cap. 'I'm going. If the Italians want to follow me, they can. Otherwise, halt here. I'm not bothered either way.' Suddenly his mood changed and he smiled at the Italian marshal. 'From now on, my dear Bastico, I'll invite you to breakfast in Cairo.'[133]

At 2pm on Tuesday 23 June, *Panzerarmee Afrika* struck eastwards once more. The *Afrika Korps* could call upon just 50 working tanks, the Italians barely a dozen. The objectives were distant: the border lay 70 miles east of Tobruk, Alexandria another 300 miles, Cairo 400. Supply lines were stretched. Urging one motorised company of mountain infantry to make for the border, their commander warned them he was running low on fuel. 'You'll have to get it from the English,' the field marshal replied. The men were tired too, but they were also confident. 'We already half imagined ourselves in Cairo,' reconnaissance patrol leader Hellmuth Schroetter remembered. His fellow Germans talked of *Rennen zum Nil* – the race to the Nile. Italians, wrote Vittorio Vallicella, were 'possessed by a single thought: Alexandria, Cairo, the Nile, pyramids, palm trees, women'.

In the east the sky darkened with black clouds as British forces in the border zone blew up their supplies and fell back towards the fortress of Mersa Matruh on the Mediterranean shore. Just after sundown, at 7.22pm, Rommel's army reached the three wire fences which stretched more than 125 miles into the desert in an almost straight north–south line and marked the frontier. Pioneers quickly cut through the three 6ft-high barriers, cleared lanes through the minefields on the other side and, as they had done on the first day of the Gazala battle four weeks earlier, marked the route with dimmed lights. The advance continued. 'We crossed the Libyan–Egyptian border,' wrote Horst Sonnenkalb, 'and were in the land of the Pharaohs again.'[134]

3

VICTORIES WITHOUT VICTORY

The further east we advance, the weaker we become.

Arthur Schmidt, Sixth Army

Exactly 12 months since he had crossed the River Bug and begun the march into Galicia, Catholic corporal Gustav Böker wrote to his family in the village of Oberg in Lower Saxony. 'One year ago today, we entered Russia,' the anti-tank gunner reminisced.

> Now we've been in the workers' paradise for one year. Who would have thought that back then? Like many others, I'd expected about four weeks of war. And how different everything turned out. Nobody expected such a military power as Russia. I think if someone had told us on June 22nd 1941: 'You'll still be in Russia in a year's time', we would have declared them crazy.
>
> But it has become reality. We are still in Russia. And who knows how much longer.[1]

The anniversary of the war caused men on both sides of the front to take stock. For Fedor Nikolaevich Krizhanovskiy, a junior officer serving with the security forces on the southern sector of the Eastern Front, it had been a year 'of hard trials, bloodshed, suffering, destruction and the deaths of many people' at the hands of the 'the worst enemies of humanity – Hitler and his pack of dogs'.

> But Hitler will pay dearly – an even greater, terrible and merciless retribution awaits him, Hitler and his hounds will pay one hundredfold for all their inhuman crimes. One year of war has passed, the second year is coming, which will mark

147

the victory of the Red Army over the Nazi troops and the final defeat of German Fascism, the triumph of progressive mankind over Fascist slavery!...

I feel good and confident. I work calmly, I know that we will win. During this year of war I've had to endure a lot, but I never doubted that we would defeat the Nazis nevertheless... Now joyful days are coming, the days of our victories![2]

Six days later Axis forces unleashed their summer offensive. Within two months German troops would stand on the banks of the Volga and on the summit of Europe's highest mountain.

Germany staked its bid for victory in the East on a single card. There were no reserves, no 'plan B'. Just *Fall Blau – Case Blue* – an offensive in four stages which would see a Soviet Union, deprived of its principal supply of oil, sue for peace before the onset of winter. *Blue* would open with the capture of Voronezh, followed by the destruction of Red Army units between Kharkov and the Don. The third phase would focus on capturing Stalingrad and Rostov and crossings over the Don. With their flank secured, Hitler's troops could then march into the Caucasus to seize the oilfields. In a few weeks German soldiers would stand on the Volga, the western shore of the Caspian Sea and on the Russian and Georgian coasts of the Black Sea.[3]

To deliver that victory, Germany mustered more than one million men, placed in the hands of Fedor von Bock and his Army Group South, supported by another 300,000 troops from allied nations – principally Romanians, Italians, Hungarians, but also small contingents of Croats and Slovaks. Offensive action would be almost exclusively the preserve of German arms; their allies would be expected for the most part to defend and pacify the captured territories, particularly those along the Don.

Bock presided over a force of 90 divisions, 65 of them German, and all but 15 of those infantry units. Eleven panzer divisions provided the armoured fist, four motorised infantry divisions the mobile foot soldiers. Despite the shock appearance of T-34 and KV heavy tanks in the opening days of the war in the East, the Mk3 and Mk4 remained the mainstay of the *Panzerwaffe*, though large numbers had been 'up gunned' to face down the Soviet armoured threat. On paper, Army Group South should have mustered more than 1,900 armoured vehicles, but many were unserviceable as the offensive began, while German industry had been unable to keep pace with losses at the front. The motorised infantry – increasingly becoming known as panzer grenadiers – suffered from a shortage of tracked vehicles, which limited their movements in rugged terrain, while infantry divisions would be even more reliant on the horse to haul their supplies across the steppe. Alongside the peerless 88mm flak/anti-

The German plan of campaign in the East

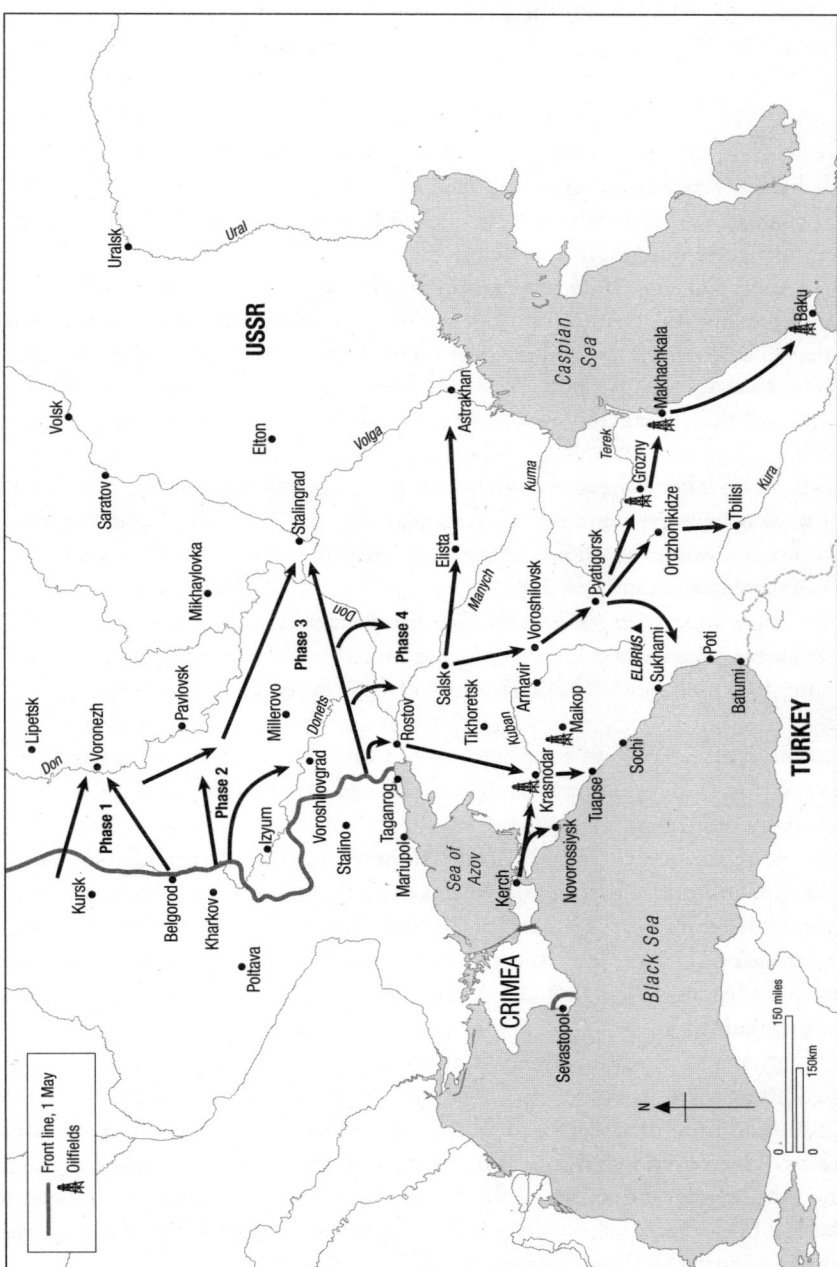

tank gun, German factories had produced the 75mm anti-tank gun in large numbers over the winter. Munitions works were rather less efficient, forcing 75mm gun crews to limit consumption of shells in the opening stages of the offensive.

As for what the Germans called *Menschenmaterial* – manpower – one third of Bock's divisions were at full strength and fully refreshed. The gaps in another 27 divisions had been filled, but had no time to rest and recuperate, leaving 17 infantry divisions which were short of men, especially leaders and non-commissioned officers, not to mention shortfalls in equipment. Men called up from the 1923 and 1924 year groups – 18- and 19-year-olds – had received barely two months' training and enjoyed no combat experience. They were spread around the divisions to dissipate the potential dilution of fighting power. Even a doctor such as Horst Rocholl, serving with the newly raised 24th Panzer Division, realised the German Army was not what it had been in June 1941:

> I find our infantry's changed compared with last summer. There's a type of soldier who's quite magnificent, for whom age plays no part, he could be 20 or 35 years old, he is weather-proof, always happy, still in a good mood even if wounded. He's delighted that he's not yet dead. He's an optimist. The small fry, mostly from the younger year groups, who make fools of themselves with nerves wrecked by nicotine, who see 100 Russians, not ten, and 200 of their own dead instead of one, play no part at all. They are forced along by the others.[4]

Commanders complained, only to be rebuked. Friedrich Paulus, in charge of Sixth Army, told his officers to stop carping and 'get the most out of the troops'. Germany was attacking with the troops it had, whatever the shortcomings.[5] Still, in the summer of 1942, Army Group South was the tip of the German spear, the strongest, best-equipped force the Wehrmacht could commit in the field. But it was a sign of the toll of the war in the East that Germany was about to unleash a smaller, less ambitious offensive on a much shorter front with fewer, less effective, less mobile forces than it had possessed during the previous summer campaign.

Only in the air did German arms enjoy parity with Soviet forces opposing their plans: three in every five Luftwaffe aircraft on the Eastern Front, around 1,600 machines, were deployed in support of Army Group South. Otherwise, the Soviets enjoyed superiority in numbers in all areas: nearly half a million more men on the relevant sectors of the front, more tanks – at least 3,000, perhaps nearly 4,000 – and more artillery pieces (16,000). In the skies, the two sides were roughly equal: 1,600 aircraft apiece.

But quantity does not equal quality. Even now, 12 months into the war, the Russians were still sending obsolete tanks into battle. Barely half the 1,600 armoured vehicles facing the initial German assault were newer models. The Red Air Force would demonstrate it knew how to sacrifice itself for the Motherland in the first few weeks of the enemy's onslaught, but little else.

And then there were the *frontoviki*, the rank-and-file Red Army conscripts – 'Ivan' to his German foe. Morale in newly raised units, such as the 284th Rifle Division, was high – the men yearned to prove themselves in battle. But Nikolai Aksenov reckoned only one in three of his fellow Siberians was ready for battle. Training had been perfunctory: wooden blocks instead of live grenades hurled at plywood tanks, just three rounds of ammunition for rifles and a solitary bullet for the anti-tank rifle. No-one in the regular ranks had any combat experience: soldiers returning home on leave from the front or convalescing were urged to share their stories of life in the line with recruits. 'How many untrained men were sent to the front – and then into combat,' Aksenov wrote. 'The law of war is simple: He who is ill-trained pays in blood.'[6]

The final days preparing for *Blau* were hindered by heavy rain. The frequent cloudbursts – short, but heavy – turned the roads and tracks of the central Russian plains into a morass which brought vehicles to a halt. 'Road conditions here really are odd,' observed Horst Rocholl, deploying around the town of Shchigry, 100 miles west of Voronezh.

If it rains for ten minutes, the roads already seem like they're freshly polished. Vehicles slide all over the place. We too fall flat on our faces as we move around. After half an hour the dirt, which until then was like a layer of ointment, sticks like a thick paste to every wheel. After that there can be no thought of getting through. After one hour there are already deep gutters. At best, when it rains all driving promptly stops. After several hours – at most after a day – the road is dusty again like it was before.[7]

Just 50 miles to the east, the Siberians of 284th Rifle Division were disembarking at the station in Kastornoye, a large village straddling the River Olym. The men were disheartened. They were itching for a fight – 'a big battle where everyone could "scratch their fists properly",' one rifleman remembered. Kastornoye was a sleepy backwater. Life went on as normal. Children with satchels headed to school while their mothers walked through the streets. The soldiers paddled in the muddy waters of the Olym. They badgered railway workers for news from the front. And they pestered their commanders for a more fitting assignment than occupying some unimportant village in the rear.

'Calm down, the time will come and we will fight, don't worry,' their officers assured them.[8]

<hr>

At 2pm on a wet Friday 19 June, staff officer Joachim Reichel climbed into a small Storch reconnaissance aircraft at 23rd Panzer Division's headquarters and headed off on a short flight to the front. With just days to go before the beginning of the summer offensive, the 34-year-old operations officer wanted to inspect the terrain allocated as the division's marshalling area ahead of the attack. It was raining – again. The ground was sodden, the roads and tracks bottomless. The inspection would take hours by car. To save time, Reichel decided to fly to the front.

In the bad weather and poor visibility, Reichel's pilot Erich Dechant lost his way and strayed over enemy territory. Russian troops took aim, peppered Reichel's body with bullets and pierced the Storch's fuel tank. A few minutes later the small aircraft came down in marshland near the village of Surkovo as it tried to reach German lines.

Search parties subsequently found the wrecked Storch and, perhaps 30 feet away, two fresh graves. The bodies were recovered – but not the papers Reichel had been carrying. They were already on their way to Moscow.

Contravening all orders, Joachim Reichel had been carrying the plans for the impending offensive. Hitler was incandescent, drew up a list of offences committed, and summoned Fedor von Bock – Reichel's ultimate superior as commander of Army Group South – to his East Prussian headquarters to account for them. As far as Bock was concerned the fault lay with Reichel – and Reichel alone. He believed he had assuaged his Führer, but on his return to his headquarters in Poltava in Ukraine, he found that Hitler had sacked not only 23rd Panzer Division's commander, Hans von Boineburg-Lengsfeld, but his superior in charge of XXXX Panzer Corps, Georg Stumme, and its chief-of-staff.[9]

Adolf Hitler need not have worried himself. Stalin dismissed the captured plans as a ruse. Soviet intelligence had surmised since March that Germany would deliver its main blow in 1942 on the southern front, to Rostov, Stalingrad, the Caucasus and the Caspian Sea. They might find time, if they succeeded, to take Moscow and Leningrad as well 'as a matter of prestige'.[10] But the *vozhd* was convinced Moscow was the prize – and the documents seized from Joachim Reichel were nothing more than a 'big trumped-up piece of work by the intelligence people'. He ordered Filipp Golikov – whose Bryansk Front would bear the brunt of the German onslaught – to prepare a counter-stroke. The first draft of the plan was completed in the small hours of Sunday 28 June.[11]

Late on Saturday afternoon, the vehicles of 24th Panzer Division received the codeword 'Skat is being played' – the signal for them to occupy their jump-off positions around Shchigry by nightfall. The terrain was still too soft, the roads still bottomless, but the land had dried sufficiently for the order to attack to be given. Soldier Wilhelm Roes watched an endless line of panzer silhouettes move towards the front as the sun went down. 'No-one can withstand such force,' he thought. 'We were so certain of victory. For so long we had known nothing but victory.' The men's mood was 'fabulous', one infantryman recalled. They all gave three hearty cheers before checking their equipment and uniforms one last time and heading up to the line. Karl Josef Wintereder, commanding a bakery unit in Sixth Army, was certain of 'final success' in the East in 1942. The 25-year-old had followed the spring fighting in the Crimea and taken part in the victory outside Kharkov – both of which, he wrote confidently to his family in Lower Austria on the first anniversary of the German invasion, set the scene for 'truly big decisions in the near future'. The Luftwaffe had the measure of the Red Air Force ('of very little importance'), while the Red Army ('howling masses') was no match for the well-led, highly disciplined Wehrmacht. 'If only we were on the Volga,' Wintereder mused, 'then the battle would be practically decided...'[12]

At 3.15 on Sunday morning, 28 June, Ernst Schwörer watched mesmerised as the sky to his left turned red. Arrayed on the front of his 16th Motorised Infantry Division – barely two miles wide – were 16 artillery batteries, plus six 210mm mortar batteries, and *Nebelwerfer* rocket launchers. The latter opened fire first – 'You can't hear the volleys as with a cannon, but the sound pierces to the bone' – followed by the artillery. It was, Schwörer recorded, 'a barrage like I've never heard before. In the air there is rattling and roaring and then shell after shell landing. On the Russian side all that can be seen is a bright glow as the many explosions combine.' So loud was the cacophonous symphony that men in jump-off positions could not hear each other, even if they shouted.[13]

Twenty-five-year-old Sepp Prentl revelled in the 'hurricane of fire' and the thunder of battle. 'One scene after another was played out like in the movies: swashbuckling and thrilling,' he wrote. The flak battery he commanded was 'only a small, but important, wheel in this tremendous war machine', charged with knocking out Soviet bunkers with its 88mm flak guns. It did so, with aplomb. Ten enemy strongpoints were neutralised within ten minutes.[14]

The howl and screech of the rockets leaving the rails and tearing through the night sky sounded, one infantryman recalled, 'as if someone has stood on the tails of one thousand cats'. The Germans watched these 'glowing balls' fizz and hiss before impacting among the enemy positions.[15]

The commander of a platoon of half-track troop carriers stood on top of his vehicle and watched the bombardment in front of 24th Panzer Division's lines.

> At first light, when the black sky is covered with silvery-grey wisps of cloud, the air is filled with a deep rumbling. A Stuka squadron approaches in close formation from the west. Then the aircraft break formation and the first ones fall like falcons on the enemy positions. Again and again – the ground trembles under the impact of the explosions.
>
> The rifle regiments attack. The dull rumble of artillery begins. We watch the rockets from the *Nebelwerfer* in a shallow arc moving with a fiendish howl towards the enemy.

Bearing the brunt of this cataclysmic opening bombardment was Mikhail Parsegov's Fortieth Army – a powerful force, ready to strike the enemy – and when it did, its general was 'certain of success'. But what if the enemy struck first, Bryansk Front's commander Filipp Golikov asked. Parsegov's response was as certain as it was unequivocal: 'Not even a mouse will get through.' His confidence was infectious, as Filipp Zhmachenko discovered when he arrived as the army's deputy commander in the third week of June. But there was much which troubled Zhmachenko. Life in Fortieth Army's headquarters – too far behind the front for his liking – continued as if it were peacetime and 'did not understand the tragedy of war'. Officers rose late, dined formally, and rarely visited the front or spoke to the men holding the line, preferring to receive written reports or converse over the telephone. Had they done so, they might have interrogated the German prisoners brought back by raiding parties who confirmed that a summer offensive was imminent.[16]

Now, that offensive was seemingly upon Fortieth Army, Zhmachenko headed to an observation post to follow the battle. So dense was the smoke and dust thrown up by the Germans' opening barrage, he could see nothing.[17]

In Fortieth Army's front lines and forward positions, hell had been unleashed. According to the diarist of 1109th Artillery Regiment, 'a hurricane of fire' fell upon its batteries. 'A sea of fire fills the sky. Explosions merge into a continuous rumble. Smoke and dust from the explosions fill the horizon and it is impossible to see what is happening behind this veil.' The air, one Russian gunner remembered, was permeated 'with the smell of burned soil and dust from the earth flying upwards'. The men cowered in their foxholes or trenches or sought shelter in dugouts and bunkers. Unable to see their foe to grapple with him, they simply waited for the barrage to end. When it did, the gunner remembered, 'we felt depressed and devastated. The expression on our faces was confused and a slight shiver ran through our bodies'.[18] The artillery supporting 160th Rifle Division complained that the moment one if its batteries began shooting, 'up to a squadron of enemy aircraft descended upon it. Some guns failed to fire more than two or three rounds before they were destroyed – and some were destroyed without firing a single shot.'[19]

After the bombardment, the ground assault. As day dawned, pioneers and the first infantry wave fell upon the battered Soviet lines. To Ernst Schwörer, the enemy seemed to evaporate. The attacking troops fired flares to signal their success. 'None of us has seen anything like this before,' Schwörer wrote. 'It looks wonderful and horrible at the same time.'[20]

Finally the signal came for 24th Panzer Division to move off. This was its baptism of fire – the division had spent the winter and spring in France being converted from a cavalry into an armoured formation, a fact acknowledged by its 'leaping horseman' insignia. 'The attack rolls!' excited junior officer Gert-Axel Weidemann wrote. 'The sun is high in a cloudless blue sky and beneath it the open, rolling terrain with its pale brown steppe vegetation, several bare fields and crossed by various hills.'[21]

Horst Rocholl found the experience exhilarating. 'Stukas roar, diving on enemy positions, artillery's shooting and we're driving in a long column,' the doctor wrote. 'At our side – clearly visible through binoculars – infantry and artillery attacking. Guns, limbered, are brought forward. Our artillery is in position behind us. What might all this is combined!'[22]

The division's grenadiers found the *Nebelwerfer* barrage had decimated the enemy. 'Most of the Russians are dead, their lungs torn apart, blood gently running out of their mouths and noses,' one wrote. 'A few survivors climb out of their foxholes completely distraught and covered in dirt and are taken prisoner.'

By 9am, 24th Panzer had punched a hole a dozen miles deep in Soviet lines, overrun the headquarters of a Red Army division and reached the banks of the River Tim – the first natural obstacle on the road to Voronezh.[23]

'We're advancing everywhere!' wrote excited mortar crewman Hans Heinz Rehfeldt, serving with the motorised infantry of the *Grossdeutschland* Division. 'Panzers, assault guns, armoured personnel carriers, half-tracks, flak guns – everything is rushing forward. It's like we're on a high!' Soviet resistance was negligible – much to Rehfeldt's surprise. 'With such a mighty war machine unleashed here with such élan and impetus against the Russian positions, this war in the East must be won soon by us. We didn't expect such a success!'

As the day progressed, the terrain, heat and exertion of advancing rapidly began to slow the *Grossdeutschland*'s attack. With the sun high in the sky, the Red Army evidently woke up and began to engage its foe. 'We see shells landing right next to our panzers, then they respond with fire and score a direct hit!' Rehfeldt continued. 'Two T-34s soon go up in flames. Extremely black smoke from burning crude oil rises. We can see many such Russian tanks knocked out in the terrain in front of us.'[24]

24th Panzer Division's advance was rapid, exhilarating, almost uncontested. The Tim was quickly crossed. So too the next river, the Kshen, before the armour rolled into the nondescript village of Yefrosimovka – the first day's objective – on the main road to Voronezh as dusk fell. 'With a hiss, the panzers' glowing tracer rounds strafe the village,' the half-track platoon commander noted.

> A Russian ammunition dump explodes somewhere. In a short, swift assault we penetrate the village. We overtake the panzers here. I drive along the village street in the lead. My groups go to my left and right through gardens. Every house is burning. Suddenly around a corner, there's a Russian gun, the limber at its side and the gunners sitting on it, all dead. The horses too are dead. We advance as far as the end of the village. In the distance we can see several Russian trucks disappearing, leaving trails of dust behind them. I chase them with my anti-tank gun which sets the last truck on fire.

The panzers and half-tracks halted on the edge of Yefrosimovka, forming a makeshift camp in a large circle. The field kitchen eventually caught up with the attacking spearhead and warm soup was distributed as heavy rain fell.[25]

With his army subjected to the full force of the German offensive, Mikhail Parsegov's response was at best nonchalant, at worst irresponsible. Initial reports reaching Fortieth Army's headquarters had been encouraging: the divisions were holding the line. But as Sunday morning progressed, the Luftwaffe's superiority in the skies of central Russia began to make itself felt. Fortieth Army's line was battered. One commander pleaded: 'Please send me aircraft.' Headquarters had nothing to offer. 'The enemy is playing with us as he wants,' Fortieth Army's chief-of-staff Zinovy Rogozny fumed. Yet neither he nor his general went anywhere near the front to direct the battle – relying entirely on the telephone. Even when Parsegov was given two tank brigades to parry the enemy assault, he did not brief them in person but sent deputies.[26]

Such half-hearted actions were not uncommon. One Soviet tank brigade commander ordered to crush a German bridgehead over the Kshen remembered that the attempts to force the enemy back were unnecessarily half-hearted. 'Instead of driving the enemy from his bridgehead by striking him with an armoured fist, we tried to push him with our finger,' he recalled. The Soviets possessed more than enough tanks and men to crush the small bridgehead, but wasted them in piecemeal attacks rather than wait to mass their forces. As a result, each counter-attack was brushed aside by the Germans – until they enjoyed superior numbers.[27]

Some units defended their positions doggedly. 1109th Artillery Regiment – sorely battered in the opening barrage – recovered its poise and took a heavy toll of enemy motorised troops. In doing so, it drew the attention of German gunners who began to zero in on its fire positions. Then panzers began to appear; the regiment's diarist counted 79 and claimed his guns knocked out at least 13. But by mid-day, with one battery commander mortally wounded, a battalion commander dead, 200 enemy aircraft circling overhead, the moment had come for 1109th Artillery Regiment to fall back. In the chaos of retreat, its guns would not fire again until it regrouped on the outskirts of Voronezh.[28]

As Fortieth Army's lines buckled then broke, many units began streaming for the rear. The Luftwaffe hounded every movement and especially concentrations of fleeing troops funnelled through the few bridges spanning the many streams and rivers dissecting the terrain. Vehicles which tried to bypass such jams by fording waterways became stuck and all manner of equipment was abandoned. Military columns became intertwined with long lines of Soviet citizens also streaming east. The Germans bombed them mercilessly, leaving the roadsides littered with the dead and dying, crying children and women huddled over them. Fortieth Army's deputy commander Filipp Zhmachenko was incensed: 'I had tears in my eyes and wondered when we would take revenge on the enemy for these monstrous crimes...'[29] The disorganised remnants of 121st Rifle Division fled through Kastornoye. 'People ran with a frightened expression on their faces, often without belts and weapons,' one Soviet soldier recalled. They passed through positions held by 284th Rifle Division, whose ranks briefly considered incorporating some of the stragglers in their units – then dropped the idea, largely at the insistence of a non-commissioned officer. 'A cowardly friend is worse than an enemy; you rely on a friend, but you fear an enemy,' he reminded his comrades. 'If we have even one coward in our company, he will let us all down in the heat of battle. Good riddance to them!'[30]

All Mikhail Parsegov heard from his superiors were terse instructions – 'act more vigorously', 'take action', 'restore the situation' – and assurances that the Red Air Force was in action, that 200 commissars and political workers were being sent to give his army an ideological backbone. The only decisive action Fortieth Army's commander took on the first day of the German offensive was to move his headquarters 20 miles to the rear.[31]

Joseph Stalin was, understandably, incandescent. His generals had once again failed to blunt a German offensive. Convinced Bryansk Front outnumbered its opponent more than two to one in tanks – the reality was in fact the opposite – he overruled his front-line commanders and demanded his armour attack, complaining 'this is no way to fight'.[32]

Under such pressure from their leader, some Soviet commanders threw their units into the battle pell-mell. Two tank brigades attacked along the River Oskol without any information on their enemy and without any co-ordination with the infantry, artillery and air force. Their attack ended in disarray, falling back behind the river.[33]

And so the settlements of the Kursk region burned like those of Byelorussia, Ukraine and along the roads to Leningrad and Moscow before them. Daylight robbed the flames of their spectacle, but not their fury. Fanned by the steppe breeze, the fires razed village after village while their inhabitants fled to the relative safety of earth bunkers and slit trenches. 'You can see that our leadership and our men are far superior,' Horst Rocholl noted. 'The heaviest Russian tanks are knocked out, even if it costs God knows how many rounds. Afterwards these ugly monsters stand there and burn. Their burned crews, youthful-looking Mongolians, lay next to two of them.'[34]

Joachim Stempel, a 22-year-old junior officer with 14th Panzer Division, was convinced he was taking part in a great victory march. '*Ja*, things will definitely end here in Russia this year,' he wrote. 'By the end of this year, we'll have occupied all the territory we need. Perhaps we'll even meet Marshal Rommel somewhere. Over the Caucasus, Iran down to Syria, Arabia and into Egypt! Well, dreams!'[35]

On the morning of 1 July, the vanguard of 9th Panzer Division approached Kastornoye, still held by the untried ranks of 284th Rifle Division. Reconnaissance the previous day had warned the men the Germans were just a dozen miles away. They prepared themselves for battle – mentally and physically. They checked and re-checked their ammunition, stocked up on water for themselves and their horses. A few jokers tried to lighten the mood. Political officers handed out leaflets, reminded men of their duty, and held rousing lectures after which the men vowed to fight to the last round.[36]

When the first vehicles of 9th Panzer appeared in their sights, the gunners let the Germans close to within 600 to 700 metres of their lines before opening fire, spurred on by a gruff senior sergeant. 'Let the Fascist bastards know how Siberians fight!' They did – and repulsed the first wave. But they paid for their effrontery. German mortar shells crashed down on the 284th's lines. The senior sergeant was soon lying in a pool of blood, cut down by shrapnel. German aircraft bombed and strafed the battery positions. A mortar round wiped out all the horses which hauled the guns. Crews – such as were left or still able to fight – continued to fire at the oncoming panzers and, when ammunition ran out, resorted to grenades and Molotov cocktails until the German armour rolled into the battery's position and crushed the remaining guns, breaking and twisting them with their tracks. 'The enemy was only able to pass through the area that the gunners were defending by passing over the corpses of the heroic crew,' one survivor of the 284th recalled. 'None of them took a step back. The heroes fought to the death and gave their lives to carry out the orders of the leadership.'[37]

Fewer than a dozen panzers were damaged or knocked out. Reports passed up the line suggested 284th Rifle Division had knocked out 80 enemy tanks and left 800 enemy dead on the battlefield. Post-war Soviet accounts exaggerated the fallen still further to 3,000.[38]

Fifteen miles away, 200 panzers waited 'like some great steel herd which is resting' in the pre-dawn mist which lingered in the hollows on the first day of July. Engines stuttered into life as the armour moved out to meet the Red Army straddling the Kursk–Voronezh highway. A not-insignificant force of heavy Soviet tanks was preparing to block 24th Panzer Division's advance eastwards. Standing in the way of the 'leaping horsemen' were not just T-34s, but also huge, lumbering, heavily armed and armoured KV tanks: KV-1s equipped with 76mm guns, the even heavier KV-2s with 152mm howitzers. Twelve months before, their appearance had terrified panzer crews and German anti-tank gunners who possessed virtually no weapon to halt the Soviet monsters. But in 1942, the German Army fielded several weapons which could penetrate the KVs' thick armour.

'The first light of dawn reveals the outlines of the steppe landscape surrounding us,' Gert-Axel Weidemann wrote. 'Nature's silence is suddenly shattered by the noise of panzer engines starting. We are ready for battle.' Under a blanket of artillery fire which stunned the Russians, the panzers seized the high ground and engaged the well-camouflaged enemy tanks at a range of 800 metres. The sound of tank guns firing reverberated around the hilly terrain. Dense smoke from burning KV-1s and concentrations of armour in the Soviet rear attacked by Stukas soon began to obscure the battlefield. The Red Army lines began to falter, then gave way.

By 2pm, the German vanguard was approaching the village of Maksimovka. 'The sun's rays, like sharpened blades, pierced the blue through the clouds that were gathering in the west,' wrote an officer from the newly formed 4th Motorised Rifle Brigade who left a fanciful – and rather bloodthirsty – propaganda account of the encounter which followed. The Red Army men observed 'drunken SS men' walking through the tall, rich fields of rye outside Maksimovka, leading columns of panzers, behind them motorcycles, then half-tracks packed with infantry, and finally trucks.

'Are they going to a parade?' brigade commander Lieutenant Colonel Shchekal asked rhetorically, then turned to his artillery chief: 'Prepare a worthy greeting for these rats...' The brigade let the attackers draw closer, close enough for German voices to be heard. The account continues:

> It seemed to them that the Russians were about to get up and run aimlessly, and they, like hunters, would pick the Russians off at will. Each of them was already thinking of rich booty, but the front line was still calm. Then it seemed to the Germans that the Russians were so entranced by the menacing sight of their advance that they were finally confused, and in dumb fear and terror, like an animal waiting for their unenviable fate to fall into their hands.

Finally, with the range down to just 400 metres, Shchekal seized his moment and ordered his men to open fire.

> The Germans had not expected such an encounter, they moved forward for a few more minutes but could not endure, abruptly turned and ran. Confusion broke out in the enemy's ranks, the panzers turned about and quickly turned back, crushing motorcyclists under their caterpillar tracks. Armoured personnel carriers moving behind the motorcyclists in turn crushed the infantry running towards them. German hubris vanished and all that had been living and formidable lay helplessly in one huge heap. Precise direct fire from our artillerymen, mortar men, gunners, machine-gunners, tank crews turned the menacing tanks and armoured vehicles into piles of metal, and the Germans into bloody fat pieces of disgusting German meat.
>
> 'Fire, fire! Shoot for the Motherland, shoot for Stalin!' – And a flurry of fire from all kinds of weapons rolled behind the fleeing Germans. The entire field in front of the front line was strewn with hundreds of dead German corpses. Unbearable cries and groaning from the wounded Fritzes. When silence suddenly descended and the acrid powder smoke cleared, the battalions were short of men. There were killed and many wounded, but the battalions remained in the defensive lines.
>
> 'Fight to the death for our Motherland, fight to the death!' was passed along the line by the men with a kind of shrill resolute agitation. And this oath rolled menacingly along the whole front line.

The brigade claimed it thwarted three waves of German attacks on the undulating terrain around Maksimovka, leaving the fields strewn with 4,000 dead and at least three dozen knocked-out vehicles.

There were no SS men – drunken or otherwise – leading the German advance astride the Kursk–Voronezh highway, and if the attackers were held up at

Maksimovka it mattered little for the high ground around Bykovo, just six miles to the north, was now firmly in 24th Panzer Division's hands. From the hilltops, the Germans surveyed the brown, undulating steppe stretching eastwards, a landscape dotted with fires where Stukas had struck. The most incredible sight of all, Gert-Axel Weidemann remembered, was the Soviet armour, barely a kilometre away, fleeing eastwards – 'a herd of elephants trying to escape the rifle of a big game hunter'. Fatally, they presented their more vulnerable sides to the German guns in trying to escape. 'Gunpowder smoke, the glistening bursts of tracer and then the explosion of enemy tanks which have been hit are signs of success,' Wiedemann wrote. As the panzers rolled past 100 abandoned or disabled enemy tanks, they noticed names painted in Cyrillic on numerous turrets. 'We learn later these were the names of heroes from Russian history, clear signs of the Great Fatherland War proclaimed by the Kremlin,' Weidemann wrote. After driving through Gologusovka, still thick with smoke from burning whitewashed cottages, the German armour paused. 'On our panzers, the hatches are open,' Weidemann noted. 'Crews wave at each other while they check their vehicles are ready for action once more.'[39]

Failure to blunt the German attack along the Kursk–Voronezh highway once again enraged Joseph Stalin. This time his ire was directed at Nikolai Feklenko, whose XVII Tank Corps was supposed to parry the enemy offensive. 'Feklenko is acting like a coward, lying all the time, and if you do not immediately move him towards Bykovo or south of Bykovo, you will answer to Stavka,' the Soviet leader railed at Bryansk Front's headquarters. Perhaps the corps commander should be replaced, Stalin opined, 'but it would be better to force Feklenko to advance immediately and wash away the disgrace he has covered himself with…'[40]

Having held the Germans at bay for two days, 284th Rifle Division was finally forced to abandon Kastornoye, reluctantly falling back through the small town. 'Tired, hungry, exhausted by long battles and sleepless nights, soldiers and officers entered Kastornoye, leaving their combat positions, drenched in blood,' one veteran recalled.

> The town was on fire. Tongues of flame eagerly devoured dry buildings, spreading from one house to another. Smoke spread. No-one put out the growing fire.
> Not a single inhabitant was to be seen: some had gone to the east, abandoning all their wealth acquired over many years to the mercy of fate, while others hid in cellars, fleeing from the enemy's bombs and shells. As if a tornado swept through the village: not a living soul was seen, not even any dogs.[41]

The stand at Kastornoye held up the German offensive no more than two days. It reduced 284th Rifle Division to just 3,000 men. Many were dead, others were taken prisoner, but a sizeable number, including commissars, had panicked and, in some instances, fled the field of battle – stopping only when they were half a dozen miles behind the front.[42]

The Germans would encounter the 284th Rifle Division again in Stalingrad.

Another town pitchforked into the path of the German onslaught was Stary Oskol, 15 miles south of Maksimovka, where Soviet forces had supposedly scored a defensive victory on the first day of July. On the 2nd, the Luftwaffe was sent in to flatten Stary Oskol ahead of the ground assault. Anyone not involved in the war effort or defence of the town had been ordered to abandon Stary Oskol for nearby villages. No assistance was given. Young and old moved on foot, pushing their meagre possessions in wheelbarrows. The remaining inhabitants took to slit trenches, where they cowered all day. 'We saw the bombs flying down from the aircraft with a wild screech, the ground shook from the explosions and immediately things came down on our heads,' one recalled. 'All around there were fires, metal cracking, roofs falling down, dogs howling. It was truly frightening.' The Red Army compounded the destruction as it fell back through the town after dark on the 2nd; mills and warehouses were set ablaze. After a day of bombing, many of the remaining inhabitants resolved to flee. They spent the night packing items to take with them and burying what they could not in vegetable gardens or in barns. But when morning came and they tried to leave Stary Oskol, the Germans had already entered the town.[43]

Those who did manage to flee on foot made it no further than a few miles before being overtaken by the advancing Germans. Others abandoned their exodus in Sorokino, just six miles away, where engineers from Fortieth Army were preparing the village mill for demolition to prevent it falling into German hands. Sorokino's inhabitants pleaded to remove the sacks of flour, piled high inside. The soldiers refused and threatened to shoot villagers for disobedience. The mill was blown up. 'It went up in the air and collapsed, blazing like a torch,' one eyewitness recalled. 'The inhabitants, risking their lives, tried to take out some of the burned flour, but were shot at by the sappers...'[44]

The engineers were enacting a scorched earth policy imposed by the Soviet leader, leaving to the enemy a wasteland 20 miles deep immediately behind the front line where there was to be nothing of use to the German war effort: no cattle, no men of military age, no trains or railway lines, no bridges, no tractors or agricultural equipment. The only thing the invader should find, Stalin demanded, were anti-tank and anti-personnel mines to wreak havoc with his advance.[45]

Except for now, the enemy was advancing too rapidly for the Red Army to strip the land bare. After less than one week of the German summer offensive, Voronezh was within striking distance. Indeed the only people more eager to enter the city than the attackers were the staff of Fortieth Army, who had established their field headquarters just 20 miles west of Voronezh – but had no intention of remaining there, as rifle division commander Ivan Sevastynov discovered when he visited on 3 July. Safes and typewriters were being loaded aboard trucks while clerks burned or shredded documents, while their commander Mikhail Parsegov seemed more interested in his personal appearance, calmly shaving in his staff car, carefully trimming his moustache, while his army disintegrated. There was talk of making a stand on the Don – which meandered through the plains just five miles west of central Voronezh – but, given the state of Parsegov's army, Sevastyanov concluded, 'it was crystal clear that it would be impossible to halt on the river. We'd have to retreat to Voronezh and start fighting in the city.'[46]

Defeat on the ground was mirrored by defeat in the skies. 'Where is our aviation?' one artillery regiment commander fumed. 'The newspapers write about our aircraft. It's all bullshit. German aircraft are good – and we have coffins. Several times I've seen with my own eyes as soon as our planes go up, they are shot down instantly and burn...' During one air raid a platoon commander railed at the Luftwaffe. 'They fly knowing all too well that our planes will not appear – and even if they do, it's no good. The Germans aren't afraid of our aircraft and destroy them immediately.' Such lamentations are borne out by Luftwaffe records. In the first ten days of the German offensive, it downed 432 Soviet aircraft – and lost just 16. The tally could have been so much higher, as frustrated fighter pilot Heinrich Setz observed. 'Day after day we throw ourselves at the masses of Russian aircraft – the only sad thing about it is that I can only commit a couple of aircraft.'[47]

Whatever impetus Fortieth Army lacked, the German spearheads possessed in abundance. The tanks of 24th Panzer Division pushed through a cold, pitch-black night of 3–4 July in their relentless drive to the Don. A platoon commander spoke to his men every 15 minutes to ensure they did not fall asleep. They did not, but their voices grew increasingly weary. By daybreak on the 4th, the panzers were moving along at more than 20 miles an hour at times, overtaking the division's motorcyclists. A *Propaganda Kompanie* reporter painted a vivid – if triumphalist – picture of the Soviet collapse on the right bank of the Don.

A few tanks, which had tried to stop the disaster, stand burning beside the churned-up road. The contents of cars and motor vehicles lie in colourful shreds and curled-up tangles in the dust. Ammunition, fuel canisters, gas masks, shirts, uniforms and blankets. And lots of paper, files, pay books. Sacks full of grain and bad bread burst open under the force of the bombs, allowing the wind to play with the grains. Dead Bolsheviks, abandoned guns – wherever we look. The closer we get to the river, the denser the crowd becomes. Many of those who tried to save themselves by crossing the miserable wooden bridge met their fate here.[48]

The advance was brought to an abrupt halt. 'Suddenly, beyond one village, the Don valley opens before us,' the platoon commander noted. 'Far below we see a wide blue ribbon of the river, whose waters gleam in the rays of the rising sun.' The sight of one of Russia's great rivers was equally intoxicating to the motorised infantry of the *Grossdeutschland* Division. 'Like the Ancient Greeks once cried "Thallata, thallata" – The sea, the sea – so we cry out with joy: "The Don, the Don! And Voronezh!"' mortar man Hans Heinz Rehfeldt recalled.[49]

24th Panzer Division sent an advanced detachment of eight motorcyclists ahead to scout for a crossing over the Don. Twenty miles south of Voronezh it found a ferry carrying Soviet troops back and forth over the 400ft-wide river and seized the crossing point in a lightning raid, capturing a Red Army rear column and forcing enemy units on the far shore to scatter. Again the Soviet response was lethargic. Yakob Tetushkin, commanding the newly committed 141st Rifle Division, warned three senior staff officers: 'I am not a prophet, but if the Front does not take immediate action to push this German platoon back to the west bank of the Don, we will lose Voronezh.' The Great War veteran urged them to throw whatever forces they could muster at the small enemy bridgehead. 'Let a regiment die in the process, but we must smash it, for tomorrow the Germans will replace this platoon with tanks and an infantry division.'[50] There was no counter-attack and, as Tetushkin predicted, by 5.30am on 5 July the first German armour was on the far bank. There were just nine miles to the city centre.[51]

Having largely been spared by the war to date – one of the Red Army soldiers taking up positions on the western and southern outskirts observed that 'it felt as if the breath of war had not touched it'[52] – Voronezh was now subjected to its full fury. The Luftwaffe sent 120 Stukas against its four most important armament works: one gun, one tank and two ammunition factories. Intelligence reports suggested all were still working at full capacity. The dive-bombers circled 5,000 metres above the city 'like an angry swarm of hornets', out of reach of the formidable anti-aircraft defences. Paul-Werner Hozzel led *Stukageschwader* 2 against the raid's principal objective, the tank works.

I gave the signal to attack, and dived at our target, staring into the muzzle flashes of every barrel below us as they spat their hatred towards us. But during the dive we offered the flak a small and very fast-moving target. The roof of the factory was getting closer and closer, and we plunged towards it at a constant speed of 560km/h: 1,500 metres, 1,200 metres, 800 metres – now the signal to release came. Bombs away. Retract the brakes. All in a matter of seconds. Then full throttle, and using the terminal velocity of the dive, we flew low over the roofs and away from the flak zone. Then we pulled up again and observed the effects of our attack. We were satisfied.

The previously pristine sky above Voronezh quickly became filled with clouds from the exploding bombs. For all the ferocity of the flak, not a single Stuka was brought down, nor did a single Soviet fighter attempt to intercept the enormous formation of sluggish dive-bombers. It was, wrote Hozzel, 'a miracle'.[53]

Voronezh's factories were working because no effort had been made to evacuate more than 300,000 souls. Even with the enemy at the gates, Soviet authorities had agreed only to begin limited evacuations: the staff and property of technical schools and colleges, and 30,000 military families. The latter move alone would require 750 railway carriages – on lines bombed and strafed daily by the Luftwaffe – and Party leaders were to make sure that evacuees were amply provided with food and hot meals on their journey.[54]

By the time the orders to evacuate even these select groups were issued, there was already fighting in Voronezh's suburbs. One Soviet-era chronicler of the city wrote wistfully that 'the outskirts of Voronezh were now inhabited mainly by soldiers and those townsfolk followed the call of their hearts to join them'.[55] In fact, the city was almost defenceless. There was not a single regiment in Voronezh – and not much outside it. Militia ('few in number but relatively combat ready') defended key buildings while workers' battalions were hurriedly mobilised to protect their factories. All that stood in the way of 24th Panzer Division southwest of Voronezh were the untried Siberians of 232nd Rifle Division. Its ranks were full, but neither fully equipped nor fully trained. It was completing its preparations for battle when it was alerted by passing refugees and moved to block the Germans' onslaught. The Luftwaffe raids had turned the woods on the western outskirts of the city, where the 232rd had trained just days before, into matchsticks and ploughed the ground – now littered with fallen trees and black smoke rising from craters. The attacks also knocked out the divisional headquarters in the city centre and unnerved its shell-shocked commander Ivan Ulitin. Nevertheless – and despite the absence of the armoured support they had been promised – Ulitin's men fought desperately. The advancing panzers ran into defensive fire 'of a fury never before experienced', especially around the airfield where – in a nasty shock for the attackers – German 88mm flak, captured during the winter, bolstered the defence. Damaged panzers fell back, carrying the dead and wounded, many suffering from horrific burns. Mortar and artillery shells were directed at the neighbouring woods, exploding in the tree tops and showering German tanks with shrapnel, forcing crews to close their hatches. 'The heat is unbearable, sweat is pouring down,' Gert-Axel Weidemann wrote. 'We long for the cool of night and the chance of opening our hatches.' The fighting raged to and fro. Attackers traded battle cries – 'Hurrah!' and 'Urra!' Before dusk set in Weidemann and his comrades watched in amazement as cadets from Voronezh's officer school launched the final attack of the day. 'Walking arm-in-arm, singing the *Internationale*, they storm towards our panzers before they are mown down by the panzers' guns,' the junior officer recorded. It reminded him of the sacrifice German students made at Langemarck, near Ypres, in the opening weeks of the Great War. Communists, Weidemann realised, were just as willing to sacrifice themselves for their Motherland.[56] Late in the day, Soviet tanks finally entered the fray, only to run into 'a hurricane of fire from enemy anti-tank weapons'. The Siberians fell back, having halted their foe a couple of miles outside the city limits. They had prevented Voronezh's rapid fall, largely sacrificing themselves in the process.[57]

Soviet accounts almost always ignore the big picture and celebrate the deeds of individuals or specific units, spurred on to heroics by inspirational Communist Party members and political leaders, always inflicting heavier losses on their foe than they suffered. Six times the 212nd Rifle Division, for example, drove back 'insane' attacks by 'drunken Hitlerites', leaving the battlefield strewn with 1,000 German corpses 'piled up in mountains' for the loss of just 13 Red Army men. Enraged by the loss of their beloved commander, 14th Tank Brigade fought 'with even greater ferocity and energy', encouraged by a wounded commissar who reputedly told his men: 'I will not leave my post until I am unconscious' and supposedly saved the entire brigade by finding a petrol tanker with his vehicles almost out of fuel. And 110th Tank Brigade 'deserves the title of guards brigade,' one officer suggested, for its 'high patriotism, courage and steadfastness' for killing 600 Germans and knocking out four dozen tanks and nearly 40 guns in two days of battle.[58] The figures were pure fantasy. Even on the heaviest day of fighting for Voronezh, 24th Panzer Division lost only 70 men.

With the onset of darkness on 5 July, the panzers formed their nightly 'hedgehog', corralled in a broad semi-circle. 'The warmth of the day radiating from the earth mixes with the coolness of the night,' Weidemann wrote. 'The smell of the steppe begins to replace the smell of gunsmoke and heat of the battlefield, exhaust fumes and fire which still lingered in our noses. Above us Luftwaffe bomber formations are attacking; from the direction of Voronezh streaks of colourful tracer from Russian flak fizz into the night sky.' Mechanics carried out urgent repairs, while officers – some with their microphones still around their necks – discussed the day of battle over a cigarette or pipe, and a glass of wine or brandy 'liberated' when the division was re-forming in France.[59]

Shortly before daybreak on the 6th, *Nebelwerfer* batteries hurled their rockets into Soviet positions on the southwestern edge of Voronezh. The foremost units of 24th Panzer Division had pulled back a safe distance – but the shock waves from the projectiles' impacts could still be felt behind the panzers' armour. Having stunned the defenders, the Germans moved out at daybreak and encountered no resistance. Nevertheless, the panzers edged cautiously into the city, fearing barricades and hidden anti-tank guns and tanks. Entire blocks burned furiously, set ablaze either by the *Nebelwerfer* barrage or Luftwaffe raids.[60] Schools and administrative buildings were reduced to shells. There were still pockets of ferocious resistance. In the centre, 'fanatical and well-armed' NKVD troops were refusing to surrender a handful of civic buildings, while in the western suburbs, the battered 232nd Rifle Division and the remnants of a tank brigade continued to frustrate the attackers before they fell back through the centre of Voronezh. 'Clinging to houses, hiding in the bushes, running across open ground, we left street after street behind us,' rifleman Evgeny Golovin recalled. 'And somewhere, very near, the Germans were walking, marching in formation, loudly calling to each other, walking with the air of victors…'[61] The withdrawing troops left the west of the city in ruins, but as one Soviet account proudly declared: 'All approaches to the meat-packing plant were littered with the corpses of enemy soldiers, there were wrecked guns lying around, and burnt-out tanks were on fire.'[62] The city's principal hospital witnessed some of the fiercest fighting where each storey, each ward, each room became a battlefield over six bloody hours. Still occupied by hundreds of patients, the defenders evicted them from their beds, which were then pushed up against windows as makeshift barricades. And when the Germans entered the building, the defenders often lay in the remaining beds, pretending to be sick, hiding their pistols and rifles, attacking their foe from behind at an opportune moment.[63] Before mid-day on 7 July, the Germans controlled the left bank of the river, which gave Voronezh – now 'one big sea of flames' – its name. Panzers were sent to block any Red Army units fleeing over the last crossing of the Voronezh in the north of the city. Navigating by the sun on the occasions it could be seen through the swathes of smoke drifting over the city, they reached the last intact river crossing and immediately engaged the Russian detachment on the far bank. With the first shells impacting, the Russians blew up the bridge. 'We're around 150 metres away and watch as the pillars of the wooden bridge spin through the air like matches,' Gert-Axel Weidemann wrote.[64]

War correspondent Gustav Staebe accompanied the second wave of German soldiers into the city. Voronezh straddles the river which gives it its name. The west bank – by far the larger and more heavily populated part of Voronezh – had suffered terribly. Staebe passed numerous abandoned and burned-out tanks, their gun barrels fixed in the direction which they had fired their last shots. He then drove through gaps smashed in the anti-tank barriers and barricades thrown across city streets and past trams stopped where their drivers had fled from them. Now the summer wind blew through their shattered windows, while electric wires and telephone lines hung limply in twisted balls from poles lining the streets. Any multi-storey building, with the exception of the occasional office block, colleges and hospitals, had been almost completely burned out and reduced to ruins. Individual houses – often made of wood – had been razed, while most factories were largely wrecked, sabotaged by the retreating Red Army. The remaining inhabitants – relatively few in number, it seemed – appeared to welcome the occupier, or at least not oppose him. Yet Gustav Staebe's overriding impression of Voronezh was its stench. The fighting had been brief, the German occupation swift, but in the summer heat the countless cadavers of horses quickly decomposed. A plague of flies descended on the rotting carcasses and on the bodies of Soviet soldiers, militia and civilians, while overhead crows circled, occasionally diving to dine on this harvest of death.[65]

Outside Voronezh, junior officer Bernhard Rademacher watched the native population bury 300 Red Army dead left in the open for more than a week.

> There was a dreadful smell and thousands of flies surrounding the corpses which are already half-putrefied... Mass graves were dug for them. The women held cloth over their mouths and noses but still threw up. How dreadful it would be if our women and girls had to do this. Thousands, *ja*, millions of Russian soldiers have been buried like this somewhere in the vast Russian earth without anyone at home learning when, where and how they died. The Russian people accept this as inevitable destiny, however. 'Kaputt', they say with a gesture and life and nature go on. What is such a small, shrivelled-up corpse in the middle of the infinite vastness of the flowery steppe? It is soon forgotten, disappears, overgrown by the natural fertility of the land and the people. What is man? Whether he's a poor nameless Russian or a German soldier with a life of his own and creative powers, corpses all look the same after eight days.[66]

By early evening on 7 July, Second Army regarded the battle for Voronezh over 'with the exception of a few small pockets of resistance'. The city's capture brought the curtain down on the first phase of *Blau* and prompted a celebratory communiqué informing the public of another victory for German arms: over 1,000 tanks and upwards of 1,700 guns destroyed, plus nearly 90,000 prisoners taken. 'The number of prisoners of war and amount of booty is growing by the hour,' it assured people.[67]

The Soviet leadership laid the blame for the loss of Voronezh squarely at the door of Fortieth Army which, one official report stated, was plagued by 'exceptional promiscuity and criminal indiscipline'. Soldiers of all ranks, of all branches, had simply melted away, wandering around the woods and villages behind the front. Commissars and political officers had failed to rally the troops, had failed to instil in them 'faith in Soviet arms and in Soviet victory', had failed to champion 'examples of bravery and selfless devotion to the Motherland' or arouse 'burning hatred of the enemy'. The rot set in at the top. Mikhail Parsegov and his staff fled the battlefield precipitously, even leaving behind four safes containing confidential documents. 'The perpetrators of this shameful crime shall be held strictly accountable,' the report stated. They were not. But Parsegov never again led troops in battle against the Germans. Dismissed on 3 July, he spent the remainder of the war commanding artillery in the Far East.[68]

Yet more astute observers realised the problems went deeper than one supposedly rotten army. On his way to the front with his 141st Rifle Division, Yakov Tetushkin had witnessed scenes reminiscent of the previous summer: groups of stragglers, often without shoes, almost certainly without weapons, but still carrying their kit bags and canteens. Aged nearly 50, Tetushkin was perhaps ten years older than most divisional commanders. He sensed a deep-rooted malaise in the Red Army – and passed on his observations to one of Stalin's lapdogs, Communist Party chairman Georgy Malenkov. Staffs and rear services were bloated. Tetushkin reckoned no more than one in five men fought in the front line. The rest – cooks, clerks, vets, mechanics, medics, headquarters – 'supported' at a safe distance. 'Literally tens of thousands of men on the front line can go to bed during the battle, sleep for a week and no-one will miss them, because no-one needs them for the battle.' A veteran of the Great War, Tetushkin remembered regiments with a headquarters of just a commander and his adjutant, perhaps three or four men directing the actions of a division. Now a regimental headquarters numbered dozens of personnel, 'hundreds' at a division and directing an army or front 'clouds of people'. As for the rank-and-file soldiers, tank crews, aviators and artillerymen were 'not bad… The same cannot be said of the infantry.' The infantry were poorly trained and ill-disciplined. Their officers, from commanders down to those in the line, lacked backbone and above all lacked respect. Discipline and respect, however, did not mean terror and fear. Tetushkin had spent the winter outside Moscow, serving under Mikhail Yefremov's Thirty-Third Army, whose leadership style consisted of telephone tirades: 'You bastard, you bastard... motherfucker... why can't your regiment take the village, I'll come and shoot you all today.' He didn't – though he did punch some of his commanders in the face. Were the troops any more successful as a result? Tetushkin asked rhetorically. 'Quite the contrary.'[69]

Konstantin Rokossovsky, who had taken charge of Bryansk Front in the wake of Voronezh's loss, had come to similar conclusions after less than a week in command. Fear of panzers and Stukas was endemic – all too often the Red Army infantryman did not fight back, even if he possessed the means to do so. Nor was he much better when facing the German soldier. Rarely did he fight to the weapon of last resort – fixing his bayonet. And when it came to retreating, there was no organisation or co-ordination, merely chaos, which usually left men and matériel at the mercy of the Germans. Put bluntly, Konstantin Rokossovsky conceded there had been 'major shortcomings' in the way the Red Army had been both led and fought.[70]

Worse was to come before the Soviet Union's leadership acted.

At a hot and humid Wolf's Lair in East Prussia, staff officer Adolf Heusinger noticed that there was widespread satisfaction. 'The old élan has returned and we can once again happily look at the situation map,' he recorded. He even thought that the Russians had 'perhaps taken on too much during the winter' and were 'now reaching the end of their strength'. Yet all was not well in the High Command. Franz Halder, the Chief of the General Staff, could not decide whether the Red Army was deliberately avoiding battle or had been decisively crushed by the summer offensive. Certainly, destroying Soviet forces was far more important to Adolf Hitler than capturing Voronezh, a battle he never wanted. He had issued strict instructions *not* to occupy the city – the prize of pursuing and crushing the fleeing enemy over the Don was far more important. He had clashed repeatedly with Army Group South's commander Fedor von Bock – arguments in the daily conferences were followed by 'highly-disagreeable' telephone conversations with the 61-year-old marshal, whom the Führer thought too slow and too easily swayed by his subordinate commanders. For his part, Bock was exasperated by the almost daily interference in his operations – even down to the actions of individual divisions – and the constant 'whining' from Hitler's headquarters.

Hitler had 'made fun of the English for sacking every general when something went wrong' when he visited Bock's headquarters in Ukraine on 3 July. Just ten days later he dismissed the marshal, ostensibly for the sluggish handling of two divisions in Voronezh. To some, like Adolf Heusinger, Bock was *längst überständig* – well past his sell-by date – ill and vain and his dismissal long overdue. Others were appalled, such as Helmuth Groscurth, operations officer of 295th Infantry Division advancing towards the Don. 'The treatment meted out to commanding officers – and us – is so shameless that I can't describe it.'[71]

Perhaps less important than the fate of Fedor von Bock was the fate of his army group. Even before he sacked the field marshal, Hitler had decided to split his force. Bock – and subsequently Maximilian von Weichs – was left with the secondary mission of capturing Stalingrad with an eviscerated Army Group B, while all the armour was diverted to the new Army Group A under Wilhelm List for the main prize: the drive into the Caucasus, over the mountains to the Black Sea and as far as Baku and the western shore of the Caspian Sea. Worse, Hitler tore up the original plan for the summer campaign. The initial goals, he decided, had 'largely been achieved'. Franz Halder was appalled. 'The constant tendency to underestimate the enemy's capability is gradually assuming grotesque proportions and is becoming dangerous,' he noted with alarm.[72]

Then again, maybe Adolf Hitler was right. With German forces sweeping down the Don, the Red Army's Southern Front – which had hitherto firmly held its heavily fortified line, anchored on the northern shore of the Gulf of Taganrog – began to fall back, without waiting for the enemy to attack it. When Army Group A opened its offensive, all too often it struck at thin air. The haul of prisoners when it linked up with Weichs' group and closed a pocket around the town of Millerovo was a disappointing 40,000. 'We have not succeeded in forming a large pocket,' the commander of a platoon of motorcycle infantry wrote in frustration. 'In a masterful manner, the enemy has extricated himself from the sack.' The eastern industrial powerhouse of Voroshilovgrad – today Luhansk – fell with barely a shot being fired, while the advance to Rostov did not seem to be an offensive, or even a pursuit, but a lunge into a void. 'Yesterday we drove 160 kilometres through territory free of the enemy,' radio operator Peter Dimt wrote. 'The only obstacles are the roads themselves.' Bone dry, they shook vehicles to bits; when it rained they became an impassable sludge into which trucks vanished up to their axles. Occasionally the advancing troops passed through 'a small collection of miserable huts'; otherwise the land was devoid of human presence, though men had passed this way. Littering the roadside everywhere were the rotting carcasses of horses, which had collapsed in the heat – either accompanying the fleeing Russians or advancing Germans. Though the cadavers were hideously distorted by gasses, everyone nevertheless filed past. No soldier could spare the time to bury them.[73]

Only on the southern extremity of the Eastern Front, along the River Mius which emptied into the Gulf of Taganrog, did the Soviet line still hold firm. But those manning it were growing increasingly uneasy. By day, the men of 30th Rifle Division worked to reinforce their defensive positions. By night, they watched the sky to the southeast light up as Rostov was bombed. 'Deep alarm filled our consciousness, our hearts,' wrote commissar Lev Dyachkov. 'It was as if this alarm of expectation of something inevitable, approaching us like a stalking avalanche, spread through the air, although at least we in our regiment could not yet imagine the true extent of the disaster.' Yet even he was 'thunderstruck' when he was summoned to the divisional headquarters on 19 July and informed the Mius front was being abandoned to prevent encirclement. The men withdrew towards Rostov reluctantly. 'The hardest part was passing through villages and hamlets,' Dyachkov remembered. The inhabitants of the villages the 30th Rifles marched through – mostly teenagers, women and the elderly – stood in front of their homes 'silently looking at us with long, wistful looks, full of unspoken bitterness'. The men quickened their pace to lessen the torment. 'No jokes, no laughter, no talking,' the commissar wrote. 'A heavy feeling of shame was pressing on their hearts.'[74]

Rostov-on-Don – 'the gateway to the Caucasus' – extends along the right bank of the Don for ten miles just upstream of the estuary. A major port and industrial centre, its defences were formidable: the terrain outside the city had been turned into a killing field 25 miles deep unlike anything the Germans had encountered before – 'one huge line of resistance,' recalled Johannes Mühlenkamp, commanding a panzer unit in the SS *Wiking* Division. 'After one obstacle, more ditches and obstacles.' Lev Dyachkov's division was pitchforked into one of these positions northwest of the city on 21 July as the first German armour approached. It held off six waves of attacks by panzers until last light, leaving a dozen disabled or wrecked enemy vehicles behind. Despite the success, the 30th Rifles were ordered to abandon the field of battle. In the darkness the men packed their wounded on carts, hastily buried the fallen without ceremony, and headed into the night in the direction of Rostov.[75]

The next morning the German onslaught resumed, preceded by a Luftwaffe concert. Panzer gunner Willi Kubik was in awe of the Stukas which repeatedly threw themselves at the Soviet defences, each aircraft making seven or eight attacks, dropping one bomb at a time. 'An impressive sight – mushroom clouds rise everywhere,' he noted. 'Half a dozen mounds are simply levelled. The effect of the bombs is incredible.' The defences were too numerous and too well camouflaged for the Luftwaffe to eliminate them all. Automated flamethrowers built into the terrain spewed jets of fire, burning the earth and anyone who dared to cross it. Mühlenkamp watched his panzers lose their tracks in the entanglements. It prompted Russian soldiers to emerge from the anti-tank ditch and attack the stranded armour with mines, or else send German shepherds carrying explosives to blow themselves up – knocking out the panzers in the process. The animals were either shot dead by the panzer crews – or by their own handlers when, terrified by the noise of battle, many dogs turned around and fled towards their own lines. 'My heart bleeds at the sight of these fine animals,' wrote Wilhelm Tieke, a teenage messenger in the *Wiking*. 'The lips hang from mouths flashing their teeth and their eyes are dull. Their virtues: devotion and faithfulness, obedience and docility are ruthlessly exploited by man. The dogs are now dead without fulfilling their fiendish orders.'

Lev Dyachkov and his battalion had spent the night in a gully about ten miles outside Rostov. Exhausted, the men slept where they sat down to rest. They were roused by the sudden noise of battle on the adjacent road. Still half-asleep, the men automatically grabbed their rifles without understanding why. An officer ran through the gorge, shouting at troops to get ready for action. Dyachkov looked down the road and saw 30 or 40 panzers approaching, their tracks glistening in the rays of the morning sun. The battalion took up positions on both sides of the highway, but the young commissar knew his comrades could not halt the approaching enemy armour. 'What can we do to these hulks of steel?' he asked himself. 'Yesterday we were occupying trenches behind the anti-tank ditch, but here…! There's flat open steppe all around here…' And so it proved. When the panzers were no more than 300 metres away, they opened fire – and the order to retreat immediately spread through the battalion. The soldiers sought salvation in the gully. They ran into it headlong, followed, or preceded, by horses pulling carts, field kitchens, ammunition wagons. Most became bogged down in the mud which flanked a stream flowing gently along the gully bed. The sole bridge over it gave way under the weight of men and matériel trying to cross it, throwing all into the sludge. As Dyachkov struggled free of the gorge and entered a field of ripe wheat, panzers appeared at the edge of the gully and opened fire. 'Panic, very real panic, seized us,' he recalled. 'Everyone simply ran, fleeing from the machine-guns and cannon of the panzers. In a few minutes, the regiment ceased to exist. It turned into a disorderly bunch of men, fleeing to save their lives.'

A couple of hours later, the commissar rallied a group of 60 men from various units and was directed by an artillery commander to make a stand near the village of Krasny Krym, just half a dozen miles from the outskirts of Rostov. The group of 60 was soon reduced to just 38 as men without rifles simply continued down the road towards the city. Amazingly, the rag-tag group of soldiers thwarted the first wave of panzers which attacked a short time later. 'Urra, you bastards, take it!' one man yelled triumphantly, while another climbed on to the parapet of the trench waving his rifle.

Their joy was short-lived. Within half an hour, Stukas appeared over the village and hammered Soviet positions mercilessly, first with bombs, then with cannon. When the attack was over, the defences of Krasny Krym were shattered. Lev Dyachkov surveyed the scene: 'Bombed, overturned cannons, the remnants of two burning vehicles, which had not managed to leave before the air raid, trenches now straddled by huge, still-smoking craters, bodies of dead soldiers and small groups of survivors, men panicking, scattered about.' When the panzers resumed their attack, the defenders of Krasny Krym fled in panic. Dyachkov joined a group of dispersed soldiers and mingled with 'the stream of people, carts, artillery harnesses, and cars moving towards the Don'.

The panzers were not far behind. By dusk, German armour had reached a range of small hills from where crews could observe the suburbs of Rostov. The panzer crews refuelled and re-armed their vehicles as they watched the city burn, filling the sky with thick black smoke. Wearily following them were the infantry of the 'Weasel' Division, 125th Infantry, who had covered 42 kilometres since moving out of their assault positions at 4am. 'In terms of physical exertion,' battalion commander Karl Göbel branded 22 July 'the hardest day of the entire Eastern campaign'. His men had advanced 'through grass as tall as a man, through cornfields, over hills and through swampy streams. Exhausted, brave men collapsed and stretched their weary limbs. The effort had been worth it. The outer cordon around Rostov had been broken. The way into the city was clear.' Though the ranks of the 'Weasel' Division – a nickname it took from its emblem – were exhausted, Göbel observed, 'the mood was fantastic. Everyone wanted to be in Rostov.'[76]

One hundred miles upstream of Rostov, near the village of Nikolayevskaya, the panzers were already rolling across the Don. Pioneers in assault boats ferried the vanguard of 23rd Panzer Division across the 150-metre-wide river and the panzer grenadiers spilled on to the far bank before spreading out across the extensive flood plain with its labyrinth of dead arms of the Don, ponds and pools. While they expanded their foothold on the left bank, engineers were throwing a bridge across the Don. Before the sun set on 22 July, the first vehicles of four motorised divisions were rolling over the temporary crossing.[77]

The final obstacle facing the Germans before Rostov was the third and last anti-tank ditch. When pioneers reached it they used explosive charges to collapse the walls, then grabbed shovels and flattened the embankments to allow the armour to pass. The SS *Wiking* rolled into Rostov's western suburbs, while 13th Panzer Division entered the eastern outskirts early on the afternoon of 23 July. The latter sent a small detachment of motorcyclists ahead, supported by a few half-tracks and armoured cars under a junior officer, Eick, to seize the Don crossings. The direct route to the river was blocked by fires raging in factories and warehouses near the central station. Instead, the Germans followed the fresh tracks left by retreating Soviet tanks towards the waterfront – only to find Rostov's iconic railway bridge, with its movable central span to allow Don shipping to pass, wrecked. The search for a crossing went on until the reconnaissance party came across a makeshift ferry: semi-naked Russian soldiers stood in the Don, pulling a truck to the south bank using ropes. Eick decided to attack. The truck mid-river was destroyed, the Russians hauling it either died under a hail of German fire – or took shelter – and the ferry was abandoned. But then the Germans suddenly found themselves cut off as Soviet troops emerged from houses and factories leading down to the river. After a 50-minute firefight, the scouting party reluctantly fell back and left the crossing to the Russians. The Don would be forced elsewhere.[78]

Red Army war correspondent Vitaly Zakrutkin observed the desperate efforts made by his countrymen to reach the left bank of the Don. 'Under constant bombardment and heavy artillery fire people dismantled wooden houses, barns, fences and carried timbers to the shore,' he wrote. There, pioneers – covered in blood and dust – built rafts strong enough to ferry guns to the distant bank, or patched up the punctured hulls of fishing vessels. Horses were driven across the river – their masters forced them to swim. They dodged all manner of detritus carried towards the Gulf of Taganrog by the Don: logs from destroyed pontoon bridges or rafts, the bodies of wrecked cars, bloated corpses.[79]

Lev Dyachkov's column of misery – retreating soldiers mixed with refugees – followed one of the main thoroughfares leading to the river, but got no further than three blocks before the Luftwaffe attacked and blocked progress. Making a detour, the commissar eventually reached the Don, glistening in the summer sun.

> Before our eyes is a picture of devastation, destruction. Fires caused by bombs, glass crunches beneath our feet, piles of broken bricks, vertical remains of sooty walls belonging to burned-out warehouses and stores. To our right, half a kilometre away, is a pontoon bridge. Troops are streaming towards it in a dense column. Six Junkers approach on a bombing raid. A lone anti-aircraft battery fires at them from the left bank.
>
> Breaking through the anti-aircraft fire, the Junkers start diving at the pontoon bridge. Exploding bombs thunder, huge columns of water fly up on both sides of

the bridge. And in spite of the bombing the flow of people, carts and cars on the bridge does not stop.

A couple of engineer officers bumped into Dyachkov's group, led it to a ferry they had set up and carried everyone across to the town of Bataisk, where the young commissar was eventually reunited with the political department – or what remained of it – of Fifty-Sixth Army.[80]

The panzers were still tentatively advancing through Rostov's residential districts. They found each block had been turned into a fortress as dogged Soviet troops hurled Molotov cocktails from windows, skylights and balconies while bunkers and barricades blocked the narrow streets. 'Occasionally, a civilian emerges from a hole in the ground,' panzer commander Ewald Klapdor wrote. 'The hell they've gone through over the past few days is written all over their faces.' Cameraman Hans Ertl watched an infantry gun fire into the side of an apartment block at point-blank range. 'Out of a cloud of dust and the remnants of a wall, a balcony falls down and the bodies of two Russian machine gunners tumble out, landing with a thud three storeys below on the rubble-strewn pavement,' he wrote. 'I filmed several such hideous scenes, but gradually, you lose your disgust, you're unavoidably numbed.' As Ertl focused on a neighbouring balcony awaiting its collapse, a burst of machine-gun fire rippled through the doorframe above him. He dragged his camera and tripod to safety and faked death by lying motionless on rubble before abandoning the building to re-join his crew. 'A shiver went through me afterwards at the thought that the Russians could have just as easily shot lower. Life and the future often hang on a silk thread!'[81]

There are several accounts of fighting raging in the numerous wine cellars of Rostov, with Germans and Russians trading blows and bullets, wading in alcohol. In one basement, the rising tide of wine lifted the corpses of two Soviet soldiers off the ground. The Germans ignored them, filling their canteens with red wine and a gold-sparkling, sweet muscatel. The soldiers joked and laughed, pushing the bodies around the sea of wine until someone decided to haul them on to a lawn across the street, where thousands of flies immediately descended on the dead.[82]

Unable to bivouac safely for the night in the city centre – sniper, anti-tank rifle and heavy machine-gun fire was directed at the armoured spearhead from three sides – the panzers withdrew to Rostov's northern suburbs, where they would remain until the infantry had cleared the streets. The tanks were corralled and, despite the danger of being attacked by Red Army stragglers, the crew posted guard fell asleep after the exertions of the preceding days.[83]

It was even more dangerous in the city centre. Although the fighting died down, Soviet troops used the cover of darkness to move back into buildings they had abandoned during the day, slitting the throats of Germans who'd dared to find billets in them.[84]

The battle for Rostov raged throughout the 26th before fading out the following day, though fires burned into August. Not one house or building had escaped some form of damage. Multi-storey Soviet-era buildings had been reduced to rubble and ash, twisted and broken metal supports protruding from the ruins. Road surfaces had been ripped up by bombs from Stukas aimed at the numerous bunkers. Tram lines were thrown up in the air, while telephone and trolleybus wires hung limply from poles – if they were still standing at all. Karol Virsík, a doctor with the Slovak Rapid Division which followed German troops into the city, was horrified by the number of dead – soldiers and horses – littering the streets, accompanied by 'a pervasive, putrid stench everywhere'. 'If someone doesn't bury them quickly,' he noted, 'packs of starving dogs will soon be on them.' Non-commissioned officer Hans Keller was shocked by the destruction. 'No house is intact,' he wrote as he moved through still-smouldering streets. 'Horror lives inside the empty windows and the clouds look in from above. Bare, crumbling walls, thick T-beams bent like sewing needles.' A handful of Rostov's inhabitants scurried around with pails, carrying water from the still-working wells. Keller drove past shot-up enemy tanks, the carcasses of horses left in the street, and the corpses of German soldiers – still awaiting burial – covered in tarpaulin, weighed down by bricks. 'The destruction, the death is terrible,' Keller noted. There was nothing but a continuous pile of rubble from the outskirts of Rostov down to the Don, where war correspondent Walter Nowak found a 'mini Dunkirk' at the approaches to the railway bridge: tractors, heavy guns – some fresh from the factory – and other military vehicles had been reduced to a confusing tangle of metal by German bombs. As for the river itself, it presented 'a perfect picture of destruction,' junior infantry officer Wilhelm Eichner remembered. 'Wrecked iron girders and bridge parts stick out of the water as if they're begging for help.'[85]

There were perhaps as many as 300,000 people still in Rostov – many of them 'intimidated' after eight months of brutal Soviet rule, during which security forces had exacted revenge against anyone suspected of collaborating with the enemy during Germany's brief occupation in late 1941. The city's Armenian and ethnic German population had been deported, and at least 800 people were executed for siding with the Nazis. As spring came, the civilian populace was pressed into service helping to dig some of the extensive trenches and fortifications on the approaches to the city. Finally, as the Germans neared the city again, inhabitants were forced to cower in their cellars and basements for 11 days until tentatively emerging. Slovak troops found themselves warmly welcomed by Rostov's remaining civilian populace. 'It was a strange occupation,' Lieutenant Jan Čelar remembered. 'In some places they were killing and in others Slovak soldiers were dancing with the local women.' The Germans, too, reported that the people of Rostov were 'very willing'. They would quickly prove to be as ruthless as the Soviet authorities. Within a week, at least 400 Communist Party officials and 'partisans' had been executed, many shot in a large city park. Although most had been denounced by fellow citizens, the mere failure to produce identity papers frequently resulted in a death sentence for some. Due to racial and language similarities, Slovak soldiers felt, if not a bond with Soviet civilians, then perhaps an affinity for them. They turned a blind eye to transgressions, shared wine with the local populace, released prisoners – some as young as eight – from the city's jail, and handed out food to youngsters. Yet there were Slovaks – those in rear units especially – who 'threw themselves into plundering', forcing their way into homes, looking for Red Army troops in hiding or concealed weapons, but emerging with record players, musical instruments, clothing. A few even stooped to stealing watches from the corpses of their fallen comrades. There was vast legitimate booty to be had in Rostov too, abandoned by the fleeing Red Army and Soviet authorities: food, wine, harmonicas, medical instruments, horses, carts, trucks, almost every infantry gun imaginable. Never before had Slovak soldiers enjoyed such spoils of war.

The front-line troops had moved into the Caucasus by the time the Nazi authorities turned their attention to the 2,000 Jews estimated to be still in Rostov. On 4 August posters appeared city-wide calling for Jews of all ages to report at assembly points one week later for resettlement. Those who dutifully followed the instructions were herded into trucks and transported to a ravine north of Rostov known as the Snake's Gorge. After undressing in a house and surrendering any valuables, they were led to the gully and shot, their corpses tumbling into mass graves freshly dug in the sandy soil. The bodies were joined by at least 300 people gassed in trucks whose exhaust fumes were directed into the rear cabin; their disfigured corpses were unceremoniously tossed into the pits. It went on like this for three days, ending only when the *Sonderkommando* or execution detail was forced to re-join the troops now pushing into the Caucasus to 'pacify' towns and villages occupied in their wake.[86]

The terrain on the left bank of the Don opposite Rostov – marshland, lakes, streams, and dead arms of the river – hardly supported a large-scale breakout. Worse, it was spanned by a solitary embankment carrying a railway line and road.

It could – and should – have been a major obstacle to the German advance, especially as the main rail bridge spanning one of the arms of the Don was prepared for demolition and heavily defended. All the same it was stormed by an elite German unit, Brandenburgers – troops who could speak Russian and were equipped with Red Army uniforms and kit. They surprised the Russians holding the bridge, then held out for more than 12 hours in the face of repeated counter-attacks. Red Army men waded through the swamp and got to within 200 metres of the precarious bridgehead when Stukas brought their assault to a halt, the bombs landing so close to the Brandenburgers that they were showered with earth and stones. When they were eventually relieved, the Brandenburgers buried their dead under the pillars of the bridge as panzer after panzer rolled southwards overhead.[87]

Among the armour heading south was Ewald Klapdor's regiment. After three days' rest on the outskirts of Rostov, the *Wiking* Division was let off the leash. Having crossed the Don on a pontoon bridge, Klapdor's panzers mingled with motorised supply columns and horse-drawn carts of the infantry divisions, while motorcycle messengers weaved in and out of the heavy traffic in both directions. Groups of sullen Russian prisoners marched south, occasionally watched by the local populace. Beyond the ruins of Bataisk, the terrain opened up. Klapdor wrote:

> We are absorbed by the vast plain, which extends to the south and east seemingly without end. Its growing expanse makes our columns, which hitherto seemed dense and mighty, become ever smaller…
>
> We overtake infantry units on the march which had attacked south via Bataisk. Elements of a bicycle unit watch us roll past with a little envy. The advanced divisional command post, established around three large haystacks, is now also behind us. From now on, there is only the enemy in front of us.[88]

The gateway to the Caucasus was open.

Perhaps Rostov was the trigger. Perhaps it was the succession of defeats from Kerch to Kharkov, Sevastopol to Voronezh, but after a month of battle which had cost the Red Army well in excess of half a million casualties and brought nothing but failure, Joseph Stalin was furious – furious not only with his commanders, but with the ordinary Red Army soldier. The Soviet leader sought to stop the rot. Recalling a draconian order issued the previous summer which forbade officers and politruks from surrendering by threatening to arrest their families, Stalin determined the time was ripe for extending it to cover the entire Red Army. The resulting Order No.227 – drawn up by the recently appointed Chief of the

General Staff Aleksandr Vasilevsky but heavily modified by the *vozhd* himself – chastised the Red Army as never before. Stalin spoke of soldiers abandoning a string of towns and cities, 'soiling their banners with shame' in the process. 'The people of our land, who love and respect the Red Army, are becoming disillusioned with it,' he warned. 'They are losing faith in the Red Army. Many curse the Red Army for fleeing to the East, surrendering our people under the yoke of the German oppressors.' He lashed out at those who sought refuge behind the Don, or the Volga, or even the Urals. The tirade continued:

> Every officer, every soldier, every political officer must understand that our resources are not limitless. The territory of the Soviet state is not some desert, it is people – workers, peasants, intellectuals, our fathers, mothers, wives, brothers, children…
>
> To continue to retreat means to ruin ourselves and to ruin our homeland. Every strip of territory we abandon will strengthen the enemy and weaken our defences, our homeland.
>
> Not one step backwards! That should be our rallying cry now.

And so it became. On the penultimate day of July, the Communist Party organ *Pravda* screamed: 'Soldiers of the Red Army, it is your sacred duty to the Motherland to halt the enemy's advance with all you have got! Not one step back!' That same day the Red Army's daily newspaper *Krasnaya Zvezda – Red Star* – published a paraphrased version of the order under the headline '*Stoyko zashchishchat rodnuyu zemlyu!*' – Defend the Motherland stubbornly! Stalin had approved the draft of the article, prepared by the newspaper's editor David Ortenberg, with one exception. He underlined two sentences in red pencil – which told Ortenberg to print them in bold: 'Not one step backwards! We must defend every position, every metre of Soviet soil, cling to every last sod of Soviet earth to the last drop of blood, to the very end.' Ortenberg got the message – as did any soldier who read his front-page article:

> Not one step back – this is the homeland's appeal to every soldier, to every regiment and division. The Germans must advance no further! We must stop and then repel and defeat the enemy, no matter what it costs us…
>
> Not one step back! This is the iron law of discipline for every commander, political officer, Red Army soldier…
>
> Not one step back! This is the order of the Motherland, this is the demand of the People's Commissar of Defence, our leader and commander, Comrade Stalin. To accomplish this task means to defend our land, to exterminate the hated enemy, to ensure our victory.

But Order No.227 was more than mere rhetoric. The second half of the document outlined the draconian measures being introduced to make the Red Army stand fast. Henceforth, any officer or commissar who abandoned their positions without orders would be dismissed. So-called 'blocking detachments' were formed behind 'untrustworthy units' with orders to shoot any panic-mongers and cowards who fled the front on the spot – a tactic employed since the Winter War with Finland. And, borrowing from his foe, Stalin ordered the formation of penal companies of 150 to 200 men apiece – rank-and-file soldiers and junior officers who'd displayed cowardice in battle. They would 'atone for their crimes against the Motherland with their blood' by carrying out the most dangerous missions on the battlefield.[89]

For many Red Army men – at the time and in post-war memoirs – Stalin's order was both 'fair and timely' (some even thought it had come one month too late). The staff of Stalingrad Front reported that the 'overwhelming majority' of soldiers approved of the order. 'This should silence those unstable people who do not yet understand our just cause and flee the battlefield in panic to save their skin, bringing disgrace on their comrades and the entire Red Army,' a soldier in Fifty-Seventh Army declared. To rifle division commander Pyotr Lashchenko, the order underlined the gravity of the Soviet Union's plight: 'there is nowhere to retreat, not one step back, otherwise we will destroy ourselves and the Motherland. This, I would say, was the thrust of the order, and it was taken by heart and mind.' An officer undergoing training was struck by the honesty of the order. 'It spoke about failures... nothing like it could be found in the vague reports of Sovinformburo, or in most newspaper correspondence, the meaning of which was reduced to the fact that everything was running to plan, the victory would be ours.' The Soviet Union stood at a crossroads. 'A lot of people understood or felt that we had to get out of the terrible hole in which we found ourselves at any cost, otherwise we would perish, everything would collapse.' One Jewish soldier was inspired by his leader's words: 'Every day we beat the Fascists under the slogan "Not one step back," and we will fulfil this slogan with honour,' he told his family. The commander of a machine-gun detachment promised to 'call cowards and panic-mongers to order. If the motherland goes under, so shall we. If we die in battle, the enemy will suffer heavy losses as a result of our resistance. Only through stubborn resistance can we defend the motherland, and the motherland will remain ours...' Lev Dyachkov had endured 'days of terrible suffering, days of recognition of our powerlessness, of burning shame and grief'. Not once during his bitter retreat from the Mius to Bataisk had the commissar seen either a Russian tank or aircraft. 'How could it be? How could all this have happened?' he asked – then answered. The fault lay entirely with the Red Army's leadership.

There were also dissenters – as agents of the Soviet interior ministry, the NKVD, reported. Their tentacles extended into every unit of the Red Army, every company, every platoon. Negative observations, or remarks critical of the regime, were noted, reported and invariably led to arrests and punishment. Some men regarded the Germans as invincible. 'No matter how much equipment and manpower we send to the front, everything is destroyed,' one tank commander fumed, while a staff officer complained: 'The Germans have now snatched the initiative from our hands, and if we can't hold on to the Don, we can't hold on to the Volga. We'll have to fall back to the Urals...' Some men, like one company commander, felt the only hope was 'to raise your hands' and surrender to the Germans. 'They woke up late, there is no hope for victory,' one soldier in 127th Rifle Division told his comrades. 'German troops have already taken half of the Soviet Union. There's nowhere left to retreat to. All that's left to do is surrender.' Many more, however, felt trapped between two ruthless regimes. 'There's only one way out: to raise your hands,' a company commander commented. 'If you attack, the Germans will kill you,' one soldier in 218th Rifle Regiment said, 'and if you run backwards, our own side will kill us, so we're all screwed one way or another,' while one senior sergeant simply observed: 'We'll die one way or another at the hands of our own side or the Germans...'[90]

By the time Stalin issued his order, the spearheads of Army Group B were bearing down on Kalach – just four dozen miles west of Stalingrad – having advanced 300 miles in three weeks, tearing through the Don steppe. 'The terrain is like a completely bleak lunar landscape,' the artillery commander of 44th Infantry Division observed. 'Sand, loam, enormous expanses in undulating hilly terrain on a scale which is almost fantastic. Not a village, not a wood, not a tree, not a bush. Canyons, the so-called balkas, are gouged in the terrain.' Temperatures were now reaching 55°C by day, ten degrees cooler in the shade. Aside from quickly emptied canteens, tomatoes and melons provided the only refreshment. Scattered Red Army troops hid among the tumbleweed, waiting for opportunities to ambush passing German vehicles or perhaps surrender. The roadsides of the dusty tracks which carved yellow-brown strips across the steppe were sprinkled liberally with the dead: dead Russian soldiers, or dead horses, the cadavers now bloated in the heat. Roads and settlements were few – the former were rarely paved; the latter were generally inhabited by Don Cossacks, hostile to the Bolsheviks and usually friendly to the Germans. 'You can travel 120 to 150 kilometres without seeing a village or scrap of woodland,' a corporal in 3rd Motorised Infantry Division wrote. 'You cannot imagine anything like this in Germany... I have a 20-litre jerrican on the vehicle because, as in the last few days, you can go 40 to 50 kilometres before you come across another half-dried-out well.' 'Here you could feel the land in its vastness and desolation,' Doctor Herbert Valentin, commanding a medical company with the motorised 29th Infantry Division, remembered. 'As far as the eye could see, there was nothing but wasteland.' There was little, if any, shade and few features by which the men could orient themselves. The armada of vehicles ground the soil to dust, ten to 15 centimetres deep. Stirred up by wheels and tracks it swirled around the advancing columns, while 'under the glaring sun, the hot air shimmered as it would in front of an oven,' Wolfgang Werthen of 16th Panzer Division remembered. Staff officer August Schlusnus was struck by the 'scorching heat, burning steppe, whirlwinds of ash and dust sweep across the land. Columns on the road disappear in the swirling dust – only the first vehicle remains visible. All the rest – men and machines – just dust.' Only in the final days of the advance were Karl-Heinrich Timpe and his fellow assault gun crews allowed to relax their uniform discipline by removing caps and unbuttoning the collars of their jackets. One junior officer wrote to a female penfriend: 'My skin has been thoroughly burned by the sun and peels constantly. For weeks I have not washed, not shaved and am totally covered by the indescribable dust.'[91]

Where the retreating Russians – or perhaps a crashed aircraft, or even a discarded match or cigarette – had torched the steppe, there was just a blackened surface and smell of burned wormwood. Freshly dug graves flanked the route of advance, decorated with hastily picked summer flowers found among the weeds of the steppe. Motorised medical units accompanied the panzer divisions, the staff in a modified, obsolete Panzer Mk2, the doctor and wounded in the *Krankenpanzer* – a half-track which carried stretchers rather than troops. The standard Phaenomen ambulance was no match for the terrain; its engine lacked power and in first gear it simply ground to a halt in deep sand, mud or steep slopes. Captured Russian Ford ambulances proved slightly better suited to the terrain. It was much worse for casualties in the infantry divisions, transported to the rear in horse-drawn ambulances fitted with pneumatic tyres. On bone-dry, rutted tracks, it was unpleasant. When it rained, it was painful for man and beast, who might cover no more than a couple of miles as wheels slithered or sank into the mud. For a while it was 'as hot as Africa' when the sun appeared. Corps commander Karl Strecker told a friend that occasionally 'thunderstorms dump buckets of rain on us. Then everything floats and finally sinks into the mud.'[92]

The deeper Strecker's corps advanced into the steppe, the more melancholic he became. 'This is a land of great and incomprehensible contrasts,' he wrote. 'I often get the feeling that one could drown in this sea of land.' Reservist officer

Udo von Alvensleben was troubled by 'a never-ending advance into limitless, unknown spaces,' while one Iron Cross holder complained: 'We'll all go mad in this cursed, desolate Steppe.'[93] And after marching 'another 700 kilometres into the incredible expanse of Russia,' 33-year-old bridging engineer Karl Thomas wrote to his family in the Eifel mountains of western Germany:

> These distances allow me to say things which I would otherwise not say when I am together with my loved ones. But this endless land also makes the silent talk and quiet lovers express themselves. The sun blazes, the steppe is silent, and my love is great. So great that it overcomes the sun, the steppe, the expanses and speeds to where it is at home: with my little wife and the boys...
>
> Darling, when I am sad, I always think of you! And I am always sad here, separated from you and the little ones. So now I don't need to write that I'm always thinking of you. *Ja*, and that's how it is. I don't believe there are five minutes which pass when I don't think of you at least once, my little girl, and you, my little one. You are always so close to me and I'm delighted whenever I have a little time to look at the small photograph of the three of you in the snowy landscape...
>
> Now the sun is almost beyond the horizon. Another quarter of an hour and it will be gone. Then it will head for you and bring greetings from me, kissing you right on the mouth. The rays of the sun which greet you at 7am will bring it. When the time comes when we can be together again, we'll make up for lost time. But now enough. Greetings and kisses and a firm hug.[94]

The advance was breathless. Infantry divisions might be expected to march three dozen miles a day – providing it was dry. Distances of more than 60 miles in a single day were not unheard of in motorised units, which were often on the move until around 11pm, when they pulled off the road or track into a field and formed a circle like on some Wild West wagon trail. The men threw blankets on the ground and tried to snatch a few hours' sleep, never more than five. 'Sleep had become rare with this rapid advance,' Herbert Valentin recalled. 'It was like an escape that led to oblivion. One slept deeply and soundly.' The red disc of the sun appeared in the east as early as 3am. Motors started. Men hurriedly tried to wash the dirt and sweat from the previous day's advance out of their ears, eyes and noses, grabbed a little breakfast if there was time, and moved off once more. The heat was so great that some officers turned a blind eye to regulations and let their men march and work wearing nothing but their swimming trunks. 'The sun is scorching hot in these steppe-like regions where you'll go 30 to 40 kilometres without water and only have clear running water in the river valleys,' an officer in 44th Infantry Division wrote. 'We are so tired that we fall asleep standing up or almost fall asleep when walking.' Wolfgang Pickert, commanding 9th Flak Division, was stirred by 'thrilling scenes' – the 'constant stream of a motorised army in pursuit, heading south!' Pursuit was an apt word: 24th Panzer Division 'crossed the entire Don steppe without encountering serious resistance', while 16th Panzer Division was convinced the Red Army was 'tired of fighting' and had 'lost its spark' as a result of constantly retreating. Dr Franz Muth, commanding the communications section of 94th Infantry Division, had reached a similar conclusion. The war in southern Russia was 'fizzling out', the Red Army melting away in the summer heat. There was little resistance. It was like the final days in France two years earlier. The enemy was 'wandering around this way and that, in utter confusion, without leadership… its spine broken'. As for the advancing German Army, it was like an avalanche sweeping unstoppably through the Don valley. 'This really clear knowledge gives us the strength to drive ourselves and our men forward again and again, so that the enemy just cannot settle down and inflict any more damage on us. So we look to the efforts of the coming week with great confidence.'[95]

After the monotony of the steppe, the terrain as the motorised spearheads approached Kalach – one panzer corps from the north, a second from the south – was a welcome change: hills with slopes covered with lush green oak bushes, ravine-like valleys or balkas, even meadows.

Less welcome, however, were worsening shortages of fuel and ammunition which hampered the panzers' ability to pursue the enemy, coupled with growing Soviet resistance as the still-forming Stalingrad Front increasingly began to make its presence felt. Its raw, untried formations were thrown across the Don to blunt the advance. Southwest of Kalach, the new Sixty-Fourth Army stood in the way of Fourth Panzer Army. The front-line units held firm, but not its rear units. When rumours spread that German armour was only a couple of miles from the Don, there was a rush for the crossings. Nikolai Gribachov watched 'a stream of retreating people, cargo, vehicles, trucks, and tractors. Gaunt soldiers and officers, unshaven, in filthy or torn uniforms, black with soot and dust, their nerves stretched to the limit, hastened to the other side, no-one daring to stop and wash or drink from the Don.' Traffic jams quickly built up on the right bank and soon drew the attention of the Luftwaffe, which promptly attacked the bridges and ferries. Vladimir Tendryakov saw 'burning vehicles, bodies falling into the water, wounded soldiers on stretchers, forgotten by everyone. They called out for no one; they maintained a doomed silence. Wounded people might have been quiet, but the wounded horses screamed with terrifying, hysterical, almost female voices.' It took the destruction of the crossing and the energetic intervention of Sixty-Fourth Army's commander, Vasily Chuikov, to restore some semblance of order.[96]

A couple of dozen miles to the northeast, Colonel Pyotr Lebedenko's 55th Tank Brigade was heading west over the Don at Kalach to meet the Germans head-on on the right bank. The river crossing and town were already under enemy artillery fire as the brigade rolled gingerly over the bridge. The vanguards of two German motorised infantry divisions, 3rd and 60th, were perhaps no more than two or three miles from the river. In company with the equally raw 56th Tank Brigade, Lebedenko drove his foe back a good half a dozen miles in two days of fierce fighting – at particularly heavy cost to the Soviet units. Lebedenko was preparing to send his tanks into action again on the morning of the 27th when the sudden appearance of huge KV-1 tanks – 'dwarfing our 34s' – brought joy to his depleted brigade: reinforcements.

Except the heavy armour did not halt – despite attempts to flag them down. Instead, the 12 KVs brushed past the colonel and assumed battle formation as they climbed a hill, ready to engage the enemy on the other side of the crest.

'Where the hell are they going without reconnaissance?' Lebedenko's furious commissar asked. 'They need to know that the Germans over there are on their guard.'

Barely had the dozen tanks disappeared from view than Pyotr Lebedenko and his comrades could hear the sound of battle, the thunder of enemy guns clearly audible, those of the KVs less so. The noise of battle lasted for several minutes before silence once more descended on the Don valley. After a few minutes, one KV re-appeared and rolled back down the slope. Its turret had been hit at least three times and a shell had torn a huge hole in the armour. An officer lay on top of the hull, barely able to raise his head, his left arm hanging limply, the occasional tear carving rivulets in cheeks smeared with oil, gunpowder, soot and blood. He was barely conscious – or coherent. 'Ta-a-nks… ta-a-nks g-g-gone…' he muttered.

Slowly Lebedenko began to piece together the disaster: the KVs had crested the hill, raced down the far slope then run into a minefield. In the chaos, the tanks were picked off one-by-one by the enemy's artillery.

The officer cried like a child, ground his teeth and thumped his good hand repeatedly against the armour.

Lebedenko lost his patience.

'Stop!' the 44-year-old Ukrainian snapped. 'Who are you? An officer or a cry baby?'

'Sorry, Comrade Colonel. Nerves…'

'Who are you?' Lebedenko asked.

'I am a staff officer of the 158th Heavy Tank Brigade. Our battalion received orders to break through this hill as far as Lipo-Lebedev...'

'Why didn't you stop when we were signalling?' Lebedenko asked.

'The commander was in a hurry. He was ordered to occupy Lipo-Lebedev before enemy aircraft appeared.'

55th Tank Brigade's commissar was livid. 'You deserve to be court martialled for such actions.'

'There, beyond the hill, was worse than any trial,' the wounded officer sobbed.[97]

Over the course of three days, 3rd Motorised Infantry Division accounted for 131 Soviet tanks – so many that the men labelled the area northwest of Kalach the '*Panzerfriedhof*', the tank cemetery. 'In some places they are so dense that I counted 100 knocked-out heavy tanks in about one square kilometre,' panzer mechanic Fritz Huber wrote. Hitler was sceptical of the claims and sent an officer to investigate. One platoon accounted for 52 enemy vehicles, the heavy 88mm flak another 11, and one sergeant's anti-tank gun finished off 11 tanks. He added one more to the tally when his position was overrun, destroying the tank with a mine, but killing himself in the process. Karlartur Apitzsch, a 21-year-old junior officer, serving with the artillery regiment attached to 3rd Infantry, provided his parents in Neustettin in Pomerania with a near-daily update of the progress of the fighting. On 1 August, he calculated the division had knocked out 150 enemy tanks in a week. 'One only has to wonder where the Russians keep getting men and matériel from.' Three days later: 'The Russians have hurled almost all the crap imaginable against us to annoy their foe. Only their infantry have no desire to attack. Thank God.' And the next day, 5 August: 'Stubborn as a tank, the Russians continue to attack daily. Their losses in tanks alone are incredible. We cannot afford such a thing! But the Russians, with their tremendous reserves of men and matériel, don't worry about that at all.'[98]

Russian resources were not infinite, however. After nine days of battle on the right bank of the Don, Pyotr Lebedenko's 55th Tank Brigade had been reduced to just 11 vehicles. Yet he thought only of attack, not withdrawal. He watched as what remained of his recently formed brigade battered itself against the enemy repeatedly for four hours, making the same attack – and the same mistakes – every 30 to 40 minutes: first the tanks, then the infantry moving behind them. Each time they advanced about 150 metres. And each time enemy artillery fire and aircraft brought the attack to a standstill. His commanders finally snapped and refused to attack again.

Pyotr Lebedenko was unapologetic and unforgiving. 'Why aren't you making any progress?'

'You can't get through the fire, Comrade Colonel. They won't let us raise our heads.'

'Go! Get your people up and go! You'll answer with your head if you don't follow orders!'

'Yes, we'll go!' the battalion commanders responded and repeated their attacks – with identical results, as Lebedenko remembered:

> And again I watch through my binoculars as tanks advance in different directions, the infantry rises and rushes forward in short leaps, I watch as devastating tornadoes pass through their ranks and men fall down, they lie down briefly, before somewhere on the flank and slightly in front the figure of the company commander stirs, gets up again and with terrible desperation tries to break through the continuous curtain of fire.
>
> The sounds of battle merge into one almighty, continuous roar: guns pummel and pound, mines explode with a terrible crash, sub-machine and machine guns splutter, and from above, bombers dive and fly away with a howl which tears at your heart.
>
> Even Me-109 fighters have bombs. They drop some special bombs which explode in the air, 15 or 20 metres above the ground, and hit people from above with shrapnel. We have never seen such 'aerial shrapnel'.[99]

When the jaws of the two panzer corps finally closed around Soviet forces in the 'great Don bend', they trapped the Sixty-Second Army and elements of 12 rifle divisions and ten armoured brigades. It was a much smaller haul than anticipated. 'Once again, the Russians have successfully avoided our attempts to encircle them,' Udo von Alvensleben observed, while a platoon leader in 24th Panzer Division conceded that the Red Army had 'extricated itself from the sack in a masterful manner'.[100] Among those who escaped was Pyotr Lebedenko, who retreated across the Don in the small hours of 7 August on a battered, makeshift bridge barely able to bear the weight of the armour. When the brigade's staff reached the far shore, they stopped and turned to face the river 'as if ordered to'.

> We stand in silence for five minutes. We say goodbye in our minds to what was left in the darkness, on the other side of the Don: to the days and nights filled with the explosions of shells and bombs, the rattle of machine-guns and automatic rifles. We say goodbye to those who laid down their heads there. The first of the

fallen – Berkovich and Mischenko, Peter Dovtolyuk, Ivan Grabovetsky, Vasily Pertsev, Ivan Yakovenko and many, many others – are swept in memory. Some I knew well, others less so. But irrespective of this, all of them were and remain equally dear and close to my heart.[101]

Sixty-Second Army had entered the battle on a high. 'We are certain that the enemy will suffer the same cruel defeat here as they did near Moscow,' one *frontovik* wrote. 'Every soldier is determined to die the death of the brave – and take the enemy with them.' Even in encirclement, it succeeded in maintaining its spirit and cohesion at first. 'If I am killed,' an infantryman in 186th Rifle Regiment vowed, 'let my sons repay this damned enemy tenfold... There has never been such a sworn enemy in the world, and no country has waged such a war as ours now. I've been surrounded, I've seen them slaughter civilians, plunder everything, kill wives and children...' And so the units caught in the sack made desperate attempts to bludgeon their way through German lines and reach the Don in scenes reminiscent of the final days in the Kharkov pocket at the end of May. 'Like in the Apocalypse, against the glow of fire from burning huts, we saw vehicles with women in them shooting wildly in every direction. There were guns and, behind them in dense columns on foot, Russians spurred on by their officers,' wrote Jochen Löser, a regimental adjutant. Artillery engaged the Russians at point-blank range, while their infantry comrades fought a hand-to-hand battle of pistols and bayonets. At the command post, still wearing his slippers, 230th Infantry Regiment's Erich Abraham demanded his men hold out. Only a few enterprising Soviet soldiers managed to slip across a small river using reeds as makeshift snorkels. As ever the nights were the worst. 'It's almost impossible to distinguish between friend and foe in the pitch-black night,' a soldier in 9th Infantry Regiment wrote. 'We have to identify each other by shouting.' Columns of Russian vehicles thundered into the village the regiment was holding – driving straight into its artillery, which opened fire at point-blank range, turning the Russian armour into 'burning barricades'. 'Mountains of dead Russian soldiers are the result, but we too have suffered losses,' the soldier noted. 'Shaken, we bury them the next day; we have no idea that one day all that will remain of these soldiers' graves are photographs.' Outside Skvorin, a village a dozen miles from Kalach, panzers overran a column of Soviet horse-drawn artillery. 'There were about 60 or more dead horses lying close together next to the road, a few guns were lying around and 50 dead Russians were lying in a thick pile on and around a few panje carts,' 44th Infantry Division's supply officer Karl Ludwig Renschhausen noted when he passed the site a few hours later.[102]

The fate of the 33rd Guards Division is typical of those trapped in the Don pocket. From the moment it was attacked on 23 July, Alexander Utvenko's unit was on the back foot. Communications with headquarters were frequently interrupted and, after 6 August, non-existent. Utvenko tried to hold his ground, certain he was tying down two German divisions. His men lived on a diet of porridge until it ran out on the 9th – along with most of the 33rd Guards' ammunition. When it was finally ordered to fall back to the Don – which came *after* the pocket was sealed – Utvenko's division had been reduced to just 3,000 men, supported by a dozen light tanks and just 17 field guns, now hauled by the men, for the horses were either dead or exhausted. Attempts to break through the German lines failed bloodily: one foray cost 300 lives, another perhaps 1,000. Commissars and officers shot at any man who tried to desert. Utvenko, a veteran of the retreat before Moscow the previous autumn, regarded that ordeal as 'child's play' compared with what he experienced on the Don. 'If we wanted to get water, we had to fight,' he told war correspondent Konstantin Simonov. 'We threw hand-grenades just to take a cooking pot full of water from the Germans, and we had nothing at all to eat.'[103]

Radio operator Paul-Hans Voss found himself involved in some of the most bitter fighting, finally eliminating Soviet resistance in his sector and forcing his way through to the Don opposite Kalach before dawn on 9 August. Some platoons had been reduced to just nine or ten men. There were dead Russians everywhere – possibly murdered after surrendering, more likely killed because they refused to give up. And now Voss stood on the shore of the Don. He reached down and filled his canteen. 'The dirty Don water, in which the dead float and which you fetch at risk of death, tastes like champagne.'[104]

To Udo von Alvensleben it seemed as if German and Soviet units were taking it in turns trying to surround each other. Frequently cut off from their supply columns, German armour had to fend off wild enemy onslaughts accompanied by rockets, artillery and tanks, while stubby Rata fighters hammered them with bombs and cannon fire. At times he felt as if he was in 'the middle of hell'. His 16th Panzer Division destroyed 41 enemy tanks – an entire Red Army regiment – in a single day of battle, 8 August, despite furious activity by the Red Air Force. The division's rear columns were mauled – ammunition trucks and fuel tankers flew up in the air, while incendiary bombs set the steppe on fire and the breeze drove the heat and acrid smoke towards German lines. Amid this maelstrom, Alvensleben marvelled at the energy and decisiveness of his Great War comrade Hans Hube, 16th Panzer's commander. Having weathered the storm, Hube wanted to exploit his success and send his panzers over the Don and into Kalach, but his superiors forbade it. Instead, Alvensleben stood on the high bluffs of the right bank and surveyed the scene:

Here the war becomes a spectacle on a grand scale once more. The infantry combs through the balkas and climbs the heights on the banks. The sapphire ribbon of the river, across which the enemy flees to the east on ferries under our artillery fire, basks in the evening light. Stukas attack the ferries, which look like gunboats, and go up in flames, while those rescued run off across the sand on the bank. On the eastern shore shells land among the fleeing columns and tanks. One bridge is set on fire by the enemy himself.

Kalach itself burned and then the bone-dry steppe beyond it, while birds of prey squawked in terror as they sought to escape the flames.[105]

A short distance away, war correspondent Clemens Podewils watched Russian vehicles on the far shore flee, disappearing into the 'bare, treeless steppe stretching to the horizon'. The panzers opened fire but the Russians moved too quickly – the shells crashed into the earth behind the fleeing vehicles. There was more sport in the waters of the Don: a couple of ferries carrying troops and equipment to the east bank. Traffic on both was brought to a halt by a combination of panzer and Stuka, while an incomplete temporary bridge over the Don was torched by the retreating Soviets. The flames were reflected in the waters of the river while, above, Kalach, set alight by errant artillery rounds, burned. Even the slopes of the right bank with their tawdry clumps of dry heather burned. 'The fire grows into rings and fiery wreaths,' Podewils wrote. 'They seem to float between heaven and earth – night has erased the border between the two.' The Don valley was aflame.[106]

The encircled troops fought to the last round – if not the last man. A Luftwaffe reconnaissance aircraft flying over the pocket at first light on 11 August sighted 'several divisions with their hands up'. Having consumed all their ammunition, 2,000 men surrendered to 16th Panzer Division 'from hunger, thirst and hopelessness'.[107] The battle in the Don bend ended a few days later some 40 miles upstream of Kalach, where a Red Army rearguard attempted to hold open the last bridge over the Don. At nightfall on 15 August, armour of 16th Panzer Division crested the high ground overlooking Trekhostrovskaya. 'Suddenly the wide valley of the river spreads out at our feet, with the silver ribbon of the river glistening between villages on this side and extensive forests on the other,' war correspondent Herbert Rauchhaupt wrote. The panzers rolled down the gentle slope to either seize or destroy the crossing.

Bursts of machine-gun fire whip between the surprised Bolsheviks. One high explosive shell after another tears into the village – and soon one thatched roof after another goes up in flames. The fires spread from house to house. Ammunition explodes, a tremendous sea of flames lights up the night. The panzers by the river report: 'The bridge is burning!' Our vehicles halt at the edge of the village for safety, shooting again and again. Burst after burst. Shell after shell. For minutes, hours. Their outlines stand out sharply against the blazing village.

In the darkness, the panzers fell back and awaited reinforcements. Crews allowed themselves a gulp of warm coffee and slice of bread from the field kitchen before wrapping themselves in their blankets and crawling under their vehicles for four hours' fitful sleep.

At 4am on the 16th, 16th Panzer renewed its attack. As by night, so by day: Soviet resistance was as dogged as it had been the previous evening, only now the panzer crews could see what darkness had hidden: the meandering river, the now-burned-down bridge, and beyond, the flat, eastern bank covered by forests of dark green, stretching for miles. As the day progressed, the Red Army finally yielded. 'A long column of prisoners finally marches past us, and the hill is littered with dead Bolsheviks, destroyed guns and abandoned vehicles,' Rauchhaupt wrote. The sight of flares rising above Trekhostrovskaya signalled the village's capture. 'At this moment, the last narrow strip on the western bank of the Don falls into German hands.' From the water's edge, Herbert Rauchhaupt watched German shells crash down on enemy troops just a couple of hundred metres away on the opposite shore. 'A naked Bolshevik climbs out of the river and quickly disappears into the forest,' the war correspondent observed. 'He is one of the last Soviets to flee to the eastern bank of the Don.'[108]

Corps commander Walther von Seydlitz considered the battle in the Don bend a 'master stroke by Sixth Army and our panzers'. The west bank of the Don was scarred by evidence of a heavy defeat. 'From a distance at first you thought there was an enormous herd of elephants in front of you; only when you got closer did you see that these were very heavy knocked-out Russian tanks.' And yes, the toll of destruction was impressive: around 1,000 tanks and 750 guns destroyed or captured. Some 88,000 prisoners had been taken. Provision for them was no better than 12 months earlier after the great battles of encirclement outside Minsk, Kiev or Vyazma. The 8,000 soldiers who surrendered to 44th Infantry Division were crammed into part of an abandoned collective farm barely two thirds the size of a typical football pitch. There was no barbed wire to hold them in – the area was simply marked off with unused medical bandages. A handful of German soldiers and a few anti-Communist Russian volunteers stood guard, watched over by a young soldier behind a machine-gun. In the stable, captured Red Army doctors and medics tended to 300 wounded, while seized Russian field kitchens and empty petrol barrels provided 'a hearty soup' made with horse ribs.[109]

Many more *frontoviki* escaped their fate, either evading encirclement on the Don or breaking out of the pocket. Given the size of the pocket and the effort expended in crushing it, the battle in the Don bend proved to be a disappointment. The Red Army forces which extricated themselves would re-form and regroup. Alexander Utvenko and around 120 comrades swam the Don and regained their composure. In time, the stragglers would grow to number 600. They would defend the approaches to Stalingrad until their 33rd Guards Division was all but wiped out in early September.[110]

The advance into the Caucasus exploded from three bridgeheads along a 100-mile stretch of the lower Don. Roads were few, paved roads fewer, so the panzer divisions were funnelled towards the towns of Salsk and Armavir, the infantry concentrated in the west, moving on foot towards the key oil-refining and industrial city of Krasnodar, 150 miles south of Rostov. The panzer and motorised spearheads made astonishing progress. 23rd Panzer Division smashed the newly raised North Caucasus Independent Cavalry Corps – despite its title, equipped with T-34s – when it was trapped in a village east of Rostov. The cavalry corps' chief-of-staff was found buried alive in a half-collapsed anti-tank trench. Still suffering from shock, he was led into captivity through the burning village – and past the knocked-out hulks of his tanks. He broke down in tears. He counted three destroyed panzers, but his North Caucasus Independent Cavalry Corps had ceased to exist; all that remained was a graveyard of 68 tanks. In company with 3rd Panzer, the 23rd made for the first major natural obstacle, the Manych, barring the German armour's way to the heart of the Caucasus. The river was forced north of Salsk. War correspondent Günther Heysing accompanied the pioneers of 3rd Panzer Division who struck across a 1,200-metre-wide stretch of the Manych in a combination of rubber and assault boats. As the Luftwaffe and artillery provided cover, the motorcycle infantry and pioneers in the boats were 'covered by the salty spray as the assault boats struck the waves of the blue water whipped up by the steppe wind,' Heysing wrote. 'It was a journey similar to crossing the lower Elbe, past islands and steep banks over which the tall steppe grass fluttered like yellow shocks of hair.' By the next day, the Germans had a sizeable bridgehead over the Manych and were ready to advance on Salsk in pursuit of the fleeing Red Army. What Heysing called 'the third gate to the Caucasus' had been 'smashed open'.

The river seemed to possess some mystical power to the Germans, a symbolic as well as a physical barrier. The Soviets had attempted to tame the river and harness its power by building sluice gates and a lengthy embankment – a 100-metre stretch of it blown up by the Red Army in retreat. German pioneers patched it up so their comrades could pass, then erected a sign: *Manytsch-Damm: Grenze Europa – Asien*; Manych embankment: border between Europe and Asia.

'At 5pm today we left the good European earth and set foot on the soil of Asia,' Peter Dimt wrote after crossing the river, while the men of XXXX Panzer Corps re-christened it *Das Deutsche Asienkorps* – The German Asia Corps. 'Officers and men cherished great expectations,' Heysing wrote. 'The joy of the adventure and the hope of getting away from the steppe helped us to carry out our duty and inspire the lunge forward.' One officer leading the advance told his men: 'Comrades, the desert of the steppe will soon end, now we're entering a beautiful, rich land where the war will assume a different face.'[111]

Within three days of crossing the Manych, the Berliners of 3rd Panzer were approaching the city of Voroshilovsk – today Stavropol – 100 miles to the south. There was little evidence that Stalin's 'Not one step back' order had any effect on the enemy forces in the division's way. 'The senior commanders fled first, then the officers, finally the leaderless troops,' it reported. The armour passed through villages and towns at speeds of 20 miles an hour or more, leaving dense trails of dust in its wake which 'crossed the steppe like lines drawn by a ruler'. The closer the division's vanguard got to Voroshilovsk, the more evident the signs of war: the Luftwaffe had hammered the roads and railway lines running into the city, leaving behind burned-out vehicles and trains. Voroshilovsk itself was aflame: homes were burned or badly damaged, the railway station was on fire, while the bodies of soldiers and civilians and cadavers of horses – all victims of German air attacks – had to be moved aside as the panzers and accompanying motorised infantry advanced deeper into the city. The roads in the centre were so badly blocked by retreating Red Army columns that there could be no organised resistance. In little more than two hours, Voroshilovsk was in German hands. So quickly did it fall that the fuel reserves were seized at the airfield on the edge of the city and Soviet aircraft continued to land. Civilians began to emerge from their hiding places, welcoming their new masters in many cases, offering them food, while the Germans raided Voroshilovsk's still-intact warehouses and depots, where the booty 'exceeded all expectations', especially deliveries from the United States: shoes, shirts, trousers, sugar and flour.

3rd Panzer Division would advance no further this Monday, however. The tankers and supply columns lagged far behind the spearhead which had captured Voroshilovsk 'with its last ounce of strength – and also with the last litre of fuel in the tank'.[112]

Forty miles to the west, 13th Panzer Division paused on the hills outside Armavir after an exhilarating drive, vividly described by regimental commander Walter Kühn:

Thrusting into the fleeing rearguards, the advance continues at a relentless pace – sparing neither man nor machine. We race all over the place following our compasses, through fields of corn and sunflowers for mile after mile. The drivers were naked, dripping with sweat like stokers on ships. The radiators, clogged with sunflower seeds and bits of fruit, cooked at temperatures of up to 120°C.

From the hills above Armavir 'an endless view' lay before the panzer crews. 'In the distance the heights of the longed-for Caucasus shimmered in the haze,' Kühn continued. 'On the opposite bank of the river, squinting eyes could make out enemy columns trailing huge clouds of dust – some on foot, some horse-drawn, some motorised – a train under way, aircraft landing and taking off: targets for the artillery it could barely imagine.'[113] The division's gunners reported that 'every road was black with enemy columns'. Frustratingly for them, there were more targets than shells to hand; batteries could only engage the enemy piecemeal. Half a dozen panzers raced down into the Kuban valley and hurriedly formed a bridgehead over the river just north of Armavir, only for the bridge to be blown up behind them. After an uncomfortable few hours, the panzers were joined by infantry who crossed the Kuban in rubber boats, but it took another day before engineers had a bridge over the river ready for armour to cross and the advance could continue.[114]

The collapse which began on the approaches to Rostov continued into the northern Caucasus for a good fortnight. Resistance seemed to melt away. Soviet forces before First Panzer Army disappeared 'in wild flight'. German motorised units regularly covered 30 miles in a day, simply bypassing any Red Army formations in the surrounding countryside – thus leaving 'enemies all around'. Behind the front, the Germans moved in columns, rather than individually, to avoid being surprised by scattered Russian soldiers. Those who ignored the warnings, like a reservist officer in charge of XXXX Panzer Corps' headquarters, were never seen again. The greatest obstacle to the advance was the vastness of the Kuban steppe, extending as far as the foothills of the Caucasus. Temperatures and conditions were desert-like, as almost every soldier crossing it observed. 'I am not even human anymore,' exhausted regimental doctor Karol Virsík, with the Slovak Rapid Division, confided in his diary. 'I feel like part of a machine that knows only one thing: to rush from battle to battle… We are all tired to death, sweaty and dirty. In the tropical heat and in the dust which permeates everywhere, we are being driven forward like cattle.' Only the presence of horses, which needed to rest by day with temperatures frequently hitting 50°C, prevented the men being driven on even harder. Advancing on foot towards Krasnodar, Leo Leixner, war correspondent with the Viennese edition of the *Völkischer Beobachter*, complained of 'Africa-like heat'. Some days an easterly breeze from the Caspian Sea 'took away some of the furnace-like heat', blowing away the fine clouds of dust vehicles rolling along the bone-dry tracks left trailing in their wake, making it easier for the marching troops to breathe. But most days, the men were tortured by 'a withering, merciless sun... blazing down on us with its scorching rays making our overheated brains spin'. The Kuban steppe reminded Wilhelm Eichner of the Old Testament. 'It feels like we've been transported back in time thousands of years,' he wrote. Skirmishes with Red Army rearguards left houses and farms burned-out shells, haystacks burned, but for the most part the men marched relentlessly. 125th Infantry Division averaged 24 kilometres every day. The thermometer hit 57°C on a least one occasion. 'Lips cracked,' battalion commander Karl Göbel recalled. 'The dirt made it impossible to recognise individuals. Water was so salty that even tea and coffee tasted of it. It merely made the men even thirstier.' The constant dust which shrouded marching and motorised columns turned the land between the Don and the Kuban into 'a smoking, murky world which never seemed to end'. A pioneer corporal described the advance to his grandmother in Munich:

> Our shirts are always drenched in sweat. Thick dust lies on the roads – our feet stir it up and we breathe it all day long and have to swallow it. Our throats become sore and dry and we think we're going to die of thirst – our canteens are always empty.
>
> There's only one thought in our heads: when's the next rest? We march by day and night. Barely have we fallen asleep than we're woken again. And then it's march, march again. Many men are ill, suffer from diarrhoea or a temperature or both. All of us are so dog tired that we'd prefer to fall down and remain by the roadside. But the non-commissioned officers always hound us: 'Forwards, forwards! Anyone who stays behind will be shot dead.'[115]

Infantry units were expected to 'march to the last breath of man and horse'. German maps of the Caucasus were poor – invariably dating back to the Tsarist era and rarely more detailed than 1:200,000. Units frequently took a wrong turn – adding to the daily toll. To men like Franz Müller, an artilleryman with 1st *Gebirgs* Division, the advance was torturous:

> We're woken in deepest sleep between 1am and 3am. The heat is strangely oppressive, almost tropical, as early as 7am. But the most annoying thing is the dust, which almost takes our breath away. Thick as a finger, it lies on the skin, clogs up your eyes and fills lungs with all the dirt. We puff our way from one rest to another, our feet are leaden and kick up yet more dirt in addition to that from

the cursed speeding cars, which are our true enemies during this period. The mid-day heat is unbelievably oppressive, it parches our throats such that not even another two drinks suffice. During the 60-kilometre march, men drop like mosquitoes, and the detachment commander organises an ambulance shuttle service, supported by the quartermaster's trucks, which takes foot patients. With barely an hour and a half for rest at mid-day, we are on our feet from early morning until evening. Darkness falls as early at 7pm and the malaria-carrying flies spoil our evening hours.[116]

Motorised units were spared the exertions of marching, but little else, as the SS *Wiking*'s Wilhelm Tieke wrote:

The dust covers the men in the vehicles with a fine, grey layer; when they laugh, their white teeth stand out sharply. Some wear sunglasses. Every man is lightly dressed. The grey field jacket has been packed away somewhere. The camouflage jacket sleeves are rolled up. Only occasionally are steel helmets and gasmasks carried into battle. The men's gaze roams across a land which is very different from the one which they have borne in their hearts since childhood. They miss the green trees and woods, the colourful summer meadows. Villages with red tiled roofs, firm roads with trees by the side giving shade. Before their eyes the golden brown sea of grain of the Kuban steppe stretches to the horizon. Heavy and plump, the overripe ears nod and wait for the reaper.[117]

The dust, monotony, poor maps and tracks made orientation extremely difficult. 'Everything is the same far and wide,' wrote Hermann Ochsner, commanding *Nebelwerfer* rocket units. 'There are no roads. The paths, simple tracks, are random and lead from village to village, changing each year.' Night fell rapidly – there was no lingering dusk as in more northerly latitudes – and brought a temporary end to hostilities. 'You simply have to stop and wait until day comes again.' Ewald Klapdor yearned for night to fall. He and his men would gather around a radio set to listen to the evening news reports. 'In this summer of 1942 they link us with the big picture.' They heard about the destruction of Soviet forces in the Don bend, about 13th Panzer Division crossing the Manych and U-boats sending half a million tonnes of Allied shipping to the seabed. 'On every front, success,' wrote Klapdor. 'The will to attack and the power of that attack appears to be unbreakable.' For his *Wiking* Division comrade Hans Dorr, a company commander, the bold lunge into the Caucasus was spellbinding. 'There has never been a German soldier here before between the Caspian and Black Seas,' he wrote. 'The Russians are fleeing. We're hot on their heels.'[118]

Regimental commander Ivan Kovalev concurred with the damning German assessment. The Red Army 'retreated in disarray,' he remembered. 'This retreat turned into a flight. Even the dead could not be buried.' Lazar Kaganovich, on the military council of the North Caucasus Front, reported that 'tank fever, panic and defeatism' were endemic in the North Caucasus Front. Wherever the troops made a stand – typically along rivers – the line collapsed as soon as the Germans broke through. First the men at the front panicked, then the rear, while the panzers raced ahead sowing confusion and chaos with every mile they advanced. Rather than rigidly adhering to Stalin's order, 'staffs and even individual officers often look for a way out – not through fighting, but by drawing "new lines" on the map which, unfortunately, means retreating'. An arch Stalinist, Kaganovich had been sent by his master as his enforcer. He dutifully reported that cowards were being shot – 37 deserters to date – or rounded up into penal units. Yet even a lackey like Lazar Kaganovich conceded that terror and threats alone would not halt the German advance. 'I beg of you, Comrade Stalin, to help us with shells and tanks…'[119]

For now, however, the leaders of the North Caucasus Front fell back on tried-and-tested Stalinist principles, reinforcing the *vozhd*'s 'Not one step back' order with a carbon-copy instruction of their own. Almost everywhere else in Russia, the front's military council told its troops – inaccurately – the Germans had been brought to a halt. It continued:

> Only our Northern Caucasus Front has failed to carry out Comrade Stalin's order. Instead it retreats in the face of the brutish and impudent enemy, surrendering one *rayon* [district] after the next, one town after the next, to be plundered and pillaged.
>
> It is time that commanders and political leaders as well as all honourable warriors put an end to this disgrace! It is time to halt the Fascist brute! Everything that Comrade Stalin said in his order about the atmosphere of retreat, about soldiers, commanders and politruks abandoning positions on their own initiative, about cowards and panic mongers who over-estimate the enemy's strength and run away as a result, all this applies to the North Caucasus Front in particular.

Henceforth, anyone who fled the front or spread panic would be shot; any officer who withdrew his unit without orders would be regarded as a traitor. The time had come, the council declared, to make a stand in the mountains. The weather, landscape, few roads and local knowledge – all were to the defenders' advantage. But these factors alone could not save the Caucasus. 'We must doggedly defend every position, every metre of Soviet soil to the last drop of blood, clinging to each clod of earth until the last moment.'[120]

13th Panzer Division was determined there should be no such resistance blocking its path. Having been held up outside Armavir for more than a day – the city's capture would be left to the infantry – the division focused its efforts on the prize: the oilfields of the western Caucasus, centred on the city of Maykop, 50 miles away. It was spurred on by its commander, Traugott Herr: 'The rapid execution of the division's mission could have a decisive impact on the course of the war. Every officer and non-commissioned officer must understand this. Avoid towns where possible during the pursuit. Forwards!'[121]

Herr promised that crossings and fords would be captured in advance of the division's arrival to prevent any hold-ups. Ahead of his panzers were two groups of Brandenburger commandos, in this instance Baltic Germans and men from the Sudetenland who spoke Russian, all dressed in the uniforms of the NKVD and riding in captured Russian vehicles. Both attached themselves to the stream of retreating Red Army units heading into Maykop. The first, led by Adrian von Fölkersam, headed for the city itself, the second for the bridge over the Bielaya, the last natural obstacle before the city. It was shown over the crossing by a Soviet general and a traffic policeman. But as soon as the Brandenburgers reached the far bank, they halted, jumped down from their vehicles and began shooting at the Soviet troops behind them, as well as cutting the wires to the demolition charges on the bridge. They then continued into Maykop. In the chaos of retreat, their vehicles covered in dirt, the Brandenburgers passed through the city 'unnoticed' by their enemy.[122]

The 27-year-old son of an aristocratic Baltic German family which had served the Tsar before the Russian Revolution, Adrian von Fölkersam was so convincing that he persuaded Maykop's NKVD commander to take him on a guided tour of the city's defences. When Herr's panzers were no more than 24 hours away, Fölkersam set his men to work, blowing up a communications exchange, persuading some of the troops defending the city to withdraw, and occupying a command centre from where they spread general unease and issued fake orders to evacuate Maykop. When 13th Panzer Division entered a few hours later, crews found 'no fires, no smoke, no destruction – apart from the black cloud around a small oil tank near the railway station,' Peter Dimt noted. 'Otherwise, Maykop is one of the best-preserved towns which has fallen into German hands.' But in its principal objective – seizing the oilfields outside the city – the division failed. The troops charged with protecting – and, if necessary, sabotaging – the pumps and wells grew suspicious of fresh orders they received from the Brandenburgers to abandon the facilities and hand them over to the NKVD for 'demolition'. In rapid succession, the oil wells of Maykop were blown up. So comprehensively destroyed were they that only a handful of drilling rigs could be assembled from the twisted and tangled remains.[123]

It wasn't merely the fields at Maykop which were thoroughly demolished by the retreating Soviets. Power stations were destroyed, roads, railway lines, pipelines – the entire oil industry infrastructure. A couple of days after Maykop was captured, German troops moved into Krasnodar, 80 miles to the northwest, and the heart of the refining industry for the fields of the western Caucasus. As in Voronezh, Communist Party officials only took measures to fortify the city with the enemy at the gates. The sluice gates on the irrigation system which fed the fields on the lower Kuban were opened to flood the valley and roads to the west of the city. The Party called on the entire populace to build barricades and fortifications and attempted to mobilise workers' battalions, while teenage boys – unarmed, untrained, straight from school, invariably still dressed in civilian clothing – were drafted and thrown into the ranks of Fifty-Sixth Army. 'Son, fight, but do not leave the Kuban,' was the slogan of the hour. Vladimir Biryukov, a village teacher before the war, moved with his anti-tank unit through the 'dead streets' of Krasnodar on the eve of the main German assault, passing 'smoke-filled windows of burnt-out buildings' and 'tram tracks in the main street, on which the occasional abandoned tram stood'. Looming over everything was a 'thick veil of black smoke' from the oil refinery, 'burning like a huge torch'. So thick was the smoky haze hanging over Krasnodar that even though the sky was cloudless, the sun was blurry – 'as if you were staring through smoked glass during an eclipse'.

Hermann Stiefvater led the German advanced detachment bearing down on the city from the northwest. Awarded the Knight's Cross for his bravery in the Balkans in the spring of 1941, the 39-year-old led the assault on Krasnodar with the same dash, puncturing the anti-tank ditch outside the city – the last major obstacle facing the attacker. 'We've found a gap, we're pushing through,' he reported. It was a strange force Hermann Stiefvater commanded, typical of the ad hoc units – *Kampfgruppen* – the German Army scrambled together for specific short-term missions: assault guns, pioneers, anti-tank guns, flak and bicycle infantry who struggled in the heat and dust to keep pace with the motorised troops. The vanguard, war correspondent Leo Leixner wrote lyrically, seemed to be 'spit out of a gigantic dust cloud, spreading panic and terror' among the Red Army holding the northwest approaches to Krasnodar. At last light, Stiefvater's men reached the outskirts of the city. Exhausted, they halted by a bend in the Kuban where they were plagued more by swarms of mosquitos than by the Soviet forces on the opposite bank. As they settled down to sleep, the nearby gasometers exploded 'with a tremendous clap of thunder,' Leixner noted. 'A blazing torch of doom shoots in the sky – and for a few seconds the landscape is bathed in a bright orange light.'

Krasnodar at first light on Sunday 9 August was a city 'frozen in anticipation'. Long lines of trams stood empty at the main depot. No-one dared venture into the streets, except for curious young boys who peered through railings and gates at the troops filing past. Vladimir Biryukov's unit was ordered to take up position by the Kuban, which meanders in great loops on the southern edge of Krasnodar. In searing heat – it was already above 30° Celsius before mid-day – crews hauled their guns until they reached the river. There the men hurriedly camouflaged their guns with whatever foliage they could find and tried to dig fire pits. The work was unfinished when the crews heard the sound of battle coming from a leather factory to the west. A few minutes later Biryukov watched as infantry jumped off advancing panzers and attempted to storm the Kuban crossing. 'A tremendous explosion was heard,' Biryukov wrote. 'The trusses of the adjacent bridge swayed. Logs and planks flew into the air. Many people looked up apprehensively to see if something heavy would hit them. But they felt better. The Germans did not break through. The pioneers had acted in time.'

Leo Leixner claimed no more than 70 men, supported by a handful of assault guns, anti-tank guns and pioneers, spearheaded the assault on Krasnodar – far in advance of any other German unit. His account of the fighting for the city, published in the *Völkischer Beobachter* in September, details only German successes: barricades penetrated, Red Army soldiers surrendering when *Landsers* called out 'Ruki vverh!' (Hands up!), bewildered Soviet citizens dressed in their nightclothes standing in front of their homes watching German troops file past, offering them refreshments. The kindly attackers, so Leixner wrote, even ceased fire when they saw civilians wandering in the streets.

Where Russian and German accounts agree is that the sight of the burning oil refinery complex on the edge of Krasnodar dominated the cityscape that Sunday. Leo Leixner watched oil spill out of one punctured tank 'like a waterfall', spreading out, burning and flowing like lava. On the south bank of the Kuban, Vladimir Biryukov looked past 'the charred remains of trees' at 'mangled, smoking fuel tanks where what oil remained was still burning'. All the surrounding buildings were covered by a thick layer of ash, while 'oil slicks floated on the muddy waters of the Kuban'.

With one crossing gone, the German attack shifted focus to a still-intact railway bridge which panzers now attempted to roll across. 'The first shell hit the first German panzer,' Biryukov recalled. 'It went up in flames like a bonfire. The mounted infantry were blown from the vehicle as if by a gust of wind.' Another gun engaged the last panzer in the column which promptly vanished amid 'a huge shower of sparks'. Despite these setbacks, the momentum lay with the attackers, who avenged the deaths of their comrades by promptly smashing Biryukov's gun at point-blank range.

By the end of 9 August, Hermann Stiefvater's scratch formation was joined by other German units fighting their way into Krasnodar from the east and northeast. The city was now 'firmly in our hands,' a satisfied Leo Leixner recorded. Stiefvater's men bedded down under the eerie glow of 'a huge petroleum lamp – the city's burning oil refinery'.

So much for the propaganda. Racked by illness which had dogged him for weeks – phlebitis, scurvy, hair loss, liver disease and especially depression – Leo Leixner actually spent his first night in Krasnodar in a field hospital. He had collapsed through exhaustion in a park, where his comrades later found him surrounded by corpses and the carcasses of horses and carried him to a first-aid post. Leixner asked his headquarters for permission to return to the Reich to recuperate. It refused. 'Shirkers' were not tolerated in the German Army. At 5am on Friday 14 August, the war correspondent climbed into an assault boat with ten comrades and set out across the Kuban. Standing up in the rubber boat, Leixner was shot dead instantly. His bullet-ridden helmet was delivered to his wife of just five months a few weeks later. On 2 September, Leixner's colleagues at the *Völkischer Beobachter* in Vienna published a eulogy alongside his final despatch. It closed with the following words:

> Dark clouds continue to gather in the sky, an abysmal black, and the purple of the raging flames unite in a gloomy duet of destruction.
>
> But the wind which stirred last night drives the gigantic clouds towards the enemy bank, where a ghastly curtain descends, obscuring the sun, as if it were the end of the world. If there were still augurs as in ancient Rome, they would probably know how to read the signs in the heavens and interpret them.[124]

Two hundred miles to the east, 3rd Panzer Division was fighting its way into the spa town of Pyatigorsk. It seemed as if the Russians were throwing their 'last levy' into the battle: 2,000 17- and 18-year-old students from the tractor school, led by their headteacher, who'd been armed the previous day. They were crushed by the Berliners, as was a cavalry regiment whose ill-trained officers deserted or fled while their men were 'scattered to the four winds'. There was just time for the retreating NKVD troops to kill all the inmates of the prison – mirroring their murderous actions in the first days of the invasion in June and July 1941 – before the Germans entered the town as the sun set. Silence descended on Pyatigorsk – total silence. No birdsong nor even the hum of insects. And definitely no people. 'It seemed as though a storm had struck and finished everything,' mother-of-two Elena Skrjabina wrote in her diary. Skrjabina had escaped the blockade of Leningrad with her two sons and joined her sister-in-law in the apparent safety of the Caucasus. Now she cowered with neighbours in her temporary home. The unmistakeable sound of a tank moving down the street tempted the civilians to tentatively look out of the window. 'Ours, ours,' a teenage girl yelled in delight. Despite the fading light, and the soldiers mounted on the vehicle, a large black cross could be seen on the tank. An entire column followed. 'After just a few hours, Pyatigorsk had already completely changed,' Skrjabina noted, as the town's new masters erected signs at every road junction while cars and motorcycles flashed by. There were several dead Russian soldiers in the streets. They remained there for days. The Germans were preoccupied with their advance; the civilian populace were too frightened to bury them. Otherwise Pyatigorsk – the 'town of five mountains' – had largely been spared the effects of war. Despite near-tropical heat, all the trees were in bloom – beech, apricot, chestnut, magnolia, cypress. Posters on the walls of hotels and public buildings showed that the spas were still in business just days before the Germans entered. Cultural life quickly resumed: concerts, operettas, variety shows, even ballet performed by dancers who had also fled from Leningrad. To Oskar Munzel of 6th Panzer Regiment, with its well-kept villas, paved roads and sanatoria, Pyatigorsk presented 'a thoroughly "European" picture'. The men were more interested in the rich booty discovered in a huge warehouse. Food and wine were plentiful. Their billets surpassed anything found elsewhere in the Soviet Union. For a few days, they lived like lords. 'It is a land of eternal spring,' wrote one officer in 3rd Panzer Division.[125]

There was something else inescapable about Pyatigorsk: the landscape. The terrain was no longer a flat, endless, featureless arid beige expanse, but undulating, the vegetation rich, the fields a lush green. 'This land between the two seas is a wonderful and fertile region,' wrote 19-year-old Fritz Trautwein, a former forestry student from southern Germany. There was fruit aplenty – apricots, mirabelles, plums and peaches – and a friendly populace even willing to pick it for their new masters. Trautwein was billeted with local families. 'When I leave people often give me an egg or even a glass of milk and a thick slice of wonderful white bread.' Rudolf von Bünau was astonished by the richness of the land. 'Oh my, what we could extract from this soil,' he wrote. 'Apparently we've arrived in a land of fruit – the branches on every tree are full to breaking point.' There were oats, vegetables, fruit and grain to supply his 73rd Infantry Division for weeks. For now, his men gorged themselves on all the fruits of the land their stomachs could hold. Though few and far apart, the small towns and villages often contrasted sharply with those of central Russia and Ukraine: neat, tidy, well-kept cottages with well-tended gardens. The soldiers scooped fresh, clear mountain water from wells – 'not the marshy water of the steppe which has frequently caused us terrible intestinal problems,' wrote radio operator Peter Dimt. And all the fruit the soldiers could wish for. 'People come out of the huts, hand us clean towels for drying and bring bowls full of fruit – oh fruit, wonderful pears, apples and greengages,' Dimt continued. 'What friendly people there are here!'[126]

And on the horizon, crowned by Elbrus just 50 miles to the southwest, the central ridge of the Caucasian mountains. Running roughly northwest to southeast, the range stretched from the Black to the Caspian Sea with more than 30 peaks rising 4,000 metres, and eight with summits above 5,000 metres. 'It is,' one contemporary guide put it, 'as if someone has pushed the Alps together to make them much steeper and more rugged.' There were just two major roads over the range – the so-called Ossetian and Georgian 'military highways' – and only the latter, linking the cities of Tbilisi and Ordzhonikidze, was passable all year round. In short, the Caucasus were a formidable obstacle – 'an enormous mass of granite rock stretched as a stone barrier 1,200-kilometres long and on average 130 kilometres wide', an officer on the staff of XXXX Panzer Corps observed. Overcoming it 'was a task roughly equivalent to seizing the entire chain of the northern Alps from Switzerland to Semmering – but without having a network of roads and passes even remotely as good'.[127]

Like most mountain infantrymen, recently promoted junior officer Werner Jacobi yearned to fight among the peaks and passes. 'Sometimes we reach the limit of sanity, but man can withstand a great deal,' the 22-year-old Saarlander wrote. 'The men know what's at stake and that we have a single objective: the Caucasus... the objective of all our dreams.' The mountain troops pictured a world of 'mountains, woods, snow, spring water, strange peoples, strange customs' and dreamed of Caucasian girls ('hot-tempered, with smouldering eyes'). Above all they longed for 'all that is exotic and romantic, bound up with the name "Caucasus"'. An officer in 198th Infantry Division chewed over the idea of two Caucasus, one 'a land of romantic books about wild struggles for freedom and adventurous mountain journeys', the other 'the rough reality, a great and difficult military task facing the division'.[128]

After a few days regrouping in Pyatigorsk, 3rd Panzer Division struck eastwards – and into the Caucasian foothills. There were so many mountain streams and rivers to cross – each one in flood as meltwater from the glaciers merged with walls of water moving down the valleys from dams blown up by the retreating Red Army – that panzer crews dubbed the region 'the damned aquarium'. Traffic jams built up at each crossing point, drawing the attention of the Red Air Force, which attacked the armoured spearheads in swarms of up to 40 aircraft.[129]

The German thrust into the Caucasus was beginning to run out of momentum. XXXX Panzer Corps' columns were stretched over a distance of 250 miles. There was much to admire and celebrate about the advance, but the corps was approaching the limits of endurance. 'We had rolled along the oil pipeline from Rostov to Baku. We had a great deal of booty – but among the rich stores in the conquered towns, the most important commodity was missing: fuel,' one staff officer lamented. 'There were huge petrol tanks in every station, but they were burned-out.' The days of pursuit were over. The advance into the Caucasus had become 'a slow, time-consuming trudge'.[130]

Hitler's Army adjutant Gerhard Engel had come to the same conclusion after a dispiriting visit to the Caucasus convinced him the offensive had run its course, the troops 'more or less at the end of their strength'; the mountainous terrain with its dense, jungle-like undergrowth and tracks suitable only for mountain troops and mules meant the panzer divisions were 'in the completely wrong place'. Hitler dismissed his report out of hand. 'That Engel allows himself to be swayed by anything he's told,' he sneered.[131]

The advance into the Caucasus was faltering, but had not yet stalled. And the Germans still had time to play their trump card.

In the last week of July 1942, as his battery moved through the ruins of Rostov, artillery commander Max Gämmerler was ordered to report to the commander of his 4th *Gebirgs* Division. 'Fly to Munich, gather maps and literature about the Caucasus, study them until you know how to cross the routes through the Caucasus like the back of your hand and come back as quickly as possible with the necessary documents,' Karl Eglseer told him, and beckoned the 42-year-old Bavarian to a waiting Ju52 transporter to fly him to Germany.

For the next fortnight, Gämmerler surrounded himself with all the material on the Caucasus held in the library of the alpine association. Maps were poor – the available 1:500,000 and 1:200,000 charts would prove too inaccurate for use in the high mountains, while more detailed 1:100,000 sketches would turn out to be dangerous because they were sloppily drawn and littered with mistakes. Mountain guides, climbers' memoirs and geographical and topographical studies proved more fruitful.

After two weeks in Munich Max Gämmerler returned to his unit as a 'walking dictionary of the Caucasus'. His mission, he found, was to raise the swastika on Elbrus, Europe's highest mountain. Scaling the taller of its two peaks, rising 5,642 metres – more than 18,500 feet – above sea level was not a particularly challenging climb by Alpine standards, although its upper reaches were often plagued by storms and blizzards. Nor did the mountain possess any military significance. But to any soldier fighting in the central Caucasus, Elbrus was both an imposing – and inspiring – sight. The Reich's battle ensign flying from its higher, western summit would spur the German soldier on to greater deeds – and undermine Soviet morale.

Operation *Elbrus*, as it became known, got under way on 12 August. Max Gämmerler led a ten-strong group of mountain troops, among them a couple of photographers, with two dozen pack animals and Caucasian donkeys and a handful of vehicles up the Kuban valley. After two days the group doubled in size when it was joined by Heinz Groth and a motley assortment of soldiers, mountaineers, an author and a war correspondent. Groth, a 36-year-old reservist from Hanover, took charge – ahead of the more experienced Gämmerler. A competent rather than outstanding mountaineer and self-confessed '*Muss Soldat*' – a soldier because he had to be – Groth yearned to return to his family once the fighting was over. But he also hated staff work and sitting behind a desk and was seized by an 'insatiable urge to go into the mountains'.

As the group continued up the Kuban valley, it was soon forced to dispense with its vehicles and continue on foot. There was 'something of a reckless Sunday outing feeling' to the mission, mountaineer, novelist and newspaper editor Josef Martin Bauer observed. It was more adventure or expedition than military operation. There would be little the group could do if it encountered the Red Army, the 41-year-old Bauer noted: 'no protection, not a single weapon which, in an emergency could bolster our defence and lift it above an otherwise absurd riflemen's club outing.'

Beyond Khurzuk, the last major village, they left the Kuban behind and climbed through the Ullu-Kam valley, past several collective farms. The valley narrowed, its sides rose sharply. The lower slopes were covered with huge Caucasian fir trees which towered above the oaks and beeches, while the upper reaches were bare rock. After establishing a base camp at the head of the valley – an altitude of 2,241 metres – the attempt on Elbrus could begin in earnest. Plans to reach the summit by the western route were thwarted when a reconnaissance team reported a mountain hut vital for any push to the summit simply did not exist, despite being marked clearly on the map. Instead, the mountaineers pushed east towards a hotel-cum-weather observation station, an imposing structure built just 1,500 metres below the double summit. Intended to host mountaineers from around the world hoping to scale the mountain, the aluminium-clad structure – known by the Soviets as Priiut 11 and by the Germans simply as 'the Elbrus House' – was garrisoned in time of war.

To reach it, the Germans had to cross the Khotju-Tau Pass and then negotiate a 'sea of glaciers' spread out over Elbrus' lower slopes. From here on the burden of carrying kit fell exclusively on the soldiers. The mules were left behind and the men continued carrying all the clothing, equipment and provisions needed – up to 30 kilogrammes per man. The group split into three as it made its way over the glacial field to the Elbrus House. Heinz Groth reached its first – and was shocked to find it occupied by Russian troops, who immediately took him prisoner. Making gestures with his hands and feet, Groth suggested to his captors that the area was occupied by a substantial German force and offered the small garrison a deal: be taken prisoner or abandon the building. A junior officer and 13 men chose the latter and fled; the remainder willingly went into captivity and would go on to serve the mountain troops as auxiliaries.

The booty in the building – which the Germans now renamed 'General Lanz House' after the commander of 1st *Gebirgs* Division – was rich: plenty of food, especially condensed milk, and mountaineering clothing and aids, including fur coats and yellow grease – 'all first-rate quality,' Josef Bauer noted. Otherwise, the hotel was a bleak structure in an even more bleak setting. 'A cutting wind continuously sweeps around the light metal walls and taps at windows, bringing the cold inside,' Bauer wrote. 'It seeps through the entire house down to the last corner.'

After a day holed up in the Elbrus House, Heinz Groth made his first attempt at the summit on 19 August, aborting the climb just an hour short of the summit due to a storm which rendered many of the troops 'almost completely blind'. Conditions were no better the next day, but Groth resolved to raise the German flag on the summit on the 21st, come what may – spurred on by a short radio message: 'The summit must be conquered, SS approaching from the north!'

Around 3am on 21 August, 21 men left the Elbrus House with rucksacks, ropes, ice picks, crampons, the *Reichskriegsflagge* and divisional standards. The weather was no more forgiving than it had been two days earlier: first thick fog, then driving snow. Nevertheless, at first the group climbed at a rate of 200 metres every hour. Conditions worsened, rather than improved. The fog grew denser, the wind became 'hurricane-like'. Once again, the mountain troops considered abandoning the climb. 'No-one wants to turn around,' wrote Gämmerler. 'So forwards!' They paused 300 metres short of the summit in a tiny hut. Its floor was covered with snow and ice, the surroundings were far from comfortable, yet it offered at least some protection from the maelstrom. A drink – condensed milk, coffee and chocolate – was quickly heated on a Primus stove before the mountain troops resumed their attempt. The storm had intensified during the hour-long rest, reducing visibility to no more than five metres. 'The storm attacks us with inordinate force,' wrote Groth. 'It hurls snow crystals into our frozen faces, stinging our foreheads and cheeks, sticking to the lenses of our goggles.' The climbers separated, stumbled around in the blizzard like blind men for at least half an hour, then were finally reunited. 'Without any visibility, merely going in the approximate direction, we tread closely behind each other, remaining so close to the next man that our eyes can see where his feet have got a foothold,' wrote Bauer. Finally, as the ridge grew less steep – the only clear sign the men were nearing the peak – Sergeant Willi Kümmerle was ordered to the front of the group. 'This is the summit, the flag will be hoisted here now,' Groth told the 29-year-old Bavarian police officer. Kümmerle was baffled. 'There was, of course, no sign of the summit far and wide, but it was probably simply too dangerous to continue,' he recalled. He rammed the *Reichskriegsflagge* into the firn, anchored it using laces and ice picks while his comrades thrust the pennants of 1st and 4th *Gebirgs* Divisions into the neighbouring fine snow. The men shook numb hands in celebration, then turned their faces into the wind and began their return to the Elbrus House.

The descent proved far grimmer than the climb. Every man was exhausted, his face encrusted with ice. One *Jäger* collapsed and had to be carried by his comrades. Gämmerler and Groth quarrelled over the best course of action while near revolt broke out in the summit party. 'There are signs of a mood of "every man for himself",' a worried Gämmerler observed. 'In bad weather a relatively easy mountain wears down even the strongest men.' But the closer they got to their mountainside refuge, the more the men recovered and morale rose. After 11 hours on the upper reaches of Europe's highest mountain, the troops – bar one who got lost and spent another night on the slope in his tent – reached the Elbrus House, from where Heinz Groth radioed a terse report to Hubert Lanz: *Mission accomplished – Reichskriegsflagge hoisted on the summit of Elbrus, 11am, August 21st. Divisional standard flies beside it. We salute our general.*[132]

Lanz responded by heaping praise upon Groth and his men:

[This accomplishment] will go down in the history of mountain warfare and Wehrmacht for all time.

Our proud 1st *Gebirgs* Division has ensured the swastika and our edelweiss have triumphed over the Soviet star on the icy peaks of the Caucasus.

We will storm down from the Caucasus passes towards the Black Sea with boundless energy and there, after 3,500 kilometres of marching, fighting and winning, we will reach the Russian border and win Germany's ultimate victory in this theatre.[133]

Quick to seize upon the success, Lanz requested his division be named in the daily communiqué emanating from Hitler's headquarters. 'My *Jäger*, who have achieved so much in Russia over the past 14 months, deserve that,' he pleaded. He made one further request – suggested by his men – that the highest mountain in Europe now bore the name 'Adolf Hitler Spitze', Adolf Hitler Peak. There is no record of the Führer's reaction to naming Elbrus in his honour – but there is to his response to Lanz's mountaineering feat. He railed at the 'crazy mountain climbers' and their 'idiotic' stunt, demanding their court martial, armaments minister Albert Speer remembered. 'For hours he raged as if his entire plan of campaign had been ruined by this bit of sport.'[134]

Barely two dozen men were involved in Operation *Elbrus*. They were away from their units no longer than a fortnight. None received either a medal or promotion for the exploit. Being allowed to take part was reward in itself. Years later Max Gämmerler looked back fondly on 'a series of experiences that could not have been more rich in content'. Nor was there a special mention for Hubert Lanz's division when Hitler's headquarters announced the feat, rather tersely, in the daily military communiqué on 25 August. 'No mountain is too high, no ravine too deep' for Germany's mountain troops, the *Völkischer Beobachter* gushed the next morning as it celebrated the conquest of the 'Mont Blanc of the Caucasus' – 'a symbolic act whose meaning extends far beyond the plain facts of the advance of German troops in the Caucasus'.[135]

The news was a surprise to most people – German troops had made much greater progress than they had suspected. The public had to wait another ten days for the first graphic accounts from Elbrus and even longer – mid-September – for film from the Caucasus. The photographs and footage of the flag raising were as good as useless. The scenes, veteran cameraman and mountaineer Hans Ertl remembered, 'could just as easily have been filmed in a steamy laundry or on the Taubenberg,' a popular hill for hikers in Bavaria. Worse, in the atrocious conditions, Germany's ensign had been planted in the wrong place, a good distance short of the summit. On 7 September, armed with colour film, Ertl 'recreated' the ascent 'in magnificent weather'. Despite never seeing the swastika raised atop Elbrus, the public were nevertheless deeply moved by the scenes filmed in the mountains: snow-covered mountain peaks and vistas of the Caucasus – all set to the rousing closing bars of Liszt's *Les Préludes*. Cinemagoers found it 'unparalleled' and 'particularly impressive'.[136]

Though fewer than the previous summer, the still-frequent bursts of Liszt's fanfare – which had trumpeted special announcements from the Eastern Front since the first days of the campaign – failed to excite the public as they once had. There were still those who followed the official communiqués, newspaper accounts and newsreels avidly. But there was also a growing proportion of the German populace which had begun to question how long the war might last.

Many doubted whether Germany could still deliver the knockout blow in 1942. Some even feared the war would run for years. Inhabitants in the west of the Reich – subjected to increasingly heavy British air attacks since March – were more concerned by 'the trials and tribulations of everyday life, food shortages, the fear of heavier enemy air raids' than news from the front. 'Even major successes only temporarily jolt them out of their indifference towards military events and provoke feelings of joy or even enthusiasm.' As one German put it succinctly: '*Wir siegen zwar, aber wir gewinnen nicht*' – 'We keep on enjoying victories, but we're not winning.'

Nevertheless, despite the relatively low number of prisoners, 'the victorious conclusion of the battle of annihilation west of Kalach has unleashed widespread joy,' the regular security service report on public morale noted in mid-August. The number of people counting on victory in 1942 suddenly rose. And there were widespread rumours that Stalin might sue for peace. Most prescient Germans looked at the maps of southern Russia printed in the newspapers and concluded that the next objective of the summer offensive would be Stalingrad.[137]

It was – and Adolf Hitler expected its capture in a matter of days, no later than 25 August. The Führer was – as his propaganda minister observed on a visit to his new headquarters in Ukraine – 'obsessed with this city' and set upon 'smashing it completely. Not one stone will rest on top of another.' Treated to an endless *tour d'horizon* – which he dutifully recorded in his diary as if it were the Sermon on the Mount – Joseph Goebbels marvelled at the scale of Hitler's ambition.

> The Führer is pursuing an enormous plan. When he's reached the Russian border in the Middle East, he'll punch through, occupy Asia Minor, take Iraq, Iran and Palestine by surprise; in doing so, he will cut England off from her last oil reserves after the loss of her sources in the Far East. When the Bolsheviks and English lose their oil, when the Bolsheviks have lost their grain fields in the Don, Donets and Kuban, when they have lost their coal region in the Don bend – coal which is suitable for coking, a prerequisite for producing steel, of course – then we'll be strangling the enemy.[138]

Iraq. Iran. Palestine. Friedrich Paulus doubted he had the forces to reach the Volga – and Sixth Army's commander certainly didn't have the troops to capture Stalingrad, as he complained to Hitler's military adjutant Rudolf Schmundt. Paulus' chief-of-staff Arthur Schmidt was just as blunt: 'The further east we advance, the weaker we become.' It wasn't that they doubted victory – there was an air of 'subdued optimism' in the upper ranks of Army Group B, Gerhard

Engel observed. But they did question whether anyone at Hitler's headquarters understood the strain of advancing to the Volga, the distances involved, the summer heat and, not least, the enemy. Too much was expected of too few troops. Walther Seydlitz, commanding one of Paulus' infantry corps, still believed both Stalingrad and Leningrad – 'the two famous cornerstones' of the Eastern Front – would soon fall. But that would not bring victory in 1942. Soviet forces were still too strong ('they've managed to scrabble so many forces together again that one would hardly think it possible after the losses of this summer'). Sixth Army would spend the winter on the Volga, then turn northwards in 1943 while German arms launched a final, decisive onslaught against Moscow. 'So much for big politics,' he told his wife. 'It's not possible to predict exactly what the immediate future will bring.' A few ordinary soldiers were also beginning to question victory in 1942. 'The day when we are victorious is drawing ever closer,' wrote 30-year-old Karl Bühler, serving with 113th Infantry Division. 'Still, we have to be a little less optimistic because from what we hear, we will not be spared a second winter of war in Russia, for better or worse.'[139]

The extra troops Friedrich Paulus pleaded for came in the form of Hermann Hoth's Fourth Panzer Army. Pulled back from thrusting into the Caucasus, Hoth was instead ordered to strike across the vast, desolate Kalmyk steppe and attack Stalingrad from the south, while Paulus' men advanced from the west, trapping the city in the jaws of two mighty armies. If the land between the Don and Volga was barren and bleak, the Kalmyk steppe was a borderland 'between desert and steppe'. There were no roads, no railway lines, few sources of water, the terrain 'barren, burned black and broken apart by the heat' which, one junior officer recorded, reached 58° Celsius one day. The sun was 'merciless,' a soldier in 21st Panzer Grenadier Regiment wrote, 'and there is no protection from it in the treeless steppe. The grass is withered and large areas are scorched by the frequent steppe fires – an eerie sight at night. Where we or the panzers are advancing, you can't get out of the yellow floury dust. Uniforms, faces, vehicles, everything is constantly covered in yellow dust, eyes are inflamed.' With minimal reference points, the troops navigated by compass. The roar of vehicles driving in low gear through the sand mixed with the rumble of caterpillar tracks. 'The landscape here is ghastly,' wrote Horst Rocholl. 'All steppe, often 40 kilometres between villages, no shade, no trees, blazing sun, when we march there's a filthy dust which penetrates everything such that often we can only see outlines just five metres away.' The few settlements seemed like oases in a desert to the advancing troops – a rare flurry of lush vegetation and trees in an otherwise barren, featureless land. The houses, frequently built of clay, and the camels roaming around – often pressed into service by the Germans to replace their exhausted horses – reminded junior officer Hubertus Schulz 'how close we are to Asia'.[140]

And yet, the men of 14th and 24th Panzer Divisions entered this wilderness full of confidence. Gert-Axel Weidemann was transfixed by the sight of his 24th Panzer Regiment on the move. 'The panzers move through the steppe, spread out, the panzer squadrons sweep from hill to hill, as far as the eye can see clouds of dust caused by advancing panzers whose tracks carve broad strips through the arid steppe grass.' An officer in 14th Panzer Division wrote in a similar vein: 'Ahead of us now is nothing but steppe, where everything is lost in glistening sunlight and a shimmering infinity. We trail huge clouds of dust behind us which cover the entire landscape and darken the heavens. Now we're coming. Now it's our turn.' One day, the vanguard of 14th Panzer Division covered more than 90 miles – 'a daily total which had never been achieved in Russia by the panzer regiment to date,' it proudly reported. It also exhausted the division's fuel reserves for 24 hours, leaving it temporarily stranded deep behind enemy lines.[141]

Equally exhausted were the ranks of 94th Infantry Division who tried – and ultimately failed – to keep pace with the panzers. Spirits were high – the men of its signals detachment called themselves 'the Rommels of the Eastern Front' and composed a marching song to sustain morale through the monotonous steppe.

And as we marched through Russia,
Filled with holy wrath,
There were some who stayed in the rear,
And there were some who were right at the front.
At the very front the signaller was in the vanguard
And the swift major who led.
The *Landser* observed it full of astonishment
And said with a deep mumble:
'Now the Rommels of the Eastern Front
Are rambling around here at the front again!'[142]

The 'swift major' was the unit's commander, Dr Franz Muth. While he admired his men for trying to keep up with the motorised troops, it was, he realised, 'bound to have some sort of effect'. By 6 August, the 'Rommels of the Eastern Front' were exhausted. 'Every day 30 to 40 kilometres of marching in the storms on the desert steppe,' he recorded. 'The sand causes eye infections as it penetrates every crack, no water during the day's marches except for salty deep wells and a few pools of foul water.'[143]

Ahead, the foremost units of 24th Panzer Division had reached high ground, from where they could survey the lower Volga valley by dusk on 21 August. As the fires in burning villages captured during the day died out, the men admired the view of Beketovka, Stalingrad's southernmost suburb, no more than ten miles to the north. In the fading light, 'shimmering like old silver' were salt lakes and beyond them, barely visible, a bend in the Volga. When darkness set in, the northern horizon flickered constantly as Stalingrad burned.[144] With any luck, German soldiers would stand on the Volga the following day.

The Red Army had other ideas. 94th Infantry Division found the road to Stalingrad blocked by a tenacious foe who 'clung to every tuft of grass in this desolate desert'. For three days, an estimated 1,500 Russians held off the attackers, despite being surrounded and pounded incessantly by Stukas and artillery. 'Without rations, cheered on by officers, they fought to the last round in the truest sense of the word. Their commander then shot himself in front of his men when the ammunition ran out,' Franz Muth wrote, impressed by a display of 'the finest soldiering'. Others tried to break out, but no more than one in five men succeeded; 1,200 Red Army troops fell into the hands of 94th Infantry Division. Even in captivity they refused to give up, attempting a breakout, their only weapons sticks and stones. 'Some' were shot, but the uprising was ended not by the gun but by a rare act of humanity: every prisoner was issued water and a hot meal.[145]

24th Panzer Division never even had the opportunity to advance. A reconnaissance aircraft sent up at first light reported 15 Soviet tanks bearing down on the division's weak vanguard. Barely was the report noted than the crash of tank guns announced that the enemy armour was within range. Panzers and tanks traded shells at close range. Columns of black smoke scarred the cloudless sky. Russian infantry attempted to storm the German positions, while Soviet artillery peppered any suspected enemy headquarters or concentrations. Stukas joined in the battle as it dragged on, pouncing on the Soviet tanks and infantry until their lust for attacking faded. The Russians had failed to drive the German armour back – but they had prevented it advancing. No German soldier would reach the Volga on 22 August.[146]

If Fourth Army could not reach Stalingrad from the south, perhaps Sixth Army might from the west. Friedrich Paulus' infantry had forged bridgeheads over the Don on the 21st. His pioneers had thrown bridges over the river by mid-day on the 22nd, allowing the armour of XIV Panzer Corps to cross. Long before dawn on 23 August, Sixth Army burst out of its bridgeheads around Kalach. Armour had rolled continually over the river since the engineers completed their pontoon bridges. Stalin's organs hammered the villages and surrounding area overlooking the crossings. The rockets arced over the Don with a howl 'like a pack of dogs', journalist Clemens Podewils remembered. 'Then the first impact, not too far way, rips through the air, the other 35 follow like hail.' The howl of the rocket launchers was soon drowned out by the rumble of aircraft engines as the Luftwaffe appeared 'in numbers never previously experienced'. The ferocity of the assault stunned Red Army troops on the Don. Soon the attackers had left the green of the Don valley behind and were once again advancing over the steppe, a great plain of earth 'hardened to stone by the summer drought' extending three dozen miles. There were occasional fields of grain, clover and sunflowers, otherwise a sea of steppe grass parched by the sun. Streams and rivers were few – and mostly dried out or reduced to a trickle. But the land was scarred by countless balkas, ravines and gullies carved in the rock, some as deep as five-storey houses, difficult to see until the vehicles were almost upon them. Some troops compared it with the landscape of the moon.[147]

Leading the charge from the Don to the Volga was 16th Panzer Division under Hans Hube. Short, stocky and missing his left arm – he lost it on the Marne in the first weeks of the Great War – Hube was popular with his men, who called him '*der Mensch*' ('The Man') or, simply, Papa Hube. He demanded the same dash and verve from them as he himself displayed. He listened to subordinates and tolerated, though would not endorse, criticism of Hitler's leadership, convinced as he was in Germany's ultimate victory. He dismissed dissenters curtly: 'The Führer will do it.' Today, he had no doubt his men would carve their names in the annals of German military history. 'This is the decisive mission facing this division in this war,' he told his men.[148]

As he conferred with his staff mid-morning, a tiny Storch reconnaissance aircraft rolled to a stop next to Hube's command vehicle. Wolfram von Richthofen – only slightly less certain of Hitler's infallibility than his own – clambered out. Arrogant, ruthless, unforgiving, the commander of Luftwaffe forces on the southern sector of the Eastern Front was frequently critical of the lack of verve shown by commanders on the ground. Now was one such moment. 'Today you're supported by 1,200 aircraft,' the Luftwaffe general told the panzer commander. 'I cannot make them available for you tomorrow. Seize the day!'[149]

Papa Hube got the message. Flanked by 3rd and 60th Motorised Infantry Divisions, his panzers made for the Volga. 'The advance was like a parade ground manoeuvre,' remembered Dr Erich Weber, accompanying a field hospital. All day long, as Wolfram von Richthofen had promised, the Luftwaffe provided a protective blanket for the advancing ground forces 'just like a sandtable exercise'. Udo von Alvensleben watched Stukas 'ominously forming in circles' before falling upon their prey, 'nipping any enemy lunges into the flanks in the bud'. German aircraft attacked anything perceived to be a threat, firing cannon equipped with armour-piercing and incendiary ammunition into vehicles, buildings, even haystacks. The steppe burned. Both sides would accuse the other of setting it ablaze – the Germans to drive the Red Army out of its positions, the Russians to halt the enemy advance. The westerly breeze certainly favoured the attackers, driving the flames inexorably across the plains. In the shimmering haze, it seemed as if the steppe burned for kilometres on end, as far as the horizon. Armoured vehicles could drive straight through, almost impervious to the fire. Infantry units were not so fortunate. 'It's extremely difficult to describe the horrific scene,' one Soviet infantryman recalled more than half a century later. 'Terrible heat, showers of sparks and dense swathes of smoke forced their way into our positions.'[150]

By the early afternoon, Hans Hube's panzers were within sight of the imposing silhouette of Stalingrad, stretching for 25 miles along the Volga: the towers of coal mine lifts, towers, chimneys. Then, at 5pm, the division sent the following electrifying signal: '1700 Hours. Volga reached. There are opportunities for crossing to form a bridgehead on the east bank.' The opportunity – if it ever existed – was short-lived. The Russians on the distant shore noticed the Germans observing them on the higher west bank – which stood perhaps 20 metres above the river. 'The enemy did not approve of our brazen observation,' Clemens Podewils noted as he scurried for cover in an abandoned Russian trench to escape flak rounds fired from the other side of the Volga. The panzers immediately turned their attention to the lively river traffic – steamers, ferries and gunboats. A monitor was driven on to a sandbank in flames; three gunboats and a barge were sunk. The Volga emptied.[151]

No German would forget his first sight of the Volga. Some men were reminded of a popular song from Franz Lehár's operetta, *The Tsarevich*: 'A soldier stands on the shores of the Volga.' Others were struck by the power of Nature. To Dr Erich Weber, the river 'stretched like a glittering ribbon through the landscape', while radio operator Joachim Porzig was stunned by the Volga's sheer size. 'I'd never seen a river as wide.' When Rudi Stigge's motorised infantry unit first caught sight of the Volga, 'there was jubilation and a joyous mood among comrades'. 16th Panzer Division's Wolfgang Werthen noticed 'pride, joy and astonishment etched on the faces of the men' as they looked down from the towering west bank of the Volga. 'Quiet and majestic, the wide, black river flowed on its way, carrying lighters downstream, and on the other side the endless Asiatic steppe stretched out.' The war had to end here, 25-year-old Austrian Karl Wintereder, in command of a bakery unit in Sixth Army, convinced himself, if only because 'there's no further we can advance, and then there's the danger that we'll burn ourselves out. If you look at the atlas, then you can hardly think of an end, because the space extends to infinity.' The more pensive German soldier, like Wintereder, was seized by a sense of unease. He looked *beyond* the Volga to unconquered Russia 'where the Russians can do whatever they want'. Panzer company commander Bernd Freytag von Loringhoven remembered: 'We stared at the vast steppe in the direction of Asia and I was overcome,' while Sixth Army officer Heinrich Meidinger asked himself: 'What are we doing here, on the Volga, a couple of thousand miles from home? What was the point of this war, why should we defend our homeland here? That's when I realised the pointlessness of this war.' Clemens Podewils was filled with a sense of foreboding. 'If I cast my gaze from the hill into the endless steppe opposite, then I feel that here begins Asia – the ultimate, shapeless gloom which still lay in store for us.'[152]

With an hour or so of daylight left, Richthofen's aviators headed off on their final sortie of the day. Kurt Ebener raced low 'over the burning steppe' to the northern suburbs of Stalingrad before banking his Me109 over the Volga to turn back to base near Kalach. 'Brimming with joy and gratitude for our comrades beneath us, we perform rolls and other aerobatics over the route of advance used by the following divisions.' Stuka pilot Herbert Pabst flew over the same terrain at dusk after supporting the panzer spearhead. 'The cornfields and steppe areas burned far and wide, and the columns rolled eastwards in enormous dust clouds – prisoners trudged towards them, heading west, in packs, without escorts. An unforgettable picture of war.'[153]

Having brought a temporary end to river traffic, Hube's panzers turned their attention to Stalingrad itself. Wheeling to the south, they entered the northern suburb of Spartakovka, where anti-aircraft gunners were defending the tractor factory and Volga ferry. In bitter fighting, three dozen flak cannons, some crewed by women – described as 'girl warriors' in contemporary Soviet reports – were knocked out.

That was as far as 16th Panzer Division would penetrate Stalingrad this first day. The panzer crews established themselves for the night, corralled with their leader at the centre. Radio operators sat in their vehicles in front of the green-illuminated dials of their humming equipment and sent reports about reaching the Volga through the night in Morse code, while motorcycle messengers constantly arrived or left with fresh orders or reports from the units. At the centre of it all, Hans Hube and his operations officer Walther Müller in the command tent poring over the latest maps and charts. With 3rd and 60th Infantry Divisions lagging far behind, the panzer men were on their own. 'We'll probably learn how risky this operation was in the coming days if the enemy recovers and does everything in his power to encircle us here in our isolated position on the bank of the Volga and cuts us off from our supplies,' Clemens Podewils observed. As he recorded the day's momentous events in his diary, Udo von Alvensleben wondered if his comrades had missed an opportunity. Prisoners brought in that evening reported panic in the city. Stalingrad, he reckoned, could have been 'easily taken if we had sufficient troops for its occupation and defence. But we are too few in numbers.'[154]

4

TOMORROW WE'LL BE DRINKING COFFEE IN CAIRO

We English have lost many battles but we'll win the last one – and with it the war.

English officer captured at Mersa Matruh

The grandly titled *Panzerarmee Afrika* did not so much march and roll into Egypt as stumble and stutter. Flak commander Josef Hissmann likened it to 'a panting pack of hounds which are hunting – but also completely exhausted'. The panzers stopped at the border to refuel. The reconnaissance units pressed on. 'An avalanche of steel and dust' moved through the night, Hissmann remembered.

> No radio, no light and rocket signals. Not easy. When you think about the weeks of uninterrupted marching and fighting behind them, the demands on commanders, drivers and the men on the front wings is hard to beat. Darkness, dust whipped up by the tracks and wheels and sporadic patches of ground fog deprives us of almost any visibility. We only see silhouettes. We are practically driving 'blind'.[1]

Drivers fixed their eyes on the night lights of the vehicle in front which 'danced like fireflies'. Motorcycles ran up and down the side of each line of vehicles to ensure no column broke up in the night. Hinrich Warrelmann drove at the head of his machine-gun battalion. Soon the noise of motor engines in the night faded and the silence of the desert enveloped his staff. Warrelmann sent his adjutant to find the rest of the battalion. He soon discovered that a driver had fallen asleep at the wheel – as had the driver of every vehicle following them. 'The tired warriors were given a pep talk and on they went.'[2]

With first light around 5am on 24 June, the land of the Pharaohs revealed itself to its latest would-be conquerors. 'It's the same, dreary desert terrain as in Marmarica,' staff officer Hellmuth Frey wrote. Flak gunner Rudolf Hubalek agreed. 'As far as the eye could see there was nothing but a stony desert plain out of which several steep rocky hills occasionally rose in the distance.' Near the coast the ground became harder, interspersed with a few clumps of lush grass, and the heat of the sun was tempered somewhat by the salty dampness in the air. Otherwise, Egypt was 'just as desolate as Libya'.[3]

Axis forces entered Egypt in June 1942 with few working tanks and exhausted men riding on a wave of high morale. '"In a few days we'll be at the Nile" is the hope luring us to victory and rest, rest, heavenly rest,' Josef Hissmann wrote. Flak officer Helmuth Köhrer brashly dismissed the Eighth Army as a spent force. 'Our only obstacles are the climate and Nature,' he recorded in his diary. 'We'll smash through anything we run into.' He borrowed a phrase from his Italian comrades-in-arms to brush aside his foe. '*Piccole pesce* – little fish – as we're accustomed to saying scornfully.' Italian soldiers were equally confident. 'Victory on our front cannot be delayed any longer, it is now a matter of weeks, perhaps days,' a junior officer in the *Ariete* Division wrote. 'Soon it will be the turn of Alexandria.' His division crossed the border with just seven working tanks of the 250 vehicles with which it had begun the offensive four weeks earlier. German divisions were similarly depleted. On the 24th, Rommel reported just 80 panzers still running. The following day he was down to around 60. 'The panzer situation grows worse by the day,' the diarist of the *Afrika Korps* recorded. By the end of 28 June, the vaunted corps was reduced to only 41 working panzers.[4] The men crewing them were in no better shape. 'We take each day as it comes,' 15th Panzer Division's Werner Bobe recorded in his diary:

> We don't know what date to write or what time it is. When the field kitchen arrives, then it's mid-day, when it comes a second time it's evening. And if we're on sentry duty, then it's night. In the morning we are woken by the sun and gigantic swarms of flies...
>
> Drivers work day and night to make sure the vehicles are ready for action. They really are good, hard-working chaps. Our repair parties – who are always with the combat units, even in battle – deserve special praise too! We often work deep into the night to keep the company ready for action. But we're utterly exhausted – we could drop on the spot and sleep, but there's always something else going on.[5]

The men marching and rolling eastwards were the same men who had been in battle constantly for a month, without rest, with few chances to wash, relax or eat a hearty meal. To Hellmuth Frey it seemed none of this mattered to Erwin Rommel. 'He yells at everybody: Forwards, even if you have to do so without fuel!'[6]

Rommel was right. However tired his men were, he was in a race against time to prevent Eighth Army regrouping. Intelligence reports confirmed it. Officials at the American Embassy in Cairo expected enemy troops in the capital 'within the next few days', although the ambassador himself, Alexander Kirk, still hoped 'the scales might be turned even now'. It was the last report Axis intelligence would intercept. The Americans finally changed their code. Henceforth, Rommel would be denied the 'good source' which had served him so well for the past six months.[7]

For now the enemy was retreating faster than Axis units could advance. 'Prisoners are still being brought in constantly,' Frey noted in his diary. 'British pride has vanished. Yesterday our division captured the staff of a Scottish regiment. The colonel and his officers were drunk. The former merely said: "I am *Herr Oberst*." That was all the German he could speak.'[8]

Britain's commander in the Middle East theatre Claude Auchinleck, who had taken charge of Eighth Army after sacking its hapless commander Neil Ritchie, attempted to steady nerves. 'The enemy is stretching to his limit and thinks we are a broken army,' he declared in an order of the day. 'He hopes to take Egypt by bluff. Show him where he gets off.' It had no impact. 'This disaster goes on and on and now it has raised a sort of impetus which takes a lot of stopping,' one junior officer wrote. 'For no good cause chaps sort of say: "Where do we retreat to next?"'[9]

The panic – it became known as 'The Flap' – was infectious. It spread behind the lines, first to Alexandria, then to Cairo, as people fled the port for the capital. Palls of smoke hung over the British headquarters as soldiers piled four bonfires with maps, papers, reports and confidential documents. Long queues formed outside banks. Packed columns headed east towards Palestine, while the wives and families of British officials and officers were advised to pack their belongings and be ready to leave the country. Fighter pilot Merton Naydler clearly noticed the behaviour of the Cairo populace towards its rulers was changing: 'Shopkeepers quickly stopped giving me the little cup of green tea every first customer of the day was entitled to, instead brazenly swapping photographs of Churchill, Roosevelt and King George VI for those of Hitler and Mussolini.' Driving out of the capital in the direction of the front, war correspondent Alan Moorehead passed 'guns of all sorts, RAF wagons, recovery vehicles, armoured cars and countless lorries crammed with exhausted and sleeping men' streaming into the

Egyptian capital. The closer Moorehead got to the front, the heavier the traffic heading in the opposite direction. 'Vehicles were pressed bonnet to tailboard, all coming back from the front, all full of desperately weary men who slept piled on one another, oblivious of the discomfort and the jolting. The traffic crawled slowly eastward, an immense lizard over 100 miles in length, a fantastically easy target for enemy aircraft. Yet no enemy machine appeared.'[10]

Axis troops were still 300 miles from the Egyptian capital when it was gripped by 'The Flap'. In the house of a road inspector in the coastal village of Sidi Barrani – where walls were still daubed with graffiti left by the Italians 18 months earlier: *Ritorneremo* ('We will return') – Ugo Cavallero, Albert Kesselring and Ettore Bastico waited for Erwin Rommel to discuss exactly how far they could – or should – advance on Cairo. The trio had conferred the previous day – and agreed to limit Rommel's plans. Whatever the directions from Rome and Berlin, all three remained sceptical of the drive to the Nile. 'Smiling Albert' was an optimist by nature, but he could see the day – not long off – when the enemy outnumbered his aviators tenfold. The deeper Axis troops were drawn into Egypt on some 'rabbit hunt', the longer their supply lines became, while the enemy's grew ever shorter. Kesselring was prepared to support an advance to El Alamein – but no further. 'I feel responsible for this judgment in the face of history.'[11]

As usual, the newly promoted field marshal was late, in a foul mood, and his uniform was dusted with fine white sand. There were no apologies, no pleasantries, just business. Rommel quickly outlined his next move: to destroy the coastal fortress of Mersa Matruh – 'a tough nut to crack,' he conceded, but when it did, its depots and stores would 'feed an army'.

'And after Mersa Matruh?' Cavallero asked.

'I will go as far I can,' Rommel snapped. 'I don't have much petrol and very little water, but in this mood of success, the soldiers don't ask about water or even food. They just want to advance.'

But advance how far? Rommel provided the answer: Alexandria, Cairo within ten days, then the Nile.

Kesselring shook his head. He guessed the ground troops were tired, their vehicles in need of an overhaul. But he *knew* his airmen and aircraft were exhausted.

Rommel stuck to his guns, hoping flattering the Italians might persuade them. 'Even the Italian soldiers under my command were magnificent,' he gushed. 'On the battlefield there was no difference between them and the Germans.'

Whether by flattery or by the strength of his argument, Rommel won the day. Cavallero and Bastico consented to a drive towards the delta.

'For now, I'll advance to El Alamein, but the real objectives are Alexandria, Cairo and the Nile. If the army is able to get through the narrows at El Alamein – and

I believe it will – we'll be in Cairo on June 30th.' Then, with the hint of a smile, he added: 'I'll be waiting there. We'll be able to talk more comfortably.'

This 'conference of marshals' lasted little more than an hour. Upon its conclusion Ugo Cavallero sent a single-word telegram to Rome: *Tiber* – the fall of Alexandria, Cairo, even the Suez Canal, was a distinct possibility.[12]

———

Exactly one month had passed since Rommel had unleashed his offensive, a month in which he had demonstrated all the traits and characteristics – good and bad – which his superiors had observed earlier in his career: desire to lead from the front, boldness bordering on recklessness, possession of an almost unparalleled grasp of the battlefield, but also his 'knee-jerk reactions' at times and especially his demands for 'a great deal of independence, which he justifies through his successes'.[13]

Erwin Rommel had not been the German Army's first choice to lead its desert adventure, but he was Hitler's, whose eye he had caught first commanding his security detail during the invasion of Poland but especially leading 7th Panzer Division from the Ardennes to the Atlantic shore in May and June 1940. He knew nothing of war in Africa – 'Can you drive a panzer on sand?' he asked intelligence officer Hans-Otto Behrendt before departing for Libya in February 1941. Behrendt, who had spent the late 1920s exploring Egypt, assured him it could. Eighteen months later, Rommel was lauded as the 'master of desert warfare'.[14]

The ordinary soldier – German *and* Italian – admired him. Rommel was a general 'who led from the front, who carried his men forward,' junior officer Meinhard Glanz recalled. 'For young men like us, he was the ideal of a military commander.' Hans von Luck, in charge of a reconnaissance unit, observed how his men 'speak only of "Rommel", not "the general". That's how popular he is among the men. He's one of them.' He was 'much loved' by Italian troops, Hans-Otto Behrendt remembered, 'because he cared more about them than anybody else in the desert'. Hellmuth Frey noticed how his allies had 'tremendous respect for Rommel. They won't hear a bad word said about him.' They referred to their German commander as *Santo Rommel* (Saint Rommel) or *Romolito* (Little Rommel). 'Rommel became a sort of myth to the Italian soldiers just as much as to the German soldiers,' junior officer Paolo Colacicchi recalled.[15]

Nevertheless, Rommel 'was not an easy man to serve,' *Afrika Korps* intelligence officer Friedrich von Mellenthin recalled – although he conceded that his master possessed 'nerves of steel' and 'spared those around him as little as he spared himself.' Staff officers bore the brunt of the field marshal's demands. 'He could not tolerate insubordinates who were not as enthusiastic and active as himself,' adjutant Heinz Werner Schmidt wrote, 'and he was merciless in his treatment of anybody who displayed lack of initiative.' He dismissed at least one general for his unwillingness to risk the lives of his men. And with his watchword of 'speed first, not safety', Rommel's impulsiveness frequently bordered on recklessness. 'He took us into situations that often threatened the survival of the entire *Afrika Korps*,' complained one company commander who was convinced Rommel 'sacrificed thousands of lives' at the altar of his personal ambition. And yet, time and again, the 'master of desert warfare' triumphed. 'That,' wrote Walther Nehring, who commanded the *Afrika Korps* through the summer of 1942, 'deserved admiration.'[16]

Admirers in the upper echelons of the German Army were few and friends fewer still. Franz Halder, the Chief of the General Staff, was appalled by Rommel's 'pathological ambition' and 'character defects which make him appear particularly unpleasant. No-one dares to openly challenge him because of his brutal methods and support he has on high.' Fellow generals found his hunger for publicity vulgar and were wary of the patronage he enjoyed of senior Nazis. Goebbels thought him 'the best leader of men in the entire Wehrmacht', wished there were more such generals and wanted to elevate Rommel to the pedestal of 'a kind of national hero', while Kesselring observed how Rommel 'exercised an almost hypnotic influence over Hitler'. And Rommel in turn fell under his leader's spell. 'If we didn't have the Führer, I don't know whether there would be another German who so brilliantly masters the art of military and political leadership in equal measure,' he gushed on the eve of the campaign in France.[17]

Rommel's exploits in the West had brought him to the attention of the German people, thanks in part to two members of Goebbels' staff serving in his division. Every opportunity for publicity was milked, even down to re-writing the popular song '*Auf der Reeperbahn nachts um halb eins*':

On the *Rommelbahn* at half past midnight
Ghosts race past at 80 kilometres an hour
Rommel himself in the lead
Everyone else has to keep up
On the *Rommelbahn* at half past midnight.[18]

As Christmas approached, Germans could buy a stylised portrait by leading propaganda artist Wolfgang Willrich to raise money for the winter relief fund. Hagiographies and pictorials appeared in flagship news magazines such as *Signal* and *Das Reich*. 'No general was as imbued with the importance of propaganda in war as Rommel,' observed Joseph Goebbels, who allowed one of his most trusted officials, Alfred-Ingemar Berndt, to serve as the general's adjutant in Africa. After Tobruk – 'Rommel's magnificent victory' – the eulogising reached new heights. He appeared in the weekly newsreels almost as frequently as his Führer. Newspapers called him *Marschall vorwärts* – Marshal Forwards, a nickname he shared with Blücher, victor of Waterloo – or else dubbed him the 'hero of Tobruk'. They celebrated the fall of the 'Verdun of the desert' and trumpeted that his blow had 'taken England's breath away'. In the summer of 1942 Erwin Rommel was arguably 'the most famous German after Hitler' – and not merely in the Reich.[19]

English newspapers which landed on the desk of Joseph Goebbels were filled with 'the greatest praise' for the desert general. 'He's as well known today in the USA as he is in London or Berlin, one of the few figures in the German Army with worldwide appeal,' the propaganda minister noted, although his fame in enemy quarters was not simply magnanimity. 'In England, you only praise your foe when you lose because it provides you with a better explanation for defeat.' Hitler told his entourage that mere mention of Rommel's presence on the battlefield was as powerful 'as several divisions'. But praise – coupled with the repeated ineptitude of their own generals – was turning Erwin Rommel into 'some sort of magician or bogeyman,' Claude Auchinleck realised. He rubbished talk of Rommel as 'superhuman', labelling his opponent 'a run-of-the-mill German general' instead. He ordered his men to refer to 'the Germans', 'Axis Forces' or 'the enemy', 'rather than going on and on about Rommel', adding unconvincingly: 'PS I am *not* jealous of Rommel.' Yet officers and men alike complained that 'Rommel seems to be a better general.' Soldier Douglas Walter remembered senior officers repeatedly telling the men, 'he is *not* invincible. But we didn't believe them.' Even Winston Churchill was becoming obsessed with his foe in North Africa. 'Rommel, Rommel, Rommel, Rommel,' he muttered. 'What else matters but beating him?'[20]

For now, Allied troops would settle for merely halting Rommel. Perhaps the coastal fortress of Mersa Matruh – 160 miles from Alexandria – was the place to make a stand. In peacetime, it had been the favoured beach resort of Egyptian high society. In war, it had become a key British base, protected by more than 200,000 mines in fields more than five miles deep to the east, and eight to the west, marked with menacing metal signs: 'Mines – Keep out'. There were extensive barbed-wire barriers and anti-tank trenches, although the latter had been allowed to silt up in places. Concrete blocks barred the way down most roads leading into the town, or else the path was blocked by iron girders chained firmly into the ground, while bunkers protected by walls of sandbags and sprouting guns and machine-guns peppered the town. The battered Eighth Army had managed to make good some of its losses – a division of New Zealanders had been transferred from Syria, while tanks had been hurriedly dispatched to bolster the front… only to be committed far to the south of the port. Once again, the British expected a direct assault on the fortress from the south or west. Once again, Erwin Rommel fell back on tactics which had served him well at Gazala and Tobruk: he would surround his enemy, then attack them from the rear. 'Up to now, that's always worked,' Hellmuth Frey noted. 'It will work too at Matruh.'

It did. Late on the afternoon of 28 June, the infantry of 90th Light Division began their assault on Mersa Matruh under a hail of artillery shells from the British guns. The sky was filled with palls of black smoke from the fuel dumps to the east of the fortress, set ablaze by the defenders. For the first 30 minutes, the 90th Light struggled to make headway. But then the German artillery belatedly cleared its throats. The British guns fell silent. The 90th Light made ground rapidly – an advance of more than two miles in just two hours. As night fell, British resistance stiffened. The staff of one makeshift German unit was cut off in the darkness. Its men found themselves fending off the enemy in hand-to-hand combat 'with pistols in hand'.[21]

Night was the signal for Mersa's garrison to break out. Despite the moonlight and the glow of fire bringing light to the desert night, the British tried to slip out of the fortress in groups small and large. Most of the vehicles were shot up. Some were set ablaze by their crews – with the corpses of their comrades still inside – as they tried to escape on foot. Abandoning the vehicles was to little avail. Silhouetted against the fires, the besieged were quickly rounded up by the besiegers. Even when dense fog descended in the small hours, the Indian troops trying to slip through the German cordon were cut down – although in the swirling mist, the fighting became particularly confused at times.[22]

Come daybreak, near-silence ruled in Mersa Matruh. Only the occasional shot was fired, while 'a thick curtain of black smoke hung over the town'. By mid-morning Italian light infantry had entered the main square and seized 6,000 prisoners, including one defiant officer who told his captors: 'We English have lost many battles but we'll win the last one – and with it the war.' A column of British trucks – loaded with and driven by captured South Africans – headed west out of the town, guarded only by a couple of Germans armed with machine-guns in the first and last vehicles. Rommel wished they had been New Zealanders, but the bulk of the Dominion's 2nd Division had slipped through his encircling ring. 'I would rather have seen this division – one of the elite units in the British Army – in our prison camps than facing us again,' he rued.

The Union Flag still flew defiantly in front of the former British headquarters. A nimble Italian soldier 'climbed the pole like a squirrel' and ripped it down, while a comrade handed him the Italian standard in its place. As the Mediterranean breeze caught the tricolore for the first time, a guard presented arms. Their comrades in the *Ariete* found enough guns, food, fuel and all manner of kit, to equip an entire division, and enough whisky to serve the tank men through the summer.[23]

But otherwise, the booty was 'pretty pathetic compared with what was captured at Tobruk,' a disappointed Hellmuth Frey noted. Shells continuously 'cooked off' in ammunition dumps set ablaze by the British, who had also sabotaged most of their trucks and torched their food warehouses. 'Thousands upon thousands of tinned cans lie in smoking and burning black piles,' Frey wrote. His men were only able to save a few pallets – mostly tinned fruit, bananas especially.[24]

Matruh's new occupiers found a couple of signs at the cinema. 'Today for the last time: *The Exodus*, with General Ritchie'; and 'Desert sweepstakes: Rommel 100:8, Ritchie 2:3'. Elsewhere, German graffiti artists had been at work. The name of 'Smuts Way' had been crossed out and chalk scrawled above it: 'Rommelstrasse', while 'Wavell Way' became 'Rommel Weg'.[25]

With Mersa Matruh, 'the last fortress and port on the coast of western Egypt had fallen,' Rommel noted.[26] His men were given just four hours to enjoy their latest prize. They longed to halt, if only briefly, take a dip in the Mediterranean and catch up on sleep after five weeks on the move. But in the late afternoon of 29 June, they were moving east again. 'With the order to move, it was back to the east!' an excited Lieutenant Manilo Leone recorded. 'Mersa Matruh has been smashed like a pomegranate, off to the Nile Delta!' He continued:

> As far as the eye can see the interminable column of the Italo-German Armoured Army. To the right of the road, above ground, on trestles, is the pipeline which carries water from the Nile Delta to Mersa Matruh. Every now and then, tall spouts can be seen gushing out of it, far away: for a sip, to freshen the face, to fill a canteen; a few bayonet blows to the pipe, and who cares if tonnes of rare, precious water are lost.[27]

As the vehicles raced along the coastal highway, the men could see columns of fire rising on the horizon and, as they drew closer, they could hear the sound of explosions as the British blew up their ammunition and fuel dumps at El Daba, an airfield 100 miles from Alexandria. The goal – for now – was the small railway halt of El Alamein where the enemy was expected to make a final stand before the ancient heart of Egypt.[28]

That same evening, 350 miles to the west, two three-engined SM81 Italian bombers banked over Derna airfield in the quickening gloom of the Cyrenaican dusk. At the controls of the first, Benito Mussolini, dressed in his finest colonial uniform – a Saharan khaki adorned with all the finery of the First Marshal of the Empire (a title only he and the king enjoyed). Assisted by his personal pilot Angelo Tondi, the Duce set his bomber down safely. But the second SM81 collided with an Italian bomber returning from a sortie. Three of the Duce's bodyguards, plus his cook and barber, were killed. It was a tragic beginning to a frustrating visit.

Mussolini came to Africa expecting imminent victory. He imagined himself riding on his white charger – safely ferried across the Mediterranean – through the streets of Cairo, carrying the Sword of Islam which had been presented to him in Tripoli five years earlier when he'd been hailed as a protector of the Muslim cause. Two hundred barrels of boot polish were on hand so his soldiers could march smartly in passo *Romano* – the Italian goose step – behind him. The ordinary Egyptian would cry '*Avanti Rommel*' – Rommel advance – and welcome the Axis troops as liberators. In time, Italian soldiers would march back into Ethiopia – seized by the British in 1941 – where local leaders were supposedly waiting for them with open arms. For now, however, the Duce settled into his quarters, a cottage on top of a hill in the small town of Berta, and began 'a useless wait for the advance'.[29]

At that very moment, a personal visit from Mussolini may have been just what his men needed to carry them forwards. The troops were at the end of their strength, vehicles barely serviceable, nerves strained. Orders and reports continued to talk of corps, divisions, regiments, battalions. It would have been more accurate, Rommel's Italian liaison officer Giussepe Mancinelli believed, to think in terms of numbers. There were three times as many panzers in the repair shops as there were in the front line as June ended, while Italian XX Corps was reduced to barely 2,000 men and little more than a dozen working tanks. When it was unnerved by a surprise attack in its rear by a British brigade desperately trying to break through to Eighth Army's lines, Rommel snapped: 'Trust your Corps will now find itself able to cope with so contemptible an enemy.' The Italians regrouped and resumed their push eastwards. Moving along the Alexandria–Mersa Matruh highway, *Bersaglieri* – elite light infantry – of the *Trieste* Division reached the 111-kilometre post. 'In everyone's eyes the mirage of Alexandria begins to flash,' one *Bersaglieri* wrote. It would prove to be the high-water mark of the Axis advance.[30]

The milestone – today long gone – stood somewhere near El Alamein, a nondescript village on the coastal highway and railway line, 60 miles west of

Alexandria. Beyond the sparsely inhabited coastal strip there was no longer an endless expanse of desert, but hills, ridges, rocky outcrops stretching no more than three dozen miles to the south where they gave way to the Qattara Depression. Vast – twice the size of the Lebanon – its salt lakes, cliffs and powdery sand made it unsuitable for armoured warfare. At Alamein, unlike Gazala, Tobruk and Mersa Matruh, there was no hope of outflanking the enemy. To reach Alexandria, Cairo, the Nile and beyond, Erwin Rommel would have to bludgeon his way through Allied lines.

He began at dawn on the first day of July. 'Drive with your men to Alexandria,' Rommel told Georg Briel, commander of a makeshift group drawn from 90th Light Division, as it moved out. 'The Tommies will have gone anyway. Tomorrow we'll be drinking coffee in Cairo.' Instead, the 90th drove into a sandstorm, stumbling headlong into a series of strongpoints where men came under heavy machine-gun fire. For the first time during the summer campaign, the German soldier cracked. There was panic in the division's ranks. The rear columns turned first, followed by some front-line units as British shells crashed down. It took the intervention of the division's commander, Ulrich Kleemann, to restore order.[31]

When Rommel headed up to the front line late in the afternoon, however, the battle seemed to be going his way. A strongpoint had fallen, 2,000 Indians had been taken prisoner, 30 guns had been captured or destroyed. The moment had come to force the issue: the field marshal threw what reserves he had into battle, leading the attack in person. A commander in the *Littorio* Division, attacking on 90th Light's flank, was sceptical of his orders. '*Littorio* has fuel for only 20 kilometres,' he scribbled on a signal. 'To Alexandria is 150 kilometres!'[32] He need not have fretted. The attack ran into trouble almost immediately. 'British shells howled towards us from the north, south and east,' Rommel recalled.

> Flak tracer whizzed through the unit. The attack ground to a halt under very heavy fire. We immediately scattered the vehicles and took cover. Shell after shell came crashing down nearby. For two hours Bayerlein [*Afrika Korps*' chief-of-staff] and I lay there in open ground. To cap it all, a large formation of British bombers but it was forced to turn around by fighters escorting our Stukas.

Only as the sun went down and the enemy fire slackened off did Rommel feel it safe to withdraw 'as quickly as possible'.[33]

As night fell, the repair units moved up to the front to fix vehicles which had broken down or been damaged during the day's fighting. In the pale light of the moon mechanics inspected engines, fixed carburettors, replaced caterpillar chains, repaired cannons and machine-guns. The sound of hammer against metal filled the desert night – drowning out the curses of the engineers as they toiled in the cold. Kurt Wolff watched long supply columns moving up the coastal road towards the front. 'When English bombers roar towards them, they veer off to the side into the desert, but then continue their journey at 40 or 50 kilometres an hour: water, fuel, supplies of ammunition,' he wrote. 'Everything is moving. Forwards. And the darkest night is no different from the hottest, brightest day.'[34]

It was morale carrying the exhausted Italians forward now – and little else, driver Vittorio Vallicella realised. 'Every division is in a bad state – many are ghosts divisions,' he wrote.

> The will to get out of this terrible desert gives us the strength to resist everything. We are, you could say, at the gates of Alexandria and very close to the Pyramids.
>
> Our spies report that there's chaos in Cairo and Alexandria, all the European citizens are packing their bags and the Arabs are looting the stores. Such reports give us hope, but we're still filled with trepidation. What will tomorrow's battle bring? Let's hope for the best!

In the evening rations were handed out for the coming day. The order passed down the line: no smoking, no light escaping from field positions. 'With the onset of darkness,' wrote Vallicella, 'there's a feeling of foreboding of a thousand dangers.'[35]

The night of 1–2 July was among the worst many Axis soldiers could remember in North Africa. The battlefield was lit by flares dangling beneath parachutes. Italian troops tried to shoot them out of the sky – without success. Any movement was targeted by British artillery. Lieutenant Gerardo Salinardi's column of motorised infantry was caught in the open. The men scrambled out of their trucks and into improvised foxholes as the British gunners found their range. Cries for help filled the night. Ammunition in burning trucks 'cooked off'. Salinardi moved among the casualties, dressing minor wounds, leaving the men fresh bandages. 'A sergeant with no legs begs for help from a soldier holding his head: there's nothing more that can be done for him.' The bombardment continued until shortly before dawn, when the horrors of the night were gradually revealed. The legless sergeant was still alive – and still in agony. Salinardi was shaken by this 'night of horror and terror'.[36]

Nearby, British troops had broken through 21st Panzer Division's southern flank during the night, forcing 5th Panzer Regiment to be committed as a last resort. With the early morning mist still clinging to the featureless terrain, the armour overran the positions of the vaunted New Zealanders who had escaped Rommel's clutches a few days earlier. Panzer against truck. Anti-tank gun against anti-tank gun. And finally, tank against panzer, as the feared Grants joined battle. The shock of the first encounter with the American-built armour of late May had passed – 5th Panzer took the fight to the enemy.

> What happened next was like a mirage [Kurt Wolff wrote]. While one company continued forwards and several attacked the Grants about 1,500 metres away on our left, the rest of the unit drove into the English positions. And where before there had just been several guns, anti-tank guns and trucks, now ten, then fifty, then 100 and finally 600 yellow and brown Tommies appeared from invisible foxholes, waved at us, half of them greeting us, half of them defending themselves. Some pointedly threw their weapons away, others approached us walking arm-in-arm in rows, the entire New Zealand force surrendered to us when we were already right in their midst.

The regiment pushed on to the Ruweisat Ridge – a barren lump of limestone rising some 200 feet above the desert – where it ran into 60 British tanks moving along a hollow. In the resulting firefight, Wolff claims every panzer knocked out at least two or three enemy vehicles, some scored as many as seven kills, for the cost of just two dead. The bulk of the enemy force, Wolff wrote, 'had been destroyed, set on fire, the rest of the tanks which escaped ended up exploding in a minefield, through which they'd probably tentatively driven at dawn courtesy of a narrow passage, now proved to be their undoing'. The armour of 5th Panzer Regiment drove across the battlefield, 'almost shocked by our victory', Wolff wrote, and back to the positions it had occupied in the morning. 'It was as if the morning hadn't happened: the Grants which had first occupied our rear had been driven away by anti-tank guns and a howitzer battery. Sweat streamed down our filthy, unwashed faces, but it ran deservedly after a great deal of work.'

Kurt Wolff's at times breathless account suggests 2 July was a day of triumph for 21st Panzer Division. It wasn't. The radio reports the division sent to *Afrika Korps* tell of a day of confused fighting, of large numbers of British tanks and, ultimately, of 'very little progress'. The division advanced barely two miles that Thursday. More accurate is the melancholy entry Wolff made in his diary at the end of the day.

> And tomorrow will be another day, hot, muggy. We don't know how we bear it. One hundred thousand flies crawl around our faces, we lost our mosquito nets a long time ago – who knows where. All we have left is our patience. The armour plate becomes glowing hot, the water is almost undrinkable. When sandstorms stir at around mid-day, yellow, impenetrable, all that's left is hope...

Now it's night again and we're standing guard. Tired, unwashed, covered in oil, wet from the nightly dew in the desert. We stand guard for Germany in the middle of the starry African night.[37]

In fact, 2 July had been a terrible day of battle for the Axis forces. 15th Panzer found itself almost encircled by British armour – it counted at least 100 enemy tanks in front of it at times. As the day progressed, a flurry of curt, but frantic, reports were flashed to *Afrika Korps*. 'Panzer spearhead engaged in a defensive action against a semi-circle of tanks enveloping it.' 'Tanks pressing us hard.' 'Defending ourselves desperately.'[38]

As for the sorely tested 90th Light, it had regained its composure after the panic of 1 July. But at the end of the day's fighting, its commander Ulrich Kleemann realised what Erwin Rommel had not yet grasped: the Axis offensive had finally run out of steam. That evening he recorded in his diary:

It seems as if the German units, exhausted by the fighting and exertions – marching by day and night – in the past few days and weeks, are no longer able to force this last English fortress before the Nile delta. The enemy has committed all his available aircraft against our attacking army. Every 20 to 30 minutes, 15, 18, often even 21 bombers with fighter escort attack. Although the physical effect of these heavy, constant bombing raids and low-level attacks is negligible given the wide dispersal of fighting and baggage units, the effect on the troop's morale is much greater. Each man longs for German fighter cover but he also knows that the German air force in Africa cannot move forward so rapidly. When German fighters appear, they are cheered on by the troops – even when they're on their own – but they are unable, of course, to attack such strong bomber formations. The last hopes now are the little-used – and hence fresh – Italian divisions. But little is expected from our comrades.[39]

As the sun went down, Vittorio Vallicella ate a meal of dry pasta, Emmental cheese and bread, accompanied by a quart of wine, reflecting on being 'stuck in this vast, desolate plain at El Alamein, exhausted, dejected, hungry, with little water and covered in lice and dirt. We know that our great leader is in the Barge area – 410 miles from the front – furious because we've not yet been able to open the gates of Alexandria for him.'

Thankfully for the exhausted Vallicella, it was a quiet night. 'No flares, no aircraft. We sleep soundly. For our exhausted bodies, this is a blessing.'[40]

Perhaps encouraged by an intercepted radio message – 'Hold on at all costs – reinforcements are on their way from Alexandria' – which suggested his foe was close to breaking point, Rommel ordered one last effort to smash through the enemy's line. 'The attack shall continue whatever happens with everything you've got – and it will be successfully executed.'[41]

Rommel could exhort all he liked. His divisions made no headway. Worn out, facing superior numbers, they stumbled, faltered and finally caved in. Having been plastered by artillery all day long, late in the afternoon the Italians were subjected to an attack by four-engined Allied bombers: 54 B-24 Liberators, escorted by P-40 fighters, 'glittering in the sun like insects in an evening dance'. For the first time, Rommel's forces experienced carpet bombing. Manilo Leone and comrades with Italy's elite assault engineers, the *Guastatori*, 'thrust their elbows and knees into the ground, lifted their stomachs to save their insides from dangerous injury, held their mouths open, their hands cupped to protect their ears. 4th Company was hit by the full force of the explosions, men were sucked into the air, into clouds of sand, losing one dead and two wounded.'[42]

The final straw was a determined attack by the New Zealanders on the southern end of the Axis front. The position of Lieutenant Alberto Coglitore's company of *Bersaglieri* was soon desperate. 'We are lost; we can no longer fight,' he wrote. 'There is no more ammunition, the weapons are destroyed or jammed.' When the battalion on his left flank was overrun and New Zealanders began attacking his lines, Coglitore ordered his men to fall back. He grabbed hold of a passing truck, hanging off its door, his feet on the running board.

> With every metre we cover, we gain a little more hope… I watch the driver, leaning forward, his eyes wide open and hands nervously clutching the steering wheel, pushing the vehicle to its top speed, crossing the only track leading out of this cursed trap for more than a kilometre… Tense faces, stunned by the explosions and gunshots, still in disbelief at what had just happened, we meet up at the regimental command post, where we report on the vicissitudes of the battalion.[43]

The *Ariete*, Hellmuth Frey complained, 'headed for home at full speed'. It lost 350 men – 'a dirty, greasy, unkempt mob without fighting spirit' was captured by the New Zealanders – as well as a sizeable number of trucks and guns. For the first time there were grumblings in the *Ariete*'s ranks. 'Perhaps the favourable moment has passed!' someone said. It took a counter-blow by 15th Panzer Division to restore some semblance of order, but at the cost of more than 100 men.[44]

Rommel was furious with the *Ariete* for offering what he called 'little more than token resistance' before surrendering to 'insignificant enemy armoured forces'. But he also realised that having battered against the 'Alamein position', as he called it, unsuccessfully for three days, there was no point attacking for a fourth. With his divisions down to barely 1,500 men, supplies strained to the limit, and the enemy offering dogged resistance, his forces needed time to rest, recuperate, regroup. Half an hour before midnight on Friday 3 July, he reported to his masters that he had called off his offensive into the heart of Egypt.[45]

Orders passed along German and Italian lines: dig in. 'Every soldier from the division commander down to the lowliest *Landser* realised that the assault which had begun so confidently on May 26th had come to a halt for the time being,' wrote reconnaissance unit commander Hellmuth Schroetter.[46]

As German and Italian soldiers dug in, newspaper readers across the Reich learned that Rommel had 'broken through' the Alamein position in a 'brilliant feat of arms by German and Italian troops'. The next morning the *Völkischer Beobachter*, promised the end of 'a 60-year tyranny' was at hand in Egypt. Other headlines talked of 'Marshal Rommel's advance to the heart of Egypt' or reported 'Alexandria naval base evacuated by the British'. 'Spoiled by Rommel's previous victories' and with enemy defences on the road to Alexandria described as 'hardly to be taken seriously', many Germans expected the fall of Alexandria 'over the weekend'.[47] Yet again the German propaganda machine had gone too far. Hellmuth Frey wrote:

> If those people at home who pin little flags on a map and who are already picturing Rommel continuing his advance on the Suez Canal or to India knew that our rifle company numbers barely 30 or 40 men, that our panzers and artillery possess only a fraction of their authorised strength, then they would change the speed of our advance from fourth gear to second. Our men have not had one day of rest since 26 May. Always fighting! Forward march! The men are now at the end of their strength.[48]

The previous autumn the Propaganda Ministry had proclaimed the war in Russia 'decided'. In the heady days of late June and early July 1942 it tantalised the German public with dreams of Alexandria, Cairo and the Nile. And now, as Joseph Goebbels realised, 'the people have far-reaching expectations from the African campaign which cannot be realised at present'. There was a 'certain degree of surprise – and fear' – among the public that the enemy had halted Rommel's advance but also widespread confidence that he would resume. After all, 'Rommel's triumphant march is generally considered to be unstoppable.'[49]

Although the front line was gradually solidifying at Alamein, intelligence reaching Rome and Berlin continued to suggest the entire edifice of British rule in Egypt was tottering. Cairo was 'under a state of siege' with martial law proclaimed, British soldiers patrolling the streets while Egyptian troops were confined to barracks. An intercepted telephone conversation from an American reporter told of 'a total collapse of order' in the Egyptian capital, of people who'd 'lost faith in victory'. British officials had abandoned the capital, but not King Farouk who had reportedly declared that his place was in Egypt, 'close to his people' apparently 'eagerly awaiting' the arrival of Axis troops – as were his subjects.[50] From Berlin, The Voice of Free Arabism addressed these *fellaheen* – peasants – calling on them to hamper Eighth Army's retreat by cutting telephone lines, attacking columns, blowing up railway lines or bridges. 'Into action. Into action.' Thousands of posters and leaflets were printed, while every hour appeals were broadcast in Arabic to stoke the flames of seemingly imminent revolution, under the watchword: 'Egypt for the Egyptians.' 'The British have always laughed at the Egyptians and now is the time to prove to the world that Egypt is alive. Prove that the Egyptian blood is running in your veins and fight for your country.' 'Egyptians, your moment has come! Free yourselves from English tyranny! We guarantee…' The native populace was encouraged to welcome Rommel – 'the Lion of the Sand' – into their hearts 'as the harbinger of a new era and the friend of the Egyptian people!… Rommel comes as liberator from the English yoke.' 'The British have always laughed at the Egyptians and now is the time to prove to the world that Egypt is alive. Prove that the Egyptian blood is running in your veins and fight for your country.'[51]

Whatever the promises, Egypt would be no more independent under Axis rule than it was under British. Hitler showed little interest in the country – he was more than happy for his ally to be a modern-day pharaoh,[52] leaving Rommel as military commander in this addition to the new Roman Empire, in charge of a force capable of repulsing every effort the British might make to re-take Egypt. The German Navy sent officers to Rommel's headquarters to form a flotilla of dhows to patrol the Nile. A director of the Reichsbank arrived to take over the Bank of Egypt. More ominously, a middle-ranking SS officer appeared ready to 'monitor' Egypt's Jews – especially the large populace in Alexandria. In fact, Walther Rauff was the vanguard of a killing squad – *Einsatzkommando* – mirroring similar groups which had murdered hundreds of thousands of Jews in occupied Russia. The two dozen men assigned to Rauff were too few to deal with more than 60,000 Jews on their own. As in Ukraine and the Baltic, the Germans turned to the indigenous population to help them. 'Rise as one man to kill the Jews before they have a chance of betraying the Egyptian people,' Berlin radio urged the country's Arabs. 'It is the duty of the Egyptians to annihilate the Jews and to destroy their property.' Jews were planning to rape Egyptian women, the broadcast continued, kill Egyptian children and finally Egyptian fathers. 'Kill the Jews, burn their property, destroy their stores, annihilate these base supporters of British imperialism,' the appeal from Berlin ended. 'Your sole hope of salvation lies in annihilating the Jews before they annihilate you.'[53]

The advance to – and failure to break through at – Alamein left *Panzerarmee Afrika* in a pitiful state. The *Afrika Korps* was down to 50 panzers and 600 motorised infantrymen. Divisions were no longer worthy of the name: the 90th Light could muster just 1,500 men. Italian units were just as depleted: barely 50 working tanks and a little over 4,000 troops. Until the gaps were filled, the best Rommel could hope for was to improve his position at Alamein. But even these localised attacks miscarried. On the 13th, Stukas smashed British strongpoints and silenced their guns, only for the subsequent attack by 21st Panzer Division to drive headlong into a sandstorm and eventually falter, prompting Rommel to complain that a 'unique opportunity has gone begging'. A plan to strike two days later was forestalled by a large-scale British attack which rattled several Italian units and unnerved Rommel. Allied aircraft ruled the skies – Rommel's command post was attacked nine times on 16 July alone – while their infantry and armour mauled Italian units in particular. Cut off from the rest of the *Pavia* Division by British armour, Sergeant Major Mario Venieri's understrength company – it had never recovered from the beating it suffered at Bir Hakeim six weeks earlier – fought to the last man when infantry followed in the tanks' wake. Venieri jumped out of his foxhole, seized a machine-gun and opened fire on the advancing enemy. 'It is a matter of life or death; kill or be killed: that is the law of war!' The infantry assault faltered, but as the British fell back Venieri's eye was caught by a group of Axis artillerymen walking towards enemy lines with white handkerchiefs tied to the top of their rifles. The incensed sergeant major yelled at them: 'Come back, you cowards, traitors!' The *Trieste*, *Trento* and *Brescia* Divisions also suffered badly, but none as much as the *Sabratha*. 'You think we're poor soldiers, don't you?' one officer from the *Brescia* told his captors. 'Well, you should see the *Sabratha*.' Raised from Italian settlers in North Africa principally to defend Libyan soil, the division was scorned by other Italian units and dismissed by Rommel as 'shitty'.[54]

Under attack in July 1942, it melted away. After ten days of fighting, it simply ceased to exist. At least 1,600 men were taken prisoner by the New Zealanders. Despite the slurs of their comrades and Rommel, many stood their ground. 'There was also a very large number of dead, more dead Italians than on any other battlefield that I have seen,' brigade commander Howard Kippenberger recalled, 'and many Germans, as the German gunners mostly fought to the death.'[55]

The British attack was only brought to a standstill on the 17th after Rommel threw in his last reserves. 'It can't go on much longer like this,' he conceded to his wife, 'otherwise the front will collapse. From the military viewpoint, these are the worst days of my life. You know that I'm an incurable optimist. But there are situations when things look completely bleak.'[56] A few hours later the field marshal conferred with his superiors. To Ettore Bastico, Rommel was a broken man. His eyes filled with rancour, he was unable to look anyone in the eye. 'I can't wait a week longer for the supplies you promised me,' he told them. 'If the enemy attacks, he'll break through. If he breaks through, it's the end...'[57]

As usual, he blamed the failings of his allies – a standard German tactic which would be repeated later in the year when the front around Stalingrad was shattered. He claimed – incorrectly – that four Italian divisions had been all but wiped out, that some Italian troops had abandoned their trenches or foxholes under the British barrage, while others were captured in their sleep, or fell into the enemy's hands because there were too few trucks to transport them to the rear.[58]

Rommel reserved even harsher criticism of his ally for German ears only. The diary of his interpreter, Wilfried Armbruster, is peppered with references to the 'shitty Italians' in July 1942. 'The Italians deserve a damned good thrashing,' Rommel fumed after one battalion surrendered en masse. 'You might as well line up this nation of shits against a wall and shoot them.'[59]

In his memoirs, Rommel described the everyday Italian soldier as 'willing, selfless, a good comrade who had given more than could be expected of him given the circumstances,' let down by a 'worthless' officer corps.[60] Too many commanders failed to form a bond with their men. They lived apart, ate apart and all too often failed to carry their men forward in battle. Collectively, however, their failings were even greater. Time and again, Rommel wrote, the Italian leadership failed its troops in North Africa. There was no popular support for the war in Italy – and too little appetite for it among the country's political and military leaders. They failed to train the men they sent across the Mediterranean adequately. But above all they failed to equip them. 'For this reason alone, they could not stand firm without German support.'[61]

Some German soldiers dismissed their ally out of hand. 'The Italians have no sense of honour,' one complained. 'They'll sell their honour for five slabs of chocolate and then eat it up. They are only good warriors on the radio.' Another grumbled: 'Here in Africa we've been more hindered than helped by our allies.' And Ludwig Crüwell, *Afrika Korps*' commander before he was captured during the Gazala battles, had sneered to Hitler: 'Three of them are not worth one German.' Others viewed the Italians as fair-weather allies. Rommel branded them 'useless except for defence – and even then they're useless if the British infantry attacks with fixed bayonets'. One incredulous junior officer observed an Italian corporal during a British attack. He simply yelled: '*Inglesi!*' and threw away his rifle. A flak officer was impressed by the sight of motorised Italian infantry riding into battle in trucks, the men repeatedly shouting in unison: '*Avanti – avanti! Noi sono in Guerra – noi vuolo combattere – noi vuolo vincere!*' – Forwards, forwards! We're at war. We want to fight. We want to win! 'But that lasted only as long as they were advancing,' he observed. 'When they really did have to fight and the fortunes of war were against them, their morale sagged dramatically.'[62]

German attitudes towards their enemy – almost always referred to as English, rather than British – swung between admiration and hatred. Memoirs and interrogations of *Afrika Korps* veterans are littered with references to a 'decent' foe, of fighting 'a gentleman'. Fighter pilot Armin Köhler talked with downed enemy aircrew – 'all splendid guys with whom you cannot get angry. Too bad that we have to wage war against the English,' he mused. But others despised their Anglo-Saxon foe. 'There is one race that I really detest and that is the Jewish – but the English are not far behind,' one major fumed. 'I could strangle any Englishman in cold blood, here and now.' Panzer driver Horst Sonnenkalb felt he was fighting 'against nearly half the world: Australians, New Zealanders, South Africans, Indians, Canadians, French, Poles, Greek, Englishmen, but also Spaniards, Portuguese, warriors from the Balkans, Russians, Sudanese, Algerians, Iraqis, Lebanese, Moroccans, Czechs, Jews, Scots and Americans.'[63]

Bernhard Ramcke, in charge of a newly arrived brigade of paratroopers, told his men they had two enemies: the climate and the British. 'There's no need to fear the latter,' he insisted. 'We will defeat them where we encounter them – to be more accurate we will annihilate them, whether we are attacking or defending. We feel thoroughly superior to any enemy thanks to our better fighting spirit, our better equipment and training.'[64] Ramcke's judgment of his foe was commonly held. The British were not masters of war, Hellmuth Frey observed, but they were masters of organisation.

Fuel and food dumps are established at regular distances. Signposts several miles apart point the way to them. The food stores are arranged in an exemplary fashion like a wholesale grocer's. Barbed wire offers protection against theft. Everything inside the store is partitioned. Precious commodities like tinned fruit, chocolate, cigarettes, are locked behind bars. Our commissariat department can learn from this. The English are masters of labelling things. There are signs all over the coastal road: 'Are you ready if an attack is carried out?' Or: 'Kill flies but not your engine!' And: 'Caution! Mines!' At the end of the mine barrage: 'You got through this time, but continue to watch out!' The railway is also well constructed. Standard gauge.

The coastal road is excellent. And yet despite this incredibly good organisation, the combat troops rarely received their goods. The English merchants worked well, the soldiers failed. In that final kilometre the courage to break through failed them.[65]

They would demonstrate as much on 22 July.

Before dawn, a ferocious barrage crashed down on the Axis lines. With a thick smokescreen obliterating the battlefield, the British made rapid progress, their armour especially. In places they punched a hole four miles deep in Rommel's positions, even reaching the rear columns. The field marshal ordered every unit to stand and fight 'to the last round, even if surrounded'.[66] Nineteen-year-old Günter Halm was among those who stood firm. His Russian anti-tank gun – nicknamed the 'crash-boom' for the noise it made – claimed nine enemy tanks this day. His deeds would earn him the Knight's Cross and admiration across the Reich, but in the aftermath of the battle, the teenager struggled to comprehend the sights in front of him.

An Englishman got out of the tank which had been knocked out by the second gun and was lying in the sand, badly wounded. Two comrades went to help him, but it was too late for any help. The Englishman asked for a revolver. When he was alone once more, he shot himself in the head. That was war, cruel and remorseless, but the fate of this enemy deeply affected us.

The battlefield was littered with burned-out and abandoned Matilda and Valentine tanks. The British had fought with particular ferocity – nine rounds passed through the shield of Halm's gun, its telescopic sight lay somewhere in the sand, and the desert floor was strewn with empty shell cases as well as unused rounds waiting to be fired. Halm's gunloader had been wounded in the leg and died on the way to the field hospital, while another exhausted comrade was sent to the rear; he died of diphtheria a few days later. 'When death so quickly surrounds you, you sometimes think what will happen to you, when will it be your turn, will the endless expanse of the desert once again spare you?' Halm recalled seven decades later.[67]

In all, nearly 150 British tanks and armoured vehicles were destroyed, while more than 1,000 troops fell into German hands. German losses, on the other hand, were 'insignificant', prompting a congratulatory message from Rommel: 'I know the same treatment will be meted out to every fresh attempt by the enemy to attack.'[68]

In fact, the fighting of 22 July had severely shaken Erwin Rommel. *Panzerarmee Afrika* could not withstand another day of battle like it. The next

British attack might 'cut the army in two', leading to the destruction of the entire force if he chose to stand and fight – or he could try to save the bulk of the troops by retreating as far as the Libyan border. Now it was the Italians who steeled Rommel, not the other way around. The situation was 'tense but not serious,' Ettore Bastico assured him. 'Our air force is very efficient. Reinforcements from the motherland are flowing into Tobruk and Mersa Matruh.' Any suggestion of falling back from Alamein was rejected. Instead, Bastico appealed to the German marshal's vanity. 'I am sure that, with his valour and perseverance, Marshal Rommel will be able to overcome the temporary crisis.'[69]

Benito Mussolini had not waited for the outcome of the July battles. After three restless weeks in Libya, a furious Duce had finally decided to return to Rome, convinced his generals had 'made a fool of him' by summoning him to Africa for a victory which they never delivered. Far from riding his charger triumphantly through Cairo, he spent his days visiting supply bases, meeting German and Italian casualties in Tobruk's military hospitals where, according to observers, he had a charming manner and gave those convalescing strength. He presented medals to fighter pilots, whose comrades provided cover from 6,000 metres overhead throughout the 80-minute ceremony. He strode around 'dressed in colonial uniform with a Tommy gun slung over his shoulder,' chastising soldiers who treated British prisoners favourably – 'You must hate the enemy,' he admonished them. He cashiered a tank officer who complained about the lack of spare parts and seriously considered a suggestion from one of his entourage to equip troops with bicycles to make good their shortage of trucks. He visited one prison camp separated into two distinct sections by barbed wire: on one side of the wire, white South Africans; on the other, British troops. The South Africans were sullen, did not recognise the Italian leader and refused to rise from tents to acknowledge their visitor until Cavallero barked 'Stand up!' at them. A few hours later a column of trucks carrying British troops passed Mussolini and his entourage. The Duce asked for a machine-gun and, juggling it in his hands, declared: 'If anyone gives me the sign of victory, I'll shoot him.' No prisoner did. And when he was bored by such excursions, he went partridge shooting.

Not once did Mussolini visit the front – he refused to venture anywhere near the Via Balbia, as the highway was constantly attacked by enemy aircraft. Rumours began to circulate among the troops that the Duce was ill, that he was forced to sit in an armchair for hours on end, motionless, his knees pressed against his chest.

He betrayed none of this on his return to Rome. Instead, Mussolini boasted to Fascist Party grandees that he had directed the battle and taken charge of the situation. In reality, all he did was pen a lengthy memorandum on the situation in North Africa. Still dreaming of the Nile and Suez, he ordered the offensive resumed, promising 'the Italo-German Armoured Army will have the forces and means which will enable it to face the enemy victoriously in a few days' – new divisions, fuel and ammunition – confident that the booty seized in Alexandria would 'fuel the advance' towards the Egyptian capital. Leaving his personal baggage behind – he would return to Africa in two or three weeks to witness the triumph – he declared bombastically: 'The battle of Tobruk is over; tomorrow's battle will be the Battle of the Delta. The time to prepare for this battle must be numbered in weeks, but not a single minute must be wasted in preparing for it in this race between the enemy and us.'[70]

There was a gulf between the Duce's rhetoric and the lives of his men in the Alamein position. 'We can't fight, we can't even survive,' the once-confident Vittorio Vallicella complained. 'And all this while our intelligence services report that all manner of supplies arrive continuously in Egypt from far-away America, breathing life and fresh forces into the sorely-tested troops of the English Eighth Army.'[71] Some Italian troops became fatalistic, convinced 'the only liberation is death, serious injury or prison'.[72] One soldier wrote home: 'Here it's getting ever worse – not only to be exposed to danger but also to fight against hunger and thirst. We're exhausted and we're no longer good enough, not only to advance but also to retreat, and we lack the strength to stand...'[73]

Water was severely limited – men in some units were restricted to one litre per day, which was clearly inadequate to sustain them. When a pipe which ran through the desert alongside the railway line from Alexandria broke near Fuka and gushed water, there was 'a race against time to take on supplies before the British woke up to what had happened,' pioneer officer Paolo Caccia-Dominioni recalled. 'Inevitably, an enormous Bavarian sergeant was already on the spot supervising the distribution, notebook in hand.' Tankers carrying between 1,000 and 6,000 litres made the run to wells and oases daily. They delivered it to units where it was stored in 20-litre petrol drums – marked with white crosses to distinguish them from fuel – in front of every tent. Food was just as bad. A shortage of stoves, which panzer crews carried but their Italian counterparts did not, meant hot meals were rare. The men ate the tinned English goods they had captured in Tobruk. The food did not fulfil their nutritional requirements. 'Almost all of us began to suffer from intestinal diseases because of the terrible English canned food,' remembered aviator Giorgio Bertolaso, who was struck down by a pneumonia-like fever. The Italian soldier would have suffered his poor diet more willingly had his commanders shared his plate. 'What pisses us off the most is the disparity between the officers and the men,' driver Vittorio Vallicella wrote. When the fighting died down, the first thought of his officers was to set up a mess where they were served 'excellent lunches washed down with good wine and liquor', while their men were given soup, bread, a lemon, perhaps a spoonful of jam. And then there was the water: for the rank and file, at best, a canteen full of brackish water, for officers, bottles of mineral water flown in daily from Italy.[74]

German soldiers too complained about their 'wretched' and 'monotonous' food. Tins of corned beef seemed endless, while fresh fruit or vegetables were almost unheard of. Occasionally the men might enjoy fresh meat – 'some bones surrounded by tough, dry scraps of meat from a sheep and a camel', edible only after being put through the mincer. Fatty gammon was too much for most *Afrikaner* in temperatures of 50°C. Fresh bread turned mouldy in a day rather than three; dry bread was simply rock hard. Dried vegetables – dubbed 'barbed wire' by the men – softened overnight were hard once more by the time the men came to cooking them. Occasionally fruit was delivered from Cyrenaica – but invariably went off on the lengthy journey.[75]

Men living in close proximity, in filthy conditions with few opportunities to wash, plagued by flies, suffering from a poor diet and dehydration all meant there was a constant stream of patients for Alfons Selmayr, a doctor in 5th Panzer Regiment. He treated 80 men a day – soldiers suffering from diarrhoea, wounds which refused to heal, a few cases of diphtheria. The longer a man had spent in North Africa, the worse his health. Beyond the usual complaints, they invariably suffered from high blood pressure and heart conditions – 'probably caused by the heat,' Selmayr, a sufferer himself, deduced. Cuts and scratches from the sharp thorns of camel thorn bushes often festered – the first sign of tropical ulcers. By far the most common illness – 'African sickness' – was dysentery, particularly among new arrivals. 'All the time you had the feeling you'd produce a great deal – but all that came out was a teaspoon of blood and gunk,' flak officer Heinrich Dammann remembered. For most *Afrikaner*, unpleasant thought it was, dysentery soon passed. But not for Otto Scharrer from the South Tyrol. When the symptoms persisted, he was sent to a first-aid post – a clusters of tents behind the front, with 20 or 30 men convalescing in each one. The latrine was a deep ditch which ran for a good 30 feet behind the tents, where ten to 15 men at a time often sat on wooden boards, while medics tossed in lime to prevent the plague of flies spreading disease. Scharrer spent several days recovering – and all the while, the cemetery next to the aid post 'grew larger and larger. The dead were wrapped in blankets or tarpaulin and laid in ditches one and a half metres deep.

Next to the "operating theatre" there was a hole which was wrapped in swaths of smoke all day long. Amputated arms and legs were cremated there.'[76]

Italian soldiers suffering from more serious wounds or illness were transported to the hospital in Benghazi – more than 550 miles behind the front. Mario Zucchetti was horrified by the sight of fellow patients whose nerves had been shattered by artillery barrages or bombing raids. Each evening, one of the patients would suffer a fit, triggering copycat fits by other patients. 'The strength they possessed during these attacks, which lasted about a quarter of an hour, was incredible,' Zucchetti wrote. 'They gnashed their teeth, stiffened with their body arched and then snapped, and sometimes they managed to free themselves from those pinning them down and fell off their beds on to the floor, feeling the consequences when they woke up.' Another patient stared constantly at the ceiling, convinced there were bombers overhead, a young officer moved his limbs constantly and pulled faces, while a soldier who lost his mind was given a room to himself. He smeared the walls and used his finger to write one word: 'Mussolini'. Men who retained their faculties yearned for a hospital ship to transport them to the Italian mainland 'from one day to the next,' wrote Zucchetti. 'But it never comes.'[77]

The only Axis troops to see Alexandria, Cairo, Suez and the Nile Delta did so through a bombsight or crosshairs. Egypt's glittering prizes may have been beyond Rommel's grasp, but not Luftwaffe bomber crews. Throughout the summer they raided Allied airfields and Egyptian infrastructure, occasionally by day, usually by night. Each mission placed 'tremendous demands' on aircrew – who normally operated from bases in Crete and therefore faced up to eight hours in the cockpit and a good 400 miles each way over the Mediterranean. 'A night-time take-off with a fully-laden aircraft means damned awful nervous tension,' Junkers Ju88 pilot Wolfgang von Bergh told his parents.

> You have nothing in front of you apart from the instruments and even the slightest movement of a needle demands your attention. The bird only lifts off the ground with difficulty and slowly climbs. Then off over the island. We know that to our left and right are mountains which are higher than we're flying but we cannot see them. Next the coast with its gusts and the instruments begin a wild dance. Then finally we're over the open sea.

The flights were long, tiring, tense. 'For hours on end the engines sing the same monotonous song,' one Heinkel He111 pilot wrote. Although the autopilot was switched on, crews always kept one eye on the instruments – and another on the heavens, looking out for enemy fighters. There was little conversation. Occasionally the cockpit would be lit briefly as the navigator checked the course and marked the aircraft's location on a map under the beam of a torch. Particularly long missions would be interrupted with a stop at a forward airfield in North Africa such as Hagag el Quasaba, a couple of dozen miles from Mersa Matruh, for resting, refuelling and re-arming.

And then it was on to the target: the airbase at Alexandria, or maybe Heliopolis – site of Cairo's international airport today. Heinkels dropped mines in the Suez Canal, Junkers attacked the fuel storage tanks for shipping using the man-made waterway. Crews grew to know the unmistakeable sights of Egypt, even in the darkness: the northern, straight, stretch of the canal, lined with searchlights; the arms, channels and irrigation ditches of the Nile spread out across the delta; the gigantic stone blocks of the Pyramids; the lights of the spa town of Helwan a dozen miles south of Cairo still blazing, while over the capital itself searchlights in clusters of 30 groped the night sky, 'snatching at us from the depths like the tentacles of an octopus,' one He111 pilot remembered. Having evaded the searchlight beams and 'red Ottos' – flak tracer – the bombers attacked their target: on this particular night for von Bergh's formation, the airfield at Bir Hooker, between Alexandria and Cairo. 'First a hail of incendiaries falls,' von Bergh continued. 'Countless lights suddenly flash there on the ground in the most concentrated of spaces. Then the second pass: bombs – a dive or horizontal attack depending on the target. The impact of the bombs which our comrades have already dropped flash beneath us and then our bombs are away too.'

Now crews faced a return flight of nearly 400 miles. With the first glimmer of dawn in the east, the bombers headed back out over the Mediterranean at low altitude. Tired, but finally able to relax, crews would enjoy breakfast – *Startverpflegung* (sortie rations) of bread, butter, eggs, biscuits, chocolate, some milk, perhaps even red wine – less to sustain them physically, but mentally, 'because the nervous strain often surpassed all known concepts,' one aircrew member recalled. For three hours there was nothing but water below them until perhaps the Turkish coast or Rhodes appeared. Finally, after a landing which demanded 'total concentration' and a mission report, crews at last had the chance to get their heads down.[78]

The raids took a terrible toll – though not necessarily of their targets. The constant attacks left aircrew mentally and physically exhausted, their ranks worryingly thin. Crews based in Crete enjoyed the best quarters and medical facilities, but repeated sorties left them 'weary and tired'. Wolfgang von Bergh was badly affected by the death of his friend Werner Doll. 'A gap has been torn in our circle of friends which can never be closed,' von Bergh wrote home to his family. 'Werner has left an excellent letter. The last lines of it are just as he lived: honest, straight and a little self-deprecating, no euphemisms. Among other things, he wrote: "We must all live life quickly, that's why we're airmen!" – and he's spot on. Life – and the struggle – go on, hard and relentless, never pausing for a second.'[79]

Morale and energy were sapped further by sandfly fever – commonplace on the island – which also left them dizzy and nauseous. The men lost up to a stone in weight. They should, the doctor recommended, be granted at least three weeks' leave or rest. There was no let-up. Veteran crews wore out; new crews out of training suffered punishing losses. Radio operator Emil Leuthner was the sole survivor of his Junkers Ju88 crew shot down over Suez at the end of July. It was the seventh of nine which left the bomber school at Hohensalza in occupied Poland after Easter 1942 to be lost. As one member of *Kampfgeschwader* 100 observed: 'We had to accept that our casualty rate was higher than any other arm of the Wehrmacht – apart from our comrades in U-boats.'[80]

Axis fighter pilots were in Egyptian skies five or six times daily, offering 'outstanding cover' to the bombers in the face of increasing interference from Allied interceptors, whose formations were frequently driven away 'in tatters', Rommel's Luftwaffe commander Otto Hoffman von Waldau noted with satisfaction. The best Axis fighters – the Italian Macchi 202 and upgraded variants of the Messerschmitt 109 – were faster than all but the latest Spitfires and generally outgunned their opponents. Pilots enjoyed a feeling of superiority over their opponent – losses were relatively low and Allied tactics often appeared cumbersome and outdated as they tried to create defensive formations of 20 or 30 aircraft at a time. German and Italian fighters simply could not match such numbers and, though undaunted by such large enemy formations, and attacks would invariably break them up, kills were few. 'Often we took off with two or four fighters, shot down three enemies, but 30 or 50 escaped untouched,' remembered Werner Schroer.[81]

With more than 30 kills to his name by the late summer of 1942, Werner Schroer was second only to one man in the skies of North Africa: Hans-Joachim Marseille. The 22-year-old Berliner missed much of the fighting in the summer of 1942, sent back to Germany partly to recuperate from exhaustion, partly to support the Nazi propaganda machine which had helped make him a household name. 'The Star of Africa' as he was dubbed was the poster boy of the Third Reich: young, with boyish good looks, charismatic. He appeared on the cover of the *Berliner Illustrirte Zeitung* and in the pages of *Signal*, the glossy news magazine distributed across occupied and neutral Europe. He'd been singled out for his accomplishments in the Wehrmacht daily communiqué three times and filmed for the weekly newsreel. Now the cameras followed him to Hitler's headquarters in East Prussia where he received the Oak Leaves with Swords to add to the Knight's Cross presented in Africa back in February. Cinemagoers watched the fighter pilot take a stroll with his Führer through the grounds of his headquarters and chat over a table indoors. They also studied the facial features of the 'young hero' and felt sympathy for him – the strain of battle was obvious.[82]

For, as so often in the Third Reich, there was a gulf between the propaganda image and reality. The real Marseille was brash, outspoken – even, or perhaps especially, in the company of senior officers – and impudent. He was indeed charismatic and good looking – and he knew it. His philandering became an open secret in Luftwaffe circles. His female conquests were many: the Italian singer Nilla Pizzi, Swedish-born actress Zarah Leander, Hitler's favourite director Leni Riefenstahl – all fell under the spell of the young fighter pilot. But then so too did Joseph Goebbels. Just like schoolboys across Germany, the propaganda minister followed Marseille's success, recording his victories in his diary as if they were scores in a sporting fixture. Goebbels also fell for the young Berliner's charm. He found Marseille 'extremely modest and shy' and, above all, 'very likeable. He's not that type of raffish, brazen fighter pilot we're used to – there's something of the dreamer about him.'

The fighter pilot told the propaganda minister about the inexperience of the Americans – 'shot down like rabbits' – and spoke of his respect for the British – 'they bravely join battle and do not surrender'. But it was also an exhausted, war-weary Marseille who returned to Germany. When Hitler suggested the Reich would need men of his ilk after the war, the young Berliner told him he didn't expect that he – or many of his comrades – would survive the war. Goebbels too was reluctant to see the pilot return to North Africa. He was reminded of the last fighter ace from Berlin he had hosted, Hans Strelow, back in May. A fortnight later, Strelow had been shot down over Russian lines.[83]

For now, however, the propaganda apparatus would milk Marseille's celebrity for all it was worth. He signed photographs, toured schools, visited the wounded in hospitals, was filmed sharing his experiences with schoolboys. He was, observed Artur Axmann, the head of the Hitler Youth, 'the ultimate role model for German youth – until he opened his mouth.'[84]

***

Hans-Joachim Marseille had arrived in Africa after a few weeks on the Channel front in the late summer of 1940. There two things had become apparent: his skill – he downed seven British fighters – and his love of the good life. He was cashiered for his long, non-regulation hair but above all for frequently boasting about his sexual exploits.

It took him time to adjust to the war in North Africa. Transferred with *Jagdgeschwader* 27 in the spring of 1941, it would be the end of the year before he began to make an impression. The winter of 1941–42 proved a fruitful killing ground. By the end of February, Marseille had more than 50 kills to his name, earning him the Knight's Cross. Rommel's spring offensive proved even more fruitful. In May 1942, 14 enemy aircraft fell victim to Marseille's Messerschmitt 109. The following month, the tally was 33 – taking him over the 100-victory threshold. A few days before the fall of Tobruk, he was sent home for two months.

Marseille owed his success in African skies to innate skill. He downed his opponents as they – and he – turned. Marseille shared his tactics with his comrades, 'but only a few pilots were able to gain from his experiences in combat because they lacked the natural talents,' his *Jagdgeschwader* 27 comrade Eduard Neumann recalled. Most pilots took at least 80, perhaps as many as 120, rounds to shoot down an enemy fighter. Marseille required perhaps 15. His opponents were wary of him; comrades on the ground listening in to chatter between Allied pilots heard them warn 'Careful, Marseille is in the air.' He – and many of his comrades – relished the *freie Jagd* (free hunt), chasing victories as they swept the skies. One group of just four '*Experten*' claimed 63 enemy aircraft shot down in August 1942, while entire units comprising three dozen fighters scored barely a third of that total over the same period. Although, as it turned out, the figures had been falsified, it was symptomatic of the problem: every fighter pilot wanted to be a Marseille. It was, observed Werner Schroer, 'a bacillus which could never be eradicated'.[85]

The greatest service Marseille's squadron rendered in August 1942, however, was to the British. On the afternoon of the 7th, Rhinelander Emil Clade was leading a formation of four Messerschmitt 109s on a free hunt east of Alexandria. Clade already had a dozen 'kills' to his name, all but four of them earned in the skies of North Africa. Suddenly, there was opportunity for number 13. Somehow, from 6,000 metres above the desert outside Alexandria, Clade spotted a sole British bomber sluggishly making for Cairo. Normally, the aircraft would hug the terrain in a bid to remain undetected, but its teenage pilot had been forced to climb to 150 metres to cool an overheating engine. The Bristol Bombay was crippled by the first bursts of fire – fired either by Clade or his wingman Bernhard Schneider, who was later credited with the victory – and forced to put down in the desert. The ruthless Schneider then strafed the transporter repeatedly until flames licked from the peppered fuselage and black smoke tumbled skywards. Most of the men aboard were sick or wounded being transferred to Cairo for treatment. Joining them for what should have been a short flight to the Egyptian capital was General William Gott, leaving the front for a few days' leave. Unbeknown to the 44-year-old general – or Clade and Schneider – he was due to be appointed the new commander of Eighth Army. He was almost certainly the wrong man for the job, but his death in the bullet-ridden fuselage paved the way for another British general: Bernard Montgomery.[86]

Given the right leader, the ranks of Eighth Army always felt they would 'prove more than a match for the Axis forces'. Bernard Montgomery seemed to be that man. 'The defence of Egypt lies here at Alamein,' he told his commanders. 'If we lose this position, we lose Egypt... There will be no further withdrawal... We will stand and fight *here*. If we can't stay here alive, then let us stay here dead.' There were still some weary units in Africa, such as the Scots Guards, exhausted after '18 months in the desert without a really decent break'. But the 'Gazala gallop' and 'the Flap' were long past and Montgomery seemed to strike the right note. 'A breath of fresh, invigorating air has swept through the British Troops in Egypt, and the mail has altered in tone almost overnight,' one report on morale noted. 'Renewed optimism and confidence were everywhere apparent, and the old aggressive spirit... is in the process of being recovered.'[87]

By mid-August, life in the Alamein position had settled into an uneasy routine – 'nerve-racking monotony,' as one gunner put it. 'One day passes just like any other,' infantryman Hans Hesse wrote. 'Sun, sand, heat – and a million flies circling over everything. The only variety is provided by the daily barrage from the British artillery. What's also depressing is that our artillery only responds to these greetings sporadically because of the lack of ammunition.' The first couple of hours after dawn were the most bearable. 'It's normally still cool,' 20-year-old Walther Weber wrote to his family in Lower Saxony. 'You can see through the damp in the air an incredibly long distance and every shadow stands out sharp and dark on the yellow sandy soil.' Occasionally the day might begin with a *Ferntrauung* – marriage by proxy – for an enemy attack was least likely. It was invariably the only time the German soldier in Africa wore formal dress. Three rifles standing on end formed a makeshift pyramid while a table covered with a swastika flag and adorned with a couple of steel helmets and the obligatory portrait of Hitler, flanked by a couple of cans, served as the 'altar'. While comrades acted as a guard of honour, the betrothed men stood in front of the table while the commanding officer performed the ceremony, explaining that, if possible, at the same time the men's fiancées were standing before a registrar going through identical proceedings back in Germany. The whole affair was rather surreal. 'When the commanding officer mentioned "loyalty in marriage", the men laughed,' Rudolf Hubalek remembered. 'No chance of anything going wrong here in Africa!'[88]

Men in the line worked to improve their positions and tried to remain alert. There was no front in the traditional sense, but a series of 'hedgehog positions' dug out of the stony ground using pickaxes and spades, pockmarking the otherwise barren desert landscape. Some of these foxholes – brigade commander Bernhard Ramcke called them 'stone caskets' – were for individual soldiers; others were large enough for a mortar troop or anti-tank gun. Conditions were unforgiving. As the sun rose, so too did the temperature, rapidly. By 8am, the heat was uncomfortable, by 9am unbearable – upwards of 55°C, when activity in the open invariably ceased. The only shade was man-made – tarpaulins stretched out next to vehicles, although erecting these sunbreaks exhausted any soldier. Aside from the heat, men were plagued by flies which clung to any exposed skin, hands and faces especially, in large black swarms. Rivulets of sweat ran down arms and legs. There was a clammy feeling between fingers and toes; mixed with sand, it caused sores. Shirts and trousers rubbed against the skin, forcing men to scratch all the time, driving them, one German gunner wrote, 'to the edge of despair'. The men left their holes only to relieve themselves: to defecate, they crawled across the stone and sand to the latrine trench before dropping down into it; for urinating, they simply scrambled a few yards from their foxholes and lay down in the sand. The brief period of dusk – around 6.30pm – was by far the soldier's favourite part of the day: a cooling breeze wafting in from the Mediterranean, the heavens filled with brilliant colours. 'When the sun goes down in the west, when the desert glows red and the wadis cast bizarre shadows, then you stand still, struck by the beauty that the desert can offer so suddenly,' 19-year-old Martin Penck told his parents in Leipzig. Italian troops, who'd received just half a litre of water to last through the day, were given a quarter of a litre to accompany their evening meal. For assault engineers like Manilo Leone that meant 'a sliver of Dutch cheese peeled from a two-pound tin, after the finger-long ants, who lived in the canteen with it, had come out', accompanied by British biscuits – all captured at Mersa Matruh – and a few sweets. After dark, men read or wrote letters – newspapers and mail were flown in daily; Italian journals reached the men within 36 hours of publication, letters – once checked by the censor – no more than five days after being posted, or whiled away the evening playing cards, skat especially, sometimes even for money, although there was nothing on which to spend the winnings. The front cinema once again provided limited entertainment: two musical comedies on a seemingly endless loop. Soldiers sat down on lumps of rock, sweated horribly and stared at the canvas. 'How distant the things flickering on the screen seemed: well-dressed people, comely women, snow and ice!' machine-gunner Heinz-Dietrich Aberger wrote. 'We barely knew things like that still existed.' The nights were pitch black – the only artificial light from the occasional parachute flare which bathed this alien landscape in a ghostly light. The temperature dropped rapidly. Men reached for their overcoats or blankets. Stuka crewman and *Propaganda Kompanie* reporter Hans Gross found the nights at Alamein 'filled with tension and danger', but brigade commander Ramcke enjoyed 'the strange magic' when there was a full moon. 'Not a sound interrupts the sublime silence of nature. Such magical nights reconcile us with a landscape which otherwise is so awful.'[89]

The men holding the line at Alamein probably envied aircrew. They enjoyed regular meals and, for those based in Crete, well-kept quarters. But the life of fliers was hardly enviable. During the drive on Alexandria they had endured just as nomadic an existence as soldiers, hopping from one makeshift airfield to the next, flying by day, sleeping under their aircraft by night with parachutes for pillows, living on whatever rations they carried with them – a canteen full of water, canned meat, some bread. 'We pilots – especially we fighter pilots – live in the realm of the temporary, this living without tomorrow, constantly moving from one airfield to another, pitched into battle by orders which always arrive suddenly,' Giulio Lazzati wrote. As the front at Alamein solidified, life became more stable and air and ground crews began to make themselves at home. Conditions were spartan, but slightly more bearable than in the line. Between missions, Hans Gross and his Stuka unit comrades drank coffee which tasted of salt, wrote letters home and, most importantly, listened to the radio. With mail sporadic – often ending up at the bottom of the Mediterranean – radio was a constant link with home, especially in the evenings. '*Ein rheinisches Mädel beim rheinischen Wein* comes from the loudspeaker while outside there's the constant rhythm of the waves striking the cliffs and the nightly breeze rippling the sides of the tent.'

By day, the sun cracked the earth; the Macchi fighters in Lazzati's 4th *Stormo* (Wing) roasted under their covers. The smell of evaporated petrol made pilots vomit when they climbed into the cockpits on a scramble. 'You look at each other before you go into action to receive strength, to hope for your return,' Lazzati wrote. 'Never in the evening, or else you'll get a lump in your throat and despair will come over you.' They made sure they carried their oily, swollen wallets – crammed with letters from home and photos of their family, wives, girlfriends, a reminder of what they were fighting for. In the evenings, sometimes after half a dozen sorties in a day, pilots gathered in small groups and reminisced about 'whatever soldiers at the front talk about: women's legs, magnificent and firm breasts, our wives, children.'[90]

To family back home, the word 'Egypt' possessed 'a strong touch of Oriental magic,' Hellmuth Frey remembered. There was nothing magical about Alamein – 'just sandy desert,' a disillusioned Federico Vallauri told his family. 'The Egypt that I'm talking about must be something else entirely.' The landscape was 'utterly monotonous – nothing but endless, fine white sand and dunes. No bushes, no stalks, nothing!' Hans Gross noted. 'The sky is constantly blue, the sun is an eternal gold, the sea glows an azure blue. Day after day! What we wouldn't give for the sight of German woods or for a refreshing proper downpour!' Even to men like junior officer Ralf Ringler, who'd spent the summer of 1941 advancing through the steppe of Ukraine, the vastness of the desert was 'unspeakably enormous'. It was hardly surprising that supply officer Hellmuth Frey found soldiers were 'often apathetic', having spent day and night in their hedgehogs. 'Everyone imagined the land of the Pharaohs to be more beautiful. The only beautiful landscape here is the blue Mediterranean – and that's not much different here than it is in Tripoli.' The magic – the Pyramids, Arabian belly dancers, the Alabaster Mosque, Mena House Hotel – were distant dreams, yet gave the men hope, Frey observed. 'Everybody feels and thinks: as soon as we are through the El Alamein position, better days will begin. For the time being, however, our *Landsers* occupy their foxholes surrounded by the shimmering desert and look through their green veil to the east, to the plains of the Nile.'[91]

The build-up made sluggish process. The battles of May, June and July cost more than 27,000 casualties, to say nothing of the matériel losses. Replacements slowly began to fill the sorely depleted German and Italian ranks. The new arrivals were a mix of men fresh out of training and 'old hares': veterans of other fronts. They mingled with elite units – both Berlin and Rome had dispatched paratroopers to Africa. They expected to be dropped far behind British lines to raise hell. 'They were bitterly disappointed,' Enrico Frattini, commander of the *Folgore* Division, recalled. 'Barely had they landed and they were ordered to give up their parachutes. They were drafted to normal infantry units, dug in in the sand behind minefields. The disappointment was huge – but it was quickly overcome.'[92]

Veteran or novice, all new arrivals were taught the skills they would need to keep them alive: keeping canteens cool by winding damp rags around them; turning cans into small cookers by making holes in them and filling them with sand soaked in petrol; defusing mines so that their explosives could be used; tying scarves under the shirt collar to avoid rashes which could turn into awful tropical sores. Old hands drove the newcomers up to the front where they could observe enemy armoured cars and tanks, watch the impact of shells, see the effects of anti-tank shells on shot-up panzers abandoned on the battlefield.[93]

Just days after arriving in Africa at the end of June, 20-year-old Austrian medical student Robert Röhlich found himself at Alamein under heavy enemy artillery fire. 'Things have reached their climax. We're barely able to lift our heads out of the dirt for five minutes. I'm hit by five splinters – thank God, nothing major.' In less than a week at the front, Röhlich's spirit had been broken. His only salvation, he believed, was the Mother of God of Mariazell – Austria's holiest Catholic shrine. 'I'm an old sinner who's turned religious,' he continued in his diary. 'I've never prayed as much in my entire sinful life as I have these past few days. I hope for the intervention of the holy virgin. This thought gives me fresh strength again and again. I have changed completely. Through my faith I find the strength to endure all the terrible things. God, continue to help me! I have faith in you!'[94]

The young student was among many replacements who were quickly disappointed by their experiences in the desert. 'Everyone who came here over the past 14 days has been surprised and astonished by the tremendous amount of fighting going on in this sector of the front,' Hellmuth Frey noted. 'They believed – as many at home believe – that they'd arrived too late for the entry into Cairo.' Now all they could do was look upon the Promised Land 'as Moses once did' or turn in the direction of the Pyramids using their compasses. 'Many of our latest replacements did not even have the chance to do this,' Frey recorded. 'They are already resting beneath the Egyptian sand or are on their way back to the homeland as wounded.' The dead included Robert Röhlich. He'd been at the front barely a fortnight.[95]

The losses of the advance into Egypt would never be made good. Come the end of August, German units were still short of 15,000 men. Troops could at least be flown in. All other supplies – food, fuel, ammunition, spare parts and replacement vehicles – came by sea. Not once during the summer of 1942 did ships deliver the 75,000 tonnes of supplies – not including tanks and vehicles – and 30,000 tonnes of fuel *Panzerarmee Afrika* needed to survive each month. Only if the Axis forces won 'the first battle at sea' could there be any victory on land, as Ugo Cavallero realised. Even when the merchant vessels reached Africa they were not safe – one British air raid on Tobruk destroyed nearly two and a half million litres of fuel and 2,000 tonnes of ammunition. From the ports, supplies faced a torturous road journey – 1,350 miles from Tripoli, 750 from Benghazi, 320 from Tobruk – to Alamein. Wear and tear on trucks and constant enemy air attacks meant, Rommel complained – perhaps with a touch of hyperbole – that re-supply efforts 'barely had any effect on the front line'.[96] In fact, units gradually recovered from the nadir of mid-July. One month later, there were now 450 working tanks – far fewer than in May but, intelligence reckoned – wrongly, as it turned out – still stronger than the Allies. There were shortages throughout the German-Italian Army: trucks, spare parts, ammunition – some artillery pieces had fewer than 150 rounds – and especially fuel which reduced Rommel's forces to a hand-to-mouth existence.

And yet both Berlin and Rome determined their forces in Egypt sufficiently replenished to resume the drive on Alexandria – and beyond – 'within a few days'. 'Rommel's reserves grow by the day,' a relieved Hitler told Goebbels. 'Sooner or later we'll smash through the El Alamein position and thrust to Cairo.'[97]

But was Erwin Rommel the man to lead that thrust? After 18 months in the desert, the strain of battle, poor diet and unsanitary conditions had taken their toll. Every other officer aged over 40 had succumbed to some ailment. Now so too the field marshal. On 21 August, he fainted. His personal physician urged the field marshal to return to Germany to recuperate, reporting bluntly, 'At present he's in no state to command the offensive.' For once, Rommel heeded the advice and suggested Hitler replace him with Heinz Guderian, the foremost proponent of armoured warfare. Hitler brushed the suggestion aside; the general was out of favour after retreating before Moscow the previous December. The response from Führer headquarters was swift – and curt: 'Guderian unacceptable.' The rejection prompted a miraculous recovery. Within days, Rommel's doctor was reporting that his patient was 'much better' and able to direct the battle 'under constant medical supervision'.[98]

When it came to beginning that battle, however, Rommel had 'continuously wavered' through late August, his chief-of-staff Siegfried Westphal remembered. A lengthy meeting with Albert Kesselring on the 27th ended the indecision. Kesselring promised two tankers would arrive in Tobruk imminently, providing all the fuel Rommel needed. If the tankers delivered their cargoes as promised, Westphal reckoned there would be enough fuel for two or three weeks. If not, the army would run out of petrol on the third day of the attack. For the 40-year-old staff officer, the margin was too fine, the risks too great. Kesselring dismissed his protests, saying Westphal wasn't looking at the big picture. Besides, even if the tankers were sunk, 'Smiling' Albert promised to fly the fuel Rommel needed across the Mediterranean. Westphal objected again – the Luftwaffe did not have the capacity, let alone the weather or enemy 'throwing a spanner in the works'. Kesselring lost his patience and dismissed the impudent colonel, continuing his conversation with Rommel in private. Whatever was said between the two, at the end they shook hands firmly as Rommel said simply: '*Topp*' – We're on.[99]

The attack would begin after dark on Sunday 30 August. Calling on 'every soldier to give his all', Rommel promised 'the ultimate destruction of the enemy'. This was the Rommel of old, exuding confidence, promising the Italians 'the probability of success is considerable' and assuring his own staff, 'We'll reach Cairo this summer, even if I have to push the vehicles myself' or joking of 'milking' captured enemy vehicles. 'Rommel's lucky star may still shine on him,' supply officer Hellmuth Frey hoped.[100] Yet there were many shortages and shortcomings which had not been solved or overcome – not least fuel, for Kesselring's tankers failed to arrive.[101] As one formation of tanks in 21st Panzer Division moved up to their jump-off positions, its commander told his men to 'save fuel and ammunition'. 'How is an attack supposed to go well like that?' one officer wondered. Rommel himself knew the attack was a gamble, as he told his wife, 'but I've taken the risk, for it will be a long time before we enjoy such favourable conditions – moonlight, relative strengths and so on – again.' Leaving his quarters on the morning of the attack, he bumped into his doctor. 'The decision to attack today is the hardest of my life,' the field marshal confided. 'Either we succeed in driving on Grozny in Russia and reaching the Suez Canal here in Africa or...' His voice trailed off and he made a dismissive gesture with his hand.[102]

On Sunday morning, the men of Vittorio Vallicella's battery gathered around an altar made from ammunition crates to celebrate Mass for the first time in two months. By holding the service at 8am the men hoped to escape the attention of Allied aviators. 'Finding us all gathered in the open would be a proper massacre,' a worried Vallicella noted. His commander pleaded with the priest to speed up proceedings. 'For us a "shortened mass" is fine because, even if we're believers, we've never found a God who'll stop the bombs or aircraft machine-guns,' Vallicella continued. 'We receive a blessing and soon we're all in our bunkers once more.'[103]

Eighteen-year-old artilleryman Sergio Bresciani was convinced of victory. 'I'm more than certain that I'll soon be sending you a postcard from Cairo,' he assured his father, Bortolo. 'If you go a few days without hearing from me, don't think the worst of it. I am sure everything will go well.'[104]

After Mass and 'religious preparation, which involves the sacrifice that we will all offer to the Motherland in a few hours,' Major Enrico Bigliani, commanding the *Littorio*'s pioneers, was handed his orders for the coming night: to clear a gap through the minefield for the division's armour to drive through. As dusk fell, he showed half a dozen volunteers how to safely remove first German Teller mines, then enemy explosive devices. At 8pm, Bigliani's truck moved towards the front and the path cleared through the Italian minefield the previous evening in preparation for the new offensive.[105]

Vittorio Vallicella reported to his headquarters after dark to receive orders. 'Here we go! Our life of Riley is over,' he wrote. 'We're off to an unknown destination. Goodbye sea, goodbye peaceful days, goodbye deep sleep.'[106]

At 7.28pm precisely, Captain Davide Beretta ordered his men to start the engines of their 75/18 assault guns. 'A deafening roar of engines rose on the vast expanse flooded by the pale moonlight,' he remembered. 'The reconnaissance vanguard of the *Littorio* Armoured Division began its march towards glory and towards death.'

The column moved into the desert night, following the compass: 110 degrees. 'The nightmare of waiting had finally ended,' Beretta wrote. 'The shapes of the moving self-propelled guns cast long trembling shadows on the expanse of sand, shadows which seemed to chase each other from dune to dune.' The vehicles kicked up clouds of sand which reflected the white moonlight; the constant, monotonous rattle of their tracks and low rumble of their motors were the only sounds for miles around. As the vehicles passed the foxholes of the *Folgore* Division, the paratroopers stood up and waved, spurring the crews on to glory and victory.

Beretta halted his guns on the edge of no man's land. Despite the full moon, despite the noise of motors and caterpillar tracks, despite a column stirring up the desert for the past two hours, the vanguard of the *Littorio* had reached its jump-off position. It stood outside 'the enemy's lair, without having been sighted'.[107]

Vittorio Vallicella's motorised gun battery moved out on the stroke of midnight. 'A wonderful night,' he wrote. 'The moon has never looked so beautiful. We head slowly south into the desert, driving further and further into it.'[108]

5

THREE AXIS ARMIES ON THE DON

What are we looking for here? Who and what are we fighting for? It's woe to us.

Romanian officer

At the end of 30 October, Lieutenant Emilio de Marchi prepared to move up to the front line for the first time. Aged 29, the lawyer was older than many of his fellow junior officers in the *Tridentina* Division – many were just 20 or 21. De Marchi felt no hatred towards his Russian foe yet volunteered out of a strong sense of duty: 'Italy is at war and therefore my place is there.' His place was a 20-mile stretch of front which followed the course of the River Don, anchored on the small town of Pavlovsk. The Alpine infantry of the *Tridentina* had expected to fight side by side with the Germans in the Caucasus. Instead, they found themselves unprepared and ill-equipped in the unfamiliar flat surroundings of the Don steppe. Emilio de Marchi did not expect to return. 'You will not receive this message until after my death,' he wrote to his parents and sisters at home in Milan. 'I think it will be in the coming months.' He continued:

I have the honour of fighting for my homeland with a weapon in my hands and I ask that you do not mourn my death.

My heart only trembles when I ask you for the ultimate sacrifice. Forgive me if I have preferred my duty as an Italian and my love for the homeland, which I must love like you, but I believe that I am acting consciously and will not change my fate.

Continue your lives as if I were still with you, work as hard as I have done, with a firm conviction in victory for the greatness of our Motherland.

My last thoughts are with you.

One last kiss.

If they ever sought his grave, his family would find it 'far from the roads, close to the Don, a wooden cross with a plaque, name, date, city of Milan and my helmet. It will be the grave of an Alpine rifleman like those I have already seen, which mark the path of Italians who came here to complete their soldierly duty.'[1]

There was no grave for Emilio de Marchi. He simply vanished, swept away as the Red Army launched a succession of counter-offensives over the winter – a fate shared by one in every three Italians sent to the Eastern Front in 1942.

Three Axis allies followed in the wake of the Germans advancing on Stalingrad, each charged with safeguarding their gains, holding the front for hundreds of miles. Each nation – Italy, Hungary and Romania – had a different motivation for committing the flower of their youth to Hitler's crusade in the East. Each would pay a terrible price for siding with Berlin.

The vanguard of Hungary's Second Army reached the front in time to support the opening stages of the German summer offensive. The ferocity of the fighting and scale of the casualties – one fifth of the troops committed – in the fighting west of Voronezh shocked every participant. Lajos Kónya discovered he was the only officer left in his company after his first action – and was promptly placed in command. 'Shrapnel and shells were falling, machine-guns were mowing down our men, the land was full of wailing,' he wrote. 'Our company lost 84 men.' Miklós Kiss Nemeskéri was repulsed by the smell of the battlefield. 'Half-burned corpses gave off an awful stench,' he recalled. 'I didn't know that so much burned human flesh could smell so bad.' Dr Lajos Somorjai had to deal with the aftermath of the fighting. Up to 130 wounded per day passed through the administrative building that served as his field hospital, so many that emergency tents were erected in the grounds. 'Casualties filled the halls, blood flowed, hands and feet were taken out of the operating room, and we worked, we worked until we were exhausted,' he wrote. 'There were scenes as if penned by Dante. I will never forget this horrible night.'[2]

Budapest had been browbeaten into sending its army east. Like Rome, it had already made a substantial commitment in the summer of 1941 to support the advance through Ukraine: 90,000 men, spearheaded by the grandly titled Rapid Corps, which, despite its name, was almost as reliant on the bicycle and horse as it was on the motor vehicle. It returned home a spent force as the Russian winter set in, having worn out or lost most of its equipment. Yet just weeks later, Field Marshal Wilhelm Keitel – Hitler's boorish, sycophantic and arrogant military chief-of-staff – was in the Hungarian capital to demand an even greater commitment in 1942. Keitel screamed, thumped his fists on the table and threatened reprisals. In the end, Hungary's leader Miklós Horthy acquiesced, believing that, like Germany's other allies, his nation had to 'take part in the "war for the future"'. But he warned Hitler not to expect or demand too much of his men.

> The Second Army lacks the appropriate equipment. It fights in territory which lies as far from our historic borders as it does from our world of thought. The Hungarian feels tightly bound inside the borders of his homeland. At the same time these borders serve as the limits of his political and military efforts. He will summon all his strength if he is committed in battle on the soil of his homeland or in its immediate vicinity.[3]

Despite its reluctance, the Hungarian Army began assembling the largest force ever sent beyond its borders – more than 200,000 men in one armoured and six infantry divisions. It took nearly six months to raise and three and a half months to transfer to the Eastern Front in more than 800 trains. Its leaders claimed that the mobilisation 'affected every part of the land proportionally'. It did not. The wealthy and higher social classes avoided or somehow deferred their military service. Instead, most of the army's ranks were filled with 'little men': farm hands, labourers, factory workers. The majority were married and generally older than soldiers in the other Axis armies in the East – the average age in some units was well over 30. All underwent six weeks of basic training before being shipped east. They were drilled repeatedly – but not necessarily usefully. They might know every part of their rifle, or be able to assemble a gun instinctively in a matter of minutes. But rarely did they fire them, due to a shortage of ammunition. And they knew nothing of other arms: an infantryman learned solely how to fight with rifle and bayonet, an artilleryman how his battery worked, never how they might co-ordinate their efforts on the field of battle. 'There were soldiers who only saw a tank for the first time on the battlefield,' one report stated. 'The appearance of these mechanised monsters provoked such a psychological effect that they completely lost their minds and were able neither to destroy the tanks nor save themselves.' While the majority of soldiers were of peasant stock, officers hailed from towns and cities. More often than not reservist officers worked in offices, knew little of leadership, even less about their men and possessed meagre or no experience of battle. Their education was frequently below par – as was their training. 'They possessed no self-confidence,' Ferenc Szombathelyi, Chief of the Hungarian General Staff, noted with alarm. 'Officers trusted neither themselves nor their soldiers because they did not know them at all.'[4]

The light infantry divisions they formed were weaker than their German counterparts in every respect: two regiments rather than three, and even more reliant on the horse. By Hungarian standards, they were well, if not lavishly, equipped with machine-guns, mortars and anti-tank guns, provided largely by raiding units left at home. The sole armoured division accompanying them received 100 obsolete Czech-built 38T tanks and a couple of dozen Panzer Mk4s.

Equipment was less of an issue than morale. The majority of Second Army went to war not merely reluctantly, but filled with resentment, its ranks all too aware that 'only a fraction of their countrymen are risking their blood and lives,' as its chief-of-staff Gyula Kovács observed. Worse, few Hungarians believed in their mission in the East. They knew nothing of the Don, and little of why they had to fight there. 'They told us that we would defend our homeland there – our freedom was at stake,' artilleryman Lajos Vollner recalled, though few men believed the propaganda. In the end, the men resigned themselves to their fate. 'One way or another, we had to go to the front – without there being an alternative,' he wrote. 'There wasn't much point thinking about it, we were here, far from our homeland.' Ferenc Szombathelyi drew up guidelines for the army, based on the German model, intent on impressing on his men that 'Bolshevism is Hungary's mortal foe', while its leaders were bent on 'destroying Europe'. As one officer observed, however, 'it's difficult to explain to the ordinary man that he is defending the borders of Hungary here. He only sees and feels that he is fighting for German interests, and this has a big impact on him.' As far as most ordinary Hungarians were concerned, they were fighting the wrong war. 'Our true enemies are, and remain, the Romanians,' Vilmos Nagy, Hungary's Defence Minister, told Hitler. 'We still have to fight our own private war in the Balkans as Antonescu's constantly stirring up hatred against us.' Lieutenant Dénes Bárány found his men were 'not as enthusiastic about fighting along the Don as they would be having to fight for Transylvania. They don't feel the need to defend their homeland here.'[5]

There was a grand send-off for the first units of Second Army: bands, parades, speeches. Children were granted the day off school. Pennants and flags were blessed then ceremoniously presented to regimental commanders, who laid wreaths on monuments to heroes past before departing. In Kaposvár, south of Lake Balaton, girls from the local convent presented the soldiers with modest gifts: packets of cigarettes and sewing boxes. The men marched off singing patriotic tunes such as 'I am a soldier of Miklós Horthy' and the train pulled out of the station 'with cheerful songs on the men's lips', according to the local newspaper. A few days later János Somogyi passed through Kaposvár as his rifle unit was mobilised. 'The departure was regarded by the man in the street as normal, like a daily event,' he remembered. 'No flowers were scattered, no farewell speech was given. No bells tolled.' There were crowds at the station – relatives of the men, mostly women, who rushed at the train when the bugle sounded for it to depart. 'Don't cry, we'll be back!' Somogyi and his comrades shouted. 'But this did not dampen the growing cries of mothers, wives and brides. As the train gathered pace, the runners alongside began to fall behind, leaving only the waving of the shawls.' Sergeant István Solymosi left his wife and son on the platform at the station in Félegyháza, a provincial town 60 miles southeast of Budapest. 'Do not cry, God will help us all,' he assured them as his train pulled out to 'heart-rending' scenes: 'crying family members, girls, wives, mothers and brides. At the same time, many soldiers were hiding their tears, sitting on straw thrown on the floor, with all their worries and doubts.'[6]

When they reached Russia, the soldiers faced a march of up to 600 miles to the front – and found it every bit as monotonous and laborious as their German ally had. To doctor Lajos Somorjai the steppe was 'an endless sandy desert, like the Sahara'. Soldiers and horses sank to their knees in sand. Each step by man or beast threw up dust which accompanied the marching columns for miles on end. Stirred by the wheels of vehicles and motorcyclists, at times it was so thick men could not see more than ten steps ahead of them. 'And in this dust, knee-deep sand, a mass of sweaty, swearing, exhausted, groaning men march, one column after another, a mass of trucks, tanks, cars.' In the occasional villages the troops passed through, the men often rested. Lajos talked with the indigenous population. 'When you dig a little deeper, a number of individual tragedies unfold before your eyes,' he wrote. A mother told how she had just buried her daughter – bomb shrapnel had taken her head clean off. Nearby Hungarian soldiers were burying a comrade; his horse had stepped on a mine. As the doctor and his staff settled down to rest, two more mines exploded a couple of hundred metres away as German infantry caught their breath. 'We were to have rested there, but they got there ahead of us and took our place.' As the troops approached the front, they encountered their first real taste of war. 'Strewn along the road for seven or eight kilometres, wrecked guns, mortars, anti-tank guns, tractors, tanks and trucks,' teacher and reservist officer Géza Lukács wrote as he neared Stary Oskol. 'Masses of shells, mines and hand-grenades are scattered all along the road. The stench in the area is terrible.' One group of Russian soldiers had been killed while playing cards. Elsewhere corpses and cadavers of horses lay on the ground. Jewish labour detachments were put to work burying them. Vet Pál Lévay was forced to kill horses exhausted by the march rather than allow the animals to fall into the hands of partisans. He shot 12 in a single day, prompting an acid remark from his commanding officer: 'Doctor, you are a butcher, not a vet.'[7] After 42 days of marching, Captain Bálint Juhász's unit finally reached the front near Korotoyak, on a bend in the Don 50 miles south of Voronezh. 'The combat formations arrived here tired. We were all expecting some kind of secondary duties or occupation work,' he recalled. Instead, they were ordered to prepare for an attack.

The Don bend at Korotoyak was one of three bridgeheads over the river held by the Soviets on the 125-mile stretch of front assigned to the Hungarians, each one a potential springboard for a counter-attack. Over a period of ten weeks until the end of September, the Hungarians – sometimes supported by German forces – made repeated attempts to crush the bridgeheads, while the Red Army strove to consolidate and expand their positions.

Lacking ammunition, adequate artillery support and above all combat experience, Bálint Juhász was convinced his worn-out division was doomed to failure as it attacked over open ground towards Korotoyak. 'We are responsible for people's lives,' he protested to his superiors. At first, despite Juhász's misgivings, the Hungarians prevailed: Korotoyak was captured. Rather than attempt to swim across the Don to re-join their comrades, trapped Russian soldiers slipped into civilian clothes and then pounced on the town's new masters when the Red Army launched a counter-attack. Now Juhász's fears were confirmed. 12th Light Division disintegrated in panic, most of its men fleeing for the woods and sunflower fields outside the town where groups of Hungarians 15 to 20 strong stumbled around without food for several days. Lieutenant Miklós Kiss Nemeskéri encountered a platoon leader who 'spoke of such horrors and was so confused, it was as if the enemy was already in Budapest. It was a perfect example of how helpless a group of men demoralised by panic can become.'[8]

Sergeant Lajos Béres' motorised unit faced an attack by Russian infantry during these opening clashes on the Don. Advancing through steppe grass as tall as a man, the enemy enjoyed an advantage – promptly squandered by the 'usual cries of "Urra! Urra!"' as the Soviet troops stormed forward. After Hungarian artillery made huge gaps in the advancing enemy lines, Béres' men jumped up and drove back attackers 'completely drunk on vodka. In the face of our unexpected attack and the glint of bayonets, they run away and seek refuge in the tall grass.' For men new to the front like István Simon, these first encounters with the Red Army introduced them to a war for which they were prepared neither physically nor spiritually. 'There is no more horrific sight than a battlefield,' he wrote. 'Destruction, death everywhere. The fields are full of the unburied dead. Nobody cares about them because they don't have time. We walk past them indifferently… The most frightening thing about this war is that there is no pity or mercy. We used to hear about chivalry. Today it's just a dream.'[9]

Hungary's generals regarded these opening battles as a failure – and berated the men accordingly, led by Second Army's commander, Gusztáv Jány. Capable, brave but also hot-headed, Jány threatened to 'decimate' any unit which panicked and fled the field of battle, while Ferenc Szombathelyi complained the men were lacking in daring and heart when they attacked, too quick to run when pressed by the Red Army. 'I want to put an end to such conduct and I will not shy from using the most ruthless means to do so,' he warned. 'This is my first and final warning.'[10]

To many observers, however, Second Army's leaders were to blame for the failures, not the men. Uniforms were already falling apart. Letters and parcels were not reaching the front, nor were basic supplies: alcohol, tobacco, fodder for the horses and especially food for the soldiers, who were expected to march or perform duties for up to 16 hours a day on a diet of 500 grammes of food – jam, butter, tinned meat – washed down with just one third of a litre of coffee.[11] And when they entered battle, all too often poor reconnaissance, stubborn orders, unrealistic objectives and terrible tactics all but ensured any attack miscarried. 'I want to cry and shout with bitterness that I am Hungarian,' Lieutenant Dénes Bárány complained in his diary after watching a failed attack. 'We will shed our blood again without purpose and meaning, and we will remain here, in this bleak, barren land.' Cavalryman Martin Ferenc was ordered to make an attack through 'the valley of Death,' as the men dubbed it. He was promised an enemy strongpoint was ripe for the taking. Instead, Ferenc noted bitterly, 'we come under tremendous fire from the hilltop opposite and we gallop forwards over a large, sloping field, presenting an excellent target. It was a stupid order! Leading a cavalry attack against heavy infantry fire is impossible!' István Simon watched in horror as Hungarian infantry 'strolled helplessly over the battlefield. They didn't take cover, they walked.' Casualties were horrific. 'It was a painful sight to watch,' Simon continued. 'Many Hungarians stood there helpless, without any leadership…'[12]

Lessons were not learned. When Second Army made a third attempt to crush the Uriv bridgehead on 9 September, the infantry attacked over open ground, bunched up, failed to co-ordinate its actions with the artillery and tanks – and suffered horrific losses as a result. Ferenc Szombathelyi would complain that the troops displayed no élan when they attacked – more often than not they 'left their officers in the lurch and got rid of their weapons and uniforms'. Such criticism is not borne out by accounts from the front line. One battalion commander reckoned that he lost two thirds of his officers and three quarters of his men, while the man in charge of 13th Light Division told friends: 'Within an hour, not a single platoon leader was left alive, 70 per cent of the section leaders were also killed.'[13]

The heavy casualties were not solely the fault of poor tactics, as Lajos Somorjai found. 'Hungarians will only fulfil their obligations if they leave at least

100,000 dead here,' his division's chief-of-staff told him. The doctor was shocked at the callousness. 'You're filled with rage when you realise that saving a few pengos is more important than saving the mass of human lives.'[14]

By the end of September 1942, Hungary was well on its way to meeting its obligations. Second Army had lost at least 20,000 men – ten per cent of its total strength, and one in every five of its officers – in the battles on the Don.

Benito Mussolini needed no cajoling to send more men to Russia. He longed for the opportunity – for his and Italy's glory. He had already committed 60,000 men in three partially motorised divisions of the *Corpo di Spedizione Italiano in Russia* – Italian Expeditionary Corps in Russia or CSIR – which fought its way through Ukraine side by side with the Germans in the summer and autumn of 1941. It acquitted itself well – enough to earn its commander the Iron Cross from a grateful ally – but it was not enough. Mussolini was desperate to prove the Italian Army's 'striking power' to his Berlin ally – not least because he wanted a seat at the table rather than allowing the Germans to dictate terms if the Soviet Union was defeated. Worse, he felt Italy's position as the 'second power of the Axis' threatened by the Romanians, especially after the latter captured Odessa. Even before a formal request for more troops in Russia came from Berlin, his foreign minister Galeazzo Ciano told Hitler it was 'something most dear to the Duce's heart: our participation in the war on the Russian front'.[15]

Thus was born the *Armata Italiana in Russia* – shortened to ARMIR and known in the field as the Italian Eighth Army. Over the winter of 1941–42, plans crystalised to send nearly 230,000 men to the Eastern Front: nine divisions, three of them specialist Alpine infantry, plus a couple of brigades of Fascist militia. They were 'well-equipped in every department by Italian standards', supported by nearly 900 guns (many of them obsolete), over 20,000 vehicles, 25,000 horses, 300 anti-tank guns (again mostly out of date) and 30 L6 light tanks. There were too few radios, telephones were antiquated and struggled with the humidity, and the men's standard-issue rifle, the Model 91, was more than 50 years old. Only one division was motorised, making the Eighth Army suitable for defensive tasks only, while supporting air power was almost non-existent: a mere 64 aircraft.[16]

Command fell to Italo Gariboldi, old beyond his 63 years, lacking in verve or ideas, frequently pessimistic. Gariboldi's record was unspectacular, his appointment purely political – to pull the rug from under the popular commander of the CSIR, Giovanni Messe. At 60, Messe was younger and abler, liked by the Germans – 'put in a German uniform, everyone would have believed him to be a German general,' one observer noted – but out of favour in Rome. Ugo

Cavallero, Italy's senior military figure, decided Messe was becoming too popular, too important – and needed to be cut down to size.[17]

Not only had Giovanni Messe been usurped, but his was the loudest voice against committing the Eighth Army on the Eastern Front. He pleaded with Mussolini: Italy had trouble sustaining the 60,000 men of the CSIR. An army 200,000 strong would be short of everything: up-to-date weaponry, suitable tanks, trucks and vehicles. Mussolini brushed the objections aside – Hitler had promised all the support his new army in the East needed. Messe reminded him that the Germans had never once met their obligations to date, that people in Italy had played down the hardships of the winter of 1941, when only a miracle had saved his corps.

'We cannot let ourselves be outnumbered by Slovakia and other smaller states,' the Duce explained. 'I must stand at the side of the Führer in Russia just as the Führer stood at my side in the war against Greece and as he stands at my side now in Africa. Italy's fate is bound with Germany's in the closest sense.

'My dear Messe, an army 200,000 strong will weigh more heavily at the peace negotiations than the 60,000 men of the CSIR.'

Giovanni Messe disagreed. 'I am convinced that an army of more than 200,000 men will find itself in a very sticky situation in Russia.'[18]

In late July 1942, the barracks of garrison towns around Turin began to empty as the Alpine infantry of the *Tridentina* Division embarked on a journey of nearly 2,000 miles to the front in Russia. It would take 48 trains to move the *Tridentina* alone – one of three divisions of *Alpini* dispatched east. The mountain infantry were battle-hardened – all three divisions had seen extensive action in Greece and Albania – and while at least one artilleryman in the *Tridentina* shot himself rather than face the front again, most men headed east on a high. 'We intend to pass through the Caucasus and go to the Black Sea where the temperatures are like those in Italy and we'll spend the winter there,' gunner Corporal Luigi Manzone wrote enthusiastically. 'The war here will end before the winter.' As his battery prepared to leave Chivasso, on the Po 15 miles upstream of Turin, 21-year-old Livio Macchi observed that there were no complaints among his comrades, only 'a spirit that will overcome any obstacle. The attitude of all the men, even in these hours of the greatest tension, shows total discipline and awareness of their responsibility,' the junior officer told his father. 'This is the finest proof of what these superb troops will be able to do and will do in the field.'[19]

Mario Rigoni Stern and his comrades could still taste the previous night's wine as they marched out of Turin's Monte Grappa barracks early one Sunday in late July. The occasional passer-by stopped briefly to watch as the *Alpini* headed for the city's main Porta Nuova station, the only noise the repetitive clash of nails in the boots and the hooves of the mules on the asphalt. Once loaded aboard the train – 40 men or eight mules to each goods wagon, whose comforts extended little beyond the straw on the floor – a trumpeter sounded the advance, the locomotive driver blew his whistle and slowly pulled away. A soldier burst into the opening lines of a folk song: 'I won't be able to forget you, beautiful little Piedmontese girl…' and the entire company joined in.[20]

Priest Don Mario Lerda accompanied men leaving the small town of Avigliana, just west of Turin, 'singing their way through the streets, entering and clearing out all the taverns'. Mothers clung to their sons for the last time, brides cried, tearful girls pinned badges on rookies and veterans alike. 'At the station, indescribable and unforgettable scenes,' Lerda continued. 'Hearts clench and a lump rises in the throat. The locomotive moves slowly, puffing. Another rose, another farewell, and the tearful eyes of those who remain are lost. The shadows of evening descend slowly and the parting is felt more deeply than ever.'[21]

Such scenes were repeated at every railway station in northern Italy as more *Alpini* joined the procession of trains heading to the Eastern Front. Single men exchanged addresses with the young women who jostled with family members on platforms to bid their loved ones farewell. The family of radio operator Aristide Rossi accompanied him to Verona's Porta Vescovo station. 'When the time came to leave, the train moved and after hugs and a few comfort packages, we set off with death in our hearts,' he recalled. 'We all hoped to return, but we knew that not everyone would be able to do so.'[22]

For the next ten or so days, the trains rolled on a far-from-direct route to the front – through the Alpine passes, Vienna, Brno, Kraków, Warsaw, perhaps Lvov or Minsk, then into the steppe. 'We were all silent, absorbed in our own thoughts,' 20-year-old Aristide Rossi remembered. 'No-one could see anything, the only sound we heard was the rhythmic beating of the wheels on the rails and the beating of our hearts: we had a lump in our throats that no one could remove.' Radio operator Camillo Stenico and comrades chatted about home, girlfriends, their jobs before the war. The men inscribed good-luck phrases on the leather band of their caps – normally something religious: 'Madonna protect me' or 'St Maria help me'. Stenico chose '*Mamma ritornerò*' – Mama, I will come back. Their commanding officer was not amused. 'What's going on?' he bellowed. 'Are we an army or a group of pilgrims?' Occasionally the company comedian might attempt to raise the mood, such as impersonating Mussolini and delivering a Duce-like speech – 'full of gibberish and platitudes' – to entertain comrades and distract them from their brooding momentarily. And Don Mario Lerda sought to break the monotony by celebrating Mass – his carriage served as the church, two boxes the altar, his comrades the congregation. One of the soldiers picked up a worn-out mandolin and provided the musical accompaniment. The ruins of Warsaw gave the men the first taste of devastation in the East – and Nazi occupational policy as they watched Jews with large yellow Stars of David on their backs being forced to work by their German masters. The more the trains pressed on through Byelorussia or Ukraine, the more the signs of war: overturned, burned-out railway carriages reduced to their skeletal metal frames, tanks, trucks and cars – all victims of the battles of 1941, all left by the sides of roads and railway lines. Several wagons were moved in front of the locomotives because of the threat of partisans blowing up the track; mules and men were deemed less valuable than the engines. Otherwise, the journey continued in monotony. 'What can I say about the Russian landscape?' Livio Macchi wrote. 'It always looks the same: steppe as far as the eye can see.'[23]

The train ride for most ended in the Donets Basin of Ukraine – typically the industrial city of Gorlovka – from where the road to the front continued on foot, at least a couple of hundred miles, for some units as many as 550. After a few days on the roads of eastern Ukraine and then Russia, it dawned on the *Alpini* that they were heading not for the peaks of the Caucasus but rather the Don steppe. A feeling of 'anger and disappointment' came over officers and men alike. They considered their deployment on the Don 'dishonourable, as well as absurd,' one *Alpino* remembered. The division was trained, armed and equipped for fighting in the mountains, not 'in an environment where the tallest objects as far as the eye could see were telegraph poles'. Marching across the Don steppe, the *Alpini* looked 'like fish out of water,' wrote junior officer Nuto Revelli. 'The worst thing is that our weapons, our equipment, our entire military stock is unsuitable for war on the plains.' The baggage train hauled pitons, manilla ropes, ice axes, crampons, avalanche ropes – ideal for the Caucasus, 'a useless burden' on the Don. A clear sign of the men's mood was that they no longer sang as they marched. 'The *Alpini* are talking – they're worried,' Revelli noted. 'We are all tired and demoralised.' The *Tridentina* was hit the hardest – it was already beyond Rostov and heading into the Caucasus when it received orders to turn about and head for the Don, which proved to be a terrible disappointment, as one soldier recorded. 'There were only endless expanses of sunflowers waiting for us. What desolation before my eyes! There was nothing to observe but endless steppe without farmhouses, trees and relief, there was a view where monotony reigned supreme.' The *Julia* Division's artillery commander Pietro Gay complained the Alpine troops were utterly unsuited to war on the steppe: they lacked tanks, anti-tank guns, their howitzers and mortars – ideal in the mountains – were badly outgunned in open terrain, and ammunition and food would quickly run out, as the divisions relied on mule trains. 'I speak with the heart of a veteran *Alpino* and for the love I have for my soldiers,' Gay warned. 'The employment of these troops on the steppe exposes them to catastrophic consequences.'[24]

Misgivings among the regular ranks of Eighth Army appear to have been far fewer. Fed a constant diet of Fascist propaganda and less-than-honest newspaper and newsreel accounts, some men were even promised that 'victory was now a foregone conclusion', that 'the surrender of the Russian Army was thought to be imminent' and their units would never be committed at the front. Company commander Ottorino Béttiga was convinced the campaign in the East 'was just a walk in the park' and 'once we got there it would be all over'. More generally, most Italian soldiers expected to grapple with the Red Army – and they expected to be victorious. 'The Russians are not advancing – and nor will they,' one soldier assured his family. 'Instead, we will advance with all our flags unfurled and we will show to the world that the Italian soldier knows how to fight and be victorious.' A non-commissioned officer remembered that the 'news coming in from the Russian front had created a euphoric mood in all of us. The Germans were going from one success to another. Ours should have been a long, risk-free stroll.'[25]

In August 1942, that 'risk-free stroll' brought the divisions of Italian Eighth Army to the Don. The sight of the broad, slow-moving river – which was anywhere between 300 and 1,300 feet wide – from the high southern bank left many Italians with 'a melancholy feeling'. Yet here, a 200-mile stretch of the Don between Voronezh and Stalingrad, they were expected to stand, holding the line of the river through the winter while the Germans captured Stalingrad. In the spring, Giovanni Messe assured them, they could return to their homeland. As Eighth Army settled into its positions, the Red Army began probing them – a breakthrough here would strike at the rear of the German Sixth Army and wreak havoc with the advance on Stalingrad. After a few minor skirmishes and the occasional attack by raiding parties, the confidence of the newly arrived Italians was tested for the first time in earnest at 2.30am on Thursday 20 August. The muzzles of artillery pieces and mortar barrels flashed briefly with orange and yellow tongues of fire, and the Don night was filled with the shrill sound of rockets leaving their racks as the Stalin organs of Sixty-Third Army opened fire. The projectiles came crashing down on the positions of the *Sforzesca* Division. In Russia for no more than two months, it was exhausted when it entered the line on the south bank of the Don after marching nearly 200 miles. The *Sforzesca*'s commander, Michele Vaccaro – 'small, round; the helmet he wears looks like a cap because the general's plump, smooth cheeks are barely held by the chin strap' – seemed untroubled by the Soviet offensive initially and more interested in his breakfast, 'a hearty omelette sandwich'. Vaccaro's men were outnumbered three – and in some situations four – to one and unable to prevent the Red Army forging a bridgehead on the south bank. Otherwise, however, the terse, incomplete initial reports reaching his headquarters were both optimistic ('We are containing them', 'the enemy attack has been deprived of its impetus') and desperate: 'The battalion is in a terrible state', 'I don't know how many company commanders are still alive', or 'The infantry are fighting stone by stone!' By mid-day, at least one battalion was encircled, its supporting artillery overrun, its fighting ranks now filled not with infantrymen but cooks and clerks. With bayonets fixed, they bludgeoned their way through the Soviet ring of encirclement, leaving 'a bloody trail of dead and wounded unaccounted for, writhing on the ground in pain, screaming in despair: "Mama, mama... Don't leave us..."' The breakout succeeded, but the battalion ceased to exist. It had begun the day with 680 men. By early afternoon it numbered barely 100 souls, and 30 of those were wounded.[26] Nevertheless, 20 August ended with the Italian line battered, driven back, but still intact.

The Soviet offensive resumed with undiminished fury at first light on the 21st. 'It's a slaughterhouse,' one experienced non-commissioned officer told his commander. 'The battalion is defending itself with everything it has, the Russians continue to attack, dozens of them fall every time, but there are too many of them, too many of them, *Signor* Major, and they're still coming.' The cavalry of the Savoy looked on helplessly. They could see the muzzle flashes of cannon engaged at the front and hear the distinct cries of their countrymen: 'Mama!', 'Help!', 'Savoy!', 'Italy!' Soon the *Sforzesca*'s front collapsed, its men streaming to the rear. Cavalry officer Lieutenant Franco Toja was appalled by the 'total chaos' he found in the village of Chebotarevskii – eight miles from the Don:

> Panic has gripped everyone, soldiers and officers alike; men are only looking for a way out, on foot, by car, by cart, any means for escaping will do. It's frightening, like a suicidal herd; people who are no longer thinking, unarmed, screaming, gripped by terror, convinced they have the Russians just a few metres away. There are officers without ranks, mixed up with the troops, only concerned about fleeing: what a pity, my God! A major to whom I turned asking for information about the regiment replied: 'What are you doing, you fool, go back and get yourself to safety: don't be a hero!' I couldn't stand it any more and let him go with a whip across the face: he stood in the dust touching his wound, without reacting.[27]

Cavalryman Nino Malingambi picked up a soldier from the *Sforzesca* who begged to be taken to the rear. 'I asked him how things were, but he didn't respond,' Malingambi remembered. 'He was holding on to my waist, like a child, and shaking. It was only after a few minutes of silence that he seemed to remember my question and answered: "Up there is death."'[28]

The collapse of the *Sforzesca* shook the cavalrymen. 'The encounter with these troops was depressing,' senior corporal Aristide Bottini recalled. 'Warehouses destroyed, magazines in flames, men disbanded and without weapons, without helmets, without muskets, men in shirtsleeves running this way and that, crying, their faces distraught with terror.' A battalion commander tried to put a stop to the panic, pistol in hand, but to no avail. The men – some of them without boots – were finally halted far behind the front, packed on to lorries and sent back into the line. A good number jumped off before they returned to the front.[29]

While the ill-fated *Sforzesca* crumpled, their neighbours in the *Tagliamento* – a legion of militia and Blackshirts loyal to the Duce – stood firm. 'You can never rely on the *Sforzesca*,' one Blackshirt major sneered while his men fought 'tooth and nail' and preferred to be 'slaughtered on the spot' than give ground. If they retreated it was only because more than half had been wiped out.[30]

For the first four days of Sixty-Third Army's offensive, the Savoy cavalry had observed the fighting at arm's length, probing, scouting, but never engaging the enemy. As one of the oldest regiments in the Italian Army, the Savoy prided itself on its history, traditions and discipline. Morale was high. The men rode to the Don singing:

> When the Savoy enter Milan
> All the women clap their hands
> Clap their hands out of joy
> Long live the Savoy Cavalry![31]

Officers expected the highest dress standards of their men – even in battle. Mid-gallop, one soldier was rebuked for daring 'to walk around without a tie', while after another action a messenger was given a dressing down for delivering a report with his uniform still covered in dust and sand. The cavalrymen both admired and dismissed the new divisions imbued with ideological zeal. 'These lads have tremendous guts,' one officer said of the *Tagliamento* – its ranks filled with Fascist youth – 'but their discipline, gentlemen, their discipline is reckless…'[32]

When darkness fell on 23 August, the Savoy's 2nd Squadron camped outside Izbushensky, an otherwise nondescript farming hamlet of a dozen or so wooden huts barely two miles from the Don. Around 3.30 the next morning, the cavalrymen were surprised by machine-gun and mortar fire from Russian troops, who used the cover of sunflowers and bushes to approach the camp. With the first rays of light beginning to bring day to the Don valley, the cavalrymen's artillery pieces flashed while the riders mounted their steeds and began to move towards the enemy lines. Emerging from a slight hollow, they caught the Russians by surprise. There was the cry 'Galoppooo!' followed almost immediately by 'Caricaaat!' – Charge! – an order, junior officer Pietro Crespi observed, 'unthinkable a few moments before'. To a man the riders responded with a thunderous chorus: '*Savoia!*' 'The long-awaited cry, the cry that we have dreamed of in childhood, which we have believed for years, which has already consecrated many other cavalry heroes, is given!' Captain Francesco De Leone remembered. 'And it rises above the din of battle, the bangs, the screech of machine-guns.' De Leone was reminded of the paintings on the walls of the regiment's mess, except there were more horrors than heroics on the field at Izbushensky. Horses fatally wounded 'kept galloping like ghosts before crashing to the ground, suddenly, like oaks struck by lightning'. Others, deprived of their riders, continued to gallop at full canter through a field of sunflowers or trotted back to the Italian line. Distraught, raising their heads and neighing constantly, they were put out of their misery by heartbroken cavalrymen.

After what seemed an eternity, despite machine-gun fire raking the field, the cavalry fell upon the Soviet positions. 'Sabres strike enemy infantry furiously,' De Leone wrote. 'The horses' hooves trample machine-guns, belts, boxes and men, hand-grenades hit enemies who crouch in foxholes.' Some cavalrymen wielded heavy Cossack sabres, tightly bound to their wrists. A blow to the head from one was fatal – even if a soldier was wearing a helmet. The skulls of those without 'burst like a pomegranate'. Vitaliano Tufano leaped into a Russian machine-gun position and dispatched the gunner with three slashes of his sabre. Another soldier found he was unable to draw his sabre, so rode into battle with a hand-grenade held high – then dismounted to throw it at his foe. Machine-guns, mortars, field guns, the slash of a sabre, shrapnel from grenades – the toll on man and beast was horrific, as were the scenes played out on the field of Izbushensky that Monday morning. A fine white stallion, beloved by the entire regiment, galloped to his last breath before collapsing, soaked with blood, while one short-sighted mare stumbled repeatedly because it couldn't see the obstacles – dead and wounded Italians and Russians, as well as the cadavers of the Savoy's horses. A bugler, struggling with his instrument and his pistol, accidentally shot his horse in the head and it collapsed to the ground. A Russian bullet ricocheted off Lieutenant Carlo Scarpelli's helmet and struck the man riding by his side. There were even occasional acts of humanity. One corporal rode through a gauntlet of Soviet troops to rescue a comrade, picked him up, then charged back through the enemy lines – taking several Russian prisoners with him. A female Soviet medic was captured after a sabre blow shattered her shoulder and breasts. She tended not to her own injuries but those of an injured Italian. 'The cavalryman died in her arms and she died soon afterwards,' De Leone wrote. His own steed was shot from under him, but the officer resolved to make a stand on the field of battle with his orderly. 'First we will use up all the ammunition, then we will kill ourselves rather than be taken prisoners,' he told him. The orderly nodded: 'As you command, Captain.' The Savoy charged the Soviet lines at least twice. They would have attacked as many times as their commander Colonel Alessandro Bettoni ordered, except that Bettoni didn't have the heart. A bullet had pierced his jacket, but otherwise the regimental commander had survived the charge unscathed – physically, that is. White as a ghost he returned to his command post, put his hand on the regimental banner, and greeted each man as he returned. 'The Savoy charged!' they said excitedly. Bettoni nodded. 'The Savoy charged!' Major Dario Manusardi begged Bettoni to commit his reserve. '*Signor* Colonel, this is Savoy's moment of glory! The whole regiment can charge, routing the last enemy resistance…' Alessandro Bettoni did not respond.

It didn't matter. The Savoy carried the day. By mid-morning the battle for Izbushensky was over. Pietro Crespi surveyed the battlefield: 'Russian and Italian soldiers lie on the ground, together, reconciled by a common death even if under a different flag; and the horses, our horses, dozens of them, amidst bloody saddles and torn saddlebags.' Wounded Italian cavalrymen were collected by their comrades and laid out on tent cloths, while other men collected personal effects – a cap, a blood-covered sabre, a saddle – to send to the families of the deceased riders, and regimental chaplain Don Passeri sat on an ammunition crate, scrupulously recording the names of the dead.

Among some of the 500 Russian prisoners, some were found wearing the grey-green of the *Sforzesca*, killed a few days earlier and worse, carrying the photographs and letters from families of the Italian dead. Their captors were incensed and 'started hitting the prisoners with their fists and slapping them,' Pietro Crespi wrote. 'I should have intervened to prevent such reactions, but I couldn't, I too let myself be dominated by resentment. The prisoners suffer, they do not defend themselves; but some cry, they are frightened.'

The Italian cavalry had driven off a force three times their size and inflicted tenfold casualties on their foe, who left behind 150 dead (Soviet sources say 'several dozen') at Izbushensky as well as guns, mortars, machine-guns and rifles. Yet far from being buoyed, the Savoy's commander seemed heartbroken, having lost 32 men and more than 100 horses. His friend Cesco Casanova found Alessandro Bettoni sitting on the step of his command vehicle, his face in his hands, tears welling in his eyes. 'Casanova, do you think that the parents and relatives of these boys will understand that I had no other choice?' It was the fate of the regiment's horses which struck Pietro Crespi, who watched them watering after the action. 'Even the horses have their fallen, their missing,' he noted. 'There was no Vallestura, no Discepolo, no Nemi. Nemi was the oldest horse in the squadron; he never distinguished himself in equestrian competitions, he was not part of the line of horses of high lineage or great breeding; he was just an ordinary military horse, strong, generous, ardent, faithful.'[33]

Though little more than a footnote among the titanic clashes on the Eastern Front in 1942, Izbushensky was a tonic to Italian morale – 'the names of these very daring regiments are on the lips of every warrior, as they are on the lips of the Germans who never cease singing their praises,' a delighted Giovanni Messe noted. He presented more than 50 medals to participants in the victory. German officers – otherwise highly critical of the Italians' performance on the Don – did not hold back in expressing their admiration to Bettoni. '*Herr Colonel*, we do not know how to do these things any more.' 'The praise was, unwittingly, bitter,' war correspondent Indro Montanelli observed. 'The Italian Army knew how to do well things which were no longer needed, and badly those which would have been necessary in the war it was fighting.'[34]

Praise or not, the day after the cavalry charge the Germans decided to take the situation on the Don in hand, insisting: 'No-one is to retreat from their present positions. Anyone ordering this is liable to severe penalties,' before taking charge of the *Sforzesca* 'to stop the retreating movements at all costs'. The Soviet attacks on the Don petered out in early September after a combination of Italo-German reinforcements and Axis air power blunted Sixty-Third Army's offensive. Alpine units were blooded in its closing stages – Mario Rigoni Stern was convinced they were being deliberately sacrificed in the unfamiliar steppe by the Germans to see if they could be trusted to hold the line away from the mountains. It was a view shared by the *Alpini*'s commander, Gabriele Nasci, who feared his men would be plagued by 'low morale' if they were not sent to the mountains. His protest fell on deaf ears – and Soviet shells fell on his Alpine troops as, for the first time, they experienced a Soviet artillery barrage, which turned the steppe into 'a sea of fire', before they drove off enemy attacks in 'fields of sunflowers which reached up to the chest'.[35]

The battles on the Don at the end of August cost Italian Eighth Army 5,000 casualties – more than half of them in the battered *Sforzesca*, which all but ceased to exist. The *Tridentina*'s Captain Gaetano Maggi lost four fellow officers in this first encounter with the Red Army. 'This is the hard law of war, which we obey and which we are prepared for,' he told his wife Teresita. 'My heart and mind ache, of course, when I think of a lost colleague but, in us, there is an acceptance of sacrifice which is amazing.' While Maggi wept for his comrades, the loss of friends and compatriots drove some Italian soldiers to acts of vengeance. 'We swear to avenge them,' one vowed. 'Our fallen can rest in peace, we will avenge them.' Another wrote: 'All of us Italians in this land thousands of kilometres away from the Motherland are animated by a single will: to vindicate all our glorious fallen, who bathed this cold land with their blood.' Atrocities provoked 'an irrepressible hatred,' one soldier wrote, 'which reveals our most bestial instincts of revenge, revenge and more revenge! Merciless killing!' There were numerous instances of Soviet wounded or soldiers 'pretending to surrender by raising their hands' – then continuing the fight. 'Never trust raised hands, fake wounded and fake dead,' one Italian general warned his men. The experienced Eighth Army soldier soon learned to 'finish off' enemy wounded 'with bayonets – because even if they appeared dead, they could not be trusted'. A colonel remembered that one group of Russian soldiers was 'put to death' when it refused to surrender, while the ranks of the elite light infantry, the *Bersaglieri*, gained particular notoriety for shooting captured Russians on the spot – indeed, at least one unit received specific orders 'not to take prisoners'.[36]

As far as the men of Eighth Army were concerned, however, they had fought courageously, honourably and victoriously on the Don. 'How many humble and heroic acts were performed by soldiers of all ages and conditions,' Gaetano Maggi gushed. 'Not a single one wavered or flinched under enemy fire. And yet, among them, many were young men of the last draft. Everyone has done their duty and perhaps even more.' While there was 'widespread belief that our soldier was inferior to the enemy as far as weapons were concerned,' Arrigo Pintonello, the senior Italian chaplain on the Eastern Front, reported, most Italian soldiers felt superior to their foe. Fascist politician Aldo Vidussoni toured field hospitals in September and found morale 'high'. 'No-one complains, not even at the most painful moments: all are proud at shedding blood for the cause and want to return to their units soon,' the 28-year-old reported. Any fighting, Piedmontese pioneer Osvaldo Curato reassured his family, was 'always decided in our favour. We showed them who the Italians at war are.' Bruno Carloni, the 21-year-old commander of a company of *Bersaglieri*, wrote to his father in a similar vein. 'Here there is always marching, advancing, fighting – and always victory. The enemy withdraws and leaves destruction. We chase him, and we will keep chasing him until final victory.' Corporal Francesco Zanetti rejoiced in the capture of 'an immense territory that was the heart, the life of Russia' – thousands of square miles of land, great industrial cities, rich seams of coal, and millions of people liberated from the Bolshevik yoke. 'Still this is not over,' he wrote. 'We have not stopped. Every day new ground is seized, this now tottering Russian Army is annihilated. These are the final blows it will receive.' One week later, he added: 'Here the news

'The German soldier has shown to the entire world that his attacking spirit is as alive as ever…'
Kharkov, Kerch and Sevastopol, May–July 1942

(Above) An 88mm flak cannon engaged in ground combat against Soviet armour outside Kharkov.

(Left) German assault troops scramble over the Tatar Wall, one of the historic defences brought back into use by the Red Army to hold the Kerch peninsula in the Crimea.

(Above) 'It was almost as if the devil had created the terrain…' German troops comb through a smashed goods yard on the barren northern shore of Severnaya Bay.

(Below left) German soldiers by the waters of Severnaya Bay with warehouses burning on the waterfront in the last week of June.

(Below right) 'The battle carved runes on the faces of the men…' Two Germans crawl along a ravine to avoid the shrapnel of Soviet guns while delivering food to their comrades at the front.

'With such a mighty war machine unleashed here… this war in the East must be won soon by us…' *Fall Blau* **unleashed, end of June 1942**

(Above) 'The attack rolls…' A Panzer Mk3 follows German armour moving across the Don steppe in formation.

(Right) 'Everything is rushing forward. It's like we're on a high…' Troops of the *Grossdeutschland* motorised infantry division leave a village in flames as they support the drive to the Don.

'Rommeling again…' From the Gazala line to Alamein, May–August 1942

(Above) Rommel's favourite Italian division, the *Ariete*, manoeuvres in formation.

(Top left) 'Not an easy man to serve…' Erwin Rommel (second right) confers with his chief-of-staff Fritz Bayerlein, *Afrika Korps* intelligence officer Friedrich von Mellenthin and *Afrika Korps* commander Walther Nehring.

(Bottom left) 'We cold-bloodedly walked past the bodies of our comrades…' A British Grant tank passes a knocked-out – and long-obsolete – Panzer Mk2 destroyed in the battle of the Cauldron, 6 June.

(Below) 'Salvoes of exploding shells spewed out death a thousandfold…' Armour burns in the Cauldron, 5 June.

(Above) 'We crossed the Libyan–Egyptian border and were in the land of the Pharaohs again…' Columns roll into Egypt past a Panzer Mk3 of 21st Panzer Division at the end of June.

(Right) 'Death reaped his harvest indiscriminately…' A dead soldier lies next to a knocked-out Panzer Mk3 at Alamein.

The war for oil: The battles for the Caucasus and Stalingrad, July–November 1942

(Above) 'The destruction, the death is terrible…' Assault troops supported by a Panzer Mk3 attack a fortified position in central Rostov, 26 July.

(Left) Pack horses and *Gebirgsjäger* (mountain infantry) file along a mountain pass ferrying supplies to the front line; the animals died at the rate of 30 a day.

(Below) 'As if someone has pushed the Alps together…' Elements of a panzer division move through the Caucasian steppe with the mountains around Pyatigorsk in the distance, circa 10 August.

(Above) 'As if you were staring through smoked glass during an eclipse…' A panzer commander watches the oil wells of the Kuban burn.

(Right) 'Our feet are leaden…' Weary German infantry march through the Caucasus foothills.

(Below) 'Like a parade ground manoeuvre…' 16th Panzer Division races towards the Volga, 23 August.

(Above) 'The fighting strength of the units melted like butter in the sun…' A mortar team and infantry from 577th Infantry Regiment approach Stalingrad's Barrikady gun works, 16 October.

(Left) 'The last act of one of the greatest epics in German history…' Battalion commander Karl-Heinz Fricke raises the German ensign on the burned-out façade of the Univermag department store in Stalingrad's Red Square, 26 September.

is always excellent. Slowly, however, ever forward. The Russians are taking some really heavy blows.' And a few days later: 'The victorious march of our troops continues. Every day, we see an increasing debacle, the disaster which is happening in the Russian Army.'[37]

While Giovanni Messe was publicly delighted with the performance of his men and the outcome of the Don fighting, in private he was appalled by the heavy-handedness of his ally – and the response of his spineless superior, Italo Gariboldi. Not only did he have the situation in hand when the Germans weighed in and took charge of his divisions, but the order to do so, Messe protested, was a slur on men:

> … who, under my orders, harshly, valiantly and bloodily fought for six days against an overpowering enemy without receiving any outside help.
>
> In the name of the dead and the living, as a commander, as a direct witness and as an Italian, I must raise the most vehement protest against the insinuation that the retreat of these heroic, exhausted and decimated troops was voluntary and that a German commander is needed to call them back to duty.[38]

Gariboldi refused to intervene. Relations between the two men, never good, broke down irreparably. Messe turned to Mussolini and asked to be given a new command 'so that you can employ me where it suits you best'. He gushed: 'You know that I have only one ambition: to serve as a soldier in Fascist Italy and you who are its Great Leader.'[39] On 24 September, Giovanni Messe was relieved of his command.

Of the three Axis armies on the Don in 1942, the Romanian was arguably the best: brave, battle-hardened, dogged. Adolf Hitler may have dismissed him as 'no good at all', while his officers haughtily looked down on him as racially inferior and 'never able to live up to the German soldier', but the Romanian was the staunchest ally on the Eastern Front, committed to the struggle against the Soviet Union since the very first day. The country's leader, Ion Antonescu, had vowed to 'erase the stain from our history' and liberate the provinces of Bessarabia and Bukovina, occupied by the Red Army in the summer of 1940. Once he had done so, the Romanian soldier continued east, along the Black Sea coast to Odessa and, after it fell, he marched into the Crimea, then the Caucasus. But he yearned to strike *west* and grapple with his country's mortal foe: Hungary. 'We didn't want anything from the Soviets – we wanted Transylvania from the Hungarians!' was a common sentiment, while the slogan 'Now on to Budapest!' was seen painted on at least one Romanian tank. One senior German officer was stunned by the response when he asked Romanian soldiers if they knew what they were fighting for: '*Jawohl, Herr* General! For Transylvania!' This wasn't merely the talk of the rank-and-file. Romanian generals were convinced the two nations would clash eventually and feared the army would be bled white 'in the distant lands of Bolshevik Russia'. The Chief of the Romanian General Staff, Iosif Lacobici, had even resigned over the issue, warning Antonescu not to commit more forces to the Eastern Front in 1942. 'The Romanian soldier will not fight enthusiastically far from home,' he warned. 'Participation in an offensive which takes our forces far from the country is not popular.'[40]

Having thrown his hat in the ring with Hitler, Ion Antonescu now realised he could not retrieve it. The campaign in the East continued 'because we cannot act otherwise. The war against Russia must be ended.' As one regimental commander reminded his men, 'if Germany is defeated, we are also defeated'.[41] And so in January 1942, Antonescu overruled objections and committed to deploying the flower of the Romanian Army – 16 divisions and half a million men – to the Eastern Front that year.

The vast majority of those men – like the ordinary Hungarian soldier – were drawn from farming stock: simple, often illiterate, but also hard-working, good-natured and dogged. Above them was a meagre cadre of non-commissioned officers, most of whom were assigned to administrative duties rather than leading the men at the front. Career officers were few; reservists were the backbone of front-line units. Their training, tactics and methods were outdated. Relations with the men were poor, discipline was severe, bordering on the brutal. While waiting for a flight out of Stalingrad, junior officer Edgar Klaus watched a Romanian fighter squadron fall in. The commander paced up and down in front of the men, 'reading out several orders, shouting like a madman'. He grabbed one ground crew engineer and slapped him down, continued down the line and seized a second man by his tie, shaking him repeatedly. It was, Klaus remembered, 'an unusual sight for us – but an everyday experience for the Romanians'. It wasn't the only injustice he suffered. Rations depended on rank – and the ordinary soldier lost out, Edgar Klaus observed, reduced to 'only the bones left to pick'. The men frequently begged their German ally for extra supplies – bread and cigarettes especially. Leave was a moot point, as Fourth Panzer Army's commander Hermann Hoth found out. 'Talking to individual Romanians is depressing,' he wrote. 'You ask how long they've been away from home and they say they've not seen their families for two years.' On the rare occasions Romanian soldiers were allowed home, little help was afforded them: some men had to walk hundreds of kilometres because no means of transport were provided – and when it was, the troops were packed into 'goods wagons where they crammed on top of each other, rather than in heated passenger carriages like German soldiers'.

Provisions at the front were no better. Equipment was 'inconsistent, poor and in some cases outmoded'. Motor vehicles were in short supply: 200 in each infantry division, five times fewer than in a comparable German formation. The horse took their place: one for nearly every two men, upwards of 8,000 animals hauling an average of 1,600 carts, wagons and limbers.[42]

Their leaders were invariably equally unsuited to the war of movement in the East. Staff officers and commanders had taken their lead from Paris, not Berlin, between the wars. They were neither especially pro-German, nor schooled in the art of Blitzkrieg. They were, their German ally observed, somewhat unstable – prone to extremes of optimism or pessimism in difficult situations. Ion Antonescu was no less critical of his country's military elite, especially the General Staff, dismissed by the self-styled *conducător* (leader) variously as 'robotic', 'bureaucratic', 'rigid' and 'stupid', the plans it drew up 'ridiculous'. 'Everyone will ask: are these the brains of the Army?' As a career officer and later defence minister, he felt justified in such withering criticism. Named Romania's premier in the wake of Moscow's 'land grab' over the summer of 1940, he had then relied on German support to overcome his rivals. As a result, Antonescu always felt unsure of his position. 'Your Führer – like the Duce – has a great movement behind him, one almost encompassing the entire nation. I have nothing like that behind me,' he told German officials.[43]

The fates of two Romanian Armies were bound with German forces at Stalingrad: the Third, which initially marched into the Caucasus before being transferred to the Don west of Kalach, and the Fourth, built around the experienced and trusted VI Corps, which advanced side by side with German units across the Kalmyk steppe towards Stalingrad from the south and found crossing 'the Russian Sahara' every bit as dispiriting and disorientating as its ally. Constantin Kirițescu painted a vivid picture of his comrades marching for mile upon mile along primitive tracks through the largely featureless terrain:

Feet bury themselves in the thick, black dust. The air is full of dust which penetrates eyes, mouths, lungs. Skin and clothes are covered with a thick sticky, powdery layer. Trucks and carts are buried up to their axles in the sand. Horses make futile efforts, carters curse and swear, engines whine constantly. At any moment, it is necessary for people to intervene, to use their arms to unload, to lighten and free the vehicles. Bodies, soiled by dust, are soaked in sweat... Exotic, unexpected sights sometimes add a picturesque note to this desolate monotony. From time to time, the curiosity of the soldiers is attracted by the appearance of caravans of camels, ridden by women raised on the two humps. Only the nights when there is a moon offer a fairy-tale spectacle to a few who still have the soul to detach themselves from the miseries of life, to forget the fatigue of marching and to overcome the cold of night, to taste the delights of the nocturnal aspect of the immensity of the Cossack steppe, under the silvery brilliance of the moon's rays.[44]

Dr Iosif Lazăr stared at the night sky during breaks in the advance and pondered life. 'We can't believe that we really are Romanians, out pursuing an enormous front which seems to run away from us the more we strive to reach it.'[45] It was the vastness of Russia which troubled Captain Dumitru Păsat's commanding officer. 'What are we looking for here, Păsat?' he asked. 'Who and what are we fighting for? It's woe to us. Either we will die and our bones will be left behind in this steppe, or we will be taken prisoner and starved to death.'[46]

The Hungarian soldier had always questioned why he was fighting the Russian on the Don rather than the Romanian in Transylvania. A few subscribed to anti-Soviet propaganda, like Sergeant Zoltán Árokszállási, who saw 'bestial cruelty' in the eyes of Russian prisoners and concluded it 'truly is time to wipe them off the face of the earth for good'. But the vast majority of Hungarian soldiers, Second Army's chief-of-staff Gyula Kovács conceded, were unprepared mentally for the war in the East and, above all, neither hated Bolshevism nor their Russian foe. 'Without hatred, we cannot demand the dash, tenacity and cruelty which are just as indispensable in modern warfare as they were in ancient times.'[47]

While many Italian soldiers regarded 'the war against the Bolshevik as their ally's war, not their own', the ARMIR's senior chaplain, Arrigo Pintonello, observed, they also wholeheartedly supported it – largely on religious grounds. On the very day the conflict began, Rome journalist Vittorio Gorresio noted that his fellow countrymen 'seemed to have found the true enemy to beat, the Bolshevism of the godless, deniers of private property'. War in the East assumed the importance of a 20th-century crusade, where the Italian soldier would 'overthrow Bolshevism in the interests of civilisation and the Christian and Catholic world'. 'This war is the continuation of the March on Rome,' corps commander Francesco Zingales told his men. 'It is our war, yours, Blackshirts, you who started the March on Rome.' The Soviets were 'without God, without religion, the pure delinquency of the race,' one committed Fascist wrote. It was a recurring theme. 'We are fighting the greatest battle ever between peoples and nations,' one soldier wrote. 'The crusade of a new world against the darkness of the godless ones...' A soldier from the 80th Infantry Regiment was determined

to 'completely destroy' an enemy 'which has suppressed us for millennia [*sic*]...
planting the insignia of Imperial Rome on this land made filthy by the Bolshevik
stench'. And viewed as a crusade, it made many an Italian more committed to the
cause. 'We will win – at any cost,' one soldier assured his family, 'even if it means
sacrificing our lives for the greatness of the Fascist homeland.' A mechanic in a
vehicle repair unit was convinced the Soviets intended to sweep across Europe
and 'enjoy you and every Italian woman,' he told his wife. 'I would rather be torn
to pieces than witness such things. Religion and Christian civilisation must
triumph over Russian barbarity and the dangerous Judeo-Jewish-Masonic
minorities.' Junior officer Nicolino Perrotta believed 'in all our work there is the
seal of our civilisation, of Italian culture, of the greatness of our immortal
homeland,' while Lino Berti was convinced he was fighting 'the holiest war that
has ever been fought'. He told his family in Trentino in northern Italy: 'How
many young men are fighting here in Russia, sacrificing themselves with great joy
for the most sublime cause that exists, civilisation, the faith of Christian virtues.
Here is our cause, here is our holiest duty.'[48]

And so many an Italian set foot on Russian soil certain he was liberating 'a
people enslaved and deprived of all freedom'. But the ground was not as fertile as
he had hoped. A quarter of a century of Soviet propaganda, of Soviet schooling,
of sidelining religion, had sowed the seeds of Communism – especially among
the young. 'They don't seem to understand that this war can bring them liberation
from Bolshevism,' one Italian soldier observed. From conversations with the
local populace, Pasquale Grignaschi felt that Communism was 'tolerated as a
necessary evil'. People cared little for Stalin, yet they fought with such
determination 'for an ideal that they do not fully share, on behalf of leaders they
begrudgingly tolerate'. The answer was obvious, Luigi Guerrieri Gonzaga, a
captain in a horse-drawn artillery unit, offered: 'We are foreigners – and the
invader is never welcome. They think everything is about changing masters and
that the new one is a foreigner.' Gonzaga came to admire the Russian people,
their strong sense of morality and order, their love of family, punctuality, their
gentle, quietly stoic attitude. 'All in all, they are a people as good as their soul, full
of kindness, who have suffered incredibly over the centuries and still do... They
suffer in silence, they die in silence.' They could also be 'cruel to the point of
bestiality. Used to the harshest suffering, they are indifferent and merciless to
their fellow man.' The *Pasubio* Division found the populace 'welcoming,
hospitable towards the occupying troops and especially towards the Italian
soldier, noting the humanitarian sense with which it is treated'. A soldier in the
Julia Division remembered how 'women ran into kitchens and came out holding
cups of milk to offer to the men' as they marched through villages, or brought

food out for the wounded. The people of the Don steppe, like the Italian soldier, were mostly solid peasant farming stock. They shared their quarters – simple, overcrowded *isbas* (thatched cottages) – with their hosts, whereas German troops forcibly evicted the original inhabitants. Life behind the front could almost be idyllic, as the occupier was readily welcomed into the *isbas* in the evening. 'The whole family would gather around the Italian soldier, and they never tired of asking about Italy, about anything that was not Russian,' one Italian soldier remembered.[49]

The key factor for the ordinary Russian was that the Italian was *not* a German. '*Italiantsi khoroshi, nemtsi ne khoroshi, nemtsi kaput*,' an elderly Russian repeated to Egisto Corradi. 'Italians good, Germans no good, death to Germans.' A historian who lived in Rossosh recalled that the 'Germans would take anything they wanted from us without asking. Italians, on the other hand, bartered with their produce – lemons, wine, cigarettes, holy images – to get food.' In fact, despite his assertion, the Italian soldier plundered and looted at will, as one German liaison officer observed, swinging between 'currying favour with the civilian populace and senselessly threatening them with weapons'. There was a lively black market in cigarettes and food – some of it intended for the front line – as unscrupulous troops raided warehouses and depots. In some towns, the troops slaughtered not merely livestock, but even dogs and cats. 'We confiscate and steal anything edible in the villages on our way through because if we were to live on what we receive as daily rations, we would have been starving a long time ago,' an artillery officer wrote unashamedly. Oliderio Rattenni was appalled by the devastation wrought by his comrades in the *Ravenna* Division in the Don villages. 'It is no longer about stolen potatoes, but about goats, lambs, chickens and other things which the infantrymen eat,' he wrote. 'At the mere sight of the grey-green troops, inhabitants secure their animals and take refuge in their homes, closing the doors. Poor people, who knows what they think of us.' One female former collective farm labourer remembered that Italian troops 'preyed on the inhabitants, stealing bread, cattle and other property. Everyone – officers and men – began to send parcels containing flour, clothing, and vegetable fats to their families; they even sent home wheat, millet, rye and so on.' *Cuneense* Division commander General Emilio Battisti was forced to order his *Alpini* to stop stealing tomatoes, potatoes, vegetables, chickens and eggs, while the civilian official overseeing agriculture in the Boguchar district, about 140 miles south of Voronezh, felt compelled to complain about the ongoing looting. 'If they had given us only half of the promised aid, we would not now have a land completely bled dry, with abandoned fields,' he reported with frustration. Instead, he watched some Italian units plunder unimpeded, such as the *Torino* Division, which had become 'an utter embarrassment' after a year in Russia, stealing at will, taking oxen and horses, setting fire to hives to steal honey. Some men progressed from theft to rape – five assaults on women were reported in a single night. One mother of three complained that rapes by Romanian and Italian troops were commonplace – sometimes repeatedly 'taking it in turns to satisfy their desires'; sometimes the women's children or relatives were forced to watch. The Italian authorities did at least intervene. Antonio Zanfagnini was forced to fall in with the rest of his unit after three Italian soldiers raped a young mother. The victim identified the perpetrators, who were led away in full view of their comrades. 'Too bad that such disgusting episodes take place and dishonour our uniform,' Zanfagnini wrote. 'Unfortunately the war also brings ugliness as well as destruction and slaughter.'[50]

Though reprisals and punishments could, on occasions, be as harsh as those carried out by the Germans – one farm labourer unable to work because her children were ill was strung upside down in a well, for example – most Italians were appalled by their ally's treatment of civilians in the East. On his way to the front, Lino Moroni's train halted in Warsaw where he watched Jews being packed into goods wagons. Shots rang out occasionally as uniformed Germans tried to corral people into the waiting cattle trucks until finally the train pulled out. 'On the platform, there is just a heap of dead,' a horrified Moroni wrote. 'These poor people... We looked at each other, intimidated and upset.' Nuto Revelli watched a group of Germans pounce upon an elderly Russian 'in a beastly manner, kicking and punching him, knocking him down'. The man attempted to protect himself, repeating: 'Not a partisan, not a partisan.' Bleeding and numb, he staggered to his feet only to face another onslaught of blows. Finally, having had their 'fun', the attackers let the man go. 'The Russian struggles to get up, almost failing to believe the order to go away,' Revelli observed. 'He takes a few uncertain steps, as if he were afraid that a volley of fire would strike him in the back, then flees like a rocket, disappearing into a field of sunflowers.' Jews suffered the most. A small number of Italians thought their maltreatment justified. 'Hanging the Jews only deserves a brief mention here,' Sergeant Francesco Zito wrote. 'We have dealt with them as they deserved – no sympathy for this race of hangers-on, who have done nothing but bad things for the entire human race.' A soldier from the *Celere* Division branded Jews 'the standard bearers of death' and was convinced that 'the sword of justice wielded by the Axis will fall upon them'. Private Pietro Mascarello was astonished by the Germans' openness about – and indifference towards – the daily atrocities. 'One soldier told us that every day they kill 70 or 80 Jewish prisoners,' he wrote home. 'They take them to a large pine forest near here, and then they make them dig the hole, and when the pit is ready, they shoot them in the back of the head.' No attempt was made to hide the crimes from their ally – or the scale of them. After a three-week visit to Eighth Army, Fascist politician Aldo Vidussoni reported to Mussolini that 'no pity is shown to the Jews – they are treated mercilessly'. Mass shootings were 'the order of the day' as Jews were 'eliminated', reducing 'the populations of entire towns and villages by one third – or up to a half'.[51]

Though Jews suffered at the hands of the Italians, they suffered more under the Romanians and Hungarians. Both used labour detachments extensively – the former mostly in their homeland or in occupied Transnistria on the Black Sea coast. Supporting Hungary's Second Army were nearly 40,000 Jewish forced labourers, ordered to build or clear roads, repair rail lines, construct defensive positions and bury the dead. Lajos Somorjai's unit was assigned a detachment of Jews to build a secondary defensive line. 'These wretches are skinny, pale, exhausted, starving,' the doctor noted in his diary. 'They are slapped, kicked, and work like animals.' Among the men forced to build barbed-wire fences on Somorjai's front was the former Olympic champion fencer, Attila Petschauer – 'already deprived of his arrogance,' Somorjai noted with some satisfaction. 'None of these men will return – they will be handed over to the Germans after we leave. At least we have the hope of returning home when this circus is over.' Few Hungarian soldiers pitied these Jews. Most shared the view of Corporal Péter Pál Kecskés that they were now 'making amends for the great many crimes committed'. The labour companies were also forced to work on the front line, ordered to clear minefields or recover casualties. Miklós Kiss Nemeskéri reckoned one in every 20 Jews was wounded by triggering mines, some of them fatally. He felt no pity. 'We have achieved two goals at once: on the one hand, the number of Jews diminished, on the other hand we managed to save the lives of Hungarian sappers,' he wrote. 'Even the Germans were saying jealously, on several occasions, that they had certainly not been thinking of this before! We were smarter in this respect.' Officers reported to regimental commander Béla Vécsey that these Jewish units 'act bravely on the front line and do not leave anyone behind, neither the wounded, nor the dead Hungarians. We may live to see that they are regarded as heroes, while our infantry is constantly routed.' And so it happened. When one division fled during the fighting at the end of August, the unarmed Jews returned to the battlefield to recover casualties under heavy enemy fire. Fifty Jews were killed; twice as many were wounded.[52]

All too often Hungarian treatment of the civilian populace was equally pitiless. Even by rural Hungarian standards, the Soviet Union seemed a primitive world filled with 'misery, dirt, flies and lice everywhere,' Sergeant István Solymosi noted. 'We dare not go into the hovel-like huts, afraid of lice and millions of flies.' All he found in Russia was 'poverty and misery'. Sergeant Major János Fejős felt the Russians 'live rather like animals. They spread straw on the floor and lie down on it.' Propaganda had told men like János Kristóf that the Russian people would welcome the Hungarian Army 'as liberators from red tyranny. Somehow this is not very visible on their faces!' It was hardly surprising. In attempting to instil order behind the front, the Hungarian soldier instead spread fear and terror. He was frequently 'undisciplined and utterly tyrannical,' one German liaison officer reported. 'Looting, rape and other excesses are the order of the day.'[53] Certainly Second Army's gendarme battalions – sent to maintain order behind the lines and keep partisan activity in check – proved more adept at stealing from the native populace (silver samovars were especially prized). Such behaviour helped swell the ranks of the partisans operating in their thousands behind Second Army's front. Those civilians not persuaded to take up the fight against the Hungarians were often coerced. Leaflets and verbal propaganda promised Soviet victory – as well as 'terrible retribution' facing anyone who collaborated with the occupiers. One poster displayed in a village held by Hungarian troops warned:

> He who does not appear to fight against the occupiers without a compelling cause, such as illness, will be treated like a traitor, like a Jew.
>
> Whoever still serves the Germans ten days after receiving this letter will be shot dead.
>
> Whoever passes this letter into the hands of the enemy will be shot dead together with his family.[54]

Death at the hands of partisans or death for siding with partisans. The choice was stark. Dr Lajos Somorjai witnessed executions of partisans almost daily – and almost always carried out with their families watching. 'They start crying and tearing at their hair,' he wrote. 'Awful. Poor people, they too are victims of circumstances.' Many were simply unfortunate bystanders, seized when their villages were razed during counter-partisan operations. Sometimes every male aged between 15 and 60 was executed; on other occasions everyone barring children faced the firing squads. Over a six-month period spanning the winter and spring of 1941–42, one Hungarian division reported more than 8,300 partisans 'eliminated' at a cost of fewer than 300 dead. Former manual labourer János Fejős took part in a partisan sweep through woodland. The search resulted in scores of Russian dead, packed into three trucks. 'It was a horrible sight,' 22-year-old Fejős remembered. 'Stripped naked, covered in blood. Blood dripped from the vehicle. On this day, I vowed that if I returned home, I would live an exemplary life.'[55]

The civilian populace suffered too when the front line passed through their villages. Red Army stragglers often hid in cellars and basements, then pounced on the invader from behind. After several such attacks, Hungarian troops simply torched the buildings. 'Entire rows of streets were set on fire,' János Fejős wrote. 'Plenty of ammunition and explosives were stored in the houses, which "cooked off" as a result of the fire.' Platoon leader István Gyerák pitied civilians still living in villages 'burned to the ground, levelled, and yet... underground, in the ruins, bearded old *muzhiks* [peasants], hunchbacked women, flat-nosed, large-breasted, freckled, blonde, and dirty children.' When the front stabilised, a 'dead zone' up to half a dozen miles deep was created behind the line, with every inhabitant evacuated. They were left with only a few essential items, tools, clothing and livestock. 'We feel sorry for them when we watch a caravan fleeing,' platoon leader László Pakulár wrote to his parents. 'It's a sorry state of affairs. Each family has a small two-wheeled cart with all their belongings on it. The man in front pulls it, the woman pushes it, and the older children carry the little ones.' The abandoned villages became a haunt for deserters and spies looking to cross the lines. Lieutenant Lajos Hőbe's unit shot two Russian women found wandering near the front line without good reason or papers. Their bodies were left on display with a sign in Hungarian and Russian: *They were shot dead because they were wandering without permission.* 'Such severity may seem repulsive at first,' wrote Hőbe, 'but anyone who's at the front knows that the Russians know our every move, all our plans, and the information is passed on by these "wanderers".'[56]

Lajos Hőbe was not a brutal occupier, however. He allowed the local populace to make flour in the village mill, ordered his medics to treat ill Russians, allowed them to pray once more in the church which had served as a warehouse during 20 years of Soviet rule. 'Usually we give them everything we can,' he wrote. 'Their confidence in us will grow stronger by the day because we take care of them.' Reservist officer Ferenc Kállay received strict instructions from his commander 'not to hurt the populace as long as it acted properly'. Leftovers from the field kitchens were distributed among the Russians – two dozen at every meal time. 'These people were very grateful to us,' Kállay remembered. 'You could say we almost made friends with them.'[57]

Many Romanian soldiers approached the campaign in the East with the same crusading zeal as their Italian comrades-in-arms. As they headed towards the Don, the magazine *Sentinela* proclaimed: 'The definitive victory of the soldiers of the Cross against paganism approaches with giant steps.'[58] Some units reportedly marched behind the Romanian Orthodox cross in the Caucasus, and it was not unknown for Romanian chaplains to preside over services for the local populace or baptise Russian children in desolate churches which the Soviets had transformed into stables, warehouses, depots and the like. 'I found the great love of this oppressed people,' Friciu Octavian, a priest serving with 20th Infantry Division, recalled. 'When it came to religious services the young and especially the elderly cried tears of joy because they could worship God again and thank God that he sent the Romanian armies to have released them from bondage, kneeling humbly before the icons they kissed with such veneration.' When 2nd Mountain Division captured Nalchik in the last gasp of the advance in the Caucasus, its commander Ioan Dumitrache allowed his men to enjoy its meagre delights – but warned them against committing crimes 'of which we are ashamed' – convinced he was still waging a crusade against Bolshevism. 'These people, who look up to you with gratitude because you have liberated them, must not see anyone who acts criminally and shames the name of Romania.' One major stressed to his men: 'We are Romanians, not Germans', while General Emanoil Bârzotecu urged the ranks of his infantry division to act in a manner which 'attracts sympathy for our army and country. Every Romanian officer, non-commissioned officer and soldier should remember that wherever they are, they are acting on behalf of the honour and reputation of our army and nation.' Not that Romanians were averse to taking hostages – or executing them in the wake of partisan attacks. But such reprisals were not widespread – unlike those perpetrated by the Germans. Indeed, the insensitivity, the indifference to human life, the ruthless actions of their ally perturbed many Romanians. Medical officer Petre Sava was appalled by the Germans' indifference to the sanctity of life. When his 1st Cavalry Division relieved a German unit on the Don in mid-September, he found the terrain littered with Soviet dead, killed by a *Nebelwerfer* barrage during fighting over the summer. The corpses had been hideously burned, veins had burst, gas masks lay scattered around as well as personal effects, including family photographs. 'My mind is in a daze,' Sava noted, 'and although I am doing my duty to my country, I cannot approve of this. If only they had them buried, for the Germans have been here for two months. But…' When a German officer was killed by insurgents in Rostov, 'a whole street of men women and children were executed,' one junior Romanian officer complained. 'An action of this type produces a reaction of hatred, creating in the rear a permanent festering source of revenge.' Gheorghe Avramescu, commanding the Mountain Corps in the Crimea during the winter of 1941–42, told Ion Antonescu curtly: 'We did not come here to wage war on the civilian population.' Avramescu was no soft touch – he believed in the crusade against Bolshevism, and had threatened to shoot his own men if they deserted during the ferocious winter battles in the Crimea. But he was appalled by the brutal methods the Germans employed in response to partisan activity in the mountains, burning down any trees or buildings lining the main roads. In

Simferopol, one of his men's field kitchens fed around 2,000 civilians – the young and elderly especially – every day, prompting one member of the city council to thank Avramescu in gushing terms. 'Most of us are wretched, most children are orphans and they had no support from anywhere, and we have found refuge in you,' the official wrote. 'So far, since your entry into Simferopol, we are very, very happy with our lot... Please, general sir, continue to take care of us, showing the care you have shown to date. Long live Mr Avramescu!'[59]

But again, all too often, the Romanian on the Eastern Front acted as ruthlessly as his German, Italian or Hungarian ally. Constantin Brătescu, commanding the Transylvanians of 1st Cavalry Division who arrived on the Don in mid-September 1942, reminded his men they were defending their country, their loved ones, here, on the right bank of the river, more than 1,000 kilometres from home. 'Our women and children, our brothers and sisters, our parents must not feel the vengeance of the Communist Jews,' he reminded them. 'Our homes must not be desecrated.' And in 'defending' their Motherland, Romanians frequently offered no quarter to the enemy. On the Kerch peninsula, at Sevastopol and Novorossiysk, he earned a reputation for executing Red Army prisoners, Jews especially, supposedly on the pretext of trying to escape. In the Caucasus a Belgian volunteer watched a group of Soviet soldiers attempt to desert by wading across a river to Romanian lines. 'The poor devils who splash around in the water, arms raised, are mown down before they set foot on the bank,' he reported from the Baksan front. 'If they manage to get through the bursts of fire, they are shot the next morning amidst great bursts of laughter. The assassins from the Danube toss the bodies into the water riddled with bullets.'[60]

By mid-November winter had arrived on the Don, a blanket of snow covering the sectors of three Axis allied armies holding a 250-mile front along the river. Temperatures remained below freezing, even in the middle of the day. For some soldiers, it was an idyllic period filled with childhood pleasures – sledging, snowball fights, perhaps a little skiing. Most, however, were unprepared mentally or physically for the Russian winter. To keep the cold at bay, men were given underpants, plus shorts, a sweater and a pair of gloves. Their leather boots froze, 'making it feel like we were standing barefoot on ice,' former weaver György Igali remembered. Russian fur boots were prized – but were in such limited numbers that only guards could wear them. However insubstantial, at least the Hungarian soldier received *some* winter clothing. The Jews in their labour detachments did not. 'The unfortunate Jews are freezing to death,' an appalled István Simon, a lawyer and reservist officer, wrote. 'They are living through the most awful tragedy of human fate. It is not without good reason that the Scriptures tell us that they are a people tossed about by Fate!' Jewish prisoners were accommodated in snow huts, wore clothing reduced to rags which was utterly unfit for winter on the Don, and suffered frostbite. Several died every night, their final ignominy to be dragged behind a column, hauled by a piece of rope to their last resting place 'like a dead dog'. Simon was no Semite – he was convinced Hungary's Jews needed to 'atone for the sins of their kind. But I cannot believe that anyone can be so guilty as to sink as low as they are now.' Platoon commander Imre Gróf observed a group of Jews ordered to dig a trench – in full view of the Red Army across no man's land, who promptly shot three dead and wounded eight more. 'They didn't get any work done, of course,' Gróf wrote. 'In the tremendous cold, their soaked clothes froze on them. In the morning the frozen corpses of eight to ten Jews were found next to the trenches.'[61]

Life in those trenches in November 1942 was only slightly less bleak for the ordinary Hungarian soldier. 'Not only were the men cold, but their guns froze,' János Somogyi remembered. Troops placed their machine-gun on a baking tray warmed by embers to ensure it could still be fired in temperatures of −30°C. Senior officers seemed not to care. At a service to remember his regiment's dead, Colonel Antal Ludányi told his men they were defending Hungary 'on the banks of the Don at the side of the glorious German Army'. The regiment's dead had to be avenged, he continued. 'Until we were satisfied with our vengeance, we could not go home,' János Somogyi recalled. Morale plummeted. 'It became quite clear that we would spend winter here. The funeral oration and sight of numerous graves did not reassure us.' Conducting an inspection tour of a unit which had spent three months in the line on the Don, one Hungarian general was appalled to discover that the 'battalion commander had not bothered to visit his companies even once, because when he took me to the front with him, he didn't even know the way there.'[62]

Broken promises, poor leadership, wretched conditions, inadequate food, uniforms and equipment unfit for the war in the East – all gnawed at the physical and moral strength of Second Army daily. Soldiers could not wash or relax, were plagued by lice and fed a wretched diet of cabbage and potatoes. Some units were down to one third of their original strength. Leave – or rather lack of it – was the men's biggest concern. As early as late August soldiers had begun to ask when they might go home – or worse, wondering if they might have to spend the winter in Russia. It quickly became the principal topic of conversation. 'It's what we talk about every hour of the day,' Dr Lajos Somorjai wrote at the beginning of September. 'It keeps us alive and makes us forget everything else. The news is: we're going home in September.' Somorjai had an ominous feeling that perhaps he would not be returning to Hungary that month. 'Nevertheless, I'm certain we'll be repatriated in October or November.' Imre Gróf longed to 'get home for half an hour, just half an hour. If only I could breathe the air at home, see a view of home, that would be enough. God, it seems, created Russia in a terribly bad mood, because there is a colourless, joyless landscape here. There is an all-pervading monotonous misery here...' Lajos Somorjai was convinced the struggle in the East was 'hopeless... Such a people and such a large country can never be completely defeated or occupied.'[63]

Families in Hungary learned little, if anything, of the men's weariness. Mail was heavily censored – and often took a month or more to reach its recipients. It was much faster to have national radio broadcast missives in its popular weekly shows *Honvédeink üzennek* (Our Men Send a Message) and *Üzen az otthon* (Messages Home). When the editor of the *Kecskeméti Közlöny* – representing a small city 50 miles southeast of Budapest – offered to publish messages from families to their loved ones in the line, he was inundated with more than 1,000 submissions inside a week. Newspapers also chose to print letters from front-line soldiers – selectively edited to feature only positive news. A survivor of the bitter fighting in the Korotoyak bridgehead 'told' readers of the *Tolnamegyei Újság* that he had turned down a period of leave in Tolna. 'I cannot bear to be at home while my comrades are fighting outside in the Russian winter against those who want to invade our calm, peaceful, beautiful land, who want to deprive us of our churches, who do not want us to know God and want to condemn us to live the animal life of Bolshevism,' he supposedly wrote.[64]

The account bore no relation to life at the front in the autumn of 1942. Spending day after day in damp, cramped underground bunkers meant that after just a couple of months in the line, more than half the men in some units were incapacitated by some illness or other. Artilleryman Lajos Vollner 'celebrated' a joyless 30th birthday in the line – without any gifts from home, for the postal service had failed again. 'We had a rather unsettling feeling of homesickness and heard little from home,' he remembered. Transportation was a growing problem. With little shelter and roughage on the Don front, up to three-quarters of Second Army's horses were sent up to 100 miles to the rear, starving units in the line of mobility or the ability to re-supply. Lajos Vollner's battery lacked everything: food, soap, ammunition, winter clothing. Mortar platoon commander Dr Sándor Szabó had been promised his regiment would be relieved 'in the autumn at the latest – unless the war on the Eastern Front was already over by then'. News that Second Army was 'preparing for the defence of the river and winter on the Don' filled 'the entire army with depression'. Staff officer Captain Tibor Zetelaky noticed that 'among the men the belief gradually took hold that the Army on the Don had already been written off by the homeland', while Defence Minister Vilmos Nagy believed the ranks of Second Army 'had the feeling that they had been sentenced to death'.[65] Hope was replaced by cynicism, encapsulated in a song:

> From Budapest to the Don
> There is a well-known saying:
> Fear not, my friend, fear nothing,
> We're going home, we're going home!...
> But all his wishes are in vain,
> A cry that reaches to heaven,
> But the fucking cold winter's coming...[66]

The Soviets did their utmost to compound the melancholy and undermine morale. Every evening at 8pm, a propaganda truck drove up to the Don and blasted Hungarian folk music across the river. When the music ended, the loudspeaker announced: 'Death to the murderous Germans, long live Hungary!' Almost every night Russian aircraft dropped leaflets over Hungarian lines, urging them to surrender, promising fair treatment in captivity. Corporal Sándor Barna remembered one particular leaflet which featured the fate of his friend who'd been mortally wounded at Uriv. The Russians printed a photograph of his widow and infant daughter, plus a final note from her husband: 'Sell your wedding dress and boots and buy kitchen furniture, goodbye.'[67]

With understrength, demoralised divisions holding up to a dozen miles of front apiece, the Hungarian front on the Don was little more than 'a thin veil', Ferenc Szombathelyi, the Chief of the Hungarian General Staff, conceded. Worse, his men were suffering 'from a very deep emotional crisis – his fighting spirit is broken'. And yet, he convinced himself that the Hungarian Army had learned the lessons of 1941 and made preparations accordingly. 'There is the hope that the Army will accomplish its mission – without major losses and difficulties.' German observers thought otherwise. Hermann von Witzleben, the senior German officer attached to Second Army, realised 'the troops and leadership did not see any sense to their mission'. To von Witzleben, 'it was clear that the Hungarian Army would not be able to withstand a serious Russian attack – but also that it didn't want to'. Hans von Salmuth, in charge of German Second Army which held the front at Voronezh, had 'grave misgivings' about the Hungarians on his right flank and expected 'nothing' of them when the Soviets attacked. The grumbling reached the ears of Adolf Hitler, who dismissed them out of hand. 'He knows the Hungarians better,' his army adjutant Gerhard Engel noted. 'They are good fighters, if well led.'[68]

Sergeant Mario Rigoni Stern and his comrades had settled into a routine in their strongpoint, built in the ruins of a former fishing village on the Don. Every day they stared at a Red Army bunker, not 50 metres away on the opposite bank of the river. 'Where we were must have been a beautiful country,' Stern opined.

> Now, instead of the houses, only brick chimneys remained standing. The church was half [demolished] and in the apse were the company headquarters, an observation post and a post for the heavy machine-gun. Potatoes, cabbage, carrots, pumpkins emerged from the earth and snow along paths in the gardens of houses which were no longer there. Sometimes it was good stuff and soup was made.[69]

The Italian soldier on the Don suffered almost as much as the Hungarian. 'The wild nature of the country, the remoteness of the homeland, the frequent lack of mail, life in a doubly foreign world' constantly chipped away at Italian morale, Arrigo Pintonello, Eighth Army's senior priest, reported. In letters home, men told their families: 'we live underground like rats', 'we have made our home in foxholes' or 'we are like moles'. Cesarino Colombo, holding the front line with the *Ravenna* Division, reckoned the temperature was at least 20 degrees below zero, perhaps much lower. 'A sharp frost penetrated our bones, making movement difficult, while it froze the muscles on that part of the face not covered by the balaclava,' he recalled. Nearly one million woollen socks and a quarter of a million pairs of gloves had been stockpiled as early as the end of August, but distributing them to the troops proved challenging – and Eighth Army was still short of thousands of fur coats and upwards of half a million blankets. Inadequate footwear was a common complaint. 'Whoever planned this equipment for the expedition to Russia must have been a criminal,' one infantryman fumed. 'The boots especially – he should have tested them first at 20 degrees below zero!' Lieutenant Carlo Vicentini complained that the cheap leather boots 'became soaked like rags when it rained and when they froze, they turned to wood', while the nails in the sole were 'perfect for transmitting the temperature outside'. Giovanni Matteucci suffered 'near-frozen feet every day, at night we shiver from the cold,' he told his mother. 'I don't feel like I'll survive this life much longer.' Rations which might have sufficed under normal circumstances failed to provide the men with the vitamins and calories they needed in winter. Supplies of meat, bread and pasta were all inadequate. 'You can't imagine the hunger,' one soldier wrote to his parents, begging for food parcels. 'Sometimes we cook a few cabbage leaves that they throw away in the kitchen and then we eat them without salt or oil and as it seems to us that they are good, we have eaten some beets and not only the beets, but also their leaves. Many times even our officers have pity on us seeing us like this…'[70]

The men were battered by propaganda from both sides. Fascist and German leaflets and letters warned that 'being taken prisoner was tantamount to death', filling men with 'the terrible fear of falling into enemy captivity', one report noted. 'Far from awakening the soldier's fighting spirit, it rather upset him and made him extremely restless.' Red Army prisoners told their captors they regarded the Italians as 'a flock of sheep sent to the slaughter' – a message reinforced by Soviet propaganda. At night Soviet biplanes peppered the Italian lines with leaflets. 'Welcome to the Don, *Alpini*. Too bad none of you will see your beautiful Italy again.'[71] Or:

> Save yourselves!
>
> Italians, save yourselves before it is too late. Break the alliance with the Germans and surrender in entire battalions and regiments. Or abandon the front and go home.
>
> Know what the whole world knows: if you continue to fight, the Red Army will exterminate you and the Russian winter will deliver the *coup de grâce*.[72]

Still, there were some Italians who were impressed by the immense effort made to fortify the Don front and prepare for winter. Pasquale Grignaschi regarded the defences as 'an enormous, almost incredible achievement': a series of strongpoints, linked by trenches, surrounded by minefields and barbed-wire fences. The men lived in underground bunkers, which they attempted to gentrify with religious icons, pictures of family, clippings from magazines. 'This winter,' *Alpino* officer Captain Roberto Missiroli wrote, 'will be very different from previous ones. We are absolutely convinced that the Russians will no longer be able to cross the Don. I don't really believe that the Russians have a burning desire to attack here, beaten as they are, and winter will be much worse for them than for us.' Having seen the effectiveness of his weapon during a raid – 'toasting more than one Russian on guard' – flamethrower operator Gino Garuffo was in no doubt that his unit would 'deal the Russians a good blow' if they attacked.[73]

There were far more Italian soldiers in Russia who looked to the coming weeks at best with concern, at worst horror. 'I think I can put the idea of an easy and quick victory aside, and in my heart I have already resigned myself to spending the winter here in the East, albeit reluctantly,' Sergeant Lorenzo Pardini wrote to his former school teacher. 'I was certainly far from imagining Russian military strength to be so formidable when learning from newspapers. Either our newspapers were lying or they were extremely ignorant of affairs in Russia.'

Arrigo Pintonello found there was a widespread feeling that 'nothing could be done against Russian tanks' and that if the Soviets unleashed an offensive on Eighth Army's front, it would not be able to hold the enemy back. The conversation in field hospitals behind the front confirmed the priest's observation. 'Pessimism is growing day by day,' Antonio Zanfagnini wrote. 'When the discussion turns to our weapons, a sense of mistrust, of disheartenment seizes everyone. For the soldier, weapons are more important than bread. We have certain tanks that would look good in toy shop windows.'[74]

Losing their best leader did not help either. The popular Giovanni Messe had been dismissed in late September and there was widespread belief among Italian troops that it wasn't Italo Gariboldi who was commanding them, nor his 'out of his depth' chief-of-staff Bruno Malaguti, rather the German liaison officer General Kurt von Tippelskirch, mockingly dubbed the 'Rommel of Russia'. Unlike North Africa, however, the ARMIR was very much the junior party in Russia – and frequently treated as such by condescending Germans of all ranks. Far from being 'particularly amiable', Giovanni Zanghieri, who commanded II Corps, observed how German soldiers attacked, abused, snubbed, insulted and threatened his men, regarding them – and every other allied army on the Eastern Front – as nothing better than 'auxiliaries'. The Italians were dismissed as *fünfzigprozentigen Kämpfer* – 'half soldiers' – by the liaison officer with the *Ravenna* Division, one Lieutenant Pernter. Relations between 298th Infantry Division and the *Ravenna* deteriorated so badly at one point that the Germans set up machine-guns and threatened to shoot their allies. 'It is clear that the German soldier is superior to the Italian soldier in every respect,' Pernter reported. 'But it must not be forgotten that the German soldier is better armed, better equipped, better educated and better fed.'[75] Such attitudes – burned into the very soul of every German soldier – prevailed over official instructions which admonished the *Landser* not to be 'superior towards our Italian allies who came here fearlessly into hard and unfamiliar conditions to help us', while a leaflet for company commanders offered this reminder:

> [The Italian soldier's] climate, his upbringing and life under the southern sun are different from ours… It would therefore be wrong to judge him by our standards and to demand of him what we demand of ourselves. The Italian soldier is fighting as best he can. He recognises the bravery of the German soldier. But the German soldier must also appreciate the efforts of his comrade in arms.[76]

Friction was often sparked by Italian shortcomings: poor leadership, poor supplies, poor equipment. 'We don't see any German soldiers on foot,' Lieutenant

Egidio Franzini of the *Cuneense* Division complained as he marched to the front. 'They all pass haughtily on their vehicles, staring at us with contempt, making us swallow masses of dust. We want to put holes in their tyres, not to mention their heads.' Andrea Garatti with the Alpine *Edolo* battalion admired the Germans' ability to improvise and adapt to the hardships of the Eastern Front. 'In a situation which destroyed us both physically and morally, they could continue to live as men,' he wrote. 'Those who took charge of them had thought of everything, even to send them planes to drop them food and ammunition. Those who should have taken care of us hadn't thought about it and were not thinking of anything.'[77]

Yet where they served – and fought – side by side on the Don, a bond developed between the German and Italian soldier. 'I could describe many examples of why our Italian comrades will always remain dear to me,' one German liaison officer wrote, struck by their bravery and spirit of comradeship. 'And, when I return to my homeland, I will tell everyone of the great deal of enthusiasm I encountered and how much faith I have in my Italian comrades. I will never forget them as long as I live.' Luigi Marras, Italy's military attaché in Berlin, noted that German soldiers talked of their Italian comrades 'with admiration' and praised the effectiveness of Italian gunnery ('better than German artillery'). 'This feeling of admiration for our troops, vivid and spontaneous among German soldiers in this sector, fades, however, the further you go up the command chain, where it seems to completely disappear.'[78]

One thing German observers did notice as winter descended on the Don was morale plummeting with the temperatures. Events in North Africa and increasing air raids on Italian cities weighed heavily on the men's minds. The mood in Eighth Army in mid-November 1942 was 'rather depressed'. Official Italian reports suggested otherwise: the morale of the troops 'consistently high', the men themselves as determined to stand firm on the Don as if it were the Piave – the river outside Venice where the Austrian offensive of 1918 had been decisively stopped. In reality, the Italian soldier on the Don was melancholy. The weather mirrored his mood. The opaque, milky sky seemed to merge into the surrounding landscape which was blanketed by snow at least half a metre deep. Each night the men listened to the noise of engines on the far side of the Don, convinced the Russians were planning an attack. 'A strange, terrifying calm made us nervous,' Cesarino Colombo remembered. 'A terrible omen hung over us.'[79]

'There was something unsettling in the air,' junior officer Stan Gheorghe observed in mid-November. 'A kind of psychosis was being transmitted from the high commands down to the units, from which it was felt that something must happen…'[80] And if it did, Stan Gheorghe knew – like every Romanian officer – that his countrymen were in no position to hold the line.

Gheorghe's 20th Infantry Division defended a stretch of front south of Stalingrad with the rest of Romanian Fourth Army. Behind the thin veneer of a front, there was little beyond the expanse of the Kalmyk steppe. A second Romanian Army, the Third, defended the Don front for a good 125 miles to the northwest of Stalingrad. Neither was fit mentally or physically for the task.

The Romanian Army was exhausted. It had been fighting tirelessly for 18 months. But by the late autumn of 1942 it was approaching breaking point. 'Everyone is tired of fighting, everyone wants to go home,' former carpenter Constantine Stefanescu complained. 'Soldiers do not go into battle because they have a strong military spirit or they see Russians as their enemies. No, the main reason is fear of German machine-guns, fear of being shot.' Life on the Don seemed particularly bleak, as 1st Armoured Division's Faranga Dumitru wrote: 'The work I am doing, the headaches, the broken bones, the depressing grey squalid houses, full of weeds, poor, covered with straw or even with mud stuck on the roof where puddles form, the hunger and cold, plus the misery of the low temperatures and prospects for the future, make me think all sorts of thoughts...'[81]

Men like Stefanescu and Dumitru were poorly fed, poorly led and poorly equipped. The troops' diet was woeful. There were occasional cases of starvation and many more of weakness, apathy and jaundice. Some soldiers were so weak they could not get out of bed for bodily functions. Others took to cutting meat from horses killed by bombardments. Such desperation was unsurprising. The Romanian soldier was invariably provided with just one hot meal a day. Rations varied by unit. Some men might enjoy half a bowl of soup or stew, plus 400 grammes of bread, accompanied with a tablespoon of honey or jam if they were fortunate. Sometimes there might be mushrooms or preserved fish, perhaps 100 grammes of cold tinned meat, and maybe half a dozen cigarettes and a few grammes of tobacco.[82] Their uniforms were falling apart: nearly half the men needed new boots or trousers. There was no change of undergarments for troops in the line, little soap and few opportunities to wash, so lice thrived. Belatedly, Romanian Army leaders responded. 'Tens of thousands of coats, hats, boots, cloaks, and the like were sent, but they never reached those for whom they were intended,' Stan Gheorghe remembered. The clothing got no closer to the front than railheads and supply depots, where they either fell victim to the Soviet advance when the counter-offensive was launched, or Soviet shells and bombs which set the stores on fire while Romanian soldiers 'watched the flames from afar'.[83]

Fourth Panzer Army commander Hermann Hoth was appalled by the sight of a company from 2nd Infantry Division which had fought with distinction south of the Don and was finally granted rest after 80 days in the line. The men gave the impression of prisoners sentenced to death. Officers cried, soldiers struggled to stand up, their uniforms hung off their bodies like rags. Hoth ordered 'rest and more rest – as much as possible'. The ranks of 1st Infantry Regiment resented facing 'the horror of fighting another winter in this Russian steppe, while many in the rear, who have not seen a single day of action, stand by the fire or are used as occupational troops.' Replacements drawn from rear units were no better than 'padding'. Disease and ailments were rife. Men reported every day to the regimental doctor. 'Their physical state is quite worrying,' he reported. 'Exhausted physically, dirty, covered in lice, some are in a state of indescribable weakness – they give you the impression of shadows.' One infantry regiment had no commander, no adjutant, no battalion commanders and no captains. It was somehow held together by a sole regular officer and 15 reservists, while the ranks were so badly thinned, companies were the size of platoons and platoons no bigger than squads. Defending the front near Kletskaya, 75 miles northwest of Stalingrad, was 1st Cavalry Division. As it relieved the Germans of 113th Infantry Division, battalion commander Erwin Jetzl chatted with the Romanian officer who would now defend the same sector. He was appalled by what he learned: barely 200 men were moving into the line, equipped with a handful of machine-guns and a couple of mortars – all Great War vintage. The only modern weapon the Romanians possessed: two 3.7cm anti-tank guns given them by the Germans. Jetzl deduced the Romanians could barely form a weak covering position, and certainly could not hold the line if the Red Army attacked in force. And once the Don froze, they would throw tanks across the river – and a couple of medium anti-tank guns would hardly stand in their way. 'You don't need to worry here,' the Romanian officer assured Jetzl. 'The Germans have promised that panzer divisions will be behind us.' Weak armament was compounded by physical weakness. Food was inadequate, men were overworked and, as summer turned to autumn, they were utterly unprepared for the hardships of a Russian winter. Still living in tents in October, water in the men's canteens now regularly froze overnight and dysentery was widespread – the result of a monotonous diet 'of too many preserves, artificial jams, dried vegetables' and the onset of cold weather which weakened the troops' resistance to disease, medical officer Petre Sava noted. 'And yet our morale remains firm,' he added. 'We laugh, we swear, we criticise and we do our duty. I don't think there's another nation like us. Really, here, on the edge of the trench, I see and am proud to be Romanian.' Sava and his comrades knew their division was weaker than the German unit it replaced on the Don, 'but we have great confidence in ourselves and I hope that everything will end with our success'. General Constantin Sănătescu, commanding the cavalrymen's parent IV Corps, did not possess such a rosy view of the men under him. The front was too long, the men too far from their homeland, their officers exhausted, forever 'running up and down the line' rallying the ordinary soldiers, whose ranks thinned daily, 'even if there's no fighting'. His corps was plagued by 'very low morale'. If the Red Army attacked in force, Sănătescu warned, 'the entire front will collapse'.[84]

Sănătescu's superior was all too aware of Third Army's shortcomings. From the very outset its commander General Petre Dumitrescu protested about the mission given his men. Holding a front 100 miles long was beyond the capacity of Third Army – especially in the looming Russian winter, with troops living in the barren steppe, with no raw materials to build defensive positions, bunkers and quarters – leaving them fully exposed to the elements. Third Army's front was 'at least twice as long' as it could cope with. Its artillery possessed barely half its quota of ammunition, its vehicles just one third of their fuel supplies. Along its entire front there were just 60 anti-tank guns – and only half a dozen of those could effectively engage a T-34. German observers warned that *Panzerschreck* – fear of tanks – was so bad that some Romanian officers were openly admitting 'that they'll flee when the first Russian tanks appear'. The lack of guns was compounded by a shortage of ammunition. On a typical day, Romanian forces on the Don might send 20,000 shells into Soviet lines, rising to 50,000 on days of intense fighting, but it was no match for the enemy's matériel superiority. Battery commanders sent back inflated reports of shell consumption in the hope they might receive extra supplies and build up a stockpile. An infuriated Captain Emil Stolerii of the 9th Infantry Division observed Soviet troops 'foraging everywhere, building shelters, walking from one place to another, sometimes 20–30 of them, even with carts behind them, and I was not allowed to fire, while the enemy, as soon as he saw me, shot immediately.'[85]

Neither the Romanian nor German leadership were oblivious to the precarious state of the armies either side of Stalingrad. 'It is unfair to expect the Romanian people to defend the most threatened sector of the Eastern Front,' Romania's Foreign Minister Mihai Antonescu complained to Hitler. 'This task is too difficult for our soldiers.' His leader – unrelated, despite their surname – was furious that the Germans had failed to provide any of the weaponry or build any of the strongpoints behind his front. 'I do not want the glory of the Romanian Army to be stained by faulty steps taken by the leadership,' Ion Antonescu fumed. Protests and warnings were brushed aside. 'The Russians lost enormous forces and matériel this summer and it seems that the decline of their resistance is growing by the day,' their ally assured them. General Ilie Şteflea, the Chief of the Romanian General Staff, hoped so. His armies were 'stretched like beads on a thread… Wherever the thread is cut, all the beads will be scattered on the floor.'[86]

6

WE'RE HOLDING ON TO WHAT
WE'VE GOT

Certainty in victory is deeply rooted in all soldiers in North Africa... Victory cannot fail to come.

Italian Morale Report

The evening of 30 August 1942 was 'a beautiful lunar night,' Major Enrico Bigliani remembered. Standing in the turret of an armoured car, he surveyed the scene as the vanguard of the *Littorio* Division rolled through a gap in the labyrinthine minefields at the southern end of a front line which wiggled and wended its way through the Egyptian desert from the Mediterranean shore to the edge of the Qattara Depression. Entranced by the moonlight and glittering array of stars, Bigliani was struck by 'the strange silence of the enchanting night'. The only sound came from 'the rattling of tank tracks and the panting of our engines'. The exhausts of the *Littorio*'s vehicles spluttered glowing sparks into the darkness. Enrico Bigliani was convinced they betrayed the column's position to the enemy, unaware they already knew the enemy was coming.[1]

The *Littorio* was one of five Axis armoured or motorised division advancing through no man's land as Sunday 30 August turned to Monday 31 August. To the north, their comrades feinted an attack along the coastal strip and centre of the 25-mile-long front while they delivered the main blow in the south. Once through the minefields and far behind Eighth Army's lines, the armour – 450 tanks, supported by more than 500 guns and nearly 700 aircraft – would turn north towards the coast, trapping the Allies between

Axis lines in the west and the armoured fist of German and Italian tanks in the east. It was Gazala all over again.

The morale of *Afrika Korps* was 'good and confident', its panzer regiments now wielding nearly 250 working vehicles, though the ranks of its infantry were still thin. Its two divisions – 15th and 21st Panzer – made solid progress until around 2.30am, a little over four hours into the attack. The battlefield was suddenly bathed by the eerie light of parachute flares – one British company commander reckoned there were rarely fewer than 20 in the sky at any one time. 'It was one of the most awe-inspiring sights I shall ever see,' he wrote. 'The whole valley, with its mass of the *Afrika Korps* stationary, was lit up like a huge orange fairyland.' It heralded a torrid 90 or so minutes. Allied aircraft raided 21st Panzer Division 18 times. Evasive action was impossible – the division was hemmed in on either side by mines. Artilleryman Martin Penck lay pressed to the ground, half buried in a hurriedly dug foxhole. 'A raging, roar of explosions filled the air,' he wrote. 'Clouds of dirt and gunpowder fumes slowly moved eerily over the earth in the night, which was illuminated by flares and the glow of burning vehicles. Wounded people screamed, ambulances sounded their sirens, it was hell!' The division's commander, Georg von Bismarck, was killed by mortar fire, his deputy wounded. The leadership of the *Afrika Korps* was similarly decapitated. A bomb landed next to Walther Nehring's command vehicle, throwing the corps commander against the body, while shrapnel pierced the thin armour shell, killing Nehring's adjutant and supply officer. The blood-covered general, wounded in the arm and head, insisted on his driver being driven to the first-aid post before he himself left the battlefield, handing command to his chief-of-staff, Fritz Bayerlein. 15th Panzer Division's attack had begun promisingly – no man's land was just that, barren terrain. But as soon as it encountered the first minefields, the attack began to go awry. The belt of mines was much deeper than expected. Pioneers were still clearing it when the enemy's artillery and machine-guns opened fire, their aim made all the easier under the light of the parachute flares. Having finally wriggled free of the minefield, the panzers ran straight into 100 British tanks which brought their thrust to a halt.[2]

Italian units fared no better. Captain Davide Beretta, commanding a column of self-propelled guns, remembered 'thousand upon thousand ribbons of fire, which rose up as if by magic from the horizon', trapping his unit in a 'web of fire'. Beretta was convinced he'd been lured into a 'diabolical ambush' by the British who threatened to wipe out the entire vanguard of the *Littorio* Division with an 'armoured avalanche of Sherman and Grant tanks'.[3]

Enrico Bigliani and his detachment of pioneers were removing the last of around 20 mines in the path of the *Littorio* Division when British artillery opened fire. 'Shells explode with a demonic crash and shrapnel flies all around… like some hellish blizzard,' he wrote. The men crawled behind the burned-out hulk of a tank, but it offered little protection as shells soon began to rain down around its lifeless body. Bigliani was thrown against the caterpillar track by one blast wave. Still dazed, he looked around him:

> One pioneer is lying face down, his back literally ripped in two. Next to him is his comrade, the pioneer Romualdo Tassi, with his right leg completely torn off and who seems to be now dying; close by, lying on his back and motionless is Lieutenant Donnarumma, who seems to be asleep. I gently touch his face and then I try to shake him, but he doesn't move: he is dead even if I can't see how or where he was hit.

The pioneer officer subsequently recovered his composure and continued on foot, only to step on a mine by accident and trigger it, shattering his left leg. He succeeded in crawling to an abandoned tank, but no-one noticed him; his *Littorio* Division comrades were too consumed by the battle to spot a wounded officer clinging to the wreck of a vehicle. Bigliani passed out. He awoke after dawn in the division's first-aid post, where he was treated and offered sips from a flask of cognac.[4]

Around the same time as Enrico Bigliani was gravely wounded, Davide Beretta's self-propelled guns were locked in a hellish battle with enemy Sherman and Grant tanks. 'A thick dust loitered around our defensive position and the air we breathed, soaked with burned petrol, burned the throat and took our breath away,' he wrote.

> Dawn was still hours away and the enemy artillery barrage did not cease its ruthless and macabre harvest of human lives. The tall flames of burning trucks, just behind the battery, looked like torches lit in a bedlam of the damned. In front of our now chaotic lines, the mighty silhouettes of the enemy tanks drew ever closer, like a curse, so much so we could feel the rattle of the tracks… shaking the ground like a distant earthquake.

Beretta reckoned upwards of 60 tanks were trying to smash their way through to the core of the *Littorio* Division. One Sherman closed to within 800 metres of Beretta's position before erupting in flames. The Italian counted three shadowy figures – silhouetted against the fire – clamber out of the blazing tank, while a fourth collapsed on the ground. The fifth crewman, the driver, did not escape. Beretta's comrade 'honoured him with the sign of the cross – as a good Christian'.

With the counter-attack seemingly stopped, there seemed to be a brief interlude and Beretta found himself transfixed by this sight:

[a] vast plain littered with dead and wounded amidst a tangle of twisted carcasses of still-smoking trucks: here and there, the torn bodies of pioneers, tank crews and *Bersaglieri*, clinging to their weapons in the spasm of death, lay collapsed on this stretch of sand. Almost as a joke, a mass of barbed wire tangled those poor mangled bodies in bizarre spirals, along with twisted metal sheets and blood-soaked strips of cloth. Those faces, contracted and turned white by death, those eyes wide open with a desperate expression, seemed to stare at us to ask us the reason for that useless holocaust…

Several dead or dying soldiers lay in a pile. Some dumbstruck survivors wandered among the corpses and the smoking carcasses of the vehicles, almost as calm as if what they saw and heard was a show in a cinema…

The body of a legless soldier was wrapped in a tangle of barbed wire: with his stiffened hands he still clutched the large wire cutter: the swinging light of the flares seemed to give life to his task; his arms moved as if they were about to break through the tangle of cable…

Inhuman moans, curses and screams mingled with the deafening roar of explosions. Near our self-propelled vehicles, some hideously-mutilated *Bersaglieri* tried to sink into the sand or slip under the vehicles to escape the shower of furious shrapnel.

The desert had turned into a charnel house for the vanguard of the *Littorio* Division, Beretta concluded. 'Death reaped his harvest indiscriminately.' And now the enemy zeroed in on Beretta's formation. His vehicle was hit three times by glancing blows or shrapnel. Others suffered direct hits. The men's cries were carried over the radio. Through viewfinders, their comrades watched crew stumble out of their wrecked vehicles and collapse on the ground. A junior officer lay on the sand, clutching his chest which had been ripped open by shrapnel. Beretta was with him as Lieutenant Rolando Del Piano whispered a faint lament, then a name: 'mamma, mamma, mamma…', and expired under the pale light of a flare which had settled next to the vehicle and gradually went out.[5]

To driver Vittorio Vallicella the battlefield looked like 'an enormous volcano erupting'. He was mesmerised by an 'awesome show' as tracer raced through the night in a near-continuous bead, landing directly on the enemy's positions. The first rumours swirling around his battery were encouraging: there was talk of an Indian division being routed, large numbers of prisoners taken and vital supply and fuel dumps seized. 'There's euphoria.'[6]

No euphoria seized Erwin Rommel and his staff. By first light on Monday, German and Italian forces should, by his plan, have been 30 miles behind the British lines and ready to strike towards the coast. They were not, as the field marshal learned visiting the still somewhat shell-shocked headquarters of the *Afrika Korps*. He considered calling the offensive off, but the corps' staff persuaded him to persist a little longer.[7] Abandoning his original plan – the most advanced units had pushed forward no more than ten miles inside enemy lines – Rommel now ordered them to turn *north*, towards the ridge at Alam Halfa to the southeast of El Alamein.

The change of plan did not bring about a change of fortune. Vittorio Vallicella – now disabused of his initial delight as daylight lifted the veil over the horrors of the night – watched German armour blunder into enemy anti-tank guns. 'It's a massacre,' he wrote. 'The panzers burn like torches.' As infantry tried to silence the British guns, the enemy's air force appeared. A sandstorm swept over the field of battle. It brought respite for the attackers from the Allied air forces, but it added to the confusion on the ground, reducing visibility to barely 350 feet. German and Italian units groped their way through the minefields 'like ships in a North Sea fog', navigating not by chart but by compass. Davide Beretta's formation of self-propelled guns had been locked in a life-and-death struggle with British armour when the storm engulfed him. 'Like robots in a dark storm, the gunners continued to fire, frequently changing the direction of shot against an invisible target, masked by the hurricane stirred up by the *ghibli*,' he wrote. 'It was a strange battle, fought in a sinister fog of dust and smoke, to compete for a share of sand or to occupy some enemy stronghold.'[8]

The storm finally died out when the sun went down – as did the fighting. 15th Panzer Division's reconnaissance force now hoped to make up lost ground. Fortune and the enemy's air force had other ideas. An inexperienced staff officer sent to the front accidentally set off a flare, revealing the unit's position, bringing down the full wrath of Allied air power. 'Explosions, fires, shrapnel, smoke, dust! Chaos. How can I describe the scene?' wrote Werner Bobe.

I wince with every explosion. My eardrums are sore. Bombs land very close – a huge, bright flash. Our fuel truck has exploded! And it's just 20 metres from my vehicle. On the left the ammunition truck. I'm seized with horror. With one leap, I'm out of the hole and run as if I'm possessed past the burning vehicles. I'm seized by a single thought: away from the vehicles, into the desert! Bombs rain down with a howling whistle – lie down! I throw myself into the sand and press my face into my blanket. Splinters and stones patter. Steel rattles on the stone. Gunsmoke forces it way up my nose. Onwards, onwards! I run like a madman, my gums stick together, my lungs pant, sweat runs down my forehead. Everywhere *Landsers* are running around as if they're being hunted, shouting, screaming. Many are wounded or are shot as they run by the aircraft cannon – and stay lying down. More bombs land! One after another! I can clearly see them landing. Huge fountains rise up from the ground. Columns of smoke shoot into the sky, there are fires and crashing and explosions as if it's the end of the world!

The bombing that night lasted eight hours without a break, 5th Panzer Regiment's Dr Alfons Selmayr remembered, surpassing 'everything that had happened to date'. Parachute flares constantly lit the battlefield 'as bright as day. Bombers buzzed around like poisonous bumble bees and bombs fell non-stop. Vehicles burned everywhere, ammunition and petrol went up in flames. My small Panzer II really shook. Something to shatter your nerves.'[9]

Seven of *Afrika Korps'* staff officers were killed in the raids. Rommel himself was showered with hot shrapnel from a near miss. When the air attacks ended around an hour before dawn, Werner Bobe and his surviving comrades returned to their vehicles – or what remained of them. Hardly any had been spared. More than 30 were reduced to burned-out wrecks and steel skeletons. The sand, soaked with phosphorus, was in flames. Tyres still burned, the acrid smoke stinging the men's eyes. And between the eviscerated armour, charred corpses.[10]

When daylight came on the first day of September, there could be no thought of resuming a general offensive. Only 15th Panzer Division was in any condition to attack, sent to capture the highest point on the Alam Halfa ridge, Hill 132 – named for the number of metres it rose above sea level. It almost succeeded, parrying a blow by upwards of 150 enemy tanks. In doing so, it all but exhausted its reserves of fuel. It had begun the offensive with enough to carry it to Cairo. Now its range was reduced to just two dozen miles. 'Troops are screaming for fuel,' Rommel's quartermaster Major Otto noted worriedly, a situation not helped when Stukas bombed a column of trucks moving petrol up the line from the base at El Daba 30 miles behind the front, convinced they were British and leaving behind little beyond 'gigantic black clouds drifting through the sky over the battlefield'. Worse still, neither vessel carrying the petrol promised to sustain the offensive arrived: one tanker was damaged, another, the *Picco Fascio* and its 1,100 tonnes of fuel, ended up at the bottom of the Mediterranean. Unless supplies arrived, Axis forces in North Africa would be immobilised by 5 September. Coupled with another hellish night of air attacks – 1,600 bombs fell on *Afrika Korps* alone on 1–2 September – and with the enemy firing ten shells for every one his guns could manage, Erwin Rommel concluded there was no prospect of success. Late on the morning of the 2nd, he called off his offensive.[11]

There were some convinced Rommel had lost his nerve, calling off the battle at the very moment of victory, when he had outflanked the enemy. Albert Kesselring was certain the 'old' Rommel – fit, tireless, healthy – would never have given up.[12]

It certainly caught the motorised infantry of 15th Panzer Division off guard. Ordered to move out, the men were convinced they were being sent to secure the ridge at Alam Halfa. 'We thought of Cairo, the Great Pyramids of Giza and Sphinx, belly dancers and celebrating Egyptians,' one machine-gunner recalled. Two hours later, trucks appeared and the infantry were told to clamber aboard.

'Are we going to Cairo?' one man asked.

'Whatever gave you that idea?' came the answer. The trucks were heading *west* – to counter an expected enemy counter-offensive.

And so, the machine-gunner conceded, 'the dream of Cairo, the Pyramids and Suez Canal was over!'[13]

The view of Rommel's staff was rather more realistic. His intelligence chief, Friedrich von Mellenthin, believed the 'whole existence of the *Afrika Korps* was in jeopardy'. The shortage of fuel was critical and, as Mellenthin put it succinctly, 'an armoured division without gasoline is little better than a heap of scrap iron'. The offensive – Germans named it the 'Six-Day Race' after the famous Berlin cycling event, the Allies 'Alam Halfa' or 'second Alamein' – had miscarried for numerous reasons: it had failed to attain surprise; poor reconnaissance had sorely misjudged the scale of the enemy's minefields; the enemy enjoyed matériel superiority – tanks, aircraft, guns, ammunition – and, for the first time, had not squandered his advantage; and Rommel had gambled on deliveries of fuel which never arrived. In his official report on the action, the field marshal himself – almost entirely unfairly – laid most of the blame for failure at the door of the Italians. Their commanders were simply 'not equal to the demands' of modern desert warfare, troops were being led into battle by men who had not seen action in the Great War, and the rank and file were poorly trained, poorly fed – they frequently turned to their German comrades for food and drink – useful in defence only when supported by their allies, useless in the attack. 'In attack, the German soldier has to bear the burden of the battle alone.' Whatever his prejudices, Rommel's decision to break off the battle had been the right one, but it still cast a shadow over his headquarters. 'Everyone here knows that the final battle for Cairo is over,' Max Clauss, diplomatic correspondent of the *Deutsche Allgemeine Zeitung* wrote, 'and perhaps everything which has been attained on African soil with sweat and blood over the years is lost, if not more…'[14]

The Six-Day Race cost Germany more than 1,850 dead and wounded. The Italians suffered 1,050 casualties, Eighth Army 1,750. Over the coming days, Axis units largely fell back to the positions they held on 30 August – save for some of Eighth Army's minefields, which were now incorporated in German and Italian defences. They left behind the burned-out, twisted and mutilated hulks of four dozen tanks, scarring a land probably untouched since Biblical times with the detritus of 20th-century battle. 'Everywhere there were corpses, hastily-planted crosses, wrecked vehicles, tanks, guns, aircraft,' wrote Italian pioneer commander Paolo Caccia-Dominioni. Otherwise, as Hellmuth Frey observed, 'had it not been for the losses, then you could console yourself by saying: It's as if nothing has happened.'[15]

Though Allied air power had mauled the attacking Axis formations – especially at night – outnumbered German fighters still enjoyed a qualitative superiority over their foe, led by the peerless Hans-Joachim Marseille. On the first day of September he claimed 17 aircraft – all fighters, including eight P-40 Curtisses – destroyed in a devastating ten minutes of aerial combat, 'a feat that no fighter pilot has ever achieved before and that no-one else will be able to match in the near future,' his comrade Hans-Arnold Stahlschmidt wrote admiringly. 'It's just like a fairy tale with him. But as well as his skill, his luck is also almost superhuman.' The next day Marseille and Stahlschmidt – who had 50 victories to his name at the age of just 21 – were drawn into 'an incredible tangle of enemy fighters': 60 Hurricanes, Curtisses and Spitfires. 'In spite of infinite enemy superiority there was no chickening out, rather a dogfight,' Stahlschmidt recorded in his diary. The two men helped each other: Marseille downed a Spitfire hanging on Stahlschmidt's tail; his young wingman returned the compliment. Each man scored three kills before finally breaking off the action, 'utterly' exhausted, their machines peppered with holes left by cannon and machine-gun shells. 'We embraced each other afterwards, for there were no words for what we had done for each other,' Stahlschmidt wrote. 'It seems to me that no word is good enough to describe it. I would have been shot down without Marseille, and he without me. That it did not turn out that way makes us both proud. It is an incomparable experience of wonderful comradeship for us.'[16]

Four luckless Curtisses fell victim to the 'Star of Africa' that day, plus a solitary Spitfire. On the third, a couple of Spitfires and another four Curtisses. 4 September was a day without killing for the young Berliner. That evening, he ate with his fellow pilots in silence – roast corned beef and bread, followed by jam, washed down with tea which tasted of salt and Bakelite. As the paymaster issued wages to men who had no opportunities to spend them on a desert airfield far from civilisation, a sergeant major handed Marseille a radio message from Hermann Göring, confirming him as only the fourth recipient of Germany's then-highest decoration, the Knight's Cross with Oak Leaves, Swords and Diamonds. 'Rest assured, dear Marseille, that the entire German nation sees in you one of its greatest heroes of this war,' the Reichsmarschall gushed. 'In this spirit, favoured by everlasting soldierly fortune, continue to fight for the final victory of our arms.' Of far greater meaning to the young ace were letters of congratulation – and gratitude – from Rommel and from Walter Sigel, whose Stukas Marseille and his comrades so often protected. 'Our wishes on the path to future glories accompany you just as closely as the safe and reliable escort you have flown has always been,' Sigel wrote.[17]

Individual successes could not, however, mask collective failure. Defeat at Alam Halfa underscored the importance of securing the supply lines to North Africa – permanently. Both Rome and Berlin understood Malta was the key. Too late, Germany's Naval Staff realised the error of their ways; the strategy for 1942 should have been Malta first, *then* strike at Tobruk. Benito Mussolini had reached a similar conclusion. 'You know, all things considered, I've come to the conclusion that instead of advancing on Mersa Matruh, it would have been better to carry out the operation against Malta,' he conceded to Ugo Cavallero. The Italian marshal, a long-time advocate of occupying Malta, agreed entirely. 'If we neutralise Malta, we will win every battle in Africa,' he told the Duce. 'If we don't, we will lose them all.' A despondent Mussolini feared the war at sea was already 'lost'. And there was no prospect of an invasion of the island in 1942, probably not until the following summer, Albert Kesselring told him. The best the Axis powers could hope for was to pound the island into oblivion and step up supplies to Africa. Except that neither Germany nor Italy possessed the ability. The means were too few, the defences now too strong. The British had not only reinforced the island, but their pilots had begun to adopt the same tactics which had served the Luftwaffe so well for three years, pouncing on their foe with the sun behind them, inflicting increasingly heavy losses. In doing so, they wore down German and Italian formations already inadequate for the task in hand. Not only did they lack the numbers, but increasingly they lacked the fortitude. Aircrew were exhausted by frequent sweeps over the Mediterranean which had shredded their nerves – they dubbed it 'the Malta evil'. Kesselring turned to Hitler for fresh blood and the Führer agreed. He would send fighters, bombers and transporters by the dozen to the Mediterranean 'two or three days after the fall of Stalingrad'.[18]

In the meantime, the burden continued to rest on Italy's navy and mercantile fleet – supported and protected by Italian and German fliers. After a lacklustre first half of 1942, the Italians made a supreme effort to build up supplies in the desert following the fall of Tobruk. More than 80 ships crossed the Mediterranean in July, with just two lost. Although they could not maintain that tempo, sailings over the summer remained high: 57 in August, 49 the following month. But losses too were on the rise: two ships sunk in July, four in August, seven in September. More than half the vehicles shipped in August ended up on the seabed. In September, 20 of 38 tanks transported were lost. Even when ships did not sink, they often returned to ports in Italy and Greece for repairs, while some vessels scurried for the nearest haven at the mere sight of a periscope – denying the front line in Egypt their cargoes. In September 1942, three in every ten ships which set out for North Africa never reached their destination.[19]

Aviators attempted to provide a protective umbrella to convoys as they sluggishly crossed the Mediterranean. Sorties of five hours or more were typical. The missions were monotonous and stressful – hours on end over the ocean, often in bad weather, day after day. 'We're slowly turning into proper bundles of nerves, something I hadn't believed was possible,' Wolfgang von Bergh told his family. 'When we return from a mission we're so tired and broken – and there's still the prospect of flying once again tomorrow at the crack of dawn.'[20]

Even if the tankers and cargo vessels arrived safely, offloading was sluggish. It could take as long as two weeks to turn some ships around ready for a return journey. Tripoli was the only port of any appreciable capacity in North Africa – and the only one capable of dealing with substantial deliveries of fuel. Alamein was a journey of nearly 1,200 miles from the Libyan capital, half that from Benghazi, half again from Tobruk.

Even with a static front, *Panzerarmee Afrika* was a moloch, requiring upwards of 30,000 tonnes of supplies every month, more than one third of that fuel, plus at least 9,000 tonnes of ammunition and 6,000 tonnes of food.[21] During concerted fighting, German and Italian troops' consumption topped 1,500 tonnes of fuel, ammunition and food *every* day – an increase of 50 per cent.

With Axis forces unable and Eighth Army unlikely to take the offensive for several weeks, Erwin Rommel was finally persuaded to take the rest and recuperation he had postponed in late August. He felt 'pretty much recovered,' he assured his wife. But many of his senior officers were suffering: his chief-of-staff Siegfried Westphal had jaundice, his head of intelligence Friedrich von Mellenthin dysentery. It was obvious to any man who knew him that Rommel was not well. 'He doesn't swagger around as he did before at the height of his glory,' Hellmuth Frey observed. Rommel's doctor was insistent, prescribing a few weeks in the Alps. The marshal reluctantly agreed – but not before his replacement arrived. Having rejected Heinz Guderian outright, Hitler had approved sending Georg Stumme, a man whom just months earlier he'd court martialled after plans for the summer offensive in Russia were lost behind enemy lines. Sentenced to five years in prison, Stumme was almost immediately pardoned and rehabilitated – typical, one observer noted, of 'the grotesque game of tin soldiers which Hitler plays with the generals'.[22]

Five years older than Rommel, Georg Stumme was a competent if stolid leader who had handed over command of the new 7th Panzer Division to the future field marshal in the autumn of 1939 then watched as Rommel seized the initiative – and limelight – while he continued his own less spectacular career as a corps commander in the West, Balkans and Russia, until the incident in the summer. Stumme lacked the dash and verve of his predecessor, though he proved popular with his men, was less demanding on his staff, less prone to mood swings and less hostile towards the Italians. There was one trait he shared with Erwin Rommel, however: he was not in good health.

Rommel knew the British, the desert, the Alamein position, the Italians, his men. Seasoned warrior though Georg Stumme was, he knew nothing of the war in North Africa. Though Rommel left his successor detailed plans for improving the defences – especially his 'Devil's gardens', the intricate network of minefields in front of German-Italian lines – he had no intention of relinquishing command permanently. 'By the time *it* comes, I'll be back again,' he reassured Wilhelm Ritter von Thoma, *Afrika Korps*' new commander, as he left Africa on 23 September. To Ettore Bastico – still nominally his superior – he was even more defiant. 'I'm not finished,' he declared. 'I still have a glimmer of hope: if things take place as I hope, the situation can be turned around...' Suddenly Rommel's expression and voice changed. 'If they send me what I have requested,' he told the Italian marshal, clenching his fist, 'and I'm assured of adequate reinforcements in Germany and Rome, I am sure that my men will be able to teach Montgomery a hard lesson...'[23]

Before joining his family in Wiener Neustadt and then heading into the Alps, Rommel first had to pay his respects to the Duce at his summer retreat outside Ravenna, then the Nazi leadership in Berlin. Mussolini found Rommel 'shaken – physically and mentally', while the field marshal was convinced the Duce had 'failed to grasp the true gravity of the situation'. At Hitler's headquarters, Rommel's star was still high. His failure to break through the Alamein line was regarded as little more than a temporary setback. Even the out-of-favour Franz Halder – a longtime critic of Rommel – was convinced the field marshal 'would regain the initiative once again'. It was certainly not 'a serious turning point in the war'. Hitler planned to name him Commander-in-Chief of the Army 'after the war,' Joseph Goebbels noted as he hosted the field marshal. The propaganda minister was entirely under his guest's spell. Rommel possessed 'modesty and candour which makes him one of the most charming companions I know' and spoke of the fighting in Africa 'with panache and flair'. He blamed the Italians for all his failures, branded them 'just about the worst allies we could find', condemned their 'cowardly weakness and lack of courage' and complained that 'entire Italian units surrendered and deserted at the slightest contact with Australians or New Zealanders'.[24]

At the Reich Chancellery, Hitler presented Rommel with his field marshal's baton before receiving a detailed overview of the war in Africa from his desert commander. At times, Hermann Göring interrupted. He dismissed Rommel's accounts of the latest weapon in the skies, 40mm cannon, which ripped apart German armour. 'That's utterly impossible,' the head of the Luftwaffe assured him. 'Americans only know how to make razor blades.' Rommel flashed back: 'We could use some of those razor blades, *Herr Reichsmarschall…*'

The overly optimistic mood of both Fascist leaders troubled Erwin Rommel. It was reassuring they had faith in his ability – there was a widespread attitude of 'You'll pull it off, all right' but, as Rommel conceded, 'without the matériel conditions in the first place, I couldn't pull anything off.' It would take a supreme effort by both Axis powers to save Africa. If the supply lines were secured, Rommel assured Hitler that his men would 'successfully hold this theatre of war in the long run against the best troops in the British Empire'. If not…[25]

In public, Erwin Rommel was nothing but cheerful and optimistic. Paraded before the international press corps at the Propaganda Ministry, he told them that the world would be amazed when the history of the fighting in North Africa was written one day and it learned how small Axis forces were compared with those of their enemy. 'Today we stand 100 kilometres from Alexandria and Cairo and have the gate to Egypt in our hands – and naturally we intend to open it,' he assured the journalists. 'We've not come all this way to let ourselves be thrown back sooner or later. And you can be assured of this: we're holding on to what we've got.'[26] Before thousands of Berliners packed into the Sportpalast to hear Hitler open the annual winter relief campaign, he acknowledged the cheers and applause, then took his seat for the Führer's first public address since April. As Hermann Göring had done in private, so Adolf Hitler did in public, contemptuously brushing aside the industrial might of the Anglo-Americans:

> Our enemies continue to perform nothing but 'miracles'. There is no tank they
> build that is not, of course, 'the best in the world', no aircraft about which they

do not claim the same. If they build a cannon, a very simple cannon at that, it is *the* cannon, the most incredible cannon in the world. When they make a new machine- or submachine-gun clearly it too is also the very best. They claim that the new Sten pistol is the greatest invention in the world.

When you look at this rubbish, you can only say that we wouldn't put it in the hands of a German soldier.

They are far superior to us in everything. They are superior in their incomparable generals, they are superior to us in the bravery of their individual soldiers. Any Englishman could easily take on three Germans…

That provoked widespread laughter.[27]

By the autumn of 1942, the qualitative gap was narrowing and the numerical gap widening. It was clear to any Italian or German aviator in Egypt, like Stuka pilot Erhard Jähnert, that 'air supremacy was lost'. Worse, Jähnert noted, 'the morale of our fighters had obviously reached a low point'.[28] It had, not least because Hans-Joachim Marseille was no longer with them.

Despite an astonishing rate of kills since his return to Africa, it was increasingly obvious to comrades that Marseille was not the man he had once been. His 158th kill – and 151st over the desert – would underline that, a bruising, nerve-wracking encounter with a Spitfire late on the afternoon of 26 September. It ended with the British fighter breaking apart in mid-air under the German's cannon, and the Messerschmitt pilot returning to base shaken to the core. Accustomed to quick victories, Marseille had come against the most spirited and skilful opponent of his career. When he climbed out of his cockpit, he was shaking, white as a ghost, sweating. His commander grounded him for several days to recover.[29]

He returned to African skies late on the morning of 30 September, a routine mission to escort Stukas back to base after a raid against British positions. He had no opportunity to add to his tally – enemy fighters baulked at the sight of Marseille's formation of 15 Messerschmitts and turned around. For the next few minutes the mission continued uneventfully as the fighters and dive-bombers returned to their bases – though they were still over British lines. Suddenly, there was a terse radio message: 'My engine's on fire!' Still two dozen miles from Axis-held territory, Marseille's Me109 trailed white smoke, which grew ever denser, while the aircraft continually lost altitude. After five minutes, and using the white mosque at Sidi Abd el Rahman as a reference point, Marseille knew he was safely over German lines – but also that his crippled fighter would never make it back to base. 'I've got to get out – I can't stand it any more.' He threw the cockpit canopy back and rolled his Messerschmitt on to its back before jumping out.

'Jochen's got out,' a comrade reported excitedly. Several seconds passed until the next voice was heard. 'He's dead!'

The parachute never opened. Marseille's body landed on its stomach as his horrified comrades circled the site in disbelief. When recovered shortly afterwards a severe wound was found across his left breast; he'd struck part of the aircraft as he bailed out. The blow at best knocked him out, at worst killed him instantly.

Marseille's commander, Eduard Neumann, made the final entry in the fallen ace's logbook: '388 sorties with 158 kills. Number of the flight: 482. Duration 49 minutes.' Next to the space for the landing time, Neumann simply marked a black cross. The other pilots sat around in their tent. Not a word was spoken. A comrade walked in with a fig tart – the galley's speciality – in an attempt to raise morale. 'You can't go on like this forever! If Jochen saw it...'[30]

Every public pronouncement stressed that Marseille had been unbeaten, a victim of a tragic accident, not the enemy's guns. 'Marseille died an airman's death, undefeated,' the *Völkischer Beobachter* screamed. 'Hans Joachim Marseille is dead! Undefeated – he did not die in aerial combat, this is the most infuriating thing, the aircraft suffered a technical failure.' His funeral a few days later ensured he entered the pantheon of fallen Nazi heroes. His body was flown to Derna airfield and laid to rest in the small military cemetery by the Mediterranean, alongside panzer division commanders Heinrich von Prittwitz und Gaffron and Georg von Bismarck, killed before Tobruk and Alamein respectively. German and Italian airmen attended, as well as senior officers, led by Hans Seidemann, the ranking Luftwaffe officer in North Africa, and Albert Kesselring, who laid a wreath on behalf of Hitler and Göring. As rifles fired in salute, aviators tossed handfuls of reddish sand into the grave. 'His heart continues to beat in the hearts of a thousand airmen,' wrote war correspondent and Stuka rear gunner Hans Gross, who covered the funeral for newspapers at home in the Reich. 'That is the legacy of the fighter pilot Hans-Joachim Marseille, who departed this life, undefeated by the enemy, as one of the greatest and bravest men in this war, who fought to his last breath for the future of the Reich.'[31]

There was no Italian equivalent of Hans-Joachim Marseille – just one *Regia Aeronautica* pilot achieved more than 20 kills in the entire war; only around three dozen aces attained double figures. And it was only getting harder. By the autumn of 1942, Italian squadrons were short of aircraft, fuel, spare parts, and found themselves increasingly outmatched by faster, better-armed opponents. Even if it was quiet at the front, the skies were never empty. Driver Vittorio Vallicella watched Me109s and Macchis grapple with a sizeable formation of Allied bombers and fighters – but only *after* the latter had raided Axis ground positions. The bombers turned for home, leaving the fighters to contest the sky in a furious dogfight. Vallicella was unable to determine who won, or how many aircraft were downed on either side, only that when it was over 'the desert was all smoke and blinding flames'. The balance in such dogfights was tipping increasingly against Axis pilots. 'They always outnumber us,' fighter pilot Giulio Lazzati wrote worriedly. 'Christ, where do all those aircraft come from? We shoot down five, ten, and at the next scramble, 30 will arrive, the next one, 40.' Lazzati reckoned he and his comrades were outnumbered five, perhaps ten, to one. And the gap was widening. Most of his squadron's Macchi fighters were worn out. Spare parts – replacement engines particularly – were non-existent. The number of serviceable aircraft fell by the day. Night offered no respite, as the Desert Air Force laid on an 'evening concert' for the Italians. First flares, dangling and swaying beneath tiny parachutes, to light the airfield, followed by the shrill whistle of bombs dropping. 'Head tucked between your shoulders, eyes closed, you curl up in the trench,' Lazzati wrote. 'Fuka is one huge explosion: bombs fall everywhere, on dumps, on the runway, between aircraft, near the barracks. Splinters and sand whirl through the air. We're seized by the anger of impotence.' Ground crews, remembered Vittorio Lana, the squadron's technical officer, waged 'a truly personal struggle with the Anglo-Americans – them to destroy, we to rebuild'. The strain of battle, the lack of spare parts and the constant enemy raids on his airfields reduced the fighter squadron to just a single operational aircraft on some days. Lana marvelled at 'unbelievable repairs, carried out in the middle of the sand, amid continuous alarms accompanied by formations overhead and machine guns'. The workshop – a large tent – was hit several times, but rebuilt and put back in operation to effect repairs once more.[32]

Air attacks and the occasional raid or reconnaissance party into enemy lines aside, life at Alamein in September and October 1942 was as monotonous and wearing as it had been before the 'Six-Day Race', only the days were slightly shorter, the temperatures more bearable. Dense fog was not uncommon at first light – 'a smoky, damp blanket' burned off by the sun after a couple of hours. Temperatures were now a more bearable high 20° Celsius. With the refreshing breeze, conditions reminded soldiers from northern Italy of autumn in the Po valley. Sunset was all too frequently scarred by 'desolation and death' – smoke rising from wrecked air force vehicles bombed by the British, coupled with the crash and thunder of heavy artillery. But when the fires died out and the barrage faded, the desert soldier was treated to a 'wonderful spectacle,' Vittorio Vallicella remembered: 'a firmament studded with stars… We cannot describe the emotion that its appearance in the immense desert causes in us, despite the tremendous harshness of life in a merciless war and the suffering of thirst.' Bernhard Ramcke was similarly bewitched by the 'strange magic of nights with a full moon in the desert... Not a sound interrupts the sublime silence of nature. Such magical nights reconcile us with a landscape which otherwise is so awful.'[33]

There was little to break up the monotony – certainly not in the Alamein position. When news reached the *Trento* Division that 'young ladies' had arrived in Mersa Matruh 'to bring a bit of cheer to the men', entertaining the troops with variety shows – 'and the rest, too,' Vittorio Vallicella noted – he was unable to avail himself of either 'distraction', being a good 250 miles away. A few days later a party of young female Red Cross volunteers visited the front. 'After 20 months in the desert, seeing these beautiful ladies – kind, smiling, caring – handing us gifts is a glimmer of light,' Vallicella wrote. Their gifts were 'a feast': soap, razor blades, chocolate, biscuits, sweets, writing paper, plus a signed photo from a young woman willing to correspond with the recipient.[34]

Normally rational men grasped at the most fantastical rumours. For weeks over the summer, there had been talk in German units that the war would end on 13 September. Belief was widespread 'at the front and in every branch of the Wehrmacht,' an exasperated Ralf Ringler wrote. 'With a serious face, people everywhere talk about this "prophesy from the grotto in Lourdes".' Even when the date arrived – 'like every other day in the desert, only not so hot' and plagued by a sandstorm – those who believed the rumour refused to give up hope. 'The thirteenth only ends at midnight,' one soldier pointed out to the 21-year-old Austrian.[35]

Deployed at the southern end of the front, Ringler spent the days checking the defences of his company – spread out across more than half a kilometre of desert. The individual strongpoints were so widely dispersed they could not help or communicate with each other. 'In the desert a man is more on his own in battle than on any other front,' he observed. 'Not only his life, but the outcome of the whole battle will depend on his courage, nerves and prudence.' Ringler's sector of the line was particularly desolate. Only the time of day altered the view of the jagged ridge south of his position – the northern edge of the Qattara Depression. 'In the morning you think that this long rim is only one thousand metres away,' he wrote. 'In the midday haze, you think you see lakes instead of desert, and the distance seems to increase tenfold. In reality, it is barely three and a half kilometres.'[36]

Ringler's superior, Bernhard Ramcke, was worried that the enemy would take advantage of poor visibility – dawn, dusk, sandstorms – to raid German lines. 'The troops have to be taught to the last man to be alert and to observe no man's land with increased vigilance for any movement and noise,' he ordered. He expected his paratroopers to defend their foxholes 'to the last round'. If any man was taken prisoner he was threatened with being condemned to death by immediate court martial.[37]

By day, those foxholes and underground shelters became the men's retreat when not working on improving their positions such that beyond the burned-out armoured vehicles and wrecked fuselages of fallen aircraft, the desert appeared empty. One dawn, Vittorio Vallicella scanned the landscape with his binoculars. 'I sweep across the immense expanse of sand without seeing a guard, only every now and then do I manage to catch a glimpse of a few re-supply vehicles,' he wrote. 'The sight is stunning, but at the same time tragic, thinking that they live underground like rats, thousands and thousands of human beings, waiting for "x" hour.'[38]

This troglodyte existence did nothing for the men's health. Artillery officer Alighiero Bottaro watched as flies and disease bedevilled his men. Fresh out of the academy, the 20-year-old had been put in charge of a battery serving alongside the *Folgore* when its original commander feigned – or overplayed – a stomach ulcer and returned to Italy for treatment. The battery comprised four pre-Great War French 75mm cannon – the only difference being now they were hauled by tractors, not horses – crewed by 80 men, mostly in their 30s from the Venice area. 'Until a month ago, dysentery was considered an illness to be treated in hospital,' he wrote. 'But now in the line, because of the shortage of men, you have to endure it. And, in battle, you had to continue to shoot, to command, to set the artillery coordinates – very often, with your trousers down.' After three months, Alberto Bechi no longer recognised the 'magnificent athletes' he had arrived in North Africa with. The ranks of his regiment of elite *Folgore* paratroopers were now filled with 'ragged, bearded men'. The division had already lost 1,000 men – two thirds of them to illness. 'Dysentery was literally killing them,' Bechi observed. 'Those who remained in the line held on through sheer force of will.'[39]

There was a surge for the mail truck every time it delivered letters from loved ones, but the news they brought was not always welcome. Vittorio Vallicella noticed a comrade in his battery visibly change after a disturbing letter from his wife. A few days later he took his own life – one of 17 suicides Vallicella knew of during his 18 months in the desert. The soldier's family – indeed the families of every suicide victim – were simply told loved ones died in action. Chaplains attempted to address the men's concerns – but they were often dismissed as pawns of the Officer Corps. 'The chaplain tries to give us courage, telling us that the ways of the Lord are infinite,' Vallicella wrote after a fireside chat with one of the *Trento* Division's clerics. 'We tell him that they are so infinite that they allow the massacres that are taking place here and around the world: they are so infinite that they allow us to witness shameful injustices between officers and men, so infinite that we say that the enemy is not only in front of us, but also among us.' Before departing, the chaplain handed the men holy pictures and a packet of cigarettes. As he left he said with a smile: 'Goodbye Bolsheviks.'[40]

Despite the growing enemy superiority, privations, the inequalities between officers and men, and monotony of life in the line at the Alamein position, Italian morale remained consistently high through September and into October. They were eager to hear Mussolini address the nation – Hitler and Göring had both delivered major speeches in recent weeks, why not the Duce? And while there were the usual grumblings about the harsh conditions of desert life, the Italian Army's censors concluded – having pored over nearly 70,000 letters – that 'certainty in victory is deeply rooted in all soldiers in North Africa. Everyone is convinced that the war may be short or long, may become easier or harder, but victory cannot fail to come.' Morale among newly arrived and elite units like the *Folgore*, who delighted in being named in the official communiqué and were convinced the mere sound of their battle cry sent shivers down the enemy's spine, was especially high. 'I am waiting for orders to hurl myself against the last obstacle in Africa,' one soldier wrote. 'Very soon we will be in Cairo.' And while some men were concerned by the enemy's widening numerical and matériel superiority, many were certain that Fascist conviction and élan would compensate. 'Those dogs can do things on a grand scale,' wrote one junior artillery officer. 'We may lack the means, but fortunately we do not lack heart and guts.' There was even talk of attack, not defence. Rumours were circulating that the advance on Alexandria and Cairo would resume in a few days. 'They will be hard days, of death, of unspeakable sacrifices,' Vittorio Vallicella wrote. 'But we are willing to endure anything as long as it ends, as long as we get out of these immense plains of sand, full of flies and fleas.'[41]

By the third week of October 1942, 'those dogs' had almost completed their preparations. Within days of Rommel's failure at Alam Halfa, Bernard Montgomery and his commanders had begun drawing up plans for a great counter-stroke. From the outset he was under pressure from London to attack as soon as possible, but stood firm. He would attack on his terms, when he was ready. 'I won't do it in September. But if I do it in October, it'll be a victory.'[42]

He used the time not merely to build up Eighth Army's reserves, but to prepare its men like never before mentally, physically, operationally. It enjoyed a substantial numerical and matériel superiority over its foe. It had thrown away similar opportunities in the past. But not this time. If every tank or anti-tank gun disabled its opponent, Allied armies could not fail to win, Montgomery insisted. Extensive fake radio traffic and dummy units – tanks, cars, trucks, with associated depots and camps – attempted to confuse the enemy about the size, scope and location of the looming offensive. Models of sectors of the front were provided for engineers and infantry to study. Sappers practised clearing minefields 'under conditions as nearly approaching battle as possible', while armoured units drilled on passing down the cleared channels and fanning out at the far end. Tank crews assigned to the new Shermans had no more than six weeks to learn how to operate – and maintain – them.

Eighth Army's morale had been raised immeasurably by the enemy's failure to puncture the Alamein position at the end of August. 'Mr Rommel got a bloody nose,' one British soldier gleefully observed, while a junior officer wrote simply: 'Our tails are up.' But what Montgomery wanted was killers. Every soldier had to want to go into battle 'imbued with the burning desire to "kill Germans" – even the padres, one per weekday and two on Sundays,' he instructed.[43]

The battle he wanted them to fight – codenamed *Lightfoot* – owed more to the First than Second World War, a Western Front battle of attrition but fought with the means of the next war. Under an intense barrage, engineers would clear paths through the extensive German minefields to allow the bulk of Eighth Army to pass. But after flowing through these gaps, the infantry and armour would not fan out, striking deep into the enemy's rear in some grand plan to outflank and encircle the Italo-German Army. Instead, they would entice their foe to attack, to wear himself out – Montgomery called it 'crumbling' – 'beating the guts out of the enemy'. He wanted the enemy armour to attack, but on Eighth Army's terms, drawn under the barrels of its more numerous tanks and anti-tank guns, where it would be defeated. It would be a slogging match, most definitely not a pushover – Montgomery ordered his men to rule out any thoughts of their foe surrendering en masse – but after a dozen days, Eighth Army would be victorious. 'The eventual fate of the *Panzerarmee* is certain,' Montgomery declared. 'It will not be able to avoid destruction.'[44]

At the southern end of the Alamein front, scouting parties of Panzer Reconnaissance *Abteilung* 33 regularly raided enemy lines, 'trying to find out whether Tommy is about to attack or not,' one junior officer noted. 'Very rarely do we succeed.' Otherwise, the two armies traded artillery blows. 'It won't stay like this for long,' the officer noted. 'The Tommies are not happy that we are here, so close to the fleshpots [of Egypt].' He observed the methodical build-up of Allied forces and was troubled: 'Tommies, Americans, South Africans, Australians, New Zealanders, Indians, Poles, Greeks and French are about to finish us off for good this time.' A little to the north, Ralf Ringler was summoned to Bernhard

Ramcke's command post, where a map had been laid out and every enemy unit identified to date marked on it. 'At the moment the enemy is about one third stronger,' Ringler noted with concern. 'New units are added daily, armoured forces especially are massing opposite us. Our reinforcements barely cover losses from wounds or illness.' The young Austrian was overcome by 'an uneasy feeling of powerlessness'.[45]

Few Axis commanders in North Africa felt more impotent than Hans Seidemann, commanding Luftwaffe forces. His airfields had been under attack by day and night since the beginning of October. Though not as devastating as they could have been, the raids nevertheless cost Seidemann around a quarter of his forces. Those who remained were *ausgeflogen* – exhausted from flying – fewer than half his aircraft were serviceable, his Stukas were now 'antiques' which could only be committed with a strong fighter escort and frequently ditched their bombs and fled for home at the first sight of enemy interceptors. Seidemann was in no doubt. 'For the first time, the British demonstrated clear air superiority against which we were powerless and which could only be put right with the provision of new, more advanced aircraft.' None were forthcoming. And so even before the Eighth Army struck, the battle, Hans Seidemann lamented, 'had already been won in the air' by his foe.[46]

Georg Stumme's mood swung between confidence and frustration. He relished the chance to prove himself. 'For me, all this is new and therefore highly interesting – getting to really know Africa and the theatre of war,' he told Rommel, updating the field marshal on progress. Privately, however, he was racked by doubt. 'Field Marshal Rommel's name is so closely associated with Africa,' he confided in Albert Kesselring, 'that I cannot but welcome his return in a few weeks.'[47]

Otherwise, the Desert Fox's temporary replacement prepared to defend the Alamein position as best he could, in line with his predecessor's instructions. The 'Devil's gardens' were becoming the formidable killing ground Rommel had hoped they would: a barrier of nearly 450,000 mines – mostly anti-tank – which would slow, perhaps even halt, an attack by Eighth Army. If the British did break through, Stumme now had more than 560 operational tanks to counter them – though fewer than a quarter of them were Panzer Mk3s and Mk4s. *Afrika Korps* – held in reserve behind the front line – would serve as the 'striking force' to smash the enemy. Should it succeed, Stumme mused, he might even unleash a counter-stroke 'to destroy the Eighth Army and, later, take Alexandria'. He found the Italians willing allies. 'But they're always an uncertain factor and you never know whether they truly mean what they say,' he told the field marshal. 'Most make an effort and that's quite something.' But the supply situation remained precarious. 'We are living from hand to mouth,' he complained. 'We fill one gap, only to see

The 'Six-Day Race', Rommel's last offensive in Egypt, 30 August–4 September

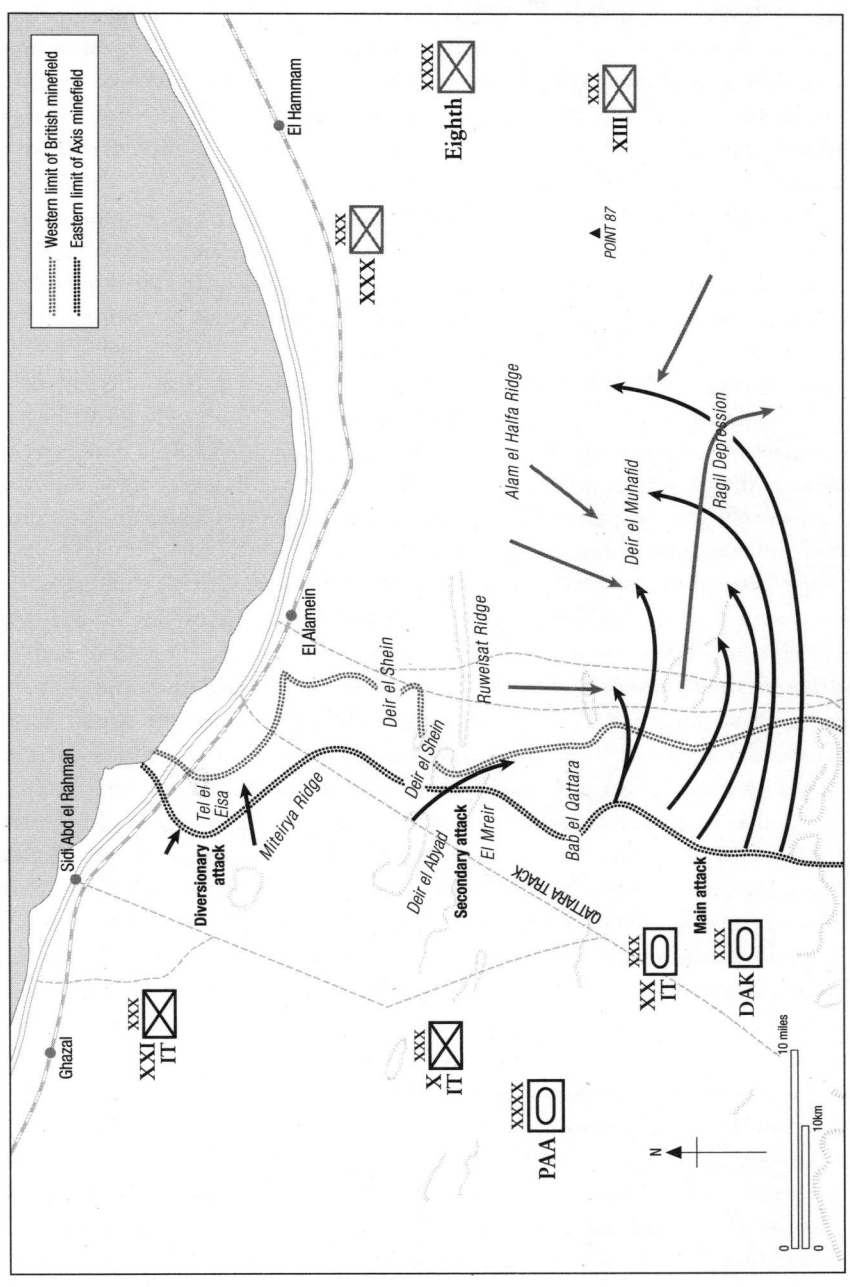

another one open.' *Afrika Korps* wasn't receiving enough fuel for its supply vehicles, let alone its panzers at the front. Petrol was rationed, limiting numerous vehicles to only what they carried in their tanks. Still, for his predecessor, Georg Stumme put on a brave face. 'Don't think too much about Africa and the fighting, concentrate on your health,' he urged Rommel. 'We'll smash the English if they suddenly attack us with their masses – which might happen any day, but may also be some way off yet.'[48]

And that was the question German intelligence could not answer. All the evidence – a new commander, political pressure to deliver an Allied victory, the arrival of reinforcements, the build-up of armour and aircraft, sabotage activity behind the front and the interrogation of Indian deserters – pointed to an impending major offensive. But where and when?[49]

All through 22 October, Giacomo Guiglia was troubled. Enemy radio traffic was suspiciously quiet, so too his air force. To the intelligence officer, these were clear signs that Eighth Army was about to attack. Guiglia spent the day roaming Italian and German command posts, warning them not to let their guard down. German officers were particularly sceptical, but Guiglia was adamant. 'Mark my words, it's a question of hours, not days.'[50]

Ulrich Liss, the usually well-informed head of German Army intelligence in the West, could offer no certain answers, dismissing talk of an enemy offensive out of hand. The 45-year-old found himself at something of a loose end at Stumme's headquarters and passed his time visiting units at the front. On the morning of Friday 23 October, he headed out into the desert with *Afrika Korps'* commander Ritter von Thoma to inspect the Qattara Depression. There was, Liss assured him, 'no danger of a major enemy attack in the near future'.[51] Stumme's intelligence section was rather better informed, predicting a British attack between 20 and 25 October, probably on the 23rd. The lack of radio traffic on the enemy side suggested an imminent attack, while prisoners expected Eighth Army to strike 'any day now'.[52]

Across the lines, officers were passing – or reading – out an order of the day from Eighth Army's commanding officer. 'The battle which is about to begin is one of the decisive battles of history,' Montgomery began.

> It will be the turning point of the war. The eyes of the whole world will be upon us, watching anxiously which way the battle will swing. We can give them the answer at once: 'It will swing our way'…
>
> Every officer and man should enter this battle with the determination to see it through – to fight and kill and finally to win. If we do this there can be only one result! Together we will hit the enemy for 'six', right out of North Africa.

As the sun went down this Friday, Ralf Ringler was invited to the battalion command post to celebrate his commander's birthday. A large tent had been erected specially to mark the occasion; inside was a display and a liberal supply of alcohol. One soldier brought his concertina; another performed folk songs. 'Everyone present sways,' the junior officer wrote. 'Alcohol has lifted the mood. In the desert just a drop of wine is enough to warm people up. Perhaps this will be the last joyful evening for some.' The merriment lasted a couple of hours before the men dispersed and returned to their foxholes somewhat intoxicated and fell into a deep sleep.

It did not last long.

Ringler was startled by a loud crash shortly before 10pm. 'The entire desert horizon seems to burn and twitch,' the Austrian noted. 'There's drumfire, the shells land so close that you can hardly tell them apart. There's whistling, banging, shaking, the ground shakes and explosions shake me all over the place.'

Eighth Army had begun its offensive.[53]

7

WE HAVE JUST TAKEN ON
TOO MUCH

Animals flee this hell, the hardest stones cannot bear it for long. Only man endures.

Officer in 24th Panzer Division

An hour before sunset on the penultimate Sunday of August 1942, six-year-old Vladislav Mamantov heard the thunder of anti-aircraft guns, then the drone of aircraft engines approaching from the direction of Mamayev Kurgan, Stalingrad's highest point. 'We didn't make it to the dugout,' Vladislav remembered.

The whole house shook from the explosions, all the windows blew out, the front door was torn off, everything was filled with dust and it smelled of burnt wood. My aunt and grandmother pushed me under the heavy old-fashioned table. They protected me from the flying splinters, pushed me to the floor. Whispering prayers, they crossed themselves after each explosion. Outside there was continuous thunder, we heard the sirens of the dive-bombers and the screams of the wounded. Small fragments of shells and bombs flew in from time to time through smashed windows and doors. Some bore into the floor and wall near us with a dull sound.

And this hell, it seemed to us, lasted a long time, a few hours. Then there was an ominous silence. Slowly, cautiously, we crawled out from under the table and peered outside. Our house was still standing, only the roof had been torn off. All around, however, the bombs had destroyed every building. The entire street was covered with boards, tree stumps, iron roof panelling, broken pipes, shattered glass and tiles. Large smoking bomb craters gaped…

I began to cry, 'Where is mama?' Weeping and wailing, my grandmother and my aunt turned over the bodies of some women. They were all strangers. Screaming and crying filled the street. People cleared away the ruins and carefully pulled dead and half-living people out from under the rubble.

Throughout the city, people had been caught out. Lev Yushchenko, a photo-journalist for *Komsomolskaya Pravda*, had spent Sunday afternoon wandering lazily through the southern fringe of Stalingrad's centre. A hot, dry wind whipped up the dust in the streets – no rain had fallen in weeks, such that the poplars lining the wide boulevards had turned yellow. Women and children with buckets and cans formed long queues at standpipes to collect water. Even though fighting was raging barely 40 miles away on the Don, life seemed to continue as if in peacetime. Women hung out washing to dry in courtyards or gardens, children played ball games or ran around. As he made his way to a telegraph office to file his latest despatch, the bespectacled war correspondent – a veteran reporter at the age of just 20 – noticed dark, turbulent clouds swirling over Stalingrad's southern suburbs, and flashes of lightning within them.

Yushchenko never heard the air raid warning – or if he did, he failed to record it in his memoirs. But sirens and the whistles of factories, locomotives and Volga steamers all announced the approach of enemy aircraft. It was also the signal to 15,000 people assigned to the city's air raid defence to take to their posts. Most Stalingraders failed to heed the warning, however. Only when the anti-aircraft guns opened up did they belatedly grasp this was not a false alarm. Bearing down on their city from the southwest were 200 bombers – Heinkels and Stukas – escorted by 50 fighters. They appeared one after another 'like a conveyor belt', the howl of the dive-bombers' sirens chilling Stalingraders to the bone. 'The screaming of bombs raining down from above mingled with the thunder of explosions,' one recalled. For the next hour more than 1,000 tonnes of bombs fell upon the city – and changed its face forever. The newly rebuilt tyre factory in the city centre was among the first structures burned to the ground – before anything had even run off its production lines. Neighbouring houses and public buildings followed suit, then the rail yard. The sky over the city 'turned black with enemy aircraft,' remembered Dmitry Pigalev, chairman of the city council. 'One wave of enemy vultures followed another.' Soon his city was 'burning like a huge bonfire' as far as the Volga – three quarters of a mile away. The water mains were among the first victims of the raid, making it almost impossible to keep the fires in check. 'It was a complete waste of time,' one official Party report noted. Even where wardens and militia succeeded in extinguishing the flames, they flared up again within minutes.

Far from taking shelter, Lev Yushchenko sought a high vantage point from which he could record Stalingrad's darkest hour with his camera. Summoning a passing truck, he raced through streets now littered with corpses, shattered glass and debris, and then scrambled up the fire escape to the roof of the civic theatre. 'Only there did I realise the scale of the tragedy,' he recalled.

> The wreckage of wooden houses was flying through the air, barns and dried trees caught fire, dry grass in front gardens burst into flames. And people who ran out of houses, out of tents, out of makeshift huts – with children, with bundles, half-dressed – were already rushing through yards and alleys, looking for salvation, and falling, cut down by shrapnel...
>
> Entire neighbourhoods were burning. Fires merged, the blaze raged as far as the horizon, and a strong and hot wind from the Volga region fanned this infernal furnace. Through the flames and smoke the figures of people could be seen, darting through the streets and squares.
>
> Feverishly clicking, I tried to photograph these round, dark objects, whistling to the ground, into the very depths of the fires. And I saw how, where they fell, everything again shook and shuddered, throwing earth, bricks, burning wood, fragments of buildings and iron beams around with monstrous force; and the red-hot, roaring flames, shooting skywards like a fountain, fell from on high with renewed force on to the burning neighbourhoods.

Seventeen-year-old Lidia Vernigora was convinced 'the end of the world had begun'. Bombs 'whistled and howled' as the populace ran for shelters built in the courtyards of apartment blocks, cellars or slit trenches and foxholes dug in open spaces. Windows shattered either from the heat or the pressure wave of explosions. The result was the same: shards of glass flew through the air like crystal daggers. The asphalt on the paved roads melted, telegraph poles 'went up in flames like matches', while the lines they carried snapped, bringing an end to orderly communications. Oil tanks fell victim to the bombs, spilling their burning contents which now flowed like lava through Stalingrad's streets, down the balkas and into the Volga, where they continued to burn on the surface. Natalia Tikhonova – celebrating her 24th birthday – abandoned all hope of reaching the far side of the Volga when she found 'the entire river on fire'. And amid the horrors, surreal sights: in one district, a cannery was hit, starting fires which caused the tins of food to explode. 'The most terrible aspect was seeing people dying in front of our eyes,' remembered Lev Yushchenko, who had now climbed down from the theatre roof. Stalingrad burned 'like a furnace', the heat from blazing buildings enough to burn the flesh of anyone standing in the middle of a street. 'A woman began to dash across the road, covering her face from the sparks, and suddenly, like gunpowder, her lush, beautiful hair went up in bright flames,' Yushchenko remembered.

There was someone writhing on the ground, bleeding or already a charred corpse. Others suffocated from smoke in the sewers where they hid from the fire. And those who still tried to flee – with children, half-clothed, almost naked after ripping off their smouldering clothes. They all ran in one direction: towards the Volga, even though everything there also burned – wharves, steamers, warehouses, fuel barges.

If the sights were horrifying, the sounds were blood-curdling – not just the Stukas' sirens or even the bombs bursting, but a constant, deafening tumult of fires crackling, buildings and walls collapsing, the cries of people. 'Everyone lost their minds,' Vernigora recalled. Children screamed out of fear; adults fared no better, tearing at their hair and 'howling like wolves'. The hot air, in places gusting through the streets at hurricane speeds, was dry, acrid, filled with soot and ash, making breathing difficult. There was no day or night now in Stalingrad. Just fire, sparks and billowing clouds of acrid red-purple-black smoke spiralling over the city and obscuring the stars.

Every now and then front commander Andrei Eremenko stepped out of his command post to survey the devastation. The war had spared the 49-year-old little since its first days, but the sights this evening were among the worst he had experienced: 'Stalingrad drowned in the glow of the fires.'

To Wolfram von Richthofen, 23 August was 'a great day'. The skies had belonged almost entirely to his airmen, who'd flown 1,600 sorties and downed 91 Soviet aircraft for the loss of just three planes – though Soviet accounts would claim 90 German bombers downed over Stalingrad alone.[1]

But 23 August was merely the overture. For three more days Richthofen's bombers pummelled Stalingrad. Lev Yushchenko was wounded by the first raid in the city on the 24th. When he regained consciousness, he was in an overcrowded cabin on a ship, rapidly filling with pungent smoke; the walls were on fire, Yushchenko's clothes were smouldering. He – and 600–700 other casualties – had been packed on to *Kompozitor Borodin*, a veteran Volga paddle steamer and sent on the 200-mile journey upstream to Saratov. The sluggish paddle boat had travelled barely 20 miles by mid-afternoon when it came under artillery fire from German guns drawn up on the west bank to disrupt river traffic. The *Kompozitor Borodin* was soon ablaze and out of control. The scenes aboard were every bit as hellish as those Yushchenko had witnessed not 24 hours earlier. Serious casualties did their best to crawl to the ship's side, but many burned alive, unable to escape, their screams piercing the roar of the fires raging through *Kompozitor Borodin*. The master succeeded in running the paddle boat aground on a sandbank where the Volga was little more than waist-deep. Yushchenko crawled on deck, removed his clothes and jumped – or fell – into the river and struggled to reach another sandbank where other survivors had gathered. There, exhausted, he rested his head on the body of a dead soldier.

> He was lying face up in the water, in a soldier's underwear, without an arm, cut off up to the elbow, and the current was moving his unwound bandage with its yellowish blood stains. And the wind carried shouts and groans, smoke and cinders from the burning steamer, which was stuck in shallow water about two hundred metres away. The river carried past us burning heads, fragments of benches, flakes of foam, burned mattresses, scraps of paper, empty sanitary bags, lumps of crumpled, dirty bandages. It carried burned corpses and wounded men, still alive, calling for help.

Again Lev Yushchenko passed out. He awoke two days later in a hospital 30 miles east of Stalingrad. It was four more months before he returned to the front as a war correspondent – but he never again reported the fighting on the Volga.[2]

While Lev Yushchenko recuperated, Stalingrad continued to endure its ordeal by fire from the skies. The attack on 25 August – a deliberate fire-bombing raid which turned the city centre into 'a sea of flame' – left two huge palls of black smoke rising upwards of 12,000 feet. Aircrew needed no navigational aids to find Stalingrad. An enormous cloud – 'snow white, rising from a base of black smoke' – could be seen for miles in an otherwise matchless sky. Below, Stalingrad's inhabitants quickly adapted to their new, terrible routine. Those who had not sought salvation on the shore of the Volga retreated to the city's cellars and basements. The first raid had left medical student Natalia Tikhonova with only the briefcase she carried, containing her identity papers, study book and a volume of Pushkin. Otherwise, neither she nor anyone else she knew possessed anything. Having abandoned her attempt to reach the river, she joined strangers in cellars, scavenging for 'anything that was at least half-way edible' and water during breaks in the bombardment. 'Sometimes we found a dead horse,' she remembered. 'That was a great feast for us.' Anna Yakovlevna Mokrova's family had also lost everything. They took refuge in various slit trenches – but never more than one family member in each trench or foxhole 'so that they could dig each other out if anyone was buried'.[3] They would never be caught unprepared again.

The battle for Stalingrad, September–November

Front line, 14 September
Front line, 16 September
Front line, 28 September
German attacks, 14–26 September
German attacks, 22–28 September

Orlovka

Spartakovka

Dzerzhinsky

Gorodishe

Orlovka

Dzerzhinsky
tractor works

Rasguljajewka

Red Barricades
ordnance factory

Red October
metalworks

LI XXX

Lazur chemical
works

Mamayev
Kurgan

62 XXXX

Volga

Ostrow
Bobrow

Tsaritsa

Central
Station

The Volga
ferry

Ssadowaya

Krasnaya
Slobada

Jelschanka

Southern
Station

Grain elevator

Minina

Kuporosnoye

XLVIII XXX

N

0   3 miles
0   3km

323

Nor too Stalingrad's defenders. On the second day of the aerial onslaught, fighter pilot Heinrich Graf von Einsiedel already reckoned the Luftwaffe was outnumbered 20 to one over the city. 'An aerial battle develops the likes of which we've only experienced to date in the West, over the Channel,' he wrote. His commanding officer in *Jagdgeschwader* 3, Günther Lützow, had grown increasingly pessimistic about the course of the war. The Luftwaffe was chasing 'five rabbits simultaneously', each running in different directions – Stalingrad, Leningrad, Baku, El Alamein and the air defence of the West – and bound to come up short. 'Gentlemen, flying for sport and seeing who can score the highest number of kills stops here,' he ordered his pilots. 'Every aircraft, every drop of fuel, every hour's flying is irreplaceable.' Lützow's admonishment fell on deaf ears. Just a couple of days later, Einsiedel found himself sucked into a dogfight with at least 20 stubby, obsolete Ratas and even biplanes. Individually, they were no match for the Messerschmitts of *Jagdgeschwader* 3, but they compensated by making near-suicidal passes at the Germans, aiming at their opponents head-on. 'In the blink of an eye the muzzles flash and it's solely down to chance whether or not we hit the enemy,' Einsiedel wrote. After one such duel, his cockpit was filled with an acrid smell as coolant emptied from a radiator, followed first by oil, then smoke, until the propeller stopped 'with a nasty jerk'. At the mercy of its enemies now, the Messerschmitt was hit several more times until it made an emergency landing – far beyond German lines. Swiftly captured, Einsiedel was promptly interrogated – where his captors struggled to comprehend that he was a descendant of Bismarck – then driven into Stalingrad for further questioning. He was pushed into a spartan room in the basement of an apartment block furnished only with an iron bedstead which he shared with a couple of drunken Soviet officers and several soldiers from Russia's far eastern regions. 'Suddenly I'm struck by a feeling of utter loneliness,' he recorded in his diary. 'I try to imagine my comrades in front of their tents at the airfield, talking about my fate. Did the major see that I made an emergency landing, that I got down safely? What will he tell my parents? And then a fresh shock shoots through me: what will my mother say when she learns I'm missing?' The 21-year-old had only questions, no answers, not least: 'How long will my captivity last?'[4]

By the time Heinrich Graf von Einsiedel was in Soviet hands, the Luftwaffe's city-wide bombardment was over. Stalingrad, Richthofen concluded, was 'destroyed – no more targets of value there!' One Soviet soldier passing through agreed. 'The hairs on our necks stood on end,' he recalled. Stalingrad was 'naked ruins – and nothing else'.[5]

Fifteen-year-old Vladimir Samoilov thought his city had been turned into 'a giant funeral pyre'. In the centre, nine out of ten buildings had been destroyed or were burned out, including almost every major industrial plant, office complex and administrative centre. More than 1,000 homes and apartment blocks now were hollow shells. The central bank, post office, the headquarters of the NKVD, city council and Red Army, printworks, breweries, bakeries, dairies, canneries, factories were in ruins. Entire neighbourhoods on the edge of the centre had been flattened. City-wide water and sewage systems, the electricity grid and telephone network were knocked out, railway lines destroyed, and wharves and jetties along the Volga wrecked. The tractor factory which just days before produced T-34s for the front was struck more than two dozen times, while the Red October works, which supplied the steel to the tractor factory to build those tanks, suffered widespread destruction. The Iylich hospital was overcrowded, unable to treat any more casualties. And yet the death toll was surprisingly low. For decades, Soviet accounts cited a figure of 40,000 – putting Stalingrad on a par with the later firestorms in Hamburg and Dresden. In fact, contemporary Communist Party documents suggest just 1,017 people in the central and northern districts of Stalingrad were killed in the four-day bombardment and fewer than 1,300 wounded.[6]

The blow delivered to Stalingrad in the last week of August galvanised the city's military and political leaders. Concerted efforts had been made to ensure little of value fell into the invader's hands as he swept across the Don steppe: collective farms had been stripped bare and all manner of cattle, plus more than 2,000 tractors, shipped across the Volga; in many cases only the ripening harvest was left behind. But no similar attention had been paid to Stalingrad's inhabitants – apart from the families of some Party leaders, that is. The bombardment on 'black Sunday' – and the spontaneous actions of thousands of Stalingraders who made for the waterfront – forced the hand of the civic authorities who now ordered the large-scale evacuation of women, children, plus the patients and staff of city hospitals.[7] The Volga offered the only escape route – either the short crossing to the east bank, or a journey of a good 450 miles upstream to Kuibyshev. Three Volga steamers were commandeered, crammed with refugees and sent upriver, but as they passed close to the German-occupied right bank just north of Stalingrad, they were engaged by enemy cannon. Two vessels managed to slip through the gauntlet, but not the *Joseph Stalin*. Peppered with shellfire, she was soon out of control and ablaze. Passengers threw themselves into the Volga before the burning hulk ran aground. Fewer than one in six of the 1,200 souls aboard was rescued. The crossing to the left bank – though it took only a matter of minutes – was just as fraught with danger. Dmitry Pigalev observed the evacuation on 25 August:

> Thousands of helpless, homeless people who had lost relatives and friends crowded on the Volga shore; the Fascist vultures continuously attacked the wharves. Oil tanks on the river bank burned, the burning oil spilling across the river. Flames engulfed the jetties. The dead and hundreds of wounded begging for help lay everywhere. Children without mothers were screaming and crying.[8]

The two principal crossing points – one in the city centre, near the statue of a fabled aviator, the other near Stalingrad's main waterworks – were quickly overwhelmed with thousands of women and children, the latter often orphans rescued from abandoned apartments blocks, basements and courtyards by young Communists. A flotilla of more than 1,000 rowing boats and motor launches was hurriedly mustered to carry them over the river, joining the two civic ferries which ran regular services. All came under attack. The waters were churned by bombs – teenager Anna Andreievna Makarova was convinced they made the Volga boil – causing waves which often swamped overladen craft. Boats were blown apart by direct hits or capsized by near misses, their passengers tossed into the Volga where they struggled to swim to shore. If they were not drowned by those who panicked, all too frequently they were strafed by German aviators, or carried away by the current. Junior officer O. K. Selyankin made four crossings, embarking far more people than his river trawler could safely carry; his freeboard was so low that he avoided sharp turns to prevent capsizing. As his boat crossed the Volga a fifth time it suffered a direct hit and sank in seconds. The blast hurled Selyankin off the bridge and into the river. When he surfaced he found he was one of just eight survivors. Nevertheless, most craft reached the east bank, where scenes were no less chaotic. Rowing boats were largely abandoned rather than sent back across the river, while little provision was made to either care for refugees – children rummaged along the bank for scraps of food, especially bread – or onward transport. Still, at the height of the evacuation in the final days of August, as many as 40,000 civilians were shipped to the far side of the Volga every day.[9]

Those who remained behind were left in no doubt about the seriousness of the hour. A state of siege was immediately imposed. Looters were to be shot on the spot, while anyone else who stepped out of line would face a court martial. That very night, the first six plunderers were executed, including a housewife, and their names listed on posters plastered across the city. Sabotage groups were formed to slip through German lines and cause havoc in the enemy's rear, destroying fuel tanks, food stores and ammunition dumps, blowing up trains and cutting telephone lines. Stalingrad's citizens were expected to defend their city to the death, standing shoulder to shoulder with the Red Army to keep the 'frenzied enemy hordes' at bay. 'We will not surrender our hometown, our homes, our families,' civic leaders declared defiantly, calling on inhabitants to rip up rail lines and paving slabs, and to overturn trams. 'Fill every street in the city with impassable barricades. Turn every house, every block, every street into an impregnable fortress.' For, at the end of August 1942, Stalingrad was no fortress. Efforts over the summer had been concentrated outside the city as upwards of 30,000 civilians – almost all of them women – had dug a series of defensive lines – defensive lines which had proved little or no obstacle to the Germans. The city itself, however, was 'unprotected,' commissar Ivan Vasilev remembered. 'There were no fortifications – nothing to fall back on.' There were some hurriedly thrown-up barricades blocking streets, but it only needed a vehicle to bump into them for the rampart to fall to pieces, Vasily Chuikov acidly remarked. NKVD blocking detachments had been established on the outskirts of Stalingrad to round up stragglers – and seized more than 1,000 men in just two days as the front crumbled. Employees of the Barrikady gun factory wheeled cannon out to the front line, while every tank completed at the nearby Dzerzhinsky tractor works – nearly 60 machines – was immediately sent to the front, often crewed by the men who had assembled them. Another 1,200 of the plant's staff were hastily armed with machine-guns. In fact, any man or woman who could bear arms was swept up in the makeshift militia units and workers' battalions to defend the industrial district in the north of the city. Nevertheless, the speed of the German advance stunned the city's leaders as much as it did the Red Army. 'We never imagined they'd get here from the Don in a single day,' city council chairman Dmitry Pigalev conceded.[10]

In fact, these were difficult days for both sides. Only 16th Panzer Division stood on the Volga and its fate hung 'by a thin thread' – the rest of Sixth Army was still trailing in its wake. Scratch Red Army and militia units from workers' settlements on the northern outskirts of Stalingrad were hurled against the division which, for several days, was on its own, the bulk of its supplies still behind the Don. Even when reinforcements arrived, the position remained precarious as Stalin cajoled his generals into launching premature counter-attacks to keep the enemy at bay. 3rd Motorised Infantry Division parried successive waves of tank and infantry assaults. 'You cannot imagine how the Russians let their regiments bleed out,' an astonished German company commander wrote. Hurriedly scraped-together units – ill-trained, ill-armed and ill-prepared – were thrown into the fray immediately. 'They often send us into battle with only our bare hands, such a fate has befallen not just our division, but others as well,' complained a baker who claimed he'd been forced to become an infantryman and sent into action with 120 men, armed with just ten rifles between them. 'Men who are hungry, exhausted after marching, go into battle with their bare hands.' A regiment formed of cadets from the Grozny Infantry Academy lasted just nine days in the line trying to blunt the German drive on the city from the south. The cadets threw themselves against the invader with cries of '*Za Rodina*' or '*Za Stalina*' – For the Motherland, For Stalin – when they counter-attacked, and when surrounded, held their ground to the last man and last round. When their commander was fatally bayoneted, his wife, who had run the regimental first-aid post, shot herself. The Germans took just 18 cadets prisoner.[11]

Blood bought time. But it could not stop Stalingrad being cut off by land as a dozen German divisions bore down on the city from the north, west and south, where Hermann Hoth's panzer army had finally punctured a formidable anti-tank ditch on the edge of the Kalmyk steppe – a wide trench, mined, overlooked by numerous bunkers. The position appeared unoccupied as Egon Reifner led a company of pioneers up to it. There was no sound, no sign of movement, just a lark overhead singing. One of Reifner's half-tracks drove into the middle of the ditch and hell was unleashed. A dozen flamethrowers, built into the trench and controlled remotely, spewed fire from every direction at the vehicle. 'It was hell,' Reifner wrote. 'The crew screamed in terror. Skin burned, the vehicle burned.' The men jumped out and rolled on the ground next to their blazing vehicle whereupon they came under ferocious fire from every bunker. But the Russians aimed too high. Reifner's men regained their composure, used surprise, the cover of dense clouds of smoke and shaped charges to knock out each bunker. As the pioneers rounded up a couple of dozen prisoners, 'panzer after panzer rolled past'. 24th Panzer Division captured most of a Red Army rifle brigade, then brushed aside an armoured brigade before reaching the main railway line between Kalach and Stalingrad. Just north of there, on the evening of 2 September, the panzers ran into 71st Infantry Division and the jaws of two German armies closed around Stalingrad.[12]

The news provoked one of Joseph Stalin's customary rages. 'Stalingrad could be captured today or tomorrow,' he chided Georgy Zhukov, the ablest of his marshals who had been dispatched to the city to bolster the resolve of its defenders. 'Tell the commanders of the forces to the north and northwest of the city that they must attack the enemy and come to the aid of the people of Stalingrad. Delay is tantamount to a crime.' Zhukov responded with a premature counter-attack against the troublesome corridor XIV Panzer Corps had driven to the Volga on the northern edge of Stalingrad. The assault failed to smash through the corridor, but it did unsettle both the corps – on the receiving end and soon protesting it was 'strained to the limit' – and Sixth Army, which decided to postpone its main assault on the city.[13]

Beyond the terrible bombardment the city had suffered, the actual fighting for Stalingrad had gone no further than the fringes of the city. Yet there was a growing realisation – on both sides – that the war in the East would be decided on the Volga. The river, one Red Army engineer decided, was the 'last frontier, here you have to die or defeat the enemy and advance westwards – there is no other choice.' War correspondent Vasily Grossman, newly arrived at the front, sensed that there was 'nowhere further to retreat. Every step back is now a big, and probably fatal, mistake. The civilians in the villages beside the Volga feel it, as well as the armies that are defending the Volga and Stalingrad.' One German flak gunner was convinced that the Russians were 'staking everything on Stalingrad. On it the outcome of the Russian campaign surely depends. Stalin will personally lead the defence of the city. But that will not affect the fate of the city when it goes up in smoke and flames like Voronezh.'[14]

Udo von Alvensleben had reached a similar conclusion – though for different reasons. He'd spent the past fortnight watching his comrades batter themselves against the defenders of Stalingrad's northern suburbs to little avail… and the enemy do likewise in response, underscored by Zhukov's hastily launched counter-attack which had now run its course with nothing gained, perhaps beyond buying time to shore up the city's defence. It dawned on von Alvensleben that the battle had already turned into a duel to the death, unparalleled in its scale and intensity. 'It becomes ever clearer to me that not only the success of the summer campaign but also the entire eastern campaign will be decided here.'[15]

The ferocity of the propaganda campaign reinforced Udo von Alvensleben's observations. Troops in Fourth Panzer Army came across an appeal to Soviet soldiers – originally published in the Red Army newspaper, *Krasnaya Zvezda* – entitled simply 'Kill'. 'If you have not killed at least one German during the course of a day, then that's a wasted day,' its author Ilya Ehrenburg told his readers. 'If you don't have any bullets left, kill him with your bayonet.' He continued:

If you let a German live, he will hang Russian men and rape Russian women. When you've killed one German, kill another – for us there's nothing we like more than German corpses. Don't count the days. Or the kilometres. Just count one thing: the number of Germans you've killed. Kill the Germans – your elderly mother begs you. Kill the Germans – your children ask of you. Kill the Germans – that's the cry of the earth of the Motherland. Do not miss an opportunity. Do not make a mistake. Kill.[16]

Stalin appealed more to patriotic duty. 'The enemy is advancing towards the old Russian river, the Volga,' Moscow radio declared on 8 September. 'Our continued existence depends on the outcome of the battles which are now so fiercely raging. Not one step back! Stand to the death! This is the cry of our nation. Russians have always defeated the Prussians.' Commissars and politruks passed on their leader's words to inspire the ordinary *frontovik*, explaining and embellishing their meaning. 'We are prepared to sacrifice everything for the Motherland, including our lives. Stalingrad must be ours and will be!' marine Viktor Barsov wrote. Soldier Mikhail Gusev observed that his comrades grasped the importance of Stalingrad and the Volga for the future of their Motherland. 'None of the men who are fighting here for Stalingrad give a thought to surrendering or retreating,' he wrote. 'We want victory. Today we want it even more than two or three weeks ago.' In the steppe just outside Stalingrad, a rifleman stared at a field littered with German corpses. 'It does you good,' he wrote, 'even if the smell is unpleasant.' As he waited for orders to attack, he wrote to his wife. 'Right now I'm in rude health and go into battle with gusto because I know that if I die, I do so for the future happiness of my small children. Think only of our victory...' Artillery officer Lieutenant Vitali Rumianchev dropped 'thousands of kilos of iron on the heads of the Fascist dogs every day'. Rumianchev was prepared to die defending Stalingrad. 'If I am destined to fall, one hundred Fritzes will lay down their lives for me.' But not every Soviet commander demanded a hero's death of his men. 'You don't have to die pointlessly, it's not heroic or valiant,' Nikolai Batiuk, the youthful commander of 284th Rifle Division, told his staff as the unit re-formed after its baptism of fire at Kastornoye, west of Voronezh, at the beginning of July. Now the Siberians were about to be thrown into the furnace of Stalingrad. 'You have to inflict a big defeat on the enemy, you shouldn't die cheaply.'[17]

But there were also Soviet soldiers convinced Stalingrad would fall. 'The shells have run out, but the fiends – the panzers – get ever closer,' one wrote to his mother. 'There's no sign of reinforcements. Not a drop to drink for three days and nights and the Volga flows next to me. I die for Lenin's great party.' He stuffed the note in his canteen – from where it was subsequently recovered by comrades upon his death. Pessimism even infected the political ranks. 'No-one believes that Stalingrad will be held any more,' one regimental commissar noted. One of the unit's junior politruks tried to rally the troops by declaring: 'We will not surrender Stalingrad.' 'The mood of the men is exactly the opposite,' the young commissar noted. 'It's rare that anyone hopes or believes in victory.'[18]

He might not have been so fatalistic had he known how weary his foe was. It was a tired Sixth Army which stood at the gates of Stalingrad in September 1942. 'In a few days we will have spent four months in permanent action, attack after attack, stress, no relief,' a non-commissioned officer in 71st Infantry Division complained. 'It was not even like this in the World War. And against *this* enemy.' 60th Motorised Infantry Division, committed on Stalingrad's northern outskirts, was haemorrhaging troops. In the six-week advance to the city, it had lost 50 men every day. In just a fortnight's fighting for Stalingrad, the rate had doubled. By the second week of September, it was no longer an effective fighting force. 295th Infantry Division was just as exhausted. Once 13,000 men strong, it was reduced to barely half strength by the time it reached the outskirts of Stalingrad. 'The heavy losses are hitting the morale of our soldiers,' one staff officer complained. 'The men have become listless, they did not expect such hard resistance. They believed they would be in the city in a few days and finally able to rest. But now most of the men consider it highly unlikely whether we will ever reach Stalingrad at all.' Radio operator Paul-Hans Voss found his comrades equally downbeat. 'As for marching into Stalingrad as victors – nobody thinks of that,' he wrote. 'The mood is bad everywhere. The bad nerves, the unresolved question of leave, the knowledge that we can hardly expect to get out of here alive, everything weighs down the men.'[19] Infantryman Karl Bühler knew, once again, that the heaviest burden would fall upon him and his 261st Grenadier Regiment comrades. He entered the city convinced his days were numbered:

> Those who have been in Russia from the beginning and have not been wounded or fallen to this day can thank their Lord God. I see it clearly in our regiment... Wherever you go, everywhere, you see new faces. Not a day goes by without fresh losses. Our divisional priest, for example, was killed by shrapnel from a bomb, so even for people who are merely putting charity into practice, there is no stopping the enemy's bullets.[20]

Soldiers who fell into Soviet hands suggested German Army morale was waning, that the ordinary soldier had been told repeatedly that the fall of this city or that region would force Moscow to throw in the towel. 'The war is endless,' one signaller sighed to his Red Army captors. 'We're going to be disappointed again – and not for the first time...'[21]

What few, if any, *Landser* considered was defeat on the Volga. He might die on the Volga, but Stalingrad would still fall. 'We advance because each man gives his all and if he has to give his life, each soldier knows that Stalingrad must fall,' Radio operator Anton Erl – later posted missing – wrote to his fiancée Resi Böhm. 'I don't yet know when that great moment will be. But this city too will fall.' Karl Bühler felt he had a sacred duty to defeat the Red Army at Stalingrad. 'I cannot imagine one day having to leave this theatre of war as a beaten man, because then we might as well put a bullet through our heads,' he wrote. 'If we do not succeed in destroying Communism, then we ourselves will be destroyed. What unspeakable misery would then befall our German homeland and all of Europe.' Artilleryman Kurt Deistler had crossed 'so many rivers': the Elbe, Oder, Vistula, Dnieper, Donets, Don. 'Now we want to reach the Volga. Only Stalingrad still stands in the way.'[22]

The task facing both attacker and defender was formidable. Occupying the high bluffs of the west bank of the Volga for more than a dozen miles, but extending only a couple of miles inland, Stalingrad had been home to around half a million people in peacetime. For most of its 350-year history, until its citizens 'chose' to rename it in honour of Stalin's role in the Civil War, it had taken its name from the Tsaritsa, the river which carved a steep gorge a couple of hundred yards wide through the landscape before spilling into the Volga. South of the Tsaritsa lay railway yards, industries and tenement blocks, all dominated by the brutalist new grain elevator complex. Most of the city was located on the north side of the valley. The historic red-brick heart of old Tsaritsyn had been largely overwhelmed by Soviet-era structures, which made Stalingrad something of a model city: the centre with its Red Square, Party Headquarters, flagship Univermag department store, NKVD complex and administrative buildings, plus gleaming inter-war apartment blocks. The centre stretched as far as Mamayev Kurgan, an ancient burial mound which rose more than 300 feet to become the highest point in Stalingrad. North of the hill, sandwiched between the main rail line and the Volga cliffs, was the factory district which made the city an industrial powerhouse. It stretched for at least four miles, a jumble of goods yards, oil tanks, mighty construction and assembly halls, power plants, canteens, administration buildings, workshops, and dozens of smaller factories and industrial concerns: the Lazur chemical plant, the Red October steelworks, the Barrikady gun factory and finally the Dzerzhinsky tractor works, a showpiece of Stalin's Five-Year Plan to drag the Soviet Union into the 20th century. A good mile long and, like all the major industrial plants, with its own extensive internal railway, since the outbreak of war tanks, not tractors, had emerged at the end of the production line.[23]

The first set-piece attempt to seize Stalingrad began at first light on Sunday 13 September as Sixth Army's commander Friedrich Paulus threw an entire corps – three divisions – against the heart of the city. The Luftwaffe and artillery had subjected the city to such a hammering in the hours leading up to the attack that one non-commissioned officer from 389th Infantry Division was convinced he would not find 'even a mouse still alive'. Herbert Pabst was not so sure. He and his Stuka squadron struggled to find targets, so well camouflaged were Soviet positions. 'When we arrive all movement stops, no muzzle flash gives them away – even the flak often waits until we've dropped our bombs.'[24]

War correspondent Clemens Podewils watched the depleted ranks of 295th Infantry Division attack in the direction of Mamayev Kurgan. The men were hopeful – they reckoned they'd be on the Volga within two days – and gave the attack their all. They quickly overran the bunker defences with the help of assault guns and pressed on to the city. The colourless, dull yellow dust of the Volga steppe soon gave way to wooden huts, then allotments, where sugary-sweet fiery red peppers remained unharvested, then finally the factories of northern Stalingrad and the workers' quarters. In the occasional pause in the bombing and artillery barrage, the inhabitants climbed out of foxholes they'd dug in their gardens or clawed in the sides of a ravine 100 feet deep. Clothed in rags, the occasional young girl with a bright yellow or red headscarf, they looked to the Germans for salvation but received only pity. 'Poverty here seems total and without consolation,' Podewils noted. The advance halted just short of the railway embankment which carried the main north–south line parallel to the river. From a nearby still-intact wooden cottage, Clemens Podewils could see beyond the railway line into the heart of Stalingrad. Along the banks of the river, oil refineries burned, sending enormous pitch-black clouds skywards. The afternoon sun pierced the thin veil of rain now falling and a rainbow arched over the ruined city. But the Volga, no more than a kilometre away, remained hidden from view. Perhaps the division might reach it with one more push; then again, its ranks were decimated – the company Podewils joined was just 20 strong. Its objectives for the first day of the attack achieved, it halted.[25]

All day long, Kurt Deistler's battery had supported 295th Infantry Division's advance from its initial positions ten miles west of the city, advancing first towards, then into Stalingrad to keep pace with the attacking infantry until the guns too were fighting in the suburbs. 'Tomorrow we'll be on the Volga,' a company commander assured Deistler.[26]

Observing the advance of the 295th Infantry through his stereoscopic binoculars from his command post on top of Mamayev Kurgan was the man who had led Stalingrad's defence for barely 24 hours, Vasily Chuikov. The bombardment left him cut off from his men – telephone lines were frequently cut, radio communications little better. It left the 42-year-old reliant on messengers, the naked eye and his instinct as a leader. And it was clear: the battle was going against him.

Of fine peasant stock, with wiry black hair, a temper as fiery as his laugh was hearty, Vasily Ivanovich Chuikov had arrived in Stalingrad at dusk the previous day, put in charge of Sixty-Second Army in good part because his character had impressed Nikita Khrushchev during the summer battles on the Don steppe. 'We will hold Stalingrad,' he vowed, 'or die trying.' Yet even he was shocked by what he found as he stepped off the Volga ferry: terrified civilians, desperate to escape a city of the dead, the horrors of the past few weeks were carved on their faces, black with dirt, streaked by tears. The fires of August had stripped the trees of all traces of green, reduced wooden houses to piles of ash and solitary brick chimneys, while the more substantial structures were burned out, their windows and doorways hollow, roofs collapsed. When he eventually found the headquarters of Sixty-Second Army, he was shocked by the state of its commander and the units he led. Armoured brigades possessed only a handful of tanks, or none at all, while disabled tanks were buried in the ground and turned into strongpoints. The best of the divisions could muster 1,500 men, the worst barely 250. And the Luftwaffe flew ten times as many sorties as the Red Air Force. The army's sacked commander, Anton Lapotin, was a broken man, convinced his shattered army could not hold Stalingrad in a protracted fight. Several of his subordinates felt likewise. Morale in the ranks was similarly low. 'Many soldiers wanted to retreat beyond the Volga to escape the hell of Stalingrad,' Chuikov observed. His first task was to banish such thinking from the minds of officers and men.[27]

While Chuikov sought a more suitable location for his command post, the plight of his army continued to worsen. In the centre of the German attack, 71st Infantry Division had made spectacular progress for minimal losses on the first day of the offensive, encouraged by stirring cries from its commanders. 'Soldiers of 71st Division! We are approaching the climax of the battle for Stalingrad,' Alexander von Hartmann assured his men. 'Forwards to the Volga!' His words were passed down by his officers, such as battalion commander Karl-Heinz Fricke. 'Everything for Germany! Then we'll take Stalingrad!' By nightfall on the 13th, the division was in the suburbs, and by noon the next day, its lead groups had reached the railway line just north of the central station. The building had changed hands three times before mid-day – and would change again twice more before the 14th ended. The tracks outside the station were littered with the remnants of abandoned trains, the wrecked carriages and locomotives a haven for snipers. Beyond the tangle of twisted rails, smashed engines and burned-out wagons, Lieutenant Colonel Friedrich Roske was electrified by the sight of 'the magnificent 1,800-metre-wide strip of the Volga'. Gerhard Münch, the young captain leading the attack, requested Stukas clear a path for his men, but the dive-bombers did not appear at the assigned time. Münch waited another 15 minutes, then decided to attack. 'I decided, if we wanted something, we needed to do it ourselves,' he recalled nearly 70 years later. 'It wasn't far from the railway station to the water – just 600–700 metres. If we wanted to do it, then we would have to do it now.' As Münch's battalion moved out, the men heard the trademark howl of the Stukas' sirens. Friedrich Roske watched violet smoke rise above the ruins beyond the railway tracks as Stukas supported the drive to the Volga: *German troops are here.* 'Our men got cold feet in the face of our Stukas more than they did in the face of the enemy,' Roske recalled – with good reason, for the bombs not only kept Russian troops pinned down in their foxholes, but also landed on the German spearhead, decimating one of Münch's companies – reducing it to just four men. 'For normal troops, this would have been the breaking point, a reason to panic,' wrote Roske. And the air raid had also demoralised the defenders, who far outnumbered their attackers but now lay down their arms. It gave Gerhard Münch's assault the renewed impetus it needed. His men rallied, swept over the still-stunned enemy and made a beeline for the river, largely ignoring the imposing buildings lining the streets running down to the Volga – and any 'garrison' lurking within until Münch was able to send a terse radio message back to Friedrich Roske, who picked up the telephone to 71st Infantry Division's headquarters.[28] 'At 3.15pm 194th Grenadier Regiment reached the Volga,' Roske reported proudly to operations officer Hugo Günther von Below. 'W-what, pardon?' von Below stuttered. 'Please, *Herr Oberstleutnant*, say again!' Roske repeated his report and hung up the receiver.[29]

The news was the trigger for a widespread conviction that Stalingrad was on the verge of falling. Sensing victory, Friedrich Paulus appeared at Roske's makeshift command post, established in a chapel on a hill near the central station, hoping to sample some water from the Volga. They expected Gerhard Münch's comrade Gerhard Hindenlang to deliver, but when the young captain finally appeared at the makeshift headquarters he had neither water nor even any Volga frogs to offer Sixth Army's commander. 'We cannot go down in daylight,' Hindenlang reported breathlessly. 'As soon as we raise our noses above the high banks, bullets whizz around our ears.' Paulus and his staff, Hindenlang remembered, seemed 'quite disappointed'.[30] Otherwise, Sixth Army's leaders were delighted with the battle's progress. 'Now all the propaganda folk are dashing to prepare their special reports,' Walther von Seydlitz wrote to his wife. The commander of 71st Infantry's parent LI Corps, Seydlitz concurred with the journalists. 'I reckon it will be September 21st or 22nd,' he continued. 'It's taken us days to get this far and there's one more difficult piece of work to be done. But the main thing is that we've done it.'[31]

The very night Friedrich Roske's troops reached the Volga, the Red Army unit which would prove to be their foil crossed the river. 'Crossing wasn't the right word for it,' the commander of 13th Guards Rifle Division, Aleksandr Rodimtsev, remembered. 'More accurately, it was forcing the great river under the hurricane of enemy fire,' he remembered. Covered with burning oil, the Volga was a 'ribbon of fire', while its waters 'boiled' from the German shells and mortar rounds constantly crashing down. The impact thew up columns of water which obscured the boats momentarily. As the craft neared the west bank, tracer fire raced over the river's surface, 'drawn to the first boat as if drawn to a magnet', Rodimtsev observed. The flares, tracer and burning oil turned night to day – 'the ominous, hellish light of war, destruction, death'. One launch carrying a company of machine-gunners took a direct hit to the bow. A tug was quickly on the scene, but there were too many men floundering in the water, the weight of equipment, weapons, ammunition, dragging them under. The screams for help drifted across the Volga, then faded. On the east bank, Aleksandr Rodimtsev watched – as did hundreds of others – 'and nobody could do anything to help'. Unable to see, the divisional commander could only assume what was happening from the sounds of battle carried across the Volga. There was the crack of rifle fire, bursts from machine-guns, individual bangs as grenades exploded. Tongues of fire licked at the far shore, suggesting Russian mortars were now in action. And then the sporadic but distinctive clang of a tank – or anti-tank – gun followed shortly afterwards by the 'crash-boom' of Rodimtsev's guns, hauled by hand up the sandy west bank. His division had joined battle in Stalingrad 'literally through fire and water'.[32]

By first light on the 15th, five battalions of Guards were on the west bank of the Volga, committed immediately in the central district: three square miles of streets, factories, shops, government buildings and apartment blocks sandwiched between the main railway line in the west and the river to the east. The central station was seen as the lynchpin of the defence not just of the centre, but the city as a whole – second only to Mamayev Kurgan.[33] 194th Infantry Regiment's push to the Volga shore had left its men strung out and in a precarious position until reinforcements arrived. Whatever garrison it possessed, it was driven out by a forceful – and well-executed – attack by a company of Guards under Anton Dragan ('first a grenade, then a soldier went in. The Fascists shot blindly in every direction and fled'). Dragan then held off several attacks before a 'barely noticeable' dawn brought a Luftwaffe and artillery barrage. The station burned, walls collapsed, rails buckled, but Dragan's company held on. Indeed it withstood every attempt to dislodge it until the small hours of 17 September when, threatened with encirclement, it forced its way into an imposing three-storey building on the corner of the large square in front of the station. With remarkable prescience, Dragan's men dubbed it the 'nail factory' – for that is what it was – after scouts discovered a large supply inside. It would be the scene of several days of the most visceral fighting – soldiers on both sides frequently reverted to using knives, spades and rifle butts as small groups fought for the right to occupy individual buildings, workshops or halls. A second company of Guards riflemen, led by Vasily Koleganov, bolstered Dragan's thinning ranks – though it had been reduced to barely 20 men by the time it fought its way through. 'Arrived in the nail factory,' Koleganov reported. 'The situation is bleak, but as long as I am alive, the scum won't get through.' He was gravely wounded the next day by a grenade tossed through a factory window. The small 'garrison' clung on for two more days, in hellish conditions. The Germans tried to outflank the defenders, slipping through attics, ruins and sewerage pipes to reach beyond the nail factory. By late morning on 21 September, Anton Dragan could withstand the enemy pressure – now supported by panzers – no longer and withdrew, but Koleganov resolved to stay, penning a note for his battalion commander which was more a valedictory than combat report:

> The enemy is trying to encircle my company, deploying machine-gunners in its rear, but all his attempts have been unsuccessful. Despite the enemy's superior forces, our officers and men show courage and heroism over the Fascist jackals.
>
> As long as they don't pass over my corpse, the Krauts won't succeed. Guardsmen do not retreat, let officers and men die the death of the brave, but the enemy must not overrun our defences.
>
> Let the whole country recognise 3rd Guards Company, 13th Guards Division. As long as the company commander is alive, no bastard will pass. They may only pass when the company commander is killed or severely wounded. The commander of 3rd Company is under pressure and is physically unwell, weak and his hearing impeded. He suffers bouts of dizziness, falls over, suffers nose bleeds. Despite all these difficulties, the Guards – 3rd and 2nd Companies – will not retreat, we will die as heroes for the city of Stalingrad, may the Soviet soil be our grave.
>
> The commander of 3rd Company, Koleganov, personally killed two Fritz machine-gunners and captured the machine-gun and documents…
>
> I rely on my soldiers and commanders. So far not a single Fascist has passed over my corpse. Guardsmen have no regrets; until complete victory we will be heroes of the liberation of Stalingrad.

In fact, Vasily Koleganov would survive and the nail factory *did* fall into German hands, but the rest of his regiment and its parent division doggedly continued to stand firm in the streets leading away from the railway station and the buildings of the central district.[34]

Two miles away, a beleaguered garrison of exhausted Red Army troops was contemplating abandoning another hotly contested structure. Rising more than 100 feet, nearly 300 feet long and 65 feet wide, the grain elevator on the edge of the city centre dominated Stalingrad's southern skyline. It would become one of the iconic sites of the battle – and another signal to the invader that he would have to conquer Stalingrad one building at a time. Briefly occupied by the Germans on the 15th – they were driven out the following day – the monolithic structure held out for a week, even though its 'garrison' never numbered more than 100 Soviet soldiers (the attackers were convinced the figure was fourfold). Conditions inside the elevator were infernal. Communications had been knocked out on the first day and the entire building was encircled, making re-supply of food, water and ammunition impossible. The defenders lived on the wheat in the silos – it was their only sustenance, although quite often it had been set on fire by the fighting, or else rendered inedible by the decomposing corpses tossed in. 'The grain burned, the water cooling the machine-guns evaporated, casualties begged for water, but there wasn't any anywhere – just heat and smoke,' Andrei Khosyainov, commanding a platoon of naval machine-gunners, remembered. 'Our lips cracked from the thirst.'

The protracted fighting for the grain elevator troubled German soldiers – both those in the front line and staff officers at headquarters. Repeated assaults left the men of 29th Infantry Division 'physically and mentally *kaput* and no longer capable of attack', its command reported with alarm. 'Our old soldiers have never experienced such bitter fighting before,' exasperated non-commissioned officer Wilhelm Hoffman recorded in his diary. His superiors in the 94th Infantry Division were similarly concerned. They had entered Stalingrad convinced it would fall 'in a few days'. 'Now the battle has been raging for almost 14 days for every square metre,' wrote Dr Franz Muth, in charge of the division's communications. Every cellar, every water tower, every high-rise building had been fortified somehow, to the attackers' horror. 'The whole of Stalingrad is a smoking, stinking pile of rubble, which serves – as only rubble can – as the embodiment of the inferno', yet its defenders 'would rather surrender their lives than these mountains of rubble'. The fighting on the Volga was costing Germany the finest of her youth, Muth feared. 'We have to be very hard on ourselves, on the troops, to achieve what is often really beyond our strength.'

The battle for the elevator reached its climax on 21 September. It began at dawn with a concerted effort by the Germans to persuade the defenders to surrender. First a panzer drove up under a white flag, demanding the Soviets evacuate the complex, 'otherwise no mercy will be shown. In an hour we'll bomb and crush you.' The response was to tell the besiegers to 'go to Hell'. A second attempt using captured Soviet soldiers fared no better. Senior Lieutenant Mikhail Polyakov, leading the defence, ordered the parliamentarians to drop their white flags, take up arms and join the defenders. They refused. Polyakov ordered them shot. There followed a concerted bombardment from panzers and the Luftwaffe.

'One shell carried away a Maxim with its gunner, while in another part of the elevator shrapnel ripped the cooling jacket off another Maxim and bent the barrel, leaving us with just a light machine-gun,' Khosyainov recalled. 'The concrete shattered as the shells exploded. We could barely see as a result of the dense smoke produced by the burning grain.' The Germans were now in the elevator – so close that Khosyainov and his comrades could hear them not merely moving, but even breathing at times. 'Still we could not see him in the thick smoke.' Nevertheless, the defenders fended off more than half a dozen assaults before the Germans called off their attack.

The defenders took stock – no more than 25 rounds left for their sub machine-guns, barely ten rounds for their rifles – and decided upon a breakout, while the Germans decided upon simply razing the enormous structure. That was until a feint attack at dusk on the 21st caught the Soviets off guard. One soldier scrambled up the fire escape to raise the swastika flag on the roof while his comrades, like Ernst-Ludwig Hofmann, rounded up the last defenders. 'Totally famished and exhausted figures, half dying of thirst, came towards us with faltering steps and raised hands,' he recalled. 'It is barely imaginable what inferno these men had survived.' Nevertheless, around 20 Soviet troops succeeded in slipping out of the building in two groups, through the German ring of encirclement, making their way to the Volga a good half a mile away and then, in some cases, swimming across it to reach their comrades.

As 84 Soviet troops were led into captivity, 94th Infantry Division's operations officer Martin Boriss telephoned the command post of 274th Infantry Regiment. If its men failed to take the elevator, Boriss haughtily explained, another division would eagerly take on the challenge. '*Herr Oberstleutnant*, that's not necessary,' the regiment's adjutant interrupted. 'For the past five minutes, our flag has been flying from the elevator.'[35]

The fighting for the grain elevator, central station, nail factory and countless other buildings tore huge gaps in the ranks of attacker and defender alike. Non-commissioned officer Edmund Schaden lost two close friends in 21st Panzer Grenadier Regiment in quick succession. 'This is a harsh reality,' he told his wife Else at home in Duisburg. 'New military cemeteries are being built here every day. Between 30 and 100 comrades are buried here, far, far away from home, and no wife or mother can visit their graves. Many of my comrades are buried here.' Some of the companies in radio operator Paul-Hans Voss's regiment numbered just 26 men. His comrades consoled themselves by convincing each other that the enemy was 'bled white' and had run out of infantry. In the most recent fighting, they had grappled with artillerymen in the front line. But the attacker was also being bled white. 71st Infantry Division was understrength when it began its attempt to reach the Volga on 14 September. After 12 days in the line, its eight infantry battalions had been reduced to seven, and three of those were unfit for offensive action. Casualties numbered more than 1,300 dead and wounded. Rodimtsev's division lost four times as many men in the same fighting – and it fared better than many Red Army units in Stalingrad in September 1942. Colonel Mikhail Pesochin complained that the line held by his 131st Rifle Division – down to just 100 infantrymen and almost out of ammunition – was no better than a 'sieve – the enemy seeps through at will'. The position of 36th Guards Division was equally parlous, having suffered 70 per cent losses – 90 per cent in officers and political workers. Stalingrad, recalled former *frontovik* Vladimir Kharchenkov, 'wasn't war, it was a meat grinder'.[36]

When Hubert Menzel, the General Staff liaison officer at Paulus' headquarters, headed up the line to spend a day at the front with 71st and 295th Infantry Divisions, he was impressed – and perturbed – by what he found. Both units were 'very good fighting divisions' but they were bleeding out by the day. Infantry companies had been worn down to no more than 15 men, almost all of whom were 'overtired and jaded', weakened by poor diet, lack of sleep and the incessant fighting for the city. Rear units had been combed out, but produced little more than cannon fodder for the front line, while replacements from the Reich lacked the experience, training and mental agility to deal with the demands of Stalingrad. As soon as a company commander or platoon leader was killed or wounded, attacks invariably ground to a halt. As for Sixth Army's foe, Stalingrad's defenders were alert, dogged and resolute. Man for man the *frontovik* was 'no match' for the *Landser*. But then he didn't need to be, for there was a constant injection of fresh blood into the front line through reinforcements crossing the Volga. Unless new German divisions were committed, the imbalance would only grow worse.[37]

The ordinary *Landser* – or *frontovik* for that matter – may well have challenged Menzel's assessment of the Red Army. After the initial shock of the German lunge to the Volga and the ferocious bombardment of the city, the defenders had 'composed themselves,' soldier Hubert Hüsken wrote. More than once in a letter to a friend – never delivered, for it was found on his corpse – Hüsken used the word 'panic' to describe German troops, admitted 26 men had been punished for fleeing from the enemy and conceded that the nerves of even the most resolute soldier were sorely frayed. 'I've never been in a situation like this,' he admitted. 'Every day we wait for our relief.' It never came. The Soviet soldier, staff officer Winrich Behr observed, 'fought for Russia with national élan and truly defended himself to the last moment, allowing himself to be beaten to death in his positions. Our troops in Stalingrad were ill-prepared from the outset to be able to sustain such a battle on their own.' The stubbornness of the Soviet defenders shocked veteran soldiers like Wilhelm Hoffman. His battalion – reduced to the size of a regular company by the time the grain elevator fell – could not dislodge them. They preferred to die rather than be captured; the only prisoners now brought in were those unable to move. Hoffman referred to his foe as 'wild beasts', 'barbarians', 'fanatics', their actions insane or barbaric, their tactics 'gangster methods' – his comrades were picked off in buildings long since seized by German troops. 'In Stalingrad,' he noted, 'anyone can die at any moment.'[38]

And yet for now the impetus still lay with the Germans. No matter how heroically – or stubbornly – the Red Army soldier fought in the rubble of the city, the enemy advanced irrepressibly. Rodimtsev's Guards were subjected to a 14-hour onslaught on 22 September as 71st Infantry Division sought to tighten their grip on the centre of Stalingrad. 'It truly was hell,' Rodimtsev recalled.

> I had been in more than one battle, but this was the first time I had ever been in such a fight...
>
> The roar of battle did not cease. The grinding of metal, the whistling of shells, the howl of bullets, the explosion of grenades, the deafening explosion of mortars – all this merged into some kind of eerie symphony. The consumption of ammunition was so great that by the afternoon the regiment had neither mortars nor cartridges for anti-tank rifles, and grenades were running out.

According to Soviet accounts, one regiment was attacked 15 times, another at least half a dozen, leaving behind hecatombs of German dead. Whether true or not – the daily casualty report is missing from Sixth Army's papers and the 71st's divisional history is strangely silent on the fighting, though it did report to Paulus that resistance was 'much tougher than in other parts of the city' – the 13th Guards were 'melting away'. The Germans bludgeoned their way to the Volga for a second time, this time seizing the main ferry landing and most of one of Stalingrad's showpiece plazas, January 9th Square.[39] Still, Rodimtsev's men clung to every house, every factory. Defenders of cellars were flushed out – or wiped out – by jets from flamethrowers or explosive charges. One by one, the Germans seized the buildings in the centre of Stalingrad: tenement blocks, the water works, the flour mill. The defenders of the theatre – from where Lev Yushchenko had observed the early stages of the devastating air raid on 23 August – proved to be a particular thorn in the Germans' side. Soviet troops poured fire down on their attackers from the circle and upper stalls, while those holed up in the basement were smoked out – literally – by using burning seats from the main auditorium. Two blocks away, battalion commander Karl-Heinz Fricke determined Red Square sufficiently secure for a propaganda set piece with the burned-out façade of the Univermag department store serving as the backdrop. At mid-day on 26 September, Sixth Army could report that the swastika was flying above the centre of Stalingrad.[40]

Symbolically, raising the Nazi standard suggested victory, but newspaper editors in the Reich were told to resist announcing the fall of Stalin's city – although it was still a certainty, merely 'a question of time'. For nearly three weeks, the German people had been bombarded with one frenzied headline after another. From the Nazi's daily mouthpiece, *Völkischer Beobachter*: 'Hurricane of fire and iron descends on Stalingrad' (7 September); 'Stalingrad in the pincers' (12th); 'The battle for Stalingrad reaches its climax' (17th); the next day, 'Fighting in the heart of Stalingrad'. And on the 19th: 'Fight to the last ruins'. Provincial newspapers – further from the direct influence of the Propaganda Ministry – were the worst offenders. Readers of Bavaria's *Rosenheimer Anzeiger* on 18 September learned of 'Stalingrad's final hours', while anyone in Düben, between Leipzig and Berlin, who picked up the village newspaper that same Friday read a lead article entitled, 'On the fall of Stalingrad'. Even in larger towns, such as Augsburg, editors could be prone to hyperbole. 'The city of Stalin and the large Soviet armies encircled there with vast quantities of equipment' were doomed, according to the *Augsburger National Zeitung*. 'The last act of one of the greatest epics in German history has begun.' Newspaper editors were ordered to prepare for Stalingrad's fall – and mark its capture appropriately by publishing special editions. After the capture of the central station, German radio suggested that trains might soon be running between Berlin and the Volga. It all reassured the German people that Stalingrad would not become a 'Soviet Verdun' or turn into a 'permanent siege' with heavy losses; rather that the city would fall 'at any moment'. But they were also growing impatient.[41]

So too was Joseph Goebbels. 'There's no-one who seriously believes any longer that Stalingrad won't soon be in our hands,' Goebbels noted. He had dispatched one of his senior propagandists, Hans Fritzsche, to record Stalingrad's capture and the hoisting of the swastika. Fritzsche – 'a disagreeable man,' staff officer Alexander Fürst zu Dohna-Schlobitten noted – kicked his heels at Paulus' headquarters for eight days before being recalled to Berlin – long before Karl-Heinz Fricke's *coup de théâtre* at the Univermag store.[42]

Goebbels could sustain the propaganda campaign no more than Germany's soldiers could maintain their attack. His mood swung violently in September 1942. One day he was convinced of Stalingrad's immediate fall, the next he feared the campaign in Russia was stalling, the media painting the situation in

342

the East 'in much too rosy a light'. Hans Fritzsche convinced him that the battle was 'almost decided', that the capture of Stalingrad was 'only a question of days'. Mindful of the mistakes his ministry had made the previous autumn, when headlines had declared the Red Army beaten and the war in the East all but won, the propaganda minister erred on the side of caution. 'The people are on tenterhooks – and we won't be able to sustain that for a long time,' he decided. He reined in his propaganda machine. Newspaper editors were ordered to find stories about subjects *other than* Stalingrad to fill their front pages. Goebbels' intervention came too late. Having 'eagerly anticipated the fall of Stalingrad for days,' the German people now felt cheated. 'The fall of Stalingrad was presented as a foregone conclusion', yet 'despite all the headlines' it had still not been captured – and if it were to fall into German hands it would no longer provoke widespread joy and celebrations, merely relief.[43]

Joseph Goebbels was slowly beginning to grasp that Stalingrad would become the iconic battle of the titanic struggle between Nazism and Bolshevism. 'Stalingrad or life!' was Moscow's rallying cry. The city would be defended to the last man and it would take a superhuman effort from the German soldier to prevail. 'Maybe the homeland expects more from them than is possible. In fact – and on this point public opinion in the Reich is right – we're dealing here with something which will decide the war. No sacrifice here is too great to reach our objective.'[44]

The swastika had been battered by the elements atop Europe's highest peak for more than a month by the time it was hoisted in central Stalingrad. But since the propaganda stunt on the summit of Mount Elbrus, little progress had been made in any direction by Wilhelm List's army group as it fanned out across the Caucasus, seeking goals more than 400 miles apart. Only in the very west had List's troops scored any notable successes. They had crossed the Kerch Strait in force and seized the Taman peninsula, before pushing down on the Black Sea coast from the west and north. Romanian forces seized the ruins of the first major port, Anapa, planting the blue-yellow-red of their national flag in the hands of a statue of Marshal Voroshilov, staring out over the waters. Anapa residents – according to contemporary propaganda accounts – greeted their new masters 'joyfully', repeatedly telling them: 'Communist not good...'[45]

Three dozen miles along the coast lay Novorossiysk – since the loss of Sevastopol, the Soviet Union's most important Black Sea port and naval base. The Germans struck from the north, advancing over the western foothills of the Caucasus. At dusk on 29 August, the men of 419th Infantry Regiment spied the waters of the Black Sea glinting in the evening sun. With a nod to ancient history – echoing the words of Greek soldiers after a 600-mile march from the Euphrates around 401 BC – their commander Helmut Friebe radioed two words to his superiors: *Thalatta, Thalatta!* – The sea, sea! A couple of days later, the regiment sighted Novorossiysk itself after seizing one of the hills which ringed the port like a horseshoe. 'It is fantastic!' one *Landser* wrote. 'I've never been there, of course, but Naples must be like this!'[46]

It took several more days for German guns to move into positions on the ridges. Battery commander Rudolf Witzel ordered his guns to target the southern mole when he noticed a large group of troops moving along the harbour wall and boarding a ship. Witzel immediately shifted his aim. 'We were lucky with a direct hit on the ship, followed by a tremendous explosion and mushroom cloud; the tub flew up in the air!' he recalled. 'There was a great howl of joy.' The disaster did not prevent another steamer entering harbour, quickly embarking a large group of people, then departing. Witzel tried to bring his guns to bear again, but to no avail. The vessel escaped. Among its passengers, the future Soviet leader Leonid Brezhnev.[47]

Red Army commanders had been slow to recognise the growing danger to Novorossiysk. The city was weakly held – no more than 15,000 defenders – and its fortifications mostly incomplete. Nevertheless, the men of 125th Infantry Division reported that Novorossiysk had been 'turned into a fortress like Rostov' as they moved into the suburbs on 7 September, with every street barricaded or mined, bunkers at key junctions, trenches dug in gardens and parks, buildings fortified. Stukas and heavy mortars reduced entire rows of houses to rubble, shook the ground like an earthquake and left 'a wall of smoke, a hazy, dirty curtain' in front of the city. Pioneers with flame throwers and assault guns reduced each strongpoint, every bunker or block.[48]

After four days, Soviet resistance collapsed. Expecting another day of fierce combat, patrols sent out at first light on 10 September found the Russians had evacuated the bulk of their forces overnight, leaving only weak rearguards behind. By 8am, the city was in German hands; by 10, artillery officer Heinrich Lipfert had raised the *Reichskriegsflagge* at the tip of the southwest mole. The rest of the day was spent mopping up, accounting for prisoners, who ran into hundreds rather than thousands, and securing booty, including more than 30,000 litres of fuel abandoned in a dump and hundreds of tonnes of refrigerated food seized in the port: jam, barrels of butter, chickens, sausages, ham and bacon.

Yet as with Stalingrad, merely raising the Nazi standard did not mean Novorossiysk was in German hands. 213th Infantry Regiment spent another six weeks clearing up the city's industrial quarter – 'a battle which had to be fought metre by metre, house by house against an enemy who, in his stubbornness, literally preferred to be beaten to death before giving up,' the unit's chronicler

The Caucasus campaign, August–November

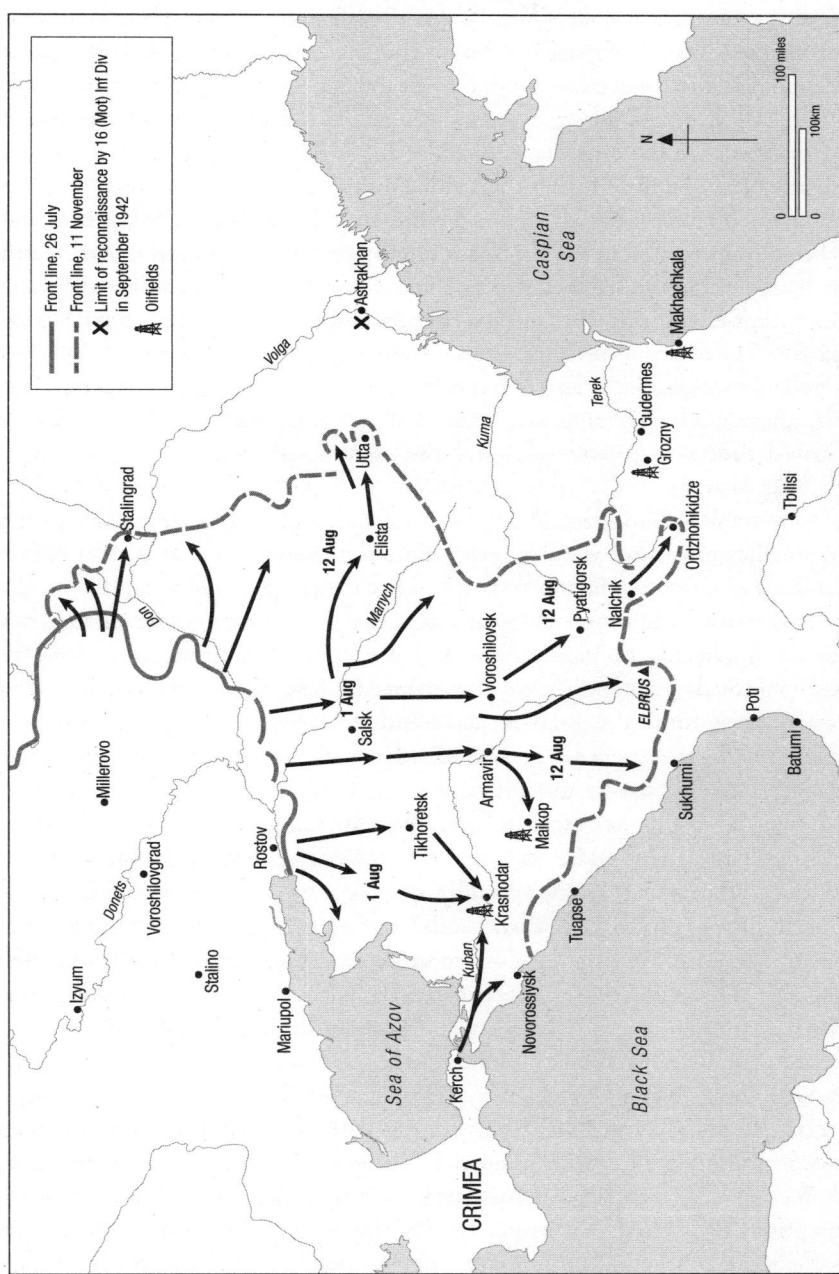

Anton Gruber wrote. 'In many cases we had to resort to the last possible means of setting fire to the houses and burning them down to be able to get at the enemy, who was still entrenched under collapsed walls and collapsed trenches.' Veterans of Sevastopol drew parallels with the fighting for the port back in June and July – although when it was finally pulled out of the line at the end of October with Novorossiysk largely secure, the 213th's losses in the Caucasus had actually been one third higher than in the Crimea.[49]

125th Infantry Division suffered similarly high casualties. In seven weeks' fighting from Rostov to the Black Sea it had been reduced to just 1,700 men fit for battle. Wilhelm Schneckenburger complained his unit had 'not enjoyed a single day's rest all this time and has been in battle every day. The fighting is not yet over. The physical exertions, in the mountains especially, were incredible.' He hoped his men would be hauled out of the line and allowed to regroup, pleading: 'The division urgently requires a lengthy rest before fresh action.' The next day he received orders to prepare to move out to support the advance on Tuapse, 75 miles away.[50]

No German soldier would ever set foot in Tuapse, yet the failure to capture the small, relatively insignificant port would provoke the greatest crisis at Hitler's headquarters since the failure before Moscow the previous December.

For many *Landsers* marching through the Caucasus, the lure of the coast proved as enticing as the Volga had appeared to their comrades driving on Stalingrad. 'The final destination – the Black Sea – seemed within reach,' said an excited Adolf Klinger as his 13th *Gebirgsjäger* Regiment advanced up the Bysb valley towards the spa resort of Sukhumi. After the monotony of the steppe, the advance initially brought reminders of home for *Gebirgs* troops: the cool, fresh mountain air, the pine trees, large herds of cattle grazing in alpine pastures, jagged peaks piercing the clouds, towering over the raging waters of the mountain streams. 'What a relief to the eyes after the glistening of the endless fields of the Russian steppe,' artilleryman Franz Müller wrote. 'Every minute offers something new to the eyes.' And the ears – 'almost every valley with a different race and language,' Müller observed. The populace were hardy mountain dwellers, Muslims, who had never embraced Bolshevism and whose customs and traditions prevailed. Heading up the Teberda valley, Müller and his comrades could sense the Black Sea was now close – barely 40 miles away. 'There in a few weeks we will probably bring the curtain down on an entire theatre of war after we've brought Ukraine and the Caucasus under the banner of the Reich,' the gunner noted with satisfaction.[51]

Yet not even experienced troops like Franz Müller were prepared for the conditions they faced the further they pushed into the mountains. The maps were poor: heights and contours were incorrect; roads were at best paths, at worst tracks. The undergrowth in the woods was jungle-like. Valleys were virtually impassable with the slightest rainfall as mountain streams and rivers flooded, sweeping away bridges and turning dirt tracks into a morass which devoured soldiers' boots and prevented anything on wheels making headway. The few passes allowed for no flanking movements or clever tactics. The terrain almost entirely dictated the direction and manner of an attack. The men simply had to batter their way through.

Supply lines became increasingly difficult to sustain, with railheads as far as 70 miles behind the front. From there single-lane roads, tracks and finally paths, climbing thousands of feet, passing through a series of temporary supply dumps, eventually led to the front line. Trucks could only cover the first leg of the journey. Thereafter, the burden of moving 30 tonnes of supplies required by a typical *Gebirgs* regiment *every day* fell upon oxen-drawn carts and motorcycles, then 2,000 pack animals and finally nearly 1,000 porters, mostly Russian prisoners. Thirty pack animals died each day in mountain formations, while losses in regular army units – reliant on horses thoroughly unsuitable for the task – were even higher. The ranks of the porters were similarly decimated by falls, frostbite – above 7,200 feet there was snow to contend with from the beginning of September – and general exhaustion; if they weren't drenched by the rain, then they were soaked in sweat. As for the men at the vanguard of the German advance, their uniforms were no match for the rugged terrain and undergrowth: the rocks, scrub and bushes tore boots and jackets apart. Meals – cooked in the safety of the rear – were invariably delivered cold to the front line. Not that they possessed much nutritional value, for the makeshift dumps could not protect food stores from the elements: bread, dried vegetables, potatoes and the like went soft thanks to the persistent rain, while fats, sugar and salt simply turned to liquid. Any fighting was reduced to confused skirmishes involving small groups of men. Cries of 'Urra!' and 'Hände hoch!' reverberated around the rockfaces as Red Army troops repeatedly tried to re-take lost passes – and were usually repulsed. 'Anyone who was wounded at the front in the passes or in the woods in the mountains had to go through hell,' one mountain infantryman remembered. It took between two and four days to transfer the wounded – up to 16 porters or stretcher bearers were required for *each* serious casualty – from the front to the second base camp from where they could at least be flown back to the field hospital at the railhead, weather permitting. The lightly wounded and sick – including anyone who could still walk – had to make their own way back, trekking for days until they reached hospital.

The burden was just as heavy on the Luftwaffe. Günther Rall's squadron moved seven times in a month to ensure the relatively short-ranged Messerschmitts could keep pace with the advance. It had begun August 75 miles east of Rostov. It ended the month just 50 miles from Grozny. With each move, 700 men and all their equipment jostled for space on the inadequate Caucasus road network with army units and their ever-lengthening supply lines. Pilots simply packed the most necessary possessions into a sack or briefcase and flew on, but with little chance to wash either themselves or their clothes, aces such as Rall soon began to resemble 'lice-ridden tramps rather than the idea they have at home of the radiant heroes of the Luftwaffe'. With more than 60 kills to his name – all but one on the Eastern Front – 24-year-old Rall was one of the German Air Force's rising stars, the latest recipient of the Knight's Cross. But having flown almost continually since the invasion of France in the spring of 1940, Rall was exhausted – and the strain would only grow worse now the bulk of the Luftwaffe was committed over Stalingrad.

> The longer we wage war, the more war leads us. We are no longer the men we were in our youth – a period in our lives which already seems an eternity away, even though it's only three or four years ago. The war has turned us into virtuosi of authorised murder. It has dominated our days and nights, our thoughts and behaviour, our conversations, our emotions, for three years now. It has become the father of all things – but a father who destroys everything he touches – including souls. The harder the fighting becomes, the more nonchalantly everyone talks about our foes and battles – a trick to hide the constant strain from others and ourselves. Our horizon hardly extends beyond the current day; we want to – and also can do nothing other than – focus all our strength on surviving between sunrise and sunset. There are no diversions: no cafés and restaurants, no cinemas, no music, no brief amusements as in France, not even a bed with fresh sheets in a proper building. Thousands of kilometres east of our homeland we have only our tents, the ubiquitous dirt and a self-contained world, eagerly trying to extract everything that our will to live needs from this wretched existence.[52]

German forces in the Caucasus gradually melted away. Fernand Kaisergruber's battalion of Belgian volunteers, heading for Tuapse, began the march into the Caucasus more than 800 strong. By the end of August, the combination of marching, exhaustion, combat and disease had whittled it down to no more than 300 men. Troops from 198th Infantry Division, making for the same objective, were encircled on a hill by the Soviets just 16 miles from Tuapse before breaking out and falling back. 'One hill more or less, what's the point!' one of the retreating infantrymen sighed. 'But one battalion more or less, that can decide a battle.'[53]

As the plight of the 198th Infantry showed, the faltering German advance wasn't due solely to the constant attrition of the advance. The defence of the

Caucasus had been given ruthless impetus with the arrival of Stalin's most loyal henchman, Lavrentiy Beria. After just one day, he decided the troops needed new leadership: the Red Army had the men to block the German advance but frittered them away, defending the wrong passes. Officers were inexperienced, communications inadequate; staff not up to the job, especially Semyon Budyonny, another of Stalin's cronies, were instantly dismissed. Beria sacked Forty-Sixth Army's commander Vasily Sergatskov – some accounts suggest he even hit the general, who in Beria had expected 'a great statesmen of the Soviet state, a great, experienced organiser' but instead encountered 'an hysterical despot – and not very intelligent to boot'.

In fact, the Communist leader barely had a good word for any senior officer in the Caucasus, branding them 'unimaginative', 'disorganised', 'clear liars'. Even Budyonny's successor, Ivan Tyulenev, failed to impress, but did at least 'give his all to his work'. Above all, Beria brought an iron rod to the defence of the Caucasus, declaring martial law, ordering NKVD troops to stop men deserting the front and putting cities on a war footing, even preparing the oilfields of Baku – a good 300 miles behind the front – for destruction.[54]

Baku was as beyond the grasp of the German soldier in the late summer of 1942 as Grozny, Sukhumi and Tuapse. 'We do not have the forces for two such large offensives as is the case here in the Caucasus and at Stalingrad,' Willi Kubik, a lowly tank gunner, conceded in his diary. 'We have just taken on too much.' Wilhelm List had the temerity to report as much to Hitler's headquarters and was ordered to Vinnitsa to explain himself. The mood at headquarters had been growing increasingly taut, the twice-daily briefings for the Führer fraught with tension and frequent outbursts – Chief of the General Staff Franz Halder was subjected to tirades 'so brutal, so filled with hate, that he simply could not respond'. List's reception was surprisingly warm. Though Hitler criticised the field marshal for squandering opportunities by dispersing his troops across the Caucasus and repeated his unrealistic orders to push across the mountains, smash the Red Army on the Terek *and* resume the drive on Grozny, army adjutant Gerhard Engel was convinced the discussion had cleared the air.[55]

If it had, it was only for a few days. One week later, still dissatisfied with progress in the Caucasus, the Führer dispatched his trusted head of operations Alfred Jodl to List's headquarters in Stalino – today Donetsk – to ensure his orders to push to Tuapse in particular were carried out to the letter.

Not only did Jodl fail to carry out his leader's instructions, he returned to Vinnitsa on 7 September convinced they would lead to disaster. The mountain troops did not have the strength to reach the coast, and even if they did, with the first snow already falling in the high passes, there was no hope of supporting them. As for plans to take the city using paratroopers, that would merely end in their annihilation. Tuapse – in 1942, at least – was a pipe dream. The troops should fall back to the mountain passes and winter there before resuming the offensive to the Black Sea the coming spring.

Jodl's report prompted a 'terrible outburst of rage' from Hitler. 'I didn't send you, Jodl, to have you report nothing but misgivings,' he yelled.

'If you want to lose your paratroopers, then send them to Tuapse anyway, *mein Führer*,' the general snapped back. 'If you want someone merely to deliver orders, send someone else.' At which Jodl claimed he left the conference room, slamming the door behind him.[56]

The break was irreparable. The Führer sulked for days. A fortnight after the clash with Jodl, the mood at Vinnitsa remained 'explosive', the morale of staff officers 'depressed', one observer noted. Hitler retreated to his windowless hut, ate alone, and refused to shake hands with his generals when they arrived for the mid-day and evening conferences, which were played out 'in an icy atmosphere' with every word recorded by a former Reichstag stenographer. 'Despite the many people around me in my headquarters, I am so lonely here in Ukraine,' he admitted to Mussolini a few weeks later. Goebbels found his master withdrawn and isolated when he visited Vinnitsa in mid-September – and naturally took his Führer's side. 'It's enough to drive you mad how little the Army's leadership agree with the Führer's intentions and are obedient instruments of his conduct of the war.' When the Wehrmacht's slavish Chief-of-Staff Wilhelm Keitel attempted to smooth things over, his 85-minute 'discussion' largely turned into one long diatribe by Hitler against Germany's generals. 'I have to have total, 100 per cent loyalty from the people who work with me,' he told Keitel. 'I need to know that the people on my staff will fight tooth and nail for my point of view… When I send one of my people somewhere, he has no right to adopt the view of the other person; he's been sent there to state my view.'

Hitler's paranoia was boundless. 'He trusts none of his generals at present and he would promote a major to general and appoint him as Chief of the General Staff, if he only knew one,' Gerhard Engel noted. 'At present everyone is against him. Sometimes he curses himself for daring to go to war with such generals.' But Engel also – correctly – realised that the cause of the rupture and Hitler's subsequent breakdown was much deeper than a mere disagreement over the progress of a few thousand troops in the Caucasus. As with his outburst over the scaling of Elbrus a fortnight earlier, the true source of Hitler's anger was failure. 'The Führer can no longer see an end in Russia – none of the objectives for the summer of 1942 have been attained,' his army adjutant observed. 'He described his tremendous fear with winter looming, yet he doesn't want to retreat anywhere.'

Still, he seized the opportunity for a changing of guard. While he assured Keitel his position was safe, Alfred Jodl would have to go, replaced by Friedrich Paulus, who had 'proved his mettle' at Kharkov and already shown 'nerves of steel' in the fighting on the Volga. 'Paulus has earned the right to have his name linked with the fall of Stalingrad, no matter what, and it would be an injustice in my eyes to remove him beforehand. He must stay until then.' Wilhelm List had already been dismissed, replaced by the only man the Führer thought capable of leading the offensive in the Caucasus – himself. He wanted rid of at least one other commander in the mountains, Seventeenth Army's commander, Richard Ruoff, and toyed with replacing Ewald von Kleist.[57]

And then there was Franz Halder, the bespectacled Chief of the General Staff, so often on the receiving end of the Führer's scorn and ire. For weeks the 58-year-old had faced Hitler in the daily conferences 'like a beaten schoolboy and filled with fear' until he was finally dismissed – on surprisingly amicable terms – on 24 September. At the end of the conference, Hitler took Halder to one side. The two men had to part company, the Führer told him. The General Staff needed fresh blood, someone who would imbue it with fanatical faith in 'the idea'.[58]

That fresh blood came in the form of Kurt Zeitzler – 'short, rotund, very ambitious, very lively and also rather forceful' and with a Hitler moustache – welcomed to headquarters by a tearful Halder, who took his successor's hand and told him: 'God be with you.' Eleven years his junior, Kurt Zeitzler was not a man in Franz Halder's mould, nor even 'a Chief of the General Staff in the traditional sense of the word' as the outgoing post-holder observed privately. While officers like Halder enjoyed relatively safe positions at headquarters behind the front during the Great War, Zeitzler had demonstrated his bravery leading troops into action, only earning the coveted red stripes of a General Staff officer in the 1920s. He was a favourite of Ewald von Kleist, serving as the panzer commander's chief-of-staff in Poland, France, the Balkans and finally on the Eastern Front. A good number of officers attributed the failure of Kleist's drive through the Caucasus to Zeitzler's absence – he'd been transferred to France in the spring of 1942. Traditional senior officers looked down on Kurt Zeitzler as a man of limited abilities – 'It's a long road from the intellectual brain of Moltke the Older to this Chief of the General Staff,' one commented acidly, while Halder thought him 'extremely high-spirited with a tendency to "boil over"'. But Adolf Hitler was impressed by Zeitzler's 'bustle and energy', convinced the 47-year-old from Brandenburg – nicknamed '*Kugelblitz*', ball of lightning – would attack the task in hand with renewed vigour.[59]

And he did. Zeitzler immediately shook up the General Staff, reorganising, eradicating posts, sending one in every ten officers to front-line units. He also demonstrated his Nazi credentials, demanding officers greet each other with 'Heil Hitler!' He did not want men 'filled with nothing but doubts, who pull a face when something unexpected happens' or 'desk-bound academics', but dogged leaders who shared the hardships at the front with their men. Zeitzler demanded every man 'give his all for the Führer' and 'radiate faith: faith in our Führer, faith in our victory, faith in our work'.[60]

In Stalingrad battle was re-joined with renewed fury the day after the government district had fallen as Sixth Army's attention shifted northwards to the 'industrial quarter'. Just before dawn on 27 September, three German divisions struck. Attached to the light infantry of the 100th *Jäger* Division was the 369th Infantry Regiment – better known as the Croatian Legion. Just three days before their Stalingrad baptism of fire, a select group of legionnaires were presented to their head of state, Ante Pavelić, in Golubinskaya on the Don – 40 miles behind the front. The *poglavnik* (leader) shook the hand of every man, told them that their deeds had carried the name of the young Croatian state around the world and regretted only that he could not visit the front line to meet every legionnaire in person. Also present was Sixth Army's commander Friedrich Paulus who regarded the Croatians as the 'best of all the lesser peoples,' he confided in a friend. 'After them came the Slovaks, then the Romanians and so on and last of all the Italians and Hungarians.'[61]

The Croatians suffered casualties even before they joined battle on the afternoon of 27 September – Stalin organs tore gaps in the Legion's lines as it moved up to the front – and their first attack, over the rutted, gullied, lower eastern slope of Mamayev Kurgan over railway lines towards the factory district almost entirely miscarried. Ivan Čorić complained that his troops came under 'strong and relentless enemy fire after a few steps – and from that moment losses in my battalion began: dead and wounded, one man after another.'[62]

Night offered the Croatians no respite. Under a clear sky, low-flying Soviet aircraft dropped phosphorus bombs on troops exposed on the battlefield. 'The men's uniforms began to burn – as did their bodies,' Čorić reported. 'The scene was awful. Healthy and even wounded men leapt on their comrades who were on fire to save them…' After just one day in the line, Ivan Čorić lost 150 men dead or wounded – half his battalion. Čorić himself was among the casualties; wounded in the head, he was relieved. The regiment was not. The following night it moved into position alongside German troops for an attack on the Barrikady works. The men were filled with 'some inner feeling of horror,' one German company commander remembered as they headed to their jump-off positions 'under almost continuous artillery and mortar fire as well as the incessant hail of bombs from enemy aircraft, when we passed through a ravine 30 to 40 metres deep, littered with the bodies of humans and cadavers of animals, wrecked vehicles, weapons and tools.' Weighed down by their weapons and ammunition, the soldiers stumbled over the bodies of dead Russians or the carcasses of horses until they reached their assault positions to the west of the factory complex. And there they waited until mid-morning on 29 September to launch their attack, pioneers equipped with flamethrowers leading the way. The Croatians had the hardest mission – an assault over open ground covered by a concrete cupola and anti-tank guns. 'As they dashed forward, many volunteers were struck down dead by a bullet fired by a Russian sniper, or were cut down by shrapnel from exploding shells,' the German company commander reported. 'Our medics hauled our wounded Croatian comrades under the heaviest enemy fire.' Still, the Croatians reached the Soviet lines, to the company commander's admiration. 'Hand-grenades exploded and, after bitter hand-to-hand fighting, the enemy began to fall back. The battle was in full swing and many of the enemy fell, their heads smashed by a strong blow from the rifle butt of a brave legionnaire.'[63]

Matthias Barth, a German non-commissioned officer assigned to the staff of the Croatian Legion, was appalled by the nihilism of the battle. 'You cannot imagine what is happening here in Stalingrad,' he wrote to a friend in Vienna. 'Stalingrad can apparently not be taken any other way than by destroying everything.' Barth was convinced he lived a charmed life: one day an artillery strike might land just feet away, killing horses; on another, shells might crash into the ground next to the ruined building which served as his quarters. 'I tell you it is no exaggeration to refer to "the hell of Stalingrad",' he continued, then listed the 'terrible abomination of devastation': the earth churned up by bombs and shells, the soldiers burrowed into it, their foxholes shuddering with every fresh impact, the roads pitted with bomb craters and the tangle of snapped telegraph wires lying on the ground, a city afire by day and plagued by Soviet bombers at night. Every 30 or so minutes Red Air Force biplanes – the soldiers nicknamed them 'sewing machines' for the noise their engines made – appeared over German lines, dropping a handful of bombs. Parachute flares drifted over the city, while Soviet searchlights groped around trying to 'catch' German aircraft in their beams. The noise, day or night, was incessant: exploding bombs, the chatter of machine-gun fire, the crack of rifles, the shells whistling through the air, impacting with a crash which caused the ground to shake constantly. 'We never got any rest, never enjoyed undisturbed sleep,' Josef Steinbauer, an artilleryman with 297th Infantry Division, recalled.[64]

Aircrew were just as exhausted, the strain of four or five sorties a day – often attacking the same target just hours apart – taking its toll. 'Meals during the breaks are brief and hurried, reports are written, the telephone rings, maps and aerial photographs are studied,' one Stuka pilot noted. Not only was it proving increasingly difficult to pinpoint targets, but by mid-September Stalingrad's air defences were assuming formidable proportions. The flak was 'unpleasant and accurate', the fighter defence daunting – up to 50 patrolling the skies over the city at times. It fell to men like Hermann Graf to hold the Soviet fighters at bay. Graf was the 'Marseille of the Eastern Front'. At 29 he was slightly older than the Star of Africa, less outspoken, and had come through more than a few close shaves with the enemy. His kill rate was astonishing. By September 1942 he was downing two Soviet aircraft a day on average. Like Marseille it was taking its toll. On the 16th – for the first time – he'd lost his wingman, Johann Kalb, a Nuremberger with 32 kills to his name. 'That hit me really hard,' Graf wrote. 'With 30 hits to the airframe I just got back to the field.' A cannon shell had narrowly missed taking off his head after striking the canopy of his Messerschmitt. A comrade suggested he remain on the ground 'otherwise I would be a corpse within a few days'. Graf ignored the advice. The next day he added his 177th kill. On the 18th, three more to take his tally to 180. By the end of September, he was physically and mentally exhausted. The Pervitin – *Fliegerschokolade* (flier's chocolate) or methamphetamine – which kept him alert also kept him awake and shattered his nerves. Yet he continued to fly – and kill. On the 25th, he scored his 198th and 199th victories. The next day, his 200th – the first Luftwaffe pilot to reach the milestone – plus two more for good measure. That evening Graf reviewed his group's achievements. In six weeks his 15 pilots had accounted for 264 enemy aircraft – 'well over half the victories over Stalingrad' – for the loss of three men. Each of the remaining dozen pilots was now an ace, while Graf himself had downed 86 enemy aircraft over the Don and Volga, 62 of them in September, a monthly tally never surpassed by any aviator. He would kill no more in the East. He was ordered back to the Reich on leave by Hermann Göring personally, followed by a propaganda tour. For the last time, his battle-scarred Me109 – callsign 'Yellow One', hit at least 100 times by enemy fire – lifted off from Pitomnik airfield, a dozen miles west of Stalingrad, and headed west. 'Good luck, comrades in Stalingrad… "Karaya One" signing off… on higher orders…'[65]

There was no relief for Herbert Pabst and his Stuka crews, pummelling Stalingrad 'all day long, non-stop. There's barely a house with a roof, smashed up, burned-out halls of factories, entire streets where there's no longer a wall still standing.' On the 22nd, the Stuka squadron was guided to Stalingrad by the smoke from burning oil tanks.

In the crystal-clear sky I could see the smoke column as a guide from more than 100 kilometres away. Pitch-black smoke billows into the sky, rising to 3,000 metres, where it was caught by a high-altitude wind and drifted to the south like a faint black flag perhaps 100 kilometres long. We could use it to approach hidden from the flak which the Russians have established in large numbers on the right bank of the Volga. You dive down following a black wall at the field of rubble below, see new clouds from explosions, new fires. An inferno![66]

Yet Pabst was beginning to wonder whether the hours he spent in the cockpit of his Stuka – seven on the penultimate day of September alone, flying five sorties against the industrial district – had any effect, beyond adding to the hell of Stalingrad. In the thick smoke which constantly enveloped the city and the proximity of friendly troops, it was almost impossible to hit Soviet lines with accuracy. And even when he did score a direct hit, he questioned its impact. 'If 50 are killed in the fire and dirt, another 100 appear and keep on coming,' he wrote. Pabst began to feel a begrudging admiration for his foe. 'The Ivans are different. They sleep in foxholes, they do not feel the dust in their hair, in all their clothes, between their teeth,' he confided to his diary. 'In this brutal fight only might, fire, cunning without any rules, killing by all means. That's where the primitiveness of these steppe people has its advantages. God knows, this is a battle between worlds – and woe to the West if it does not win the fight.'[67]

While Herbert Pabst continued to bludgeon the ruins of Stalingrad, 295th Infantry Division was still trying to force its way through to the Volga – more than a week after it reckoned it could reach the river in just a couple of days. Messenger Karl Fritz provided a vivid account of the fighting:

A cloudless night above the burning sky of Stalingrad. The glow of the bloody destruction is reflected like a glorious sunset in the raging Volga. A cool breeze blows through the clear autumn night from the bank. I stand alone in my foxhole. Only a few comrades from my company are in their positions, stretched far apart. The watch shows around midnight. Both fronts remain silent. Only individual rifle shots break the cruel silence of the night. The muffled roar of the Volga and the soft whispering of the wind sound like a funeral chorale of dead comrades over the blood-soaked battlefield. Hopelessly, but as if spellbound, I stare into the infinity of the starry night.

With tense nerves, in expectation of what is to come, the hours pass one by one. The horizon is getting even brighter. The sun casts its first rays over the dew-covered steppe grass. Startled, I look up. Long trails of fire announce a Stalin organ firing. Flocks of enemy aircraft hunt us down. Shells crash down and machine-guns race past me. A new Russian attack begins. Ineffective orders, fire commands and the screaming of wounded comrades wear down my nerves. This is Stalingrad, truly the last judgment. My lieutenant lies close to me, calling an order to the neighbouring company. My heart stops. A messenger dashes across open terrain, without protection and cover? Quick as a flash he pulls out his notepad and writes: '2nd Company: Cease fire. Advance to the right, attack from the flank, provide covering fire for 1st Company. Change of positions to prepare a new attack.' I still hesitate for a few minutes. The lieutenant looks at me with feverish, burning eyes: 'Don't waste any time, the report must go.' Without saying a word, I grasp the slip with the thought: Lord thy will be done. A leap into the rain of fire. The report must reach its destination. The company's existence depends on it. I've covered a kilometre. Bullets hurtle past me ever more closely. I observe the approaching enemy through my binoculars, working my way forward. A desperate situation, but there is no turning back. Then a blow and I lie bleeding on the ground. The fury of battle drowns out my cries for help. Who will help me too? Perplexed, I lie there, moaning in pain. With my last ounce of strength I work my way forward. The dew on the grass quenches my burning thirst. At last I see the company's post. With all my strength I shout: 'An important message. I am wounded.' Then darkness descends in front of me.[68]

Fritz ended up at a first-aid post established close to the front in the bleakest of conditions, similar to one 24th Panzer Regiment's Horst Rocholl set up next to the ruins of a school, whose walls were still adorned with portraits of Soviet leaders. Otherwise, little was intact. Every window was shattered, the classroom furniture smashed in the courtyard. He and his staff shared the dangers the infantry and panzer grenadiers faced – the bombardments, the near misses, the snipers, the stray bullets. Yet he never lost his admiration for the ordinary *Landser* taking the fight to the enemy daily. 'Our chaps are outstanding,' he wrote in mid-September. 'After twenty-three days of fighting every day they advance, do their duty and die if they have to. Each one of them is a hero, each one is one hell of a guy.' At 34, Rocholl was older than many of his comrades. He was also a committed Nazi, a Party member for nearly a decade and local official in peacetime. He took younger soldiers under his wing, in particular a stretcher bearer named Heybeck – 'a young tearaway'. Rocholl taught him basic first-aid skills so that they could work side by side in an ambulance and watched Heybeck develop into a fine young man. A random shell carried his upper right leg away one day during a break in the fighting at Stalingrad. Despite Rocholl's best efforts, he died of his injuries a few hours later. 'A lad with a lust for life,' he wrote. 'Now he goes to eternal rest in this blood-soaked earth – one of those who helped to save our people and the world from the gravest danger.'[69]

Horst Rocholl was convinced the struggle in the East was a modern-day crusade, 'at stake existence or destruction – not just of our people but all European nations'. But many fellow surgeons were beginning to question the meaning and outcome of the war. After a discussion with his comrades one evening in mid-September, 71st Infantry Division doctor Richard Burkhardt noted all shared 'an oppressive feeling which makes us serious and silent'. Three hundred miles west of Stalingrad, junior doctor Theo Hoffmann was overcome by similar concerns. The 28-year-old Rhinelander's medical unit should have been supporting the advance in the Caucasus. Instead, it had been sent to a military hospital in Ukraine to treat casualties from the Volga. 'The number of wounded is alarming,' he told his wife Rose. 'They pour in from Stalingrad continuously.' Casualties spoke of enemy soldiers offering resistance 'which surpasses everything we've seen to date,' demonstrating 'courage without equal'. Hoffmann was troubled. 'Stalingrad seems to be a new Verdun,' he wrote. 'Even if it falls, it is not the end. And our troops no longer have the guts and the élan they had in '39, '40 and even '41. They are willing, disciplined, but even those with unconditional faith are beginning to crack.'[70]

The assault on Stalingrad's factory district was accompanied by an exodus of the city's remaining inhabitants. Since the wave of air raids in late August, thousands of civilians had eked out a wretched existence in the ruins of their city. The German soldier had been warned to expect 'a fanatical population determined to the last… Even after the capture of the city, they will repeatedly try to stab our troops in the back.'[71] Instead he found wretched, apathetic people merely trying to survive from one day to the next. Staff officer August Schlusnus was moved by the fate of civilians in Peschanka, just west of Stalingrad. The village had been flattened – not a single house was left intact; shot-up vehicles, dead horses and unburied corpses littered the streets. Occasionally a civilian rummaged for some salvageable possession in the rubble, or cut meat from the cadaver of a horse which they then roasted over an open fire. The remaining inhabitants had created a new Peschanka, dug into the sides of a balka, one family per hole, every one of them 'harassed and frightened'. And on the main road through the ruins of their village 'a never-ending procession of refugees, women, children, old people', all heading west towards Kalach and beyond, perhaps with a few possessions. It was, August Schlusnus conceded, 'a picture of misery'. The road to Gumrak airfield, ten miles west of the city centre, was a scene of never-ending horrors, artilleryman

Josef Goblirsch remembered. 'Dead Russians with belts around otherwise swollen bodies and Russian horses lay bloated with their legs stretched and spread apart, emitting a foul smell,' he recalled. At night, civilians appeared from their hiding places and 'cut chunks of meat from the carcasses, which had already been gnawed by countless rats'.[72]

In the city, people turned half-collapsed basements into makeshift homes or burrowed into the sides of the balkas, even adding doors from the ruins of houses to keep the elements at bay. Conditions were primitive, sanitary provision non-existent. Filthy streams served for cooking, washing and calls of nature. The squalor was total. There was a pervading stench of stagnant manure. In the south of the city, civilians bribed prisoners of war to steal sacks of flour from the grain elevator or sent in children at night to stuff their pockets or school bags – until supplies ran dry when the complex was the subject of a week's bitter fighting. Stalingraders living near the river raided half-sunken barges; those near the railway stations, abandoned goods wagons. The grain was pounded using makeshift mortars – sometimes used shell cases sufficed – and, until temperatures dropped, cooked in front of the cave-like dwellings by mothers, while their children played in the mud and dirt. Like animals preparing to hibernate, some families began stockpiling dried pumpkin and potato skins for the winter. Cane root was considered a particular delicacy, but could only be gathered from swamps or marshes – which meant wading 'knee-deep in icy slush'. In desperation, some children ate the Stalingrad clay – and required a stomach pump. 'You at home do not have the slightest idea of all the misery,' one German soldier confided in his parents. 'When they're in a fix, the inhabitants eat dead horses. Everyone is freezing and children cry day and night. You shake your head that something like this still happens today, but that's war.' Journalist Clemens Podewils watched 'large families' squatting around 'a boiling pot in the open, indifferent to the threat of mortars'. The meal smelled of cabbage 'which a disappointed dog sniffs around. The dogs do better with the carcasses of horses. But many a foul-smelling piece [of meat] finds its way into people's cooking pots. I found just the head and legs of one dead horse left in a lane.' These balka communities were not safe havens. The soil and mud offered little protection from bombs, mortars and shells. Podewils stumbled over the bodies of dead civilians. 'A bomb has torn one in half,' he noted. 'Only the bloody mass of the torso and clothes are left. In the telegraph wires over my head, a hand.'[73]

Any attempt to move near the front line by day inevitably proved fatal. A non-commissioned officer in 79th Infantry Division watched in horror as women, cradling their children, ran through a Soviet artillery barrage. 'They screamed and rushed through the explosions in the middle of the street,' he told his wife Helga. Through his binoculars, he saw one woman collapse, hit in the neck by shrapnel. 'Blood ran down on to her tattered coat. Three children stood around her, none of them more than four years old. They stood there and stared at their dead mother. They probably had no idea of what had happened and were waiting for their mother to get up again.' The soldier conceded his heart was 'tied in knots'. The three children were orphans for only a matter of seconds. The next salvo obliterated the youngsters and their dead mother. Panzer grenadier Edmund Schaden found 'dead civilians lying everywhere in the streets, beaten to death, burned, it looks horrible'. At the first sight of German soldiers, civilians living in the ruins cautiously emerged, begging for bread. 'There is something terrible about war,' Schaden continued. 'We can thank God that we don't have something like that in our own land. I don't think the city will ever be rebuilt either.'[74]

To survive, some Stalingraders began to serve their invader – men as labourers, while women provided laundry services, worked in kitchens or field hospitals. Dr Kurt Wallischeck was astonished by their resilience, especially a 26-year-old mother of two whose husband had been killed in the first days of the war in the Minsk pocket. Now she did whatever odd jobs the men of 295th Infantry Division required – washing laundry, peeling potatoes or cleaning vegetables for the field kitchen, cleaning the officers' quarters. One day the normally reliable Marusia did not appear. The soldiers questioned one of the other Russian ancillary. 'Marusia is at home – that's what she calls the hole in the ground – and she cries,' she told them in broken German. 'Tonight the little one died… Malenki *kaput*.' It prompted Wallischeck to ponder: 'How many Russian people, old men, women and children will die next winter, die of cold, malnutrition and hunger?' Fellow surgeon Horst Rocholl warmed to the older civilians, but not the younger generation, 'especially adolescent women who give the impression of being fanatical and brutal'. All seemed convinced Germany's leader was disfigured, possessing only one eye and arm. 'When we showed his picture disproving this, they said he looked very likeable.'[75]

The 'likeable' Führer was convinced the entire populace of Stalingrad were 'Communists, through and through' and ordered them 'eliminated'. His genocidal instructions were never carried out, for although established, the German administration assigned to Stalingrad could not do much while the fighting raged. Appointed *Kommandant*, Colonel Paul Loehning and his staff – on paper responsible for basic amenities, law, order, the smooth running of traffic and welfare of the civilian populace – achieved little beyond imposing a curfew which was universally ignored and erecting warning signs: 'Entry into the city is forbidden. Sightseers endanger not only their own lives, but also the lives of their comrades.'[76]

Outside the city, on the Don and Kalmyk steppe, however, the region's new masters were ruthless: collective farm workers were whipped to harvest grain. When the head of one state farm resisted, he and his wife were executed. Spies and saboteurs were shot. 'Wherever the Germans stay in the occupied territory they are accompanied by terror and the humiliation of civilians,' one Soviet report noted. Even those who had welcomed the Germans as liberators were now openly hostile. 'Soviet rule was a thousand times better than these Herods, the Germans,' one complained. Stalingrad's inhabitants were about to experience similarly brutal treatment.[77]

By the beginning of October, Sixth Army had largely exhausted whatever supplies it had seized and harvest reaped during the advance to Stalingrad. It could no longer meet the needs of its own men, let alone any civilians. They had to be evacuated, Paulus' staff determined. Those who could work would serve the Reich; the rest would be sent to the featureless Kalmyk steppe where they would undoubtedly perish. First, however, they would have to cross more than 50 miles of the Don steppe to reach the railhead at Chir, where a makeshift refugee camp had been set up, then continue another 100 miles to a larger camp for selection. More than half would end up as forced labourers in Germany or Ukraine; one in six would be sent to collective farms. Others would work on the railways, support the German Army as engineers, carpenters, drivers, or re-build roads and bridges in the *Organisation Todt* labour/construction service.

Edmund Schaden watched civilians stream out of the city. 'In a hole I found a small child aged about four, lying there as if dead,' he wrote. 'When I touched it, it was still alive, yet no-one showed any interest in it.'[78] Little or no provision was made for the tens of thousands of civilians fleeing Stalingrad – an exodus so great, it was visible from the skies. Flying low over the Don steppe in a Storch reconnaissance aircraft, Herbert Pabst was struck by the sight of a 'torrent of refugees' moving westwards 'with huge sacks on their backs' or else 'lying wearily by the wayside, squatting around a small fire, then move on, endlessly and without a visible goal'.[79] Pabst was spared the scenes on the ground. No German soldier who witnessed them was unmoved. Junior infantry officer Alfons Metzger encountered thousands of civilians leaving the city:

[They were] wrapped in rags, pushing carts on which they have loaded their 'fortune', or squatting impassively in the road, mostly women and children, without shelter, without food. Every now and then, they can be seen pouncing on a dead horse, which has often been lying in the filth for days, cutting off its flesh and intestines until literally only the bones are left: the only thing they find to survive in the steppe apart from dirty puddles.[80]

Signs by the roadside instructed truck drivers to take civilians with them into the hinterland on their way back from Stalingrad. There were too many refugees and too few vehicles to take them all. So, most people traipsed westwards on foot, many pushing carts heavily loaded with furniture, bedding, household goods and food. 'Every now and then a collapsed cart stands at the side of the road, people waiting next to it with stoic calm,' medical company commander Richard Burkhardt noted. Soon it wasn't merely carts abandoned by the roadside. 'Several infirm elderly Russians didn't get far and have been left lying by the road,' 20-year-old Richard Wilts wrote. 'The misery is appalling, terrible – you can't help but ask: why?' Corps commander Walther von Seydlitz thought it 'the worst misery' he had witnessed in the war. 'For those who've not experienced it, all of this is unimaginable...' Hanns Neidhardt of 100th *Jäger* Division saw 'more and more corpses of men, women and children along the roads' but didn't consider their plight for too long. 'It was just a minor tragedy on the fringes of the looming major catastrophe.'[81]

As autumn turned to winter, temperatures regularly fell below zero. Refugees set the steppe grass on fire to keep warm, while mothers wandered around the steppe looking for a field of millet, where they stripped the tiny grains in empty shell cartridges: millet cooked with rainwater or melted snow would serve as their meal for days on end. Sometimes German soldiers would offer families their quarters – but countless more collapsed by the roadside 'from hunger and exhaustion and are left there – unburied initially, later wrapped in the first flurries of snow,' Sixth Army's senior pioneer Herbert Selle remembered. 'Death on the back streets of this war.' One non-commissioned officer was shocked by the sight of 'children, women, old men grandfather's age lying on the road, with scant clothing, at the mercy of the cold... Even if they are our enemies, I still feel sorry for them. I have already seen a lot of misery in this war, but Russia surpasses everything. Stalingrad especially.'[82]

For those who reached Chir, conditions were hardly any better than on the open steppe: there was no accommodation and the only meal was one bowl of soup a day. Soldier Carl Bruns watched refugees – 'old women, old men, invalids, one-legged people on crutches, young mothers with two- and three-year-olds in their arms, with babies – all the people that a burning city throws out' – packed like cattle into trains. 'More and more groups of ragged people approach with their hurriedly-gathered belongings on their shoulders, on rickety carts.'[83] In time, they too would be shipped west, some deported to the Reich, others to Ukraine to work on collective farms. In the autumn of 1942, as many as 25,000 Stalingraders passed through one of Sixth Army's transit camps such as Chir.[84]

How different the German attitude to the peoples of the Caucasus. The advance introduced the German soldier to a world beyond their comprehension – a world beyond Europe and its peoples, a world most men knew only from the adventure novels of Karl May. Passing through village cemeteries in the Caucasian foothills, 13th Panzer Division's Helmut Blume realised 'the people here are not Russians… On graves, there are wooden beams with a square base, approximately ten centimetres square, on which you can read blue or white handwriting – not Cyrillic but Ossetian, Kabardinian, Chechnyan or Armenian.' SS *Wiking* Division junior officer Günter Wanhöfer encountered tribesmen 'as wild as the landscape… tall, gaunt figures with black beards' who treasured the weapons they carried. 'If you get together with them do not be surprised if the host draws his pistol and immediately fires several bullets into the clay soil in front of your feet. This is a sign of utmost respect, really rough customs!'[85] The *Landser* was told to expect at least 40 different races and tribes among the 12 million inhabitants of the Caucasus, seven million of them Muslims.

On the northeastern fringes of the Caucasus, between Stalingrad and the Caspian Sea, lay Kalmykia, twice as large as any Nazi *Gau* administrative region, but home to just a few thousand people descended from Mongols. The Kalmyks' existence was primitive, nomadic. They bartered for all the food and goods they needed. Older Kalmyks – aged over 35 – were almost all opposed to Stalin's regime, the younger generation less so. Young or old, most Kalmyks were Buddhists – a fact exploited by the Germans, who used Buddhist priests to spread the word among the populace: the invader would smash Bolshevism, granting the Kalmyk people their freedom in due course.[86]

The western Caucasus were dominated by the Circassians and their numerous tribes – all victims of decades of first Russian, then Soviet oppression. Men with their large wide-brimmed hats or fur caps – even at the height of summer – blue, dashing breeches with fine boots, women in colourfully embroidered blouses: all lined the roads to welcome the German 'liberators'. 'Here,' gunner Franz Müller noted, 'the influence of Bolshevism is only skin deep.' Fritz Trautwein and his comrades were invited to dine with Circassian villagers outside Maykop – a feast of strongly seasoned roast lamb, potatoes, white bread and apples. 'One of them made a speech in our honour, but we didn't understand a word apart from Hitler and Stalin,' he recalled. 'The rest were in a hideous language which bears no similarity to Russian or Ukrainian.' Not every encounter with Circassians went so smoothly. On the edge of the village of Ulyap-Aul – roughly half-way between Krasnodar and Armavir – a 40-strong delegation of elders set out with bread and salt to welcome the advancing Germans, who were then shot at from the same direction. The German soldiers opened fire and killed the entire delegation, possibly by mistake, possibly deliberately – for, as one report put it, 'a populace which fights is better than one which offers uncertain friendship'. Kabardians – one of the main Circassian tribes – 'greeted German soldiers with gifts of tomatoes and large loaves of bread', Felix Steiner remembered. Devoted Muslims, they 'fell to their knees wherever they stood when the call of the Muezzin from the turrets of the mosque sounded in the evening'. This was alien to the invader, even a division whose ranks were drawn from many nationalities like the *Wiking* – 'but they showed consideration for the religious customs of the Muslim population'. And advancing through the Kura valley east of Pyatigorsk, children called out to panzer crews in German. The map of the region was peppered with German-sounding names: Friedefeld, Eigenheim, Schönfeld or Neudorf. There had once been 50,000 ethnic Germans in the Caucasus, descendants of 19th-century settlers. Almost all were now gone, deported at the beginning of the war. Only women who had married Russians had been allowed to stay. Once-thriving villages such as Karlsburg, Freudental and Gnadenburg lay abandoned, neglected, plundered, stripped of windows, doors, furniture and fittings.[87]

What united these people with their many customs, costumes, traditions, tongues was hatred of Bolshevism. German leaflets – scattered in their thousands by the Luftwaffe – and radio broadcasts assured them that the Axis armies came 'as their friends... liberating them from the yoke of Bolshevism'. The region's new rulers would allow the different nationalities to live, worship and work freely, put an end to collective farms and respect 'all creeds, customs and traditions'. The propaganda landed on the most fertile ground since German troops had entered the Baltic States and Ukraine in the summer of 1941. 'Twenty-five years of Bolshevism is all the propaganda needed for the liberation of the peoples of the Caucasus,' one report noted. Officers of LII Corps were greeted by the village elder in Deyskoye on the Terek with the words: 'You have liberated us Kabardians.' He continued: 'You have freed us from forced labour in the kolkhoz. You have given us back the freedom of belief. We can again work in our own fields, our children will be free and not the servants of the Soviet tyrants. For all this, we thank you from our hearts.'

Tribal leaders were quick to show their support for – and allegiance to – the Caucasus' 'liberators'. In Pyatigorsk, Hermann Ochsner, commanding Germany's *Nebelwerfer* rocket units, admired Circassian cavalry 'fighting for us' while two leaders or princes, who lived in the surrounding woods and remained bitter enemies of the Bolsheviks, came to pay their respects to the general. 'We greeted each other with kisses. Hopefully all the races in the mountains will go along with us.' SS *Wiking* Division commander Felix Steiner was impressed by 'bold people, full of a thirst for freedom and a thirst for action who would gladly have picked up a rifle and aimed it at the Soviets'. The ranks of auxiliaries – 'Hiwis' or *Hilfswilliger* – filling the baggage column supporting *Jagdgeschwader* 52 as the fighter squadron pushed into the mountains swelled with Chechens, Tatars, Karachays. The educated served as translators, armed tribesmen rode horses bareback providing protection, women worked in the field kitchen. Only the Armenians failed to impress. 1st *Gebirgs* Division's commander Hubert Lanz dismissed them as 'workshy, lazy and completely disinterested in their work'. Those who volunteered to serve the Germans as labourers proved no more willing to hold a shovel than hold a rifle when they'd been pressed into the Red Army. Lanz was faced with large-scale desertions. 'I feel compelled to send this rabble – as a soldier I cannot call them anything else, with the exception of some who have shown themselves to be willing to work and reasonably reliable – to a punishment camp.'[88]

The sight of 'slit-eyed' so-called 'subhumans' bearing arms, supporting the German war effort, was too much for Alfred Meschenmoser from 97th *Jäger* Division, however. It proved impossible to nullify the impact of years of Nazi propaganda which cast the peoples of the East as *Untermensch*. Even as the summer campaign began, one edition of the best-selling weekly magazine *Illustrierter Beobachter* branded Soviet prisoners 'of Turkish origin... despicable bastards of the steppe', while captured Red Army troops were paraded before the newsreel cameras as the narrator intoned: 'Look, these are the faces of the Asiatic hordes! The Wehrmacht must protect all of Europe from them!' And now, Meschenmoser wrote, 'here were the same Asiatic faces – and in a German uniform!'[89]

Such attitudes – and they were not uncommon – could easily turn friend into foe. 'It is in the troops' interests to treat the Caucasian peoples correctly,' the men of 13th Panzer Division were reminded. The *Landser* was told to honour local customs and traditions, instructed not to plunder and loot, and above all respect the female populace: 'Do not touch Caucasian women! Hands off women and girls!' Given the precarious, lengthy supply lines and rugged terrain, the 'liberators' could not afford to make enemies of the Caucasian peoples. 'Any mistake and any violation of the norms of this order will have to be paid later with German blood.' Ewald von Kleist told his panzer army it needed to reassure the native populace that 'a better future lies in store for them than under the rule of the Tsar and Stalin'. But others, such as Seventeenth Army's Richard Ruoff, had their doubts. He demanded 'constant alertness' from his men, convinced there were spies and saboteurs everywhere. 'Twenty years of Soviet education have left their mark in the Caucasus,' he warned. And then there was Gerret Korsemann, the brutal senior SS officer in the region, who dismissed the idea of harnessing the anti-Bolshevik sentiment of the mountain tribes as nothing but 'pathetic romanticism'. The Reich had 'gone too far', kowtowing to Cossacks, Circassians, Ossetians, Karachians and others, granting them 'constitutional liberties which they would never have dreamed of even if they had a fever'. As a result, 'small tribal republics with wide-ranging independent powers sprang up'. It was all wrong, Korsemann argued. 'People must be given the opportunity to fight for their freedom honestly; you cannot give a people freedom like you're giving them a tip.'[90]

Attempts were made to stir up anti-Jewish sentiment both at the front and in some of the occupied towns and cities. Leaflets were scattered behind Soviet lines, blaming Jews for 'all the terror, all the hardship, all the man-made famines' in Russia. 'The Germans are not fighting against you but against our common enemies, not to enslave you but to free you – and us – from the Jewish plague.' Or: 'Do not die for the foreign interests of Jewry. Jews plunged us into this war. Those who plunged us into this senseless war are our enemy. It's pointless shedding blood for the Jews.' In Cherkessk, the bodies of around two dozen prisoners, murdered by the NKVD before Soviet authorities pulled out, were found buried in the jail courtyard. The Germans laid the blame at the feet of Jews – though fewer than one in 200 inhabitants was Jewish. The 'martyrs' were reinterred with full ceremony by Cherkessk's new rulers, while its newspaper proclaimed: 'Citizens of Cherkessk! Here before your eyes are the atrocities of the Jews and Bolsheviks! The victorious German Army has freed us from the horrors of Bolshevik terror, from the terror of Stalin's regime which only benefitted the Jews.'[91]

There was no repetition of the 'spontaneous' pogroms which had swept through the western borderlands of the Soviet Union in the first days of *Barbarossa*, however. Instead, it fell to SS and police detachments to deal with the Reich's enemies: Communists, intelligentsia, Jews. At first the latter were assured that no harm would come to them, that the rumours about the fate of Jews spread by the Bolsheviks were false; the Jewish populace merely lived in 'complete safety' in special districts. In early September 1942, Jews in major towns across the Caucasus were ordered to report for 'resettlement' to those new districts. On 5 September between 800 and 1,000 Jewish men, women and children from Pyatigorsk and the surrounding villages were herded into trucks. The journey lasted just 30 minutes. The destination was a gravel pit where the Jews were ordered to surrender their valuables, then strip naked before being forced into a gas van which drove around for several minutes, until the passengers had been killed by carbon monoxide. Jews who were promised their lives would be spared removed the corpses and tossed them into the pit – and the murders continued 'calmly and methodically'. And when the van had completed its work, those

365

promised salvation joined their fellow victims in the pit. The murders proved no secret, as Elena Skrjabina, who fled to the apparent safety of Pyatigorsk from Leningrad, noted: 'The atmosphere around us has been darkened, however, by strange types of rumours circulating in the city about the fate of the Jews,' she wrote. The Jews of Maykop were greeted outside the former NKVD building by the jovial, almost patriarchal figure of SS officer Erich Kubiak, who chatted with young women as they waited patiently to register inside. But once through the door, the Jews were interrogated, forced to surrender any valuables, then remove their clothes before being led to gas trucks which drove a short distance to a large courtyard in the prison complex. The journey was of sufficient length that all the passengers were dead by the time the vehicle reached its destination, their corpses tossed into a large pit. Thus did 200 of Maykop's Jewish population die.[92]

The cleansing actions were not limited to Jews, or even the Nazis, political foes. Having dealt with the Reich's enemies in the small coastal town of Yeysk, its SS special detachment turned its attention to those sick and disabled. The town's orphanage was home to upwards of 270 children, more than a third of them infants and almost all refugees, evacuated from the Crimea the preceding year to escape the horrors of war. On 9 October 1942, war came to them in the form of an SS detachment and several vans. The youngsters were excited, convinced they were being transferred to a new home; some even packed their belongings in anticipation of the journey. Staff carried out babies and children with disabilities, while others dutifully gathered in the courtyard ready for their adventure. Some willingly boarded the trucks, but the older children began to suspect their fate and tried to escape. The mask of the SS murderers – who claimed most of the victims were 'deformed' or 'imbeciles who could not speak and just babbled' – now slipped as they beat any child who resisted and tossed them into the trucks like sacks. More than 200 children were promptly gassed in the back of the trucks, but there were still two dozen left alive in the home. As the trucks departed, the SS interpreter told the home's staff: 'We'll come back tomorrow.' They kept their promise.[93]

Otherwise, the spa towns of the Caucasus became backwaters of the war, places where wounded soldiers like signaller Dolf Wagner convalesced. Wagner observed life go on in Kislovodsk 'as if it were peacetime: there were shops and restaurants open'. The recovering soldiers had their photographs developed and printed and spent evenings in the cinema. After the horrors and devastation of Ukraine, the Caucasus seemed a land almost at peace to Red Cross nurse Annette Schücking. The 22-year-old was convinced that war had 'swept over this land like a storm on the plains which had no time to stop and so couldn't destroy much'. Maykop wasn't scarred by the usual burned-out tanks by the roadside, the shot-up military columns. There weren't even many graves. Just the occasional barricade swiftly brushed aside and half-finished trenches which Russian soldiers had hurriedly dug – and equally hastily abandoned. What Schücking did not notice was that the people of Maykop were starving. A skilled worker in the employment of the city's rulers might earn 25 roubles for a day's work, a labourer no more than ten roubles, yet was expected to pay 60 roubles for five apples, 100 roubles for a chicken. The realities of war – to say nothing of Nazi occupational and racial policies – meant the many peoples of the Caucasus enjoyed few benefits of German rule, but they did suffer most of its consequences: forced labour, exploitation of their land, hunger and privation. 'Looking at the big picture,' Seventeenth Army's chief-of-staff Vincenz Müller observed, 'we offer the populace little, but demand a great deal.'[94] Harnessing the crusade against Bolshevism in the Caucasus proved to be as much a false dawn as it had elsewhere in the Soviet Union.

The German people were steeling themselves for a fourth winter at war, rallying – as they did at the end of every year – to donate whatever they could to ensure less fortunate souls did not suffer in the cold. The *Winterhilfswerk*, or winter relief programme, had been a firm fixture in the Nazi calendar since they came to power, launched with bombast and pomp and ceremony by Hitler with a great speech. Twelve months before, the Führer had stood on the podium in Berlin's Sportpalast and proclaimed the enemy beaten, unable to ever rise again. He had learned nothing from his hubris. Now he told a fanatical audience that neither the name of the city nor even the capture of Stalingrad mattered – although it would be taken, of course. Blocking the Volga – even more important to the lifeblood of the Soviet Union than the Rhine was to Germany – was key. The fall of Stalingrad would follow – 'and you can be sure that no human being will shift us from this spot'. Cheers and applause echoed around the arena for several minutes.

The following afternoon, the Führer addressed Party leaders in a similar vein during a three-hour *tour d'horizon*. No-one could stop Germany triumphing at Stalingrad – 'it's only a matter of time'. After Stalin's city would come Astrakhan, the shores of the Caspian Sea, Baku would be flattened by the Luftwaffe, and ultimately German troops would march into Mesopotamia to 'present the Führer's business card to England's oil supplier'.

'Right now these are fantastic plans,' Goebbels concluded, 'but they really do lie within the realms of possibility.' The lead story of that day's *Völkischer Beobachter* left the German people in no doubt: 'No-one can deprive us of victory.'[95]

For now, the *Landser* in the ruins of Stalingrad still believed in victory on the Volga. The prevailing question was: when? Private Karl Nülsen and his comrades turned to a fortune teller, who predicted that the war would end on

24 September – Stalingrad would fall and Stalin would shoot himself. 'It would have been nice if this old woman had been right,' Nülsen wrote three days after the deadline had passed. Still, he wasn't troubled. 'She was about right in guessing that Stalingrad would soon fall.' A soldier from Hanover was convinced that, however dogged the Russians' defence of the city, 'in the long run they won't be able to hold out. It may even be the case that this Stalingrad is the grave of Bolshevism because the Russians hurl an awful lot of men and matériel into the battle.' There was every possibility the Red Army would be bled white on the Volga and 'then we'll be in Baku in four or six weeks and we'll have reached our objective in the south'. After the desperate fighting for the grain elevator and the city centre, Wilhelm Hoffman was not so sure. 'When will the Russian forces in Stalingrad be exhausted?' he asked in his diary. 'Will this bloodbath be over by Christmas?'[96]

Another factor beginning to prey on the mind of the German soldier: time. By mid-September it was clear the weather was starting to turn. It was now dark by 6.30pm. The steppe wind from the east was no longer refreshing, but cold. The radiant sunsets which all summer long had bathed the endless western horizon 'in a blaze of glowing colours every evening, from a glowing fiery red to a subdued violet,' observed Herbert Rauchhaupt, a war correspondent accompanying 16th Panzer Division, had been replaced by the dark grey of clouds. For the first time in six weeks, rain fell. Panzer crews hunkered down in their vehicles, where the wind drummed the droplets against the hull and through the slightest gap. The crew wore their jackets or overcoats, collars turned up trying to make themselves 'as "cosy" as you can do in a panzer'. The only comfort was that the wind and rain largely brought the fighting to an end – none of the usual disruptive night-time raids by Soviet aircraft and searchlight beams groping for them. There was still fighting – it *never* stopped in Stalingrad. Flares were sent up occasionally, casting the scarred cityscape briefly in a pale, flickering white light before fading. There were sporadic bursts of machine-gun fire but 'the howling of the wind and the drumming of the raindrops drown out the guns' distant hammering,' Rauchhaupt wrote. 'Only the flashing chains of tracer pierce the night like fiery threads... All that remains is the cold, wind and rain.' Although the days were still warm – the sun rose around 4am, the skies were frequently cloudless – the journalist noted that the layers of dust had disappeared from the dirt tracks which counted for roads on the outskirts of Stalingrad and the steppe grass was damp. The *Landser* could bid 'farewell to summer, farewell to the red-hot, dry days. Something hangs in the air which foreshadows the imminent arrival of autumn.'[97]

Sober officers like XI Corps' chief-of-staff Helmuth Groscurth wondered whether Stalingrad was becoming a second Verdun. 'That's what we ask ourselves here, full of worry. It's become too much of a matter of prestige between Hitler and Stalin.' Just a fortnight after predicting the city's imminent fall, Walther von Seydlitz was similarly despondent. 'I'm not at all happy with my lot,' he wrote to his wife. 'The hope that it will end quickly here is always deceptive,' he continued. 'We'd have done it long ago if we'd enough fresh forces – it's almost impossible to rally the necessary strength for battle time and again.' And it was impossible to rally those forces, Seydlitz complained, not least because Stalingrad was 'a very one-sided siege'. Hitler and the Nazi propaganda machine would trumpet the death of traffic up and down the Volga thanks to German troops investing the city. But traffic *across* the river, from the endless expanse of the Russian hinterland into the ever-shrinking bridgehead, never stopped. The Volga was the lifeblood of Stalingrad, the sole source of the defenders' strength: men, weapons, food, ammunition, equipment. All came across the Volga. 'But it was a path through fire,' regimental commander Vasily Velichko wrote. Veteran sailors reckoned it was ten times more dangerous than any traditional naval action, requiring, one senior Red Navy officer observed, 'nerves of steel and special courage'. The Germans occupied most of the high bluffs on the west bank so that the Volga 'lay before them as on the palm of their hands'. They allocated 'squares' along the river to direct concerted artillery and mortar fire. 'As soon as a black spot appeared on the river, a six-barrel mortar started barking, and heavy mortars came down on the square, throwing up huge water columns,' Velichko remembered. And there was always the possibility of the Luftwaffe attacking. Pavel Medvedev's division was pounced upon by Stukas as it crossed. 'The first bomb missed us, as did the second. We thought we'd get away with it. But no!' the 40-year-old signaller recalled. The barge was blown apart, the blast hurling Medvedev into the river. Having grown up by the Don, he could swim and reached the shore.[98]

The journey out of the city was no less perilous. P. M. Makarov ferried badly wounded soldiers to the east shore by rowing a small fishing boat, crossing in broad daylight. 'We did not have time to travel even 100 metres when the enemy opened mortar fire on our overloaded boat and a wave began to overwhelm it.' Two Stukas dived on the rowing boat, straddling it with cannon fire. Soon the blood of the wounded mixed with water pouring into the tiny craft. Exhausted, Makarov was about to pass out when a wounded officer prodded him: 'On Mamayev Kurgan, our soldiers and commanders are bleeding to death, holding back the onslaught of a numerically-superior enemy. I am a reconnaissance pilot. Here is a map, there are the enemy's firing positions, pass them to the aerial unit on the left bank of the Volga…'

'Comrade Major, you will definitely pass it on yourself,' Makarov assured him, picking up the oars and continuing to the left bank where he safely delivered his cargo.

Within an hour, Soviet bombers were attacking German positions using the wounded major's map as their guide. Makarov spent two days rowing across the Volga, saving the lives of more than 300 people. Despite the onslaught his fishing boat faced on every crossing, it was hit only once by shrapnel.[99]

For most Red Army soldiers, crossing the Volga was their introduction to the battle. They knew what was expected of them – the roads leading down to the jetties on the east bank were lined with banners and placards, imploring them to defend the city to the last man. During a halt in the journey to the Volga, a senior officer addressed the ranks of 84th Tank Brigade. 'Comrades! In a few hours' time you'll be on the right bank of the Volga. Remember, there's no way back. Before us lies either death or victory – and we will be victorious!' The first sight of Stalingrad, however, quickly dented such bravado. 'Since the first days of the war I have seen many harrowing and cruel things, but what we saw was terrible,' one veteran *frontovik* wrote. An enormous curtain of smoke wrapped around Stalingrad, fires running the length of the waterfront, burning oil still flowing from damaged tanks down the balkas and into the river, whose waters reflected this tremendous wall of fire and made the scene even more horrific. Tugs hauled lighters carrying troops from the left bank to the right as mortar shells crashed down between the craft, whose passengers were powerless to respond. 'We even stopped whispering, everyone was silent, all faces became serious,' the veteran continued. 'The boys suddenly looked transformed. We were aware that we would have to go in there shortly, in ten or 15 minutes, into those dark, unknown jaws.' War correspondent Vasily Grossman joined a ferry packed with vehicles, carts and people. The experience was 'terrifying'. A smokescreen was laid across the Volga but it served little use as Grossman's boat became stranded and drew the attention of a Junkers Ju88. Despite its stationary target, the dive-bomber missed, merely drenching passengers as the water fountain its bomb threw up crashed back down into the Volga.[100]

And there was the rub. Whatever forces the Germans brought to bear, however many shells and mortar rounds rained down on the Volga, or bombs the Stukas hurled at the ferries and launches, however much fire was concentrated every time a searchlight scanning the river's surface fell upon a vessel, the effort and expenditure of ammunition was largely in vain, for most craft reached Stalingrad. By the time the river froze, the Volga flotilla had delivered more than 90,000 men to Stalingrad, having made more than 35,000 crossings. As far as Nikolai Krylov, Chuikov's deputy, was concerned, the Volga saved Stalingrad. Krylov had escaped Sevastopol. 'It seemed to us sometimes as if we were continuing the same battle,' he recalled. But there was one key difference: the constant flow of men, ammunition and supplies from the left bank of the Volga. As a result, 'we did not feel doomed, as we did at Sevastopol.'[101]

As the boats reached the Stalingrad landing, passengers were struck by 'an oppressive smell of burning – the stench of burnt iron and something else,' poet and author Konstantin Simonov remembered. He was reminded of the smell of villages torched by the Germans the previous winter during the retreat before Moscow. Land offered no protection, for the jetty and shoreline were under constant bombardment. 'The earth beneath our feet trembles under the impacts, sometimes stronger, sometimes weaker.' This was not the pre-war Volga vista Simonov knew, the Stalingrad of gleaming white tenement blocks towering over the Volga on the clifftop, the lively quays and jetties, the rows of bathing huts interspersed with kiosks. Simonov tried to make sense of his surroundings. 'All around is an unholy mess – ruined houses, collapsed barracks, bent rails, barrels, boards ripped up, pieces of furniture and household effects.' The shoreline was littered with burned-out vehicles and the wreckage of barges driven ashore. The waters carried a charred log, the corpse of a woman, her burned, twisted fingers clinging to it. There was no clue to her identity – or fate. Perhaps she had been killed trying to cross the river; perhaps she had been blown into the water by a bomb striking a jetty. Either way, Simonov concluded from her disfigured face, 'the agony she went through before dying must have been incredible'. Her plight seemed to anger Simonov more than any of the horrors and destruction he had yet seen in the city. 'The Germans did this – they did it before our very eyes,' he wrote. 'Let them not ask for mercy from any of those who saw it. After Stalingrad, we will not spare them.'[102]

Vasily Grossman was convinced he had set foot in Pompeii in its final hours, its inhabitants cowering in basements 'half-insane' while the buildings above them burned, their walls white-hot, their window panes melted or shattered, roofs collapsed, allowing the sun's rays – turned a hue of pink by the flames and smoke – to penetrate the ruins. The ordinary soldier had no time to acclimatise to his new surroundings, sent directly to the front line to engage the enemy. And there, they were often destroyed in a matter of hours. 'Only 15–20 people out of 4,000 are soon left alive – and those are the senior commanders,' one Soviet soldier complained. 'It only takes 15 minutes to break up a division…' Despite the terrible rate of attrition, surviving letters and documents largely suggest men entered battle willingly. 'A burning hatred of the enemy burns in my heart,' a 43-year-old veteran of the Russian Civil War wrote. 'As long as we still have the strength, we will destroy the Fascist scum. The German occupiers will not leave our sacred soil with their skin intact. A shameful death is the enemy's fate.' Some men, like one Rifleman Sholoiko, seized upon the words of propagandists such as

Ilya Ehrenburg sparing the foe no mercy – or invective. 'We love our Motherland like we love our mothers, and if we have to die for this beloved Motherland, it is only so that our children, our entire nation does not become a refuge for hated Fascism,' he wrote. 'We will never allow these Fritzes to violate our women, kill our elderly and children. We will avenge them for all the agony they have inflicted upon our people. The Fascist Fritzes will be destroyed once and for all, and never again will progressive mankind see such bloodthirsty killers as German vassals. Their end is nigh…' A last letter was found on the body of Sixty-Second Army soldier Alexei Sherkachenko. 'Do not cry, father!' he wrote. 'Be proud in your heart, be proud of your son! In death, I spit in the face of the enemy. With the last strength in my finger I will send a burst of fire from my machine-gun at the Fascists.' Deaths like Sherkachenko's inspired one soldier named Panfilov, who told his wife Valentina: 'How many heroes there are in our ranks who have shown examples of heroism and courage. We will win with such people and victory will be ours…' A company commander, who claimed he had killed more than a dozen German soldiers personally, vowed he would never surrender Stalingrad. 'The blood we shed on the battlefields is not in vain – until the last drop of blood we will crush the enemy, until his complete destruction…' Other men sought to thank their wives, sisters, girlfriends or even mothers for their efforts in the factories of the Soviet Union. 'Your factory is giving us everything we need,' one soldier thanked his wife in Moscow. 'In our hands is all that the Motherland has given us to defeat the cursed enemy.'[103]

The first major attack in the industrial district petered out in a matter of days. 'Without reinforcements, the Army is not going to take Stalingrad,' a despondent Friedrich Paulus recorded on 4 October. Two days later he was forced to call off his attack because the infantry were worn out. There was no hope of occupying the city with battalions half the size of companies.[104]

At least one senior commander blamed Paulus personally for the failure. In his Luftwaffe opposite number Wolfram von Richthofen, the Sixth Army commander had his staunchest critic, a man who found fault in everyone but himself. Richthofen chided Paulus almost from the moment battle was joined; he thought him sluggish, unimaginative, lacking in inspiration and unduly pessimistic. Nor did the men around him impress. 'The generals merely issue orders and lead neither by example nor by their actions,' Richthofen fumed.

His name would forever be associated with Stalingrad, but Friedrich Paulus, one staff officer put it bluntly, was 'the wrong man in the wrong place'. He had been appointed on the recommendation of his monocled predecessor, Walther von Reichenau – a man everything the new Sixth Army commander was not: imposing, aristocratic yet gruff, an ardent Nazi. Reichenau enjoyed being an army commander, he enjoyed the responsibility, he enjoyed taking firm decisions, he attacked problems with audacity, forced ideas through with sheer weight of will. Paulus was the antithesis: tall, thin to the point of appearing gaunt, elegant, always smartly attired, yet ever conscious of his relatively humble origins – he was born into a middle-class family in northern Hesse in September 1890, though he married minor Romanian royalty. He did not make snap decisions, but 'analysed each point from every angle, carefully separating the wheat from the chaff' before finally deciding on a course of action. That diligence made him an excellent deputy for both Reichenau and, later, Franz Halder. But the qualities which made a first-rate chief-of-staff – attention to detail, organisation, carefully considering every word, every sentence – did not necessarily make a first-rate army commander. Even as a junior officer his comrades labelled him *cunctator* – the procrastinator. He overcompensated for his bourgeois background, earning him the nicknames the 'noble Lord' and the 'refined thin gentleman'. And he was certainly no leader of men. Unlike his friend of 20 years' standing, Erwin Rommel, he possessed little instinct for battle. The units in which he served may have seen action in some of the most bitter fighting of the Great War – Verdun, Flanders, the Isonzo – but not Paulus himself; he was always in the rear, always an adjutant or staff officer. Men did not warm to him. He was too analytical, too remote, fastidious bordering on pedantic. He relied on his chief-of-staff Arthur Schmidt – as much Sixth Army's commander as Paulus. Schmidt was a careerist who did not mince his words, accepted no criticism and was widely despised by Sixth Army's staff, who referred to him as a '*harter Hund*' – a tough son of a bitch. Schmidt was also a committed Nazi, convinced of Hitler's military genius, though in the late summer of 1942 he was beginning to have his doubts. 'The war,' he confided to Udo von Alvensleben, 'cannot be won militarily but only decided politically.' His master still believed he could deliver victory at Stalingrad, but the longer the battle dragged on, the more the strain on Paulus began to tell. He railed at the 'absurd orders' from above, among the more absurd of which was Hitler's micromanagement of the battle: any operation in Stalingrad involving anything larger than a company required the Führer's approval. Never a well man – he'd been plagued by illness since struck down with severe sinusitis in the opening weeks of the Great War – Sixth Army's commander was weakened by his wretched diet and lifestyle, working long into the night sustained largely on coffee and cigarettes. Dysentery compounded discomfort and exhaustion, while close family and friends noticed that the constant emotional strain caused a nervous tic on the left side of his face to become more pronounced.[105]

And yet outwardly, however unconvincingly, Friedrich Paulus tried to exude confidence. 'Progress is extremely slow, but we advance a little every day,' he assured Hitler's Wehrmacht adjutant Rudolf Schmundt. 'It's all a question of time and manpower. But we will finish off the Russians.'[106]

Kurt Zeitzler wasn't so sure. Just a week after demanding 'faith in our Führer, faith in our victory,' the new Chief of the General Staff had come to the conclusion that the German Army was being bled white at Stalingrad and dared to suggest halting the battle, sending troops to the Caucasus instead to reinvigorate the offensive there. Adolf Hitler would not hear of it.[107]

The two-pronged advance on Ordzhonikidze and the oilfields of Grozny and Baku was proving no more successful than the push towards the Black Sea ports. German and Romanian forces had forced two of the last major natural obstacles – the Terek and, beyond it, the Baksan. Having fought and marched for 750 miles, the Romanian 2nd Mountain Division was exhausted. It succeeded in crossing the deep, fast-flowing Baksan, but could do little to expand its bridgehead as the Soviets threw whatever forces they could scrape together – including cadets from a commissar school – at the attackers. After ten days the Romanians abandoned the precarious foothold on the far side of the river, having lost more than 1,500 men.[108]

The raging Terek – 800 feet wide – was stormed in one of the last set-piece actions of the summer campaign. A couple of hours before dawn on the penultimate day of August, 26 German batteries – 75 guns in all – and ten *Nebelwerfer* cleared their throats and spewed their deadly combination of iron, lead and high explosive at the far bank of a u-bend in the river at Ishcherskaya, just 40 miles to the northwest of Grozny. For ten minutes the barrage pummelled the defenders before leaping further south. Having dragged their inflatable boats through the scrub and marshy flood plain, pioneers launched themselves into the fast-flowing river. Outboard motors were started and a 'wild journey' from one bank to the other began, for the Russians had recovered from their initial shock and began to trade shells with their foe. The Terek boiled as rounds crashed down, boats were ripped apart, gaps were torn in the ranks of panzer grenadiers waiting on the north bank to be ferried across. Before the first German soldier set foot on the far bank, the staff of at least one attacking battalion were wiped out. The defenders of the Terek were ejected from their trenches in visceral hand-to-hand fighting as the Germans desperately tried to gain a firm foothold. 'Any man who reached the bridgehead took part in the battle – be he grenadier, pioneer or assault boat skipper.' After four hours, pioneers had transported several hundred men across the Terek and carved a small bridgehead. No more would follow, however.

The pioneers had lost five out of every six boats – as well as half their men – while every attempt to build a pontoon ferry and move heavy weapons across the river was thwarted by day and, when it eventually came, night, as Russian artillery shelled the crossing constantly. The men in the tentative bridgehead were ordered to dig in. Outnumbered perhaps eight to one, 'our men held like iron,' one contemporary official report declared proudly, while no man's land and the marshy riverbank were littered with hundreds of Red Army corpses.[109]

And there – with Axis forces at the end of their strength and Soviet units defending resolutely – the front largely rested for a good six weeks. 'Soldiers began to think that we have enough armament and equipment, yet victory always eludes us,' one captured German officer told his Soviet interrogators. 'They promised us the operation to capture the Caucasus would be over in July, but it is September and there is no sign of it. We are still stuck at Mozdok. The men are tired of the war, they are anxious to go home...' Ewald von Kleist was given the SS *Wiking* Division to bolster his attack and punch a hole in Red Army defences along the main road to Grozny through the twin villages of Malgobek and Sagopshin. 'The entire army looks to your division,' Kleist told Felix Steiner. 'You have the mission of carrying forward the army's attack on Grozny.'[110] As the panzers moved out in the thick pre-dawn fog on 25 September, a senior officer drove past the advancing armour, shouting at crews: 'Come on comrades, on to Baku!' The terrain – a valley floor just a couple of miles wide – did not allow Steiner to bring all his armour to bear, nor any outflanking manoeuvre. The only hope was for the *Wiking* to bludgeon their way through to Sagopshin.

As the mist thinned, the cry 'Panzer marsch!' echoed in the headset of tank commanders. Progress was slow – heavy artillery fire, an anti-tank ditch and the Red Air Force hindered the advance sufficiently to ensure Kleist's goal would not be achieved. With its ravines, balkas and hollows, 'the terrain is just not suited to tank attacks,' frustrated panzer commander Karl Jauss lamented. His observations were reinforced the following morning when his panzer was crippled, losing a track when it ran over a mine. The remaining armour continued the assault and, assisted by infantry who suffered heavy losses, battered its way into Sagopshin at the end of its strength.[111]

And there it remained for nearly three weeks, unable to muster the forces needed to capture the high ground to the south. 'You've still got one combat-worthy battalion, the Finnish battalion!' Kleist's staff insisted.

'For what?' the division's commander Felix Steiner asked.

'For continuing the attack on Grozny!'

On 16 October, the Finns moved out to take Hill 701, whose defenders had defied all previous attempts to dislodge them. 'If the operation failed, it would be our very last attack,' junior officer Tauno Pohjanletho recalled as 50 Finns moved up the slope without any artillery preparation. 'There was nothing more to lose. Our mood was utterly determined as is always the case when there's no going back.' The first Soviet defenders were surprised and overrun, but the higher the Finns got, the more determined the opposition and the more brutal the fighting, until Hill 701 was captured. 'We sat on the peak with six men and removed our steel helmets from our sweaty heads,' wrote Pohjanletho. 'We held our first cigarettes in our trembling, dirty hands.' The Finns counted just a dozen men left after the attack. They had opened the way to Grozny – barely 50 miles away – but there was no hope of exploiting their victory. Prisoners reported that the city was defended like a fortress, surrounded by anti-tank ditches filled with naphtha, or else a formidable barrier of trenches and barbed wire ready, plus petrol barrels to turn the landscape into an inferno. Only the Luftwaffe was able to reach Grozny, raiding the city in force, destroying fuel depots. The resulting fires produced a thick black cloud of smoke which 'blotted out the sun like in an eclipse', was visible to 3rd Panzer Division on the Terek. and was so intense that it prevented reconnaissance over the city for another two days.[112]

Tuapse too remained tantalisingly close yet beyond the grasp of the *Landser*, still stuck in the wooded mountains to the north of the port. 'The sights are reminiscent of 1914–18 in France,' a junior officer in 125th Infantry Division noted. Shells had carried away the tops of trees and pockmarked the foothills of the western Caucasus with craters. The dead were carried to the rear tied to panje carts; the wounded fared little better, and there was always the danger of being picked off by partisans on one of the few roads. Rain was incessant, leaving roads impassable – except by pack animal or on foot. No company in the front line mustered more than 30 soldiers; some were down to just five. Perhaps the sole consolation was that the Soviets' predicament was little better. They shared the same privations and hardships as their foe: poor food, the constant damp, the lice infestation, frostbite, hypothermia. One teenage officer cadet remembered his days in the mountains 'as a time of subhuman misery'. Despite sidelining the incompetent Budyonny, despite unifying all Soviet forces, despite the German attack losing impetus, the enemy continued to make headway – largely due to the shortcomings of the defenders. Units were sent into the line with the rank and file unable to fire their rifles accurately and with officers who 'could not handle their weapons'. Red Army commanders overestimated the enemy, counter-attacking Soviet units ended up shooting at each other by accident, communications were poor, leadership sluggish, aerial support lacking. 'We are sending people to the front – I am at the front myself – but we are not always successful, unfortunately, not even in the majority of cases,' Lazar Kaganovich, another of Stalin's paladins dispatched to the Caucasus, reported to his master.[113]

Sensing weakness in the Soviet lines, the Germans made a renewed push for Tuapse in mid-October. The port, readers of the flagship fortnightly magazine *Die Wehrmacht* were told, 'lies within reach after months of fighting'. 'Neither the terrain, nor the bitterness of the Soviet enemy can break the attacking spirit and formidable expertise of our mountain infantry.'[114] Which was ironic because by the time the photo essay 'On the road to Tuapse' appeared, the attack on the Black Sea port had broken down, irrevocably, for a good three weeks. The mountain infantry of 1st *Gebirgs* Division advanced to within 15 miles of the city – the men could *almost* see the Black Sea resort from the summit of a 3,400ft peak. They got no further. The division had reached the end of its strength. Its commander Hubert Lanz had combed out drivers, pack units, staffs, to form a 'last levy' of 200 men to throw into the front line. 'I no longer have any reserves left and must have faith in the fighting strength of my troops that they will hold the present position,' he warned. Companies were 40 men strong – a number which fell almost by the hour as the weather turned. Lanz suggested either relieving his division or withdrawing it. If it remained in the line, its very existence was at stake. 'The ground in the forests turned to a deep mire,' Lanz later recalled. 'Any movement became torture, supplies sank into the mud. Horses and pack animals perished by the dozen from exhaustion. Ammunition and rations were running dangerously low. It was a terrible period.'[115]

The plight of the divisions outside Tuapse was shared by almost every German unit in the western Caucasus. On a fine autumn day, the German soldier awoke to the morning sun streaming over the peaks and ridges and filling the woods and forests with bright colours, while a milky-white fog clung to the valley floors, gradually dispersing. But fine days were rare now. The change of season brought the rain. Tame, narrow mountain streams became raging torrents which swept makeshift bridges away. Too dangerous to ford or swim across, soldiers had to wait for the waters to subside before pioneers could throw a new bridge over. The mountain tracks turned into barely passable morasses, which brought traffic to a halt. Vehicles struggled to cover two or three miles a day. Ammunition and food failed to reach the men at the front. Battalion commander Walter Kopp complained that supplies only 'trickled through – we lived from hand to mouth', despite the best efforts of men like Rudolf Hermann who served in a 'combat baggage column' from 198th Infantry Division.[116] Each day he and his men delivered food, ammunition, weapons, equipment, mail, fodder, even furniture to the men in the front line.

Daily marches, always hard-going, always energy-sapping, heavy loads, meagre fodder, meagre fare for the accompanying men, no rest-days, losses from enemy action, illnesses, over-tiredness and exhaustion. Losses in men and animals grew by the day, the paths grew worse. Hundreds of our faithful four-legged 'tractors' died from exhaustion by the road – after a short time the roadside was lined with nothing but the cadavers of horses. There was only one hope: frost! Only it didn't come – or came much too late. And when it finally came, the conditions became even worse. The frost wasn't strong enough to freeze the ground to any depth. It merely formed a thin crust which the men and horses broke through at every step. The march thus merely became even more arduous and more painful. Horses often waded up to their bellies in the morass for hours, days, weeks, sometimes months. The life of suffering did not seem to want to end.

It would take seven, eight, nine hours for the column of men and beasts to reach the front, and it would be long past dark when the exhausted supply troops returned to their base. The division lost at least three horses every day in the autumn to exhaustion. And it was not unheard of for men to die in the mud, collapsing from exhaustion. If they were Russian prisoners, 'no-one cares about him,' Alfred Meschenmoser from 97th *Jäger* Division noted. 'Human life is not worth much here. The next column of animals will trample over him. It will trample him into the mud and soon he'll have vanished. Later someone will stumble while wading through the morass and curse the unexpected obstacle. Who will know what they've stumbled over?'[117]

Realising the 1942 campaign had failed to deliver victory, the German soldier in the Caucasus began preparing to winter in the mountains. Forests and woods were felled to make bunkers and shore up trench walls, providing protection from shrapnel and mortar shells. The trench floors were covered with fern, which also served as padding for beds. 'I'm sitting in a foxhole one metre wide, two metres long and one and a half metres deep, covered with earth and thick boards,' Gustav Kalberlah, a battalion commander in 111th Infantry Division, wrote:

A telephone in a small niche in the clay wall shows that it is a command post. A strip of canvas closes the hole to the outside world, there's a thin layer of straw on the ground. A candle lights up the room from time to time; unfortunately, we cannot let ourselves be seen outside by day because of Russian snipers. The clay dust is awful. Now after the sunshine we have drizzle, the soil clings to our boots.

My men are lying all around in similar holes. In the hilly terrain in front of us which rises up to the mountains lie the Russians.

Such positions were invariably infested with mice and rats which spread disease – the men dubbed it 'mouse sickness': a fever, bloated face, blurred vision. Peter Dimt was convinced he was in the midst of some plague from the Middle Ages. 'These cute little rodents can infest an area in vast numbers and turn into a nightmare and a real threat to humans,' he wrote. 'Wherever we climb, grab, look, it's always teeming with mice. One mouse fell into an open wound right in front of the surgeon's fingers during a stomach operation in the main first aid post.'

Damp, cold, poor diet, lack of sleep, the constant struggle to keep warm, lice and rodents, left men exhausted and vulnerable to a string of illnesses from skin ulcers, jaundice, stomach complaints, kidney complaints, colds and, as temperatures dropped, frostbite. Even water, taken from the once-pure mountain streams, could no longer be trusted due to the cadavers of animals and corpses decomposing on the slopes. Malnutrition and dysentery were rife. Men were 'severely emaciated', reduced to 'nothing but skin and bone' and beginning to die of exhaustion. Some units even reported cases of starvation.

There was winter clothing in abundance – overcoats, sweaters, vests, gloves, boots – while Hitler's headquarters reminded front-line units that every man should possess a tube of frost-protection ointment and a bag of 'Russla' – anti-lice powder made of horse hair and horse fibres. In most cases, such supplies were stuck behind the front. What the men actually wore – 'permanently drenched, covered in dirt, ripped and worn-out' was, one doctor lamented, 'utterly inadequate for the weather and cold'. What replacements there were – losses in officers and non-commissioned officers were rarely made good – were no substitute for the hardened warriors they replaced. Worse, some veteran soldiers – even officers – had become apathetic. They remained brave and would fight, 'but they can no longer carry their men forward'.[118]

Wednesday 14 October was a fine morning in Stalingrad. The Volga sparkled in the first rays of autumn sun while the silhouette of the ruined city towered above it. The peace was shattered almost immediately by the first Stuka raid of the day. Artilleryman Heinrich Schlapp watched as many as 60 dive-bombers fall upon the tractor factory complex 'in constant waves', the sirens on their undercarriage howling seemingly endlessly. Cameraman Benno Wundshammer, who recorded the attack by the Immelmann squadron from the rear seat of a Stuka, 'pulled away under the huge smoky umbrella of burning oil tanks'. He had time to observe 'white mushroom clouds caused by our heavy bombs'. Udo von Alvensleben felt he was staring at a painting of some historic siege, accompanied by 'clouds of smoke, flames and a hellish noise'. 24th Panzer Division's Ferdinand Kusterer watched 'the howling Stukas' unleash their bombs amid the factory ruins three, four or five times in the face of furious Russian flak. 'At the same time, the artillery also raised its voice until the pillars of smoke merged together over the city to form one massive cloud.' Hermann Henkes, a junior officer in 578th Infantry Regiment, described the bombardment as 'an incomparable orgy of fire': 'Dive bombers, fighters and bombers are gyrating overhead and with the ear-splitting shrieks of their sirens pounce upon the enemy from under the shifting clouds. Bursts of smoke shells harass the enemy and explosive shells are bursting with incredible violence.'

Among those on the receiving end was Pavel Strishchenko's battalion, whose positions were hammered from before dawn until past dusk. 'The earth shook from the explosion of bombs and artillery shells,' he recalled. 'A continuous roar drowned out the sounds of human voices. In the shelters, dugouts and trenches there was such a vibration that it rocked from side to side, like on the sea in stormy weather. Many people were bleeding from the ears and nose. It was hard to believe that someone could survive in this hell.' By the day's end, Strishchenko's battalion numbered just 29 men.

'The earth shook as never before in a battle,' a gun commander in 95th Rifle Division remembered. 'Clouds of smoke and dust hid the heavens and took our breath away.' The bombardment reduced the battery to just a handful of men, gunners were buried alive or else rendered temporarily deaf, but it continued to fight. 'Everything burned, everything was covered by earth, equipment and men were wiped out, but we kept on shooting.' Thus began Sixth Army's offensive 'for the total occupation of Stalingrad'.

The first assault against the industrial quarter had almost been a half-hearted affair: the men fought bravely, but the attacks themselves were piecemeal, unco-ordinated. Sixth Army had only gnawed at the sprawling expanse of railyards, factories, workshops, assembly halls, furnaces, power stations, fuel tanks, plus numerous tenement blocks for the workers. It had made *some* progress. But the attacks left the infantry 'all but exhausted' and the panzers unable to make headway because they lacked troops to secure any ground captured. Having observed the battles, liaison officer Hubert Menzel concluded Stalingrad would have to be taken house by house. 'We have to accept it will take a considerable amount of time,' he warned Hitler's headquarters.

The Führer was not listening. He wanted the attack carried forward as quickly as possible, the city of Stalin in his hands sooner rather than later. When Paulus pleaded for time to regroup, re-build and refresh Sixth Army – of his 15 divisions, none was capable of staging an all-out attack while six were better suited to defence – Hitler overruled him. The only concession the general wrung out of his leader was time: an extra week. It availed him little. As Sixth Army prepared to unleash its 'final' attack on Stalingrad, one in five of its 100 infantry battalions was '*abgekämpft*' – worn out.

When the barrage lifted this Wednesday morning, four German divisions moved out to crush Sixty-Second Army. They had orders to reach the Volga by midnight on Thursday. The pulver smoke was so dense that the men could barely breathe as the attacking waves left their jump-off positions. The sun appeared only intermittently – a grey-brown speck mostly hidden behind dense cloud. 24th Panzer Division headed towards the Barrikady factory, guns thundering. The Russians fell back initially, then stood firm. Petr Popov and his 95th Rifle Division comrades occupied the ruins of a building on the western side of the Barrikady complex. Amidst the tumult of battle Popov heard the shrill blast of a whistle – the signal to attack. The men left the relative safety of their rubble and followed their commander, who yelled: 'For the Motherland! For Stalin! Urra!' and charged forward, never to be seen again in a mist of brick dust and gunsmoke. His company drew grenades and hurled them towards the German attackers with cries of 'Urra!' The German onslaught was blunted, the enemy fell back, but it had reduced Popov's company to the size of a platoon.

Friedrich Paulus flitted around the front all day long trying to follow the assault, moving from command to observation posts, receiving snippets on progress by telephone or radio from the officers driving the attack forward. It began promisingly, his troops 'gaining ground according to plan'. But by mid-day the reports coming in were disconcerting. First the armour of XIV Panzer Corps was unable to attack. Then 14th Panzer Division ran into 'particularly fierce enemy resistance' on the approaches to the tractor factory. By the time he reached the forward headquarters of 389th Infantry Division towards dusk, Paulus realised the day's objectives had only been 'partially achieved'.

Having struggled to make ground – even with the support of assault guns – Hermann Henkes' battalion halted its advance before nightfall as the smoke, fire and mist over Stalingrad reduced visibility to zero. The night, Henkes wrote, was 'terrible'. The Soviet air force had abandoned the skies over Stalingrad during the day, but after dark 'an endless string' of bombers attacked the children's home which served as his battalion's temporary quarters, shaking with each impact. 'Sometimes we cast an anxious glance at the ceiling,' he wrote. 'Even a near hit by one those bombs would mean we had come to the end of our tether.'

And amid the carnage around the Dzerzhinsky tractor factory, Heinrich Schlapp wandered up to a statue to its namesake at the entrance where flowers still grew. He picked a small bunch and sent them home in a letter.[119]

Disappointing though the first day of the offensive had been for Paulus, the attack rattled Vasily Chuikov, who had observed the initial barrage from near his command post. He later described 14 October as the 'most critical day' of the entire battle. The howling of aircraft engines and constant detonation of bombs and artillery rounds drowned out any conversation. The bombardment disrupted communications for the rest of the day, while the German attacks succeeded in splitting his army and inflicted at least 3,500 serious casualties, men who were transported to the far shore of the Volga that night.[120] The second day of the enemy's offensive was just as brutal, just as relentless, as the terse entries in the war diary of Chuikov's army reveal:

5.30am	Like yesterday, the enemy has begun a reinforced artillery bombardment.
8am	The enemy is attacking with tanks and infantry. Fighting rages along the entire front.
9.30am	The enemy's attack on the tractor factory has been thwarted. Ten Fascist tanks are burning in the assembly hall.
10am	Tanks and infantry have overrun 19th Guards Rifle Regiment (37th [Guards] Rifle Division).
11.30am	The left wing of 524th Rifle Regiment (95th Rifle Division) has been overrun. Around 50 tanks rolled over the regiment's combat units.
11.50am	The enemy has taken the sports field at the tractor works. Our cut-off, encircled units continue to fight.
12 noon	The commander of 117th Rifle Regiment, Major Andreyev, has been killed.
12.20pm	A radio message from one of 416th Regiment's units in the hexagonal-shaped apartment block. 'We're surrounded. We've got water and ammunition. We'll die before we give ourselves up!'
12.30pm	Stukas attack the command post of General Zholudev [37th Guards Rifle Division]. General Zholudev finds himself in a collapsed bunker without communications.
1.20pm	Using a barrel, we've pumped air into General Zholudev's command post.
2.40pm	Telephone communications with the troops are cut off, we've switched to the radio, confirming orders by sending liaison officers.

4pm	Communications with 114th Guards Regiment are broken, its situation is unknown.
4.20pm	Around 100 tanks have broken into the area around the tractor factory. The enemy's air force, as ever, is overhead and attacking us with bombs dropped at low altitude.
4.35pm	Regimental commander Lieutenant Colonel Ustinov asks artillery to shoot at his command post as he's surrounded by troops with machine-pistols.
5pm	The radio operator can barely record the radio messages from units who are encircled and continue to fight.
9pm	One more radio message from 37th Guards Division. It's still fighting.[121]

The fighting of mid-October was about as close as Stalingrad's attackers came to victory, its defenders to defeat, as Vasily Chuikov's forces splintered. Sixty-Second Army's commander would subsequently play down just how bleak his position was, convinced he had weathered the storm. Front commander Andrei Eremenko was sufficiently concerned, particularly after the tractor works fell into German hands and 37th Guards Rifle Division was all but wiped out, to cross the Volga and head straight for Chuikov's headquarters near the Barrikady works to demand answers. Eremenko was all for tearing a strip off the Guards Division's Viktor Zholudev, but the pathetic impression the 37-year-old general made mollified him. 'Commander, the division performed its mission honourably without retreating an inch – most of the soldiers and officers perished,' Zholudev reported. 'Everyone held his position.'

Andrei Eremenko nodded. '*Da*, war is merciless and the enemy cruel.'[122]

In Moscow, David Ortenberg, editor of the Red Army's newspaper *Krasnaya Zvezda (Red Star)*, also sought an explanation for the loss of the tractor plant. It flew in the face of official pronouncements, rhetoric and, not least, Stalin's 'not one step back' order. Ortenberg turned to the Chief of the General Staff, Aleksander Vasilevsky, for an explanation. 'The Germans have a tremendous numerical superiority,' Vasilevsky told him. 'They are taking heavy casualties to finish the operation in the next few days. Our men are fighting day and night, selflessly, but we don't have enough strength yet. In some battalions there are only a few dozen men left.' Ortenberg returned to his compositing board, changed a headline and cranked up the rhetoric, adding a new closing paragraph to the daily report from the city: 'Now comes the decisive battle for Stalingrad. We must defend the city with all means. Demonstrate greater persistence, tenacity, and the ability to manoeuvre – and the enemy's new furious attacks will be repulsed.'[123]

In Germany, the relative success of the assault on the industrial quarter prompted renewed interest in Stalingrad. Goebbels urged caution, ordering editors not to elaborate on the terse official communiqués. The city's capture may still 'take a few days'. But in Munich – still reeling from its first heavy air raid of the war, which left more than 400 dead – the Propaganda Minister told the crowd packed into Odeonsplatz that during the summer and autumn campaign 'the right arm of the Bolshevik armed forces has been cut off' and underlined the words of Hitler a few weeks earlier: 'Today we hold what the enemy has lost.' Growing numbers of Germans were not so certain. They were beginning to appreciate 'the extraordinary reserves and great strength of the Soviet Union'. Most Germans did not question victory – particularly after Hitler's and Göring's recent bombastic speeches – but they did not expect it imminently. Stalingrad had 'turned into a second Verdun' and 'shattered illusions about the Soviet Union'. The German people were growing tired of war. All wanted it to end, though few dared to predict when it might. Most now feared 'a very long, costly and bitter struggle'.[124]

They were certainly not ready for the unvarnished truth of the fighting in Stalingrad. They saw pictures of the devastation in Stalingrad, of bombs throwing up great fountains of earth and steel in the factory district, of soldiers moving through desolate streets and *Landsers* eating from their mess tins during a pause in the fighting – invariably published without any context – in the daily papers. Photographic essays were reserved for the illustrated newspapers and glossy magazines – the road to Stalingrad, the fighting outside the city, the struggle for the tractor works.[125] Benno Wundshammer, one of the Reich's most experienced photojournalists, spent more than a month at the front with a Stuka squadron, taking part in 16 sorties over Stalingrad, capturing some of the iconic images of the battle in the process. They would go on to grace the front page and innards of the Nazi's flagship bimonthly picture magazine, *Signal* – the Nazi counterpart to the US best-selling *Life* – as well as countless books on the battle to this day. Accompanying the pictures was Wundshammer's account of the aerial battle, 'Stukas over Stalingrad', which opened with a vivid account of a dusk raid against the city. After an uneventful flight over the Don and the Volga steppe, the formation of Junkers Ju87s – constantly climbing and descending, banking and twisting – followed the Volga upstream until Stalingrad appeared, 'deadly buds of black flak' already exploding over the city as the anti-aircraft batteries on the island which split the river in two opened fire. When the Stukas arrived over the heart of Stalingrad, white specks began to pepper the dark black clouds floating above the city as light flak joined in the barrage. As the formation of dive-bombers passed through the columns of smoke rising above the ruins of a swirling abyss, Wundshammer's pilot spoke briefly over the radio: 'Let's go.' He pushed his stick forward and the aircraft began to head towards the ground.

> Then this awful howling hurricane begins, whining and hissing, growing louder by the second. It drowns out any other sound, all other sensations: the sirens are triggered. I hold on tightly.
>
> The dive seems almost easy. At first you feel like you're floating like a lost balloon, trying to hold on to space. But the body soon gets used to the accelerated plunge. I turn towards the earth to locate the target. The blocks of houses seem to fly towards us. The force of the dive blurs the contours, until I can only see sparks in the middle of a yellowish, shapeless mass. A sudden burst of speed makes me look at the aircraft. Then, in the sky, above my head, I see comrades diving from the clouds and attacking – like flowers pouring out of a basket. It's the devil's dive. A nightmare vision, buildings with a thousand windows pass between the fires! Mushrooms of smoke where the giant ferns of our bombs grow, flora of the Apocalypse. We are carried away by the furious momentum of the aircraft.
>
> The commander follows the attack of his squadron. At the places where the bombs are dropped, fires appear like magic. A bluish-white flame dazzles us, an arc lamp or magnesium. It all flashes, flickers and glows in every direction. Devilish tongues of fire of annihilation.

By the time the Stukas had finished their attack, night had fallen and Stalingrad was a blazing torch in the darkness.

The novelty and exhilaration would quickly wear off. After a month in Stalingrad, Benno Wundshammer was writing of a 'monotonous battle', of raids on the city 'morning, noon and night', of dive after dive by the Stukas, their sirens howling, the puffs of cloud of exploding flak, targets torn apart by fire and explosions – perhaps a bunker complex, or the fish canning factory, a silo, maybe a railway goods yard with its twisted, mangled chaos of wagons – those carrying fuel emitted black smoke, other cargoes white – of streets ploughed by the Junkers' cannons, above all of the German soldier struggling to prevail against a fanatical enemy:

> Every stone is a bunker. Every house a fortress. Should the bombs destroy it, its ruins will be occupied again that night. Metre by metre, the infantry move into Stalingrad. 'They don't want to abandon their foxholes. We have to force them out using guns, grenades, even shovels.' And that's what we do, always advancing. Day after day. One battle after another.[126]

Otherwise, written accounts of the battle played second fiddle to the visual in Germany. Most were little more than a re-hash – or even carbon copy – of the official communiqué from Hitler's headquarters, or a news agency report, perhaps accompanied by an 'explanation' provided by a military commentator. First-hand accounts provided by *Propaganda Kompanie* correspondents were invariably formulaic and held up by the censor by two to three weeks. They added a little colour to the terse official communiqués, but rarely scratched the surface of the battle. Readers learned of fighting 'from cellar to cellar', of grenades tossed through strongpoint embrasures to eliminate dogged Soviet troops, of defenders encouraged – or threatened – to fight to the last round and man by commissars, and plucky German non-commissioned officers whose spontaneous acts of bravery carried the day.[127] There was the occasional writer or war correspondent embedded with Sixth Army, such as Clemens Podewils, but they spent more time in the rear with staffs than at the front with the men. No-one spoke for the ordinary *Landser*. After hearing a radio account of the fighting in the city in mid-October, one furious German soldier recorded: 'What rubbish! He needs to visit the city and "stick it out in the bunkers where there's an heroic mood". Scumbag. It's a good thing not all my comrades heard this drivel!'[128]

On the other side of the front line, some of the USSR's finest writers and correspondents reported the battle for the Soviet press, men such as poet and author Konstantin Simonov, his *Krasnaya Zvezda* colleague Vasily Grossman, or *Pravda*'s Peter Lidov. But there were also many second-string writers in Stalingrad. 'The standard is much lower than on our Western Front – you can feel the provincial bohemia,' observed Lidov, who had narrowly escaped the fall of Minsk during the first days of the war, then covered the Red Army's defeats to the outskirts of Moscow. Too many correspondents were content to hang around Eremenko's headquarters on the east bank of the Volga where they embellished official reports or, worse, simply made up stories – without risking crossing the river. 'None of us has the right to write about the Battle of Stalingrad unless he has been to the city himself,' Grossman scolded them. 'There is no moral right to talk about battles that you have not seen.'[129]

Moscow, of course, wanted stories of Soviet socialist glory, of peasants killing one hundred Fascists single-handedly while pledging to die for the Motherland and Stalin. Twenty-year-old Dusya Dmitrieva – nicknamed 'the little white girl' – fitted the bill of heroine perfectly. She volunteered as a nurse serving with the fighting troops, accompanying ambulances as they rocked and rumbled over the battlefield. The Red Cross offered no protection; on one run Dmitrieva's vehicle was peppered by 22 bullets. She was also pressed into service as a spy, sent to infiltrate German-occupied districts to report on enemy dispositions. Her luck ran out on her 14th mission. Returning to Soviet lines with her friend Nadya Shurina, the pair stumbled into a minefield. Dusya lost both her legs and a hand; her friend was also badly injured. Dusya managed to crawl to her friend Nadya. Before dying in her arms she supposedly said: 'Tell my mother, friends and comrades that I am dying for my motherland, for Stalin, for Stalingrad.' Dusya Dmitrieva was posthumously awarded the Order of Lenin.[130] When Peter Lidov's editor demanded a flag-waving article based on a few terse lines in the official military communiqué about the victorious battle for a hill, Lidov laconically reported: 'Our troops occupied a hill with more than 100 German and Soviet tanks, damaged, burnt or blown up by mines. Recovering them was impossible. The hill passed back into German hands before the communiqué was published.' Such instructions were typical of what the chroniclers of the Battle of Stalingrad were expected to produce, 'serving the reader desserts when he actually asks for some cabbage soup,' the frustrated Lidov observed. 'How I long to prepare, as I did last winter, a good soup, tasty and full of information!'[131]

For all the column inches filling newspapers around the world, for all the bombast of dictators and their propaganda machines, the dramatic panoramas of Armageddon on weekly newsreels, by mid-October Stalingrad had been reduced to a great battle fought on a small scale: contests for individual buildings, factory halls – or more typically parts thereof – between clusters of soldiers on both sides. 'The metre replaced the kilometre as a measurement, the A-to-Z took the place of the general staff map,' staff officer Hans Doerr observed. 'There were no distances, just "near".' The impetus may have rested with the Germans, but it was the Soviets who imposed their will on the battle to wear down the attacker, mentally and physically. 'Every German must feel as if he's living under the barrel of a Russian rifle,' Chuikov instructed. He knew that 'the Germans did not like, or rather were no good at, close fighting. Their morale would not stand it; they did not have the spirit to look an armed Soviet soldier in the eyes.' Special methods demanded special soldiers. In late September new assault groups – each slightly larger than a platoon – began to be assigned to Chuikov's regiments, 'small, but hard-hitting and mobile'. Equipped with flamethrowers – American-made flamethrowers had a greater range than their German counterparts, sending jets of flames more than 60 feet long into cellars, bunkers and rooms – explosive charges, grenades, bayonets and daggers when needed, the groups 'literally clung to buildings and the earth, waiting until the enemy was within grenade-throwing range'. Also deployed in substantial numbers – 400 marksmen at the peak of battle – in Chuikov's divisions were snipers. 'Anyone who raised their head had to expect a sniper straight away,' Walter Loos recalled. Gerhard Münch found their methods 'inwardly revolting', akin to hunting deer and 'nothing to do with soldiership'. But they were effective, taking a mental and physical toll of Sixth Army, claiming more than 6,000 German lives by mid-November. Eighteen-year-old Hubert Kremser was observing the battlefield next to a comrade with whom he'd gone through all the travails and hardships of Stalingrad. 'He dared to appear a little too high above the breastwork and received a shot to the head. Dead straight away. For me it was an utterly demoralising experience.' The Germans attempted to counter the sharpshooter danger – although the duel between Sixty-Second Army's most famous sniper, Vasily Zaitsev, and one Major König is a creation of Soviet propaganda. 'A lieutenant was flown in, a sniper, who had a rifle with a long-range barrel,' *Landser* Vincenz Griesemer remembered. 'Our senior sergeant briefed him on where the Russian snipers were roughly located. But if he wanted to shoot them, he had to look up himself first. He didn't get a single shot away before he was killed.'[132]

And Vasily Chuikov was right. The German soldier did not like fighting at close-quarters. 'The enemy is invisible,' XI Corps commander Karl Strecker complained. 'Attacks from cellars, from behind the remains of walls, hidden bunkers and the ruins of factories inflict heavy losses on our men.' Junior officer Gerhard Dengler found Stalingrad was 'something new to all of us because the Russians did not give way, but fought in houses from one floor to the next, from one *room* to the next'.[133] The doggedness of the defenders defied belief, if not description. 'We have fought for 15 days for a single house, with mortars, machine-guns, grenades and bayonets,' a junior officer in 24th Panzer Division wrote.

> Already by the third day, 54 German corpses were strewn in the cellars, on the landings and staircases. The front is a corridor between burnt-out rooms. It is the thin ceiling between floors. Help comes from neighbouring houses by fire escapes and chimneys. There is a ceaseless struggle from morning until night. From storey to storey, faces black with sweat, we bombard each other with grenades, in the middle of explosions, amid clouds of dust and smoke, heaps of mortar, floods of blood, fragments of furniture and human beings. Ask any soldier what half an hour of hand-to-hand struggle means in such a fight. And at Stalingrad it has been 80 days and nights of hand-to-hand struggle. The street is no longer measured in metres, but in corpses. Stalingrad is no longer a city. By day it is an enormous cloud of burning, blinding smoke. And when night arrives, one of those scorching, howling, bleeding nights, the dogs plunge into the Volga and swim desperately to gain the other bank. The nights of Stalingrad are a terror for them. Animals flee this hell, the hardest stones cannot bear it for long. Only man endures.[134]

The grenade became the weapon of choice but 'once you'd thrown the four hand grenades you kept on your belt, there wasn't much left,' one soldier lamented. 'Sometimes we then threw stones or beat each other with spades.'[135] Nights were the worst. 'There's no such thing as front line, front, rear, flanks,' Aleksandr Rodimtsev wrote. 'The enemy might be anywhere: the floor above, the floor below, all around.' The fighting was primeval. Men relied less on training, skill and experience than their senses. Rodimtsev continued:

> Rustling? Someone's breath in the pitch blackness? Who's there? Friend? Foe? How do I know? Shout? What if a machine-gun fires back? Should I shoot? Or maybe it's the enemy? What's underfoot? Sliding shards of glass? Broken chairs? Ropes? Wires? A dead body? Or maybe a lurking enemy? Decide quickly! Perhaps a tenth of a second separates you from the silent throw of someone else's grenade or a blow from a knife.[136]

There were occasions when pragmatic realities trumped fanaticism. After his daring lunge to the Volga in mid-September, Gerhard Münch found his battalion sucked into the bitter struggle for buildings in the government quarter. The small groups of opposing Germans and Russians fighting in the blocks soon reached an accommodation. 'When the Russians ate, we couldn't disturb them – it would immediately become uncomfortable for us if we did that.' As soon as Münch's men heard the clatter of pots and pans, fighting ceased. 'And when we ate, they had to stop fighting too.'[137]

Rest – a couple of days in the rear – was rare, and precious. The men washed, shaved, had their hair cut, cleaned their weapons, restocked ammunition. Officers filed combat reports, wrote letters to the families of men lost under their command. Uniforms were cleaned, sewn, fixed, boots repaired, underwear changed. Mail was handed out. Perhaps there was time to scribble a few lines home in return. There were even wedding ceremonies. Alfons Metzger was asked to officiate at a *Ferntrauung* – marriage by proxy – of a doctor in his unit. His men decorated one of Stalingrad's ruined squares, the regimental band fell in, and pyramids of rifles straddled a table covered with the German ensign. Metzger gave a short address then read out the wedding script before inviting the groom to sign a form, while the band performed the bridal chorus from *Lohengrin*. It was, Metzger wrote to his fiancée, 'a wonderful experience'.[138]

Posted to 79th Infantry Division, 23-year-old Alfons Metzger had arrived in Stalingrad in late October. 'The fierceness of the battle that raged here speaks from every metre of earth,' he observed in his diary.

The impressions of destruction are shocking: stumbling through an endless cratered landscape, jumping from one pile of rubble to the next, you suddenly see a wide strip running in a straight line through the rubble, and almost with horror you realise that you are standing on the former main road, you realise that the splintered wooden stumps were once trees in whose shade people walked in front of shop windows, you realise that over there, on the hidden tracks, the tram was still sounding its bell just weeks ago. Now only piles of stones remain.[139]

Metzger was spared the horrors of hand-to-hand combat at the front – and felt all the more guilty for it. He spent most days in a command post, slept in a caravan, ate regularly, could wash and shave daily, while his men 'lived among rubble, craters and dead bodies, unwashed for weeks, always fighting for their lives, threatened every moment by treacherous steel, by tumbling concrete, by lurking death'. Metzger was appalled when he encountered them after a few days in the line: a once-proud unit whose ranks were now filled with apathetic men, their faces sullen, their hands and faces filthy, their hair unkempt, 'men who have seen hell and have forgotten how to talk'.[140]

Behind the line – if there was such a thing in Stalingrad – war correspondent Herbert Rauchhaupt found 'entire divisions living underground': in cellars and basements, former Soviet trenches and bunkers, reinforced with all manner of beams, planks and boards salvaged from the ruins of the city, while men not in the line kept warm burning splintered pieces of wood in stoves.[141] Croatian Legion supply officer Dragan Jurak was impressed by how his compatriots adapted to such primeval conditions. The unit's artillery established their command post in a cemetery north of Mamayev Kurgan, exhuming the dead to create space for the living in a subterranean world. When they could, troops raided homes for anything which might still be of use not merely to survive, but even to feel at home in these shelters. 'They covered the walls with planks, papers, paintings,' Jurak noted, 'fitted windows – from the ruins of houses, naturally – and even decorated them with flowers. And they feel comfortable inside.' Comfortable perhaps, but safe, never. 'Constant thunder shakes the earth, as if you're standing on the crater of some volcano,' Jurak continued. 'Every minute we are greeted by a shell or bomb, or we are showered with shells with a loud clap of thunder and the ground shakes. Pieces of wood, human flesh and the legs of horses fly through the air.' And so the cemetery continued to grow. While Soviet dead were left unburied, 'neat, freshly-dug mounds with some flowers and beautifully-crafted crosses, with Croatian coats of arms' marked the final resting place of 'warriors for global civilisation who were born on the shores of the blue Adriatic, the karst of Bosnia, the flat lands of Slavonia or cultivated Zagorje'.[142]

Typically, men were buried where they fell – at least in the short term. The slopes of Mamayev Kurgan were covered in corpses – in places two or three deep. If there was time – and the bodies had not decomposed too badly – the dead were carried to large shell craters, which now became makeshift mass graves. The Soviets buried their dead with full honours at night where the fighting allowed. Graves were dug, markers placed, if there was time a eulogy and volley in salute. The grimmest task was re-burial, when the battle moved on, and comrades buried days or even weeks earlier were exhumed for reinterment in a communal cemetery. 'We get tobacco and wine as extras, but I would rather dig up rocks in a quarry,' one soldier assigned the task wrote. 'I would never have believed that I'd have to carry out such work in my life – we do it because orders are orders.'[143]

Landser or *frontovik*, there was only so much and so long man could endure Stalingrad. In a rare act of compassion, battalion commander Erwin Jetzl ordered his medics to treat a gravely wounded Soviet soldier, shot in the lung and coughing up blood. The casualty was carried on a sheet of tarpaulin to the battalion's makeshift first-aid post, dug out of the clay earth. That is where Jetzl found the wounded *frontovik* a few hours later as he conducted his rounds. He chided the doctor on duty for failing to treat the Russian. 'The doctor looked at me in astonishment and then – he was wearing heavy Red Army boots – he jumped up and landed with both feet on the Russian's chest.' Jetzl was furious: 'Have you gone mad?' And perhaps he had – for the doctor stood his ground and, unrepentant, screamed back: '*Herr Hauptmann*, I am not treating an animal. That Russian, that's an animal, not a human being.' Albert Burkovskiy watched naval infantry storm a hill, accompanied by cries of 'Urra', only to be cut down by German machine-guns. The bodies were piled three deep on the slope. Burkovskiy's unit was then ordered up the same hill. 'I noticed that my feet had got stuck in the ground,' he recalled. 'I pulled my leg out and then realised that I was standing in the middle of a corpse.'[144] As the battle dragged on, Sergeant Grigori Nikolski found it increasingly difficult to summon the physical and mental strength to lead his squad in a counter-attack:

It is not easy to be the first to jump up with an enthusiastic 'Forward!' when you actually only have the desire – the only natural desire under the given circumstances – to dig in, to crawl as deep as possible into the earth. All around the roar of explosions, a hissing, howling inferno, and death greedily and with a murderous look searches for you, perhaps it wants to see you die slowly, in pain. Your comrades still press themselves close to the warming earth, and there they will remain lying, for a few seconds or… for eternity!

At that moment you stand all alone and have the feeling that all these shells and mines, all this shrapnel and bullets are for you, just you. After all, there is no-one else they could hit.[145]

The battle was, Heinrich Leonard Linssen, a priest serving in one of Sixth Army's field hospitals, told a friend, 'more terrible than the world has ever seen before… What our eyes are forced to see, what our hands do, what our nerves must bear cannot possibly be described – it ages everyone here by 20 years!' Nikolai Aksyonov, second-in-command of a Soviet rifle regiment, reckoned one month in the line at Stalingrad was equivalent to one year of the rest of his life. That was if you survived. After five days in the line the companies of 79th Guards Rifle Division counted no more than two dozen men. 'The fighting strength of the units melted like butter in the sun,' a soldier in 14th Panzer Division complained. Only five weeks after the visit of their leader, the Croatian Legion had been reduced to just 191 men fit for action. Beyond the dead and wounded, dysentery was endemic and the legion's effectiveness was undermined by talk of its imminent transfer to Germany to rest and regroup such that the men's 'thoughts were already more there than on the Volga'. Non-commissioned officer Walter Loos no longer recognised the men in his platoon – 'all of them strangers, from different units which had been wiped out. We never knew our comrades' names, where they came from, with whom they went to their deaths together.' Nor did he have time to get to know them. Ten were killed when a heavy mortar shell landed while they enjoyed a cigarette break in a shell crater. Erwin Jetzl reckoned his 'battle-weary' 113th Infantry Division only remained in the line thanks to Red Army deserters and former prisoners employed as 'volunteers' or *Hiwis* – he valued men from Turkmenistan, who'd defected on the Don during the summer, particularly highly. At first they had performed duties behind the lines: cooks, drivers, horse grooms. But increasingly, they were beginning to serve at the front, filling junior positions in Jetzl's mortar platoon. 'Only the commanders were still German,' he remembered. 'Everyone else was a *Hiwi*. We would hardly have been able to operate without them.'[146] With or without *Hiwis*, Sixth Army was bleeding to death. By mid-October, it had lost more than 40,000 men since crossing the Don. No division was able to commit more than 6,000 troops in the front line; the weakest were down to little more than 2,700 men able to bear arms. 295th Infantry Division was no longer an effective fighting formation. A new regiment was being sent into the line so the division could join in when the offensive resumed. 'Our infantry has shrunk so much that they can no longer attack,' Dr Kurt Wallischeck recorded. 'Our graveyard in front of the house is growing by the day. There are already around 250 graves. A Knight's Cross holder is also buried there.'[147]

Even the most optimistic soldier could count the days he had left. 'You can call Stalingrad "hell",' one experienced German corporal wrote in early November. 'Several days ago the company went into position and today many of them have already been killed. Our boss, a 23-year-old lieutenant, a very good man, had barely arrived in Russia and today he's already dead. If only it was over here.' More than one *Landser* entrusted his fate – for good or ill – to God. 'The meaning of life is not to live as long as possible, but as worthwhile as possible,' theology student Christian Krause wrote. 'War, like any danger, awakens prized forces. Forces of love – being prepared to lay down one's life for the other – of sacrificing comforts, of the belief that we are safe in the hands of the Father, of the hope that life is only truly worthwhile after death.' A soldier in 113th Infantry Division wrote: 'One must not lose courage and trust in God, even if the machine-guns still rattle and the bombs and shells crash. If Fate has decided that I should not get out of this witches' cauldron, then it is simply God's will.' Matthias Barth, serving with the Croatian Legion, told a friend: 'Be glad and happy that you have nothing to do with such things. So far I must thank my Lord God that he has led me through all the dangers in one piece. Lord, give us the peace we long for!' Priest Heinrich Leonard Linssen led Holy Communion for men in an enormous shell crater in the shadow of the ruins of a large building. 'It was already dark and everyone knelt in the dirt and clasped their hands like children! All that is in the men's hearts surged up towards the Lord! And a squadron of heavy enemy bombers roared over us.'[148]

The unsanitary conditions ensured disease was rife. Soviet soldiers were plagued by diarrhoea caused by poor diet and unclean water – the men either failed to boil it, or drew it from the Volga, polluted with oil, wood, corpses and cadavers. In command posts jaundice was rife. 'It is the fashionable illness in the staffs,' Helmut Welz observed, 'a creeping ghost or a rescuing angel, terror or a way out, depending on the attitude of the man affected. Jaundice in the command staffs is like a hero's death among the troops: it thins the ranks.' It was a 'ticket home' – sufferers simply did not recover in Russia. 'A replacement fills the post after a short course,' Welz continued. 'A faulty assessment of the situation – with the corresponding orders – and we must pay for it again.'[149]

Men in Erwin Jaenecke's 389th Infantry Division began 'collapsing without an obvious cause – and dying within an hour'. Jaenecke was convinced an epidemic was sweeping through his ranks until the division's doctors reported the findings of their autopsies: malnutrition and exhaustion. For the first time men who were exhausted, not wounded, arrived at 76th Infantry Division's main first-aid post, 'men who'd turned to skeletons, who simply fell down, who by our concepts at the time had nothing wrong with them,' the division's senior doctor reported. 'We simply put them in a tent, let them sleep and if they could run again after three days, were sent back to the front, because every rifle was needed there.' Poor diet – frequently cold horse-meat soup – struck down men already weakened by constant itching from the lice infestations in front-line trenches and among the rubble.[150] There were even suggestions that the Russians had resorted to the methods of a medieval siege, releasing infested vermin into the occupied parts of the city; quick-witted *Landsers* dealt with the plague by soaking them with gasoline and chlorinated lime, but elsewhere the pestilent rats rendered bunkers uninhabitable.[151]

On both sides of the line, first-aid posts were established below ground, in the basements of ruined buildings, or clawed out of the soil in the high right bank of the Volga. Conditions were barely sanitary. Earth crumbled off the walls or ceilings with each shell impact. Light was provided by makeshift lamps – shells filled with petrol which Soviet troops dubbed 'Stalingradka'. The air was thick, the galleries overcrowded. There were frequently insufficient bandages or medicines. Surgeons, nurses, medics, stretcher bearers, ambulance drivers – all were expected to give blood once a week, perhaps even every three or four days, to guarantee transfusions for casualties. At the height of the battle in mid-October, surgeons and surgical nurses in the rudimentary operating theatres worked 20-hour days. Even on a 'quiet' day of battle, such as 1 October, 295th Infantry Division surgeon Kurt Wallischeck and his colleagues could expect to treat upwards of 150 casualties. The first wounded arrived at his first-aid post around 5am that Thursday, but it was another three hours before there was a steady flow of trucks and ambulances delivering fresh casualties. 'The poor guys lie next to each other like herrings, dusty and dirty faces,' he wrote. 'Some of them groan gently, you want to help all of them first, but that won't work. Peter operates in a smaller room.' There were men with stomach wounds, men with makeshift tourniquets on leg wounds, a flak officer wounded in the eye – it was beyond saving – and a pale young sergeant bled white. 'His right upper arm is completely torn apart, the forearm stuck in the torn sleeve lies lifelessly beside it, as if it no longer belonged to the body,' Wallischeck noted. 'One glance is enough to see that the arm is lost.' By mid-day, Wallischeck reckoned his team had treated 100 casualties – and there were still another 40 men waiting to be seen. Two dead were also delivered – another 17 were at the front, but their corpses could only be recovered after nightfall. 'My last activity after this hot day before I return to the ravine is to give the Iron Cross and the silver wounded badge to the man whose right arm was amputated,' Wallischeck continued in his diary. 'Then I drive home. I am tired and exhausted, not so much from the physical work as from the impressions, the misery, the stench of sweat and blood.'[152]

The lightly wounded would be returned to their units, serious casualties shipped across the Volga in the case of the Red Army, while the Germans evacuated theirs by Junkers Ju52 transporter from Gumrak airfield, ten miles west of the city centre. Despite the constant arrival and departure of the transporters, many wounded spent several days at the adjacent overcrowded field hospital. 'Gumrak presented a scene of horror,' remembered artilleryman Josef Goblirsch, who awaited being flown back to Germany after being struck by shrapnel in his abdomen. 'Mountains of amputated limbs – all covered with tonnes of chlorinated lime; rats attacking wounded who had been operated on; overworked surgeons.' Those not requiring immediate evacuation filled the corridors, sedated only with morphine. Goblirsch was given an anti-bacterial drug and the occasional cup of tea. 'I had become so apathetic that I could no longer take everything in properly.' Ferdinand Kusterer was sent to the field hospital at Karpovka, about 25 miles outside Stalingrad, suffering from jaundice, waiting for transport west. The hospital was badly overcrowded, the misery in its corridors and rooms – they were not worthy of the word 'ward' – 'indescribable'. Men lay side by side on beds of straw, teeming with flies which crawled over their emaciated bodies and sallow, bearded faces. The staff were overwhelmed. 'A panzer driver with severe burns was so heavily bandaged that only his mouth remained free; the man next to him had lost both his eyes, another had a stomach wound, a man with one leg already in plaster was taken to the operating theatre moaning: "I'm going to die, I'm going to die!"' Prisoners of war carried out the dead and laid them to rest in the adjacent cemetery, where fellow captives were constantly digging fresh graves.[153]

To regimental commander Richard Wolf, the fighting for the industrial district was the apogee of the hell of Stalingrad. 'The heavy artillery fire, the Stukas and ground-attack aircraft constantly dropping bombs, salvoes from the *Werfer* batteries surpassed everything experienced in the fighting there hitherto,' he recalled. The heaviest shells 'turned the urban landscape into a lunar one', while the ruins of tenement blocks, houses and factory halls 'turned a walk through the terrain into a lengthy game of climbing, where death in the form of a bullet from a sniper hidden somewhere still lay in wait'. There was shooting, flashing and crashing around every corner – though it was impossible to tell who was shooting or what they were shooting at. The foolhardy decision was taken to commit 14th Panzer Division. The panzers were shaken or torn apart by mines, or else 'clambered over mountains of rubble and tangled metal, crept with a squeal through the chaotic, wrecked factory halls and fired at point-blank range into the rubble-strewn streets and confined factory courtyards,' one of the division's soldiers reported. In the spasmodic breaks in the fire, 'ghostly shadows scurried through the rubble and smoking ruins of houses. Russian civilians and our soldiers wandered around,' Wolf wrote. His men were, unsurprisingly, 'seized by terrible nervousness, provoked by a general feeling of uncertainty in this vast expanse of rubble and the horrible, cratered moonscape'. Wilhelm Traub, commanding a battalion of pioneers, was shocked that not every civilian had yet fled the city. 'They live in cellars, in sewage pipes and potter about, half-starving, pursuing their miserable existence,' he told his family. A few days earlier his men had come across a four-year-old girl, lying next to the corpse of her mother who'd been killed by shrapnel. 'There are many such shocking fates,' Traub wrote. 'But we have become insensitive to them and are no longer touched by events.' The soldiers inhabited the same hell. They lived in the cellars, basements and sewers of the workshops and factory halls. Wilhelm Gütinger, a 23-year-old corporal, lived in a vaulted cellar beneath one of the wrecked halls in the Red October works. There was no natural light, just candles and oil lamps. 'Food is brought to us in the evening under the cover of darkness,' he wrote home. 'A canteen of tea or coffee then has to last until the next evening. There's probably water very close by in a shell crater but I cannot – and will not – drink it or use it to make tea.' The men did, however, wash in it and use it to clean their canteens. 'All of us hope it will soon end in this wasps' nest,' he concluded, though the enemy showed no sign of giving up. Indeed, each night Red Army soldiers emerged from the balkas 'like some elemental force', striking at the flank and rear of the Germans. 'What in the evening had been gained after fierce fighting was lost again by morning,' a soldier from 14th Panzer Division wrote in frustration. 'And then everything began afresh.'[154]

All but immovable in defence, the Red Army proved no more effective at gaining ground in the rubble of Stalingrad than its mortal foe. A counter-offensive by Sixty-Sixth Army north of the city in mid-October should, on paper, have yielded promising results, not least thanks to overwhelming numerical superiority. But the army's commander, Aleksei Zhadov, had been in post barely a week and by the second day had convinced himself that 'nothing would come of this offensive'. Rather than attempt to rectify any shortcomings before the attack was unleashed, however, the army commander merely poured scorn on the plans and scolded his commanders. Zhadov proved to be particularly prescient. His army advanced no more than a couple of kilometres, its attacking divisions having lost upwards of 5,000 men each. Zhadov and his superior Kuzma Trubnikov, deputy commander of the Don Front, laid the blame squarely with the ordinary *frontovik*. 'Our infantry is not worth a damn,' Trubnikov complained, while Zhadov protested he'd been given men who were 'completely unprepared, many of them do not know how to use a rifle'. The official investigation into the catastrophe, however, criticised not the rank and file, but their leaders. The ordinary soldier had fought bravely, doggedly. He had been let down by his commanders, men who did not know their mission, did not know the field of battle, did not brief their subordinates – or care, for that matter. At least one political officer shot himself in his left hand to avoid leading his men in battle, the chief-of-staff of one rifle division was sorely drunk while trying to lead the assault and was dismissed. The officer cadre of 62nd Rifle Division proved particularly inept from its commander, Sergei Frolov, down. Frolov only studied the battlefield in his sector from his map, established his headquarters a couple of miles behind the front, and failed to brief either his staff or his front-line commanders on the mission. Such an irresponsible attitude was pervasive. The commanders of 123rd Rifle Regiment failed to study the terrain, the troops became disorientated moving up the line, arrived in their jump-off positions late – in daylight – were sighted by the Germans and subjected to a heavy counter-barrage. Although units became confused and unsettled, they attacked all the same, but became entangled with another regiment. The nail in the coffin of the bungled attack was rumours of an enemy advance on the regiment's flank, which sparked panic. By the time order was restored, the 123rd had lost half its strength, the 62nd Rifles some 3,000 men for no gain.[155]

Within days, 62nd Rifle Division was broken up, its remaining troops assigned to other units, evidence of the ruthless streak which permeated the Red Army in the autumn of 1942. It took time, but through September and into October, the words of Stalin's 'not one step back' order crystalised into action at the front. More than 15 blocking detachments – which had largely served their purpose by mid-October – succeeded in intercepting nearly 52,000 soldiers behind the lines of the Stalingrad and neighbouring Don Fronts. All but 4,000 of the men were simply returned to their units, but almost 2,500 were sent to penal units, and more than 1,300 men were executed. Vasily Chuikov went a step further and established a dedicated patrol of NKVD troops to scour Stalingrad for stragglers and suspicious elements. They rounded up more than 1,200 men. Again, most were sent back to their units, but more than 20 were shot. Even such iron discipline was still not enough to keep the attacker at bay. After the loss of the government quarter in late September, Sixty-Second Army's commander reminded the defenders of Stalingrad of their duty:

Explain to all personnel that the army is fighting on the last line, there is no place to retreat further. It is the duty of every soldier and officer to defend his trench and his position to the end – not a step further. The enemy must be destroyed – *whatever it takes*. Officers and men who arbitrarily leave their trenches and positions are to be shot on the spot as traitors to the Motherland.

Chuikov was as good as his word. The commissar, *politruk* and a staff officer of 399th Rifle Regiment were executed in front of the men they had once led for abandoning them and trying to leave the battlefield. Any man with self-inflicted wounds was shot, while Vasily Grossman watched the execution of one soldier for cowardice or attempting to desert. Stripped of everything but underwear, his body was tossed in a grave. That night he staggered back to his unit – and was executed a second time. There was no mercy for anyone – civilian or *frontovik* – who sided with the enemy. A German-speaking Russian woman, Volodina, had supposedly fought side by side with the invaders as a machine-gunner until wounded. 'The situation did not allow for interrogation and our troops shot Volodina.' And captured Red Army soldiers who served the Germans as *Hiwis* by carrying ammunition or food for troops in the front line were shot 'as traitors to the Motherland' if they fell into Soviet hands.[156]

On 23 October, Paulus concentrated his efforts on the Red October steelworks. It was an attack planned and executed like its predecessors: a Stuka bombardment to soften up the defenders before assault guns moved off, escorting the attacking infantry. And the results, predictably, were the same. Five of the complex's fabrication and assembly halls were seized before nightfall at a cost of 400 casualties. But there, once again, the onslaught faltered.[157]

As the fighting faded, Alfons Metzger ventured into the plant to see how his men were faring. What remained of the walls was riddled with bullets. The roofs had long since collapsed, but the iron girders, beams and supports still stood. Otherwise, the huge sheds 'presented an unimaginable scene of destruction': a succession of craters, some partially filled in by rubble or broken stones; huge steel plates 'bent like sheets of paper' and enormous machines 'reduced to scrap'. In the power plant hall, once-mighty dynamos were half buried by rubble; smashed control panels, ripped wiring and wrecked insulators littered the floor, which had turned into a greasy mulch of soil mixed with oil. Metzger found it hard to believe that just a few weeks earlier 'the sophisticated machinery of a highly-developed armaments industry was running as part of a well-ordered daily routine'. He finally located his men resting in a basement room under the ghostly flickering light of a sooty lamp. The ceiling shook frequently as shells and grenades exploded above, on the surface of the wrecked hall. 'It is a treacherous battle which lies in wait for them there,' the young officer wrote.

The men face an enemy they cannot see yet is only a hand-grenade's throw away.
True, the rubble forms an obstacle that is difficult to cross. But the close combat

with hand grenades and snipers is all the more dangerous as a result. The slightest careless movement, the slightest lapse in attention, however brief, can mean death. No support from heavy weapons and no covering fire from comrades a few craters away is of any use.[158]

The next day 22-year-old junior officer Joachim Stempel found himself leading the remaining infantry of 103rd Panzer Grenadier Regiment against 'Bread factory No.2' – sandwiched between the gun factory and steelworks. Having served on the regimental staff, this was Stempel's baptism of fire in the cauldron of Stalingrad:

> Here they come, our Stukas! We attack! Metre by metre we push forward, always following the dive bombers hurling their bombs in front of us. Howling sirens, crashing, bursting, splintering, fountains of dirt thrown up by the exploding bombs! Bursts of fire from the high-flying machines, some of which also strike around us with their sickening bang, forcing us to take cover for a while. And then our artillery roars over us – hopefully not too briefly! But also from the other side! Entire salvoes of Soviet artillery shells shake the earth, crashing into the still-standing factory walls over there and spreading a roar – like an S-Bahn train thundering into a station. Unbelievable, you can't understand anything anymore. We continue to jump from shell crater to shell crater, from the earth to the next fragment of wall! Just get to the block of houses, get to the next cover.

Stempel's attack captured neither the bread factory nor the ultimate objective – the west bank of the Volga. As night fell, the young Dresdner called off the assault and ordered his men to recover the dead and wounded from the battlefield, while he prepared a report for his superiors. There was no rest for the 103rd that night. Russian troops emerged from tunnels behind the German lines and ambushed any enemy soldier – messenger, food carrier, men taking ammunition up the line – they encountered.

The attack Joachim Stempel led the next day was a near carbon copy, yet the panorama of battle appeared even more hellish.

> Above us clouds of smoke from the burning buildings, the oil tanks to our left and the glowing remains of the factory halls. And then suddenly our Stukas appear once again! We fire white flares so that they can immediately identify our front line and drop their bombs as close as possible to the enemy in front of us! White and yellow-white flares are rising into the sky everywhere. Everywhere: 'Here we are!' How are the aircraft now supposed to determine where the German

spearheads are? So they circle and circle, then suddenly they dive! With a deafening wail of sirens they come crashing down! Far ahead of us, directly in front of us and, my God, behind us too! Huge new craters appear, clouds of smoke and fumes and the muck of earth fountains darken the terrain and temporarily envelop everything! We can't see anything. Suddenly there's machine-gun fire! Independently from the groups. Shouts, screams – the sound of engines! Counter-attack by the Soviets! And that's when I recognise them. Thirty to 40 metres in front of us, directly in front of us, crouching, moving quickly, without steel helmets, all wearing caps! We shower them with fire from every available weapon. An artillery barrage is needed! Red flare! Quick, quick! And already there's howling, our artillery blocks their path.

By nightfall, the administration block of the bakery was in Stempel's hands and the Germans had edged closer to the west bank of the Volga. The young officer wondered what he might find there: Red Army command posts and bunkers dug into the sides of the ravines and balkas, sending a never-ending line of fresh Soviet soldiers into battle. 'How long will this hand-to-hand struggle, this shooting at point-blank range, be able to last?' Stempel asked himself. 'It can't go on much longer with these losses! But maybe we'll still make it the remaining 100 metres. Tomorrow!'

Tomorrow – 28 October – merely brought more of the same. German bombardment. Infantry assault. Soviet counter-barrage. Stempel's men finally cleared the bread factory. But they did not reach the Volga – Joachim Stempel reckoned he was no more than 50 metres from the river bank. It was as close as he would get.[159]

The advances towards Tuapse and Grozny had stalled, but there was still time for one final German lunge into the Caucasus and perhaps a victory fanfare on loudspeakers across the Reich before winter set in. The objective was Ordzhonikidze, unofficial capital of the Caucasus and the end of the Georgian Military Highway which had linked the city with Tbilisi in Georgia since the early 19th century. Ewald von Kleist was able to muster an entire panzer corps – two armoured divisions plus one Romanian mountain infantry – but it was a desperate gamble by an almost-exhausted army: 13th Panzer Division, for example, had combed through its ranks, putting a rifle in the hands of any man willing to bear it. Seven Red Army divisions stood in their way, but the Soviet leadership was largely decapitated on the eve of the attack as 70 bombers struck at the headquarters of Thirty-Seventh Army, knocking out its communications centre.[160]

Long before dawn the next day, Monday 26 October, III Panzer Corps struck. The town of Baksan burned from the preparatory bombardment, while the white crest of the Caucasus mountains glistened in the moonlight. The terrain – steppe grassland, damp with the morning dew – favoured the attackers, whose 600 vehicles – panzers, assault guns, half-tracks carrying grenadiers, motorcycles and scout cars – struck under a protective umbrella of Stukas. 'Every gun, every mortar – ours and German, including the dreaded *Nebelwerfer* – fell on the enemy positions like hell on earth,' remembered Virgil Magulet, commanding a Romanian mortar platoon. 'You got the impression that everything on the enemy's bank had been lifted up, everything in the village, floating like a mirage. Brains also shook and the trembling of the ground made it almost impossible to use the observation binoculars, even holding them in my hands rather than on the tripod.' The Russians, junior officer Konrad Steidl observed, were 'completely shaken. They hadn't expected such a blow before the onset of winter.' After being stuck for weeks, the leaders of 13th Panzer Division were delighted to see that every man displayed bravado and '*Draufgängertum*' – throwing caution to the wind. When their comrades in 23rd Panzer cut the main road to Ordzhonikidze outside Nalchik, the defenders were cut off, surrounded and 'heading to their destruction'. Prisoners streamed north in their thousands.[161]

As the panzer divisions wheeled left and began the advance down the highway towards Ordzhonikidze – now under 70 miles distant – the Romanians sought to take Nalchik and secure the rear of the advance. They found the Russians had turned the town into a fortress. 'Every house, every window was defended, the streets were barricaded, and on the hills that dominated the town there were guns and mortars of various calibres shooting,' company commander Ion Mirescu remembered. 'All this turned the battlefield into a proper hell in a short time.' The Romanians were forced 'to take one house at a time' and call up specialist troops to knock out strongpoints and casemates at major road intersections. A Romanian captain observing the fighting from a captured building was attacked by three civilians, dragged into the street and murdered. His killers were quickly captured by a Romanian patrol and were disembowelled with bayonets. There was a final, desperate stand by the NKVD in their headquarters, but by 29 October Nalchik was in Romanian hands at a cost of 800 dead, wounded or missing. While the Romanian commander Ioan Dumitrache set about burying men who died 'for the motherland – far from that motherland', he received a congratulatory telegram from Ewald von Kleist: 'Onward to final victory!'[162]

However doubtful final victory perhaps seemed, at least Ordzhonikidze appeared well within reach. Crews of 23rd Panzer Division received an order consisting of just three words: Forwards! Forwards! Forwards! 'We continued in this spirit against the backdrop of the mighty panorama of the Caucasus and its giants of ice in weather almost worthy of high summer,' remembered Heinz-Joachim Werner-Ehrenfeucht, the division's deputy commander. 'Light clouds in magnificent colours greeted us in the heavens.'[163] The defenders had still not recovered from the shock of the initial onslaught. One by one the towns and villages on the main road fell. Digora. Ardon. Alagir. The route, Hans Keller noted, was lined with knocked-out T-34s, dead Russians – including one poor soul crushed by a tank's caterpillar tracks – and fresh German graves, plus a couple of wrecked armoured trains on the railway line which ran parallel to the road. But it was a perilous advance: an armoured column moving along a single road through the Terek valley whose 'every nook and cranny' was occupied by Russians trying to pick off the Germans. By 2 November, the foremost elements of Keller's 13th Panzer Division had reached Gizel, just five miles west of Ordzhonikidze, fully expecting to drive into the capital of the Caucasus that very day. 'It is unbelievable but we're still advancing,' gunner Helmut Blume wrote excitedly, while a corporal from Nedlitz, near the division's garrison city of Magdeburg, expected imminent victory. 'Our Stukas are attacking constantly and dropping bombs on the Russian positions,' he wrote to his wife. 'To my left is a long line of anti-tank guns and artillery. Behind are the units which are to storm the city. The sun is now shining above us, huge factory complexes and tall chimneys can be seen. The entire city is empty and dead.'[164] It was not. Far from it.

In peacetime, Ordzhonikidze had been a city of clean boulevards, of museums, trams whose bells sounded as they rumbled through the cobbled streets, parks with linden trees and footpaths along the banks of the Terek. In November 1942, the city had been turned into a makeshift fortress, the cobbles ripped up and piled into barricades, anti-tank guns drawn up in streets now guarded by concrete bunkers and patrolled by militia wearing armbands, the parks scarred by trenches. Its defence was directed from a once-fine villa, now fortified. From an observation post in its grounds, anyone who grabbed a pair of powerful field binoculars and scanned the horizon to the west would see the wooded mountains, the road snaking to Alagir 20 miles away and the muzzle flashes of artillery barrels.

To underline their resolve to defend their city, thousands of Ordzhonikidze's inhabitants gathered for a fiery rally. In the shadow of an obelisk crowned by a red star, erected in the southern suburbs to the 17,000 men lost in the Civil War a generation earlier, an eclectic line-up of speakers appeared on a hastily erected rostrum: Khadzhimurza Mildzikhov, an Ossetian Hero of the Soviet Union who had supposedly killed more than 100 Germans single-handedly south of Leningrad at the beginning of the year; the soprano Ragimat Gadzhieva from Dagestan; a female Cossack leader; the head of a collective farm. And opening proceedings,

Civil War hero and cavalryman Vasily Kniga, now in his early 60s, his face wrinkled, his once-fine moustache thinning, but the sparkle in his eyes undimmed. 'Fellow warriors!' he appealed. 'Mount your war horses! Draw a sharp sword! Let the enemy feel the power of an axe in the hands of a *dzhigit* [local cavalryman] and a Cossack! Let him pay with his own blood for the grief he has caused us…'

The determination of Ordzhonikidze's people impressed Ivan Tyulenev. The front commander had flown into the city from Tuapse to take charge of its defence, livid with his deputy, Ivan Maslennikov, not merely for allowing the enemy to advance so close, but also for transferring his headquarters to Grozny, 60 miles away. 'The front line is *here*, near Ordzhonikidze. The enemy is at the gates,' Tyulenev told him. 'Ordzhonikidze is a fortress, it is the key to the Caucasus, it is the gateway to the East. We have no right to surrender the city. The order of the Motherland, of the Party is to defend it to the last breath.'

Maslennikov understood. '*Da*, Comrade Commander! The order will be carried out.'

Party leaders displayed the backbone and initiative Ivan Maslennikov had not. They assured the front commander they – and the city's inhabitants – were prepared to defend Ordzhonikidze to the death, citing the words of Ossetia's most famous poet, Kosta Khetagurov: 'It is better to die a free people than to serve a despot as slaves.' Factories were still producing ammunition and Molotov cocktails for the front line, food processing plants continued to operate, printworks still published newspapers, extras and posters. Above all, the morale of the troops was high. A visiting American general had recently inspected the defenders, buttonholing a gruff Siberian rifleman. 'We shall fight not only to the last drop of blood but also to the last Fascist on our soil,' the soldier told him.

Ivan Tyulenev was impressed, but did not sugar-coat his briefing to Ordzhonikidze's leaders. The Germans would make every effort to take the city over the coming days so that Hitler could announce its fall to the world in time for the 25th anniversary of the Bolshevik Revolution. The general let his audience into a secret. 'The Fascists are already at the walls of the city, but its fate is in our hands,' he told them. 'Here is my word as a soldier: on the evening of the sixth, we will gather here again, and our voice will carry as far as Moscow. In the name of the Party our troops will go on the offensive tomorrow'.[165]

It wasn't rhetoric which halted 13th Panzer Division's attack on Ordzhonikidze but Soviet resistance. Artillery and anti-tank guns on the western edge of the city rained shells on the German vanguard. The Red Army struck at the rear of the Germans' armoured spearhead, threatening the tenuous line of communications. Gizel was reduced to rubble as the defenders doggedly clung to each house, the walls daubed with slogans: 'We'll emerge from here as victors – there's no going back.' Even when beaten back or subdued, Russian units resumed the struggle a few hours later. 'None of us have been through days like this before,' artilleryman Helmut Blume noted. 'Hell is let loose… like nothing I've experienced here in a year and a quarter.' When darkness fell at 5pm on the first Monday in November, 13th Panzer was still a good mile from Ordzhonikidze's western limits. It hoped to enter the city the next day, 'although the terrain does not remotely favour an attack'. But, as one officer observed, the division 'was like a piece of rubber shortly before it snapped'. It was two more days, at 12.40pm on Wednesday 4 November, before a scratch force led by Friedrich-Erdmann von Hake limped into the industrial district on the western outskirts of Ordzhonikidze. No German soldier had advanced further – nearly 1,800 miles from Berlin – and none would do so. Hake was ordered not to attack the city – not that he could anyway, for his men were immediately subjected to a fierce bombardment from Soviet tanks, artillery and aircraft.[166] That evening 13th Panzer Division called off the attack and went over to the defensive.

A couple of days later, Peter Dimt was sent forward ten miles from his battery to look for targets. Climbing a ridge, he grabbed his binoculars and scanned the Ossetian plain laid out before him:

We can see as far as the chimneys of Ordzhonikidze and the panzers' route of advance which stretches for miles. Almost every village where the fighting rages lies in front of us like on a board, each one as tangibly close as the next, and it seems strange to have to say: Look there at the five tanks burrowing through the cornfield – they're Soviet tanks; what's that there, a short distance away, just flashing, that must be the muzzle flash of Soviet guns, now a white signal rocket is rising up, coming towards us, revealing our front line.

The sight of Ordzhonikidze, nestling among the hills in the valley of the upper Terek, was intoxicating. 'It is the gate to Georgia, it opens the way to Tbilisi – our dream for many difficult weeks,' Dimt wrote. But as the day progressed, the fine weather turned to rain. In the increasing gloom, Ordzhonikidze disappeared from view, while the Luftwaffe disappeared from the skies above the panzer spearhead, replaced by the Red Air Force. And there was troubling news filtering through. Soviet troops had penetrated the flank of the armoured thrust. 'This could be decisive,' Dimt noted with concern.[167]

It was. The Red Army had taken advantage of their enemy's exhaustion and inclement weather – leaden skies, drizzle alternating with sleet – and, just as Ivan Tyulenev had promised, gone over to the offensive, throwing two corps at the German forces outside Ordzhonikidze. 13th Panzer Division had no answer to the onslaught. Soviet troops bypassed Gizel, pushing westwards, cutting off the German spearhead. For a couple of days the Germans managed to hold open a narrow corridor – no more than two miles wide – centred around the villages of Mayramadag and Dzuarikau, to continue to feed the troops at Gizel with food and ammunition. But the situation was precarious and the lifeline frequently cut, until finally closed for good. 'What is happening now on the outskirts of Ordzhonikidze is a real horror,' junior officer Karl Heuschild wrote to his family in Berlin. 'How any man can endure this madness. We are in the Mayramadag area and we have been cut off three times already.' In 13th Panzer's first-aid post a mile outside Gizel, medical staff struggled not merely to tend to more than 400 casualties, but to feed them. After two days cut off, with the last bread supplies used up, they begged for warm food and drinks. Finally, what was left of 13th Panzer Division resolved to break out to the west, along the road to Alagir. 'At first there were attempts to regulate the traffic,' one panzer crewman remembered. 'Soldiers were ordered to hold back the Russians while officers' vehicles passed. But nothing came of it. Our company had 38 vehicles, and now there are only four left.'[168]

In Alagir – where the elite *Brandenburg* Regiment found itself fighting alongside regular troops – the Germans had held off repeated Soviet charges, each one launched with a hoarse cry of 'Urra!', each one ending with 'brown bodies' piled up before their lines. The autumn rain turned to sleet and light snow, the earth to mud. Rations and ammunition could only be brought up at night. Finally the Brandenburgers were ordered to fall back, acting as the rearguard. 'In the evening, a huge fireworks display tells us the troops have escaped from the pocket,' one officer wrote. 'Eight hundred vehicles with ammunition go up in the air. It is an eerie scene of destruction.' With the bulk of the troops extricated from the pocket, the Brandenburgers joined the remnants of 13th Panzer Division and reached the relative safety of German lines.[169]

All through the 10th, 11th and 12th, the survivors of 13th Panzer Division re-appeared in German lines, having slipped out of the pocket. After ten days in action, unable to wash, often with inadequate rations, they were a sorry sight to non-commissioned officer Hans Keller: tattered, exhausted and nervous. They were also largely on foot – as well as the wounded and dead, the latter piled in heaps in places. 'It looked awful,' wrote Keller. 'Our division is badly battered. Is it still fit for action?'[170]

The answer, perhaps, was 'barely'. Its panzer grenadiers escaped from the pocket having not eaten for days and 'reached the limits of endurance'. The new divisional commander, Hellmut von der Chevallerie – who had broken *into* the pocket to be with his men and lead them out – reckoned the fighting outside

Ordzhonikidze was 'probably the toughest which we had to struggle through in the campaign in the East'. With no sleep, frequently no food and insufficient ammunition, the division had survived thanks to the 'brave stance of every man' demonstrating 'nerves of iron'.[171]

After the rain, sleet and persistent grey of recent days, Wednesday 11 November was a fine, clear autumn day in the central Caucasus. Ivan Tyulenev followed the soldiers of Ninth Army into Gizel. Not a single building was intact. All that remained of the cottages and houses were lonely chimneys rising above the ashes. Villagers streamed out of the woods and ravines back to their homes, hailing the Red Army as liberators and recounting the brief, but brutal German occupation with stories of capricious acts and summary executions.

Satisfied that the village was secure and its inhabitants safe, Tyulenev returned to Ordzhonikidze to thank those who had distinguished themselves in its defence. The city had changed in the ten days since he last visited. Streets and squares had been cleared of barricades, the anti-tank guns wheeled away, the cobbles returned to their rightful place in the roadway. Shops, pharmacies and civic institutions had reopened. And in front of one of the main theatres, a steady stream of trucks delivered captured German vehicles and guns, the mangled fuselage of Messerschmitt fighters, even panzers. They would form the centrepiece of an exhibition of booty from the Nazi war machine.[172]

When the bitter struggle for Stalingrad's industrial district petered out in the dying days of October, both sides again took stock. Sixty-Second Army had withstood the German onslaught – though at times it had come 'within a hair's breadth of catastrophe'. Chuikov was convinced his opponent could not mount another offensive on the scale of the October battles. But he also knew his army could not withstand another such onslaught. 'Every soldier was doing the jobs of three, if not five, men,' he wrote. 'We knew that the enemy's losses were heavier than ours, and that his reserves were running out, but the initiative was still in his hands.'[173]

Friedrich Paulus still believed not only that Stalingrad would fall, but that the battle was 'approaching its rapid conclusion'. XI Corps' chief-of-staff Helmuth Groscurth dismissed his optimism out of hand. 'Personally, I can't see it, as I have been at the front...' His counterpart at LI Corps, Hans Clausius, was more confident, but warned his wife Elisabeth not to expect a special announcement trumpeting Stalingrad's fall just yet. 'It will still take some time,' he wrote, 'because even the final tenth [of the city] not in our hands will cost heavy fighting.' Clausius could not understand his enemy. There was a steady flow of deserters every day, but the Red Army soldier who remained stood his ground 'with unprecedented tenacity' such that prisoners were few. Clausius ascribed it to the 'very stubborn, soulless, spiritless blind obedience of Soviet citizens, dead inside' and the ruthlessness of the commissar and his blocking detachments, prepared to 'gun down anyone who retreats without orders'. As far as 22-year-old artilleryman Karl Nünninghoff was concerned, Stalingrad was 'effectively' already in German hands. 'Only a factory site and a village on the outskirts of the city are still tenaciously and doggedly defended,' he assured his family in Mülheim an der Ruhr. 'When will this "thing" end?' an artillery officer in 44th Infantry Division wondered.

> Nobody knows, we don't ask about it, it doesn't matter to us, we just have to be victorious, we want to go home victorious. I certainly believe, as do my soldiers, that we will succeed, we will hold out; the big question is whether the others can hold out. After the successes of the past few days, you have to assume that they'll run out of breath one day.

Infantryman Karl Bühler assured his parents the fighting on the Volga would be over soon and he would return home to the small market town of Spaichingen in southern Germany by January 'at the latest' – a date based entirely on conjecture and hope. 'It's something all of us here are clinging to with all our hearts,' the 30-year-old wrote. 'However, every minute you have to reckon that you will no longer be among the living.'[174]

There were *frontoviki* just as determined to hold the city. 'Soon the moment will come when all these scum who have designs on our soil are destroyed down to the last man,' Sergeant Yegor Borisov vowed. Marine Viktor Barsov had lost none of the ardour for action he had possessed at the beginning of September. 'Be sure that your son will not surrender one foot of land or one house to the enemy!' he told his parents. 'Our enemies are afraid of us, marines – they call us "black commissars". In our sector, not only has the enemy not moved a step forward, he has even retreated. It will continue to be so!' But there were also Red Army men certain the city was on the brink of being lost. 'Our regiment was defeated in two days,' one Soviet soldier wrote to his wife from a field hospital bed. 'There are a lot of killed, wounded, it's sickening to see, it makes your heart bleed. The Germans are attacking with such ferocity that there's no escape anywhere.' Another soldier predicted that Stalingrad would 'obviously be in German hands in a couple of days... thanks to our weakness and poor leadership'.[175]

Many *Landsers* were equally fatalistic. After two weeks' largely fruitless fighting for the Barrikady works, Wilhelm Hoffman's regiment had made negligible progress. The unburied corpses of countless comrades rotted before his eyes. 'Who would have thought three months ago that instead of the joy of victory we would have to endure such sacrifice and torture, the end of which is nowhere in sight?' he asked his diary rhetorically. 'The soldiers are calling Stalingrad the mass grave of the Wehrmacht.' A few days later he added: 'Everyone is depressed. Stalingrad has turned us into beings without feelings – we are tired, exhausted, bitter. If our relatives and families could see us now they would be horrified.' As far as Croatian Legion staff officer Adolf Sabljak was concerned, the battle for Stalingrad and its districts had almost become irrelevant. 'It is solely a matter of prestige,' he wrote. 'The Führer and Stalin are fighting here, so to speak.' In the five weeks it had spent in Stalingrad, the Legion had suffered more than 800 casualties. It could commit just 68 men in the front line.[176]

Replacements were coming – though not for the Croatian Legion. Trains bringing troops and supplies got no closer than Chir, from where they faced a journey of 60 miles to Stalingrad, the men often on foot. 'Fresh troops were just being unloaded,' observed junior officer Edgar Klaus, returning to the front. 'Very young lads, some of them still with children's faces, straight from the parade ground, without any front-line experience, were intended for action and were to reinforce the front line.' Battalion commander Eberhard Rettenmaier was shocked by the state of 305th Infantry Division when he returned. Its sick commander Kurt Oppenländer had been replaced by a colonel, Bernhard Steinmetz. There was a new operations officer too. Gone too was Willy Winzer, commander of 578th Infantry Regiment, killed in the October attacks in the industrial district. 'II Battalion had lost every officer and the companies numbered seven, nine, twelve and thirteen men,' the alarmed Rettenmaier noted. 'To the many, many questions: "Where's so and so?" – the same answer: "Dead, wounded, missing." I had returned to strange surroundings.'[177]

Winter had now descended on Stalingrad. The first snow had fallen on 19 October – 'swirling over the city, steppe, river and roads in a wild dance,' journalist Herbert Rauchhaupt wrote. The storm obscured Soviet batteries on the far side of the Volga, making it impossible for German artillery to distinguish them, while the white blanket it cast over the city made identifying targets on the ground even more difficult for the Luftwaffe. It also hid 'all the wounds inflicted by war' – the craters, ruins and rubble – Helmut Welz observed. Wolves were spotted moving around the ravines. Murders of crows with their dull black plumage sat on the snow 'like ugly little splashes of ink on a blinding white linen cloth,' recalled Richard Burkhardt, in charge of a medical company with 71st Infantry Division. Now the soldiers in Stalingrad faced an additional enemy: 'General Winter'. The 71st was not prepared – Burkhardt's men had received 'a few lined jackets, pants and boots, but it is a drop in the ocean'. A full outfit of winter clothing was distributed among the men of 24th Panzer Division in the Kalmyk steppe 45 miles west of Stalingrad: a pair of wonderful felt boots and a special uniform.[178] Karl Bergauer thought the provisions 'truly fabulous'. He continued in a letter home: 'Now winter can come, I have no fear of it. After all, we are not little girls. Winter can come, we will master it and the Russian can come too, we will destroy him.'[179]

Others were not so sure. 'After a desolate, rainy day today with temperatures of -7 and an icy wind, we're really relishing the prospect of winter,' XI Corps' gloomy chief-of-staff Helmuth Groscurth wrote. 'The Führer has ordered us to hold our positions to the last man – something we'd do anyway, because losing our positions would not improve our position. Then we'd be sitting on the open steppe without quarters.'

Surveying the 'white wasteland' before him, a shiver ran down Helmut Welz's spine. Winter had again arrived before the German Army had achieved its objectives for the year. 'The heart tenses up, and thoughts race back one year, back to the many men who were reported missing, although each one of us knows that most of them froze, they died miserably.' Would, he wondered, things end like they did last year too?[180]

The German Army – indeed, the German nation – was better prepared for winter in 1942 than it had been 12 months earlier, Adolf Hitler declared in Munich as he marked the anniversary of his failed putsch in the city 19 years before. The previous day Stalin had marked the 25th anniversary of the Bolshevik Revolution not with a speech but an order of the day. The enemy had been 'checked' at Stalingrad and given 'a taste of the Red Army's powers of resistance'. The *vozhd* claimed – wildly – more than eight million German soldiers had been killed, wounded or captured and that the enemy's strength was on the cusp of breaking. 'The day is not long off when the enemy will again feel the weight of the Red Army's blows. Our turn will come!'[181] The speech in the Löwenbräukeller – chosen to host the annual address after a failed attempt to blow up Hitler back in 1939 rendered the original Bürgerbraukeller unusable – was the German dictator's response. As darkness fell on Sunday 8 November, Party leaders and faithful veterans of the coup, senior officers and recently decorated soldiers, began assembling. News of Allied landings in French North Africa (see Chapter 8) – announced just before guests gathered – 'electrified' the mood in the beer hall. They waited for nearly two hours, entertained by marches performed by the regional Party leadership's band.

Shortly before 6pm, they rose to a man, as former brownshirt Jakob Grimminger with his carbon-copy Hitler moustache, strode into the hall carrying the *Blutfahne* – the flag stained with the blood of a putschist. The audience had to wait a little longer until the band struck up the opening bars of the *Badenweiler March* – Hitler's favourite – which announced the Führer's arrival. The 52-minute address which followed was not one of Hitler's finest performances – though Goebbels, as ever, marvelled at his Führer's poise and stamina and the audience was seized by an 'unparalleled wave of enthusiasm' at the end. The Führer had barely slept in three days. He started limply, struggled for applause and laughter, made no reference to the Allied landings in North Africa and brushed aside Rommel's plight in Egypt as simply part and parcel of the pendulum of war in the desert. 'The decisive issue in this war is who deals the final blow, and you can be sure that we will deliver it.' As for Russia, this time German forces were prepared for the coming winter 'even if it should turn out to be as severe as last year's. Whatever happened to us last winter cannot be repeated this time around.' And then there was Stalingrad specifically.

> I wanted to reach the Volga, at a specific place, at a specific city. It happens to bear the name of Stalin himself, but don't believe I marched on it for that reason – I did so only because it occupies a vital position...
>
> I wanted to seize it. And, you know, we're modest: basically, we've taken it – there are just a couple of tiny parcels of land left.
>
> Now some people say: Why aren't you fighting more quickly? Because I don't want to have a second Verdun on my hands – I'd rather finish the job with very small assault groups. Time doesn't matter. No ships travel up the Volga anymore – that's what matters!

On a generally rather subdued evening, that sentence brought the audience to its feet with thunderous applause echoing around the hall. To the German people the speech 'once again conveyed tremendous confidence in victory', his assurances about the coming winter 'made a lasting impression', his promise not to turn Stalingrad into a second Verdun 'seemed to have a soothing effect on relatives of soldiers in particular'.[182]

'Nothing particular' occurred in Stalingrad this Sunday, recorded Helmut Welz, the 31-year-old commander of a battalion of pioneers. It was 'a day like any other': localised skirmishes for piles of rubble and entrances to the sewage system; assault troops fought their way through the ruins of factory workshops; aircraft of both sides attacked positions on the ground. The low clouds and falling temperatures – the mercury was dropping by the day – added to the growing sense of gloom. By 4.30pm it was dark – a moonless, overcast night.

> Only the brazen light of flares rising and falling in the east. Further south the heavens reflect the muzzle flashes which glint so quickly one after another that they merge into a single, awful flickering. The earth gently shakes and groans as if it were a living being suffering pain under the blows. The flickering light on the horizon – white, then yellow, then red – causes erratic light and shadows to move through the darkness. Gutters, ravines and hollows become visible – then disappear. For a second it casts light on a lunar landscape, grey and yet more grey, no vegetation. In the middle of it, black craters from bombs and shells, the parallel lines of tank tracks, in the distance signposts stick out with laconic names pointing to bunkers nestling against the edges of gulleys.

In one such bunker near the Red October steelworks Welz and his men restlessly listened to Hitler's speech, until he turned to Stalingrad. The pioneers fell silent for a couple of minutes, then began to openly criticise their Führer's words. 'No second Verdun?' one pioneer scoffed. 'I reckon we've already lost more than 100,000 men in this lice-infected hole. In two months! The number of losses rises by the day.' Welz noted widespread 'disappointment and anger' among his fellow grenadiers. 'Every soldier in this ruined city can disprove what has just been said about our successes,' he wrote. 'You can't simply trivialise the fighting here – which rages for individual houses or floors – with such remarks as we heard today.'[183]

Three days later, Friedrich Paulus rolled the dice one last time. He did so reluctantly, confiding in his friend Karl Hollidt, commanding a corps on the Don. Hitler's orders – demanding a renewal of the attack – were 'absurd'. His divisions and especially his assault troops were being 'bled white in pointless localised fighting', Sixth Army was 'quickly draining away'.[184] But the sickly Paulus lacked the mental or physical strength to stand up to his Führer. He bowed to Hitler's will and, at first light on 11 November, Sixth Army made a renewed attempt to seize the Red October plant outright and force its way to the Volga. And once again the assault ground to a halt in the tangled ruin of the steelworks. Its steel furnace – Hall Nr.4 – became the crucible of the battle. Helmut Welz left a vivid account of the assault:

> A bright yellow flash of light! The hall wall totters then gives way. A deafening blow forces everyone to the ground. A tremendous blast of air passes over us. Bits of stone, entire bricks, pieces of iron and shredded metal are already drumming

down. We're surrounded by a thick grey-black fog. The smoke stings our eyes. We cannot see one metre in front of us. The assault troops thrust right into the middle of this haze. They leap over every obstacle to the front. When the wall of smoke begins to disperse, I can see that the entire right-hand corner of the hall has collapsed. Through the ten-metre-wide gap and over the pile of rubble which has just accumulated, the first pioneers enter the hall.

The interior of the furnace building was like the set from some horror film: lumps of iron of all shapes and sizes were scattered around, while twisted metal sheets hung down from the roof. Between the thick stumps of wrecked load-bearing columns, makeshift barricades had been thrown across the hall, composed of trucks, tracks, iron bars and beams. Bombers, Stukas, howitzers, cannons, mortars had turned the furnace hall 'upside down. Not a centimetre has remained untouched.' They had created 'a world of shadows', occasionally brightly lit for a radius of around 100 feet by the yellow-orange jet of the pioneers' flamethrowers, which favoured the defender at every step. The floor of the hall was littered with rubble, ruins, steel plate, smashed bricks and a tangle of barbed wire. 'Amid all this the defenders' hand-grenades explode, their machine-guns and machine-pistols rattle,' one of Welz's men recalled. 'Dust and smoke drift around this chaos. The handful of men take cover, pressed right up to the rubble and masonry.' They could make no progress – and the battalion commander could not conceive a solution. Even if he had more men, there was not the space to commit them – they'd merely present a larger, easier target to the defenders. 'For the first time in this war I face a task which simply cannot be carried out,' a frustrated Helmut Welz wrote. 'This fact shakes me – I've overcome every difficulty in campaigns to date. Yet now, not far from the Volga, there's a shoddy factory which cannot be captured. I'm struck by a blow of disillusion. I feel utterly humbled.'[185]

The battle for Hall Nr.4 was the baptism of fire for Bertold Paulus, a former factory fitter from the Saarland and no relation to Sixth Army's commander. He arrived in Stalingrad just in time to celebrate his 19th birthday. He would not live to see his 20th. On 11 November, his platoon was ordered to capture an area just 500 metres long and 200 metres wide in the Red October complex. The defenders had created some form of strongpoint every ten metres. Paulus' friend and squad leader led his dozen-strong assault troop for 50 metres until a shot to the head killed him instantly as he approached one such Soviet strongpoint. 'He didn't say a word,' Paulus told his parents in the Saarland. 'That's how we knew he was dead,' adding a plea: 'Don't tell his parents anything until the company has written.' His squad remained continuously in action for another 50 hours.

'The hand-to-hand fighting was constant,' Paulus wrote. 'No Russian surrendered, no prisoners were taken.' When Paulus' platoon was pulled out of the line – briefly – it had been reduced to one lieutenant, a sergeant and ten men. 'We are only a small group now,' Paulus continued. 'Many of our comrades are dead, and most are wounded... I didn't know what war was before, but now I do... I never imagined the war would be so terrible. If I am lucky and make it home, I will tell you all about Stalingrad. What I have seen so far cannot be described.' Bertold Paulus' squad was due to make a fresh attempt to capture the Red October works on 20 November. 'I have been lucky so far. I hope I always will be.'[186]

The assault of 11 November wasn't a total failure. At least one assault group reached the high bluffs on the Volga's west bank. But, like so many German attacks, it delivered only a 'partial success'.[187]

Though Friedrich Paulus continued to exude optimism wherever he went, most of Sixth Army was now resigned to spending the winter on the Don. 'We have made a lot of progress, but not reached the end,' a frustrated Walther von Seydlitz, commanding LI Corps, wrote. 'And now it almost seems as if we will not succeed in taking the last remaining stretch from the Russians this year. That hurts me deeply after so many weeks of endless, truly gigantic effort.' Arthur Schmidt, Paulus' feared chief-of-staff, went even further. 'The war,' he confided to Udo von Alvensleben, 'cannot be won militarily but only be decided politically.' Pioneer battalion commander Wilhelm Traub clung to his belief in victory, convinced the Russians were 'at the end of their tether' and the battle for Stalingrad would 'end within a week at the most... The fighting here – and everyone here agrees about this – will be the high point of this present war and can certainly be compared with the battle of Verdun.' And the ever-critical Wolfram von Richthofen wanted to take a clean broom to Sixth Army. Its men and leaders were 'lifeless' and needed 'the injection of fresh blood', he told Kurt Zeitzler. 'I suggested giving tried-and-tested commanders leave and completely different commanders take their place. But no-one at the top has the balls to do that.'[188]

Adolf Hitler had no intention of making any changes at Stalingrad, nor of making any effort to appreciate the sacrifices made or the challenges faced by Sixth Army. He was convinced a final, supreme effort by German soldiers on the Volga before the full onset of the Russian winter would unseat Stalingrad's defenders and 'save ourselves a lot of blood later on'. Whatever challenges German troops faced, those facing the Russians were 'even greater', he told Paulus. 'I once again expect the leadership to make the ultimate effort with all the energy it has repeatedly demonstrated and the troops to do the same with the guts they have so often shown until they have at least pushed through to the Volga via the gun factory and metal works, having captured these districts.'[189] Having read the teletype, Friedrich Paulus told his staff to pass it on verbally to every commander down to the regimental level. 'I'm convinced that this order will give our brave troops fresh impetus,' he gushed.[190]

It's doubtful the German soldier had either the strength or numbers to attack again. But, above all, for the first time the *Landser* was beginning to lose hope. 'Stalingrad has still not fallen,' one frustrated German soldier recorded in his diary. 'Even though it's only a few hundred metres long and wide, we're unable to take this strip, despite countless divisions attacking the Russians almost every day. And yet each attack grinds to a halt and is repulsed.' Signals officer August Schlusnus noticed 'a strange mood among the troops'. After more than two months of fighting for Stalingrad, the men were physically and mentally exhausted. The unceasing losses, the unwavering doggedness of the defenders, the constant shelling and bombing, day and night, the onset of winter – all had eroded Sixth Army's confidence. 'We no longer believed in victory, that we could still take Stalingrad,' Schlusnus conceded. 'There was something in the air of impending doom.'[191] And one soldier wrote to his family: 'I have seen more German soldiers dead in Stalingrad than Russian. Our cemeteries grow bigger every hour. The war in Russia won't be over so soon. It'll take at least a couple of years. As a matter of fact, it's next to impossible to fix a date.'[192]

Some had reached that conclusion much sooner. Even as the battle for the grain elevator raged two months earlier, Karl Wintereder – just turned 26 – was certain that the 1942 campaign had failed. 'We're going to have to endure a second winter here, because I'm convinced that Russia won't capitulate in the short time that's left for operations,' he warned his family at home in Anzbach, just outside Vienna. 'Will the enemy be strong enough to launch attacks like last year, or is he finally weakened?' he wondered, then consoled himself. All the Axis armies had to do was hold the line between Voronezh and the Volga.[193]

8

ENDGAME, NOT *ENDSIEG*

What will become of us is in God's hands.

Erwin Rommel

Friday the 23rd was a day like any other in October in the desert west of El Alamein. In fact, it was probably quieter than average, a day staff officer Gavino Ledda noted of 'almost absolute calm' on the front of the XXI Corps. The mixed Italo-German force – the motorised infantry of the *Trento* Division and the newly formed 164th Light Division – held a stretch of front just inland from the Mediterranean. As he had done for several weeks now, Corporal Hans Hesse worked to improve the foxhole and small strongpoint for his 5cm anti-tank gun and mortar which he had carved out of the stony ground using pickaxe and shovel. 'One day passed like any other,' Hesse remembered. 'Sun, sand, heat and circling over everything, millions of flies. The only variety was provided by the daily shooting of the English artillery.' Lack of ammunition prevented Hesse and his 164th Light Division comrades from replying. 'It was depressing.' He, like most German and Italian soldiers, had settled in for the night in bunkers, trenches and makeshift positions when, shortly before 10pm, 'the gates of hell burst open'. A barrage 'which has no precedent on the African battlefield' hammered the forward positions of XXI Corps. Silvio Astolfi, a 30-year-old staff officer with the *Bologna* Division, who had been enjoying the cool of the evening on a small hill, was transfixed. 'There was something messianic about the show,' he wrote as he watched 'the entire line – from the coast to the Qattara Depression – lit with flames'.[1]

At the *Trento*'s command post, chief-of-staff Giacomo Ferraioli lost communications with units in the front line. Nor could he observe what was happening. 'The sky was as red as a fiery sunset, but the curtains of smoke prevented visibility of the ground ahead.' When news finally came in, thanks to superhuman efforts by engineers, it was alarming: entire companies simply ceased to exist by daylight on the 24th, wiped out where they stood, while two German battalions fighting alongside the *Trento* were overrun – to the disbelief of the German liaison officer on the Italian division's staff.[2]

Nevertheless, senior officers were not unduly concerned by the enemy's progress – or lack thereof. 15th Panzer Division destroyed 28 tanks on the first full day of the offensive. With 44 panzers still working, it felt there was a 'good chance' of stopping Montgomery's offensive while *Afrika Korps* commander Ritter von Thoma reported there was 'no great cause for anxiety'. The greatest concern was the lack of leadership, for Axis troops had been without a general since the opening hours of Eighth Army's attack. Proving himself to be as reckless as his predecessor, Georg Stumme had driven up to the front for a better understanding of the battle unfolding. Unfortunately, he did not enjoy Erwin Rommel's good fortune. His vehicle was ambushed by British anti-tank and machine-gun fire. As the driver took evasive action, Stumme was thrown from the vehicle. His body was found by von Thoma in the aftermath of a counter-attack the following night. The general was still wearing his monocle as well as his habitual short trousers. There were no signs of injury or wounds, so von Thoma's doctor concluded Stumme had suffered a heart attack.[3]

Even before Georg Stumme's fate was determined, Erwin Rommel's convalescence at a villa in the Semmering had been interrupted, first by a call from his adjutant, then by one from Hitler. The conversations were almost identical: the British had unleashed their offensive; Stumme was missing. The field marshal offered to return to Africa immediately to take charge of the situation. He was back in Africa by Sunday afternoon and back at the front before midnight on the 25th as he took charge of his army again.[4]

After receiving reports from his chief-of-staff Siegfried Westphal and then von Thoma – neither of which was especially encouraging – Rommel decided on his course of action. Despite a shortage of both fuel and ammunition – at times the enemy was shooting 500 shells for every one returned by Axis forces – he resolved to attempt to wipe out the bulge in German lines. He rallied his troops and impressed on them the gravity of the hour: any man capable of bearing arms was thrust into the front line. Any man who failed in his duty – 'regardless of rank' – would face a court martial. 'The present battle is a life and death struggle,' Rommel reminded his men.[5]

Had he possessed the fuel, Rommel would have corralled all his armour and thrown it against the breakthrough to smash it. But he did not. Hopes had been pinned on the tanker *Prosperina*, but she was set ablaze off Tobruk, leaving Rommel's forces with no more than three days' fuel. The panzers attacked piecemeal.[6]

15th Panzer Division was reduced to the role of spectators. From high ground, regimental adjutant Eilhard Bentlage watched enemy engineers methodically clear a path through the dense belt of mines, 'slowly eating their way through the field'. Then British tanks moved up. 'It was a shame we couldn't show it as a training film at school,' he wrote. 'It was just like being at the cinema.' Bentlage was troubled by the enemy's seemingly bottomless resources. Axis artillery spluttered a few rounds in response to a British barrage. 'There's no counterbalance to this matériel.' As Montgomery desired, the Axis front at Alamein 'crumbled'. 'Bit by bit, the Italian front in the north is broken.' The Italians' nerves, Bentlage wrote, 'are simply not up to it'. Then again, nor were those of German troops under the weight of enemy matériel. The Tommies, the adjutant bitterly recorded, 'slowly ate their way through'.[7]

It was clear to Erwin Rommel after just a couple of days back in Africa that the tide of battle was turning against Axis fortunes. If the fighting continued at the same tempo and ferocity, the Italians feared their ammunition would run out in two or three days, their fuel even sooner. 'The result of the battle depends first of all on the flow of supplies,' Rommel pleaded to his allies.[8]

But there were moral factors at play as well. At times, the fighting at Alamein was every bit as brutal as in Stalingrad – though never as protracted or on the same scale. 'The battle has been raging for 96 hours without respite,' one worn-out Italian soldier recorded in his diary. 'On the horizon huge fires blaze against the sky – 13 fires fed by steel and human flesh, by iron and blood, by tanks and their crews.' The next day, after five nights continuously awake and in action, he watched as the desert landscape was torn up by a rain of bombs and shells and the 'earth and sky mingled in an enormous wall of sand, noise and fire.' The grenadiers of 21st Panzer Division faced a night attack by motorised enemy infantry – Eighth Army's infantry proved particularly skilled in fighting in the dark. On this particular occasion, however, anti-tank guns knocked out six British vehicles before the infantry fell upon the German positions. 'With rifle butts, spades and fists, a scramble for foxholes begins,' a corporal recorded in his diary. 'Only gasps, groans and whimpers can be heard. The attackers are silhouetted against the night sky. The best recognition sign – friend or foe – is the flat steel helmet of the Tommies.' Such was the ferocity of the German defence that the British broke off their attack after 30 minutes, leaving the desert strewn with dead.[9]

Night offered no respite for Axis tank crews either. The *Ariete* formed its vehicles in a semi-circle after darkness fell, the outline of guards' helmets silhouetted against the African sky as they stood watch in the turrets of their M13 tanks while crews tried to sleep. But there was a constant soundtrack of enemy artillery thundering somewhere. And the enemy air force always put in at least one appearance, dropping flares which 'lit us up like daylight, exposing us to aircraft which cut us down from low altitude,' complained junior officer Vincenzo Formica, who served with the division's combat baggage column. 'In that hell it was impossible to sleep.'[10]

The Italians at Alamein – as they had been throughout the campaign in North Africa – were as dogged as their German comrades-in-arms. 'We fight hand-to-hand,' one captain noted. 'The Australians, drunk on whisky, seem to have gone mad.'[11] Captain Dino Campini took over a *Littorio* tank battalion after its commander and deputy were wounded and killed, respectively. His armour was outnumbered four to one, his 14-tonne tanks and their 47mm guns outgunned by the enemy's Shermans, twice as heavy and equipped with a 75mm main weapon. 'And yet, the enemy was driven off,' he recalled.

> Some continued to advance, even after they had been hit and set on fire, with only dead and dying men inside them, like huge, self-propelled funeral pyres, a dead man's foot pressing down on the accelerator.
>
> What a sight! A procession of blazing monsters, shaken by explosions and emitting coloured flashes as the shells inside went off – like something out of a terrifying ghost story. The souls of the dead men were trapped in their burning vehicle – how else could a smashed and blazing tank continue to advance towards the enemy.[12]

Vittorio Emanuele Borsi di Parma, an adjutant in the *Trieste* Division, was ordered to recapture an abandoned position, passing burned-out British vehicles on his way up the line.

> On one tank, a head and an arm are leaning against the turret. That head has a grin. I approach: head and arm are joined, but the rest of the body is missing.
>
> I stare at those wide-open eyes. 'I hope you didn't suffer much.' And looking at him I see his mother and father still writing to him and telling him many good things for when the war is over and he comes home. I also see a pale, sad bride and two beautiful, carefree kids. Life and death.

At the front, di Parma found anti-tank gunners engaged in a desperate battle with British tanks. The gunners 'weep in despair – their shells don't penetrate the enemy's armour'. A dozen Italian tanks, crewed by men 'full of enthusiasm' but largely inexperienced, were thrown into the fray. Di Parma urged caution, but the commander pressed on. 'They swagger forward like ancient knights and after a few minutes the 12 tanks are knocked out, they burn, and with them the bodies of those brave men.'[13]

Stanley Christopherson's regiment of obsolescent Crusader tanks ran into more than a dozen Italian M13s and destroyed every one. 'We made a horrible mess of them,' the British officer noted. And then, in the aftermath of the slaughter, a British medic 'was worked to death patching up' the enemy wounded. 'It made us think how illogical war was,' Christopherson continued. 'First of all we do our best to kill these Germans and Italians, shelling them and machine-gunning them, and then afterwards we do all we can to save their lives.'[14]

The fighting over the battlefield was as unforgiving. Axis aviators believed they were outnumbered 20 to one, flying aircraft increasingly outclassed or outgunned by their opponent. Giorgio Solaroli flew one of a dozen fighters ordered to escort a formation of nearly 60 bombers – one third Stukas, the rest Italian CR42 biplanes – attacking the enemy's front line. 'We are not even over the front line when the radio reports enemy aircraft coming at us from all directions. Our nerves are at breaking point. We have to defend those poor colleagues of ours in their outdated aircraft, slowed down by bombs, who have no chance of defence.' The battle – Solaroli preferred the term 'bedlam' – quickly disintegrated into a series of 'small duels'. The biplanes dropped their payloads and 'engaged in wild aerobatics' to avoid the machine-guns of American-built P-40s.[15]

Roman Czjzek's radio unit was overrun by Eighth Army's tanks, the truck in which he was trying to escape no match for the enemy's armour over the uneven, stony terrain. One tank directed its cannon at Czjzek and his comrades. 'I pressed my head between blankets and my laundry bag,' he recalled. 'Someone in front of me was groaning. Ulbricht, a signaller, craned his neck, slumped back – he was dead. With a lurch, the truck stopped.' The vehicle was surrounded by British soldiers and the survivors taken prisoner. 'Like an iron door which closes in front of you, like a net which you are hopelessly caught up in: captivity,' Czjzek wrote. 'It was probably only much later when we were burying the dead that the thought arose: I have escaped with my life...'[16]

As early as 26 October – the fourth day of Eighth Army's offensive – the *Panzerarmee*'s diarist noted that 'the troops are showing signs of exhaustion', and it wasn't merely the new enemy offensive to blame. Too many men had spent too long in Africa – 18 months or more – and could no longer bear the strain. Rommel's mood grew darker by the day. 'All the cards are stacked against us,' he wrote to his wife on the 27th. 'Even so, I hope we can pull it off.' He was prone to over-estimating his enemy's armoured strength, convinced Montgomery possessed in excess of 1,800 tanks – although he reckoned 300 had been knocked out to date. But he also knew that his forces could not fight a sustained battle of attrition. He had already committed his reserves – there was nothing and no-one left to throw into the fray. 'Only with the skill of a juggler is it possible to plug the gaps,' he sighed during a staff conference on 29 October, counting the lifespan of *Panzerarmee Afrika* in days, perhaps even hours. 'I have the impression that we are approaching the end of the army.'[17]

In Rome, Mussolini and the Fascist leadership were preoccupied – but not with events in North Africa. Plagued by dysentery for the past couple of months, which caused him to shed a good 40 pounds, the Duce was not just thinner than he had been for some time, but also weaker and tired. He was, however, in high spirits, looking forward to the 20th anniversary of the March on Rome and the opening of a new museum in the capital dedicated to the Fascist revolution. It devoured far more of the Duce's time than the worsening military situation. He had possessed a translation of snippets of Montgomery's order of the day – 'We now have a great opportunity to fight the enemy and end the war' – within hours of Eighth Army's offensive beginning, but dismissed the attack. 'This doesn't appear to be a large-scale offensive,' he told Ugo Cavallero, Italy's senior military commander. Cavallero fed his master nothing but wildly optimistic reports from Egypt, convinced Rommel was crying wolf, still able to muster 250 tanks. The situation was serious, *not* desperate, 'and Rommel is in a position to fix it,' he mused. 'It's *his* battle. He's got the petrol and ammunition...' Given such a wild over-estimation of Rommel's situation and under-estimation of his foe, it's hardly surprising that Mussolini was not especially troubled by the Allied offensive. Efforts to parry it, the Duce declared, were 'quite satisfactory'.[18]

Yet some of the Duce's troops shared his view. After more than a week of fighting, the British had failed to score a decisive breakthrough; they had merely gnawed at the Axis front and pushed it back. The 'euphoric' ranks of the *Ariete* Division were convinced they had weathered the storm – and Rommel was about to unleash a counter-punch. 'Officers and soldiers who had lived, fought and suffered for months and months in the middle of the Egyptian desert, during the hottest period of the year, were finally seeing all their sacrifices rewarded and all their hopes crowned with the most coveted reward for a warrior: victory,' an excited Vincenzo Formica wrote. The *Ariete*'s tank crews spoke openly of 'spending Christmas in Alexandria'. 'Would what had been denied Marshal

Graziani back in 1940, what had seemed a vain chimera to veterans of 30 months of the bitter African campaign, be given to us to enjoy?'[19] Their hopes were to be dashed in a matter of hours.

While *Panzerarmee Afrika* fought for its life, the German public were desperate for news from the Alamein front. Instead, newspaper readers in the Reich were learning 'what Rommel's soldiers eat', as war correspondent Ernst Günter Dickmann explained that a 'ready meal' from a tin was the troops' staple diet. 'And every day we are once again grateful to the homeland that it takes care to produce us tinned food whose quality is matchless,' he wrote ingratiatingly. Fellow reporter Dr Kurt Pauli painted a picture of life on the Alamein front – though not of the battle raging. Readers of the *Völkischer Beobachter* read about 'sand dunes as high as houses' and a featureless expanse of desert extending as far as the Qattara Depression: 'no trees, no bushes, *ja*, not even camel thicket'. It took 'a real man' to survive here, to endure the heat, the plague of flies – 'almost unbearable without mosquito nets'. Rommel was not immune, frequently yelling in his Swabian dialect for his fly swat. As for the fighting, war correspondent Rudolf Kettlein egged on the enemy. 'Let the Tommies come,' he wrote in the *Hessische Landeszeitung*. 'We'll beat them back.' There were no facts in Kettlein's report, only rhetoric. 'The British offensive is not yet over,' he wrote.

> Bitter fighting is still raging. Every metre of earth is bitterly contested. The battle is tough, it demands our soldiers give their all. The 'hour of reckoning' of which the Commander-in-Chief of the English Eighth Army, Montgomery, spoke, will never come, however. What Field Marshal Rommel said, his soldiers espouse more than ever now: what they have, they hold firmly.[20]

By the time Kettlein's report appeared, Axis forces were running west for their lives.

The thin crust which was the Axis front line at Alamein finally cracked, then splintered, in the small hours of 2 November as Eighth Army unleashed the second phase of its offensive, *Supercharge*. There was nothing German and Italian troops could do to respond to the enemy's barrage, which crashed down on their positions shortly after 1am – some batteries in 15th Panzer Division only had three dozen rounds left. By 3.30am, the division's weak front had been smashed. The headquarters of 115th Panzer Grenadier Regiment was overrun, its vehicles left ablaze. An intercepted radio message – 'Our tanks are through the gap in the minefield and are now advancing on a wide front' – provided more concrete information than his own units to 15th Panzer's commander Gustav von Vaerst, who conceded to his *Afrika Korps* masters that he was 'unable to cope with the situation alone'. All he heard from von Thoma were orders to counter-attack at first light. 'The enemy must be pushed back.' Von Vaerst did as ordered. In doing so, he sent 8th Panzer Regiment on a death ride which failed to halt the enemy breakout and reduced it to just eight working tanks. 'The division's backbone was thus broken,' von Vaerst rued in his diary.[21]

21st Panzer Division had escaped the battering suffered by its neighbour, but spent a fruitless night waiting for clear orders. With the early morning haze lying over the battlefield, dawn was the perfect time to strike a decisive blow. But no instructions came. As the mist cleared, so the advantage of surprise was lost. The two wasted hours proved costly. When the panzers finally moved off they ran headlong into Allied armour and anti-tank guns. 'The defensive fire is too strong and our infantry are pinned down by enemy fire,' noted Dr Alfons Selmayr, who accompanied the armour. The counter-attack made no headway.[22]

Rommel had observed the day's fighting from high ground overlooking the battlefield. He watched the two dozen anti-aircraft guns – the last he possessed – struggle to hold off the waves of British air attacks. He saw his 88mm anti-tank guns – the only weapon truly capable of stopping the enemy's heaviest armour – knocked out. He was perturbed by signs of disintegration in the Italian ranks as the *Littorio* and *Trieste* divisions were mauled; some men were no longer following the orders of their commanders and running west. And he watched the remnants of the fabled *Afrika Korps* knock out at least 40 enemy tanks but leave the field of battle with fewer than three dozen working panzers, while an enemy at least four times stronger carried the day.

Erwin Rommel had seen enough. He had no reserves. His supply chain could not keep pace even with the demands of the depleted ranks of his army. The troops had endured a relentless pounding from the enemy's artillery, tanks, infantry and especially air force, for ten days. Their spirit remained unbroken. It was about the only thing which wasn't. Put simply, *Panzerarmee Afrika* stood on the brink of annihilation. It could not withstand another British attack. The moment had come to break off the battle and fall back from Alamein. That evening, as he sent his daily report back to Hitler's headquarters, he ordered his troops to break contact with the enemy and begin falling back to the west.[23]

Still spoon-fed inaccurate, unrealistic or irrelevant news from the desert, the German public were suddenly gripped by the battle raging in Egypt – but unsure what to make of it given the frugal information in the daily communiqués. Most Germans hoped that Axis arms would triumph in North Africa – as they always had, thanks to their great commander. As one put it: 'As long as Rommel is down there, nothing can happen to us…' It was a view shared by Joseph Goebbels. 'I still place all my hopes in Rommel,' he noted. 'He will not be so easily beaten.'

As far as the propaganda minister was concerned, there was no question of defeat in North Africa for now. 'The game's only lost when there's nothing left to save – but we've nowhere nearly reached that stage yet.'[24]

Tuesday 3 November began with a sorely tested Erwin Rommel penning a letter to his wife Lucie after a restless night when his mind tried – and failed – to find a solution to his army's plight. 'The battle is going very heavily against us. We're simply being crushed by the enemy weight,' he wrote. 'We are facing very difficult days, perhaps the most difficult that a man can undergo. The dead are lucky – it's all over for them.' His men were becoming equally fatalistic. 5th Panzer Regiment was hurrying to the assistance of its comrades in the 8th as the sun rose. 'But what can we do?' a weary Alfons Selmayr asked himself. 'In total we're just 30 panzers, but facing us are a good 300.' There was nothing in the Germans' favour: the terrain was as level as a table; the enemy had better tanks with stronger armour and more powerful guns. Over the radio Selmayr heard two of the regiment's most senior officers, Otto-Friedrich Senfft and Werner Mildebrath, conversing. 'Attack, this is madness!' Senfft complained. 'True, but orders are orders.' The counter-attack made no more than 100 metres before the first panzers were knocked out.[25]

Rommel spent the morning observing the sluggish retreat along the coastal highway and the enemy's air force attack what was left of the *Afrika Korps* at least 11 times before returning to his headquarters – surviving a bombing raid on his staff car in the process. The field marshal found orders from the two Axis dictators waiting for him. Mussolini demanded he stand and fight in his current positions 'whatever the cost'.[26] Adolf Hitler was even more explicit:

> I, your Führer, and the German people have complete confidence in you as Commander-in-Chief and in the courage of the German and Italian troops who are fighting an heroic battle in Egypt under your command.
>
> In the situation in which you find yourself, there can be no thought other than holding out with utter determination, committing every weapon and every soldier capable of bearing arms in battle.
>
> Despite his numerical superiority, the enemy will squander his forces. This will happen – it has happened more than once before in history – and the stronger will triumphs over more powerful enemy forces.
>
> There is no other course of action for your troops but victory or death.[27]

To Paul Meixner, the senior German naval officer in North Africa, Hitler's order was just what was needed to rally the men. 'What a boost this gives to everyone, how it fires them up, as each man thinks now victory is already achieved. In such instances you realise the tremendous strength of the Führer,' he wrote. 'But there's just one thing to do: let yourself be killed on the spot and do not think about withdrawing under any circumstances.' But to Erwin Rommel, it meant a death sentence for his forces. His units were down to half strength. *Afrika Korps* could call upon just two dozen working panzers and would be annihilated if it chose to stand and fight, while the Italian *Littorio* and *Trieste* Divisions had already been 'practically wiped out'. Hitler's orders 'demanded the impossible,' the field marshal wrote, but he carried them out nonetheless.[28]

He did, however, dispatch his adjutant, Alfred-Ingemar Berndt – a 'rising star' in the Propaganda Ministry – to Hitler's headquarters to report in person. Perhaps then the Führer might grasp the gravity of the situation. Accompanying the 37-year-old officer, what little money the field marshal had on him (25,000 Italian Lire) and the second letter of the day to his wife, terser and even bleaker than the one he had penned that morning. 'What will become of us is in God's hands...'[29]

Wednesday 4 November was bleaker than Tuesday 3 November. 21st Panzer Division's grenadiers began the day troubled by the sound of battle coming from behind a chain of hills: the enemy had overrun much of the division's remaining armour and was now streaming westwards. The grenadiers' commander, Curt Ehle, seized the initiative. 'Our commanding officer leads the way,' battalion commander Adalbert von Taysen wrote. 'He sees the burned-out wreckage of tanks and, on the vast plain south of it recognises hundreds of British vehicles and tanks roaring westwards at high speed in a seething sea of dust. This is the great breakthrough of the Eighth Army...' Rommel's report to Berlin this Wednesday morning was a litany of woe, of overwhelming Allied superiority, of enemy breakthroughs ten miles deep in places, of Italian troops abandoning their positions and running to the rear. One by one, German and Italian units were being destroyed and the only solution to Rommel appeared to be 'a fighting withdrawal' to 'prevent the loss of the African theatre', falling back 50 miles towards Fuka on the coastal highway, making the Allies 'fight for every foot of ground' on the way. The situation worsened with each passing hour. As he drove medics, fuel and ammunition up to the still-working tanks of the *Ariete* Division, Vincenzo Formica encountered 'all kinds of vehicles from the *Trieste* and *Bologna* Divisions – and other units – crossing my path, loaded with men crammed into boxes, most of them without weapons and with pale, dejected faces.' Formica feared the entire front had collapsed, but was relieved to find his division's tanks holding the line as ordered. As Formica arrived at the front, a colleague handed him a pair of binoculars and pointed at a group of black dots in the east. 'The enemy,' thought Formica. 'He was in front of me, a couple of kilometres away, still silent and motionless like a treacherous beast, half-hidden in the morning mist. Should I live to be 100 years old, I will never forget those moments.' The young officer now watched as an entire company of M13 tanks moved out, throwing up thick clouds of dust as they advanced towards the enemy Shermans. The *Ariete*'s commander, Francesco Arena, had been reluctant to commit his armour, but was overruled by Erwin Rommel. 'General, I know your division better than you do,' the field marshal told him. 'The *Ariete* still has a chance, it will stop the British for a day.' Both were right. The *Ariete* sacrificed itself this day. Even when their tanks were disabled, crews remained with them and continued to shoot, or else sought another vehicle in which to continue the battle; one officer changed tanks three times before the day was over. As night fell on 4 November, the tanks of the *Ariete* largely stood where they had begun the day – but now they were lifeless hulks or blazing torches. Thus did the 132nd Armoured Division pass into history. 'It will not be said of it that it turned around,' Vincenzo Formica recorded with pride. Its destruction left a gap in Axis lines a dozen miles wide through which the enemy poured and could never be plugged. The remnants of the *Trento* Division – almost out of vehicles and ammunition – were surrounded early in the afternoon of 4 November. Its commander, Giorgio Masina, rejected a senseless fight to the death. Masina sent a final message to XXI Corps: 'Ammunition almost exhausted. We will fight to the last round where we stand. Everyone is fighting brilliantly. Savoia. Salute the King. Salute the Duce. Viva la *Trento*!' Having burned his confidential papers and destroyed his radio equipment, Masina offered to surrender his group, but the British simply continued rolling westwards, leaving the general, his staff and a few vehicles to escape into the desert. Joining forces with German paratroopers, they sought to remain out of sight and range of the advancing Eighth Army to reach Axis lines outside the town of Fuka. After a heroic, unequal fight all morning long, *Afrika Korps* faced an identical fate and lost its commander in the late afternoon: Ritter von Thoma was taken prisoner when his command post was overrun by British armour. For Rommel it was the final straw. He could not wait for a decision from the Wolf's Lair. He took it upon himself to order his army to wait until dusk, then head for Fuka. The third Battle of El Alamein was over.[30]

No Italian or German soldier at Alamein believed he had been outfought by his foe. 'The Englishman did not win the battle of El Alamein by superior leadership or bold decisions,' Gustav von Vaerst observed. The enemy was lacklustre, uninspired, unimaginative. Axis forces had been defeated by 'superiority in mass and matériel, not in leadership and spirit', especially prodigious expenditure of ammunition. For example, the artillery of 21st Panzer Division loosed an impressive 11,000 rounds between 24 October and

4 November – just under 1,000 shells a day. But its opponent fired 20 times as many. The elite Italian paratroop units were similarly affronted at having to break off the battle and retreat. The ever-thinning line of *Folgore* had stood firm, repulsing British and Free French forces time and again. The 187th *Folgore* Regiment alone reckoned it had killed, wounded or captured more than 375 enemy soldiers for the loss of 150 of its own. It dismissed Montgomery's offensive as a 'bloody failure', a succession 'of fierce but useless attacks'. But there were failings and shortcomings on the Axis side, too. Rommel's much-vaunted minefields, the 'Devil's Gardens', had proved surprisingly ineffective. The enemy was more skilled in fighting at night. His infantry was fresh and well rested. His tanks were better. His aircraft were better. Rather than provide reinforcements and dispatch the latest machines to North Africa, however, Hermann Göring chastised his fighter pilots for failing to keep the enemy at bay. 'Wave after wave' of enemy aircraft appeared, yet 'not one' was shot down because 'all aggressive spirit' had 'disappeared' since the death of Marseille at the end of September. But the Reichsmarschall went further: comrades in Russia and France were ashamed of their colleagues in Africa who were besmirching the good name of German fighter pilots. Göring demanded his men 'throw themselves at the enemy – even to the point of self-sacrifice. Only one thing matters: to save our honour.' The men of *Jagdgeschwader* 77 regarded the order as an insult. 'In a nutshell: the fighters are at fault for Rommel's retreat,' Armin Köhler noted. 'The fighter pilots in Africa hold a different view. Every one of us!'[31]

The retreat to Fuka was well underway by the time first Mussolini, then, five minutes later, Hitler begrudgingly gave their consent to the withdrawal. Long before nightfall, there had already been a constant flow of German and Italian vehicles streaming westwards – often crammed with all manner of items: tables, washbowls, carpets – while infantry struggled along on foot. The Messerschmitts of *Jagdgeschwader* 77 had already fallen back to the coastal airfield at Quotaifiya, a good 40 miles from Alamein. The move failed to afford the fighter pilots or ground crew even a temporary respite. 'I experience an attack by 20 or 30 aircraft,' pilot Heinz Lüdemann wrote. 'You can write off your life when you see these masses flying towards you and the explosions slowly but steadily getting closer and closer. And we're standing there – no aircraft, hardly any fuel for the rest and hardly any maintenance. It's utter chaos.' That evening, the unit was on the move again, another five miles into the desert. 'The psychosis of retreat is having a devastating effect on people. Just retreat!' Lüdemann observed. 'The front line is still holding. But everyone seems to think the British are at their heels. Such thinking probably deprives most people of sober and clear judgment.'[32]

The Italian airfield at Abu Haggag had been 70 miles behind the front when the battle began. With Eighth Army barely 30 miles away, Giorgio Solaroli received orders to abandon the base. Before dawn on the 5th, the tents were dismantled and loaded with all the men's kit on to trucks and sent 60 miles west on a wretched journey of eight hours or more. Those who chose the coastal highway – blocked in several places by burning vehicles – were continuously harassed by enemy aircraft. Other trucks 'preferred to make their way through the desert sand. Where tracked vehicles would have been necessary, the arms of our men, eager to escape capture, worked miracles.' The small number of still-serviceable aircraft began departing mid-morning. As the last Macchi fighter lifted off the ground, the first British began rolling into Abu Haggag. Solaroli doubted he would return. 'Now that we realise that we have irretrievably lost a battle – and perhaps possession of Africa.'[33]

The order to retreat came too late for the men running 5th Panzer Regiment's workshop. Thanks to Hitler's stand fast order, engineers had continued toiling on broken-down panzers rather than prepare them for towing to the rear. There was no time to consider an evacuation when they were instructed to fall back a second time. 'As a result, 40 panzers – certainly no fewer than 40 panzers – have to be blown up, half of which could have been repaired had the orders been correct,' one German soldier fumed. 'But in the Wolf's Lair they know better...'[34]

The armour of 21st Panzer Division had just enough fuel in their tanks to reach Fuka. As night fell, the armour began to head west. 'After dark we see British flares on our right and left,' one soldier wrote. 'The march turns into a race for our freedom. The drivers race like the hangman over the thankfully stony ground. What is left behind is taken under tow. A number of scattered troops from other units are also picked up.' Around first light on the 5th, the remaining vehicles of 21st Panzer Division arrived at Fuka 'in reasonable order'.[35]

Except Rommel's army did not stop at Fuka. The retreat continued, gathered momentum, took on a life of its own. 'Panic was in the air,' one flak officer remembered. Men seized whatever vehicle was still running and headed west. The main road was choked, limiting the vehicles at best to moving a mere 30 miles during the hours of darkness. By day, Allied air power made any movement almost impossible. 'Every bomb hit something,' the flak officer wrote. 'Christ it was awful! Dying, wounded, blazing vehicles – the most terrible scene I have ever experienced.'[36]

Wretched as *Panzerarmee Afrika*'s plight was, it was about to worsen considerably due to events hundreds of miles in its rear. Around mid-day on 7 November, Italian intelligence had passed an alarming report to Berlin: 'Enemy intends to land in French North Africa', accompanied by a note from Eberhard

Weichold, the senior German naval officer in Rome who warned there was the 'gravest threat for the war and victory in what is happening'.[37] The following morning, British and American troops landed in French North Africa: either side of Casablanca on the Atlantic coast, Oran and Algiers in the Mediterranean. French resistance to Operation *Torch* evaporated within 48 hours, leaving Rommel facing a two-front war, albeit separated by 1,000 miles of Libyan and Tunisian desert. German and Italian forces secured Rommel's rear, for now, by occupying Tunis ahead of the Allies, but it did little to improve the situation facing his army – or his mood. 'The end will not be long for we're simply being crushed by the enemy superiority,' he wrote to his wife on 14 November. 'The army is in no way to blame. It has fought magnificently.' The next day he dashed off another note: 'How will the war turn out if we lose North Africa? How will it end? I wish I could shake off these terrible thoughts.'[38]

Student Lore Walb was beginning to ask herself similar questions. The 23-year-old was filled with mixed emotions after her weekly trip to the cinema in Heidelberg. 'Deep down, I quite enjoyed it,' she confided in the diary she had kept since the age of 14, 'but a great weight is beginning to put us under increasing pressure. Fate seems to be confronting us with tough events.' The worst news came from Africa. Daily. Tobruk had now fallen. 'If the fighting continues like this, Africa will soon be lost,' the worried Walb noted. 'Even Rommel can't help there. Is this the beginning of the end???' After nearly three months, there was still fighting raging in Stalingrad. 'We couldn't believe this was still possible. But in the newsreel you can see that each individual house is a fortress.' It was beginning to dawn on Walb – whose family were committed National Socialists – and many of her friends that the war was turning against Germany: 'We simply cannot believe it after such victories. *Ja*, then all those countless sacrifices will have been in vain… Everyone is depressed. Everybody feels that something decisive lies in store for us.'[39]

A few days later Joseph Goebbels sought to assuage such fears, addressing Party faithful in the city of Wuppertal, close to the industrial heartland of the Ruhr. His speech was unscripted, unvarnished, raw. The retreat from El Alamein and the landings in French North Africa were part of the 'temporary ups and downs in the fortunes of war – but they are not decisive for its outcome,' he explained. He likened the war to a football match. Germany enjoyed a lead of 4 or 5-0 after the 'first half'. Her opponent might 'score' once or twice in reply, but the Reich would still triumph.

> When we've experienced the most glorious victories in this war, we have not allowed ourselves to become cocky and reckless. And if we suffer momentary setbacks in this

war, we do not allow ourselves to be weakened by them. Burdens are there to be overcome and difficulties are there so we do not give in in the face of them.

The only factor decisive for the war's outcome was whether the enemy caused 'one of the critical parts of our front to collapse,' he continued. 'And I can assure you this won't happen – I know because I've got all the facts at my disposal.' He closed his 85-minute address by citing Nietzsche. 'The war can bring whatever it likes in its future course, we will rise to each test in keeping with the words: *Praise what makes us hard*!' Rousing applause filled the city hall. Goebbels was convinced he had delivered a powerful speech. 'You can tell from the strains of the national anthem sung at the end that my audience understood me.'[40]

While citizens of the Reich read excerpts from the propaganda minister's speech in their daily newspapers the next day – Wednesday 18 November – the military council of the Stalingrad Front agreed the wording of a rousing appeal to the troops:

> The hour of reckoning with the cruel enemy has arrived.
>
> The troops of the Stalingrad Front are going over to a decisive attack against the despicable foe, the German-Fascist occupiers. Destroy them and fulfil your duty to the Motherland with honour...
>
> Death to the German occupiers.[41]

It would be issued the following day.

As Wednesday 18 November turned to Thursday, the 19th, a storm descended on the Don some 70 miles northwest of Stalingrad and did not stop. The easterly wind drove crystals of snow and ice into the faces of the Romanian soldiers unfortunate enough to be standing guard on the Don this evening with such ferocity that it burned the skin. The snow flurries were so thick no man could see more than a few metres. Ears were more use. 'But on this night, nothing could be heard,' Sergeant Alexander Andricu remembered. The previous nights had been marked by the rumble of engines on the other side of the front line near Kletskaya on a bend in the Don. 'There was a ghostly silence over the fields of snow.' The sergeant returned to his bunker, crawled into his bed and fell into a restless sleep.

Alexander Andricu was woken by the ground beneath his bed shaking. The bunker seemed to rise and fall – as if it were a ship riding the waves. Clods of earth fell from the bunker ceiling, the wooden boards propping up the shelter began to come loose, and a terrible howling filled the cramped, crumbling underground space. 'Hell had opened its gates over us,' Andricu recalled. A guard staggered into the bunker with blood streaming down his face. Pressure waves tossed the men around, throwing them against the floor or walls. It went on like this for a good two hours. Eventually the bunker roof caved in. Men prayed, the sergeant remembered, 'but God did not seem to hear them.' Ion Constantinescu remembered 'a sinister howling unleashed from the barrels of the entire arsenal of war travelled through the air – it was as if the entire front was on fire. The heavy artillery groaned, the artillery thundered with shrapnel, the mortars howled like the packs of wolves, Stalin's organs shook the ground with an infernal noise.' Valeriu Munteanu and his comrades were 'stricken with terror', huddled together in their trenches as if prepared to die together. 'The earth is shaking, it shakes, burns in flames, wails in pain,' he continued:

> We see shelters, trenches, machine-gun nests blow up. Legs, arms, pieces of flesh, intestines fall on us, we're spattered with blood. Around us there's nothing but flashes and lightning, flames and smoke, howling and shouting... There's nothing human about the men's faces any more; some desperately make the sign of the cross, others are on their knees praying.[42]

When the barrage shifted further to the rear, Alexander Andricu and his comrades dug themselves out of their wrecked bunker and ran up the narrow steps to the trenches.

> We saw terrible scenes. The ground all around us was like a lunar landscape. Our squadron chief lay in a crater. A splinter had ripped his head off. We saw dead bodies and the dying everywhere. Their shrill cries mingled with the shells hissing and wailing over our heads.
>
> Suddenly, however, we heard another sound. A rumbling like thunder approaching fast, coming from no man's land. A short time later they stood before us. The steel walls of the Soviet tanks became colossal in front of us. Like strange mythical creatures, they pushed through the black-grey wall of powdery smoke with their grinding caterpillar tracks. They drew ever closer. Their wide tracks pushed the snow aside. Crouching figures ran behind them. Not once did the rumble of the tank engines drown out the piercing battle cry of the Red Army soldiers. One of the steel monsters came directly towards us. I wanted to yell but I could not. Like the snout of a monster, the tank's long cannon bobbed up and down threateningly with the rhythm of movement.
>
> We did not think about resistance any more. We threw our guns away and ran off. We fell down in the snow, got up and ran on again. The tracks of the Soviet tanks rattled behind us. To us, they were like demonic whips, always driving us

on. They did not even shoot. Nor did they have to. Their appearance had spread panic-stricken horror. They were steel coffins which drove death through the morning.

Andricu was captured that afternoon by a Soviet cavalry patrol.[43]

Romanian Third Army was on the receiving end of the first blows of Operation *Uranus*, a two-pronged assault on Axis forces along the Don and Volga with the objective of trapping Sixth Army at Stalingrad. Five Red Army motorised and armoured corps concentrated on a front of little more than three dozen miles. Everything was against the Romanians – the weather, the terrain, the lack of local resources and, not least, their allies. Supplies for the Sixth Army took precedence. Two thirds of the trains and transport meant for Third Army on the Don were diverted to the Volga instead. As a result, only one in six of the 300,000 mines it required to fortify its lines were delivered, only a quarter of the 600 miles of barbed wire promised had been rolled out, and the four Romanian infantry corps standing in the Red Army's way possessed just 60 heavy anti-tank guns. Based on the interrogation of disgruntled prisoners, Soviet intelligence expected Third Army's front to crumble. 'When the Red Army delivers its first serious blow, we'll drop everything and run away. Let Hitler and Antonescu fight.' Some Romanian soldiers did flee. 'Everyone went crazy, they came running from behind, no helmets, no weapons, naked,' Ioan Patca recalled. 'Hearts were filled with horror. Throughout the white expanse there was nothing but chaos and blood, dead and wounded, soldiers walked around with no object.' Though outnumbered and outgunned, many Romanian units in fact fought to the end. The 13th Anti-Tank Battery destroyed around ten Russian tanks before it was wiped out to a man with every one of its guns. General Gheorghe Stavrescu's 14th Infantry Division – trying to defend a front more than 11 miles long – lost two regimental commanders, five battalion commanders and almost every company and battery commander. All that was left of his formation was the baggage column and headquarters staff. On the left wing of the Romanian front, Captain Dumitru Păsat was still holding his position. 'You no longer saw calm human figures, only tense and worried ones,' he wrote. 'Soldiers and cadets also looked at us, at the officers, and saw we had worried faces like theirs.' Occasionally they would ask Păsat about his intentions. 'What are we doing, Captain? Are we going to be caught like mice here?' His only response: orders were orders – and he too would be trapped like a mouse, just like them. The battalion had received no orders to fall back – and would not do so on its own initiative. Third Army's commander

General Petre Dumitrescu recalled that his infantry 'performed its duty; it stood firm... it sacrificed itself with unblemished honour in the positions entrusted to it, defending them "without any thought of retreat".'[44] Nevertheless, by the day's end, the Red Army had punched two enormous holes in Dumitrescu's front – each a good ten miles wide and between ten and 25 miles deep. They would never be plugged.

By the time news of the Soviet offensive reached Friedrich Paulus' headquarters in the village of Golubinskaya on the west bank of the Don it was late morning and the Red Army spearhead was no more than three dozen miles away. Neither the offensive nor its success surprised Wolfram von Richthofen. 'Now last year's mess is beginning all over again,' the Luftwaffe general fumed. Paulus failed to act. Richthofen *couldn't* act: the freezing fog, snow and icy rain kept his aircraft grounded all day. Only if the weather lifted would 'the Russian spectre be banished'.[45]

In Stalingrad itself, Joachim Stempel was still convinced that the German soldier would drive the last Soviet soldier from the right bank of the Volga. But he was also troubled by an old proverb: 'Russia can only be defeated if the enemy crosses the Volga.'

He had expected to once again lead 103rd Panzergrenadier Regiment in yet another attempt to reach the river. The men waited in their jump-off positions, but the appointed time passed without the order to attack given, nor the usual preparatory bombardment. The guns were silent, the Luftwaffe notable by its absence over Stalingrad. Only at headquarters was there lively activity – the hustle and bustle of confused staff officers who had only questions for Stempel, no answers. He returned to his men and continued preparations for the assault. As night fell on Stalingrad that Thursday, no man in 103rd Panzer Grenadier Regiment had any idea what was happening at the front.[46]

On the other side of the front line, news of the counter-stroke quickly spread among the defenders. 'Stalingraders, our friends, and also our enemies, will never forget this date,' an excited Red Army regimental commander wrote. 'It has begun!'[47]

The thrust which brushed aside Romanian Third Army alone would probably have trapped Sixth Army in Stalingrad, but to guarantee victory the Soviets delivered their second blow south of the city late on the morning of 20 November. Once again Romanian divisions were the victims, the forces hurled against them overwhelming. From his observation post on the southern end of the German front, battalion commander Bruno Gebele watched the Romanian lines pummelled by the brief, but intense, opening barrage before the armour and infantry moved out. Gebele had grown to know his comrades-in-arms during the preceding months and pitied them: the men themselves were rugged – the ranks of 20th Infantry Division were largely filled with good farming stock from Transylvania – but their officers cared little for them, rarely venturing to the front. Equipment, clothing and food were poor, bunkers and strongpoints inadequate and horse-drawn anti-tank guns useless against the T-34. Now Gebele watched the Soviets acting 'as if on the exercise ground'. A concerted bombardment from German and Romanian guns held the Red Army troops off for ten minutes. But once the Soviet tanks reached the Romanians' defensive line, 'there was no stopping them'. There was some hand-to-hand fighting between the opposing infantry, but once the Russian armour pierced the defences 'the surviving Romanian soldiers ran across the white steppe'. The front of 20th Infantry Division collapsed and two entire Soviet armies drove through the gap.[48]

With bad weather grounding aerial reconnaissance, the airwaves flooded with fake messages, and few reports reaching Sixth Army's headquarters from front-line units, Friedrich Paulus was starved of accurate information. All manner of rumours were swilling around. Staff were tense, yet their commander seemed not to grasp the gravity of his situation – even when he was informed of the second Soviet blow south of Stalingrad. Sixth Army's commander smoked constantly – the ashtray on his desk was full, his office filled with the stench of cigarette smoke and a blue haze – and seemed more interested in minutiae, such as replacing the sick commander of 14th Panzer Division, than taking decisive action. It is difficult to know whether Paulus was overwhelmed by the situation, or blasé, but more than one senior German officer was convinced that 'a brief period of good weather with a sharp strike from us will break up the Russian affair,' as Luftwaffe commander Wolfram von Richthofen predicted.[49]

The one decision Paulus did make was to begin transferring his headquarters from Golubinskaya on the Don to the town of Nizhne Chirskaya, a good 30 miles to the southwest – and *outside* the pocket the Soviet pincers were threatening to create if they met. Trucks set off in temperatures 20 degrees below zero on the night of 20–21 November carrying the advanced staff to establish the new command post. They returned a few hours later claiming the road south was blocked by Soviet forces. Paulus' operations officer Hans Elchlepp dismissed their report. 'In their worked-up state, they saw ghosts,' he snapped. A couple of staff cars and motorcyclists were sent out into the bitter night to scout the route. There were no ghosts on the road to Nizhne Chirskaya, but there were Soviet tanks on the Don highway barely 12 miles from Golubinskaya.[50]

Other German officers did not dismiss the Soviet threat so lightly. 'We are experiencing a great crisis here,' 384th Infantry Division's commander Eccard von Gablenz confided in his wife, Vita. 'The situation is extremely critical – as far as I can judge from my humble point of view, it is the same as a year ago outside Moscow. The Russians are trying to surround Stalingrad.'[51]

The spearhead of the southern pincer was closing in on the village of Tinguta, 30 miles south of Stalingrad and otherwise insignificant except that it served as the supply hub for the Romanian 20th Infantry Division. Stan Gheorghe was woken in his quarters around midnight on 21–22 November by German soldiers crying 'Ruski!' Tinguta was not heavily defended, but Gheorghe and his comrades called the enemy's bluff, sending the few 120mm shells they had left in the direction of the Russian tanks. It worked. The enemy armour halted – and did not resume its advance until dawn. It allowed the bulk of the Romanian formations – supply and administration units – to slip away. They would be pretty much the only elements of 20th Infantry Division to return home from the Eastern Front. The bulk of its fighting formations, ranks filled with Transylvanian farming stock, would be trapped.[52]

Stan Gheorghe and his staff proved rather more alert than Sixth Army's quartermaster, Werner von Kunowski, in Kalach. When Sixth Army's headquarters column passed through the town around 5am on the 22nd, the town – and its garrison – were largely asleep, 'as if the enemy were far away,' recalled a troubled Wilhelm Adam, Sixth Army adjutant. Kunowski immediately set about trying to evacuate food, clothing and mail – but without the necessary trucks and, above all, time, much would have to be destroyed just a few hours later.

Kalach became the eye of the needle through which Axis forces east of the Don were desperately trying to pass to avoid being trapped. There was no order, no control imposed on the traffic, just cars, trucks, vehicles of every kind, plus men on foot, a green-grey mass 'carried along by the tide of "every man for himself",' Stan Gheorghe observed. Half a dozen miles from Kalach, Gheorghe's column ground to a halt and worrying news began to pass along it: the bridge was already in Soviet hands.[53]

The Don crossing had been guarded by several 88mm guns positioned on the high west bank, overlooking the temporary bridge and the 1,000ft-wide river. Each day Russian tanks – captured by 71st Infantry Division and re-painted in German grey – crossed the bridge and conducted gunnery practice against shot-up hulks in the tank graveyard from the fighting of July and August. On the morning of 22 November, no German soldier reacted when he saw Russian armour crossing the bridge, except the tanks proved to be the vanguard of 26th

Armoured Brigade. The flak gunners on the heights raised the alarm, but were quickly overrun while the Don bridge fell into Russian hands.[54]

The Don crossing 20 miles to the southwest at Verkhne Chirskaya was still in German hands – for now. And the chaos mirrored that at Kalach, adjutant Wilhelm Adam remembered.

> Driven by fear of Soviet tanks, trucks, command vehicles, cars, motorbikes, riders and horse-drawn vehicles hurried westwards, colliding with each other, getting stuck, overturning, blocking the way. In between, pedestrians pushed, shoved, danced. Those who stumbled and fell to the ground never got back on their feet. They were trampled, run over, flattened.
>
> In the race to save their skin, everything which hindered them was left behind. Weapons and equipment were thrown away. Fully-loaded ammunition wagons, field kitchens and supply vehicles were left behind... Everyone had lost their head, everyone had panicked.[55]

While Adam and his comrades struggled to reach Sixth Army's new headquarters – now barely half a dozen miles away – the two Soviet pincers met on the main railway line some 25 miles west of Stalingrad. Soviet propaganda painted pictures – and filmed scenes – of pure joy, of soldiers embracing each other, of wild cries of 'Urra!', of men throwing their caps in the air. In fact, the encounter had been a bloody affair. As the two forces approached each other at dusk, 45th Tank Brigade failed to fire the correct recognition signals and a fierce firefight ensued. It was half an hour before Red Army troops stopped killing each other.[56]

Bloody union aside, the Soviet blow had been an incredible success – far beyond German expectations. They had feared a winter counter-offensive, but nothing with the vision of *Uranus*, nor executed with such verve and resolve. The Soviets had learned to Blitzkrieg. American journalist Harry Shapiro, United Press' veteran Moscow correspondent, was subsequently invited to survey the battlefield:

> The steppe was a fantastic sight. It was full of dead horses, while some horses were only half-dead, standing on three frozen legs and shaking the remaining broken one. It was pathetic. Ten thousand horses had been killed during the Russian breakthrough. The whole steppe was strewn with these dead horses and wrecked gun carriages and tanks and guns – German, French, Czech, even British and no end of corpses, Romanian and German.[57]

Trapped inside the fledgling pocket was not just the core of Sixth Army, but substantial elements of Romanian Third Army and Hermann Hoth's Fourth Panzer Army – upwards of 290,000 men. *Pravda* relished the prospect of their destruction: 'Now the Germans will start to pay the price for our blood and the tears of our people, for their crimes and plundering.'[58]

When Wilhelm Adam finally reached Sixth Army's new headquarters in Nizhne Chirskaya, he found Friedrich Paulus and Arthur Schmidt already preparing to leave the barely established command post. The army commander and his chief-of-staff had overtaken the rest of the headquarters by flying the short distance in a couple of tiny Storch courier aircraft which took off from Golubinskaya as Soviet artillery rounds crashed down. Paulus had received fresh orders – from the Führer himself – to direct the battle from *inside* the *Kessel* (literally 'kettle', but in military parlance 'pocket') in which Sixth Army found itself. The staff took to the skies again, this time for Gumrak airfield on the western outskirts of Stalingrad, where they would share the same privations and hardships as the men they led.[59]

Croatian Legionnaire Rudolf Baričević was summoned – along with numerous other officers and adjutants – to a command post where he learned Sixth Army was surrounded. But not for long. Baričević was told the army would abandon Stalingrad at dusk and fight its way out of encirclement, laying waste to anything in its path. The Croatians merely had to wait for the codeword – *Wir bauen um* ('We are relocating') to move out. It never came.[60] Though its commanders, including Paulus, mulled over a breakout, Hitler ordered Sixth Army to anchor itself on the Volga, hunker down and await rescue from outside. A relief force hurriedly assembled under the victor of Sevastopol, Erich von Manstein, would break *into* the pocket to save the day. And though it was far beyond its means, the Luftwaffe would keep Paulus' men supplied. LI Corps' commander Walther von Seydlitz was sceptical, as he wrote to his wife.

> We will do our best to get ourselves out of this situation, but *everything* else must come from outside. Time is the key – can we hold out long enough?
>
> In any case I have to reckon on this being one of my last – if not the last – letters. There's no point hiding the situation from you… I have only one wish: that our death here for Germany and the Führer will not have been in vain.
>
> Obviously, we've still not given up all hope. But, as I've said, in such a situation we have to expect every eventuality. It'll take quite some *miracle!*[61]

While encirclement troubled senior officers like Seydlitz, junior leaders and the rank and file were remarkably sanguine. 'We can probably break out any time we like,' 24th Panzer Division doctor Horst Rocholl wrote to his family. 'But that means giving up the successes we've achieved over several months – so that's not going to happen.' Rather than batter itself against the wall of the pocket, Sixth Army consolidated its positions and waited for the Führer's instructions. 'Perhaps it'll end with a pocket where we encircle rather than are encircled,' Rocholl mused. 'After two or three restless days, faith in the Führer is stronger than ever. Even in the most unsettling of moments not one soldier ever doubted him.'[62] The deeply religious Helmut Gründling, barely 19 and from Breslau, urged his family 'not to trouble themselves unnecessarily'. 'The Führer himself is in charge of operations in our sector,' he assured them. 'In fact, yesterday – or the day before yesterday – he was even nearby. One of our comrades saw him. You can imagine how calm and confident we've been since then.'[63] Junior officer Friedrich Waldhausen was equally certain. 'Yesterday Field Marshal von Manstein sent the following telegram to our encircled little group,' he told his family.

HALTET AUS
ICH HAU EUCH RAUS
MANSTEIN

Stick it out
I'll get you out
Manstein

'That really hit home. We *will* stick it out! The mood of the men is exemplary. They're all whistling and singing. Everyone is confident.'[64]

Manstein did not come. He tried – and failed. The offensive he launched on 12 December initially punched through the encircling ring southwest of Stalingrad before progress slowed and the advance finally petered out still 30 miles short of Sixth Army's lines. By then the Soviets had unleashed a second winter counter-stroke – *Little Saturn* – smashing through Italian lines on the Don, threatening Manstein's rear. Two days before Christmas 1942 the field marshal conceded defeat. The Sixth Army was doomed.

The situation in Stalingrad – not to mention Soviet resistance and winter in the mountains – had already brought offensive operations in the Caucasus to an end. Wherever they stood, German troops prepared for several uncomfortable months riding out the winter. Despite combing out the rear units, the front line was sparsely populated. Perhaps that was a blessing, for in the few hours of daylight there was barely the time, and certainly not the resources, to improve their positions. In late November night fell as early as 3pm, after which, wrote Gernot Nagel, operations officer of 101st *Jäger* Division, 'the men go into their narrow, damp hole in the earth where they've one candle per week for three people.' The wretched diet, constant damp, little warmth, left front-line soldiers emaciated and vulnerable to all manner of diseases and illnesses: jaundice, stomach complaints, cystitis, kidney conditions and constant colds. The damp and dirt – and inability to wash or shower or change clothing – caused all manner of skin complaints, rashes and ulcers, clothes were infested with lice, water was dirty or else polluted by the cadavers of animals and humans, and now, with the arrival of winter, cases of frostbite were being reported. The casualty rate was horrific. Hubert Lanz was losing 60 mountain infantrymen a day, including two men daily to hunger and exhaustion – losses twice as high as his advance through Poland and Ukraine in the summer and autumn of 1941. 125th Infantry Division lost two thirds of its fighting strength – more than 2,300 dead and wounded – during the stalled drive to the Black Sea coast in September and October. Replacements aged 18 and 19 arriving from Germany were simply no match for the men they replaced – especially the experienced non-commissioned officers. Young officers were brave – eager to take the fight to the enemy – but struggled to carry their men with them. Morale was low, apathy not uncommon. 'You can see it in every man here – officers and men – that they've been in battle,' observed Gustav Kalberlah, commanding an infantry battalion stalled on the River Terek. 'The expression on their faces is completely different from those at home.' The only consolation was that the enemy's efforts were half-hearted. 'They are driven forwards constantly, but they desert at every opportunity, particularly the peoples of the Caucasus who do not speak Russian,' Kalberlah continued. 'Unfortunately the Russians still have a lot of heavy weapons and artillery. There are many, many crosses here on the River Terek.'[65]

Gustav Kalberlah and his comrades would not spend the winter on the Terek. After nightfall on the first day of January 1943 the division fell back from the river – destroying anything of value to the Russians in key towns such as Mozdok. It did not stop retreating until it reached the southern outskirts of Rostov 26 days later – a march of nearly 400 miles in temperatures as low as -25°C on occasions, often endured without any shelter. 'We were basically nothing but machines, driven forward only by duty and iron necessity – sometimes it was only the naked instinct for self-preservation,' battalion commander Major Paul Nickel recalled. 'When we look back on those weeks, we wonder how it's still possible to laugh.' 111th Infantry Division's retreat was mirrored by *all* German forces in the Caucasus, which spent the first month of the new year rapidly falling back to the north and west. The mass withdrawal had been triggered by the Soviet offensive on the Don, 500 miles away. Though it eventually ran out of steam 100 miles from Rostov, the Red Army's *Little Saturn* operation served as a wake-up call at Hitler's headquarters in East Prussia. Had the Soviets reached the 'gateway to the Caucasus', they would have cut off all Axis forces to the east and south. At Stalingrad, the Red Army had 'merely' surrounded Sixth Army. A breakthrough to the mouth of the Don would have trapped two entire enemy army groups. Three days after Christmas – having been warned by the fiery Chief of the General Staff Kurt Zeitzler, 'unless you order a withdrawal from the Caucasus now, we shall soon have a second Stalingrad on our hands' – Hitler reluctantly ordered an evacuation. The retreat – never a rout or flight, but always difficult – was executed with remarkable speed and success, despite the terrible weather conditions. By the beginning of February, the bulk of First and Fourth Panzer Armies had threaded through the narrow gap east of Rostov – closed on Valentine's Day when the Red Army entered the city – while Seventeenth Army clung on to a small bridgehead in the western Caucasus to prevent Soviet forces crossing the Kerch Strait and liberating the Crimea. Three days later, after an eight-hour climb, a small group of Russian mountaineers ripped down the weather-beaten German ensign and the pennants the *Gebirgsjäger* had raised the previous August on Mount Elbrus and replaced them with the Hammer and Sickle. The Soviet Union once again ruled over the Caucasus.[66]

The Soviet standard now flew over Stalingrad too. The failure of Manstein's 'rescue offensive' passed the death sentence on Sixth Army. Worn down by starvation, exhaustion and a shortage of ammunition – the supply of Paulus' men worsened considerably after the Soviets seized the Luftwaffe airbase at Tatsinskaya, the hub of the air lift, during *Little Saturn* – as well as growing despondency, not to mention increased Soviet pressure tightening the ring of encirclement, Germany's largest army finally disintegrated at the end of January. First Paulus – who led resistance in the city centre from the basement of the Univermag department store over which the swastika had flown since 26 September – surrendered on 31 January, followed two days later by the defenders of the industrial district to the north.

Thus ended the Battle of Stalingrad after 164 days. No German soldier stood on the Volga. Some 91,000 traipsed into captivity. Fewer than 20,000 would ever see their homeland again. German casualties in the Stalingrad campaign are estimated at more than 350,000, while Army Group South lost more than half a million dead, wounded and missing between May and 19 November. The Red Army suffered four times that number trying to stop them. Its 'unrecoverable losses' – killed and missing – at Stalingrad were at least just short of half a million men, but may have been as high as around 675,000, with an almost identical number wounded.

The Axis armies paid a terrible price for supporting Hitler's 'crusade' in the East. The Romanians alone suffered 140,000 dead, wounded and missing during the autumn and winter, all but 30,000 of them since the Red Army's counter-offensives began in November. Hungary – whose Second Army was the last of three Axis allies to be steamrollered by the Soviets' winter counter-offensives – lost over 100,000 men. Having suffered 'only' 18,600 casualties – including 5,000 dead – in the preceding year and a half in Russia, the *Armata Italiana in Russia* was decimated by the Red Army's winter offensive on the Don. Besides most of its guns and armour, it lost more than one third of its men – over 84,000 souls – in six weeks of fighting. Of the 70,000 Italian soldiers who fell into Soviet hands, just one in seven returned home after the war.[67]

Axis losses in North Africa are difficult to calculate – and pale by comparison with the Eastern Front. But defeat in the two weeks of Alamein is believed to have cost the combined German-Italian force upwards of 30,000 men, more than half prisoners of war, and deprived those who survived the battle of around 1,000 guns and four-fifths of their armour. And the collapse of the front was even more precipitous, the hard-won gains of May and June abandoned to Eighth Army in rapid succession: Tobruk (7 November), the Gazala line (13 November). Rommel's retreat did not stop there, however. Four days later he was in Benghazi. On the 22nd, he had fallen back to El Agheila at the base of the Gulf of Sirte from where he had begun the reconquest of Cyrenaica as 1942 opened. The front temporarily lingered there for a couple of weeks before another pell-mell withdrawal began. Western Libya – 'Tripolitania', as Italian colonisers called it – proved no more defendable than the country's east. One by one the coastal towns fell: Sirte, Misratah, Homs, then Tripoli itself on 23 January. By the beginning of February 1943, Rommel's forces stood on the Tunisian border. In three months Axis forces had been driven back more than 2,000 kilometres – some 1,250 miles.

Germany's bid for victory, for *Endsieg*, in 1942 had failed utterly. It had failed even before the Allied counter-offensives. It failed to reach its geographical objectives, Suez and the Caspian Sea. It failed to deny its foes the supplies they needed to sustain the war, either by blocking the Suez Canal or denying the Soviet Union oil from its vast reserves in the Caucasus. It failed to secure those same oilfields for its own war effort. Having proclaimed – in dramatically unequivocal fashion – that he would lose the war without oil from the Caucasus, Hitler had received no more than seven tonnes from the wells around Maykop before they were abandoned in mid-January 1943. Above all, the 1942 campaign failed to deal a decisive blow to its enemies in the field. The Red Army and Allied armies in Africa were in a much stronger strategic position at the beginning of 1943 than they had been 12 months earlier, the Axis powers much weaker. A German victory was a *possibility* – and no more than that – in 1942. One year later, the best it could hope for was holding off defeat for as long as possible, as staff officer Erwin Jetzl discovered in a revelatory conversation with his superior, 113th Infantry Division's commander Hans-Heinrich Sixt von Arnim. '*Herr General*, our companies at the front are utterly exhausted. We need reinforcements, reinforcements, reinforcements,' he pleaded. Sixt von Arnim nodded in agreement. He had spoken with 'Fritz' Fromm, commander of the Reserve Army in Berlin, and told him the very same. Fromm's reply was devastating:

> My dear Sixt von Armin, it's hopeless. I know that. There are no replacements. Not now nor in the near future. There will be no more replacements in 1943 either. By that I mean replacements on a scale which would allow us to launch a large-scale offensive. We can only defend ourselves and perhaps launch an attack with limited objectives on some section of the front – if we scrape together everything that is still there. But a major offensive, such as in 1941 or 1942, is no longer possible.[68]

Perhaps Adolf Hitler had reached the same conclusion – though he would never concede so publicly. When Günther Rall reported to the Führer's headquarters – now returned to the Wolf's Lair in East Prussia after the summer and early autumn in Ukraine – to receive the Oak Leaves to the Knight's Cross after scoring his 100th victory, he found his leader still talking about resettling the East, of German farmers tilling Russian soil, of irrigating the desert-like Nogai steppe leading to the Caspian Sea, of replacing Russian railway lines with Germany's narrower gauge. The 24-year-old ace had the temerity to interrupt Hitler in full flow.

'*Mein Führer*, how much longer will the war in the East last?'

'I don't know, Rall.'

For the young fighter pilot who had idolised Hitler for a decade, the words 'planted seeds of doubt' which he was never able to remove. 'One question and we're staring into the abyss.'[69]

NOTES

ABBREVIATIONS

ADAP	*Akten zur Deutschen Auswärtiges Politik 1918–45*
AL	Archive Librarian – reference system used by the Imperial War Museum
AOK 6	*Die Anlagenbänder zu den Kriegstagebüchern der 6 Armee*
BA-MA	Bundesarchiv Militärarchiv
CAB	Cabinet Office Papers, National Archives
GASWW	*Germany and the Second World War*
IR49	*Geschichte des Infanterie- und Jäger-Regiments 49*
IWM	Imperial War Museum
KTB	Kriegstagebuch (war diary)
NA	National Archives, Kew
OKW	Oberkommando der Wehrmacht
SD Meldung	Boberach, *Meldungen aus dem Reich*
Skl	Seekriegsleitung (German Naval Staff)
TB	Tagebuch (diary)
TB Pabst	Diary of Herbert Pabst in BA-MA RL 10-802
TB Richthofen	Diary of Wolfram from Richthofen in BA-MA N 671/9
VB	*Völkischer Beobachter* (Berlin edition unless otherwise stated)

INTRODUCTION: 46° 39' NORTH, 47° 47' EAST

1 The latitude/longitude is approximately 46° 39' 3" N, 47° 47' 17" E. Memminger, pp.D1358–61; Shein, pp.72–3.
2 Letter, 2/10/42, Bähr, p.174.
3 Wendt, i, p.153.
4 Memminger, pp.D1301, D1310.
5 Shein, p.63.
6 Memminger, pp.D1317–18.
7 Memminger, pp.D1361–2.
8 Bericht, 22/8/42 in BA-MA RH 24-52/102.
9 Wendt, p.130.
10 Memminger, pp.D1307–08.
11 Memminger, p.D1302.
12 Wendt, p.150.
13 Memminger, pp.D1354–5.

14   VB, 3/9/42; see also VB, 30/8/42; Ziemke, p.440.
15   See TB Goebbels, 2/10/42.
16   Stempel, *Wir müssen ran, wir greifen an!*, p.213.
17   Buchmann, p.79.
18   SD Meldung, 3/9/42.

Chapter 1: Unfinished Business

1   Lagoda, pp.64–6.
2   KTB HGr Nord, 4/5/42 in BA-MA RH 19 III/182. Cf. Adam, p.37: 'If we don't reach Maykop and Grozny, then I'll have to end the war.'
3   Hartmann, *Halder*, p.314.
4   Losses are based on figures in Greiner, letter to his wife, 12/4/42 in Greiner papers; GASWW, vi, p.872; TB Halder, 21/4/42.
5   Author's papers and Reinhardt, pp.365–6.
6   Heinrici, report to his family, 8/5/42 in Hürter, pp.162–3.
7   Munzel, pp.218–19.
8   Ebert, *Ein Arzt in Stalingrad*, p.108.
9   Kirstein, pp.662–4.
10   The mood in Germany in the spring of 1942 is based on VB, 5/4/42, 21/4/42, 26/4/42; *Freiburger Zeitung*, 18/4/42–25/4/42; Von Weiss's reports, 2/2/42 and 13/4/42, in Schmitz and Haunfelder, pp.167, 171–2; Schminck-Gustavus, p.98; SD Meldungen, 2/4/42 and 23/4/42; and Bajohr and Strupp, p.567.
11   Ochsenknecht, p.144.
12   Based on Jasper, p.103; Hack, p.108 and Wittek, pp.345–8.
13   Based on TB Goebbels, 26/4/42, 10/6/42 and VB, 5/4/25.
14   Based on KTB Halder, 28/3/42; Directive No.41 in the author's papers; Hitler's speech to *Reichsleiter* and *Gauleiter*, 23/5/42, in TB Goebbels, 24/5/42; Conversation with Goebbels, TB Goebbels, 10/6/42; Fromm, pp.437–8 and BA-MA RM 7/990, p.61.
15   Fuchs, p.39.
16   Urbanke, p.73; TB Bock, 5/5/42.
17   Simonov, pp.86–7; BA-MA RH 26-50/43; and author's papers.
18   Stichling and Leukefeld, p.73.
19   IR49, 1942, pp.34–9.
20   Waiss, p.58.
21   Taghon, ii, p.108.
22   IR49, 1942, pp.30–3; Blanken, p.63.
23   BA-MA RH 26-50/43 and IR49, 1942, pp.30–3.
24   *Krym v Velikoy Otechestvennoy voyne 1941–1945 gg*, Doc 62.
25   Based on author's papers; *Krym v Velikoy Otechestvennoy voyne 1941–1945 gg*, Doc 62; Prien, *Einsatz des Jagdgeschwaders 77*, ii, p.995.
26   Based on Waiss, p.60; and TB Richthofen, 8–9/5/42.
27   Based on reports in BA-MA RH 26-50/43 and BA-MA RH 26-50/35; Stichling and Leukefeld, p.74; and IR49, 1942, pp.43–4.
28   Based on Blanken, p.64; Harward, pp.151, 153; Tieke, *Krim*, p.134; Manoshin, p.267; Lützkendorf, Felix, 'Die Schlacht um Kertsch', *Das Reich*, Nr.22 1942, 31/5/42; and TB Richthofen, 11/5/42.

29 Memminger, p.D1076.

30 Manoshin, pp.252–3, 261–2, 264.

31 TB Goebbels, 13–14/5/42; VB, 14/5/42; SD Meldung, 14/5/42.

32 Lützkendorf, 'Die Schlacht um Kertsch', *Das Reich*, Nr.22 1942, 31/5/42.

33 Tieke, *Krim*, p.141; *Luftwaffe over Sevastopol*, p.31; Manstein, *Verlorene Siege*, p.260.

34 Memminger, pp.D1097–9.

35 Author's papers.

36 IR49, 1942, pp.50–1.

37 Urbanke, pp.94–100.

38 Based on Atzesberger and Stahlmann, pp.73–7 and pp.B20–1; TB Halder, 13/6/42 and Fast, iii, pp.72–4.

39 KTB 28 ID, 19/5/42 in BA-MA RH 26-28/45; Tieke, *Krim*, p.146; Forczyk, *Where the Iron Crosses Grow*, p.146. Some German units in the vanguard of the attack, such as 49th Infantry Regiment, suffered heavy losses: officers 74 per cent, non-commissioned officers 50 per cent and men 51 per cent. See IR49, 1942, pp.52–3.

40 BA-MA RH 26-28/45.

41 TB Goebbels, 20/5/42.

42 Author's papers.

43 Based on Manoshin, p.267; IR49, 1942, pp.52–3; Kranz, pp.420–1; Hödl, pp.45–6; and Prien, *Einsatz des Jagdgeschwaders 77*, ii, pp.1024, 1028.

44 Scherzer, *46 Infanterie Division*, pp.391–2.

45 Abaturov and Portugalskiy, p.98.

46 Based on Stalin's Order of the Day to the Red Army, 23/2/42 and Zhukov, ii, pp.73–4.

47 Hill, pp.335–40; Bellamy, p.476; GASWW, vi, p.888; Ziemke, pp.296–7.

48 Based on author papers plus Glantz, *Kharkov*, p.114; *Stimme*, p.167; and Abaturov and Portugalskiy, p.84.

49 Abaturov and Portugalskiy, p.95; Schmitt's letter 20/6/42 in Schmitt, *Bin noch am Leben*.

50 When the division counter-attacked a few days later, they found the same guns where they had been left, still intact. The Russians had not had the time to either spike them – or take them in retreat. See Scherzer, *113 Infanterie Division*, p.192.

51 TB Gehrig, 12–13/5/42.

52 TB Bock, 12/5/42.

53 *71 Infanterie Division*, pp.176–7.

54 Abaturov and Portugalskiy, pp.125–6.

55 Ibid, p.119.

56 Lopez, *Kharkov 1942*, p.147.

57 Ibid, pp.158–60.

58 Moshchanskii, pp.199–200.

59 Abaturov and Portugalskiy, p.133.

60 Glantz, *Kharkov*, p.172.

61 Degrelle, pp.65–9.

62 Based on Glantz, *Kharkov*, p.265; Lopez, *Kharkov 1942*, p.149; Moshchanskii, pp.221–2 and Abaturov and Portugalskiy, pp.151–3.

63 Volkogonov, p.431.

64 Dollinger, pp.137–8 and Hörmann, pp.45–6.

65 Lopez, *Kharkov 1942*, pp.175–7 and *Stalingradskaya epopeya*, Doc.15.

66 Busch, *Zurück aus der Hölle*, pp.137–9.

67 Bühler, 29/5/42 and *Stimme*, p.167.

68 Author's papers and Lopez, *Kharkov 1942*, pp.209–12.

69 Abaturov and Portugalskiy, pp.162–3, 176–7.

70 Kljakič, p.61 and Werthen, pp.88–9.

71 Arnhard, pp.6–10.

72 Abaturov and Portugalskiy, pp.172–4 and Lopez, *Kharkov 1942*, p.202.

73 Arnhard, pp.6–10.

74 Rebentisch, pp.42–3.

75 Stempel, *Wir müssen ran, wir greifen an!*, pp.190–1.

76 Lopez, *Kharkov 1942*, pp.204–05.

77 Buchner, 'Die Schlacht beiderseits Charkow'.

78 Arnhard, pp.6–10.

79 Meyer, *Blutiges Edelweiss*, pp.79–80.

80 Kissel, p.111; Busch, *Zurück aus der Hölle*, pp.137–9; and Rebentisch, pp.42–3.

81 Hörmann, pp.45–6 and Ljubimye, p.524.

82 Glantz, *Kharkov*, p.218; TB Bock, 28–29/5/42; *Veteranii pe Drumul Onoarei și Jertfei 1941–1945: De la Nistru la Marea de Azov*, pp.387–8.

83 Groscurth, p.526; *Veteranii pe Drumul Onoarei și Jertfei 1941–1945: De la Nistru la Marea de Azov*, pp.387–8; and Obhodas and Mark, pp.137–8.

84 Based on Braatz, *Krupinski*, p.67; Meldung von Kleist, Fernschreiben, III Panzerkorps, 29/5/42 in BA-MA RH 20-17/125; Voss, p.114; Stempel, *Wir müssen ran, wir greifen an!*, pp.196–7; and Abaturov and Portugalskiy, pp.177–8.

85 Based on author's papers; *Das Deutsche Reich und der Zweite Weltkrieg*, Band VI, p.860 and Moshchanskii, pp.254–6.

86 Far from being executed – the fate suffered by many of his predecessors in the summer and autumn of 1941 – Kharitonov was exonerated, rehabilitated and given command of an army, which he successfully led until his death in May 1943. Abaturov and Portugalskiy, pp.138–9.

87 Sebag, p.424.

88 BA-MA RM 8/1548; Bidermann, *und litt an meiner Seite*, p.77; *Die 50 Infanterie Division*, p.219.

89 BA-MA RH 26-22/1573 and Taube, *Festung Sewastopol*, p.14.

90 Nuzhdin, pp.14–18.

91 Hofmann, pp.22–3; Laskin, pp.101–02; Bidermann, *und litt an meiner Seite*, p.68; Atzesberger and Stahlmann, pp.81–2.

92 Baumbach, pp.123–4; *Die 50 Infanterie Division*, p.217.

93 Nuzhdin, pp.28–9.

94 Sazhin, pp.431–2.

95 Karpow, *Der General und Ich*, pp.178–9.

96 Taube, *Eisenbahngeschütz Dora*, pp.72–3.

97 Ibid, p.78.

98 Ibid, p.115.

99 *Wir erobern*, pp.165–7.

100 Based on BA-MA RL 2-IV/35; Karpow, *Der General und Ich*, pp.178–9; Nuzhdin, pp.28–9; Voyetekhov, p.56; and Atzesberger and Stahlmann, p.81.

101 Nuzhdin, pp.31–6.

102 Choltitz, pp.121–2 and *Die 50 Infanterie Division*, p.219.

103 BA-MA RM 8/1548.

104 Nuzhdin, p.36.

105 Laskin, pp.112–13.

106 Emde, p.93 and Atzesberger and Stahlmann, pp.81–2.

107 Balke, pp.111–12; Buhse, p.44.

108 Freter, pp.533–5.

109 Buhse, p.44.

110 Winkler, pp.54–5, 67–85.

111 BA-MA RH 26-50/43.

112 Bidermann, *In Deadly*, pp.130–1.

113 Karpow, *Der General und Ich*, pp.181–2.

114 Ibid, p.183 and Laskin, p.123.

115 Kranz, pp.429–34.

116 BA-MA RH 26-50/43.

117 Laskin, p.123.

118 Karpow, *Der General und Ich*, p.184.

119 Manstein, p.272; Choltitz, pp.121–2; BA-MA RH 26-28/45.

120 Nuzhdin, p.63; Karpow, *Der General und Ich*, pp.184–5.

121 Bidermann, *und litt an meiner Seite*, p.83; Tieke, *Krim*, p.172.

122 Based on IR49, 1942, pp.78a–b and Kranz, pp.449–50.

123 TB Richthofen, 11/6/42; Schmidt, *Torpedo los*, pp.150–1; KTB Oberquartiermeisterabteilung, 14/6/42 in BA-MA RH 20/11-422.

124 Choltitz, p.122.

125 The battle for Maxim Gorky I is based on Hitzfeld, pp.90–1; Gruber, pp.225–31; Tieke, *Krim*, pp.182–8; Egger, pp.294, 315; Bidermann, *und litt an meiner Seite*, pp.77, 79, 81; and Nuzhdin, pp.143–53.

126 *Wir erobern*, p.198.

127 *50 Infanterie Division*, pp.230–1 and BA-MA RH 26-50/43.

128 *Wir erobern*, pp.199–203 and Nuzhdin, pp.214, 222–3.

129 Based on *50 Infanterie Division*, p.232; TB Richthofen, 19/6/42; Nuzhdin, p.174; and Skrytaia, pp.334–5.

130 Waiss, p.87 and Prien, *Einsatz des Jagdgeschwaders 77*, ii, pp.1057–8, 1061.

131 Laskin, pp.108, 151, 157; *Pravda*, 15/6/42; Tieke, *Krim*, p.180.

132 Buhse, pp.49–50.

133 Einsätze der Jäger Division auf der Krim in BA-MA RH 26-28/45.

134 Skrytaia, pp.334–5.

135 Bidermann, *und litt an meiner Seite*, pp.81–2; *50 Infanterie Division*, p.229; Prien, *Einsatz des Jagdgeschwaders 77*, ii, pp.1057–8, 1061; Tieke, *Krim*, p.155.

136 *Veteranii pe Drumul Onoarei și Jertfei 1941–1945: De la Nistru la Marea de Azov*, p.345.

137 Bähr, pp.211–12.

138 Bidermann, *und litt an meiner Seite*, pp.81–2; Giusti, p.151.

139 Dinkler von Schuber, *Feldpost: Zeugnis und Vermächtnis*, pp.77–9.

140 Winkler, p.265; Bidermann, *und litt an meiner Seite*, pp.81–2; Bruns, pp.38–9; Hödl, p.48; Nuzhdin, p.134.

141 Nemenko, p.514; Nuzhdin, p.70.

142 Nemenko, pp.445–6; Voyetekhov, pp.67–8; Nuzhdin, p.111.

143 Nuzhdin, p.178.

144 Ibid, p.192.

145 Isaev, *Bitva za Krim*, p.489.

146 Nuzhdin, p.236.

147 Ibid, pp.220, 231. Few regimental colours were evacuated. Many were burned in a dugout by Kamyshovaya Bay shortly before it was overrun. See Manoshin, p.42.

148 Laskin, p.170 and Nuzhdin, pp.244–5.

149 Choltitz, pp.125–6; Tieke, *Krim*, pp.208–09; *Wir erobern*, pp.204–05 and Gruber, pp.237–8.

150 Tieke, *Krim*, pp.210–11; Nuzhdin, pp.256–8, 262 and Manoshin, p.51.

151 Nuzhdin, pp.264, 269 and Melvin, p.525.

152 Based on *Wir erobern*, pp.196–7; BA-MA RH 26-50/43; Winkler, pp.375–6; Nuzhdin, pp.272–3; and Melvin, p.526.

153 Manoshin, p.64.

154 Nuzhdin, p.290.

155 Sazhin, p.439.

156 Samiy, pp.175–7.

157 Laskin, pp.175–6.

158 *Românii in Crimeea 1941–1944*, pp.277–8.

159 Manoshin, p.91.

160 BA-MA RH 26-50/43.

161 Oktyabrsky was supposedly received 'very coolly' in Krasnodar for failing to organise an evacuation. See Karpow, *Der General und Ich*, pp.209, 219–20.

162 Nuzhdin, pp.293–8.

163 BA-MA RH 26-50/43.

164 Fuchs, pp.42–3; Alfred Hennecke, 'Sewastopol und der Karl Einsatz, 3/9/42' in BA-MA MSg 2/6475.

165 BA-MA RH 26-50/43.

166 BA-MA RH 26-50/50.

167 *Românii in Crimeea 1941–1944*, p.279.

168 KTB 50 ID, 1/7/42 in BA-MA RH 26-50/35.

169 Scherzer, *46 Infanterie Division*, p.405.

170 BA-MA RH 26-50/43 and Scherzer, *46 Infanterie Division*, p.405.

171 Scherzer, *46 Infanterie Division*, p.405.

172 Feldwebel Gutsmann, 'After the battle', in *Wir erobern*, p.226.

173 Manoshin, pp.92, 127–8.

174 Egger, pp.172–4 and Nuzhdin, p.325.

175 Nuzhdin, pp.317–24; Karpow, *Der General und Ich*, pp.215–17 and Tieke, *Krim*, pp.221–2. Later that year Novikov was transferred to Flössenburg concentration camp in Bavaria where he died in August 1944 either of exhaustion from maltreatment, or at the hands of an SS guard. A street in Balaklava was later named in his honour.

176 BA-MA MSg 2/13245.

177 Nuzhdin, pp.313–14.

178 Skrytaia, pp.336–7.

179 Nuzhdin, p.332.

180 Atzesberger and Stahlmann, p.B17.

181 Nuzhdin, p.326.

182 Manoshin, p.174.

183 Laskin, pp.182–3; Nuzhdin, p.326; Manoshin, pp.190–1.

184 Nuzhdin, p.331.

185 Nuzhdin, pp.335–6, 341, 344; Manoshin, pp.194–6; Tieke, *Krim*, p.221 and AOK 11, interim report, 4/7/42 in BA-MA RH 20-11/466; Egger, pp.174–5.

186   *50 Infanterie Division*, p.244 and *Românii in Crimeea 1941–1944*, pp.280–2.

187   Hitzfeld, p.93; Gruber, p.240; Manstein, *Verlorene Siege*, pp.283–4; *Veteranii pe Drumul Onoarei și Jertfei 1941–1945: De la Nistru la Marea de Azov*, p.353.

188   TB Pabst, 5/7/42.

189   Based on Forczyk, *Where the Iron Crosses Grow*, p.90; Tieke, *Krim*, pp.22–3; Bellamy, p.464; BA-MA RH 26-50/44; and BA-MA RL 8/52.

190   SD Meldungen, 2/7/42 and 9/7/42.

191   BA-MA RH 26-22/157.

192   TB Goebbels, 18/8/42; BA-MA RH 26-50/44; BA-MA RH 26-28/45.

193   Based on Choltitz, pp.127–8; *Wir erobern*, pp.217–20 and SD Meldung, 9/7/42. Goebbels, on the other hand, was furious with Choltitz's address for painting the enemy as a heroic foe, bravely defending his native soil rather than the Bolshevik beast of Nazi propaganda. Choltitz had allowed himself to 'get a little worked up. But that is no reason for us to let things go off in the wrong direction. Such a mindset will gradually make heroes of the Bolshevik armies which is anything but promising for the future.' See TB Goebbels, 9/7/42, 16/7/42.

194   Based on Taube, *Eisenbahngeschütz Dora*, p.97; *Wir erobern*, p.226; Bidermann, *und litt an meiner Seite*, pp.84–5; BA-MA RM 8/1548.

195   Letter dated 17/7/42 in Angrick, pp.530–1.

196   See Nuzhdin, pp.335–6, 341, 344; Manoshin, pp.194–6, 198, 199–202, 213; Tieke, *Krim*, p.221 and AOK 11, interim report, 4/7/42 in BA-MA RH 20-11/466; Egger, pp.174–5; Bidermann, *und litt an meiner Seite*, pp.84–5.

197   BA-MA RH 26-50/50 and Fuchs, p.43.

198   Oldenburg, p.147.

199   KTB Oberquartiermeisterabteilung AOK 11, 3/7/42, in BA-MA RH 20-11/422.

200   Angrick, pp.531–2.

201   Hartmann, Hürter, Lieb and Pohl, *Der deutsche Krieg im Osten*, pp.388–90.

202   Fuchs, p.43.

203   Wimmer, p.143.

CHAPTER 2: ROMMELING AGAIN

1   Ciano Diario, 28/4/42.

2   Rommel, *Krieg Ohne Hass*, p.96.

3   Based on Salewski, ii, p.88; Greene and Massignani, pp.223, 232; Ciano Diario, 12/5/42; Radtke, p.118.

4   Taghon, i, p.392. Mussolini told the visiting head of the German U-boat arm, Karl Dönitz, he considered Malta 'ripe' for invasion. Reuth, *Entscheidung im Mittelmeer*, p.168.

5   KTB PzAOK Afrika, 24/4/42 in author's papers.

6   Rommel, *Krieg Ohne Hass*, pp.112–14.

7   Westphal, pp.159–60.

8   Ciano Diario, 28–29/4/42; Bottai, pp.303–05.

9   ADAP, E, Band 2, Docs.178, 182, 183; Cavallero Diario, 29–30/4/42.

10   Rommel's papers.

11   BA-MA RM 7/235.

12   Ciano Diario, 29/4/42 and Salewski, ii, p.67. The official communiqué of the talks was published, *inter alia*, in the *Freiburger Zeitung*, 1–2/5/42.

13   For the cancellation of *Herkules*, see Junge's letter of 22/5/42 in BA-MA RM 7/234 and KTB Skl, 23/5/42.

14   Hubalek, p.11; Ringler, p.7; Sonnenkalb, p.23.

15   Schirmer, p.60.

16   Based on KTB Köhrer, 13/5/42 and TB von Waldau, circa 13/5/42.

17   Hubalek, p.19.

18   Schirmer, pp.95–7.

19   Kost, p.76.

20   The arch was actually around 20 miles west of the historic border. Soldiers knew it simply as '*Kilometer* 1,000' – the half-way point between Libya's western and eastern frontiers, although it was actually 800 kilometres from the Tunisian and 850 from the Egyptian border.

21   Hubalek, pp.25–9.

22   Ibid, pp.33–4.

23   Letters of 1/5/42 and 11/5/42 in Frey, pp.227, 233.

24   Schirmer, pp.116–17.

25   Taysen, p.29.

26   Henning, pp.54, 62.

27   Hartmann, p.166.

28   Ibid.

29   Schirmer, p.143.

30   Henning, p.78.

31   Ringler, pp.8–9, 109.

32   Henning, p.62.

33   Frey, p.233 and Marwan-Schlosser, p.132.

34   Henning, p.54.

35   Hartmann, p.166.

36   Henning, pp.54–5.

37   Aberger, Taysen and Ziemer, p.198 and Hubalek, p.55.

38   Hubalek, p.42.

39   Based on Gross, pp.54–6 and Henning, pp.55–6.

40   Hubalek, pp.48, 52.

41   Frey, p.236; see also Henning, p.55.

42   Rommel, *Krieg Ohne Hass*, p.116.

43   Ibid, p.115.

44   See Cavallero Diario, 5/5/42.

45   It was actually a remarkably accurate guess: Eighth Army possessed 849 front-line tanks when *Theseus* began.

46   Rommel, *Krieg Ohne Hass*, pp.116–18; Behrendt, *Rommel's Intelligence*, pp.145–7; and Mellenthin, p.111.

47   KTB Köhrer, 24/5/42.

48   Frey, pp.230, 235.

49   Aberger, Taysen and Ziemer, p.164.

50   Sonnenkalb, p.97.

51   GASWW, vi, p.673–4.

52   Hubalek, p.70.

53   Based on KTB 90 Light Division, 26/5/42 in AL773; KTB *Afrika Korps*, 26/5/42 in AL833/1; Luck, p.117; Freter, pp.365–6; Henning, pp.70–1; Hartmann, p.216 and Mancinelli, p.90.

54   Behrendt, *Rommels Kenntnis*, p.188.

55   Rebora, pp.191–5; Romersa, pp.34–6; Broche, pp.153–4, 175, 177.

56   Hart, pp.228–30.

57   *Die Oase*, 2017, Heft 2.

58   Based on KTB *Afrika Korps*, 27/5/42 in AL833; KTB 90th Light Division, 27–28/5/42 in AL773; TB Armbruster, 27/5/42; Rommel, *Krieg Ohne Hass*, pp.129–32; Sonnenkalb, pp.106–08; Schroetter, pp.164–5; Paul, *Nehring*, p.132; Hubalek, p.76.

59   Mancinelli, p.106; Westphal, p.162.

60   Hartmann, p.218.

61   TB Armbruster, 28/5/42; Rommel, *Krieg Ohne Hass*, pp.132–4.

62   TB Armbruster, 29/5/42; Rommel, *Krieg Ohne Hass*, pp.134–5; KTB *Afrika Korps*, 29/5/42 in AL833.

63   Mauer, *Heiss über Afrikas Boden*, p.266.

64   Marwan-Schlosser, p.136 and Aberger, Taysen and Ziemer, p.168. Crüwell was not dead, but he was no longer in command. His reconnaissance plane was shot down over British lines. The pilot was killed; the general was taken prisoner and quickly spirited away from the battle to Cairo. In the Egyptian capital he asked his captors to show him the finest hotel, telling them: 'Rommel will be moving in shortly…' See Aberger, Taysen and Ziemer, p.169.

65   Rommel, *Krieg Ohne Hass*, pp.135–7.

66   Rommel, *Krieg Ohne Hass*, p.138; KTB *Afrika Korps*, 1/6/42 in AL833; KTB 90th Light Division, 3/5/42–1/6/42 in AL773; PzAOK Afrika Tagesmeldung, 1/6/42 in AL 866/6. Various accounts ascribe the fall of Got el Ualeb to one of Rommel's legendary bluffs. 'The enemy's weakening,' he told a battalion commander. 'Wave a white flag and he'll surrender.' The men waved scarves, a few handkerchiefs, and one soldier even stripped off his shirt to hold it up to the enemy. The British responded by surrendering en masse. See for example Carell, *Foxes of the Desert*, p.197. There's no such record in the *Afrika Korps*' diary, only that the box was overrun, and that the negotiator sent the previous day was rebuffed by the defenders. KTB *Afrika Korps*, 31/5/42–1/6/42 in AL833.

67   KTB 90th Light Division, 3/6/42 in AL773; Broche, pp.202–04, 213–14; and Sonnenkalb, p.114.

68   Based on Rommel, *Krieg Ohne Hass*, p.141; KTB *Afrika Korps*, 5/6/42 in AL833; and Mellenthin, pp.132–3.

69   Hubalek, pp.95–6.

70   Mobius, pp.104–05.

71   Based on Frey, p.254; Hubalek, p.91; Reuth, *Rommel: The End of a Legend*, p.110; OKW Communiqués, 29/5/42–5/6/42; SD Meldung, 1/6/42.

72   KTB Köhrer, 5/6/42.

73   Hubalek, p.103.

74   Bedeschi, *Fronte d'Africa*, p.137.

75   Frey, p.256; Mitchelhill-Green, pp.185–6.

76   Hartmann, p.220.

77   Hubalek, p.102.

78   Leterrier, p.100.

79   Rosso, p.100; Ceva, pp.128–9; TB Paul Walentan, 4/6/42.

80   Gross, pp.63–4, 67. Similar comments can be found from a JG53 pilot in JG53, ii, p.436.

81   Based on KTB *Afrika Korps*, 15/6/42 in AL833; Mobius, pp.101–02 and Aberger, Taysen and Ziemer, p.170.

82   Based on Hart, p.253; Hubalek, p.101; Fennell, p.69; Rommel, *Krieg Ohne Hass*, p.143.

83   Bedeschi, *Fronte d'Africa*, pp.66–8.

84   Broche, p.245.

85   Gross, pp.80–1.

86   Based on Onana, p.245; 'Der Afrika Feldzug aus Sicht der Artillerie Abteilung im Afrika Regiment 361'; Rommel, *Krieg Ohne Hass*, p.144; Bedeschi, *Fronte d'Africa*, pp.66, 68.

87   Marwan-Schlosser, pp.145–7.

88   Onana, p.245.

89   Von Waldau papers.

90   Henning, p.78; Leterrier, pp.103–05; Bedeschi, *Fronte d'Africa*, p.64.

91   The fall of Bir Hakeim is based on Sonnenkalb, pp.116–17; Westphal, p.162; Henning, p.78; Frey, p.259 and Hitler's order of 9/6/42 in the author's papers.

92   Mauer, p.268; Frey, p.247; Varco, p.320; Rosso, p.100.

93   The order fell into German hands around 5 June. *Deutsche Allgemeine Zeitung*, 23/6/42.

94   Rizzo, p.376; Hartmann, p.220.

95   Moorehead, p.363.

96   *Die Oase*, 2017, Heft 2.

97   Bedeschi, *Fronte d'Africa*, pp.134–5.

98   Rommel, *Krieg Ohne Hass*, pp.148–9.

99   Sonnenkalb, pp.118–19.

100 Based on Rommel, *Krieg Ohne Hass*, pp.149–50; Schroetter, pp.169–70; Vallauri, p.205; KTB *Afrika Korps*, 14/6/42–15/6/42 in AL833.

101 Rommel, *Krieg Ohne Hass*, pp.153–4.

102 Frey, pp.261–2.

103 BA-MA RH 53-18/292.

104 Based on Taysen, pp.30–1; BA-MA RH 27-15/70; Moorehead, pp.370–3; Fennell, pp.201–02; Mitchelhill-Green, pp.188, 211.

105 Gross, p.94.

106 Based on TB Hans Greim; Koch, p.78; Freter, p.375; Aberger, Taysen and Ziemer, p.176; Schmidt, p.144 and Varco, pp.298–9.

107 TB Goebbels, 23/6/42 and Rommel, *Krieg Ohne Hass*, p.153.

108 Gross, pp.94–5, Jähnert, pp.193–6, Koch, p.78 and Taghon, ii, pp.34–5.

109 Romersa, pp.42–3.

110 Varco, p.299.

111 Ibid, p.300.

112 Hartmann, pp.223–4 and TB Hans Greim.

113 Varco, p.300.

114 Hartmann, p.224.

115 Koch, p.79.

116 Bedeschi, *Fronte d'Africa*, pp.142–3.

117 Ibid, pp.160–1.

118 Varco, p.299.

119 The battle for Tobruk is based on Hartmann, pp.223–7; Aberger, Taysen and Ziemer, p.176; Schroetter, p.171; KTB Hans Greim; *Die 33er*, p.148; Koch, pp.78–81; Varco, p.303; and Vallicella, pp.15, 17.

120 Based on Schirmer, pp.143–4; Caccia-Dominioni, *El Alamein*, p.28; Aberger, Taysen and Ziemer, pp.177–8; *Die 33er*, p.167; Schroetter, p.173; Fattore, pp.80–1; Moorehead, p.379; Varco, p.303; Vallicella, pp.17–18 and Frey, pp.265–6.

121 Mancinelli, p.122.

122 The surrender of Tobruk is based on TB Rommel, 21/6/42; Rommel, *Krieg Ohne Hass*, p.162; Freter, pp.377–8; Koch, pp.78–81; Mitchelhill-Green, p.199; Fattore, pp.80–1; Frey, p.265; Varco, p.301; Bedeschi, *Fronte d'Africa*, pp.160–1 and Montanari, p.350n61. Some South African prisoners fluent in foreign languages were immediately flown to Berlin so they could work for the Propaganda Ministry. See Rommel's papers.

123 Based on Avagliano and Palmieri, pp.73–4; Feldpost Witzke, 2/7/42; Caccia-Dominioni, *El Alamein*, pp.32–3; *Andere Helme*, p.126; and BA-MA RH 27-15/70.

124 VB, 23/6/42; TB Goebbels, 23/6/42.

125 TB Armbruster, 23/6/42. Another account suggests a rather more laconic response to news that Hitler would send a field marshal's baton. 'It would have been better if he'd sent me a division.' See Knopp, *Hitlers Krieger*, p.46.

126 Churchill, *Hinge of Fate*, p.344; Mitchelhill-Green, pp.200–01.

127 Reports 17/6/42, 24–28/6/42 in De Felice, pp.758–9.

128 TB Goebbels, 22–23/6/42; SD Meldung, 25/6/42.

129 Kesselring, pp.127–8; Cavallero Diario, 22/6/42; and KTB Skl, 20/6/42.

130 Baum and Weichold, p.230.

131 Reuth, *Entscheidung im Mittelmeer*, pp.250–1.

132 Reuth, *Entscheidung im Mittelmeer*, p.193 and Rommel, *Krieg Ohne Hass*, p.163.

133 Romersa, pp.47–50.

134 Based on Kost, p.71; Schroetter, p.179; Vallicella, p.19; Sonnenkalb, p.126.

CHAPTER 3: VICTORIES WITHOUT VICTORY

1 Feldpost Böker, 22/6/42.

2 *Vernus*, pp.264–5.

3 Directive No.41, pp.178–83.

4 Ebert, *Ein Arzt in Stalingrad*, p.214.

5 Ziemke, pp.324–8.

6 Sdvizhkov, *V iyule 1942*, p.7.

7 Ebert, *Ein Arzt in Stalingrad*, p.176.

8 Sdvizhkov, *V iyule 1942*, p.8.

9 TB Bock, 20–27/6/42. The men of 23rd Panzer were told their commander was departing due to long-standing injuries suffered in a car crash. Boineburg-Lengsfeld would be back in charge of the division within two months when his successor was killed in action.

10 See Ziemke, pp.302–03 and Förster, p.42.

11 Ziemke, p.332; Kazakov, pp.101–05.

12 Emde, p.89; Knopp, *Stalingrad*, p.71; Senger und Etterlin, p.74; Fuchs and Rella, pp.97–8.

13 Memminger, pp.D1108–09; Sdvizhkov, *Operatsija Blau*, i, p.284.

14 Prentl, pp.53–4.

15 Senger und Etterlin, p.75.

16 Kazakov, p.98; Sdvizhkov, *Operatsija Blau*, i, pp.128–31.

17 Sdvizhkov, *Operatsija Blau*, i, p.293.

18 Ibid, pp.430–1.

19 Ibid, p.285.

20 Memminger, pp.D1108–09.

21 Weidemann, p.130.

22   Ebert, *Ein Arzt in Stalingrad*, p.177.

23   Senger und Etterlin, p.75.

24   Rehfeldt, pp.162–3.

25   Senger und Etterlin, pp.74–6.

26   Sdvizhkov, *Operatsija Blau*, i, pp.221–4; Kazakov, p.105.

27   Beshanov, pp.260–1.

28   Sdvizhkov, *Operatsija Blau*, i, pp.262–4.

29   Ibid, pp.265–6, 296.

30   Sdvizhkov, *V iyule 1942*, p.17.

31   Sdvizhkov, *Operatsija Blau*, i, pp.311–13.

32   Shamray, p.83; Sdvizhkov, *Operatsija Blau*, i, p.547.

33   Shamray, p.114.

34   Podewils, p.44; Ebert, *Ein Arzt in Stalingrad*, p.182.

35   Stempel, *Wir müssen ran*, p.213.

36   Sdvizhkov, *V iyule 1942*, pp.40, 197.

37   Ibid, pp.41–3.

38   Ibid, p.48.

39   Based on Weidemann, pp.136–9 and Sdvizhkov, *Operatsija Blau*, ii, pp.83–5.

40   Feklenko was dismissed later that day and even briefly held under arrest at his command post, but no charges were laid. Sdvizhkov, *Operatsija Blau*, ii, p.119.

41   Sdvizhkov, *V iyule 1942*, pp.122–4.

42   Ibid, pp.181–2, 236–7.

43   Sdvizhkov, *Operatsija Blau*, ii, pp.219–21.

44   Ibid, p.221.

45   Ibid, p.282.

46   Ibid, pp.329–31.

47   Beshanov, pp.286–7 and Prien, *Einsatz des Jagdgeschwaders 77*, ii, pp.1112–13.

48   Kuehn, p.24.

49   BA-MA RH 39/533; Senger und Etterlin, pp.82–3; Rehfeldt, pp.166–7.

50   Sdvizhkov, *Operatsija Blau*, ii, p.447.

51   Soviet accounts suggest subterfuge played a role in the Germans forcing the Don, claiming they applied red stars to their vehicles and laid hammer and sickle flags over the bonnets. The ruse evidently worked, for the 'Soviet tanks' overran at least one defensive position until a gust of wind caught the flags to reveal the large swastika flag painted on one of the panzers. 'For a moment,' one Soviet soldier recalled, 'everyone was taken aback.' See Sdvizhkov, *Operatsija Blau*, ii, pp.378–9.

52   Sdvizhkov, *Operatsija Blau*, ii, p.380.

53   Nauroth, pp.178–9.

54   Filonenko, iv, Docs.38 and 39.

55   Shamray, p.229.

56   Weidemann, pp.143–4.

57   For their bravery the 232nd Rifles were honoured post-war with a street named after them in Voronezh's western suburbs. Shamray, pp.233, 238, 240; Senger und Etterlin, pp.85–6.

58   Filonenko, i, Docs.48, 49; Shamray, p.295.

59   Weidemann, p.144.

60   Ibid, p.144.

61   Sdvizhkov, *Operatsija Blau*, ii, p.451–2.

62 Shamray, p.308.

63 Staebe, 'Offensive und Abwehr um Woronesh', pp.9–12.

64 Weidemann, p.145.

65 Staebe, pp.9–12 and AOK2, 'Die Angriffsschlacht von Woronesh', undated, CAMO 500/12472/44 at wwii.germandocsinrussia.org, accessed 2024.

66 Dollinger, p.146.

67 AOK2, 'Die Angriffsschlacht von Woronesh', undated, CAMO 500/12472/44 at wwii. germandocsinrussia.org, accessed 2024; OKW Communiqué, 11/7/42.

68 Sdvizhkov, *Operatsija Blau*, ii, pp.665–8.

69 Ibid, pp.441–4.

70 Ibid, pp.448–9.

71 Based on Meyer, *Heusinger*, p.185; letter 15/7/42 in Groscurth, p.527; TB Bock, 3–15/7/42; TB Halder, 3–13/7/42.

72 KTB Halder, 23/7/42.

73 Senger und Etterlin, p.92; Dimt, pp.44–6.

74 Dyachkov, pp.30–5.

75 Oosterling, p.137; Dyachkov, pp.35–8.

76 The fighting of 22 July is based on Oosterling, pp.137–9; Kubik, pp.223–4; Tieke, *Ein ruheloser Marsch*, p.111; Dyachkov, pp.39–45; Klapdor, pp.24–5; and CAMO 500/12482/136 at wwii. germandocsinrussia.org, accessed 2024.

77 BA-MA RH 24-40/191, pp.3–4.

78 BA-MA RH 27-13/92.

79 Author's papers.

80 Dyachkov, pp.45–6.

81 Klapdor, p.26; Ertl, pp.140–1.

82 Ertl, pp.139–40.

83 BA-MA RH 27-13/92; Klapdor, p.25.

84 Ertl, pp.139–40.

85 Based on TB Blume, 31/7/42–2/8/42; Mičianik, Vol.3, pp.130–1; VB, 30/7/42; TB Uffz Hans 'Hanni' Keller, 30/7/42, in BA-MA MSg 2/5611; Eichner, p.11.

86 Angrick, pp.560–5 and Mičianik, Vol.3, pp.133–4.

87 Spaeter, pp.185–8.

88 Klapdor, p.37.

89 Based on Order No.227 in author's papers, plus *Pravda*, 30/7/42 and *Krasnaya Zvezda*, 30/7/42.

90 Based on Daines, pp.80–1; *Stalingradskaya epopeya*, Docs.28, 29, 32, 33; Mann, p.64; Dyachkov, p.48 and Messe, *Krieg*, p.197.

91 Schimak, p.225; Pirschl, pp.36–7, 40; Löser, pp.188–9; Mark, *Panzerkrieg*, i, p.64; Werthen, p.98; Timpe, pp.42–3; Knopp, *Verdammte Krieg*, p.194.

92 Busch, *Stalingrad: Die stillen Helden*, pp.90–1, 152; Ebert, *Ein Arzt in Stalingrad*, pp.203–04.

93 Strecker letter, 19/7/42 in Haller (ed.), p.192; Alvensleben, 17/7/42, p.217; Adam, p.65.

94 Rossoschka, pp.102–03. Thomas was posted missing in the Stalingrad pocket in January 1943.

95 Based on Timpe, pp.42–3; Busch, *Stalingrad: Die stillen Helden*, p.152; Tagebuch Muth, 25/7/42 in BA-MA MSg 2/3282; TB Pickert, 14/7/42, BA-MA RL11/42; Senger und Etterlin, p.92; and Werthen, p.105.

96 Broekmeyer, p.93; Chuikov, pp.37–8.

97 Lebedenko, pp.77–9.

98 Mark, *Panzerkrieg*, i, p.70; Dieckhoff, p.188; Apitzsch, pp.122–4.

99   Lebedenko, pp.148–9.

100 Alvensleben, 4/8/42, p.219 and Senger und Etterlin, p.92.

101 Lebedenko, pp.171–2.

102 Based on *Stalingradskaya epopeya*, Doc.26; Löser, pp.179–80; Paul, *Potsdamer Infanterie Regiment*, pp.485–6; letter of 17/8/42 in BA-MA MSg 2/11157.

103 Simonow, *Kriegstagebücher*, ii, pp.188–91.

104 Voss, p.121.

105 Alvensleben, pp.219–21.

106 Podewils, pp.94–6.

107 Alvensleben, p.220.

108 Rauchhaupt, Herbert, 'So wurde der Donbogen ausgefegt', *Der Führer* (Karlsruhe), 31/8/42.

109 Seydlitz, pp.157–8; Letter of 17/8/42 in BA-MA MSg 2/11157.

110 Simonow, *Kriegstagebücher*, ii, pp.188–91.

111 Based on BA-MA RH 24-40/191, pp.8–10; TB Dimt, 31/7/42 in Dimt, p.66; and BA-MA RH 24-40/189, pp.34–5, 37–8.

112 Based on Hoffmann, *Kaukasien 1942/43*, p.71; BA-MA RH 24-40/191, pp.19–20, 22 and 3rd Pz, pp.311–12.

113 BA-MA RH 27-13/152.

114 BA-MA RH 27-13/92 and Tieke, *The Caucasus and the Oil*, pp.42–3.

115 Ziemke, p.362; BA-MA RH 24-40/191, pp.19–20, 22; Mičianik, Vol.4, p.276; Leixner, Leo, 'Die Attacke auf Krasnodar', *Völkischer Beobachter*, Vienna edition, 2/9/42; CAMO 500/12482/136 at wwii.germandocsinrussia.org, accessed 2024; and Ernsthausen, pp.61–2.

116 Franz Müller, pp.243–5.

117 Tieke, *Ein ruheloser Marsch*, p.116.

118 Emde, p.99; Klapdor, pp.39–40; Strassner, p.140.

119 Author's papers.

120 BA-MA RH 27-3/188.

121 Tieke, *Ziel Kaukasus*, p.77.

122 Spaeter, pp.206–08.

123 TB Dimt, 9/8/42 in Dimt, pp.83–4; Behind Soviet Lines, pp.58–62 and Eichholtz, p.98.

124 The fighting for Krasnodar on 8–10 August is based on Vladmir Biryukov's memoirs reproduced in part at 'Pamyat' serdtsa svyata!' At www.gazetavk.ru/?d=2011-12-30&r=28&s=252, accessed April 2025; Leixner, Leo, 'Die Attacke auf Krasnodar', *Völkischer Beobachter*, Vienna edition, 2/9/42; and Marion Pruckner, 'Dr. Leo Leixner – ein typischer Vertreter der nationalsozialistischen Kriegsberichterstatter? nationalsozialistischer Schriftleiter während dem Zweiten Weltkrieg', thesis, University of Vienna, 2009, pp.105–06.

125 BA-MA RH 24-40/192, pp.4–7; Skrjabina, pp.11, 28–31; Munzel, pp.123–4; 3rd Pz, p.317.

126 Bähr, pp.225–6; Oldenburg, p.268n1120 and TB Dimt, 8/8/42 in Dimt, pp.76–7.

127 Bergsteiger, pp.1–2; BA-MA RH 24-40/188, pp.1, 3.

128 Jacobi, pp.54–5; Graser, p.172.

129 BA-MA RH 24-40/189, p.41.

130 BA-MA RH 24-40/188, pp.10–11.

131 KTB Engel, 15–16/8/42.

132 Operation *Elbrus* is based on BA-MA RH 28-1/273; Kaltenegger, *Edelweiss und Endzian*, pp.185–91; Bauer, pp.73, 111–12, 118–25; Kaltenegger, *Gebirgsjäger im Kaukasus*, pp.98–9; Knopp, *Verdammte Krieg*, p.58; Groth's account in *Der Soldat zwischen Alpen und Donau*, No.10, 1942; and Kaltenegger's biography of Groth, pp.71–2.

133 BA-MA RH 28-1/65.

134 BA-MA RH 28-1/65; Speer, p.332.

135 Kaltenegger, *Groth*, p.99; VB, Vienna edition, 26/8/42.

136 SD Meldungen, 27/8/42, 17/9/42; Ertl, p.149.

137 SD Meldungen, 20/7/42–17/8/42.

138 TB Goebbels, 20/8/42.

139 Kirstein, p.718; Knopp, *Stalingrad*, p.86; Diedrich, *Nach Stalingrad*, pp.220–2; KTB Bühler, 20/8/42.

140 Kalmyk steppe based on Ziemke, p.385; Senger und Etterlin, p.110; Kuehn, p.69; Ebert, *Ein Arzt in Stalingrad*, p.213 and Stockhausen, pp.223–4.

141 Weidemann, p.157; Wijers and Stempel, *Stalingrad Tagebuch*, p.15; Grams, p.50.

142 Papers of Dr Franz Muth, BA-MA MSg 2/3282.

143 TB Muth, 6/8/42 in BA-MA MSg 2/3282.

144 Senger und Etterlin, p.112; Weidemann, pp.157, 159.

145 TB Muth, 23/8/42 in BA-MA MSg 2/3282.

146 Weidemann, pp.159–60; Senger und Etterlin, p.112.

147 Podewils, pp.105–07; Selle, p.38.

148 Dohna-Schlobitten, pp.247–8; Werthen, p.106.

149 Podewils, p.107.

150 Langsdorff, pp.193–4; Alvensleben, p.222; Timpe, p.49; Knopp, *Stalingrad*, pp.104, 108.

151 Alvensleben, pp.222–3; Podewils, pp.108–10.

152 Based on Knopp, *Stalingrad*, pp.109, 111–12; Busch, *Stalingrad: Die stillen Helden*, pp.53–4; BA-MA RH 27-16/46; Werthen, pp.106–07; Letter 24/8/42 in Fuchs and Rella, p.103; and Podewils, p.105.

153 Jagdfliegerverbände, 9/II, p.129n298; TB Pabst, 23/8/42.

154 Werthen, pp.106–07; Podewils, pp.105–07; Alvensleben, pp.222–3.

CHAPTER 4: TOMORROW WE'LL BE DRINKING COFFEE IN CAIRO

1   Freter, pp.631–2.

2   Marwan-Schlosser, p.166; Mauer, p.274.

3   Frey, pp.270, 273; Hubalek, pp.121, 127.

4   Freter, pp.631–2; TB Köhrer, 25/6/42; Rebora, p.212; NA CAB146/12; KTB DAK, 25/6/42 and 28/6/42 in AL833/1.

5   *Die 33er*, p.138.

6   Frey, p.270.

7   Kitchen, p.258.

8   Frey, p.270

9   Fennell, pp.24, 174.

10 Neulen, p.115; Moorehead, pp.383–5.

11 Based on Varco, p.305; Romersa, pp.59–61 and Cavallero Diario, 25/6/42.

12 Based on TB Rommel, 26/6/42 in Rommel's papers; Kesselring, p.123; and Romersa, pp.61–6. The decisions reached at Sidi Barrani were confirmed the following day in a directive from the Comando Supremo; see Reuth, *Entscheidung im Mittelmeer*, p.252. A decade later Kesselring complained the conference 'sealed the fate of North Africa'.

13 Taysen, pp.340–1.

14 Behrendt interview in Behrendt papers; Knopp, *Hitlers Krieger*, p.49.

15 Knopp, *Hitlers Krieger*, p.41; Luck, p.112; Holmes, pp.161, 265; Frey, p.272.

16   Mellenthin, p.54; Schmidt, p.42; Behrendt interview; Reuth, *Rommel: The End of a Legend*,
      p.112; Heckmann, pp.328–9.

17   KTB Halder, 6/7/41; TB Goebbels, 30/9/42 and 28/11/41; Kesselring, p.124; Reuth, *Rommel:*
      The End of a Legend, p.42.

18   Knopp, *Hitlers Krieger*, p.49.

19   Ibid, pp.48, 53.

20   TB Goebbels, 20/12/41 and 7/2/42; *Hitler's Table Talk*, 9/7/42; Koch, pp.60–1; Fennell, p.174;
      Knopp, *Hitlers Krieger*, p.50; Dimbleby, p.317.

21   Varco, pp.305, 308; Frey, p.273 and KTB 90th Light, 28/6/42 in AL773.

22   Rommel, *Krieg Ohne Hass*, p.171 and KTB DAK, 29/6/42 in AL833/1.

23   Marwan-Schlosser, p.178; Varco, p.308; Rizzo, p.414.

24   Accounts of the booty captured at Matruh vary. Rommel's memoirs and the diary of the 90th
      Light talk of 'enormous booty' and 'a huge supply dump'; the *Ariete's* chief-of-staff reckoned his
      men seized enough matériel to equip an entire division, while supply officer Hellmuth Frey, who
      made a detailed inventory, was far more conservative.

25   Ritchie had been sacked four days before Matruh fell. Based on Frey, pp.273–4; Freter, p.641;
      KTB 90th Light Division, 29/6/42–30/6/42 in AL773.

26   Rommel, *Krieg Ohne Hass*, p.172.

27   Varco, p.308.

28   KTB 90th Light Division, 29–30/6/42 in AL773 and PzAOK Afrika Tagesmeldung, 30/6/42 in
      CAB 146/12.

29   Koch, p.95; Bottai, p.312; Neulen, p.115; Romersa, pp.66–7; Mancinelli, p.132.

30   Based on Mancinelli, pp.141–2; Walker, p.137; and Loi, p.54.

31   Heckmann, p.379; KTB 90th Light Division, 1/7/42 in AL773.

32   Walker, p.139.

33   Rommel, *Krieg Ohne Hass*, pp.182–3.

34   Hartmann, pp.232–4.

35   Vallicella, p.36.

36   Bedeschi, *Fronte d'Africa*, pp.196–7.

37   Based on KTB DAK Appendices, 2/7/42 in AL833/2 and Hartmann, pp.232–4.

38   KTB DAK Appendices, 2/7/42 in AL833/2.

39   KTB 90th Light Division, 2/7/42 in Rommel's papers.

40   Vallicella, p.39.

41   KTB DAK Appendices, 3/7/42 in AL833/2. See similar exhortations to 21st Panzer Division in
      KTB 21 PzDiv, 3/7/42 in AL918/1–2.

42   Varco, p.315.

43   Zambon, *Ariete*, p.97.

44   Walker, p.141; Rizzo, p.418; Frey, p.278.

45   Appendix to PzAOK Afrika Tagesmeldung, 3/7/42 in CAB146/12; Rommel, *Krieg Ohne Hass*,
      pp.184–5.

46   Schroetter, p.183.

47   VB, 3–4/7/42; SD Meldungen 2/7/42 and 9/7/42.

48   Frey, p.278.

49   TB Goebbels, 7/7/42; SD Meldungen, 8–9/7/42.

50   See Cavallero Diario, 4/7/42; the report from 'Hannibal', 3/7/42, in KTB OKW, 5/7/42; and
      TB Goebbels, 2/7/42.

51   See TB Goebbels, 4/7/42, Frey, p.278, Baum, p.235 and Heckmann, p.373; Herf, pp.113, 116–18.

52   See TT, 9/7/42.

53   Note by Jodl, 3/7/42 in Rommel's papers; Westphal, p.173; Kitchen, pp.278–80; Herf, pp.125–6.

54   Rommel, *Krieg Ohne Hass*, p.186; TB Rommel, 13/7/42 and TB von Waldau, 13–14/7/42; Bedeschi, *Fronte d'Africa*, pp.64–5; TB Armbruster, 10/7/42; Moorehead, p.396.

55   Kippenberger, p.174.

56   Remy, p.102.

57   Romersa, p.74. It's entirely possible Rommel suffered a breakdown in mid-July 1942. The period, he conceded one month later, was 'the ugliest and most tormented in his military life, the most full of anxiety and moral depression'. Montanari, p.229.

58   Mancinelli, p.146; GASWW, vi, p.746 and Cavallero Diario, 17/7/42.

59   TB Armbruster, 10–11/7/42

60   Irving, p.198.

61   Rommel, *Krieg Ohne Hass*, pp.197–8.

62   Welzer, Neitzel and Gudehus, pp.198, 199; SRM73 in NA WO218/4136; Irving, p.198; Marwan-Schlosser, p.175.

63   Welzer, Neitzel and Gudehus, pp.202–03, 205; Prien, *Geschichte des Jagdgeschwaders 77*, iii, p.1263; Sonnenkalb, p.125.

64   Stimpel, pp.26–7.

65   Frey, p.277.

66   KTB DAK Appendices, 22/7/42 in AL833/3.

67   Mobius, p.137. The Knight's Cross made teenage anti-tank gunner Günter Halm a celebrity, inundated with 'fan mail' from the Reich which he had neither the time nor inclination to deal with. Some wanted photographs; others asked for his autograph, even 'the fulfilment of other wishes'. In the end his father became his publicist, sending out photographs of his son – retouched with the addition of his decoration. 'Others who were decorated received home leave but for me crossing the Mediterranean was too dangerous,' Halm recalled with frustration. 'The desert held me prisoner. The sun blazed, as on every day, the sand reflected the heat, in my canteen the coffee was still brackish, but my thoughts were at home.' One letter did at least bring good news: a philanthropist from Düsseldorf had set aside 10,000 Reichsmarks for Halm's education – should he return safely from the war. Mobius, p.175.

68   KTB 90th Light Division, 22/7/42 in AL733.

69   See Cavallero Diario, 22/7/42; Montanari, p.176 and Mancinelli, pp.155–6.

70   Mussolini's visit to North Africa is based on Monelli, pp.9–11; Rintelen, pp.171–3; Burgwyn, pp.146–7; Vallauri, p.215; Petacco, *L'armata nel deserto*, p.134; Romersa, p.70; and the diary entries of Ciano, 22–23/7/42, and Bottai, 11/8/42. For Mussolini's memorandum, see Mancinelli, pp.152–3 and Cavallero Diario, 19/7/42.

71   Vallicella, p.49.

72   Montanari, p.227.

73   Rizzi, p.73.

74   Based on Cavallero Diario, 1/8/42; Caccia-Dominioni, *El Alamein*, p.38; Gross, p.57; Neulen, p.119; Vallicella, p.59.

75   Hartmann, pp.237–8 and *Die 33er*, p.153.

76   Based on Hartmann, pp.237–8; *Die 33er*, p.153; Heckmann, p.418; Buchmann, p.169 and Frey, p.299.

77   Diario, Libyan front, 25 October 1942. Trentino, p.31.

78   Based on Taghon, ii, pp.54–5, 67–8; Balke, pp.201–02, 211.

79   Taghon, ii, p.74.

80   Radtke, p.126; Taghon, ii, p.52; Balke, p.211.

81   TB von Waldau, 17/7/42; Shores and Ring, p.231.

82 SD Meldung, 16/7/42.

83 Heaton, p.124; TB Goebbels, 1/7/42.

84 Heaton, p.125.

85 Shores and Ring, p.222; Fish, p.190; Prien, Rodeike and Stemmer, I/JG27, p.172.

86 Prien, Rodeike and Stemmer, III/JG27, p.151.

87 Fennell, pp.25, 174, 205.

88 Based on Caccia-Dominioni, El Alamein, p.86; Die 33er, p.153; Bähr, p.141; Peitz, p.115; Frey, pp.288–9; Henning, pp.130–1; and Hubalek, pp.63–4.

89 Based on Stimpel, pp.32, 49; Letter of 29/7/42 in Stimme, p.237; Aberger, Taysen and Ziemer, pp.198–9; Gross, p.117; Varco, p.325.

90 Neulen, p.113; Gross, pp.116–17; Lazzati, pp.106–09.

91 Vallauri, pp.216–17; Gross, pp.116–17; Ringler, p.35; Frey, p.307.

92 Lormier, pp.146–7.

93 Aberger, Taysen and Ziemer, pp.198–9.

94 Dollinger, p.145.

95 Dollinger, p.145; and Frey, pp.288–9.

96 Diario Cavallero, 18/8/42; PzAOK Afrika, Tagesmeldung, 6/7/42, 18/7/42 in AL866/6.

97 Montanari, p.230; TB Goebbels, 20/8/42.

98 See Rommel, Krieg Ohne Hass, p.206n and GASWW, vi, pp.751–2.

99 Westphal, pp.168–9.

100 Based on Order of the Day, 30/8/42, author's papers; Montanari, pp.227–8; Frey, pp.293, 312.

101 Of seven ships dispatched to North African ports in the final week of August, only three reached their destination. Montanari, p.239.

102 Hartmann, p.245; Letter, 30/8/42 in Rommel's papers; Rommel, Krieg Ohne Hass, p.210n.

103 Vallicella, pp.53–4.

104 Besana, p.81.

105 Bedeschi, Fronte d'Africa, p.401.

106 Vallicella, p.54.

107 Beretta, pp.91–3.

108 Vallicella, p.54.

CHAPTER 5: THREE AXIS ARMIES ON THE DON

1 Vasyukov and Tikhomirov, pp.443–4.

2 Don Bend, p.71; Pihurik, Naplók, p.349; Lajos, 30/6/42.

3 Nemeskürty, pp.32–3.

4 Ibid, pp.33–9.

5 Vogel and Wette, p.87; Vollner, p.57; Pihurik, Naplók, pp.114, 328, 334; Gosztony, Hitlers Fremde Heere, p.274.

6 Lukács Bence and Szabó, pp.32–4, 42; Don Bend, p.41.

7 Lajos, 11/7/42; Lukács Bence and Szabó, pp.61, 79.

8 Aradi and Szabó, pp.92, 99–100.

9 Szabó, Magyarok, pp.211–13; Pihurik, Naplók, p.327.

10 A második világháború, pp.234–5.

11 Filonenko, iv, Doc.97.

12 Pihurik, Naplók, pp.208, 315, 317.

13 Förster, p.224; Szabó, Magyarok, pp.244–5; Gosztony, A Magyar, p.73.

14   Lajos, 15/7/42.

15   Ciano Diario, 10/10/41 and 17/10/41; Schlemmer, *Italiener*, p.24.

16   Composition of the Eighth Army is based on Schlemmer, *Italiener*, pp.29–30, 102; Sapori, p.271; Förster, pp.269–70; and Scianna, pp.127–30.

17   Scianna, p.220; Ciano Diario, 17/5/42.

18   Messe, *Krieg*, pp.210–13.

19   Voghera, pp.270, 297; Revelli, *L'ultimo fronte*, p.151.

20   Voghera, p.344.

21   Ibid, pp.273–4.

22   Ibid, pp.285, 293.

23   Ibid, pp.271, 274, 291, 294, 298.

24   Giusti, pp.144–5, 147; Revelli, *Mai tardi*, 13/8/42 and 24/8/42; Sapori, pp.137–9.

25   Giusti, p.137; 5 Alpini, p.118; Schlemmer, *Invasori*, p.68; Pannacci, p.38.

26   Lami, pp.201, 210; Mela and Crespi, p.238; Cati, pp.260–6, 268–70.

27   Cati, p.314; Lami, pp.212, 215.

28   Lami, p.215.

29   Lami, p.213; Schlemmer, *Italiener*, p.54.

30   Lami, p.219.

31   Ibid, p.201.

32   Lami, pp.219–20.

33   The cavalry charge at Izbushensky is based on Mela and Crespi, pp.243–6, 258; Lami, pp.230–2, 239–40; Gribaudi, pp.171–2.

34   Messe, *Lettere*, 12/9/42, p.146; Lami, p.240; Petacco, *L'armata scomparsa*, p.74.

35   Longo, p.172; Stern, pp.82–83; Rossetti, p.185; Giusti, p.218; Cenci, p.21.

36   Scianna, pp.137–8; Maggi, pp.134–5; Pannacci, pp.56, 64–5.

37   Bruno Carloni was killed ten days later. Based on Maggi, pp.134–5; Giusti, p.165; Schlemmer, *Italiener*, pp.175–6; Avagliano and Palmieri, pp.99, 102–03; *Stimme*, p.169.

38   Longo, pp.172–3.

39   Ibid, pp.184–5.

40   KTB Halder, 30/3/41; BA-MA RH 31-I/96; Gosztony, *Hitlers Fremde Heere*, p.249; Axworthy, p.58; Thers, pp.63–4.

41   Ştefănescu, p.216; Harward, p.135.

42   Based on Balta, pp.185–6 and BA-MA RH 31-I/93, 22/5/41; Kehrig, p.62; Axworthy, pp.39, 61–3; Klaus, pp.23–4; Voicu, *Pentru*, p.419.

43   Kehrig, pp.62–3; Spânu pp.133–4; BA-MA RH 31-I/93.

44   Thers, pp.83–4.

45   Author's papers.

46   Negrici, p.138.

47   Pihurik, *Naplók*, p.100; Sándor, p.79.

48   Based on Giusti, p.165; Pannacci, pp.33, 34, 40; Schlemmer, *Invasori*, pp.68, 72, 284; Rizzi, p.99; Perrotta, p.114; Trentino, p.137.

49   Pannacci, p.34; Schlemmer, *Invasori*, pp.75–6, 77, 82; Grignaschi, pp.79–81; Sapori, pp.280–1.

50   Based on Sapori, pp.280, 285; Scotoni and Filonenko, pp.185–6; Schlemmer, *Italiener*, p.102; Filatov, p.105; Schlemmer, *Invasori*, pp.89–91; Scotoni, *Il nemico fidato*, pp.390–1; Zanfagnini, p.161.

51   Scotoni, *Il nemico fidato*, pp.390–1; Sapori, p.299; Revelli, *Mai tardi*, 13/8/42; Schlemmer, *Italiener*, pp.42, 173; Schlemmer, *Invasori*, p.72.

52   Lajos, 9/6/42; Pihurik, 'Hungarian Soldiers', pp.87–90.

53   Szabó, *Keleti Front*, pp.38–40; Pihurik, *Naplók*, p.109; BA-MA RH 23/176.

54   Ungváry, *Magyar Megszallo*, p.304.

55   Lajos, 2/5/42; Ungváry, 'Hungarian occupation forces', pp.81–120; Aradi and Szabó, p.80.

56   Szabó, *Magyarok*, pp.211–12, 283, 285–6; Szabó, *Keleti Front*, pp.38–40.

57   Szabó, *Magyarok*, pp.283, 285–6.

58   *Sentinela*, 26/7/42. Cited in Harward, p.159.

59   Based on Harward, pp.160, 162–3, 165; Voicu, *Sacrificiu*, p.65; Bichir, pp.134–5; Duţu, *Armata Română in Război*, pp.158–9; Iorga, p.96.

60   Iorga, p.87; Harward, pp.151–3, 157; Lienard, p.237.

61   Lukács Bence and Szabó, pp.144, 158, 164; Pihurik, 'Hungarian Soldiers', p.96.

62   Lukács Bence and Szabó, pp.150–1; Nemeskürty, pp.37–9,

63   Szabó, *Magyarok*, pp.336–7; Filonenko, iv, Doc.97; Lajos, 30/8/42 and 1/9/42; and Lukács Bence and Szabó, p.95.

64   Szabó, *Magyarok*, pp.333–4, 336.

65   Sándor, pp.88–9; Gosztony, *A Magyar*, p.83; Vollner, pp.96–7; Szabó, *Keleti Front*, p.59; Nemeskürty, pp.34, 36.

66   Sándor, p.122.

67   Szabó, *Keleti Front*, pp.60–1.

68   Förster, p.225; Gosztony, *Hitlers Fremde Heere*, pp.249, 281; KTB Engel, 27/10/42.

69   Filatov, pp.108–09.

70   Based on Rizzi, p.74; Sapori, p.160; Gooch, p.287; Giusti, p.142; Avagliano and Palmieri, p.252 and Hamilton, pp.61–3.

71   Schlemmer, *Italiener*, pp.247–8; Leonelli, p.33; Bedeschi, *Fronte Russo*, ii, p.387.

72   Leonelli, p.33.

73   Grignaschi, pp.83, 87; Avagliano and Palmieri, p.102; Trentino, p.138.

74   Avagliano and Palmieri, p.250; Schlemmer, *Italiener*, pp.247–8; Zanfagnini, p.212.

75   Giusti, p.137; Schlemmer, *Italiener*, pp.203–04; BA-MA, RH 31 IX/35, Bl.60-74.

76   Zambon, *Les Italiens*, pp.68–9 and Beevor, pp.182–3.

77   Zambon, *Les Italiens*, pp.73, 76.

78   Schlemmer, *Italiener*, pp.49, 51.

79   BA-MA RH 31-XIV/3; Pannacci, p.41; Sapori, p.160.

80   Gheorghe, p.74.

81   *Stalingradskaya epopeya*, Doc.11; Voicu, *Sacrificiu*, p.121.

82   Voicu, *Sacrificiu*, p.124 and *Stalingradskaya epopeya*, Doc.14.

83   Voicu, *Sacrificiu*, p.126; Gheorghe, p.74.

84   Based on Voicu, *Sacrificiu*, pp.127–9; Scherzer, *Stalingrad war der Anfang*, p.75; Iorga, pp.89, 104, 114 and Duţu, *Armata Română in Război*, p.191.

85   Based on Pandea, *Românii La Stalingrad*, pp.144–5, 148–50; Constantiniu, p.404; Kehrig, p.66; Iorga, p.122; and Ocoleanu, p.170.

86   Förster, p.199; Kehrig, p.57; Ştefănescu, p.227; Antonescu Jurnalul, ii, p.472.

Chapter 6: We're Holding on to What We've Got

1   Bedeschi, *Fronte d'Africa*, pp.401–02.

2   Based on KTB DAK, 2200 Hours, 30/8/42 in AL 834/1; Barr, p.226; *Stimme*, pp.238–9; KTB 21 Pz Div, 30–31/8/42 in AL 925/2; Aberger, Taysen and Ziemer, p.202; Nehring, pp.137–8; 15 Pz Div intelligence report, 17/8/42–5/9/42 in KTB 15 Pz Div Appendices, AL1656.

3   Beretta, p.94.

4   Bedeschi, *Fronte d'Africa*, pp.402–06.

5   Beretta, pp.101–06.

6   Vallicella, pp.56–7.

7   KTB DAK 0805 Hours, 31/8/42 in AL834/1.

8   Vallicella, pp.56–7; KTB 21 Pz Div, 1300 Hours, 31/8/42 in AL 925/2; Caccia-Dominioni, *El Alamein*, p.145; Beretta, pp.120–1.

9   Hartmann, *Geschichte des Panzerregiments 5*, p.245.

10   Fiebig, pp.155–7.

11   Based on Mancinelli, p.168; KTB OQu PzAOK Afrika, 1/9/42 in NA CAB 146/20; Rizzo, p.478; KTB DAK, 1000 Hours, 2/9/42 in AL834/1; Report to OKW, 2/9/42, in KTB PzAOK Afrika appendices in NA CAB 146/14.

12   Kesselring, p.131.

13   Aberger, Taysen and Ziemer, p.203.

14   Mellenthin, p.176; Mancinelli, pp.166–9; Report by Rommel, 11/9/42 in NA CAB 146/16; Dollinger, *Kain*, p.156.

15   Caccia-Dominioni, *El Alamein*, p.154; Frey, pp.315–16.

16   Hans-Arnold Stahlschmidt was posted missing five days later, having been credited with 59 victories. Dettmann, pp.179–80.

17   Dettmann, pp.186–7; Heaton, pp.141–9.

18   Based on KTB Skl 2/9/42; Cavallero Diario, 5/9/42, 7/9/42, 12/9/42, 16/10/42 and 20/10/42; Report by Rintelen, 4/9/42 in NA CAB 146/16; and report of a meeting between Mussolini and Kesselring, 7/9/42 in NA AIR 20/7703.

19   See Cavallero Diario, 20/10/42 and Baum, p.258.

20   Taghon, ii, pp.84–5.

21   NA AIR 20/7705. See also Salewski, ii, p.88.

22   Letter to his wife, 9/9/42 in Liddell Hart, p.290; Frey, pp.315–16; Von Hassell, p.267.

23   SRM75, 20/11/42 in NA WO 208/4136; Romersa, p.84.

24   Ciano Diario, 27/9/42; Baum, p.257; TB Goebbels, 29/9/42.

25   Liddell Hart, pp.294–5; Baum, p.249.

26   VB, 4/10/42.

27   Author's papers.

28   Jähnert, p.209.

29   Heaton, pp.172–3.

30   Marseille's death is based on Ring, *Chronik Jagdgeschwader 27*, pp.238–41; Dettman, p.207; Heaton, pp.176–82; Report from Luftflotte V to Kesselring, 30/9/42 in NA DEFE 3/573.

31   VB, 2/10/42; and Gross appendix, unnumbered.

32   NA AIR 20/7702; Vallicella, p.88; Lazzati, pp.151–4, 158–60; 4 Stormo, pp.312–13.

33   Vallicella, pp.77, 79; Stimpel, p.49.

34   Vallicella, pp.59, 62

35   Ringler, pp.84–5.

36   Ringler, pp.108, 118.

37   Stimpel, p.53.

38   Vallicella, p.75.

39   Bottaro, p.30; Santoponte, pp.80–1.

40   Vallicella, p.64.

41   Cavallo, p.248; Montanari, iii, pp.993–4; Avagliano, pp.74–5; and Vallicella, p.92.

42   Cited in Bierman and Smith, p.241.

43 Barr, p.261; Fennell, p.207; Dimbleby, p.369.

44 Cited in Bierman and Smith, p.264.

45 Fiebig, p.163; Ringler, p.113.

46 Seidemann papers in BA-MA N406/28.

47 GASWW, vi, pp.769–70.

48 KTB DAK, 1000 Hours, 14/10/42, 19/10/42 and 22/10/42 in AL 834/1; Stumme to Cavallero, 3/10/42 in Rommel Papers; report by von Rintelen, 22/10/42 in NA AIR 20/7705; Based on an undated letter from Stumme to Rommel in mid-October 1942 in Rommel Papers.

49 KTB 15 Pz Div Appendices, undated report, in AL 1656.

50 Caccia-Dominioni, *El Alamein*, pp.208–09.

51 KTB DAK, 1000 Hours, 23/10/42 in AL834/1.

52 Behrendt, pp.61, 197–8.

53 Ringler, pp.118–19.

CHAPTER 7: WE HAVE JUST TAKEN ON TOO MUCH

1 Bombing of 23 August based especially on the testimonies collected in *Und die Wolga brannt*, pp.61–2, 115, 129–30, 233, 266–7; Semenov, p.56; Lev Yushchenko, 'Pamyat', taken from *Letopistsy Pobedy*, digitised at www.maxima-library.com/component/maxlib/b/383519, accessed April 2024; *Stalingrad i Stalingradskaya oblast*, pp.366–7; Mark, *Angriff*, p.71; Bastable, p.43; Eremenko, pp.134–6; and TB Richthofen, 23/8/42.

2 Lev Yushchenko, 'Pamyat', taken from *Letopistsy Pobedy*, digitised at www.maxima-library.com/component/maxlib/b/383519, accessed April 2024.

3 Hellbeck, *Stalingrad Protokolle*, p.134; BA-MA RL10/802; *Und die Wolga brannt*, pp.61–2, 129–30.

4 Einsiedel, pp.7–9, 13–14, 16–23.

5 TB Richthofen, 25/8/42; *Stalingradskaya epopeya*, Doc.35.

6 *Und die Wolga brannt*, p.173; *Stalingrad 1942–1943*, Doc.501. When Sixth Army surrendered at the end of January, one of the city's Party leaders buttonholed 71st Infantry Division's commander Friedrich Roske. 'Why did you bomb Stalingrad so savagely?' Roske's reply was curt: 'War is war.' *Stalingrad i Stalingradskaya oblast*, pp.366–7.

7 *Stalingrad 1942–1943*, Doc.493.

8 *Stalingrad i Stalingradskaya oblast*, pp.366–7.

9 Bastable, p.45; Hellbeck, *Stalingrad Protokolle*, pp.142–3; Kucherenko, p.87.

10 *Stalingrad 1942–1943*, Docs.495, 496, 500, 505; Hellbeck, *Stalingrad Protokolle*, pp.126–9; *Stalingradskaya epopeya*, Doc.34; *Stalingrad 1942–1943*, Doc.492.

11 Dieckhoff, p.200; *Stalingradskaya epopeya*, Doc.36; Popov, pp.54–5; Werthen, pp.108–11.

12 Senger und Etterlin, pp.116–17.

13 Volkogonov, pp.461–2; Ziemke, p.391.

14 *Stalingradskaya epopeya*, Doc.32; Grossman, p.133; Buchbender, pp.96–7.

15 Alvensleben, p.231.

16 De Zayas, *Die Wehrmacht Untersuchungsstelle*, p.286.

17 Papers of Dr Franz Muth, BA-MA MSg 2/3282; *Auf beiden Seiten*, p.43; Karpow, *Russland im Krieg 1941–1945*, p.126; Vogel and Wette, pp.144–5; Proskouriakov, p.211; Sdvizhkov, *V iyule 1942*, pp.228–9.

18 Wette and Ueberschar, p.103; *Stalingradskaya epopeya*, Doc.44.

19 Buchbender, p.97; *Strana v Ogne*, 1942–43, ii, Doc.44; Kirstein, p.786; Voss, p.131.

20 Bühler letter, 1/9/42.

21 Semenov, p.36.

22 Knopp, *Verdammte Krieg*, p.72; Bühler, 1/9/42; Kirstein, p.827.

23 Ziemke, pp.388–91; Craig, pp.28–30, 33–7; Bellamy, pp.510–13.

24 Knopp, *Stalingrad*, p.134; TB Pabst, 9/9/42.

25 Podewils, p.139.

26 Kirstein, p.827.

27 Tschuikow, pp.104, 107–08, 114, 116–17.

28 According to Münch's testimony more than 60 years later, he reported the Volga reached at 3.50pm – almost certainly a transcription error. Testimony of Gerhard Münch in FacingStalingrad.com, accessed 2018.

29 *Die 71 Infanterie Division*, pp.239–41.

30 Testimony of Gerhard Hindenlang in FacingStalingrad.com, accessed 2018.

31 Diedrich and Ebert, *Nach Stalingrad*, p.224.

32 Rodimtsev, pp.32–4 and *Stalingrad i Stalingradskaya oblast*, pp.116–17.

33 Rodimtsev, p.61.

34 Evacuated, Vasily Koleganov was transferred to the east bank of the Volga and eventually returned to duty. He was killed two years later fighting in Poland. Kobyakov, pp.121–3 and Tschuikow, pp.155–8.

35 The fighting in the grain elevator is based on: Mark, 'Stalingrad: Battle for the Grain Elevator', pp.3–40 passim; the diary of Wilhelm Hoffman, 94th Infantry Division, 16–22/9/42, cited in Chuikov, pp.270–1; Tschuikow, pp.133–5; Kobyakov, pp.88–90; Mark, *Angriff*, pp.174, 177, 179; TB Muth, 16/9/42 and 21–22/9/42 in BA-MA MSg 2/3282; and *Erinnerungsbuch der 94 Infanterie-Division*, pp.232–5.

36 Based on a letter, 23/9/42 in Schnitzler, p.56; Voss, p.137; AOK 6 daily and strength reports, 14/9/42–26/9/42, Tagesmeldung 26/9/42; MacGregor, p.149; Kobyakov, p.73; Knopp, *Stalingrad*, p.136.

37 Report reproduced in Kirstein, pp.862–4.

38 Hellbeck, *Stalingrad Protokolle*, pp.463–4; Knopp, *Stalingrad*, p.147; Chuikov, pp.271–2.

39 Rodimtsev, pp.67–8; AOK 6 Zwischenmeldung, 24/9/42.

40 Mark, *Angriff*, pp.208–09; AOK 6 Zwischen/Tagesmeldung, 26/9/42.

41 Sündermann, pp.232–3; VB, 7–19/9/42; SD Meldung, 17/9/42, 25/9/42; Kershaw, *Der Hitler Mythos*, p.167.

42 TB Goebbels, 7/9/42, 18–19/9/42 and Dohna-Schlobitten, p.246.

43 Boelcke, pp.275, 279; TB Goebbels, 20/9/42; SD Meldungen, 10/9/42 and 25/9/42.

44 TB Goebbels, 20/9/42.

45 BA-MA RH 31-I/180(b).

46 Breymayer, pp.213–15.

47 Witzel, pp.177–8.

48 Breymayer, p.217 and Kurowski and Schlee, pp.290–2.

49 Gruber, pp.251–2.

50 Breymayer, pp.218–20.

51 Kaltenegger, *Eglseer*, p.121; Spraul, pp.252, 256–7.

52 Conditions and difficulties of the advance through the Caucasus are based, *inter alia*, on: Weinmann, pp.449–50; Buchner, *Vom Eismeer bis zum Kaukasus*, pp.76–8; Kaltenegger, *Eglseer*, pp.117–19, 121–2; Graser, pp.184–5; and Rall, pp.117, 121.

53 Kaisergruber, p.102; Graser, p.183.

54 Tyuleneva, Sablin and Timofeyev, pp.106–07, 110–11 and Sokolov, p.179.

55   Kubik, p.284; GASWW, vi, p.1046; KTB Halder, 29–31/8/42, KTB Engel, 31/8/42 and
      8/9/42 and Meyer, *Heusinger*, p.188.
56   Keitel, p.181 and Jodl, p.66. Jodl's account – given to his future wife two months later – largely
      tallies with Heusinger's memoirs, pp.198–200. See also Konrad's warnings in Kaltenegger, *Eglseer*,
      p.123 and Konrad, p.32.
57   The crisis in the High Command is based on a letter from the Naval Liaison Officer to OKH,
      22/9/42 BA-MA RM 7/990, p.140; KTB Halder, 11/9/42; Broucek, pp.151–2; ADAP, E4,
      Doc.82; TB Goebbels, 17/9/42; KTB Engel, 7–8/9/42, 14/9/42, 18/9/42 and Hürter and Uhl,
      'Hitler in Vinnytsia', pp.170–210.
58   Meyer, *Heusinger*, p.188; KTB Halder, 24/9/42.
59   Based on Greiner letters, 27/9/42; Meyer, *Heusinger*, p.189 and Hartmann, *Halder*, p.339.
60   Speech by Zeitzler, 26/9/42 in Liss Papers, AL 1669 and Megargee, pp.183–4.
61   Pojić, pp.171–3; Broucek, pp.152–4.
62   Pojić, p.179.
63   Pojić, pp.179, 186–7.
64   Letter, 1/10/42 in Schnitzler, pp.119–20; Beck, pp.155–6; Alvensleben, pp.234–5.
65   Bähr, pp.184–5; Jochim, pp.200–03.
66   TB Pabst, 22/9/42.
67   Ibid, 29/9/42.
68   Kirstein, pp.852–3.
69   Rocholl, pp.236–44.
70   Rocholl, p.243; Busch, *Stalingrad: Zurück aus der Hölle*, p.234; Rüther, pp.770–1.
71   Lübbers, p.97.
72   Pirschl, pp.60–1; Busch, *Stalingrad Überlebende*, p.69.
73   Alvensleben, pp.237–8; *Stalingrad i Stalingradskaya oblast*, p.438; Kucherenko, p.91; Wette and
      Ueberschar, p.166; Podewils, p.151.
74   Aaken, pp.113–14; Letter, 2/10/42 in Schnitzler, p.58.
75   Kirstein, pp.930–1; Rocholl, p.239.
76   KTB OKW, 2/9/42; Mark, *Angriff*, pp.202, 304.
77   *Stalingradskaya epopeya*, Docs.13, 20.
78   Letter, 27/9/42 in Schnitzler, p.57.
79   TB Pabst, 6/10/42.
80   Butz-Metzger, p.239.
81   Busch, *Stalingrad: Zurück aus der Hölle*, p.236; Dollinger, p.166; Diedrich and Ebert, *Nach
      Stalingrad*, p.231; 100th Jäger, pp.217–18.
82   Selle, p.43; Unteroffizier H.D., 6/11/42 in Wette and Ueberschar, p.166.
83   Lübbers, p.113.
84   Mark, *Angriff*, p.340.
85   BA-MA RH 24-52/102; Blume, pp.113, 125–6; Wanhöfer, pp.49–50.
86   Shein, pp.155–6 and Memminger, pp.D1307–08.
87   Spraul, p.251; Bähr, p.227; Mičianik, Vol.3, p.160; Steiner, p.168; BA-MA RH 24-52/102; and
      BA-MA RH 24-40/188, pp.15–16.
88   Based on CAMO 500/12478/89; Hoffmann, *Kaukasien*, pp.195, 331–2, 444; Emde, p.100;
      Steiner, p.160; and Rall, p.117.
89   Hoffmann, *Kaukasien*, pp.95–6; Oldenburg, pp.265n1109.
90   Based on CAMO 500/12478/89; Matiev, pp.355–6; Hoffmann, *Kaukasien*, p.465; Oldenburg,
      p.287; and Angrick, p.637.
91   Oldenburg, pp.300–01, 302n1282.

92 Fefermann, pp.185–7; Angrick, pp.582–4 and 614–15; Skrjabina, pp.42–3.

93 Angrick, pp.648–51.

94 Wagner, p.185; Paulus and Röwekamp, p.381; Oldenburg, pp.267, 275.

95 TB Goebbels, 2/10/42; VB, Vienna edition, 1/10/42.

96 Nülsen letter, 27/9/42 in Schüling; Letter 22/9/42 in Begalke, p.70; Chuikov, p.272.

97 Rauchhaupt, Herbert, 'Panzerwacht vor Stalingrad', *Salzburger Volksblatt*, 12–13/9/42.

98 Groscurth, p.528; Diedrich and Ebert, *Nach Stalingrad*, pp.227–8; *Stalingrad i Stalingradskaya oblast*, pp.116–17, 436.

99 Samiy, pp.242–3.

100 Bastable, p.118; letter dated 17/9/42 in Ebert, *Junge*, p.192; Hellbeck, *Stalingrad Protokolle*, pp.399–400; Grossman, p.135.

101 Grossman, p.176.

102 Simonow, *Kriegstagebücher*, ii, pp.183, 186 and Simonov, 'Dni i Nochi', *Krasnaya Zvevdza*, 24/9/42.

103 Based on Popoff, p.137; Bastable, pp.114–16; *Stalingradskaya epopeya*, Doc.54; Proskouriakov, p.228; *Stalingradskaya epopeya*, Doc.45 and Wette and Ueberschar, p.103.

104 KTB AOK 6, 4–6/10/42.

105 This biography of Paulus is based primarily on Diedrich, especially pp.199–200, 211–12, 226, 243–4; Knopp, *Hitlers Krieger*, pp.244–59; Alvensleben, p.247 and TB Richthofen, 27/8/42, 16/9/42.

106 Görlitz, p.170.

107 KTB Engel, 2–3/10/42.

108 Bichir, pp.93, 95–6, 98; Duţu, p.180.

109 *Geschichte der 3 Panzer Division*, pp.327–9, 331 and BA-MA RH 24-40/188, pp.17–20.

110 Tyulenev, *Cherez tri voyny*, p.185; Steiner, p.169.

111 Oosterling, pp.175–8.

112 Strassner, pp.166–9; BA-MA RH 24-40/188, pp.33–4; and *Geschichte der 3 Panzer Division*, p.339.

113 Breymayer, pp.239–40; Statiev, pp.203, 233–4; Sokolov, pp.229–30.

114 Kriegsberichter Gerspach, 'Auf dem weg nach Tuapse', *Die Wehrmacht*, 18/11/42.

115 Scherzer, *46 Infanterie Division*, p.437 and Kaltenegger, *Groth*, pp.99–100.

116 Bähr, p.228; Weinmann, p.491; Kaltenegger, *Gebirgsjäger im Kaukasus*, p.158.

117 Graser, pp.207–09 and Oldenburg, p.285.

118 Conditions in the Caucasus in the autumn are based on Graser, pp.186–7; Wanhöfer, pp.80–2; Dimt, p.209; Oldenburg, pp.270–1; Breymayer, p.223; Buchner, *Vom Eismeer bis zum Kaukasus*, pp.90–1; Musculus, pp.158–60; and AL1669.

119 The first day of the assault is based on Wijers, pp.14, 17; Alvensleben, pp.238–9; *True to Type*, p.75; KTB AOK 6 Anlagen, 5/10/42–14/10/42; Popov, pp.192–3; Tschuikow, pp.224–5; and Mark, *Leaping Horseman*, pp.273–5.

120 Tschuikow, pp.220, 226, 234.

121 Wijers and Stempel, *Stalingrad Tagebuch*, p.38.

122 *Two Hundred Days of Fire*, pp.107–08.

123 Ortenberg, 18/10/42.

124 Boelcke, p.288; VB, 19/10/42; SD Meldung, 22/10/42.

125 See, for example, *Die Wehrmacht 1942*, issues 19–23.

126 Wundshammer, Benno, 'Stukas sur Stalingrad', *Signal*, French edition, No.22, 1942.

127 See, for example, Biebrach, Hans-Joachim, 'Der Todesturm der Wolgafestung', VB, Vienna edition, 11/10/42.

128 Knopp, *Stalingrad*, p.159.

129 Ortenberg, 27/10/42.

130 *Stalingrad i Stalingradskaya oblast*, p.165.

131 Koustova, pp.115–18.

132 Knopp, *Stalingrad*, pp.133, 140, 142–3; Tschuikow, pp.182–4 and Chuikov, pp.160–1; Rees, p.160.

133 Knopp, *Stalingrad*, pp.120, 143.

134 Account by one Lieutenant Wiener in author's papers.

135 Knopp, *Stalingrad*, pp.144–6.

136 Rodimtsev, p.83.

137 Testimony of Gerhard Münch in FacingStalingrad.com, accessed 2018.

138 Holl, p.75; Butz-Metzger, p.307.

139 Butz-Metzger, pp.241–2.

140 Butz-Metzger, p.306.

141 Rauchhaupt, Herbert, *Strassburger Neueste Nachrichten*, 4/11/42.

142 Pojić, pp.183–4.

143 Popov, p.189; Grossman, p.173; Wette and Ueberschar, p.87.

144 Knopp, *Stalingrad*, p.169.

145 Karpow, *Russland im Krieg 1941–1945*, p.129.

146 Schleicher, p.279; Hellbeck, *Stalingrad Protokolle*, p.403; Grams, p.55; Pojić, pp.66, 251; Wijers, pp.128–9; Wette and Ueberschar, p.87.

147 Kirstein, pp.938–9.

148 Krause, p.247; Buchbender, pp.98–9; Letter, 1/10/42 in Schnitzler, pp.119–20; Schleicher, p.279.

149 Hellbeck, p.335; Welz, p.44.

150 Diedrich, p.242; Löser, p.212; Beck, pp.155–6.

151 Alvensleben, pp.238–9. There's no evidence in Russian accounts of such tactics being used – and there was nothing to stop the infected rats roaming freely on either side of the front line.

152 Popov, p.205; Kirstein, p.887.

153 Busch, *Stalingrad Überlebende*, p.83; Mark, *Leaping Horseman*, p.312.

154 Based on Wijers, pp.110–11; Mark, *Into Oblivion*, p.459; letter dated 29/10/42 in *Namen für Rossoschka*, p.113; Grams, pp.54–5.

155 Semenov, pp.127–34.

156 Semenov, pp.89, 116; Kobyakov, p.236; Grossman, pp.141, 149.

157 Mark, *Angriff*, pp.314–34.

158 Butz-Metzger, pp.245–6.

159 Wijers and Stempel, pp.44–7. As he recalled half a century later: 'Again and again we heard: "Another 100 metres and you're there!" But how can you do it if you just don't have the strength left?' Rees, *War of the Century*, p.159.

160 Anlagen, KTB 13 Pz Div, 14/10/42 in BA-MA RH 27-13/64; Tyulenev, *Cherez tri voyny*, p.186.

161 Cavaleri, pp.199–200; KTB 13 Pz Div, 26/10/42 in BA-MA RH 27-13/63; Duțu, p.180.

162 Duțu, pp.180–2 and Bichir, pp.121–34.

163 Werner-Ehrenfeucht, H.-J., 'Die 23 Pz Div im Kaukasus', copy in the author's papers.

164 TB Hans Keller in BA-MA MSg, 2/5611; Blume, p.140; Tyulenev, *Edelweiss*, p.111.

165 Tyulenev, *Edelweiss*, pp.104–10, 111–12.

166 BA-MA RH 27-13/63; Blume, p.140; Hoffmann, *Die Magdeburger Division*, p.180; Kaltenegger, *Gebirgsjäger im Kaukasus*, p.158.

167 Dimt, pp.245, 269–70.

168 Tyulenev, *Edelweiss*, pp.120–2.

169 Spaeter, pp.232–3.

170 TB Hans Keller, 12/11/42 in BA-MA MSg2/5611.

171 BA-MA RH 27-13/63.

172 Tyulenev, *Edelweiss*, pp.130–3.

173 Chuikov, pp.213, 215.

174 Groscurth, p.529; Letter, 2/11/42 in BA-MA MSg 2/5199; Feldpost Nünninghoff, 30/10/42; Dettmer, pp.11–12; Bühler, 30/10/42.

175 Proskouriakov, p.201; *Auf beiden Seiten*, pp.43, 44; *Stalingradskaya epopeya*, Doc.60.

176 Entries for 22/10 and 30/10 in Chuikov, pp.273–4; Pojić, p.66; Letter, 4/11/42 in Schnitzler, p.120.

177 Klaus, p.19; Hauck, pp.76–7.

178 Rauchhaupt, Herbert, *Strassburger Neueste Nachrichten*, 4/11/42; Welz, p.95; Neidhardt, p.218 and Busch, *Stalingrad: Zurück aus der Hölle*, pp.248–9.

179 Ohl, p.81.

180 Groscurth, p.529; Welz, p.95.

181 Author's papers.

182 VB, 9/11/42; TB Goebbels, 9/11/42; SD Meldung, 9/11/42.

183 Welz, pp.49, 52.

184 BA-MA N 753/40. Cited in Diedrich, pp.243–4.

185 Welz, pp.69–71, 74 and Wijers, pp.152–3.

186 Paulus was posted missing in the Stalingrad pocket in mid-January. He ended his final letter home: 'Don't worry too much about me, I'll get through it. Let's hope for the best, because we mustn't give up hope... In the hope that you will never suffer as I have.' Letters 9/11/42–18/11/42 and 9/1/43 in *Die Nazis aus der Nahe*, pp.414–16.

187 Ziemke, p.467.

188 Diedrich and Ebert, *Nach Stalingrad*, p.236; Alvensleben, pp.246–7; Mark, *Into Oblivion*, p.455; TB Richthofen, 16/11/42.

189 Author's papers.

190 Kehrig, p.69.

191 Knopp, *Stalingrad*, p.173; Pirschl, p.165.

192 True to Type, pp.109–10.

193 Fuchs and Rella, p.112.

Chapter 8: Endgame, Not *Endsieg*

1 Peitz, pp.115, 119; Santoponte, p.38; Caccia-Dominioni, *Trecento Ore*, p.25.

2 Santoponte, pp.50–1.

3 KTB 15 Pz Div, 24/10/42 in AL1657/1; KTB DAK, 2240 Hours, 24/10/42 in AL834/1; SRM76, 20/11/42 in NA WO208/4136.

4 Rommel, *Krieg Ohne Hass*, p.247; Irving, pp.199–201.

5 Rommel, *Krieg Ohne Hass*, p.250; Order of the Day, 28/10/42 in NA DEFE 3/573. Albert Kesselring similarly called on Luftwaffe crews to perform their duties 'to the limit... It is a matter of honour for each man in my *Luftflotte*'. Order of the Day, 29/10/42 in DEFE 3/573.

6 Rommel, *Krieg Ohne Hass*, pp.252–3.

7 *Die 33er*, p.167.

8 Montanari, pp.446, 509n.

9   AFHQ Mediterranean, 26–27/10/42 in NA WO 204/983, No.7; Aberger, *21 Panzer*, p.292.

10   Diario Formica, 29/10/42.

11   Avagliano and Palmieri, p.76.

12   Caccia-Dominioni, *El Alamein*, p.215.

13   Caccia-Dominioni, *Trecento Ore*, pp.87–8.

14   Christopherson diary, 5/11/42.

15   Caccia-Dominioni, *Trecento Ore*, pp.415–17.

16   Dollinger, *Kain*, p.162.

17   KTB PzAOK Afrika, 26/10/42 in NA CAB 146/7; Montanari, pp.435–6; Irving, pp.203–04; Mancinelli, pp.192–4.

18   Cavallero Diario, 2/11/42; Ciano Diario, 23/10/42–2/11/42.

19   Diario Formica, 1/11/42.

20   *Kleine Zeitung*, Vienna, 31/10/42; VB, 1/11/42; *Hessische Landeszeitung*, 5/11/42.

21   KTB 15 Pz Div, 2/11/42 in AL1657/1.

22   Hartmann, p.257; KTB 21 Pz Div, 0250–0751 Hours, 2/11/42 in AL926/7.

23   Based on Rommel, *Krieg Ohne Hass*, pp.264–6; KTB DAK, 1730 Hours, 2/11/42 in AL834/1; Irving, pp.209–10; Tagesmeldung PzAOK Afrika, 2/11/42 in NA CAB 146/17.

24   SD Meldung, 5/11/42; TB Goebbels, 4/11/42.

25   Rommel, *The Rommel Papers*, p.320; Hartmann, p.258.

26   KTB PzAOK Afrika, 1100 Hours, 3/11/42 in NA CAB 146/17.

27   Author's papers.

28   Buchmann, p.80; Tagesmeldung, PzAOK Afrika, 3/11/42 in NA CAB 146/17 and KTB DAK, 1428 Hours, 3/11/42 in AL834/1; Rommel, *Krieg Ohne Hass*, p.269.

29   Rommel, *The Rommel Papers*, p.320.

30   Based on Aberger, *21 Panzer*, pp.293–5; Formica Diario, 4/11/42; Santoponte, pp.48, 54; PzAOK Afrika, Morgenmeldung and Tagesmeldung, 4/11/42 in NA CAB 146/17; GASWW, vi, pp.785–9.

31   *Die 33er*, p.169; Aberger, *21 Panzer*, pp.296–7; Santoponte, pp.81–3; Order of the Day, 8/11/42 in NA DEFE 3/573; Prien, *Geschichte des Jagdgeschwaders 77*, iii, p.1331.

32   Montanari, p.520; Prien, *Geschichte des Jagdgeschwaders 77*, iii, p.1317.

33   Caccia-Dominioni, *Trecento Ore*, pp.424–5.

34   Aberger, *21 Panzer*, p.295.

35   Ibid, p.296.

36   AFHQ Mediterranean Intelligence Notes, No.13, 27/6/43 in NA WO 204/983.

37   KTB Skl, 7/11/42 and FS Weichold to Fricke, 2100 Hours 7/11/42 in Salewski, ii, p.166.

38   Rommel, *The Rommel Papers*, p.351; Remy, *Mythos Rommel*, p.140.

39   TB Walb, 14/11/42.

40   Heiber, pp.125–57 and TB Goebbels, 18/11/42.

41   Knopp, *Stalingrad*, p.188.

42   Voicu, *Sacrificiu*, p.145.

43   Aaken, pp.121–4; Duțu, p.192.

44   Based on Voicu, *Sacrificiu*, pp.85–6, 145–50; *Stalingradskaya epopeya*, Doc.16; Negrici, pp.135–6; Duțu, p.195.

45   TB Richthofen, 21/11/42.

46   Wijers and Stempel, p.58.

47   Wette and Ueberschar, p.104.

48   Beck, pp.170–1.

49   Adam, pp.145–7; TB Richthofen, 20/11/42 and 22/11/42.

50   Adam, p.149.

51   *Stalingradskaya epopeya*, Doc.62.

52   Gheorghe, pp.76–7.

53   Gheorghe, p.84.

54   Klaus, p.29.

55   Adam, pp.151–3.

56   Knopp, *Stalingrad*, pp.206–07.

57   Werth, *Russia at War*, p.457.

58   Reports from OQu AOK 6, 6/12/42 and Verluste der 6 Armee in der Zeit vom 21/11–5/12/42 in Anlagenbänder zu den Kriegstagebücher der 6 Armee; Knopp, *Stalingrad*, p.205.

59   Adam, pp.150–1.

60   Pojić, p.343.

61   Diedrich and Ebert, pp.238–9.

62   Ebert, *Ein Arzt in Stalingrad*, p.256.

63   Ebert, *Junge*, p.147.

64   Ebert, *Feldpostbriefe aus Stalingrad*, p.81.

65   Conditions in the Caucasus are based on AL1669; Musculus, pp.159–70; Buchner, *Vom Eismeer bis zum Kaukasus*, pp.90–1; Konrad, pp.44–5; Breymayer, p.237.

66   Musculus, p.180; Richardson and Freidin, p.155; Gusev, pp.193–203.

67   Gooch, p.296.

68   Scherzer, *Stalingrad war der Anfang*, p.115.

69   Rall, pp.134–7.

BIBLIOGRAPHY

Unpublished Sources

Bundesarchiv Militärarchiv, Freiburg

Official documents

Army

RH 19 III/182 KTB Army Group North

RH 20-11/422 KTB Oberquartiermeisterabteilung AOK 11, 1/4/42–15/9/42

RH 20-11/466 KTB AOK 11, Anlagen 29/6/42–9/7/42

RH 20-17/125 KTB AOK 17, Anlagen

RH 23/176 Wilhelm Crüwell Erfahrungsbericht

RH 24-40/188 'Aus der Kriegsgeschichte eines Panzerkorps: Im Kampf um das Kaukasusgebirge, 22 August bis 30 November 1942'

RH 24-40/189 Oberleutnant Günther Heysing, 'Von Charkow zum Terek: Kampf und Marschweg des XXXX Panzerkorps während der grossen deutschen Offensive in Südrussland 1942'

RH 24-40/191 'Vom Don zum Kuban'

RH 24-40/192 'Aus der Kalmückensteppe in das Kaukasusgebirge'

RH 24-52/102 Akten Oberst Hans Doerr, Chef des Generalstabes LII Korps

RH 26-22/157 Der Angriff der 22 ID auf Sewastopol, 2/6–1/7/42

RH 26-28/45 Einsätze der Jäger Division auf der Krim

RH 26-50/35 KTB 50 Infanterie Division, 1/1/42–10/7/42

RH 26-50/43 KTB 50 ID 1/1/42–10/7/42 Anlagen: Erfahrungs, Gefechts und Erlebnisberichte

RH 26-50/44 KTB 50 ID Anlagen 1/1/42-10/7/42

RH 26-50/50 Erfahrungs, Gefechts und Erlebnisberichte zum KTB 7 50ID, 11/7/42–31/12/42

RH 27-3/188 KTB 3 Pz Div Anlagen

RH 27-13/63 KTB 13 Pz Div Anlagen

RH 27-13/64 KTB 13 Pz Div Anlagen

RH 27-13/92 KTB 13 Pz Div Anlagen

RH 27-13/152 KTB 13 Pz Div Anlagen

RH 27-15/70 KTB 15 Pz Div Anlagen

RH 28-1/65 KTB 1 Geb Div Anlagen

RH 28-1/273 KTB 1 Geb Div Erfahrungsbericht Elbrus, 19–21/8/42

RH 31-I/93 Papers of the Deutsche Heeresmission Rumänien, 1941–42

RH 31-I/96 Deutsche Heeresmission in Rumänien, 1/10/42–21/1/43

RH 31-I/105 Bericht Frontreise Marschall Antonescu 1/4–6/4/42 und 1/6–13/6/42

RH 31-I/180(b) Deutsch Heeresmission in Rumänien 8/7/42–20/9/42

RH 31 IX/35 Deutscher Verbindungsstab beim italienischen II. Armeekorps, 1942–1943

RH 31-XIV/3 Berichte Major Wilhelm Hutzelmeyer, Deutsche Verbindungskommando zum ital II AK

RH 39/533 Kradschützen-Abteilung 4 (24. Pz.Div.): 2. Schwadron. Persönliches Tagebuch (Einsatz Sowjetunion) 15. Mai–16. Sept. 1942

RH 53-18/292 Berichte und Zeitungsartikel, Afrikafeldzug

LUFTWAFFE

RL 2-IV/35 Erfahrungen und Auswirkung beim Einsatz der Luftwaffe im Kampfe um Festungen: Erläutert an dem Beispiel des Kampfes um Sevastopol im Juni 1942

RL 8/52 Abschlussmeldung über Kampf um die Festung Sewastopol

RL 10-802 Nachkriegsaufzeichnung von Hauptmann Herbert Pabst, Staffelkapitän in der II. Gruppe

RL 11/42 Aufzeichnungen des Generalmajors Pickert, Kdr der 9 Flak Division, 25/6/42–23/1/43

KRIEGSMARINE

RM 7/234 Besondere Überlegungen zu Einzelfragen und zu den Problemen der Seekriegführung

RM 7/235 Besondere Überlegungen zu Einzelfragen und zu den Problemen der Seekriegführung

RM 7/990 Seekriegsleitung, Handakte Barbarossa

RM 8/1548 Kriegswissenschaftliche Abteilung der Marine (Marinearchiv)

PERSONAL PAPERS

MSg 2/3282 Papers of Major Dr Franz Muth, Kdr Nachrichten-Abteilung 194

MSg 2/6475 Alfred Hennecke, 'Sewastopol und der Karl Einsatz, 3/9/42'

MSg 2/5611 TB Uffz Hans 'Hanni' Keller, 13th Panzer Division

MSg 2/11157 Papers of 44 Infanterie Division/Stalingrad

MSg 2/13245 Kurt Pickart, 'Mit General Martinek in der Schlacht von Sewastopol 1942'

N 406/28 Papers of Hans Seidemann, Fliegerführer Afrika 1942–43

N 671/9 TB Wolfram von Richthofen

GERMANDOCSINRUSSIA.ORG (ACCESSED APRIL 2025)

CAMO 500/12472/44 AOK2, 'Die Angriffsschlacht von Woronesh', undated

CAMO 500/12478/89 Unterlagen der Ic-Abteilung der 13. Panzerdivision

CAMO 500/12482/136 Text des Rundfunkvortrages von Major Karl Göbel, Kommandeur des III. Bataillons des Infanterieregiments 420 der 125. Infanteriedivision

MUSEUMSSTIFTUNG POST UND TELEKOMMUNIKATION, BERLIN

Feldpost of:

Gustav Böker

Theodor Körner

Alfred Marx

Karl Nünninghoff

Rudolf Oehus

Gottfried Walther

Robert Witzke

IMPERIAL WAR MUSEUM, LONDON

AL 773 KTB 90 Leichte Division
AL 833 KTB DAK and Anlagen
AL 834 KTB DAK
AL 866 KTB PzAOK Afrika Anlagen
AL 918 KTB 21 Pz Div
AL 925 KTB 21 Pz Div
AL 926 KTB 21 Pz Div
AL 1656 KTB 15 Pz Div Anlagen
AL 1657 KTB 15 Pz Div
AL 1669 Papers of Ulrich Liss
KTB Skl War diary of the *Seekriegsleitung*, the German Naval Staff

NATIONAL ARCHIVES, KEW

AIR 20/7702 Translations from Captured Enemy Documents: Vol III
AIR 20/7703 Translations from Captured Enemy Documents: Vol IV
AIR 20/7705 Translations from Captured Enemy Documents: Vol VI
CAB 146/14 Cabinet Office Historical Section: Appreciations and Associated Papers IV
CAB 146/16 Cabinet Office Historical Section: Appreciations and Associated Papers V
CAB 146/20 Cabinet Office Historical Section: Appreciations and Associated Papers XI, Part 2
DEFE 3/573 Intelligence from intercepted German, Italian and Japanese radio communications
WO 204/983 G2 Intelligence Notes, Mediterranean Theatre
WO 208/4136 Interrogation reports on German prisoners of May 1940–Aug 1943

PERSONAL DIARIES AND PAPERS

Afrika Regiment 361 'Der Afrika Feldzug aus Sicht der Artillerie Abteilung im Afrika Regiment 361',
    Author's papers
Armbruster, Wilfred David Irving papers, Microform Ltd
Greim, Hans Diary, June 1942, Author's papers
Greiner, Helmut David Irving papers, Microform Ltd
Halder, Franz Held by the Imperial War Museum, London
Köhrer, Helmuth Diary, May–June 1942, Author's papers
Rommel, Erwin David Irving papers, Microform Ltd
Staebe, Gustav 'Offensive und Abwehr um Woronech', Author's papers
Waldau, Otto Hoffmann von David Irving papers, Microform Ltd

NEWSPAPERS AND JOURNALS

Deutsche Allgemeine Zeitung
Freiburger Zeitung
Der Führer (Karlsruhe)
Die Gebirgstruppe
Krasnaya Zvezda
Die Oase
Pravda
Das Reich

Der Soldat zwischen Alpen und Donau
Völkischer Beobachter
Die Wehrmacht

PUBLISHED WORKS

DOCUMENTS

A második világháború, Osiris, Budapest, 2005

Akten Zur Deutschen Auswärtiges Politik 1918–45, Series E, B and 2–4, 1 Vandenhoeck & Ruprecht, 1972–75

Die Anlagenbänder zu den Kriegstagebüchern der 6 Armee, Selbstverlag, 2006

Bajohr, Frank, and Strupp, Christoph (eds), *Fremde Blicke auf das Dritte Reich: Berichte ausländischer Diplomaten über Herrschaft und Gesellschaft in Deutschland 1933–1945*, Wallstein, 2011

Boberach, Heinz, *Meldungen aus dem Reich: Die geheimen Lageberichte des Sicherheitsdienstes der SS 1938–1945*, Pawlak, 1984

Boelcke, Willi A. (ed.), *The Secret Conferences of Dr. Goebbels: The Nazi Propaganda War 1939–43*, Dutton, 1970

Filonenko, S. I. (ed.), *Voĭna na Voronezhskoĭ zemle 1942–1943 gg. v dokumentakh Krasnoĭ Armii, vermakhta i voĭsk satellitov*, five volumes, Kvarta, 2014

Hürter, Johannes, and Uhl, Matthias (eds), 'Hitler in Vinnytsia: A new document casts fresh light on the crisis of September 1942' in *Hitler – New Research*, De Gruyter Oldenbourg, 2018

Kriegstagebuch des Oberkommando der Wehrmacht, seven volumes, Bernard & Graefe, 1961–65

Krym v Velikoy Otechestvennoy voyne 1941–1945 gg, Yauza Katalog, 2017

Ocoleanu, Ionuţ-Mihăiţă, and Bojor, Marius-Daniel, *Noi am luptat in Cotul Donului:Mărturiile ofiţerilor şi subofiţerilor scăpaţi din iad – Declaraţii, hărţi, rapoarte, dări de seamă. documente inedite integrale*, Editura Militară, 2023

Pandea, Adrian, and Ardeleanu, Eftimie (eds), *Românii in Crimeea 1941–1944*, Editura Militară, 1995

Pandea, Adrian, Pavelescu, Ion and Ardeleanu, Eftimie (eds), *Românii La Stalingrad*, Editura Militară, 1992

Scotoni, G., and Filonenko S. I. (eds), *Retroscena della disfatta italiana in Russia nei documenti inediti dell'8a Armata*, Casa editrice Panorama, 2008

Stalingrad 1942–1943: Stalingradskaya Bitva v Dokumentakh, Biblioteka, 1995

Stalingradskaya epopeya. Dokumenty, rassekrechennyye FSB RF, Zvonnitsa-MG, 2012

Sündermann, Helmut, *Tagesparolen: Deutsche Presseweisungen 1939–1945 – Hitlers Propaganda und Kriegsführung*, Druffel, 1973

Trever Roper, Hugh (ed.), *Hitler's War Directives*, Pan, 1966

UNIT HISTORIES

GROUND FORCES

Aberger, Heinz-Dietrich, *Die 5 (Lei)/21 Panzer Division in Nordafrika 1941–1943*, Preussischer Militär, 1994

Aberger, Heinz-Dietrich, von Taysen, Adalbert and Ziemer, Kurt, *Nur ein Bataillon*, Selbstverlag, 1972

Aradi, Gábor, and Szabó, Péter, *A tolnai hadosztály a Don-kanyarban – Hadiokmányok, harctéri naplók, tábori levelezőlapok és visszaemlékezések a szekszárdi magyar királyi 12. honvéd könnyű hadosztály történetéhez 1942–1943*, Zrínyi Kiadó, 2017

Arbeitsgemeinschaft das Kleeblatt (ed.), *Die 71 Infanterie Division 1939–1945: Gefechts- und Erlebnisberichte aus den Kämpfen der 'Glückhaften Division'*, Selbstverlag, 1973

Atzesberger, Michael, and Stahlmann, Hans (eds), *Marsch und Einsatz des IR42*, Selbstverlag, 1985

Beck, Alois, *Bis Stalingrad*, Helmuth Abt, 1983

Bidermann, Gottlob H., *...und litt an meiner Seite!: Krim – Kurland mit der 132. Infanterie-Division 1941–45*, Steinach, 1995

Blanken, Martin, *Geschichte des Artillerie Regiments 240 in der 170 Infanterie Division 1939–1945*, Selbstverlag, 1986

Breymayer, Helmut, *Das Wiesel: Geschichte der 125 Infanterie Division 1940–1944*, Armin Vaas, 1983

Bruns, Diedrich, *Regiment 16: Weg des Feldregimentes im zweiten Weltkrieg aufgezeichnet nach Tagebuch-Erinnerungen seines letzten Kommandeurs Oberstleutnant der Reserve Bruns*, Hans Münstermann, 1959

Buhse, Rudolf (ed.), *Aus der Geschichte des Grenadier Regiments Nr.47*, Selbstverlag, n.d.

Cati, Italo, *Onore di Soldato! L'epopea dei fanti del 54 Reggimento fanteria Sforzesca nella prima battaglia difensiva del Don*, Tralerighe Libri, 2022

Cavaleri, Leo, *Das 2 Regiment der Division Brandenburg: Eine Dokumentation zum Einsatz der Brandenburger-Gebirgsjäger im Osten bzw Südosten Europas*, Helios, 2017

Dettmer, Friedrich, *Stalingrad – Ein Rückblick nach 60 Jahren: 44. Infanterie Division 'Hoch- und Deutschmeister'*, Buchdienst Südtirol, 2003

Die 33er Pioniere: Versuch Einer Chronik, Verlag & Antiquariat für Zeitgeschichte, n.d.

Die 50 Infanterie Division 1939–1945, Traditionsgemeinschaft 50 Infanterie Division, 1965

Dieckhoff, Gerhard, *3 Infanterie Division/3 Infanterie Division (mot)/3 Panzergrenadier Division*, Erich Börries, 1960

Erinnerungsbuch der 94 Infanterie-Division an die Kriegsjahre 1939–1945, Kameradschaft der 94 Infanterie-Division, 1985

Fiebig, Gerhard, and Keller, Johannes, *Pz AA 33 in Nordafrika*, Selbstverlag, 1988

Fish, Kevin, *Panzer Regiment 8: In World War II: Poland-France-North Africa*, Schiffer, 2008

Geschichte der 3 Panzer Division 1935–1945, Günter Richter, 1967

Geschichte des Infanterie- und Jäger-Regiments 49, Traditionsverband Jäger-Regiment 49, n.d.

Grams, Rolf, *Die 14 Panzer-Division 1940–1945*, Nebel, n.d.

Graser, Gerhard, *Zwischen Kattegat und Kaukasus: Weg und Kämpfe der 198 Infanterie Division*, Kameradenhilfswerk und Traditionsverband der ehemaligen 198 Infanterie Division, 1961

Gruber, Anton, *Das Infanterie-Regiment 213 (Grenadier-Regiment 70) 1939–1945*, Selbstverlag der Kameradschaft des Ehem. Infanterie-Regiments 213, 1963

Hack, Franz, *Panzergrenadiere der 5 SS Panzerdivision Wiking im Bild*, Munin, 1987

Hart, Peter, *At Close Range: Life and Death in an Artillery Regiment 1939–45*, Profile Books, 2021

Hartmann, Bernd, *Geschichte des Panzerregiments 5 1935–1943 und der Panzerabteilung 5 1943–1945*, Selbstverlag, 2002

Hauck, Friedrich Wilhelm, *Eine Deutsche Division in Russland und Italien: 305 Infanteriedivision 1941–1945*, Podzun Pallas, 1975

Hoffmann, Dieter, *Die Magdeburger Division: Zur Geschichte der 13 Infanterie und 13 Panzer Division 1935–1945*, Max Schlutius, 1999

Il 5 Alpini è ancora tra noi: la preparazione e la partenza per il fronte russo dei battaglioni Morbegno, Edolo e Tirano: November 1941–Luglio 1942, Susalibri, 2009

Kaltenegger, Roland, *Edelweiss und Endzian: Die Kriegschronik der 4 Gebirgs-Division 1940–1945*, Österreichischer Milizverlag, 2006

Kirstein, Wolfgang, *Rekonstruktion eines Tage-Buches: Die 295. Infanterie-Division von 1940 bis 1945*, Selbstverlag, 1999

Kissel, Hans, *Angriff einer Infanterie Division: Die 101 leichte Infanteriedivision in der Frühjahrschlacht bei Charkow Mai 1942*, Kurt Vowinckel, 1958

Klapdor, Ewald, *Mit dem Panzerregiment 5 Wiking im Osten*, 1981

Kost, Werner, *Gebirgsjäger in Libyens Wüste*, Langer, *Infanterie-Regiments zum Jäger-Regiment 83*, Diedrichs, 75

Kuehn, Dietrich, *Geschichte des Reiter Regiments 1/Panzer Grenadier Regiments 21*, Teil III, 1942–1945, Selbstverlag, 1972

Kurowski, Franz, and Schlee, Alois, *Das Infanterieregiment 170 im Einsatz mit der 73 Infanteriedivision 1939–1945: Polen, Frankreich, Balkan, Russland, Westpreussen und Danzig*, Flechsig, 2019

Lienard, André, *Légion Wallonie: Wallonisches Infanterie Bataillon 373*, Editions Heimdal, 2015

Loi, Salvatore, *Aggredisci e Vincerai: Storia della divisione motorizzata Trieste*, Mursia, 2008

Löser, Jochen, *Bittere Pflicht: Kampf und Untergang der 76. Berlin-Brandenburgischen Infanterie-Division*, Biblio, 1986

Lukács Bence, Ákos, and Szabó, Péter, *A somogyi rosseb hadosztály a Don-kanyarban: Hadiokmányok, harctéri naplók, tábori levelezőlapok, visszaemlékezések és sajtóhíradások a magyar királyi 10. honvéd könnyű hadosztály történetéhez 1942–1943*, Zrínyi Kiadó, 2016

Mark, Jason, *Into Oblivion: Kharkov to Stalingrad – the Story of Pionier Bataillon 305*, Leaping Horseman Books, 2013

Mauer, Helmut, *Heiss über Afrikas Boden: Die Geschichte des motorisierten Maschinengewehrbataillons 2 1935–1943*, Selbstverlag, 1984

Marwan-Schlosser, Rudolf F., *Rommels Flak als Pak*, Weilburg, 1991

Memminger, Fritz, *Die Kriegsgeschichte der Windhund Division*, Heinrich Pöppinghaus, n.d.

Meyer, Hermann Frank, *Blutiges Edelweiss: Die 1 Gebirgs-Division im Zweiten Weltkrieg*, Ch Links, 2008

Mičianik, Pavel, *Slovenská armáda vťažení proti Sovietskemu zväzu: (1941–1944)*, Vol.3, *Slovenská armáda vťažení proti Sovietskemu zväzu. Rýchla divízia*, Dali, 2009

Mičianik, Pavel, *Slovenská armáda vťažení proti Sovietskemu zväzu: (1941–1944)*, Vol.4, *1. pešia divízia Slovenský vojak*, Dali, 2012

Munzel, Oskar, *Gekämpft, Gesiegt, Verloren: Geschichte des Panzerregiments 6 1740–1980*, E. S. Mittler & Sohn, 1980

Musculus, Friedrich, *Geschichte der 111 Infanterie Division 1940–1944*, Selbstverlag, 1980

Neidhardt, Hanns, *Mit Tanne und Eichenlaub: Kriegschronik der 100 Jäger Division, vormals 100 leichte Infanterie Division*, Leopold Stocker, 1981

Paul, Wolfgang, *Das Potsdamer Infanterie Regiment 9 1918–1945*, Biblio, 1983

Pirola, Federico, *Varco! Genieri all'assalto*, Edizione del Capricorno, 2023

Pojić, Milan, *Hrvatska pukovnija 369. na istočnom bojištu 1941–1943*, Hrvatski državni arhiv, 2007

Rebentisch, Ernst, *Zum Kaukasus und zu den Tauern: Die Geschichte der 23 Panzer Division 1941–1945*, Selbstverlag, 1963

Rebora, Andrea, *Carri Ariete combattono: Le vicende della Divisione Corazzata Ariete nelle lettere del tenente Pietro Ostellino Africa Settentrionale 1941–1943*, Prospettiva Editrice, 2016

Rossetti, Roberto, *La Divisione Cuneense sul fronte del Don*, Araba Fenice, 2023

Scherzer, Veit, *46 Infanterie Division: Krim-Kaukasus-Kubanbrückenkopf-Isjum-Jassy*, Scherzers Militaria, 2009

Scherzer, Veit, *113 Infanterie Division: Kiew-Charkow-Stalingrad*, Scherzers Militär, 2007

Schimak, Anton, Lamprecht, Karl and Dettmer, Friedrich, *Die 44 Infanterie Division: Tagebuch der Hoch und Deutschmeister*, Austria Press, 1969

Schirmer, Alois (ed.), *Division zbV Afrika: Alpenrose ruft Enzian*, Flechsig, 2012

Senger und Etterlin, Ferdinand, *Die 24 Panzer Division (vormals 1 Kavallerie Division) 1939–1945*, Kurt Vowinckel, 1962

Spaeter, Helmuth, *Die Brandenburger: eine deutsche Kommandotruppe*, Dissberger, 1994

Strassner, Peter, *Europäische Freiwillige: Die 5 SS Panzerdivision Wiking*, Nation Europa, 2000

Szabó, Péter, *Magyarok a Don-kanyarban: A magyar királyi 2. honvéd hadsereg története (1942–1943)*, Kossuth, 2024

Voghera, Franco, *La Tridentina in Piemonte*, Susalibri, 2018

Weidemann, Gert-Axel, *Unser Regiment: Reiter Regiment 2 – Panzer Regiment 24*, Ernst Dohany, 1982

Weinmann, Willi, *Die 101 Jäger Division in Dokumente, Berichten und Bildern*, Selbstverlag, 1966

Wendt, Kurt, *Warum: Bildband d. 116. Panzer-Division, vorm. 16. Panz.-Gren.-Division, 16. Inf.-Div. (mot) = Pourquoi*, Selbstverlag, 985

Werthen, Wolfgang, *Geschichte der 16 Panzer Division*, Podzun, 1958

Air forces

Balke, Ulf, *Kampfgeschwader 100 'Wiking': eine Geschichte aus Kriegstagebüchern, Dokumenten und Berichten 1934–1945*, Motorbuch, 1981

Duma, Antonio, *Quelli del Cavallino Rampante: Storia del 4 Stormo Caccia*, Vol.1, Rome, 1981

Fast, Niko, *Das Jagdgeschwader 52*, 3 volumes, Bensberger, 1988–89

Freter, Hermann, *Fla nach vorn! Die Fliegerabwehr-Waffe des Heeres und ihre Doppelrolle im Zweiten Weltkrieg*, Im Eigenverlag der Fla-Kameradschaft, 1973

Nauroth, Holger, *Stukageschwader 2 Immelmann*, Schütz, 1988

Prien, Jochen, *Einsatz des Jagdgeschwaders 77 von 1939 bis 1945: Ein Kriegstagebuch nach Dokumenten, Berichten und Erinnerungen*, Vol.2, *Juni 1941 bis November 1942*, Selbstverlag, 1993

Prien, Jochen, *Geschichte des Jagdgeschwaders 77*, Vol.3, *1942–1943*, Struve, Eutin, n.d.

Prien, Jochen, Rodeike, Peter and Stemmer, Gerhard, *Messerschmitt Bf109 im Einsatz bei Stab und I/ Jagdgeschwader 27 1940–1945*, Stuve, Eutin, n.d.

Prien, Jochen, Rodeike, Peter and Stemmer, Gerhard, *Messerschmitt Bf109 im Einsatz bei der III/ Jagdgeschwader 27 1940–1945*, Stuve, Eutin, n.d.

Radtke, Siegfried, *Kampfgeschwader 54 – von der Ju52 zur Me262: eine Chronik nach Kriegstagebüchern, Dokumenten und Berichten 1935–1945*, Schild, Munich, 1990

Ring, Hans, and Girbig, Werner, *Chronik Jagdgeschwader 27*, Motorbuch, Stuttgart, 2012

Schmidt, Rudi, *Achtung – Torpedo los! Der Strategische und Operative Einsatz des Kampfgeschwaders 26*, Bernard & Graefe, Koblenz, 1991

Taghon, Peter, *Die Geschichte des Lehrgeschwaders 1*, Band 1, *1936–1942*, Band 2, *1942–1945*, VDM Heinz Nickel, Zweibrücken, 2004

Waiss, Walter, *Chronik Kampfgeschwader Nr. 27 Boelcke*, Band 4, Helios, Aachen, 2005

First-person accounts

Adam, Wilhelm, *Der schwere Entschluß*, Verlag der Nation, 1965

Alvensleben, Udo von, *Lauter Abschiede: Tagebuch im Kriege*, Ullstein, 1979

Apitzsch, Frieda, *Und dennoch hast du mich getröstet!: Briefe eines Frühvollendeten*, Selbstverlag, 1970

Arnhard, Albert, 'Die Tage und Nächte an der Bereka vom 25.–27. Mai 1942', *Die Gebirgstruppe*, Heft 3, 36 Jahrgang, June 1987

Auf beiden Seiten der Front/Po obe storony fronta: Pisma sovetskikh i nemetskikh soldat, 1941–1945 gg, Sol, 1995

Avagliano, Mario, and Palmieri, Marco, *Vincere e vinceremo! Gli italiani al fronte 1940–1943*, Il Mulino, 2014

Bähr, Walter, and Bähr, Hans (eds), *Kriegsbriefe Gefallener Studenten 1939–1945*, Rainer Wunderlich, 1952

Bauer, Josef Martin, *Unternehmen Elbrus*, Wilhelm Heyne, 1978

Baumbach, Werner, *Broken Swastika: The Defeat of the Luftwaffe*, Robert Hale, 1986

Bedeschi, Giulio, *Fronte d'Africa: c'ero anch'io*, Mursia, 2004

Bedeschi, Giulio (ed.), *Fronte russo: c'ero anch'io*, two volumes, Mursia, 2016

Begalke, Sonja (ed.), *Vernichtungskrieg an der Heimatfront: Analysen und Dokumente aus Hannover*, Verlag für Regionalgeschichte, 1998

Behrendt, Hans-Otto, *Rommel's Intelligence in the Desert Campaign*, William Kimber, 1985

Behrendt, Hans-Otto, *Rommels Kenntnis vom Feind im Afrikafeldzug*, Rombach, 1980

Beretta, Davide, *Batterie semoventi alzo Zero: Quelli di El Alamein*, Mursia, 2010

Bidermann, Gottlob, *In Deadly Combat: A German Soldier's Memoir of the Eastern Front*, University Press of Kansas, 2000

Blume, Helmut, *Zum Kaukasus 1941–1942: Aus Tagebuch und Briefen eines jungen Artilleristen*, Gunter Narr, 1993

Bock, Fedor von, *Zwischen Pflicht und Verweigerung. Das Kriegstagebuch*, Herbig, 1995

Bottai, Giuseppe, *Diario 1935–1944*, Rizzoli, 2001

Bottaro, Alighiero, *Il vento del deserto*, Mursia, 2008

Broucek, Peter (ed.), *Ein General im Zwielicht: die Erinnerungen Edmund Glaises von Horstenau*, Band 3: *Deutscher Bevollmächtigter General in Kroatien und Zeuge des Untergangs des 'Tausendjährigen Reiches'*, Böhlau, 1988

Buchbender, Ortwin, and Sterz, Reinhold, *Das andere Gesicht des Krieges: Deutsche Feldpostbriefe 1939–1945*, C. H. Beck, 1982

Bühler, Karl, *Spaichingen Stalingrad: Feldpostbriefe 9.2.1941–6.1.1943*, Selbstverlag, 1982

Busch, Reinhold, *Stalingrad: Überlebende berichten*, Ares, 2012

Busch, Reinhold, *Stalingrad: Zurück aus der Hölle, Die Ärzte von Stalingrad, Teil 3 – 25 Stalingrad-Ärzte berichten vom langsamen Sterben der 6. Armee im Kessel und in der Gefangenschaft*, Band 1, Frank Wünsche, 2006

Butz-Metzger, Hedwig, *Alfons Metzger: Eine verlorene Jugend in Deutschland: Tagebuchaufzeichnungen und Briefe 1937–1943*, Geschichtsverein Zwiefalten, 2002

Buzatu, Gh., Cheptea, Stela and Cîrstea, Marusia (eds), *Pace și război (1940–1944): jurnalul mareșalului Ion Antonescu*, Vol.2, Tipo Moldova, 2011

Caccia-Dominioni, Paolo, *Alamein 1933–1962: An Italian Story*, Allen and Unwin, 1966

Caccia-Dominioni, Paolo (ed.), *Le Trecento Ore a Nord di Qattara*, Longanesi, 1972

Cavallero, Ugo, *Comando Supremo. Diario 1940–1943*, Rocca S. Casciano, 1948

Choltitz, Dietrich von, *Soldat unter Soldaten*, Europa, 1951

Christopherson, Stanley, *An Englishman at War*, Penguin, 2020

Chuikov, Vasily, *The Beginning of the Road*, Harper Collins, 1970

Churchill, Winston S., *The Second World War: The Hinge of Fate*, Cassell, 1951

Ciano, Galeazzo, *Diario 1937–1943: Edizione integrale*, L'Universale, 2016

Degrelle, Léon, *Campaign in Russia: The Waffen SS on the Eastern Front*, Crecy, 1985

Dettmann, Fritz, *Mein Freund Marseille*, Verlag die Heimatbücherei, 1944

Diedrich, Torsten, and Ebert, Jens (eds), *Nach Stalingrad: Walther von Seydlitz' Feldpostbriefe und Kriegsgefangenenpost 1939–1953*, Wallstein, 2018

Dimt, Peter, *Flammender Kaukasus: Tagebuch eines Artilleristen von Sommerfeldzug 1942*, Kurt Vowinckel, 1984

Dinkler von Schubert, Erika (ed.), *Feldpost: Zeugnis und Vermächtnis. Briefe und Texte aus dem Kreis der evangelischen Studentengemeinde Marburg/Lahn und ihrer Lehrer (1939–1945)*, Göttingen, 1993

Dohna-Schlobitten, Alexander Fürst zu, *Erinnerungen eines alten Ostpreussen*, btb, 1999

Dollinger, Hans, *Kain, wo ist dein Bruder?* Fischer, 1987

Dyachkov Lev Nikolaevich, *Ob ognyakh-pozharishchakh... Vospominaniye o voyne*, Atlant, 2020

Ebert, Jens (ed.), *Ein Arzt in Stalingrad: Feldpostbriefe und Gefangenenpost des Regimentsarztes Horst Rocholl 1942–1953*, Wallstein, 2009

Ebert, Jens (ed.), *Feldpostbriefe aus Stalingrad*, Wallstein, 2003

Eichner, Wilhelm, *Jenseits der Steppe: Tagebuch aus dem Russlandfeldzug 1942–1944*, Universitas, 1997

Einseidel, Heinrich Graf von, *Tagebuch der Versuchung*, Ullstein, 1985

Engel, Gerhard, *Heeresadjutant bei Hitler 1938–1943: Aufzeichnungen des Majors Engel*, DVA, 1974

Eremenko, A. I., *Stalingrad*, Plon, 1963

Ertl, Hans, *Als Kriegsberichter 1939–1945*, Steiger, 1985

Fattore, Fabio, *Gli Inviati di Mussolini: I correspondenti di Guerra 1940–1943*, Mursia, 2018

Formica, Vincenzo, *Diario*, www.ferreamole.it, accessed 1 October 2022

Frey, Hellmuth, *Für Rommels Panzer durch die Wüste: Als Divisionsnachschubführer beim Deutschen Afrikakorps*, Brienna, 2010

Fuchs, Martina, and Rella, Christoph (eds), *Ein 'ganz normaler' Soldat? Feldpostbriefe eines Wiener Unteroffiziers von Polen bis Stalingrad*, Kral, 2023

Fuchs, Max, *Tagebuch Russland 1.7.1941–13.5.1945*, Selbstverlag, 1989

Gehrig, Franz, *Kompanie Chef im Osten 1942–1943*, Kameradschaft es ehem Grenadier Regiment 530, n.d.

Gheorghe, Stan, *Din Cercul de la Stalingrad în Lagărele Sovietice: Memorii 1942–1948*, Editura Militară, 2018

Goebbels, Joseph, *Die Tagebücher von Joseph Goebbels*, K. G. Saur, 1993–96

Grignaschi, Pasquale, *Vita quotidiana durante la campagna di Russia 1942–1943: Il diario fotografico inedito di un alpino sul Don*, Interlinea, 2000

Gross, Hans, *Als Kriegsberichter im Einsatz: Mit Marseille und Helbig am Feind im Kampf ums Mittelmeer 1942–1944*, Druffel, 1987

Grossman, Vasily, *A Writer At War: Vasily Grossman with the Red Army 1941–1945*, Harvill, 2005

Gusev, Aleksandr Mikhailovich, *Elbrus v ogne*, Voenizdat, 1980

Hassell, Ulrich von, *The Von Hassell Diaries*, Greenwood Press, 1971

Heiber, Helmut (ed.), *Goebbels Reden 1939–1945*, Wilhelm Heyne, 1972

Hellbeck, Jochen, *Stalingrad Protokolle*, Fischer, 2014

Henning, Otto, *Als Panzerschütze beim Deutschen Afrika Korps 1941–1943: Ein 17-jähriger Kriegsfreiwilliger in der Aufklärungs-Kompanie (mot.) 580*, Flechsig, 2006

Hitzfeld, Otto Maximilian, *Ein Infanterist in zwei Weltkriegend*, Biblio, 1983

Hödl, Christian, *Bei uns wurde viel gestorben: Die Kriegserlebnisse des Frontsoldaten Josef Hödl*, Reiner Saunar, 2009

Hofmann, Klaus, and Biere, Andreas (eds), *Dr Werner Hofmann: Feldpostbriefe eines Ostfrontkämpfers*. N & W Versand, n.d.

Holl, Adelbert, *An Infantryman in Stalingrad from 24 September 1942 to 2 February 1943*, Leaping Horseman Books, 2005

Holmes, Richard, *The World at War*, Ebury, 2007

Hörmann, Anton, *Jahr des Unheils: 1942 – von Charkow nach Stalingrad*, Literareon, 2013

Hubalek, Rudolf, *Vom Sand verweht: El Alamein war die Wende*, Weilburg, 1983

Hürter, Johannes, *Ein deutscher General an der Ostfront: Die Briefe und Tagebücher des Gotthard Heinrici 1941–1942*, Edition Tempus, 2001

Iorga, Filip-Lucian (ed.), *De la Stalingrad, cu dragoste*, Corint, *iegstagebuch 1939–1945*, Selbstverlag, 1995

Jähnert, Erhard, *Als Sturzkampfpilot an allen Front: Mal oben, mal unten*, Teil I *1935–1943*, Flechsig, 2010

Jodl, Luise, *Jenseits des Endes: Leben und Sterben des Generaloberst Alfred Jodl*, Molden, 1978

Kaisergruber, Fernand, *We Will Not Go to Tuapse*, Helion and Company, 2016

Karpow, Wladimir, *Der General und Ich*, Militärverlag der DDR, 1989

Kazakov M. I., *Nad kartoy bylykh srazheniy*, Voenizdat, 1971

Keitel, Wilhelm, *The Memoirs of Field Marshal Keitel*, William Kimber, 1965

Kesselring, Albert, *Memoirs*, Greenhill, 1988

Kippenberger, Howard, *Infantry Brigadier*, Geoffrey Cumberlege, 1949

Klaus, Edgar, *Durch die Hölle des Krieges*, Frieling and Huffmann, 1991

Knyshevskĭ, P. N. (ed.), *Skrytaia pravda voiny: 1941 god: neizvestnye dokumenty*, Russkaia kniga, 1992

Koch, Lutz, *Erwin Rommel: Die Wandlung eines grossen Soldaten*, Walter Gebauer, 1950

Konrad, Rudolf, *Kampf um den Kaukasus*, Copress, n.d.

Krause, Joachim, *Fremde Eltern: Zeitgeschichte in Tagebüchern und Briefen 1933–1945*, Sax, 2016

Krausnick, Helmut (ed.), *Helmuth Groscurth: Tagebücher eines Abwehroffiziers 1938–1940*, DVA, 1970

Kubik, Willi, *Erinnerungen eines Panzerschützen 1941–1945: Tagebuchaufzeichnung eines Panzerschützen der Pz.Aufkl.Abt.13 im Russlandfeldzug*, Flechsig, 2007

Lagoda, Max, *Ein Blick in die Vergangenheit: Kriegserinnerungen eines Fernaufklärers aus Russland und dem Orient*, Helios, 2011

Lajos, Dr Somorjai, *Megjártam a Don-Kanyar: Harctéri Napló Oroszország, 1942–1943*, Rubicon, 2012

Langsdorff, Gero von (ed.), 'Jagdflieger in Stalingrad: Aus den Aufzeichnungen des Oberleutnant Kurt Ebener', in *Deutsches Soldatenjahrbuch 1973*, Schild, 1973

Laskin, Colonel Ivan A., *Na puti k perelomu*, Voenizdat, 1977

Lazzati, Giulio, *I soliti quattro gatti*, Mursia, 1967

Lebedenko, P. P., *V izluchine Dona*, Voenizdat, *no dalle sette vite sul fronte russo*, Gaspari, Udine, 2011

Leterrier, Paul, *J'étais fusilier marin à Bir Hakeim: Souvenir Iné: Le récit inédit d'un des derniers témoins*, De Taillac, 2018

Liddell Hart, Basil (ed.), *The Rommel Papers*, Collins, 1953

Ljubimye,zhdite! Ja vernus… Frontovye pisma 1941–1945, Veche, 019

Luck, Hans von, *Mit Rommel an der Front*, Mittler & Sohn, 2006

Maggi, Gaetano, *La mia naja Alpina*, Mursia, 1989

Mancinelli, Giuseppe, *Dal Fronte dell'Africa Settentrionale 1942–1943*, Rizzoli, 1970

Manstein, Erich von, *Verlorene Siege*, Bernard & Graefe, 2011

Mellenthin, Friedrich von, *Panzer Battles*, Ballantine, 1985

Messe, Giovanni, *Der Krieg im Osten*, Thomas, 1948

Messe, Giovanni, *Lettere alla moglie: Dai fronti greco-albanese, russo, tunisino e dalla prigionia 1940–1944*, Mursia, 2018

Mobius, Ingo, *Ein Grenadier entscheidet eine Schlacht: Die Erinnerungen von Günter Halm, dem jüngsten Ritterkreuzträger des Afrikakorps*, Mobius, 2019

Moorehead, Alan, *Africa Trilogy: The North African Campaign 1940–43*, Weidenfeld Military, 2000

Namen für Rossoschka: Schicksale aus Stalingrad, Volksbund Deutsche Kriegsgräberfrsurge e.V., GGP, 2007

Negrici, Eugen (ed.), *Memoriile capitanului Dumitru Păsat 1941–1945*, Humanitas, 2015

Ochsenknecht, Ingeborg, *Als ob der Schnee alles zudeckte: Eine Krankenschwester erinnert sich Kriegseinsatz an der Ostfront*, Econ, 2004

Ohl, Rainer, *Grüsse aus Stalingrad: Schicksal eines Stalingradkämpfers*, epubli, 2016

Onana, Raphaël, *Un homme blindé à Bir Hakeim*, Éditions L'Harmattan, 1996

Ortenberg, David, *God 1942*, Politizdat, 1988

Paulus, Julia, and Röwekamp, Marion (eds), *Eine Soldatenheimschwester an der Ostfront: Briefwechsel von Annette Schücking mit ihrer Familie 1941–1943*, Schöningh, 2015

Perrotta, Giuseppe (ed.), *Il grande inferno bianco: Lettere dal Don di Nicolino Perrotta, S. Tenente medico dei Granatieri di Sardegna con l'ARMIR in Russia*, Youcanprint, 2016

Pirschl, Andreas (ed.), *Von Kursk nach Stalingrad Juni 1942–November 1942*, Selbstverlag, 2022

Podewils, Clemens, *Don und Wolga: Aufzeichnungen aus dem Jahre 1942*, Carl Hanser, 1952

Prentl, Sepp, *Flak-Kampfgruppe Prentl*, Schild, 1978

Rehfeldt, Dr Hans Heinz, *Mit dem Eliteverband des Heeres 'Grossdeutschland' tief in den Weiten Russlands*, Flechsig, 2009

Revelli, Nuto, *L'ultimo fronte*, Einaudi, 2009

Revelli, Nuto, *Mai tardi: Diario di un alpino in Russia*, Einaudi, 2020

Richardson, William, and Freidin, Seymour (eds), *The Fatal Decisions*, Michael Joseph, 1956

Ringler, Ralf Roland, *Endstation El Alamein: Tagebluchblätter aus der Wüste*, Ferdinand Berger & Söhne, 1970

Rizzo, Giuseppe, *Buche e Croci nel Deserto*, Aurora, 1969

Rodimtsev, Aleksandr, *Gvardeytsy stoyali nasmert'*, DOSAAF, 1969

Romersa, Luigi, *I segreti della guerra d'Africa*, Mursia, 2005

Rommel, Erwin, *Krieg ohne Hass*, Heidenheim/Brenz Heidenheimer Zeitung, 1950

Rosso, Giovanni, *Lettere dal fronte libico e dalla prigionia in Algeria: Il cappellano militare don Giovanni Rosso*, Ass. Primalpe Costanzo Martini, 2016

Samiy pamyatnyy den' voyny. Pis'ma-ispovedi, Veche, 2018

Santoponte, Antonella, *El Alamein: Immagini, Cronache, Testimonianze*, editione Settimo Sigilio, 2005

Sazhin, Petr, *Sevastopolskaya Khronika*, Ripol Klassik, 2015

Scherzer, Veit (ed.), *Stalingrad war der Anfang vom Ende der Moral der Armee: Erwin Jetzl – Erinnerungen an meine Erlebnisse in Stalingrad*, Scherzer, 2019

Schleicher, Karl-Theodor, and Walle, Heinrich, *Aus Feldpostbriefen junger Christen 1939–1945*, Franz Steiner, 2005

Schmidt, Hans-Werner, *With Rommel in the Desert*, Harrap, 1952

Schmitt, Josef, *Bin noch am Leben: Feldpost des Gefreiten Joseph Schmitt von der Ostfront 1941 bis 1945*, Selbstverlag, 2016

Schmitz, Markus, and Haunfelder, Bernd, *Humanität und Diplomatie: Die Schweiz in Köln 1940–49*, Aschendorff, 2001

Schnitzler, Konrad, *Feldpost aus der Hölle von Stalingrad 1942/43*, Selbstverlag, Lüdenscheid, 2012

Schroetter, Hellmuth, *Panzer rollen in Afrika vor: Mit Rommel von Tripolis bis El Alamein*, Limes, 1985

Schüling, Hermann (ed.), *Kriegsbriefe des 2 Weltkrieges von der Ostfront 1941–1945*, Selbstverlag, 2012

Selle, Herbert, *Wofür? Erleben eines führenden Pioniers bis Stalingrad*, Kurt Vowinckel, 1977

Seydlitz, Walther von, *Stalingrad: Konflikt und Konsequenz*, Gerhard Stalling, 1977

Simonow, Konstantin, *Kriegstagebücher*, Band 2, Volk und Welt, 1982

Skrjabina, Elena, *After Leningrad: A Diary of Survival During World War II*, Transaction Publishers, 1988

Sonnenkalb, Horst, *Deutsche Panzer im Wüstensand: Erinnerungen an das Deutsche Afrika-Korps*, Tyr Edition, 2009

Speer, Albert, *Inside the Third Reich*, Sphere, 1971

Spraul, Gunter (ed.), *Franz Müller: Ein Gebirgsartillerist an der Front und in Gefangenschaft 1939–1945*, Frank & Timme, 2019

Steiner, Felix, *Die Freiwilligen der Waffen-SS: Idee und Opfergang*, Deutsche Verlagsgesellschaft, 1992

Stempel, Joachim, *Wir müssen ran, wir greifen an! Das Schützen/Panzergrenadier Regiment 108 der 14 Panzer Division über Bug und Dnjepr zum Don*, Selbstverlag, 1999

Stern, Mario Rigoni, *L'ultima partita a carte*, Einaudi, 2002

Die Stimme des Menschen: Briefe und Aufzeichnungen aus der ganzen Welt, 1939–1945, Piper & Co, 1961

Stockhausen, Hans-Ludwig von, *Ritter, Reiter, Russen: Erinnerungen*, Bernard Schäfer, 2004

Tieke, Wilhelm, *Ein ruheloser Marsch war unser Leben*, Munin, 1977

Timpe, Karl-Heinrich, *Der Krieg, wie ich ihn erlebte: Erinnerungen eines Sturmgeschützsoldaten*, Scherzer, 2013

Trevor-Roper, Hugh (ed.), *Hitler's Table Talk*, Oxford University Press, 1988

True to Type: A Selection from Letters and Diaries of German Soldiers and Civilians Collected on the Soviet–German Front, Hutchinson, 1945

Tschuikow, Wassili Iwanowitsch, *Die Schlacht des Jahrhunderts*, Militärverlag DDR, 1988

Two Hundred Days of Fire: Accounts by Participants and Witnesses of the Battle of Stalingrad, Progress, 1970

Tyulenev, Ivan, *Cherez tri voyny*, Voenizdat, 1972

Tyulenev, Ivan, *Krakh operatsii 'Edelweiss'*, Ordzhonikidze, 1975

Tyuleneva, N. I., Sablin, V. K. and Timofeyev, A. V. (eds), *General armii Tyulenev: Moskva v zhizni i sud'be polkovodtsa*, Izd-vo Glavaarkhiva, 2005

'Und die Wolga brannte': Überlebende aus Stalingrad erinnern sich, Verein zur Förderung der Städtepartnerschaft Köln-Wolgograd, Selbstverlag, 2002

Urbanke, Axel, *Dem Kessel von Halbe entkommen: Der Weg des Panzeroffiziers Joachim Senholdt*, Luftfahrtverlag-Start, 2021

Vallauri, Federico, *Pilota 1915–1942*, Societa Editrice Torinese, 1944

Vallicella, Vittorio, *Diario di Guerra: Da El Alamein alla tragica ritirata 1942–1943*, Arterigere-Chiarotto, 2009

Vernus tolko s Pobedoi – Frontovye pisma 1941–1945, Veche, 2020

Veteranii pe Drumul Onoarei și Jertfei 1941–1945: De la Nistru la Marea de Azov, Vasile Cârlova, 1997

Voss, Paul-Hans, *Freigegeben: Tagebuchaufzeichnungen eines Funkers von Juni 1941 bis November 1942 an der Ostfront Berditschew bis Stalingrad*, Helen M. Brinkhaus, 1982

Voyetekhov, Boris, *The Last Days of Sevastopol*, Cassell, 1944

Wagner, Adolf, *Erlebnisse: Feldpostbriefe erinnern an ein sudetendeutsches Schicksal*, Band 1, Buch&Media, 2005

Walb, Lore, *Ich, die Alte – Ich, die Junge: Konfrontration mit meinen Tagebüchern 1933–1945*, Aufbau, 1997

Walentan, Paul Johann, *Mein Tagebuch 1941 & 1942: Mit der Kolonne 651 im Deutschen Afrika Korps*, J. H. Röll, 2017

Wanhöfer, Günter, *Pioniere nach vorn! Vom Kaukasus bis Kurland*, Kurt Vowinckel, 1962

Welz, Helmut, *Verratene Grenadiere*, Deutscher Militärverlag, 1969

Westphal, Siegfried, *Erinnerungen*, Hase & Koehler, 1975

Wijers, Hans, and Stempel, Joachim, *Stalingrad Tagebuch*, Helios, 2016

Wimmer, Josef, *Ich war dabei*, H-E-K Creativ, 2011

Winkler, Walter, *Der Kampf um Sevastopol*, Kurt Vowinckel, 1984

Wir erobern die Krim: Soldaten der Krim-Armee berichten, Pfälzische Verlagsanstalt, 1943

Wittek, Erhard, *Die Soldatische Tat: Der Kampf im Osten 1941/42*, Deutscher, 1943

Witzel, Rudolf, *Mit Mörsern, Haubitzen und Kanonen: Als Artillerieoffizier im Frieden und Krieg 1936–1945*, Flechsig, 2008

Zanfagnini, Antonio, *Diario di un soldato in Russia: Un friulano curioso del mondo. Luglio 1941–dicembre 1942*, Aviani & Aviani editori, 2011

Zhukov, Georgy, *Reminiscences and Recollections*, 2 volumes, Progress, 1985

SECONDARY LITERATURE

Aaken, Wolf van, *Hexenkessel Ostfront: Von Smolensk nach Breslau*, Erich Pabel, 1964

Abaturov, Valeriy, and Portugalskiy, Richard, *Kharkov – proklyatoye mesto Krasnoy Armii*, Yauza, 2013

Angrick, Andrej, *Besatzungspolitik und Massenmord: Die Einsatzgruppe D in der südlichen Sowjetunion 1941–1943*, Hamburger Edition, 2003

Axworthy, Mark, *Third Axis, Fourth Ally: Romanian Armed Forces in the European War, 1941–45*, Weidenfeld, 1995

Balta, Sebastian, *Rumänien und die Grossmächte in der Ära Antonescu 1940–1944*, Franz Steiner, 2005

Barr, Niall, *Pendulum of War: Three Battles at El Alamein*, Pimlico, 2005

Bastable, Jonathan, *Voices from Stalingrad*, David & Charles, 2006

Baum, Walter, and Weichold, Eberhard, *Der Krieg der Achsenmächte im Mittelmeer-Raum*, Musterschmidt, 1973

Beevor, Antony, *Stalingrad*, Penguin, 1998

Bellamy, Chris, *Absolute War*, Pan, 2009

Der Bergsteiger: Deutsche Monatsschrift für Bergsteigen, Wandern und Skilaufen, 13 Jahrgang, Oktober 1942–März 1943

Besana, Antonio, *Il bambino di El Alamein: Sergio Bresciani Medaglia d'Oro*, Edizioni Ares, 2023

Beshanov, V. V., *God 1942: 'Uchebnyy'*, Kharvest, 2003

Bichir, Florian, *Cruciada Diviziei de Cremene: Viața și memoriile generalului Ioan Dumitrache*, Editura Militară, 2018

Bierman, John, and Smith, Colin, *Alamein: War Without Hate*, Penguin, 2003

Braatz, Kurt, *Walter Krupinski: Jagdflieger, Geheimagent, General*, Neunundzwanzigsechs, 2010

Broche, François, *La Cathédral des Sables: Bir Hakeim (26 Mai–11 Juin 1942)*, Belin, 2019

Broekmeyer, Marius, *Stalin, the Russians, and Their War: 1941–1945*, University of Wisconsin Press, 1998

Buchmann, Bertrand Michael, *Österreicher in der Deutschen Wehrmacht: Soldatenalltag im Zweiten Weltkrieg*, Böhlau, 2009

Buchner, Alex, 'Die Schlacht beiderseits Charkow,' in *Die Gebirgstruppe*, Jahrgang 14, Heft 4, August 1965

Buchner, Alex, *Vom Eismeer bis zum Kaukasus: Die deutsche Gebirgstruppe im Zweiten Weltkrieg 1941–42*, Podzun Pallas, 1988

Burgwyn, H. James, *Mussolini Warlord: Failed Dreams of Empire, 1940–1943*, Enigma, 2012

Cavallo, Pietro, *Italiani in guerra: Sentimenti e immagini dal 1940 al 1943*, Il Mulino, 1997

Cenci, Nelson, *Ritorno: La drammatica esperienza degli alpini sul fronte russo raccontata da uno di loro*, Mursia, 1991

Ceva, Bianca, *Cinque anni di storia italiana 1940–1945 da lettere e diari di caduti*, Edizioni di Comunità, 1964

Constantiniu, Florin, *O Istorie sinceră a poporuliu roman*, Univers Enciclopedic Gold, Bucharest, n.d.

Craig, William, *Enemy at the Gates*, Penguin, 2000

Daines, Vladimir, *Shtrafnyye formirovaniya Krasnoy Armii*, Yauza, 2022

De Felice, Renzo, *Mussolini l'alleato I. L'Italia in guerra (1940–1943)*, Einaudi, 2008

De Zayas, Alfred, *Die Wehrmacht Untersuchungsstelle*, Heyne, 1981

Das Deutsche Reich und der Zweite Weltkrieg, Band VI, DVA, 1990

Diedrich, Torsten, *Paulus: Das Trauma von Stalingrad*, Schöningh, 2008

Dimbleby, Jonathan, *Destiny in the Desert: The Road to El Alamein – the Battle that Turned the Tide*, Profile, 2013

Don Bend: An Illustrated Chronicle of the Royal Hungarian 2nd Honvéd Army, MoD Institute and Museum of Military History, 2013

Duțu, Alesandru, *Armata Română in Război*, Editura Enciclopedica, 2016

Ebert, Jens (ed.), *Junge deutsche und sowjetische Soldaten in Stalingrad*, Wallstein, 2018

Egger, Martin (ed.), *Die Festung Sewastopol: Eine Dokumentation ihrer Befestigungsanlagen und der Kämpfe von 1942*, Harry Lippmann, 1995

Eichholtz, Dietrich, *War for Oil*, Potomac Books, 2012

Emde, Joachim, *Die Nebelwerfer: Entwicklung und Einsatz der Werfertruppe im Zweiten Weltkrieg*, Podzun Pallas, n.d.

Ernsthausen, Adolf von, *Wende im Kaukasus*, Kurt Vowinckel, 1958

Fefermann, Kiril, *The Holocaust in the Crimea and the Northern Caucasus*, Yad Vashem, 2016

Fennell, Jonathan, *Combat and Morale in the North African Campaign: The Eighth Army and the Path to El Alamein*, Cambridge University Press, 2014

Filatov, G. S., *La campagna orientale di Mussolini*, Mursia, 1979

Forczyk, Robert, *Where the Iron Crosses Grow*, Osprey, 2016

Förster, Jürgen (ed.), *Stalingrad: Ereignis, Wirkung, Symbol*, Piper, 1992

Germany and the Second World War, Volume 6, Oxford University Press, 2001

Giusti, Maria Teresa, *La campagna di Russia 1941–1943*, Il Mulino, 2018

Glantz, David M., *Kharkov 1942*, Ian Allan, 1998

Gooch, John, *Mussolini's War: Fascist Italy from Triumph to Collapse, 1935–1943*, Penguin, 2020

Görlitz, Walter (ed.), *Paulus: 'Ich stehe hier auf Befehl!'*, Bernard & Graefe, 1960

Gosztony, Peter, *A Magyar Honvédség a Második Világháborúban*, Európa Könyvkiadó, 1992

Gosztony, Peter, *Hitlers Fremde Heere: Das Schicksal der nichtdeutschen Armeen im Ostfeldzug*, Gustav Lübbe, 1980

Greene, Jack, and Massignani, Alessandro, *The Naval War in the Mediterranean 1940–1943*, Chatham, 1998

Gribaudi, Gabriella, *Combattenti, sbandati, prigionieri: Esperienze e memorie di reduci della seconda guerra mondiale*, Donzelli, 2016

Haller, Uli, *Lieutenant General Karl Strecker: The Life and Thought of a German Military Man*, Praeger, 1994

Hamilton, Hope, *Sacrifice on the Steppe*, Casemate, 2011

Hartmann, Christian, *Halder: Generalstabschef Hitlers 1938–1942*, Ferdinand Schönigh, 2010

Hartmann, Christian, Hürter, Johannes, Lieb, Peter and Pohl, Dieter, *Der deutsche Krieg im Osten 1941–1944*, Oldenbourg, 2009

Harward, Grant T., *Romania's Holy War: Soldiers, Motivation, and the Holocaust*, Cornell University Press, 2021

Heaton, Colin, and Lewis, Anne-Marie, *The Star of Africa*, Zenith, 2012

Heckmann, Wolf, *Rommels Krieg in Afrika: Wüstenfüchse gegen Wüstenratten*, Bastei Lübbe, 1980

Herf, Jeffrey, *Nazi Propaganda for the Arab World*, Yale University Press, 2011

Higgins, David R., *Behind Soviet Lines: Hitlers Brandenburgers Capture the Maikop Oilfields 1942*, Osprey, 2012

Hill, Alexander, *The Red Army and the Second World War*, Cambridge University Press, 2016

Hoffmann, Joachim, *Kaukasien 1942/43: Das deutsche Heer und die Orientvölker der Sowjetunion*, Rombach, 1991

Irving, David, *The Trail of the Fox*, Weidenfeld and Nicolson, 1977

Isaev, Aleksei, Glukharev, Nikolai, Romanko, Oleg and Khazanov, Dmitriy, *Bitva za Krim, 1941–1944 gg*, Yauza, 2016

Jasper, Andreas, *Zweierlei Weltkriege? Kriegserfahrung deutscher Soldaten in Ost und West 1939 bis 1945*, Schöningh, 2011

Jochim, B. K., *Oberst Hermann Graf: 200 Luftsiege in 13 Monaten*, Moewig, 1998

Kaltenegger, Roland, *Gebirgsjäger im Kaukasus*, Leopold Stocker, 1997

Kaltenegger, Roland, *General der Gebirgstruppe Karl Eglseer*, Flechsig, 2013

Kaltenegger, Roland, *Major der Reserve Heinz Groth*, Flechsig, 2016

Karpow, Wladimir, *Russland im Krieg 1941–1945*, Weltbild, 2009

Kehrig, Manfred, *Stalingrad: Analyse und Dokumentation einer Schlacht*, DVA, 1974

Kershaw, Ian, *Der Hitler Mythos*, DVA, 1980

Kitchen, Martin, *Rommel's Desert War*, Cambridge University Press, 2009

Kljakič, Dragan, *Ustaško domobranska Legija pod Staljingradom*, 1979

Knopp, Guido, *Der Verdammte Krieg: Stalingrad 1942–43*, Bertelsmann, 1991

Knopp, Guido, *Hitlers Krieger*, Random House, 1999

Knopp, Guido, *Stalingrad: Das Drama*, Goldmann, 2006

Kobyakov, Egor, *Neizvestniy Stalingrad*, Yauza, 2020

Koustova, Emilia, *Combattre, Survivre, Témoigner, Expériences soviétiques de la Seconde Guerre mondiale*, Presses Universitaires de Strasbourg, 2020

Kroener, Bernhard R., *Der starke Mann im Heimatkriegsgebiet – Generaloberst Friedrich Fromm: Eine Biographie*, Schöningh, 2005

Kucherenko, Olga, 'Greyzone Stalingrad: Civilian Experience of the Battle', in Mann and Kucherenko, *The Eastern Front: War, Myth and Memory*, Routledge, 2024

Lami, Lucio, *L'ultima carica: Isbuscenskij*, Mursia, 1970

Longo, Luigi Emilio, *Giovanni Messe: L'ultimo maresciallo d'Italia*, Stato Maggiore dell'Esercito, 2006

Lopez, Jean, *Kharkov 1942*, Perrin, 2022

Lormier, Dominique, *Rommel: La fin d'un mythe*, le cherche midi, 2003

Lübbers, Gert, 'Die 6 Armee und die Zivilbevölkerung von Stalingrad', *Vierteljahrshefte für Zeitgeschichte*, 54, No.1, 2006

MacGregor, Iain, *The Lighthouse of Stalingrad*, Constable, 2022

Mann, Yan, *Contested Memory: Writing the Great Patriotic War's Official History During Khrushchev's Thaw*, Dissertation, Arizona State University, 2016

Mann, Yan, and Kucherenko, Olga, *The Eastern Front: War, Myth and Memory*, Routledge, 2024

Manoshin, Igor' Stepanovich, *Iyul' 1942 goda: padeniye Sevastopolya*, Veche, 2009

Mark, Jason, *Angriff: The German Attack on Stalingrad in Photos*, Leaping Horseman Books, 2009

Mark, Jason, *Death of the Leaping Horseman*, Leaping Horseman Books, 2003

Mark, Jason, *Panzerkrieg*, 2 volumes, Leaping Horseman Books, 2018–24

Mark, Jason, 'Stalingrad: Battle for the Grain Elevator', in *Kampfzone*, No.1, 2022

Megargee, Geoffrey P., *Inside Hitler's High Command*, University Press of Kansas, 2000

Mela, Luciano, and Crespi, Pietro, *Dosvidania: Savoia Cavalleria dal fronte russo alla Resistencza*, Vita e Pensiero, 1995

Melvin, Mungo, *Sevastopol's Wars: Crimea from Potemkin to Putin*, Osprey, 2017

Meyer, Georg, *Adolf Heusinger: Dienst eines deutschen Soldaten 1915 bis 1964*, Mittler & Sohn, 2001

Mitchelhill-Green, David, *Tobruk 1942: Rommel and the Defeat of the Allies*, History Press, 2016

Monelli, Paolo, *Mussolini: An Intimate Life*, Thames and Hudson, 1953

Montanari, Mario, *Le Operazioni in Africa Settentrionale, Vol III, El Alamein: Gennaio–Novembre 1942*, Stato Maggiore dell'Esercito, 1993

Moshchanskii, I. B., *Khronika okruzheniia: Demiansk i Khar'kov*, Veche, 2011

Murawski, Marek J., *Luftwaffe over Sevastopol*, Kagero, 2010

Die Nazis aus der Nahe: Im Mikrokosmos der Hitler-Diktatur. Spurensuche im St. Wendeler Land, Schaumberg, 2014

Nemenko, Aleksandr, *Sevastopol 42*, LitRes, 2023

Nemeskürty, István, *Untergang einer Armee*, Verlag der Nation, 1982

Neulen, Hans Werner, *Rommels italienische Flieger: Die Regia Aeronautica in Nordafrika 1940–1943*, Helios, 2013

Nuzhdin, Oleg, and Ruzayev, Stanislav, *Bitva za Sevastopol: Posledniy shturm*, LitRes, 2019

Obhodas, Amir, and Mark, Jason, *Croatian Legion The 369th Reinforced (Croatian) Infantry Regiment on the Eastern Front 1941–1943*, Leaping Horseman Books, 2011

Oldenburg, Manfred, *Ideologie und Militärisches Kalkül: Die Besatzungspolitik der Wehrmacht in der Sowjetunion 1942*, Böhlau, 2004

Oosterling, Paul, Erlings, Ron and Fischer, Hans, *Standartenführer Johannes Mühlenkamp und seine Männer*, De Krijger, c.2003

Pannacci, Raffaello, *L'occupazione italiana in URSS: La presenza fascista fra Russia e Ucraina (1941–1943)*, Carocci editora, Studi storici, 2023

Paul, Wolfgang, *Panzer General Walter K. Nehring: Eine Biographie*, Motorbuch, 2002

Peitz, Bernd, *Das Afrikakorps in Original Farbfotografien*, Motorbuch, 2007

Petacco, Arrigo, *L'armata nel deserto: il segreto di El Alamein*, Mondadori, 2018

Petacco, Arrigo, *L'armata scomparsa*, Oscar Storia, 2018

Pihurik, Judit, 'Hungarian Soldiers and Jews on the Eastern Front, 1941–1943', Yad Vashem Studies, Vol.35, No.2, 2007

Pihurik, Judit, *Naplók és memoárok a Don-kanyarból 1942–1943*, Napvilág kiadó, 2015

Popoff, Alexandra, *Vasily Grossman and the Soviet Century*, Yale University Press, 2019

Popov Pavlovich, Petr, *Turning Point: Recollections of Russian Participants and Witnesses of the Stalingrad Battle*, Leaping Horseman Books, 2008

Proskouriakov, Alexander, *Feldpost aus Stalingrad: Kriegswahrnehmung und soziales Bewusstsein deutscher und russischer Soldaten*, Köster, 2004

Pruckner, Marion, 'Dr. Leo Leixner – ein typischer Vertreter der nationalsozialistischen Kriegsberichterstatter? nationalsozialistischer Schriftleiter während dem Zweiten Weltkrieg', thesis, University of Vienna, 2009

Rees, Laurence, *The War of the Century: When Hitler Fought Stalin*, BBC Books, 1999

Reinhardt, Klaus, *Moscow – The Turning Point: The Failure of Hitler's Strategy in the Winter of 1941–42*, Berg, 1992

Remy, Maurice, *Mythos Rommel*, List, 2002

Reuth, Ralf Georg, *Entscheidung im Mittelmeer: Die südliche Peripherie Europas in der deutschen Strategie des Zweiten Weltkrieges 1940–1942*, Bernard & Graefe, 1985

Reuth, Ralf Georg, *Rommel: The End of a Legend*, Haus, 2008

Rizzi, Loris, *Lo sguardo del potere*, Rizzoli, 1984

Rüther, Martin, *Köln im Zweiten Weltkrieg: Alltag und Erfahrungen zwischen 1939 und 1945*, Emons, 2005

Salewski, Michael, *Die deutsche Seekriegsleitung 1935–1945*, Band 2, *1942–1945*, Bernard & Graefe, 1975

Sándor, György, *Szombathelytől a Don-kanyarig*, Szülőföld Könyvkiadó, 2017

Sapori, Julien, *Marcher ou Mourir: Les troupes italiennes en Russie, 1941–1943*, Éditions Sutton, 2018

Schlemmer, Thomas, *Die Italiener an der Ostfront 1942–43: Dokumente zu Mussolinis Krieg gegen die Sowjetunion*, Oldenbourg, 2005

Schlemmer, Thomas, *Invasori, non vittime: La campagna italiana di Russia 1941–1943*, Editori Laterza, 2019

Schminck-Gustavus, Christop, *Bremen Kaputt: Bilder vom Krieg 1939–1945*, Edition Temmen, 2008

Scianna, Bastian Matteo, *The Italian War on the Eastern Front, 1941–1943: Operations, Myths and Memories*, Palgrave, 2019

Scotoni, Giorgio, *Il nemico fidato: La guerra di sterminio in URSS e l'occupazione alpina sull'Alto Don*, Casa editrice Panorama, 2013

Sdvizhkov, Igor, *V iyule 1942. Oborona Kastornogo. Pravda i vymysel*, Piatyi Rim, 2019

Sdvizhkov Igor, *Operatsija Blau*, 2 volumes, Pjatyj Rim, 2022

Sebag-Montefiore, Simon, *Stalin: The Court of the Red Tsar*, Orion, 2007

Semenov, Konstantin, *Nepokorenniy Stalingrad*, Komsomolskaya Pravda, 2023

Shamray, V. A., *Srazheniye za Voronezh: oboronitel'nyy period (28 iyunya–11 iyulya 1942 g.)*, Tsentr dukhovnogo, 2013

Shein, Oleg, *Na Astrakhanskom napravlenii. Khulkhuta – neizvestnyy uchastok Stalingradskoy bitvy*, Rodina, 2020

Shores, Christopher, and Ring, Hans, *Fighters over the Desert*, Arco, 1969

Sokolov, B. V., *Bitva za Kavkaz*, Veche, 2021

Ştefănescu, Alexandru, *În umbra Marelui Reich*, Cetatea de Scaun, 2020

Spânu, Alin, *Bătălia de la Stalingrad (1942–1943): Studii, analize şi memorii Româneşti*, Editura Militră, 2023

Stalingrad i Stalingradskaya oblast' – Velikoy Pobede, Volgograd, 2010

Statiev, Alexander, *At War's Summit: The Red Army and the Struggle for the Caucasus Mountains in World War II*, Cambridge University Press, 2018

Stichling, Siegfried, and Leukefeld, Karl Otto, *Generalmajor Erich Bärenfänger: Ein Lebensbild*, Biblio, 1994

Stimpel, Hans-Martin, *Die deutsche Fallschirmtruppe 1942–1945: Einsätze auf den Kriegsschauplätzen Süden*, Mittler & Sohn, 2006

Strana v ogne: Korennoy perelom. 1942–1943, 2 volumes, Abris, 2018

Szabó, Péter, *Keleti front, nyugati fogság – A magyar honvédség a második világháborúban és azután, 1941–1946*, Jaffa Kiadó, 2018

Taube, Gerhard, *Eisenbahngeschütz Dora: Das größte Geschütz aller Zeiten*, Motorbuch, 1979

Taube, Gerhard, *Festung Sewastopol*, Mittler & Sohn, n.d.

Taysen, Adalbert von, *Tobruk 1941: Der Kampf in Nordafrika*, Rombach, 1976

Thers, Alexandre, *Les Roumains dans la Campagne de Stalingrad*, Editions Jourdan, 2021

Tieke, Wilhelm, *Kampf um die Krim 1941–1944*, Selbstverlag, 1975

Tieke, Wilhelm, *The Caucasus and the Oil*, J. J. Fedorowicz, 1995

Tieke, Wilhelm, *Ziel Kaukasus*, Winkelried, 2013

Il Trentino, i trentini nella seconda guerra mondiale, Vol.2, 1942–1943, Egon, 2010

Ungváry, Krisztián, 'Hungarian Occupation Forces in Ukraine 1941–1942,' in *Journal of Slavic Military Studies*, Vol.20, No.1

Ungváry, Krisztián, *Magyar megszálló csapatok a Szovjetunióban, 1941–1944. Esemény – elbeszélés – utóélet*, Osiris, 2015

Vasyukov, Petr Pavlovich, and Tikhomirov, Aleksandr Arkadievich, *Italianskiye alpiyskiye strelki na russkom fronte 1942–1943*, Knizhnyy mir, 2020

Vogel, Detlef, and Wette, Wolfram (eds), *Andere Helme – andere Menschen? Heimaterfahrung und Frontalltag im Zweiten Weltkrieg*, Klartext, 1995

Voicu, Marin, *Pentru Neam şi Ţară*, Editura Miidecărţi, 2019

Voicu, Marin, *Sacrificiu şi supravieţuire. Armata Română în Cotul Donului şi Stepa Calmucă. 1942–1943*, Editura Miidecărţi, 2019

Volkogonov, Dmitri, *Stalin: Triumph and Tragedy*, Grove, 1991

Vollner, Lajos, *Woronesch: Das Schicksal ungarischer Soldaten am Don/Russland zwischen 1942/43*, Bauer, 2011

Walker, Ian, *Iron Hulls, Iron Hearts*, Crowood, 2003

Welzer, Harald, Neitzel, Sönke and Gudehus, Christian, *'Der Führer war wieder viel zu human, viel zu gefühlvoll': Der Zweite Weltkrieg aus der Sicht deutscher und italienischer Soldaten*, Fischer, 2011

Werth, Alexander, *Russia at War*, Pan, 1965

Wette, Wolfram, and Ueberschar, Gerd, *Stalingrad: Mythos und Wirklichkeit einer Schlacht*, Fischer, 1992

Wijers, Hans, *Der Kampf um Stalingrad: Die Kämpfe im Industriegelände 14 Oktober bis 19 November 1942 – Augenzeugen berichten*, Selbstverlag, n.d.

Zambon, David, *132a Divisione Corazzata Ariete*, Caraktère, 2014

Zambon, David, *Les Italiens sur le front de l'Est: Juillet 1941–Mars 1943*, Lemme Edit, 2019

Ziemke, Earl F., *Moscow to Stalingrad: Decision in the East*, Center of Military History, 1987

INDEX

Note: page numbers in **bold** refer to illustrations.